AMERICAN LAW YEARBOOK 2011

A GUIDE TO THE YEAR'S
MAJOR LEGAL CASES AND
DEVELOPMENTS

ISSN 1521-0901

AMERICAN LAW YEARBOOK 2011

A GUIDE TO THE YEAR'S
MAJOR LEGAL CASES AND
DEVELOPMENTS

 GALE
CENGAGE Learning

Detroit • New York • San Francisco • New Haven, Conn • Waterville, Maine • London

American Law Yearbook 2011

Project Editor: Jeffrey Wilson

Product Manager: Stephen Wasserstein

Editorial Support Services: Andrea Lopeman, Natasha Mikheyeva

Indexing Services: Janet Mazefsky

Rights Acquisition and Management: Christine Myakovsky

Composition: Evi Abou-El-Seoud

Manufacturing: Rita Wimberley

Imaging: John Watkins

Product Design: Pam Galbreath

For product information and technology assistance, contact us at **Gale Customer Support, 1-800-877-4253.**

For permission to use material from this text or product, submit all requests online at **www.cengage.com/permissions.** Further permissions questions can be emailed to **permissionrequest@cengage.com**

While every effort has been made to ensure the reliability of the information presented in this publication, Gale, a part of Cengage Learning, does not guarantee the accuracy of the data contained herein. Gale accepts no payment for listing; and inclusion in the publication of any organization, agency, institution, publication, service, or individual does not imply endorsement of the editors or publisher. Errors brought to the attention of the publisher and verified to the satisfaction of the publisher will be corrected in future editions.

Gale
27500 Drake Rd.
Farmington Hills, MI, 48331-3535

ISBN-13: 978-1-4144-5802-1
ISBN-10: 1-4144-5802-9
ISSN 1521-0901

This title is also available as an e-book.
ISBN-13: 978-1-4144-6340-7   ISBN-10: 1-4144-6340-5
Contact your Gale, a part of Cengage Learning sales representative for ordering information.

Printed in Mexico
1 2 3 4 5 6 7 15 14 13 12 11

CONTENTS

The need for a layperson's comprehensive, understandable guide to terms, concepts, and historical developments in U.S. law has been well met by *The Gale Encyclopedia of American Law (GEAL)*. Published in a third edition in 2010 (in e-book format, and 2011 in print) by The Gale Group, *GEAL* has proved itself a valuable successor to West's 1983 publication, *The Guide to American Law: Everyone's Legal Encyclopedia.* and the 1997 and 2004 editions of *The West Encyclopedia of American Law*.

Since 1998, Gale, a part of Cengage Learning, a premier reference publisher, has extended the value of *GEAL* with the publication of *American Law Yearbook (ALY)*. This companion volume series adds entries on emerging topics not covered in the main set. A legal reference must be current to be authoritative, so *ALY* is a vital companion to a key reference source. Uniform organization by *GEAL* term and cross-referencing make it easy to use the titles together, while inclusion of key definitions and summaries of earlier rulings in supplement entries whether new or continuations make it unnecessary to refer to the main set constantly.

UNDERSTANDING THE AMERICAN LEGAL SYSTEM

The U.S. legal system is admired around the world for the freedoms it allows the individual and the fairness with which it attempts to treat all persons. On the surface, it may seem simple, yet those who have delved into it know that this system of federal and state constitutions, statutes, regulations, and common-law decisions is elaborate and complex. It derives from the English common law, but includes principles older than England, along with some principles from other lands. The U.S. legal system, like many others, has a language all its own, but too often it is an unfamiliar language: many concepts are still phrased in Latin. *GEAL* explains legal terms and concepts in everyday language, however. It covers a wide variety of persons, entities, and events that have shaped the U.S. legal system and influenced public perceptions of it.

FEATURES OF THIS SUPPLEMENT

Entries

ALY 2011 contains 150 entries covering individuals, cases, laws, and concepts significant to U.S. law. Entries are arranged alphabetically and use the same entry title as in *GEAL* or *ALY* when introduced in an earlier *Yearbook* (e.g., September 11th Attacks). There may be several cases discussed under a given topic.

Profiles of individuals cover interesting and influential people from the world of law, government, and public life, both historic and contemporary. All have contributed to U.S. law as a whole. Each short biography includes a timeline highlighting important moments in the subject's life. Persons whose lives were detailed in *GEAL*, but who have died since publication of that work, receive obituary entries in *ALY*.

DEFINITIONS

Each entry on a legal term is preceded by a definition where applicable, which is easily distinguished by its sans serif typeface. The back of the book includes a Glossary of Legal Terms containing the definitions for a selection of the most important terms **bolded** in the text of the essays and biographies. Terms bolded but not included in the Glossary of Legal Terms in ALY can be found in the Dictionary volume of GEAL.

CROSS REFERENCES

To facilitate research, *ALY 2011* provides two types of cross-references: within and following entries. Within the entries, terms are set in small capital letters (e.g., FIRST AMENDMENT) to indicate that they have their own entry in *GEAL*. At the end of each entry, additional relevant topics in *ALY 2010* are listed alphabetically by title.

APPENDIX

This section follows the main body and includes a selection of primary documents related to cases discussed in *ALY 2011*.

TABLE OF CASES CITED AND INDEX BY NAME AND SUBJECT

These features make it quick and easy for users to locate references to cases, people, statutes, events, and other subjects. The Table of Cases Cited traces the influences of legal precedents by identifying cases mentioned throughout the text. In a departure from *GEAL*, references to individuals have been folded into the general index to simplify searches. Litigants, justices, historical and contemporary figures, as well as topical references are included in the Index by Name and Subject.

CITATIONS

Wherever possible, *ALY* includes citations to cases and statutes for readers wishing to do further research. They refer to one or more series, called "reporters," which publish court opinions and related information. Each citation includes a volume number, an abbreviation for the reporter, and the starting page reference. Underscores in a citation indicate that a court opinion has not been officially reported as of

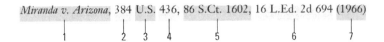

1. *Case title.* The title of the case is set in i and indicates the names of the parties. The suit in this sample citation was between Ernesto A. Miranda and the state of Arizona.

2. *Reporter volume number.* The number preceding the reporter abbreviation indicates the reporter volume containing the case. The volume number appears on the spine of the reporter, along with the reporter abbreviation.

3. *Reporter abbreviation.* The suit in the sample citation is from the reporter, or series of books, called *U.S. Reports,* which contains cases from the U.S. Supreme Court. Numerous reporters publish cases from the federal and state courts; consult the Abbreviations list at the back of this volume for full titles.

4. *Reporter page.* The number following the reporter abbreviation indicates the reporter page on which the case begins.

5. *Additional reporter citation.* Many cases may be found in more than one reporter. The suit in the sample citation also appears in volume 86 of the *Supreme Court Reporter,* beginning on page 1602.

6. *Additional reporter citation.* The suit in the sample citation is also reported in volume 16 of the *Lawyer's Edition,* second series, beginning on page 694.

7. *Year of decision.* The year the court issued its decision in the case appears in parentheses at the end of the cite.

Brady Handgun Violence Prevention Act, Pub. L. No. 103-159, 107 Stat. 1536 (18 U.S.C.A. § § 921-925A)

1	2	3	4	5	6	7	8

1. *Statute title.*

2. *Public law number.* In the sample citation, the number 103 indicates this law was passed by the 103d Congress, and the number 159 indicates it was the 159th law passed by that Congress.

3. *Reporter volume number.* The number preceding the reporter abbreviation indicates the reporter volume containing the statute.

4. *Reporter abbreviation.* The name of the reporter is abbreviated. The statute in the sample citation is from *Statutes at Large.*

5. *Reporter page.* The number following the reporter abbreviation indicates the reporter page on which the statute begins.

6. *Title number.* Federal laws are divided into major sections with specific titles. The number preceding a reference to the U.S. Code stands for the section called Crimes and Criminal Procedure.

7. *Additional reporter.* The statute in the sample citation may also be found in the *U.S. Code Annotated.*

8. *Section numbers.* The section numbers following a reference to the *U.S. Code Annotated* indicate where the statute appears in that reporter.

ALY's publication. Two sample citations, with explanations, are presented below.

COMMENTS WELCOME

Considerable efforts were expended at the time of publication to ensure the accuracy of the information presented in *American Law Yearbook 2011.* The editor welcomes your comments and suggestions for enhancing and improving future editions of this supplement to *The Gale Encyclopedia of American Law.* Send comments and sugges tions to:

American Law Yearbook

Gale

27500 Drake Rd.

Farmington Hills, MI 48331-3535

ADOPTION

A two-step judicial process in conformance to state statutory provisions in which the legal obligations and rights of a child toward the biological parents are terminated and new rights and obligations are created in the acquired parents.

Florida Court of Appeals Strikes Down Ban on Gay Adoption

Permitting homosexual individuals and couples to adopt children has been a hot-button issue in some states. Though research overwhelmingly demonstrates that adoptive children of homosexual parents do not have any more problems than children of heterosexual parents, the state of Florida continued to prohibit adoptions by gays and lesbians. However, the state did permit homosexuals to be foster parents and guardians of children. This contradiction was highlighted in a lawsuit challenging the Florida law by a gay man who had an exemplary record as a foster parent. The Florida Court of Appeals, in *Florida Department of Children and Families v. ADOPTION of X.X.G. and N.R.G.*, 45 So.3d 79 (2010), ruled that the legislature had no rational basis for imposing a total ban on gay and lesbian adoption.

F.G., a homosexual man living in Florida, had served as a licensed foster parent for several years. In 2004, X.X.G., then four years old, and N.R.G., then four months old, were removed from their home by the Florida Department of Children and Families. The removal was based on allegations of

abandonment and neglect. The department asked F.G. to accept the children on a temporary basis until a permanent home could be found them. F.G., who had previously parented seven foster children, agreed. The children had physical and emotional problems but soon thrived in F.G.'s household. In 2006 the state terminated the rights of the natural parents and placed the children for adoption. F.G. applied to adopt the children and a home study was conducted by a private nonprofit corporation that the state contracted with for adoption services. The home study was favorable but the contractor recommended against the application because F.G. was homosexual. Under Florida **statute** 63.042(3), "No person eligible to adopt under this statute may adopt if that person is homosexual." The department denied the application on that basis, though it admitted that F.G. would have been approved if not for the statute.

F.G. filed a petition in Florida state court, asking the court to find the statute unconstitutional because it violated his **equal protection** rights. An independent lawyer represented the two children and argued that the law violated their EQUAL PROTECTION rights. A four day trial was conducted, with F.G presenting expert witnesses who testified regarding homosexual and heterosexual parenting abilities. The department offered the testimony of two expert witnesses. The trial court issued a lengthy opinion, ruling that the statute was unconstitutional because it violated the equal protection

Martin Gill, left, father of two brothers, and attorney Robert Rosenwald smile during a news conference in Miami, September 22, 2010. Florida's strict ban on adoption by gay people is unconstitutional because no other group, even people with criminal backgrounds, are singled out for a flat prohibition by state law, an appeals court ruled.

AP IMAGES/ALAN DIAZ

rights of F.G. and the children under the Florida Constitution. The department then appealed.

A three-judge panel of the Florida Court of Appeals upheld the trial court ruling. Judge Gerald Cope, writing for the panel, noted that the department believed there was a rational basis for the statute and that the trial court had misinterpreted the law. Judge Cope found that F.G. had successfully argued in the trial court that the statute treated him unequally because the law created an absolute prohibition on gay adoption. In contrast, the statute allowed all other persons, including persons with criminal histories and histories of substance abuse to be considered on a case-by-case basis. Under the **rational basis test**, a court must uphold a statute if the classification bears a rational relationship to a legitimate government objective. Most importantly, the classification must be based "on real difference" which is reasonably related to the subject and purpose of the regulation. Therefore, the appeals court had to determine if the law was based on real difference between heterosexual and homosexual parents.

The adoption statute required an individual, case-by-case evaluation to determine if the proposed adoption was in the best interest of the child. Except for homosexual persons, there was not categorical exclusion of anyone from consideration of adoption. Judge Cope pointed out that individuals with a range of problems and crimes were eligible to adopt. Moreover, single adults were allowed to adopt under the law. Despite the fact that the department used homosexual foster parents and that state law permitted homosexuals to be legal guardians of children, the state categorically excluded a homosexual person from adopting.

Though this prohibition strongly suggested that homosexuals are unfit to be parents, Judge Cope noted that nothing in the present case "even hinted at" such an argument. The department instead argued that there is a rational basis for the ban because children will have better role models and face less DISCRIMINATION if they are placed in heterosexual households, preferably with a **husband and wife** as parents. The appeals court found little merit in this argument, for state law permitted adoption by an unmarried adult and statistics showed that one-third of adoptions in Florida were by single adults. The statute did not restrict adoption to heterosexual married couples.

The rational basis of the law was undercut by the fact homosexuals could serve as foster parents and legal guardians of children. Though the department contended that social science evidence justified gay adoption, Judge Cope found that the expert witness testimony at trial demonstrated that there were no differences in the parenting of homosexuals or the adjustment of their children. He agreed with the trial court's conclusion "that the issue is so far beyond dispute that it would be irrational to hold otherwise." The views of the department's two expert witnesses were discounted both by the trial and appeals courts. Other experts questioned the methodology of these two men and the appeals court agreed that the scientific data could not support a blanket prohibition on homosexual adoption. Therefore, the court ruled that there was no rational basis for the prohibition. As to the claims made on behalf of the children, the court agreed that the law violated their equal protection rights as well.

AFFIRMATIVE ACTION

Employment programs required by federal statutes and regulations designed to remedy discriminatory practices in hiring minority group members; i.e., positive steps designed to eliminate existing and continuing discrimination, to remedy lingering effects of past discrimination, and to create systems and procedures to prevent future discrimination; commonly based on population percentages of minority groups in a particular area. Factors considered are race, color, sex, creed, and age.

California Supreme Court Upholds Ban on Affirmative Action

In 1996, the voters of California amended the state constitution through the initiative process, enacting a new provision that forbids a city awarding public contracts to discriminate or grant preferential treatment based on race or gender. Article I, section 31's ban on municipal **affirmative action** plans was ignored by the City and County of San Francisco, which continued to award public contracts to minority-owned business enterprises (MBEs) and women-owned business enterprises (WBEs). A contractor challenged the legality of the city's AFFIRMATIVE ACTION programs, leading the California SUPREME COURT to rule in *Coral Construction, Inc. v. City and County of San Francisco*, 235 P.3d 947 (2010), that San Francisco could

no longer use affirmative action in awarding public contracts.

San Francisco first adopted a MBE/WBE **ordinance** in 1984, setting aside specified percentages of public contracting funds for MBEs and WBEs. It also gave bid discounts, which required the city's contracting authorities to treat bids by MBEs and WBEs as if they were lower than in fact they were. Both the set-asides and the bid discounts gave the MBEs and WBEs a competitive advantage over other bidders. In 1989 the Ninth **Circuit Court** of Appeals ruled that the ordinance violated the Fourteenth Amendment's **Equal Protection** Clause and the city charter. Following this decision the city's Board of Supervisors enacted a new affirmative action ordinance that eliminated the set-asides but kept the bid discounts and other preferences for MBEs and WBEs. A business organization filed a federal lawsuit challenging the ordinance but the federal district declined to issue an INJUNCTION.

Voters approved Proposition 209 in 1996, which added section 31 to the state constitution. Section 31 states that the state and its political subdivisions "shall not discriminate against, or grant preferential treatment to, any individual or group on the basis of race, sex, color, ethnicity, or national origin in the operation of public employment, public education, or public contracting." In 1997 the Ninth Circuit ruled that section 31 did not violate the EQUAL PROTECTION Clause. In 1998 the Board of Supervisors conducted research on the effectiveness of its affirmative action program. It found that MBEs and WBEs received a smaller share of city contracts than would be expected and that this was due to DISCRIMINATION by the city and discrimination in the private market. Based on these findings, the board adopted a new ordinance that preserved bid discounts and required contractors to use MBE and WBE subcontractors at levels set by the city or to make **good faith** efforts to do so through preferential outreach programs.

In 2000 the California Supreme Court struck down a similar affirmative action program by the city of San Jose, stating that section 31 does not tolerate "race-and-gender-conscious preferences" the equal protection clause does not *require* but merely *permits*. The following year Coral Construction filed a state lawsuit, asking the court to declare the

San Francisco ordinance invalid. The ordinance was reenacted in 2003 as the case moved slowly through the courts. The city again cited research to justify the continuation of the program. The trial court ruled in favor of Coral, citing the Ninth Circuit decision that found section 31 constitutional. The California Court of Appeals upheld most of the trial court decision, remanding for **adjudication** the city's claim that the federal equal protection clause required the ordinance.

The California Supreme Court, in a 6-1 decision, upheld the court of appeals on all points. Justice Kathryn Werdegar, writing for the majority, confronted the city's main argument that section 31 violated the political structure doctrine articulated by the U.S. Supreme Court in two cases. The court noted that section 31 prohibited affirmative action programs that the federal equal protection clause permits but does not require. However, the provision does not pose an obstacle to race or gender measures required by federal law or the U.S. Constitution. As to the political structure doctrine, the court pointed out that it is has been rarely used. This doctrine addresses a political structure that treats all individuals as equals yet "more subtly distorts governmental processes in such a way as to place special burdens on the ability of minority groups to achieve beneficial legislation." The city argued that section uses the racial or gender-based nature of an issue (preferences) to structure governmental decisionmaking; groups that seek these preferences must first overcome the obstacle of amending the state constitution, while groups that seek preferences on other bases, such as disability or veteran status, do not.

The court rejected the political structure doctrine argument, finding that the Sixth and Ninth Circuit Courts of Appeals had correctly reasoned that this doctrine was inapplicable. The Ninth Circuit, in upholding the constitutionality of section 31, had stated that "impediments to preferential treatment do not deny equal protection." Individuals do not have equal protection rights against political obstructions to preferential treatment. Moreover, while the U.S. Constitution permits race-based or gender-based preferences, that did not imply that the state could not ban them altogether.

The city also contended that the ordinance could survive because without these affirmative action programs it would not receive federal

funds. Section 31 provides an exception for programs which must conform to federal eligibility requirements. The court rejected this argument, finding that the relevant federal regulations did not require racial preferences. However, the court did agree with the court of appeals that the trial court needed to conduct proceedings to assess the city's claim that the federal Equal Protection Clause required the city ordinance as a remedy for the city's own discrimination. The court made clear that the city would have to prove that it purposefully or intentionally discriminated against MBEs and WBEs and that the ordinance was narrowly tailored to deal with this intentional discrimination.

Justice Carlos Moreno, in a dissenting opinion, contended that the majority had failed to correctly apply the political structure doctrine.

ARBITRATION

The submission of a dispute to an unbiased third person designated by the parties to the controversy, who agree in advance to comply with the award–a decision to be issued after a hearing at which both parties have an opportunity to be heard.

Supreme Court Strikes Down State Class Action Arbitration Rule

The Federal ARBITRATION Act (FAA) makes agreement to arbitrate "valid, irrevocable, and enforceable, save upon such grounds as exist at law or in equity for the revocation of any contract." The SUPREME COURT, in *AT&T Mobility LLC v. Concepcion*, 563 U.S. ___, 131 S.Ct. 1740 (2011), was called on to decide whether a state could condition the enforceability of certain arbitration agreements on the availability of **class action** arbitration procedures. The Court ruled that a state could not require CLASS ACTION arbitration.

In 2002, Vincent and Liza Concepcion purchased cell phone service from AT&T, based upon an offer of free phones. Though they were not charged for the phones themselves, they were assessed $30.22 in sales tax based on the phones' retail value. In 2006, the Concepcions filed a complaint against AT&T in California federal **district court**, alleging that the company had engaged in **false advertising** and **fraud** by charging sales tax on phones it advertised as free. This complaint was later consolidated into a class action lawsuit. AT&T moved the court to compel arbitration under the contract the Concepcions signed when they purchased service. The contract stated that all disputes between the parties must be arbitrated. In addition, the contract provided that claims must be brought in the parties' "individual capacity, and not as a PLAINTIFF or class member in any purported class or representative proceeding." Under the terms of the contract the customer could make a claim by completing a one-page form. If AT&T did not offer to settle the claim within 30 days, the customer could file a demand for arbitration. AT&T agreed to pay all costs for nonfrivolous claims and if the customer's arbitration award was greater than the company's last settlement offer, AT&T would pay a $7,500 minimum recovery and twice the amount of the claimant's attorney fees.

The Concepcions argued to the federal court that the arbitration agreement was **unconscionable** under California state law because it disallowed class-wide arbitration procedures. The court agreed with them, citing *Discover Bank v. Superior Court*, 113 P. 3d 1100 (2005). In this case the California Supreme Court ruled that most collective-arbitration waivers in consumer contracts were UNCONSCIONABLE. AT&T appealed the ruling but the Ninth **Circuit Court** of Appeals upheld the decision. The appeals court also held that the *Discover Bank* rule was not preempted by the FAA.

The U.S. Supreme Court, in a 5-4 decision, overturned the Ninth Circuit. Justice ANTONIN SCALIA, writing for the majority, noted that the FAA was enacted in 1925 in response to hostility to arbitration agreements. The Court, acknowledging this liberal federal policy favoring arbitration, has ruled that courts must place arbitration agreements "on an equal footing with other contracts." Under the FAA, arbitration agreements may be declared unenforceable "upon such grounds as exist at law or in equity for the revocation of any contract." The question in this case was whether this FAA provision preempts California's *Discover Bank* rule. This rule had been frequently applied to find arbitration agreements unconscionable, based on the fact that companies had superior bargaining power that could be used to "deliberately cheat large numbers of consumers out of individually small amounts of money." Under these circumstances, a consumer's

waiver of class-action arbitration was unconscionable and should not be enforced. Justice Scalia concluded that when state law "prohibits outright the arbitration of a particular type of claim, the analysis is straightforward: The conflicting rule is displaced by the FAA." However, the inquiry is more complex when, as here, a generally applicable doctrine like unconscionability is alleged to have been applied in a way that disfavors arbitration. He noted that California's courts "have been more likely to hold contracts to arbitrate unconscionable than other contracts." In his view the FAA provision did not suggest an intent to preserve state-law rules that stand as an obstacle to the "accomplishment of the FAA's objectives."

As to class action arbitration, the Court expressed hostility, finding that it interferes with "fundamental attributes of arbitration and thus creates a scheme inconsistent with the FAA." Arbitration is designed to be streamlined, efficient, and expeditious. The *Discover Bank* rule interfered with arbitration by allowing any part to demand class-wide arbitration after the execution of the arbitration agreement. Class-wide arbitration encourages plaintiffs' lawyers to ignore bilateral arbitration and to seek higher fees in a class action. In addition, the structural issues surrounding class-wide arbitration undercut the primary advantage of arbitration, which is informality. A class action makes the process slower, more costly, and "more likely to generate procedural morass than final judgment." Justice Scalia cited statistics that showed a bilateral arbitration resulted in a decision in six months, while class arbitrations dragged on for years without a final resolution.

The Court also found that class arbitration required procedural formality through the use of the Federal Rules of **Civil Procedure**. The FAA never contemplated class arbitration, which is a recent development. Justice Scalia found it "odd" that an arbitrator would be "entrusted with ensuring that third parties' due process rights are satisfied." He also concluded that class arbitration greatly increased risks to defendants. The risk of error in arbitration is always present because of the informality, but the costs of these errors are low in bilateral arbitration. However, when tens of thousands of potential claimants are "aggregated and decided at once, the risk of an error will often become unacceptable." In this situation the

DEFENDANT may be pressured into a settling questionable claims. Arbitration is "poorly suited" for high stakes LITIGATION because there is little chance an **appellate court** will review an arbitrator's decision. Congress could not have intended to allow a state to place a defendant in a position "where there is no effective means of review." Therefore, the California rule was preempted by the FAA.

Justice STEPHEN BREYER, in a dissenting opinion joined by three other members of the Court, argued that the *Discover Bank* rule was consistent with the FAA provision and with the purposes of the act. Moreover, "neither the history nor present practice suggests that class arbitration is fundamentally incompatible with arbitration itself."

AUTOMOBILES

State Tort Laws Not Preempted by Federal Seatbelt Law

Civil lawsuits against automobile companies by persons alleging injuries caused by design defects have become a part of the contemporary legal landscape. A contentious and important issue has been whether plaintiffs can use state laws to pursue their claims if federal laws exist that appear to preempt state law. The Federal Motor Vehicle Safety Standard 208 (FMVSS 208) requires that automobile manufacturers install seatbelts on the rear seats of passenger vehicles, but allows the makers the option of installing lap belts in the middle seats of cars and aisle seats of minivans rather than lap-and-shoulder belts. The SUPREME COURT, in *Williamson v. Mazda Motor of America*, __U.S.__, 131 S.Ct. 1131, __ L.Ed.2d__ (2011), ruled that the FMVSS rear-seat belt requirements did not preempt state **tort law**.

In 2002, Delbert Williamson was driving a 1993 Mazda minivan. He and his wife Alexa were in the front seat, wearing lap-and-shoulder belts. Their daughter Thanh was sitting in a rear aisle seat, wearing a lap belt. The Williamson car was hit head on by another vehicle. The parents survived but Thanh died. The Williamsons filed a tort lawsuit against Mazda in California state court, alleging that Mazda should have installed lap-and-shoulder belts on rear aisle seats and that Thanh died because Mazda installed the seat with a lap belt instead.

The California trial court dismissed the lawsuit and the California Court of Appeals upheld this decision. The appeals court noted that the U.S. Supreme Court had ruled that a different part of the FMVSS 208 that dealt with the installation of air bags seemed to apply to the seat belt standard. In that case, the Court held that the regulation which gave manufacturers the option of installing air bags preempted state tort lawsuits premised on the failure to install air bags. Because both standards gave manufacturers a choice, the appeals court concluded that the Williamsons' state lawsuit was preempted.

The Supreme Court, in a 8-0 decision (Justice Elena Kagan did not participate), overruled the state appeals court decision, finding that the two provisions of the FMVSS 208 were not equivalent. Justice STEPHEN BREYER, writing for the Court, focused on whether the state tort action conflicted with the federal regulation. The key question was whether a state law that "stands as an obstacle to the accomplishment and execution of the full purposes and objectives" of a federal law is preempted. In the air bag regulation case the Court found that giving automakers a choice among different passive restraint devices (automatic SEAT BELTS and air bags) was a significant objective of the regulation. In the early 1980s, when the regulation was issued, many car occupants did not buckle their seat belts. The installation of passive protection was the goal, but air bags were not required. Therefore, state tort actions that sought to impose liability on automakers for exercising their choice under the regulation not to install air bags undercut the purpose of the federal law and were preempted.

As for the Williamsons' lawsuit, Justice Breyer found that while the tort action would restrict the choice of rear seat seatbelts by automakers, this choice was not a significant regulatory objective. There was some evidence that lap-and-shoulder belts were not required in rear aisle seats because they could cause "entry and exit problems for occupants of seating positions to the rear" by stretching the shoulder belt across the aisle way. Moreover, there was, according to Breyer, "little indication" that the DEPARTMENT OF TRANSPORTATION (DOT) considered this issue a significant safety concern. Unlike the passive restraint matter, not requiring lap-and-shoulder belts for rear inner seats was driven by the belief this requirement would not be cost-effective. DOT concluded that installing lap-and-shoulder bets would be significantly more expensive for automakers to install in rear middle and aisle seats than in seats next to the car doors. The Court found that there was no preemptive intent based on cost by DOT. To allow **preemption** in this case would result in treating such federal standards as if they were maximum standards, "eliminating the possibility that the federal agency seeks only to set forth a *minimum* standard potentially supplemented through state tort law."

Justice Breyer also noted that the federal government itself believed the DOT regulation did not preempt the Williamsons' state tort action. This was important because the Court had held in the air bag case that "the agency's own views should make a difference." Congress had delegated to the DOT the authority to implement the **statute**. The subject matter was technical and the agency was likely "to have a thorough understanding of its own regulation and its objectives." Therefore, though the state tort suit "may restrict the manufacturer's choice," it did not stand as an "obstacle to the accomplishment" of the full purposes and objectives of federal law.

BANKRUPTCY

A federally authorized procedure by which a debtor–an individual, corporation, or municipality–is relieved of total liability for its debts by making court-approved arrangements for their partial repayment.

Ransom v. FIA Card Services

Chapter 13 of the Bankruptcy Code, 11 U.S.C. § 1301 *et seq.*, allows individuals to obtain a discharge of their debts if they pay creditors a portion of their monthly income in accordance with a court-approved plan. The Internal Revenue Service (IRS) uses a **statutory** formula known as the "means test" to establish the allowances that may be deducted from a debtor's monthly income, leaving a net "disposable income" available for payment to creditors. This formula is based on national and local standards. In *Ransom v. FIA Card Services, N.A., (MBNA America Bank, N.A.),* No. 09-907, 131 S. Ct. 716, 562 U.S. ___ (2011), the U.S. Supreme Court held that a debtor in bankruptcy who does not make loan or lease payments on a vehicle cannot take the car ownership deduction in calculating monthly expenses. The Court particularly noted that the Bankruptcy Abuse Prevention and **Consumer Protection** Act of 2005, Pub. L. No. 109-8, 119 Stat. 23, had adopted the means test "to help ensure that debtors who *can* pay creditors *do* pay them.

Jason Ransom filed for Chapter 13 bankruptcy in July 2006. He itemized more than $82,500 in unsecured debt, including a claim held by FIA Card Services (FIA). Among his assets, he listed a 2004 Toyota Camry, then valued at $14,000, which he owned free and clear of any debt.

For purposes of the "means test," Ransom reported monthly income of $4,248. He listed monthly expenses totaling $4,038. Based on those figures, Ransom had disposable income (available to creditors) of just $210 per month. He proposed a five-year plan that would result in repayment of about 25 percent of his unsecured debt.

FIA objected to confirmation of the plan, arguing that the plan did not direct all of Ransom's disposable income toward repayment of debt. Specifically, FIA objected to Ransom having claimed the car ownership allowance because he did not make loan or lease payments on his car. Without that allowance, Ransom would have $681 per month of disposable income available to unsecured creditors. The difference over the five-year plan amounted to about $28,000.

The bankruptcy court denied confirmation of Ransom's proposed plan. It held that Ransom could deduct a vehicle ownership expense only if he were currently making loan or lease payments on that vehicle. Ransom appealed to the Ninth Circuit Bankruptcy **Appellate** Panel, which affirmed the bankruptcy court's holding. The appellate opinion noted that such an expense amount "becomes relevant to the debtor (i.e., appropriate or applicable to the debtor) when he or she in fact has such an expense." What was important, noted the appellate panel, was the payments that debtors actually made, not how many cars they owned, because those loan/lease payments actually affected how much remained to reimburse unsecured creditors. The Ninth **Circuit Court** of Appeals affirmed.

However, three other Circuit Courts of Appeals (Fifth, Seventh, and Eighth) had previously ruled that a debtor who owned a vehicle free and clear was nonetheless entitled to the car-ownership allowance. The U.S. Supreme Court accepted **certiorari** review to resolve the conflict among the circuits.

Justice Elena Kagan delivered the 8-1 majority opinion affirming the Ninth Circuit and lower courts. The Court began by reviewing the language of the Bankruptcy Code, which defines a debtor's disposable income as "current monthly income … less amounts reasonably necessary to be expended." § 1325 (b)(2). Further, a debtor may claim only "applicable" expenses (i.e., appropriately corresponding to the debtor's financial circumstances) as listed on a National or Local Standard (the "Standards"). These Standards are in the form of tables prepared by IRS to list standardized expense amounts for basic living necessities and expenses.

The Code specifies that a deduction is applicable only if the debtor will incur the kind of expense covered by the Standards tables during the lifetime of the repayment plan. This is important because, as the Court expressly noted, had Congress not desired to separate debtors who qualified for an allowance from those who did not, it could have omitted the term "applicable" altogether. Accordingly, the **statute** is best interpreted to require a threshold eligibility determination ensuring that "applicable" carries meaning, as each word in statutory language should. Thus, because Congress intended the means test to approximate a debtor's reasonable and basic expenditures, that debtor should be required to qualify for any deductions by actually incurring those expenditures.

As to the vehicle-ownership deduction relevant in the present case, the Court noted that Ransom had claimed a car ownership deduction of $471, the full amount specified in the IRS's "Ownership Costs" table in its

Collection Financial Standards. Ransom claimed a separate deduction of $338 for car operating costs. The $471 ownership cost allowance represents the average monthly payment for loans or leases nationwide. Maintenance and driving expenses are allowed under the separate "Operating Costs" deduction. A person who owns a vehicle free and clear is entitled to the operating costs deduction for all driving-related expenses, but cannot claim the "ownership costs" deduction, which represents the separate expense for loan or lease payments. Ransom was therefore not entitled to the ownership cost allowance, but could claim the operating cost deduction he listed.

Justice ANTONIN SCALIA was the lone dissenter. He would have reversed the judgment of the Ninth Circuit and joined the three circuits that found debtors who owned their cars free and clear were nonetheless entitled to the car-ownership allowance. He disagreed with the Court's having imported the meaning behind the word "applicable" from an IRS standard into the Local Standards used for bankruptcy proceedings.

Stern v. Marshall

For years, legal experts have followed the string of cases involving Vickie Lynn Marshall (Vickie herein, but known to the public as Anna Nicole Smith) and her efforts to acquire some of her deceased husband's (former Yale professor and Texas oil billionaire J. Howard Marshall II) $1.6 billion-dollar estate. In what might be the final legal battle, the U.S. SUPREME COURT held, in June 2011, that a BANKRUPTCY court ruling in favor of Vickie did not have the constitutional authority to render such a ruling, as the issue was not a "core matter" relating to the bankruptcy code. *Stern v. Marshall*, No. 10-179, 564 U.S. ___ (2011). By the time the case had reached the Court, both parties to the LITIGATION were also deceased (Vickie herself, as well as husband Marshall's son E. Pierce Marshall, who had fought Vickie in court over the estate money), along with Vickie's only beloved son and heir to her estate, Daniel. (Even Howard Stern, Vickie's long-time lawyer and sometime lover, who was now representing Vickie's estate in the Supreme Court case, was embroiled in his own legal battles over his personal and professional relationship with Vickie and her son.)

Summarizing the history leading up to this final matter, shortly before her elderly husband passed away, Anna Nicole Smith, who now was known as Vickie Lynn Marshall, filed suit in a Texas **probate** court, alleging that Pierce Marshall (the ultimate BENEFICIARY of his father's estate) had fraudulently induced his father to sign a living (*inter vivos*) trust that did not include her. Vickie alleged that her husband had made multiple oral promises to her and had directed his attorney to redraft the estate plan to take care of her.

As this case was moving along in Texas probate court, Vickie was suddenly sued by her former housekeeper in California for SEXUAL HARASSMENT. A **default judgment** of $850,000 in that case resulted in Vickie filing for bankruptcy in California. In the bankruptcy proceeding, Pierce filed his own complaint and proof of claim as a potential creditor against Vickie's bankruptcy estate, alleging that Vickie had defamed him by telling the media that he had engaged in **fraud** to control his father's assets. Vickie responded by filing a truth-as-a-defense answer and a COUNTERCLAIM alleging that Pierce had tortiously interfered with the gift she was expecting from her husband. This was precisely the essence of the claim she had made, and which was still pending, in Texas probate court.

The bankruptcy court in California ultimately ruled that this issue in the pending case was a "core matter" for which it could render a judgment; it did, giving Vickie half of Marshall's estate. On appeal, a federal **district court** in California held the bankruptcy's ruling as proposed, not final, then ruled itself on the merits, again in Vickie's favor. Meanwhile, down in Texas, the probate court had decided against Vickie on the very same claim, and found that she was not entitled to anything from the estate. (During the pendency of this litigation, both parties passed away and their respective estates were substituted as parties in interest.)

The Ninth **Circuit Court** of Appeals reversed the California rulings, concluding that the bankruptcy court lacked authority to enter final judgment on Vickie's counterclaim; it held that the Texas state decision was controlling, and because it had been decided first, the district court should have given the Texas judgment preclusive effect.

The simplest way to characterize the issue ultimately before the Supreme Court was, which court's decision was controlling? In its **plurality** opinion affirming the Ninth Circuit, the Court essentially ruled that, although the California bankruptcy court had the **statutory** authority to render judgment on Vickie's counterclaim, it lacked the constitutional authority to do so.

Chief Justice JOHN ROBERTS delivered the opinion of the Court, joined by Justices ANTONIN SCALIA, CLARENCE THOMAS, ANTHONY KENNEDY, and SAMUEL ALITO. To determine whether the Ninth Circuit was correct, the Court needed to determine (1) whether the bankruptcy court had the statutory authority to issue a final judgment on Vickie's counterclaim, and (2) if so, whether conferring that authority on the bankruptcy court was constitutional.

The Court found that the bankruptcy court did have authority, under 28 U.S.C. § 157(b)(2)(C) (governing "core proceedings") to enter judgment on Vickie's counterclaim, despite Pierce's various arguments to the contrary. Notwithstanding, and in a strange twist of law, the Court further concluded that, although § 157 allowed the bankruptcy court to enter final judgment, Article III of the U.S. Constitution did not. Article III mandates, in part, that [t]he judicial Power of the United States, shall be vested in one supreme Court, and in such inferior Courts as the Congress may from time to time ordain and establish." It goes on to outline judges' lifetime tenure "for good Behavior" under Article III and their compensation not diminished by tenure. Article III, noted the Court, was an inseparable element of the constitutional system.

That having been said, in the case of *Northern Pipeline Constr. Co. v. Marathon Pipe Line Co.,* 458 U.S. 50, 102 S. Ct. 2858, 73 L. Ed. 2d 598 (1982), the Court considered whether bankruptcy judges serving under the Bankruptcy Act of 1978, Pub. L. No. 95-598, 92 Stat. 2549, who lacked the tenure and salary guarantees of Article III, could "constitutionally be vested with jurisdiction to decide a state law contract claim that was not otherwise part of the bankruptcy proceedings." A majority of the Court concluded that it was not so vested, and rejected the argument that such an exercise of jurisdiction was constitutional because the bankruptcy judge was merely acting as an adjunct of the district court or the court of appeals. Even though Congress subsequently revised the statutes governing bankruptcy jurisdiction and judges (1984), the bankruptcy courts still exercise the same powers they wielded under the 1978 Act with respect to "core" proceedings. Therefore, any authority exercised over a counterclaim such as Vickie's exceeds the boundaries of Article III.

Justice STEPHEN BREYER, joined by Justices RUTH BADER GINSBURG, SONIA SOTOMAYOR, and ELENA KAGAN, dissented. The DISSENT agreed with the majority's holding that the bankruptcy **statute** authorized the **adjudication** of such a counterclaim, but disagreed that it was unconstitutional under Article III. The dissent concluded that the statute was consistent with the Constitution's delegation of the "judicial Power of the United States" to the Judicial Branch of the Government, therefore making it constitutional.

BANKS AND BANKING

Authorized financial institutions and the business in which they engage, which encompasses the receipt of money for deposit, to be payable according to the terms of the account; collection of checks presented for payment; issuance of loans to individuals who meet certain requirements; discount of commercial paper; and other money-related functions.

Congress Passes Massive Financial Reform Legislation

After months of fierce partisan debate, Congress in July 2010 approved a massive financial reform bill that will have far-reaching implications on the nation's financial services industry. The driving force behind the bill was the nation's financial crisis that lasted from 2007 to 2010. President BARACK OBAMA applauded the bill, stressing that the legislation would mean that taxpayers would never again have to foot the bill in the event that a major financial firm collapses. However, Republicans have countered that the legislation is too restrictive and that the law will not prevent future bailouts.

A variety of factors led to the financial crisis in the late 2000s. One event that precipitated the recession was the sharp decline in REAL ESTATE values in 2007. Many investment banks had invested heavily in mortgage-backed SECURITIES, which were vital to allow the banks to

continue to provide short-term financing. When the real estate values fell, the mortgage-backed securities likewise fell, and the investment banks ran into problems with liquidity. The problems related to mortgage-based securities is what led to the collapse of large investment service companies Bear Sterns and Lehman Brothers in 2008.

The federal government stepped in to bail out Bear Sterns (which was eventually purchased in a fire sale by JP Morgan Chase) as well as more than a dozen other large financial firms and major corporations in 2008 and 2009. Some of these companies were deemed by the government to be "too big to fail." Use of taxpayer money to bail out these failing firms was not popular among the public, and the bailouts were part of the discussions during the presidential debates leading up to the 2008 election. Several commentators—especially liberals—noted that Washington had done too little to regulate the financial services industry since the 1980s and that the federal government needed to place more controls on Wall Street firm.

In June 2009, President Barack Obama introduced a sweeping reform bill for the U.S. financial system. His proposal met with fierce resistance from lobbyists and Republicans, however. Over the next several months, Democrats in Congress continued to work on the bill, and in December 2009, Representative Barney Frank (D.-Mass.) and former Senator Chris Dodd (D.-Conn.) introduced a new bill. The bill retained many of the reforms that the Obama proposal had originally contained, and opponents continued to fight strongly against the bill's passage. Nevertheless, the HOUSE OF REPRESENTATIVES approved the bill in December 2009, and despite struggles with Republicans and a handful of Democrats, the SENATE followed suit in May by approving the bill with amendments. A joint committee resolved differences in the two bills, and the final bill was completed in July 2010. On July 21, Obama signed the Dodd-Frank Wall Street Reform and **Consumer Protection** Act, Pub. L. No. 111-203, 124 Stat. 1376 (2010).

The final bill was nearly 900 pages long, which demonstrates its breadth. Proponents of the legislation have championed several of its highlights. One part of the legislation created the Financial Stability Oversight Council, which has been charged with identifying and responding to emerging risks in the U.S. financial system. The Council met several times in 2010 and 2011 and as of April 2011 had already considered some proposed rules. The Act also created the Consumer Financial Protection Bureau, which is an independent agency housed at the Federal Reserve. This Bureau has an independent budget and independent rulemaking authority and will have the power to examine and enforce regulations for banks and credit unions with assets of $10 billion or more. Supporters of the legislation have emphasized that this one agency will improve CONSUMER PROTECTION because one office is responsible for handling these protections.

The legislation was also designed to end "too big to fail" bailouts of large financial firms. The legislation subjected a wider range of companies to government oversight and created new systems to apply to companies that are on the verge of collapse. In the event that a firm must **liquidate** its assets, taxpayers are not supposed to be "on the hook" for any costs or expenses.

Other parts of the legislation affect the following: reform of the Federal Reserve; greater regulation of derivatives, which are contracts that are traded on exchanges; reform of mortgage practices; raising of standards that apply to private investment funds known as hedge funds; creation of new requirements to apply to credit rating agencies as well as credit scores; and changes to rules governing executive compensation. The Act also provided funding to combat the negative effects of the mortgage crisis, including $1 billion in emergency mortgage relief for qualified unemployed homeowners.

Obama praised lawmakers for passing the legislation. Upon signing the legislation, he noted, "The fact is, the financial industry is central to our nation's ability to grow, to prosper, to compete and to innovate. There are a lot of banks that understand and fulfill this vital role, and there are a whole lot of bankers who want to do right—and do right—by their customers. This reform will help foster innovation, not hamper it. It is designed to make sure that everybody follows the same set of rules, so that firms compete on price and quality, not on tricks and not on traps." Obama further added that "the American people will never again be asked to foot the bill for Wall Street's mistakes."

Republicans denounced the legislation during congressional election campaigns in 2010, and when Republicans took control of the House after these elections, several promised either to **repeal** or rewrite a large percentage of the law. Industry representatives also criticized the legislation, saying that many of the changes were done in a haphazard manner.

CAPITAL PUNISHMENT

The lawful infliction of death as a punishment; the death penalty.

Washington Supreme Court Upholds Indefinite Solitary Confinement for Death Row Inmate

In December 2010, the Washington Supreme Court held that death row prisoners may be held indefinitely in solitary confinement, although they previously had been held in a more relaxed "Special Housing Unit" (SHU) until state budget cuts forced its closure. *In re Pers. Restraint Petition of Gentry*, 245 P.3d 766 (Wash. 2010). The SHU had provided death row inmates with family visits and interaction with other prisoners. Death row inmate Jonathan Gentry had challenged the confinement as an "increase" in severity of punishment and therefore unconstitutional as a form of **ex post facto** punishment.

Gentry, who had a long criminal history, was no stranger to **appellate** challenges. Convicted in 1991 of raping and murdering a 12-year-old girl, he was sentenced to death at that time. In 1995, the Washington Supreme Court upheld his death sentence. Later in 1995, the state high court denied Gentry's request for a hearing on his appeal to overturn his conviction. In 1999, the state high court again upheld his death sentence, stating in part, "Gentry has not provided us any reasons to re-examine issues we previously resolved in

direct review. Moreover, he has not demonstrated the existence of new issues."

In 2009, Gentry again appealed, this time joining two other death row inmates, challenging Washington's three-drug lethal injection protocol for carrying out death sentences as "cruel and unusual punishment" under the Eighth Amendment. After a five-day **bench trial** in Thurston County Superior Court, the trial court upheld the lethal injection protocol, and he appealed that. In 2010, the state high court affirmed and dismissed his case, in part because the main issue was moot: the Washington Department of Corrections had since abandoned the three-drug protocol and adopted a new, one-drug protocol, effective March 2010. *Brown v. Vail, et al.*, 237 P.3d 263 (Wash. 2010). As of 2011, Gentry was the longest-serving death row inmate in the state.

Meanwhile, while the above case was still pending, Gentry initiated the present challenge, arguing that his return to solitary confinement from the previous, less restrictive environment of the SHU housing unit, through no fault of his own, constituted an ex post facto punishment.

Gentry spent his first year of incarceration in solitary confinement in the Washington State Penitentiary's highly restrictive Intensive Management Unit (IMU) (standard practice for death row inmates at that time). Later, based on a good behavior review, he was transferred to the SHU. Among other privileges and benefits granted to SHU inmates, Gentry enjoyed out-of-cell leisure time, daily contact with other inmates, employment as a tier porter, and family contact visits.

In 2008, the Washington Department of Corrections, facing steep budgetary cuts, closed the SHU and returned *all* death row inmates to solitary confinement for the duration of their stays at the prison. Since that time, Gentry's only daily contact has been with prison guards or Department of Corrections personnel.

In its decision upholding the Department of Corrections, the 7-2 majority opinion of the Washington Supreme Court concluded that Gentry's constitutional rights had not been violated by the move. More specifically, the high court held that holding death row inmates in solitary confinement was not an impermissible *ex post facto* increase in the severity of punishment. In rejecting Gentry's petition, the state high court majority opinion stated, in relevant part,

> Mr. Gentry does not challenge his conviction or general confinement to prison as … unlawful. Instead, he claims that his removal from the SHU and placement in the IMU [solitary confinement] has subjected him to more restrictive conditions of confinement in violation of the prohibition on ex post facto punishment. Gentry's claim presupposes a liberty interest in residing in the SHU or in retaining the privileges afforded there. The Washington and United States Constitutions do not create a liberty interest in a particular form of prison housing, absent allegations of **cruel and unusual punishment** in violation of the Eighth Amendment, which Gentry does not assert.

The majority opinion further noted that "a prisoner's participation in good behavior incentive programs, which confer benefits over which the DOC [Department of Corrections] has discretion, can be discontinued by ex post facto changes to prison regulations for valid administrative reasons having nothing to do with an individual prisoner's conduct."

Two justices joined in DISSENT. Justices Debra Stephens and Richard B. Sanders opined that "Gentry raises a significant question" of whether death row inmates face a significantly harsher punishment by the state after their convictions. Moreover, Justice Stephens would have remanded the case to superior court "for a reference hearing to make determinations as to several factual questions that are unanswered here."

CIVIL RIGHTS

Personal liberties that belong to an individual owing to his or her status as a citizen or resident of a particular country or community.

Prosecutor Not Liable for Withholding Evidence From Defendant

Under the federal **statute** 42 U.S.C. § 1983 action, an individual may sue local government officials and the municipality itself for injuries caused by the deprivation of the individual's constitutional rights. The SUPREME COURT has placed limits on municipal liability, requiring a PLAINTIFF to show that a municipal policymaker has acted unconstitutionally. However, the Court has created a narrow exception based on the theory of deliberate indifference. Plaintiffs can prevail if they prove that municipal officials were aware of a constitutional deprivation and failed to train employees to stop the practice. The Court, in *Connick v. Thompson*, 563 U.S. ___ (2011), limited this exception by ruling that a district attorney's office is not liable for failure to train based on a single constitutional violation.

In 1985, John Thompson was charged with the MURDER of a man in New Orleans, Louisiana. Media attention about the murder led the victims of an unrelated armed **robbery** to identify Thompson as their attacker. Harry Connick, the New Orleans District Attorney, charged Thompson with attempted armed ROBBERY. Crime scene investigators took from one of the victims' pants a swatch of fabric stained with the robber's blood. The week before the robbery trial the swatch was sent for testing and two days before trial an assistant district attorney received the crime lab's results that the perpetrator's blood was type B. Prosecutors had not tested Thompson for his blood type and the report was never disclosed to Thompson's lawyer. The PROSECUTOR handling the trial checked out the swatch as part of the physical evidence but never mentioned it or used it at trial. Thompson was convicted of robbery. A few weeks later Thompson was tried for murder. His lawyer did not put Thompson on the WITNESS STAND, fearing that the robbery conviction would be used to discredit his testimony. A jury convicted Thompson of murder and he was sentenced to death.

In 1999, a private investigator for Thompson discovered the crime lab report and had

Thompson tested. His blood type was O, thereby ruling him out as the robber. Thompson's lawyer presented this evidence to the district attorney's office, which moved to stay the execution and vacate the robbery conviction. The Louisiana Court of Appeals reversed the murder conviction, concluding that the robbery conviction unconstitutionally deprived Thompson of his right to testify in his own defense at the murder trial. He was retried in 2003 and acquitted of murder. Thompson then filed a § 1983 action against the district attorney's office, Connick, and others, alleging that their conduct caused him to be wrongfully convicted and incarcerated for 18 years. The only claim that went to trial was that the district attorney's office had violated the Supreme Court ruling that prosecutors must share all evidence that is favorable to the DEFENDANT with the defendant's lawyer. The jury rejected Thompson's claim that an unconstitutional policy in the district attorney's office caused the violation but agreed that Connick had been deliberately indifferent by failing to train the office's prosecutors. The jury awarded Thompson $14 million in damages. Connick appealed the verdict, arguing that at trial there was no evidence of a pattern of similar nondisclosure violations, which he claimed was needed to sustain a failure to train theory of liability. The Fifth **Circuit Court** of Appeals upheld the **district court**.

The Supreme Court, in a 5-4 decision, overturned the appeals court ruling. Justice CLARENCE THOMAS, writing for the majority, noted that deliberate indifference is a "stringent standard of fault, requiring proof that a municipal actor disregarded a known or obvious consequence of his action." A pattern of similar constitutional violations is "ordinarily necessary" to demonstrate deliberate indifference for purposes of failure to train. Decisionmakers need to be on notice of a problem before citing them as deficient in failing to train their subordinates. Thompson had cited four cases in the ten years before the robbery trial where the Louisiana courts had overturned convictions because the New Orleans district attorney's office had failed to disclose evidence favorable to the defendant. Thomas rejected this claim because none of them dealt with the failure to disclose blood evidence, a crime lab report, or physical or SCIENTIFIC EVIDENCE. Therefore, Connick could not have been put on notice that "specific training was necessary to avoid this constitutional violation."

Thompson also relied on the "single-incident" liability that the Court had discussed in a failure to train case. He argued that the violation in his case was the "obvious" consequence of failing to provide training on the need for prosecutors to share evidence favorable to the defendant. Justice Thomas rejected this theory because lawyers, unlike police officers, are "trained in the law and equipped with the tools to interpret and apply legal principles, understand constitutional limits, and exercise legal judgment. They must graduate from law schools and be licensed to practice, and once admitted to the bar they must take CONTINUING LEGAL EDUCATION classes. Therefore, recurring legal violations are not the "obvious consequence" of failing to provide prosecutors with formal in-house training "about how to obey the law." Thompson had failed to show that Connick was on notice that, "absent additional specified training, it was 'highly predictable' that the prosecutors in his office would be confounded by those gray areas and make incorrect" decisions as a result.

Justice RUTH BADER GINSBURG, in a dissenting opinion joined by three other members of the Court, disagreed with the majority's discussion of the conduct of the district attorney's office. Ginsburg found "long-concealed prosecutorial transgressions [that] were neither isolated nor atypical." In her view, Connick and the prosecutors below him misunderstood their duty to disclose favorable evidence and "therefore inadequately attended to their disclosure obligations." This was no "momentary oversight, no single incident of a lone officer's misconduct." Connick had been deliberately indifferent and the city should have been held liable for his actions.

Supreme Court Limits Appeals of Denials of Official Immunity

The SUPREME COURT has provided a qualified IMMUNITY defense for government officials sued for CIVIL RIGHTS violations under the federal civil rights law 42 U.S.C. § 1983. Officials will be immune from such lawsuits if the law they are accused of violating is not clearly established and if the underlying facts are not in dispute. If a government official fails to immediately appeal the denial of qualified immunity, the official will not be able to raise the immunity defense on a direct appeal of an unfavorable verdict. The Supreme Court, in *Ortiz v. Jordan*, __U.S.__, 131 S.Ct. 884 , 178 L.Ed.2d 703 (2011) provided clear guidelines for what a DEFENDANT must do to be able to raise an immunity defense on direct appeal.

Michelle Ortiz, a former inmate at the Ohio Reformatory for Women, filed a § 1983 lawsuit in federal court, alleging that a male prison guard had sexually assaulted her on two consecutive nights, and that two prison officials had failed to protect her. (The prison guard had left state employment and could not be found.) The day after the first ASSAULT Ortiz reported the matter to her case manager, Paula Jordan. Jordan told Ortiz that the guard had been reassigned to another correctional facility and was serving his last day at the reformatory. In light of this fact, Jordan suggested that Ortiz not file a written complaint. Jordan wrote an incident report that stated Ortiz had refused to name her assailant or provide any other information about the assault. Jordan did not immediately notify her superiors of the assault and did not file the report for two days. That night the guard assaulted Ortiz again in her cell. Rebecca Bright, a prison investigator, looked into the two assaults. During the investigation she placed Ortiz in solitary confinement. Ortiz maintained that Bright isolated her in retaliation for her accusations against the guard. Bright, however, stated that she segregated Ortiz because Ortiz disobeyed her order not to discuss the incidents with other prisoners.

Ortiz claimed that Jordan did nothing to ward off Schultz's second sexual assault, despite Jordan's awareness of the substantial risk of that occurrence. Bright, Ortiz charged, retaliated against her because she resisted Bright's efforts to induce her to retract her accounts of the guard's assaults. Jordan and Bright moved for **summary judgment** based on qualified immunity. The **district court** denied their motions, ruling that the qualified immunity defense turned on multiple factual disputes over Ortiz's claims. They did not file **interlocutory** appeals of this ruling and the case proceeded to trial. The jury returned a verdict of $350,000 in compensatory and **punitive damages** against Jordan and $275,000 in damages against Bright. The defendants did not file post-trial motions under Rule 50 of the Federal Rules of

Civil Procedure in which they could have asked for judgment in their favor as a MATTER OF LAW. Instead, they appealed the verdicts to the Sixth **Circuit Court** of Appeals, raising the denial of their pretrial motion for summary judgments for the first time.

The Sixth Circuit noted that appeals courts "normally do not review the denial of a SUMMARY JUDGMENT motion after a trial on the merits." However, the court concluded," denial of summary judgment based on qualified immunity is an exception to this rule." The court then ruled that both defendants were entitled to summary judgment and reversed the judgment below. The Supreme Court agreed to hear Ortiz's case because the circuit courts of appeals were split over the question of whether a party may appeal an order denying judgment after a full trial on the merits.

The Supreme Court ruled that the defendants could not appeal the issue. The Court concluded that such an order "retains its INTERLOCUTORY character as simply a step along the route to final judgment. Once the case proceeds to trial, the full record developed in court supersedes the record existing at the time of the summary judgment motion." One problem with the Sixth Circuit analysis was that it was based on evidence introduced at trial, not on the ruling by the trial judge before trial. However, the appeals court's "judgment was infirm" because the defendants failed to renew their motion for judgment as a matter of law under Federal Rule of CIVIL PROCEDURE 50(b). By not doing so, the appeals court had no authority to reject the appraisal of the evidence by "the judge who saw and heard the witnesses and ha[d] the feel of the case which no **appellate** printed transcript can impart."

The Court noted the contours of qualified immunity motions in the first stages of LITIGATION. Interlocutory appeals of denials of summary judgment are available when the appeal presents a "purely legal issue," which goes to the determination of what law was "'clearly established" at the time the defendant acted. Immediate appeal is not available when the district court determines that there are factual issues genuinely in dispute. In this case the Court found it understandable that Jordan and Bright did not seek immediate appeal of the denial order, as the court had based its decision on factual disagreements. However, the defendants did not seek relief after the verdict with Rule 50(b), which permits the **entry of judgment** for the verdict loser if the court finds that the evidence was legally insufficient to sustain the verdict. The failure to seek this relief meant that the Sixth Circuit was powerless to review the sufficiency of the evidence on appeal.

Jordan and Bright tried to avoid this jurisdictional roadblock by insisting that a qualified immunity plea raising an issue of a "purely legal nature" is preserved for appeal by an unsuccessful motion for summary judgment. There was no need not be brought up again under Rule 50(b). They contended that a purely legal issue could be resolved with reference only to undisputed facts. The Court refused to address this argument, finding that their claims of qualified immunity hardly present "purely legal" issues capable of resolution "with reference only to undisputed facts." The only type of cases that fit this approach "typically involve contests not about what occurred, or why an action was taken or omitted, but disputes about the substance and clarity of pre-existing law."

The Court noted that the pre-existing law was not in dispute. Under its precedents the Court had established that prison officials could be held liable for "deliberate indifference" to a prisoner's EIGHTH AMENDMENT right to protection against violence while in CUSTODY if the official knows the inmate faces substantial "risk of serious harm and disregards that risk by failing to take reasonable measures to abate it." The only matter in dispute was whether the facts proved that Jordan and Bright's actions had "crossed the constitutional line." There were numerous disputed facts that were relevant to the decision whether qualified immunity should be granted. Therefore, the qualified immunity defenses raised by the pair were not "neat abstract issues of law."

CLASS ACTION

A lawsuit that allows a large number of people with a common interest in a matter to sue or be sued as a group.

Settlement in USDA v. Native American Farmers Case

On October 19, 2010, the U.S. DEPARTMENT OF AGRICULTURE (USDA) announced the settlement of the 1999 **class action** case of *Marilyn KeepsEagle v. Vilsack*, No. 99-3119 (D.D.C.).

Agricultural Secretary Tom Vilsack and U.S. Attorney General ERIC HOLDER jointly announced the settlement, which ended years of LITIGATION over alleged discriminatory treatment of Native American farmers and ranchers who applied for USDA loans. The certified class covered claimants during the period from 1981 to 1999. The total value of the settlement was $760 million ($680 million in compensation and another $80 million in debt forgiveness) plus the inclusion of several non-pecuniary provisions.

The original plaintiffs were Marilyn and George Keepseagle, a Sioux couple from Fort Yates, North Dakota, who filed their lawsuit on November 24, 1999. Unable to make payments on their USDA loan, they sold 380 acres of their land in order to avoid **foreclosure**, then filed suit alleging that the USDA refused to renegotiate their loan based on their ancestry, while Caucasian farmers and ranchers enjoyed easy approval. They were joined in suit by approximately 900 Native Americans, but the certified class ultimately included several thousand persons who were allegedly denied credit during 1981 to 1999.

For years, settlement negotiations stalled on two fronts: money demands and insufficient evidence to support claims of class DISCRIMINATION. Ultimately, the final settlement agreement provided two tracks for claim reimbursement. Under the first track, persons who met the class definition and provided substantial evidence of discrimination to an impartial adjudicator would receive a uniform settlement amount of up to $50,000. For those persons who met the class definition and believed they had stronger evidence of economic loss caused by alleged discrimination, a second track would provide for damages up to $250,000 per individual. Actual monetary awards were subject to reduction, based on the total number of meritorious claims and the amount of available funding. A total of $680 million was to be placed in The Judgment Fund, maintained by the U.S. Departments of Justice and Treasury, for the payment of any monetary awards under the settlement. The USDA was to provide an additional $20 million to administer the settlement.

In addition to the monetary awards, the settlement provided for up to $80 million in debt forgiveness to successful claimants with outstanding USDA Farm Loan debts. Settlement terms also included a MORATORIUM on foreclosures for most claimants' farms, and a moratorium on loan accelerations. Administrative offsets of class members' farm loan accounts were to be established until qualifying claimants completed the claims process or the Secretary of Agriculture had been notified that a claim had been denied.

Terms of the settlement provided for other relief as well. Several programs designed to assist Native American farmers and ranchers were created, including a new 15-member Federal Advisory Council which will include Native American representation from around the country (at least ten members who are Native American or represent their interests, as well as four senior USDA officials). A new Ombudsman post was to be established to address farm program issues. The USDA further agreed to offer enhanced technical assistance services through an established network of 10 to 15 regional offices, providing intensive instruction to recipients regarding financial, business, and marketing planning skills. It also will support the placement of tribal agricultural advocates and **third party** outreach personnel as well as education providers.

After approval by the U.S. **District Court** for the District of Columbia, settlement payments were scheduled for distribution in late 2011 and early 2012.

Despite settling this lawsuit, the USDA still faced additional CLASS ACTION suits involving alleged discrimination against other class populations. One widely-publicized case involved African-American farmers, *Pigford v. Glickman.* The lead PLAINTIFF in that class action, North Carolina farmer Timothy Pigford, had his original case dismissed with prejudice. However, the case attracted thousands of new plaintiffs who were able to gain class action status and **mediation** rights (Pigford II). All was settled in February 2010 for close to $1.3 billion; still pending was additional Congressional APPROPRIATION of funds to cover the settlements. Also still pending was the class action case of *Garcia v. Vilsack,* involving alleged discrimination against Hispanic farmers, and *Love v. Vilsack,* involving female farmers and ranchers.

Secretary Vilsack commented that "[t]he Obama administration is committed to closing this chapter on an unfortunate CIVIL RIGHTS history at USDA and working to ensure our customers and employees are treated justly and equally."

Smith v. Bayer Corporation

Federal courts are generally hesitant to interfere with state-court proceedings. Under the federal Anti-Injunction Act, 28 U.S.C. § 2283, a federal court generally cannot meddle with state proceedings, though the **statute** allows a federal court to issue an INJUNCTION if it is necessary to "protect or effective its judgments." Courts have narrowly construed this provision, but in a class-action suit involving a cholesterol-reducing drug, the Eighth **Circuit Court** of Appeals enjoined a state court in West Virginia from certifying a class after the federal court had denied a class that had brought a similar claim. However, the U.S. SUPREME COURT disagreed with the Eighth Circuit, concluding in a unanimous decision that the district court's injunction was improper. *Smith v. Bayer Corp.*, No. 09-1205, 2011 WL 2369357 (U.S. June 16, 2011).

The Bayer Corporation distributed a product known as Baycol from 1997 to 2001. The drug was later linked to 31 deaths in the United States, and the company withdrew the drug as a result. Since the drug's withdrawal, tens of thousands of individuals have filed lawsuits against Bayer. The Judicial Panel on MULTIDISTRICT LITIGATION ultimately consolidated the federal cases in the U.S. **District Court** for the District of Minnesota.

One of the plaintiffs who brought a claim was George McCollins, who initially brought the case in state court. Bayer removed the case to federal court based on diversity grounds, and the case was later transferred to the District of Minnesota. However, McCollins was the only remaining class representative by 2008. He claim was not based on side effects caused by the drug, given that he had actually experienced benefits from taking the drug. Instead, he sued Bayer under the West Virginia **Consumer Credit** and Protection Act, W. Va. Code § 46A-6-101, alleging that Bayer had committed breach of WARRANTY that caused him economic loss.

Two other plaintiffs—Keith Smith and Shirley Sperlazza—brought a similar **class action** in state court in 2001. Under the federal law at the time, a one-year **statute of**

limitations to remove the action expired, and the claims remained in state court. Thus, while McCollins' CLASS ACTION ended up in federal district court in Minnesota, Smith and Sperlazza's class action remained in a West Virginia state court.

In 2003, the district court in Minnesota denied certification of a nationwide refund class for the drug. After this denial, Bayer moved for the court to deny class certification to the economic class that McCollins proposed. Bayer also moved for **summary judgment** on McCollins' individual claim. The court agreed with Bayer on both motions, concluding that the class certification was improper for reasons similar to those in the court's 2003 decision.

Smith and Sperlazza then moved for the West Virginia state court to certify their economic loss class. The proposed class in the state court proceeding based its claims on a similar economic loss argument as the McCollins' class, and Bayer moved for the district court to enjoin Smith and Sperlazza from relitigating the district court's decision that applied to McCollins. The district court granted the injunction.

Smith and Sperlazza appealed to the Eighth Circuit Court of Appeals. A panel of the court reviewed the Anti-Injunction Act, 28 U.S.C. § 2283, which prohibits a federal court from interfering in a state-court proceeding but allows the court to enjoin a case in state court if the injunction is necessary to "protect or effectuate its judgment." Although the Act's exception has been narrowly construed, the Eighth Circuit panel noted that the district court's injunction could be proper if the doctrine of **collateral estoppel** would bar Smith and Sperlazza from certifying their class in state court. The court reviewed their claims in light of West Virginia's collateral-estoppel requirement, and the court concluded that the doctrine precluded Smith and Sperlazza from relitigating the same issue. Thus, the court thus held that the district court's injunction was proper. *In re Baycol Prods.* LITIGATION,, 593 F.3d 716 (8th Cir. 2010).

The Supreme Court agreed to review the Eighth Circuit's decision, and in a unanimous decision, the Court reversed the panel. Writing for the majority, Justice Elena Kagan focused on the text and application of the Anti-Injunction Act. Noting that federal courts must construe the Act narrowly, Kagan stressed that two conditions had to be satisfied for the federal court's action to preclude the state court's class certification. First, the issue presented to the state **tribunal** must be the same as the one presented to the federal tribunal. And second, the class representative must have been a party in the federal court, unless one of a few narrow exceptions apply.

Kagan first disagreed with the Eighth Circuit panel that the issue in the federal court was the same as the one presented in state court. The federal court had adjudicated its claim based on the Federal Rules of **Civil Procedure**, while Smith and Sperlazza's certification was based on the West Virginia Rules of CIVIL PROCEDURE. Although the rules are similar, West Virginia courts do not apply the state rule identically to the way that federal courts apply the corresponding federal rule, so the issue in the two cases necessarily differed. Kagan also noted that Smith and Sperlazza were not parties to the federal action, and no exception to this requirement applied. Accordingly, Kagan and the majority reversed the Eighth Circuit's decision.

When she issued the opinion, Kagan joked, "This decision involves a very complex procedural issue. And if you understand anything I say here, you will likely be a lawyer, and you will have had your morning cup of coffee." The comment marked one of several instances in which the newest Supreme Court justice has found an opportunity to make a light-hearted joke.

Wal-Mart Stores v. Dukes

In the landmark case of *Wal-Mart Stores Inc. v. Dukes,* No. 10-277, 564 U.S. ___ (2011) the U.S. SUPREME COURT disallowed the continuation of the class-action certification of approximately 1.5 million current and former female employees of retail giant Wal-Mart Stores who had alleged gender-based DISCRIMINATION. The gist of the complaint was that pay and promotions were exercised disproportionately in favor of men, constituting unlawful DISPARATE IMPACT under Title VII of the CIVIL RIGHTS Act of 1964 42 U.S.C. § 2000e-2(k). The proposed PLAINTIFF class would have made this the largest employment discrimination lawsuit in U.S. history.

Wal-Mart employee Betty Dukes listens in her attorneys office in Berkeley, California. Dukes was involved in a sex discrimination lawsuit against Wal-Mart blocked by the Supreme Court.
AP IMAGES/PAUL SAKUMA

Wal-Mart is the country's largest employer, nationally operating four different types of retail stores: discount stores, super-centers, neighborhood markets, and Sam's Clubs. Importantly, employment decisions, including hiring, firing, pay, and promotions are handled by local managers, who also may increase hourly wages (within limits) with only limited corporate oversight. Wal-Mart also delegates to local managers the discretion to apply their own subjective criteria when selecting candidates for "support managers," (the first step toward management). However, getting into Wal-Mart's management training program involves company-wide objective criteria (i.e., above-average performance ratings, at least one year in current position, willingness to relocate, etc.). Beyond this, regional and district managers may use their own judgment when selecting candidates for management training.

The three plaintiffs selected by plaintiffs' counsel as representative of the plaintiff class alleged that a culture of gender bias existed at the corporate level of Wal-Mart, which in turn trickled down and manifested in discriminatory pay and promotion decisions by local managers in Wal-Mart stores throughout the country. Without opinion or ruling on the merits of individual plaintiffs' claims of discrimination, the Supreme Court held that all proposed plaintiffs could not be united in a single **class action** because they had not produced sufficient evidence indicating a company-wide discriminatory pay and promotion policy.

In finding the plaintiff class untenable to continue as a whole, the 5-4 majority opinion of the Court, delivered by Justice Scalia, held that Federal Rule of **Civil Procedure** 23(a) requires that a party seeking class certification prove that the class has common "questions of law or fact." Questions common to the class, sufficient to allow CLASS ACTION certification, must relate not only to the same alleged violation of law, but importantly, must relate to the same injury "of such a nature that determination of its truth or falsity will resolve an issue to the validity of each one of the claims in one stroke." Here, the court found, an estimated 1.5 million female plaintiffs could not possibly have suffered the same injury.

Quoting a lower court, the Supreme Court found that plaintiff class members

> held a multitude of different jobs, at different levels of Wal-Mart's hierarchy, for variable lengths of time, in 3,400 stores, sprinkled across 50 states, with a kaleidoscope of supervisors (male and female), subject to a variety of regional policies that all differed... Some thrived while some did poorly. They have little in common but their sex and this lawsuit.

Even the three representative plaintiffs of the class had alleged different forms of discrimination. Plaintiff Betty Dukes started as a cashier at a Wal-Mart store in California in 1994. She later sought and received a promotion to customer service manager. However, after a series of disciplinary actions, she was demoted back to cashier and then to store greeter. She acknowledged that she had violated company policy, but claimed the disciplinary actions were taken in retaliation for her having invoked internal complaint procedures. She additionally alleged that male employees had not been disciplined for similar violations. Finally, she alleged that two male greeters in her store were paid more than she was.

Fellow plaintiff Christine Kwapnoski worked at Sam's Club stores in Missouri and California for many years, holding several different positions, including a supervisory one. She alleged that a male manager yelled at her frequently and screamed at female employees, but not at men. She further alleged that the same manager "told her to 'doll up,' to wear some makeup, and to dress a little better."

The third-named representative plaintiff, Edith Arena, worked at a Wal-Mart store in Duarte, California from 1995 to 2001. She alleged that on 2000 she approached management on more than one occasion to see if she could get some management training, but was brushed off. She alleged the reason for the brush-off was gender. When she initiated internal complaint procedures, she was told to contact the district manager directly if she thought her store manager was being unfair. However, she decided not to do that and never applied for management training again. In 2001, she was fired for failure to comply with Wal-Mart's timekeeping policy.

Although different in factual scenarios, the plaintiffs claimed that the discrimination was common to *all* female Wal-Mart employees through an alleged "corporate culture" that permitted bias against women to permeate, perhaps even subconsciously, the discretionary decision-making of thousands of individual managers in individual Wal-Mart stores across the country. According to plaintiffs, this made every female employee a victim of a singular, common, and discriminatory employment practice. They, therefore, wanted to join all female employees at Wal-Mart stores in a nationwide class action. They wanted declaratory and injunctive relief as well as monetary damages and other forms of **reparation**.

The federal **district court** had certified them as a class, finding that Rule 23(a)'s "commonality" requirement had been satisfied. Moreover, the court found that the class action met Rule 23(b)(2)'s requirement of showing that "the party opposing the class has acted or refused to act on grounds that apply generally to the class, so that final injunctive relief or corresponding declaratory relief is appropriate respecting the class as a whole."

The Ninth Circuit substantially agreed that the commonality requirement of Rule 23(a) was met. It also held that the plaintiffs' back pay claims, even though they did not constitute "injunctive or declaratory relief," could nonetheless be certified as part of a Rule 23(b)(2) class because those claims did not predominate over the declaratory and injunctive relief requests. Finally, it found that a class action would not deprive Wal-Mart of its right to present **statutory** defenses if the district court selected a random set of claims for valuation, then extrapolated the validity and value of the remaining claims in the class from the sample set.

But the Supreme Court reversed. The crux of a Title VII claim, said the Court, focuses on the reason behind an adverse employment decision. Here, plaintiffs wished to represent hundreds of thousands of female Wal-Mart employees, both current and former employees, some promoted and some demoted, some disciplined and some receiving awards, some receiving discipline or awards from male supervisors, some from female supervisors. Without some glue holding together the alleged reasons for those employment decisions, said the Court, it will be impossible to say that examination of all the class members' claims would produce a common answer to that crucial question of alleged discrimination. The Court also found that back pay claims, i.e., monetary relief, were improperly certified under Rule 23(b)(2) because those requests were more than incidental to the requested injunctive or declaratory relief.

Justice Scalia delivered the opinion of the majority, joined by Chief Justice Roberts and Justices Kennedy, Thomas, and Alito. The other four justices (Breyer, Sotomayor, and Kagan, led by Justice Ginsburg), concurred on the finding of improper 23(b)(2) certification, but dissented that "the Court … disqualifies the class at the starting gate, holding that the plaintiffs cannot cross the 'commonality' line set by Rule 23(a)(2)." The DISSENT opined that the majority was thus "import[ing] into the Rule 23(a) determination concerns properly addressed in a Rule 23(b)(3) assessment."

CONSUMER PROTECTION

Consumer protection laws are federal and state statutes governing sales and credit practices involving consumer goods. Such statues prohibit and regulate deceptive or unconscionable advertising and sales practices, product quality, credit financing and reporting, debt collection, leases and other aspects of consumer transactions.

Chase Bank USA v. McCoy

The question before the U.S. SUPREME COURT in the **class action** case of *Chase Bank USA v.*

McCoy, No. 09-329, 131 S.Ct. 871, 562 U.S. ___ (2011) related to interpretation of a FEDERAL RESERVE BOARD regulation affecting when a creditor seeking to raise interest rates on a credit card, following default by the cardholder, must provide the cardholder with a "change in terms" notice.

At issue was Regulation Z, promulgated by the Board pursuant to its authority under the TRUTH IN LENDING ACT, 15 U.S.C. § 1601 *et seq.* Under the version of Regulation Z in effect at the time this dispute arose (the regulation was amended in 2009, see below), credit card issuers were obliged to provide cardholders with an "[i]nitial disclosure statement" specifying "each periodic rate that may be used to compute the finance charge." 12 CFR § 226.6. Subsequent disclosure requirements applied whenever "any term required to be disclosed under § 226.6 is changed." Further, when "a periodic rate or other **finance charge** is increased because of the consumer's delinquency or default," notice must be given "before the effective date of the change."

At the time suit was filed in California federal **district court**, McCoy, individually and on behalf of all others similarly situated, was the holder of a credit card issued by Chase Bank. His cardholder agreement with Chase specified his qualifications for "preferred rates" as long as he met certain conditions. If the conditions were not met, Chase reserved the right to raise the interest rate (up to a specified maximum) and to apply the new rate to both existing and new balances.

McCoy did not deny delinquency or default. Instead, his suit alleged that Chase increased his interest rate and applied it retroactively. McCoy argued that this action violated Regulation Z, as Chase had not notified him of the increase until after it had taken effect.

The district court dismissed the complaint, finding that an interest rate increase did not constitute a "change in terms" under § 226.6(9)(c). Therefore, Chase need not notify him in **advance** of its effective date. The Ninth **Circuit Court** of Appeals did not agree and reversed.

An unanimous U.S. Supreme Court reversed the Ninth Circuit and remanded the case. Justice SONIA SOTOMAYOR delivered the opinion of the Court in a 20-page decision, holding that the version of Regulation Z in effect at the time of, and therefore applicable to, this case did not require such advance notice.

The Court did find ambiguity in the text of Regulation Z, necessitating the Court's review of the Board's own interpretation of its text. The Court has historically deferred to an agency's interpretation of its own regulations, absent a finding that such an interpretation was "plainly erroneous or inconsistent with the regulation." *Auer v. Robbins*, 519 U.S. 452, 117 S. Ct. 905, 137 L. Ed. 2d 79 (1997). In this case, the Court accepted the agency's (Federal Reserve Board) interpretation of Regulation Z as advanced in its legal brief, finding that it was "in no sense a *post hoc* rationalization advanced by an agency seeking to defend past agency action against attack" (quoting from *Auer*). Further, there was "no reason to suspect that the interpretation [did] not reflect the agency's fair and considered judgment on the matter in question" (again (quoting from *Auer*). Here, the agency was not a party to the suit, so there was no reason to believe that its explanation was postured as a LITIGATION defense position, and therefore it was entitled to deference.

McCoy had argued that deference given to a legal brief was inappropriate because the regulation's interpretation in the Official Staff Commentary commanded a different result. However, the Court found that the relevant portion of the Commentary explaining the requirements at issue herein largely replicated the ambiguity found in the regulatory text. Therefore, there was no reason to disregard the interpretation advanced by the agency in its brief.

Congress, prior to the decision in this case, held a different view. Pursuant thereto, in 2009, the Federal Reserve Board implemented new regulations requiring credit card companies to provide 45 days notice for rate increases that were increased due to delinquency or default. This effectively rendered moot the issue presented in *McCoy*, but disposed of the potential claims of an entire class of litigants joined in the CLASS ACTION, who were cardholders with similar situations.

CONTRACT

Agreements between two or more persons that create an obligation to do, or refrain from doing, a particular thing.

Local Government Cannot Sue Drug Manufacturers for Overcharging

Some federal laws involving government programs permit private rights of action. This means a person or **entity** may sue in court, alleging a violation of the law by the party benefiting from the government program. However, if the law explicitly denies private rights of action, there may be no legal recourse. A California county sought to avoid this outcome by suing a drug manufacturer for violating the terms of the contract it signed with the federal government to sell drugs to public health entities. The SUPREME COURT, in *Astra USA, Inc. v. Santa Clara County, California*, 131 S. Ct. 1342 (2011), ruled that the county could not sue to enforce the contract.

The federal government established the **Medicaid** Drug Rebate Program in 1990. It now covers a significant portion of drug purchases in the United States. To receive payment under MEDICAID for covered drugs, drug maker must sign a standardized agreement with the DEPARTMENT OF HEALTH AND HUMAN SERVICES (HHS). The agreement commits the drug maker to provide rebates to states on their Medicaid drug purchases. The amount of the rebates depends upon the manufacturers "average" and "best" prices, as defined by law and regulation. This calculation is complex and requires HHS to examine detailed information about the company's sales and pricing. HHS, with few exceptions, may not disclose the submitted information in a form that discloses the identity of the specific manufacturer or the prices charged for drugs by the drug maker.

In 1992 Congress amended the drug rebate law to require drug makers participating in Medicaid to offer discounted drugs to local facilities that provide medical care for the poor. This new initiative, known as § 340B, employed a form contract like the Medicaid rebate program. In these contracts the drug makers agree to charge covered entities no more than predetermined ceiling prices, derived from the "average" and "best" prices and rebates calculated under the Medicaid Drug Rebate Program. If a manufacturer overcharges a covered entity, the federal government may terminate the drug maker's contract. The government used informal procedures to handle overcharge complaints but the 2010 Patient Protection and Affordable Care Act directs the Secretary of HHS to develop formal procedures. These procedures, which are not yet in place, will result in decisions that are subject to **judicial review**. The new law also authorizes compensation awards to overcharged entities.

Santa Clara County, California did not have the benefit of these legislative reforms when it sued Astra USA, Inc. and eight other drug manufacturers for allegedly overcharging 340B health care facilities in violation of their contracts with HHS. The county framed the lawsuit as a **class action** on behalf of the 340B entities in California and the counties that fund them. It claimed the federal contract sought to protect these third-party beneficiaries. The county sought **compensatory damages** for the drug makers' breach of contract. The federal **district court** dismissed the lawsuit, finding that the pricing contracts gave no enforceable rights to 340B entities. The Ninth **Circuit Court** of Appeals reversed the district court, ruling that although covered entities had no right to sue under the **statute**, the county could maintain the action as third-party beneficiaries of the pricing agreements between the drug makers and HHS.

The Supreme Court, in a unanimous decision (Justice Elena Kagan did not participate), overturned the Ninth Circuit ruling. Justice RUTH BADER GINSBURG, writing for the Court, noted that county agreed that it had no right to private action under the rebate program statute. Therefore, the only issue was whether the county, as a third-party BENEFICIARY under the pricing agreement, had the right to enforce the contract. A non-party becomes legally entitled to a benefit promised in the contract only if the contracting parties so intend. The county argued that the agreements specifically named the covered entities as recipients of discounted drugs. The object of the agreements was to ensure that these entities would be charged no more than the ceiling price. Therefore, the intended recipients acquired a right to the benefit enforceable under federal **common law**.

Justice Ginsburg countered that the county had overlooked the fact that the pricing agreements simply incorporated **statutory** obligations and recorded the makers' agreement to abide by them. These were form agreements, written by HHS, which contained no negotiable terms. Therefore, the county was "in essence" trying to enforce the statute itself. To allow a private **right of action** through a contract lawsuit would negate the intent of Congress not to allow private enforcement actions. The statutory and contractual obligations were one and the same. Justice Ginsburg found telling the fact the county based its suit on allegations that the drug makers charged more than the 340B ceiling price, not that they violated "any independent substantive obligation" arising from the pricing agreements.

The Ninth Circuit had concluded that allowing the county to sue would "spread the enforcement burden instead of placing it [entirely] on the government." The Supreme Court found this unacceptable because that was "hardly what Congress contemplated" when it placed centralized enforcement with HHS. Justice Ginsburg found that third-party suits would undermine the government's efforts to enforce Medicaid and 340B "harmoniously and on a uniform, nationwide basis." She also emphasized the confidentiality of pricing information. If Congress meant to allow third-party beneficiary suits "it would not have barred the potential suitors from obtaining the very information necessary to determine whether their asserted rights have been violated." Though the Court acknowledged that the government had not had effective mechanisms and authority to police pricing practices, the 2010 healthcare reform act had corrected this deficiency.

General Dynamics Corp. v. United States

In 2011, the U.S. SUPREME COURT involved itself in a longstanding dispute between the United States Government and defense contractors that had been hired to construct a stealth aircraft. With Justice ANTONIN SCALIA noting that "[n]either side will be entirely happy with the resolution we reach today," the Court ruled that the contractors did not have to return the money the government paid up front. However, the Court refused to reinstate a $1.2 billion damages award from the Court of Federal Claims.

With the decision in *General Dynamics Corp. v. United States*, 131 S. Ct. 1900 (2011), the Court ended a saga that involved nearly 20 years of LITIGATION. The Federal **Circuit Court** of Appeals, which had ruled in the

government's favor, referred to the case as the "American version of *Jarndyce and Jarndyce*," the fictional court case by Charles Dickens that often serves as an adage for unending litigation.

In 1988, the Navy entered into fixed-price contract with several defense contractors to develop the A-12 stealth aircraft. The ceiling price for the contract was set at just under $4.8 billion. The contract called for the contractors to design, manufacture, and test a total of eight A-12 prototypes, with the first delivery during June 1990. The contractors agreed to complete their testing by April 1993, and the contractors would provide training support for three years thereafter.

However, the contractors ran into trouble from the outset. The contractors could not meet the schedule called for in the contract so that by the time of the first scheduled flight date in June 1990, the contractors informed the Navy that the work would be delayed by 12 to 14 months. Moreover, the contractors told the Navy that the costs would greatly exceed the $4.8 billion ceiling. When the contractors missed the first flight date, the Navy unilaterally modified the contract to change the delivery dates.

Even with the modified delivery dates, the contractors continued to have problems. After several delays, the contractors were spending up to $150 million of their own money each month to try to complete the project on schedule. The contractors finally submitted a formal request to the Navy asking to restructure the contract so that the contractors could receive cost-reimbursement. Officials with the U.S. government met with representatives of the contractors several times in late 1990, and the government informed the contractors that the work had been unsatisfactory.

The parties attempted to negotiate for nearly a month. During this time, then-Secretary of Defense Dick Cheney directed the Secretary of the Navy to SHOW CAUSE why the government should not terminate the contract. The contractors admitted to the delays but denied that they were in default on the contract, arguing that the original contractual dates were based on false assumptions. On January 7, 1991, the contracting officer with the Navy formally notified the contractors that the government was terminating the agreement. A few weeks after the termination, the government demanded that the contractors return

$1.35 billion that had already been paid as progress payments.

The contractors originally brought suit in June 1991 in the Court of Federal Claims. The claims were based on the Contract Disputes Act, 41 U.S.C. § 609(a). The contractors requested several remedies, including damages for breach of contract, costs and a reasonable profit under the contract, and a denial of the government's demand that the contractors return the progress payments.

The parties litigated the case for several years before the Court of Federal Claims ruled that the government's termination based on default was invalid. The court determined that Cheney had effectively forced the Navy to terminate the contract, so the Navy did not exercise "reasoned discretion" before the termination. The court denied the government's request for $1.35 billion in progress payments and awarded to the contractors $1.2 billion in damages.

The government appealed the decision to the Federal Circuit Court of Appeals, and during the next several years, the parties went through several rounds in both the Court of Federal Claims and the Federal Circuit. One of the contractor's arguments was that the contractor's alleged default was excused because the government had failed to share its "superior knowledge" about the design and manufacture of stealth aircraft. Some military secrets were disclosed during the discovery phase of the trial, but the acting Secretary of the Air Force stepped in and informed the Court of Federal Claims that further discovery would risk the disclosure of classified information. The Court of Federal Claims eventually determined that the contractors had defaulted on the contract and that the contractors could not rely on the superior-knowledge defense because the government could assert the privilege of protecting state secrets. In 2009, the Federal Circuit affirmed the latest Court of Federal Claims' decision.

In a unanimous decision, the Supreme Court vacated the Federal Circuit's decision. Writing for the Court, Justice Antonin Scalia noted that the government is entitled to a privilege that prevent a court from ordering the disclosure of state and military secrets. When the government is entitled to the privilege of not disclosing state secrets, issues presented that involve those secrets are nonjusticiable, meaning the Court could not resolve them.

The lower courts in this case had allowed the government's claim for default but denied the contractor's the ability to raise the superior-knowledge defense. The Court concluded that those courts had erred in doing so. According to Scalia's opinion, the lower courts should not have allowed the government's default claim to proceed while refusing to consider the contractor's defense on the grounds of privilege.

The Court concluded that the best solution would be to put the parties in the position they were in on the day that the contractors filed suit. In other words, the government could not recover the amounts it had paid up through June 1991, but the contractors also could not recover the Court of Federal Claims' original award. The Court therefore vacated the Federal Circuit's opinion and remanded the case for the lower court to determine whether the government had an obligation to share its superior knowledge.

COURTS
Judicial tribunals established to administer justice.

Federal Judiciary Approve Cameras in the Courtroom Pilot Program

Although 46 of the 50s states permit cameras in trial courtrooms, the federal judiciary has been adamant in their opposition to televising or video recording of proceedings. However, pressure from Congress lead in part to the U.S. Judicial Conference authorizing in September 2010, a three-year pilot program that will allow federal **district court** judges to install video cameras in their courtrooms and record civil proceedings. The details of the program have yet to have been released, but it is clear the test will be limited in scope and subject to failure if parties or judges decline to participate. Members of the SENATE ignored the pilot program and introduced the Sunshine in the Courtroom Act, which passed its first legislative hurdle in April 2011. The bill seeks to give federal district court judges the discretion to invite the electronic media into the courtroom.

Electronic media coverage of criminal proceedings in **federal courts** has been expressly prohibited under Federal Rule of **Criminal Procedure** since the ADOPTION of the criminal rules in 1946. This prohibition stemmed from the circus-like atmosphere surrounding the Lindbergh baby KIDNAPPING trial of the mid-1930s, where newsreel and still photographers captured the proceedings on a day-by-day basis. The U.S. Judicial Conference, which is lead by the Chief Justice and is comprised of federal appeals and district court chief judges, reaffirmed this prohibition in 1972, banning photographs and television cameras from all federal courts. Since the 1970s, however, most states permit the televising or recording of trial proceedings, criminal and civil, under certain conditions. This has made the federal courts opposition more conspicuous.

In 1990, the 27-member Judicial Conference authorized started a three-year pilot program permitting electronic media in civil proceedings in six district courts and two appeals courts. The study by the FEDERAL JUDICIAL CENTER found that the program had worked well but the conference voted by a slim margin in 1996 to permit each of the federal courts of appeals to "decide for itself whether to permit the taking of photographs and radio and television coverage of **appellate** arguments." The Second and Ninth Circuit Courts of Appeals were the only two circuits to permit electronic coverage of APPELLATE proceedings.

The cameras in the courtroom issue reappeared in January 2010, when U.S. District Judge Vaughn Walker proposed to allow broadcasts of the trial concerning the constitutionality of California's Proposition 8 which banned same-sex marriage. Walker proposed close-circuit telecasting to audiences in five federal courthouses around the country and suggested that he might post the video on YouTube. The Ninth Circuit began modifying its rules on cameras in December 2009 and Walker announced his decision in early January. The proponents of Proposition 8 objected and sought a stay from the U.S. SUPREME COURT. Seven days later the Court issued a 5-4 decision granting the stay. The Court, in an unsigned opinion, stated that the Ninth Circuit and Walker had not followed proper procedures in changing the cameras in the courtroom rules and had failed to give the public sufficient time to file comments on the changes. The majority made clear that it was "not expressing any view on whether such trials should be broadcast."

Justice STEPHEN BREYER, in a dissenting opinion joined by Justices RUTH BADER GINSBURG, SONIA SOTOMAYOR, and Elena Kagan, rejected the argument by Proposition 8 supporters that televising the proceedings would subject their witnesses to harassment, economic reprisals, and possibly physical violence. Justice Breyer noted that the witnesses had not asked the court to intervene. "All of the witnesses supporting the applicants are already publicly identified with their cause," he wrote. "They are all experts or advocates who have either already appeared on television or Internet broadcasts, already toured the state advocating a 'yes' vote on Proposition 8, or already engaged in extensive public commentary far more likely to make them well known than a closed-circuit broadcast to another federal courthouse."

In September 2010, the Judicial Conference approved a three-year cameras in the courtroom pilot project. The pilot is national in scope and will be used to evaluate the effect of cameras in district court courtrooms, video recordings of the proceedings, and publication of these video recordings. The details of the project will be developed and implemented by the conference's Committee on Court Administration and Case Management. The courts that take part will amend local rules to provide an exception for judges participating in the pilot. Judges will have discretion when to use video, which will be produced by cameras installed by the courts. Recordings by the news media will not be permitted, recordings of members of a jury will not be permitted, and all parties in a civil trial must consent to participating in the pilot. The latter rule may prevent many trials from being recorded, as defendants typically do not want cameras in the courtroom.

In early 2011, Senator Charles Grassley, (R-Iowa) introduced the Sunshine in the Courtroom Act, with Democrat Senators Charles Schumer of New York and Patrick Leahy of Vermont as co-sponsors. The bill would give chief judges in federal district court and the court of appeals the discretion to decide whether cameras should be allowed in court proceedings. The purpose of the act is to provide greater transparency, which would lead to greater accountability by the federal courts. The law would direct the Judicial Conference to issue nonbinding guidelines for judges to use to assess whether a proceeding should be videographed, photographed, broadcast, or recorded. It would also require the conference to issue mandatory guidelines for obscuring vulnerable witnesses, such as undercover officers, crime victims, and their families. Unlike the pilot project, the act would not prevent cameras in criminal proceedings, yet one provision would bar cameras if it would violate the rights of the trial participants. The SENATE JUDICIARY COMMITTEE passed the bill in April 2011 on a 12-6 vote.

Televised Trials Gain in Popularity and Viewing

In July 2011, millions of Americans had their eyes and ears glued to their televisions to be the first to hear a jury verdict in the highly-publicized Casey Anthony MURDER trial. Anthony was accused of murdering her 2-year-old daughter Caylee in 2008, and a jury surprised many commentators by acquitting her. Live television coverage of the trial was available through HLN, the unit of Time Warner formerly known as Headline News. The channel's audience had more than doubled since the trial started on May 24, resulting in the channel adding more hours of coverage, led by Nancy Grace (former prosecutor-turned-TV-host) outside the Orlando, Florida courthouse. HLN boasted that it averaged 509,000 viewers at any given time, up from 239,000 in the prior four weeks. During prime time, the gains were more than 900,000, up from 372,000 in the prior four weeks.

Television ratings had also spiked in central Florida. "The trial has electrified daytime television," wrote Hal Boedeker, the TV critic for the *Orlando Sentinel.* "For many viewers, watching Casey Anthony's reactions is more dramatic than scripted drama."

Other high-profile and greatly anticipated televised trials in 2011 include that of Dr. Conrad Murray, Michael Jackson's former live-in physician, accused of giving the pop star a lethal dose of the powerful anesthetic propofol, and salesman James Arthur Ray, charged with the deaths of three paying participants of a sweat lodge ceremony in Sedona, Arizona in 2009.

The public's fascination with real trials and real persons in real-time grew by leaps and bounds following the 1995 televised O.J. SIMPSON trial on CourtTV, the cable channel that helped turn television viewers into armchair jurors and judges over the years. But CourtTV is now a reality TV channel, while the HLN division also produces "In Session," a weekday trial coverage program on CourtTV's successor, truTV.

The U.S. SUPREME COURT has never outright banned live television coverage of civil trials. Its 45-year old precedent, *Estes v. Texas,* found fault with a criminal trial being broadcast, noting its potential prejudicial effect on jurors, potential juror intimidation, and the defendant's due process right to a "fair trial." But in the 1981 case of *Chandler v. Florida,* 449 U.S. 560, 101 S. Ct. 802, 66 L. Ed. 2d 740 (1981), the Court made clear that there was no constitutional bar to televising trials. Although the Court acknowledged that trials which generated great publicity might infringe upon such rights, nonetheless, electronic media coverage of state court cases did not inherently violate the due process rights of witnesses and defendants, said the Court.

More recently, the Supreme Court stopped, by **interlocutory** Order, live audio-video streaming, telecasts or delayed broadcasts (on You-Tube) of the California **district court bench trial** (decided by a judge rather than jury) of *Perry v. Schwarzenegger,* 704 F. Supp. 2d 921 (N.D. Cal. 2010). In that CIVIL RIGHTS trial, attorneys sought to invalidate (as unconstitutional) California's "Proposition 8," which reversed a state supreme court decision permitting same-sex marriage. Without comment on the merits, the U.S. Supreme Court, by a narrow 5-4 decision, expressed concern that, given the notoriety of the same-sex trial, the public had insufficient time to comment on the decision to televise the trial. In other words, the majority asserted that its focus was not on the larger issue of broadcasting trials, but rather, on the narrower issue dealing with the lack of proper procedure in amending court rules to allow the broadcast. The Court agreed that petitioners had shown a danger of irreparable harm resulting from a broadcast, in the form of a danger of witness intimidation and harassment. This was the first time the Supreme Court ever literally stopped the televising of a trial.

Following the 1981 *Chandler* decision, several states began allowing live coverage of trials. As of 2011, 48 of 50 states (excepting Mississippi and South Dakota) permit cameras in the courtrooms in some fashion, while 37 permit televised trials. The issue remains one left to the discretion of a trial judge, who weighs the risks of a potentially prejudiced trial with that of the public's right to know and follow the proceedings.

Many of the concerns in 1981 have gone by the wayside. Bulky, noisy, and intrusive camera equipment and personnel have now been replaced with remote electronic controls that can silently transmit live real-time proceedings without interruption or even noticeable operation. Technology also allows videofilming to pan in or out, leaving jurors and witnesses faceless and anonymous, as a judge may so rule. In any event, with the **advancement** of social media tools such as FaceBook and Twitter, the availability of instantaneous real-time messaging about trial proceedings would defeat, or at least surpass, most arguable concerns about televising live trials anyway. Further, judges continue to make good use of juror sequestering to avoid any influence in their decision-making by media.

At 2:15 p.m. EST on July 5, 2011, the Florida jury announced its verdict in the Casey Anthony trial to a live and riveted international television audience, as local stations streamlined the coverage in real-time. Television and Internet viewers anxiously watched Anthony's face as the verdict was read. Fifteen minutes later, the verdict would be "old news," having already been tweeted, e-mailed, and announced on the radio in literally hundreds of thousands of information messages across the globe. Most would have it no other way.

CRIMINAL LAW

A body of rules and statutes that defines conduct prohibited by the government because it threatens and harms public safety and welfare and that establishes punishment to be imposed for the commission of such acts.

Federal Habeas Review Limited to State Court Record

Federal **habeas corpus** review of state court criminal cases remains a bedeviling area of the law for the U.S. SUPREME COURT. Federal laws have sought to restrict the ability of prisoners to file more than one habeas petition and to impose limitations on the time to file and the issues to be raised in a petition. As for the **federal courts**, the Antiterrorism and Effective Death Penalty Act of 1996 (AEDPA), 110 Stat. 1214, placed limitations on what federal courts could consider when reviewing a state court decision. The Court each term deals with the interpretation of these laws. In *Cullen v. Pinholster*, 131 S. Ct. 1388 (2011), the Court considered whether a federal court could consider new evidence introduced by the DEFENDANT in the federal court action. It concluded that habeas review is limited to the record that was before the state court that adjudicated the claim on the merits.

Scott Pinholster was convicted by a California jury for the 1982 MURDER of two men. Pinholster and two accomplices broke into a house of a local drug dealer in the middle of the night looking for drugs. The three men, who were armed with buck knives, did not find the dealer at home. When two of the drug dealers arrived at the house, Pinholster repeatedly stabbed the men with his knife, brutally killing them. The **robbery** of the house netted just $23. The California trial court appointed two lawyers to defend Pinholster on charges of first-degree murder, ROBBERY, and **burglary**. Pinholster testified on his own behalf and presented an alibi defense. He also boasted that he was a "professional robber," not a murderer, and that he had committed hundreds of robberies over the previous ten years. He insisted he always used a gun, not a knife. The jury convicted him on both counts of first-degree murder.

During the penalty phase, Pinholster's lawyers sought to exclude any aggravating evidence on the ground that the prosecution had failed to provide notice of the evidence to be introduced, as required by California law. At the hearing on this issue, one of his lawyers in reliance on the lack of notice stated he was not "presently prepared to offer anything by way of mitigation." When the trial court offered a continuance, the defense lawyer declined, explaining he could not think of a mitigation witness other than Pinholster's mother. The court ruled that the defense had received notice and denied the motion to exclude. The same jury that convicted Pinholster was present for the penalty phase. The PROSECUTOR produced eight witnesses that detailed Pinholster's long history of threatening and violent behavior. The defense called Pinholster's mother, who recounted his troubled life and called her son "a perfect gentleman at home." The defense did not call a psychiatrist, though they lawyers had consulted with one six weeks earlier. He concluded that Pinholster had "psychopathic personality traits" but "was not under the influence of extreme mental or emotional disturbance" at the time of the murders." The jury unanimously voted for the death penalty.

The California Supreme Court upheld Pinholster's conviction and sentence in 1992. The following year Pinholster filed his first state habeas petition, alleging ineffective assistance **of counsel** at the penalty phase of his trial. His new lawyer asserted that the two defense lawyers had failed to adequately investigate and present mitigating evidence, including evidence of mental disorders. The lawyer introduced school, medical, and legal records, along with declarations from family members and testimony from a different psychiatrist. This doctor criticized his colleague's report as incompetent, unreliable, and inaccurate. The California Supreme Court denied Pinholster's petition on the substantive ground that it was without merit. In 1997, Pinholster filed a federal habeas petition that asserted the same claims and evidence as in the **state action**. However, he also included new allegations that this trial lawyer had failed to furnish the first psychiatrist with adequate background material. The doctor now asserted that had he known this background he would have conducted further inquiry before concluding that Pinholster suffered only from a personality disorder.

The federal **district court** stayed the proceeding to allow Pinholster to bring this new evidence in a second state habeas petition. The California Supreme Court summarily denied the petition and Pinholster restarted his federal habeas action. The district court granted an evidentiary hearing. At the hearing the first psychiatrist stated that none of the new material he reviewed altered his original diagnosis.

Pinholster presented the testimony of two new psychiatrists who claimed he had an organic personality syndrome and that he suffered from partial epilepsy and brain injury. The district court granted habeas relief, finding there was ineffective legal counsel. The Ninth **Circuit Court** of Appeals upheld this ruling, finding that the evidentiary hearing was not barred by AEDPA. The evidence introduced in the federal proceeding demonstrated that the California Supreme Court had unreasonably applied the Supreme Court rules governing ineffective counsel claims.

The Supreme Court, in a 5-4 decision, overruled the Ninth Circuit. Justice CLARENCE THOMAS, writing for the majority, noted that the federal courts must be highly deferential to state court decisions and that these decisions must be given the benefit of the doubt. Under AEDPA, federal courts must focus on what a state court knew and did. Therefore, federal habeas review is "limited to the record that was before the state court that adjudicated the claim on the merits." The AEDPA provision used the past tense to refer to a state-court **adjudication** that "resulted in" a decision that was contrary to, or "involved" an unreasonable application of established law. This "backwards-looking language" meant that the federal court had to examine the state-court decision "at the time it was made." Therefore, the record under review is the one that was before the state court.

Justice SONIA SOTOMAYOR, in a dissenting opinion joined by two justices, argued that AEDPA did allow the introduction of new evidence. Pinholster was unable to develop the factual claims in state court through no fault of his own. Introducing new evidence under the limited circumstances of another AEDPA provision did not "upset the balance that Congress struck in AEDPA between the state and federal courts."

DEPARTMENT OF THE TREASURY

Congress Creates the Financial Stability Oversight Council

Faced with public backlash over the government's bailout of large American financial firms that were "too large to fail," Congress in 2010 created the Financial Stability Oversight Council (FSOC or Council). The Council was charged broadly with identifying risks and responding to emerging threats to the country's financial stability. However, the Council came under fire in 2011 for failing to give companies a chance to comment about which of the large financial firms would be subject to enhanced oversight by the Federal Reserve.

During the financial crisis that began in 2007, Congress was forced to come to the aid of several of the nation's largest financial firms. In an effort to ensure future financial stability, Congress passed the Dodd-Frank Wall Street Reform and **Consumer Protection** Act, Pub. L. No. 111-203, 124 Stat. 1376 (2010). Subtitle A of this Act created the FSOC. The FSOC's purposes under the Act fell into three broad categories. First, the Council is to "identify risks to the financial stability of the United States that could arise from the material financial distress or failure, or ongoing activities, of large, interconnected bank holding companies or nonbank financial companies, or that could arise outside the financial services marketplace." Second, the Council is required "to promote market discipline, by eliminating expectations on the part of shareholders, creditors, and counterparties of such companies that the Government will shield them from losses in the event of failure." And third, the Act requires the Council "to respond to emerging threats to the stability of the United States financial system."

The financial crisis worsened, in part, because of inconsistencies in how regulatory bodies oversaw the various financial sectors. Moreover, no single **entity** had responsibilities related to the nation's financial stability. The authors of the Act intended for the FSOC to perform a number of functions so that it could serve as the principal entity for overseeing these financial institutions. The Act charged the Council with a number of duties, including: (1) facilitating coordination of regulatory bodies; (2) facilitating information sharing and collection among various agencies; (3) designating nonbank financial companies for consolidating supervision by the Council; (4) designating systemic financial market utilities and systemic payment, clearing, or settlement activities; (5) recommend stricter standards governing large banks and financial firms; (6) break up larger firms that post a threat to financial stability; and (7) recommend that Congress close specific gaps in regulation.

Members of the FSOC include the following: the TREASURY DEPARTMENT secretary (who serves as the FSOC chair); the chair of the Federal Reserve; the **comptroller** of the currency; the director of the Bureau of Consumer Financial Protection; the chair of the FEDERAL DEPOSIT INSURANCE CORPORATION; the chair of the COMMODITY FUTURES TRADING COMMISSION; the director of the Federal Housing Finance Agency; the chair of the NATIONAL CREDIT UNION ADMINISTRATION Board; and an independent member appointed by the President. The Council also has five nonvoting members, including the director of the Office of Financial Research; the director of the Federal Insurance Office; a state insurance commissioner; a state banking supervisor; and a state SECURITIES commissioner.

The FSOC is required to report directly to Congress once a year. In its first year, the Council's plans were to "establish processes for designating nonbank financial companies and financial market utilities, recommending stricter standards, for monitoring and reporting on systemic risk, and for monitoring the financial system for emerging risks. The Council promised accountability through the requirement that it report to Congress annually. The Council also promised transparency by holding open meetings whenever possible.

The FSOC held its first meeting on October 1, 2010. During its third meeting on January 18, 2011, the Council reviewed several reports regarding rules established in the Dodd-Frank Act. One of these reports focused on certain trading activities and private fund investments prohibited by the Act. Another report focused on a rule that restricted financial firms from creating entities with large liabilities. A final report discussed a rule that would affect companies whose failure would threaten the financial stability of the United States. At its March 17 meeting, the Council considered a proposed rule that would give the FSOC the authority to identify and designate the companies that would be subject to the rule. Under the proposed rule, the designated companies would be subject to heightened supervision by the Council.

The rule regarding heightened supervision of these larger firms drew fire from members of Congress. According to some congressional members, the Council did not give companies a sufficient opportunity to comment on the proposal. Other critics noted that the Council

had forged ahead with its activities even though some of its members have yet to be appointed. Some members of Congress threatened to approve legislation that would weaken or **repeal** the financial reforms in the Dodd-Frank Act. The chief executive officer of JPMorgan said he thought that the Act and the Council's activities would "stifle economic growth"

Representatives of the Treasury Department struck back, though, arguing that had reforms been in place in 2007, the country could have averted the financial collapse. Other supporters of the Act and the Council have added that the Council may crucial as part of the administration's efforts to reduce the federal deficit. In particular, commentators have suggested that because the Council operates outside the political process, members of Congress may pay more attention to the Council's recommendations and assessments.

DNA EVIDENCE

Skinner v. Switzer

Advances in the use of **forensic** DNA testing have led to LITIGATION by convicted criminals asking courts to order additional testing that may reveal the convicts' innocence. One means for a prisoner to seek testing is through a petition for **writ** of **habeas corpus**. Other prisoners, though, have asked courts to order testing by relying on the CIVIL RIGHTS **statute** contained in 42 U.S.C. § 1983. In 2011, the U.S. SUPREME COURT ruled that a death-row prisoner could request DNA testing by filing an action under § 1983, thus sparing the prisoner's life just hours before his scheduled execution.

In 1993, police officers arrived at the scene of a brutal MURDER of Twila Busby and her two sons. The officers found blood and blood smears in several places throughout the house where the murders occurred. The officers also found an axe handle stained with blood and hair along with a trash bag containing a knife and towel. The officers found more blood in a bedroom where the sons slept. The officers additionally collected fingernail clippings, additional hair samples, and vaginal swabs from Busby. Busby's boyfriend, Henry Skinner, was hiding in a closet, and when he was found, he was wearing blood-stained blue jeans and socks. Skinner was charged with capital murder for the killings.

The State of Texas tested fingerprint evidence and the blood on some of the items in preparation for Skinner's trial. Only some of this evidence implicated Skinner. For instance, bloody palm prints in the room where one victim was killed belonged to Skinner. However, fingerprints on the trash bag that contained the knives and towels did not belong to Skinner. Moreover, the state did not test blood in several items, including the knives, the axe handle, the vaginal swabs, the fingernail clippings, and additional hair samples. Nevertheless, a jury in Gray County, Texas in 1995 convicted Skinner and sentenced him to death.

Skinner acknowledged that he was in the house, but he claimed that he had taken large amounts of alcohol and codeine, resulting in his incapacitation. He also claimed that Busby's uncle, Robert Donnell, had committed the murders. Donnell was an ex-convict with a history of physical and SEXUAL ABUSE. Donnell died after Skinner's conviction. After Skinner's conviction, the State conducted additional testing on some of the evidence, though Skinner was not involved with this testing process. The results of this testing were inconclusive, with only some of the evidence pointing to Skinner.

For years, Skinner sought post-conviction relief in both the state and **federal courts**. Six years after his conviction, the State of Texas enacted Article 64 of the Texas Code of **Criminal Procedure**. This statute allows for post-conviction testing in some limited circumstances. Pursuant to this statute, Skinner twice filed motions in Texas state court requesting DNA testing of the untested biological evidence. However, in one opinion, the Texas Court of Criminal Appeals determined that Skinner had failed to demonstrate that he would not have been convicted if the DNA test result were exculpatory. *Skinner v. State*, 122 S.W.3d 808 (Tex. Crim. App. 2003). In another opinion, the Court of Criminal Appeals concluded that Skinner could not prove that the evidence was not tested through no fault of his own. A principal reason for the second decision was that Skinner's trial counsel had testified that he was concerned that the DNA on the evidence would point to Skinner. *Skinner v. State*, 293 S.W.3d 196 (Tex. Crim. App. 2009).

Having lost in the STATE COURTS, Skinner filed an action in the U.S. **District Court** for the Northern District of Texas. In 2007, the district court denied Skinner's habeas **corpus** relief, and the Fifth **Circuit Court** of Appeals affirmed the decision in 2009. Skinner then filed an action under § 1983, arguing that district attorney Lynn Skinner had violated his constitutional right by not having the DNA tested. Skinner specifically alleged that Switzer had violated his FOURTEENTH AMENDMENT due process right. However, the district court dismissed the suit after concluding that requests for DNA EVIDENCE were only available through HABEAS CORPUS proceedings. The Fifth Circuit affirmed the decision on January 28, 2010, and Skinner was scheduled for execution in March. However, the Supreme Court agreed to do review the case and stayed the execution.

In a 6-3 decision, the Supreme Court reversed the Fifth Circuit. Writing for the majority, Justice RUTH BADER GINSBURG noted that the federal circuits were split on the issue. However, in other cases, the Court had considered circumstances in which a party could seek relief under § 1983 instead of a habeas CORPUS proceeding. If the prisoner were to seek a "immediate or speedier release" from confinement, the prisoner would have to file a habeas petition. However, if the claim would not necessarily lead to a speedier release, the prisoner could pursue a § 1983 action. Ginsburg concluded that access to DNA testing would not lead to a speedier release, and so the § 1983 action was proper. Ginsburg noted a limitation, though: "Success in the suit gains for the prisoner only access to the DNA evidence, which may prove exculpatory, inculpatory, or inconclusive." Ginsburg also rejected the argument that the decision would lead to a proliferation of litigation. She stressed that Texas prosecutors had failed to provide evidence showing "any litigation flood or even rainfall."

The case had become a celebrated cause among death penalty opponents. A group of journalism students in Chicago had found new witnesses expressing Skinner's innocence, leading to calls for DNA testing of the remaining items.

DRUGS AND NARCOTICS

Drugs are articles intended for use in the diagnosis, cure, mitigation, treatment, or prevention of disease in humans or animals, and any articles other than food intended to affect the mental or body function of humans or animals. Narcotics are any drugs that dull the senses and commonly become addictive after prolonged use.

DePierre v. United States

Under the Anti-Drug Abuse Act (ADAA) of 1986, Pub. L. No. 99-570, 100 Stat. 3207, a person convicted of distributing five kilograms of powder cocaine receives a mandatory minimum sentence of 10 years in prison. The same **statute** provides that a person who distributes 50 or more grams of a substance containing cocaine base receives the same mandatory minimum 10-year sentence. A DEFENDANT who was convicted of distributing 50 or more grams of cocaine base challenged his 10-year sentence, arguing that the sentence should only apply to distribution of crack cocaine. In *DiPierre v. United States*, No. 09-1533, 2011 WL 222426 (U.S. June 9, 2011), the U.S. SUPREME COURT ruled that the statute applies to any form of cocaine base and not just crack cocaine.

Congress responded to growing concerns about illicit drugs by enacting the ADAA. Members of Congress were particularly concerned about crack cocaine at the time of the enactment in 1986. The ADAA revised penalties for crimes involving drug offenses. One section establishes a 10-year sentence for drug offenses that involve five kilograms or more of "a mixture or substance containing a detectable amount of" certain kinds of cocaine, particularly cocaine in a powder form. Another section establishes a sentence for offenses involving "a mixture or substance ... which contains cocaine base." Thus, a person must be convicted of an offense involving 100 times the amount of powder cocaine to receive the same sentence that a person convicted of an offense involving crack cocaine or another form of cocaine base.

Frantz DePierre in 2005 contacted a confidential informant and offered to sell the informant crack cocaine. The informant was a former drug dealer who had been working with police during a crackdown of firearm and drug sales in the Boston area. The informant recorded a subsequent telephone conversation in which DePierre confirmed that he had the "cookies," which is a street term for crack cocaine.

DePierre and the informant agreed to meet about the purchase of powdered cocaine.

DePierre told the informant that DePierre could cook the powder into crack. The two completed the sale in February 2005, but federal agents investigating the case decided to have the informant engage in further discussions with DiPierre about selling crack. In April 2005, DePierre sold the informant two bags of a substance described as "off-white [and] chunky," though it was disputed whether the substance was crack or some other form of cocaine base.

DePierre was indicted on several charges, including several for selling firearms and one for selling the substance containing cocaine base. Before the U.S. **District Court** for the District of Massachusetts, he asked the judge to instruct the jury that his offense had to involve the distribution of "the form of cocaine base known as crack cocaine." He proposed an instruction that would have limited the jury's focus to crack and not to other forms of cocaine base. However, the court rejected his argument and instructed the jury that it had to find whether the substance was cocaine base and not specifically crack. The district court sentenced DePierre to 120 months in prison.

DePierre appealed the decision to the First Circuit. He made several arguments, but his main focus was on his 10-year sentence for distributing crack cocaine. At the time of the decision, several courts of appeals had concluded that "cocaine base" only included crack cocaine. However, the First Circuit was already among a group of circuits ruling that cocaine base as a term was broader than simply crack cocaine. DePierre was unsuccessful in persuading the panel of the First Circuit to rule otherwise.

He attempted to persuade the panel that the U.S. Supreme Court's decision in *Kimbrough v. United States*, 552 U.S. 85, 128 S. Ct. 558, 169 L. Ed. 2d 481 (2007) should affect how the lower courts read the provisions of ADAA. The Court in *Kimbrough* concluded that judges had the discretion to impose sentences outside the range recommended by the Federal Sentencing Guidelines for crimes related to crack cocaine. That case was based in part on the disparity between sentencing for powder cocaine and crack cocaine. However, the panel noted that the guideline in question referred specifically to crack cocaine, whereas the ADAA referred to cocaine base and not specifically to crack.

Because of the split among the lower courts, the Supreme Court agreed to review the case. In a unanimous vote, the Court affirmed the First Circuit's opinion. Justice SONIA SOTOMAYOR wrote for the majority and focused on Congress' use of the terms cocaine and cocaine base. Her analysis noted that the chemical composition of cocaine in a powdered form is different than a cocaine base. However, the different forms of cocaine base—including crack, coca paste, and freebase—are chemically identical.

The Court acknowledged that the language Congress used in the ADAA is confusing. Nevertheless, the Court disagreed with DePierre's argument that Congress only intended for the sentencing provisions to apply to crack. Sotomayor's textual analysis of the ADAA along with the statute's LEGISLATIVE HISTORY provided support for the Court's conclusion that cocaine base applies to "cocaine in its base form."

Justice ANTONIN SCALIA filed a concurring opinion in which he agreed with the Court's conclusion (the "obvious" holding that "the term 'cocaine base' refers to cocaine base) but disagreed that the Court needed to refer to legislative history to support this conclusion. According to Scalia, even if the legislative history had clearly supported DePierre's position, it would not have changed the outcome because the text is unambiguous.

Michigan Law Does Not Prevent Employment Discharge of Medical Marijuana User

As of 2011, there were 16 states, including Michigan, with medical marijuana laws. **Statutory** language varies in each state, and courts generally interpret the laws on a case-by-case, fact-specific basis. In early 2011, a Michigan federal court interpreted the state's 2008 Michigan Medical Marihuana Act (spelled as such) (MMMA) as not protecting an employee who was terminated from employment after testing positive for marijuana, despite his possession of a medical marijuana registry card issued pursuant to the MMMA. *Casias v. Wal-Mart Stores,* 764 F. Supp. 2d 914 (W.D. Mich. 2011).

PLAINTIFF Joseph Casias was a five-year employee with retailer Wal-Mart Stores, assigned to work in a Battle Creek, Michigan store. He was by all accounts a good worker,

being promoted into inventory management after three and a half years, and being named "associate of the year" in 2008. Nonetheless, Casias was an "at-will" employee (one who can be terminated from employment "at the will" of the employer, with or without good reason), as most retail hourly workers are.

Casias's employer, Wal-Mart, had a written drug use and drug testing policy in effect for its employees. Wal-Mart required Casias to take a drug test when he was first employed, and he passed. Thereafter, he and other employees were required to be tested again under certain situations outlined in Wal-Mart's policy.

In June 2009, Casias had qualified for and obtained a medical marijuana registry card under MMMA to treat chronic pain and he began using marijuana outside of the workplace and after work hours. Later that year, Casias injured his knee at work and was required, under Wal-Mart's mandatory policy, to take a post-accident drug test in November 2009. He tested positive for marijuana.

At the time of the drug test, Casias had informed his manager, Troy Estill, as well as drug testing staff, that he possessed a medical marijuana registry card pursuant to MMMA. Mr. Estill advised Casias that drug testing after a workplace injury was mandatory under Wal-Mart policy, and not discretionary for any particular store or store management to decide its administration or application. One week later, following the positive test results, Mr. Estill informed Casias that Wal-Mart had terminated his employment.

Casias filed a complaint in Calhoun County **Circuit Court** (a state trial court) in June 2010, alleging **wrongful discharge** under the MMMA and in violation of **public policy**. He named both Wal-Mart and Mr. Estill as defendants. Defendants removed the case to federal **district court**, asserting diversity jurisdiction, based on the fact that it was Wal-Mart corporate offices in Arkansas, and not the local Michigan store, that made the decision to terminate Casias. In fact, Wal-Mart had a specific drug-screening department located in its Arkansas corporate headquarters to precisely handle these cases and situations.

Before a trial could even commence, the federal court needed to rule on two crucial pre-trial motions. Casias moved to have the case remanded back to state court for lack of jurisdiction (based on diversity of parties), as DEFENDANT Estill was also a Michigan resident. Defendants, meanwhile, had moved for summary **disposition** (dismissal of the case) for failure to state a **cause of action** under the MMMA. As pertinent here, the issue before the court in this case of **first impression** under the MMMA was whether the Act provided employment protection for medical marijuana users.

The court first looked to the language of the MMMA, the preamble to which states that it "provide[s] protections for the medical use of marijuana." The court concluded that notwithstanding, this statement did not imply protection from all possible consequences of medical marijuana use. In a previous 2010 state case, *People v. Redden,* the state court had noted that "The MMMA does not codify a *right* to use marijuana; instead, it merely provides a procedure which seriously ill individuals using marijuana for its palliative effects can be identified and protected from prosecution under state law."(emphasis in original). The referenced "state law" would mean arrest and prosecution for possession or use of marijuana. So, for example, the MMMA does not protect a person from federal prosecution for marijuana use, as federal law prohibits *any* use of marijuana, excepting rare and very limited circumstances, said the court.

Moreover, nothing in the language of the MMMA indicated a general policy, on behalf of the State of Michigan, to create a special class of citizens (i.e., medical marijuana users) to be protected against *civil* causes of action related to their drug use. Michigan's protective statutes for employment (and other) DISCRIMINATION expressly identify the categories of protections, e.g., religion, race, color, national origin, age, sex, height, weight, or marital status (and under separate statutes, disability, whistle-blowers). If the voters of Michigan meant to enact such sweeping legislation, said the court, they needed to do so explicitly, as in the other statutes.

Finally, Casias had argued, in support of his claim for violation of PUBLIC POLICY, that the term "business" in the MMMA, to wit, language stating that registry cardholders cannot be "denied any right or privilege, including but not limited to civil penalty or disciplinary action by a business or occupational or professional licensing board or bureau, for the medical use

of marijuana in accordance with this act," referred to his employer. The court also rejected this argument, holding that the term "business" did not stand alone, but was instead merely a modifier for a "licensing board or bureau."

After noting that no other medical marijuana **statute** (in other states) had been held to regulate private employment, the court concluded, "Whatever protection the MMMA does provide users of medical marijuana, it does not reach private employment. Accordingly, the court dismissed Casias's motion to remand and granted Defendants' motion to dismiss.

In February 2011, the AMERICAN CIVIL LIBERTIES UNION (ACLU) filed an appeal on behalf of Casias with the U.S. Circuit Court of Appeals for the Sixth Circuit.

DUE PROCESS

Los Angeles County v. Humphries

In the 1978 case of *Monell v. New York City Dept. of Social Svcs.,* 436 U.S. 658, the U.S. SUPREME COURT held that CIVIL RIGHTS plaintiffs who sued a municipal **entity** under 42 U.S.C. § 1983 (the Civil Rights Act of 1871, codified) must show that their injury was caused by a municipal policy or custom. Section 1983 provides:

> "Every *person* who, under color of any [state] **statute**, **ordinance**, regulation, custom, or usage ... subjects, or causes to be subjected, any other person ... to the deprivation of any rights secured by the Constitution and laws [of the United States], shall be liable to the party injured in any action at law, suit in equity, or other proper proceeding for redress."

The *Monell* case directly involved money damages. In the 2010 case of *Los Angeles County v. Humphries,* No. 09-350, 131 S.Ct. 447, 562 U.S. ___, the Court was asked to decide whether the same "policy or custom" requirement applied to prospective relief, such as injunctions or declaratory judgments, as well. The Court, in its unanimous 8-0 decision, held that the same requirement did apply, whether the relief sought was monetary or prospective. (Justice ELENA KAGAN took no part in deliberations or decision.)

As background, it had already been determined, in the 1961 case of *Monroe v. Pape,* 365 U.S. 167, 81 S. Ct. 473, 5 L. Ed. 2d 492 (1961), that municipal entities were not "persons" under 42. U.S.C. § 1983. This earlier conclusion was largely premised upon the history behind the 1871 Act itself, and Congress' rejection of what was known as the Sherman Amendment. That amendment would have made municipalities liable for damages done by private persons "riotously and tumultuously assembled."

However, 16 years later, in the *Monell* case, the Court reexamined the liability issue and the LEGISLATIVE HISTORY behind the Act. The *Monell* Court then determined that Congress had previously rejected the Sherman Amendment *not* because it imposed municipal liability, but because it imposed liability upon a municipality for the act(s) of *others*. The *Monell* Court then overruled *Monroe v. Pape*, concluding that a municipality could indeed be liable, tantamount to the general rules regarding **vicarious liability**, when its own actions, e.g., policies or customs executed by its agents/employees/representatives, resulted in civil rights violations under § 1983.

Now, in the present case, the Court needed to further define the limits of § 1983 liability for municipalities. A California couple, the Humphries, had been initially accused of CHILD ABUSE, but were later exonerated. Under the California Child Abuse and Neglect Reporting Act, law enforcement and other state agencies are required to report all instances of alleged child abuse to the California DEPARTMENT OF JUSTICE. In turn, the statute requires the Department to include all the reported cases in a Child Abuse Central Index, where the names remain available to various state agencies for at least 10 years.

The Humphries, after **exoneration**, attempted to have their names removed from the Index (above), but the Los Angeles Sheriff's Department would not comply. The Humphries sued the Los Angeles County sheriff, two detectives in the sheriff's department, the County of Los Angeles, and the state attorney general. The **cause of action** alleged civil rights violations under 42 U.S.C. § 1983 in that defendants had deprived them of due process by failing to create a procedural mechanism through which they could contest their inclusion on the Index. Neither California nor Los Angeles County had created any such procedures to allow the Humphries to object. They sought damages, an INJUNCTION, and a declaration that defendants had deprived them of their constitutional rights of due process.

The federal **district court** granted **summary judgment** for all defendants, but the U.S. Court of Appeals for the Ninth Circuit reversed. The appeals court held that the FOURTEENTH AMENDMENT to the U.S. Constitution required the state to provide those on the Index with notice and a hearing; thus, the Humphries were entitled to declaratory relief. The **appellate court** further found that, as prevailing parties, the Humphries were entitled to attorney's fees, to be apportioned between county and state defendants.

DEFENDANT Los Angeles County objected to the $60,000 attorney's fees assessed against it. It argued that, being a municipal entity, under *Monell*, it was liable only if its "policy or custom" had caused the deprivation of Humphries' federal rights. But the Ninth Circuit, among other things, found that the Humphries did prevail against the county on their claim for declaratory relief, and that *Monell* did not apply to claims for prospective relief.

The U.S. Supreme Court unanimously disagreed and reversed the decision of the Ninth Circuit. It held that *Monell*'s "policy or custom" requirement applies to all § 1983 cases, whether the relief sought is monetary or prospective. Justice STEPHEN BREYER, writing for the Court, noted that nothing in § 1983 suggested that the causation requirement changed according to the relief sought. In fact, to the contrary, the actual text states that a person who meets § 1983's elements "shall be liable ... in an action at law, suit in equity, or other proper proceeding for **redress**. Since the Court had previously held that a municipal could be a "person" for purposes of § 1983, the question here was whether Los Angeles County did have a "policy or custom" that proximately caused constitutional deprivation to the Humphries. The case was remanded for reconsideration in light of this holding.

EDUCATION LAW

The body of state and federal constitutional provisions; local, state, and federal statutes; court opinions; and government regulations that provide the legal framework for educational institutions.

The Healthy, Hunger-Free Kids Act of 2010

In December 2010, President BARACK OBAMA signed into law the 111th Congress' Healthy, Hunger-Free Kids Act of 2010 Pub. L. No. 111-296, 124 Stat. 3183. At the signing ceremony, Obama noted that he was following in the tradition of President HARRY S. TRUMAN, who signed the first federal school lunch program into effect, and President LYNDON B. JOHNSON, who signed the Childhood Nutrition Act of 1966, 42 U.S.C. § 1771 et seq. The proposed meal requirements in the new 2010 law represented the first rise in nutrition standards for children in fifteen years. (In January 2011, the USDA followed up with proposed new rules to update nutritional standards for meals served through the National School Lunch and School Breakfast programs.)

The new law was immediately dubbed by media reports as Obama's "cookie law." In fact, however, it was a bipartisan Congress that created and passed the bill: first the SENATE in August 2010, followed by a Republican-controlled HOUSE OF REPRESENTATIVES in November 2010, with a vote of 264-157. Notwithstanding,

Republicans attempted to send the bill back to the Senate for amendments regarding background checks for CHILD CARE workers (a procedural maneuver to kill the bill in the last few weeks of the congressional session before it adjourned for the year). But Democrats passed a separate bill on background checks, thus bypassing any return to the Senate. The law, administered by the U.S. DEPARTMENT OF AGRICULTURE (USDA), increased spending on school nutrition programs by $4.5 billion over ten years. Many Democrats initially opposed it because it is partially funded with $2.2 billion in future food stamp dollars.

The Healthy, Hunger-Free Kids Act provides that the federal government may subsidize and regulate what children eat during school hours (and during summers in federally-funded school-based feeding programs). Additionally, the law provides the federal government with power to decide what kind of foods and beverages may be sold in school vending machines (a measure already adopted in many states) and in after-school food programs.

While critics saw the new law as government overreaching, many members of Congress viewed it as one way to contain rising health care costs caused by diets rich in grease, fat, and sugar. Government data indicates that nearly one in three (32 percent) of children aged 6 to 19 are overweight or obese, a number that has trebled in the last few decades, reported the

Fairmeadow Elementary School third grade students Ellery Carlson, left, and Tatiana Aboytes, right, pick chocolate milk during a school lunch program in Palo Alto, Calif., Thursday, Dec. 2, 2010. More children would eat lunches and dinners at school under legislation passed Thursday by the House and sent to the president, part of first lady Michelle Obama's campaign to end childhood hunger and fight childhood obesity.
AP IMAGES/PAUL SAKUMA

USDA. These children are more likely to have risk factors associated with chronic disease such as Type 2 diabetes, high cholesterol, and higher blood pressure.

With national child obesity on the rise, the legislation was designed to improve the quality of foods provided to over 31 million children in school lunch programs, as well as educate children regarding healthy food choices. While it is likely that hamburgers and pizza will remain in school cafeterias, new guidelines may require using leaner meat, whole grain crusts, no trans fats, etc. Additionally, schools will be required to limits levels of saturated fats, sodium, and overall calories.

Specifically, the Healthy, Hunger-Free Kids Act will increase school lunch reimbursements by 6 cents per meal for schools meeting updated nutritional standards. It will also provide enhanced technical assistance regarding more nutritious meals. Other provisions expand access to drinking water in schools, particularly during meal time. Outside of school, the new law helps communities create school gardens, make more use of locally-grown foods in the school setting, and establish local farm-to-school networks. (The USDA also must work to improve the nutritional quality of commodity foods that schools receive from the USDA for use in their school meals.)

The new law increased the number of eligible children enrolled in school meal programs by approximately 115,000 nationwide by using **Medicaid** data for certification. It also allows more meal access for eligible students in high-poverty communities by eliminating paper applications and instead using census data to determine school-wide income eligibility.

The Healthy, Hunger-Free Kids Act coincided with President Obama's Childhood Obesity Task Force, working with the USDA. The proposed rule published by USDA in January 2011, which adds more fruit, vegetables, whole grains, and fat-free milk, is based on recommendations published by the National Academies' Institute of Medicine (IOM) and released in October 2009 in their report, *School Meals: Building Blocks for Healthy Children.* The USDA sought public input through April 2011 before finalizing its rule.

Several programs within the new law do not specify an expiration or completion date. However, the law tasks Congress to periodically review them and reauthorize funding as needed.

In an effort to respond to mounting criticism of for-profit COLLEGES AND UNIVERSITIES, the U.S. DEPARTMENT OF EDUCATION released proposed regulations that would end or limit federal financial aid for for-profit institutions that produce graduates who are unable to find employment and repay their loans. Representatives of for-profit schools heavily criticized the regulations and even brought a lawsuit to prevent the EDUCATION DEPARTMENT from implementing the regulations. On the other hand, an effort by members of Congress to block the regulations failed during budget negotiations in April 2011.

For much of the twentieth century, for-profit schools struggled to compete with publicly subsidized colleges and vocational schools. However, in 1972, Congress approved amendments to Title IV of the Higher Education Act of 1965, 20 U.S.C. §§ 1070 **et seq.**, increasing the amount of federal financial aid that students at for-profit schools could obtain. Between 1976 and 2006, the market share of for-profit schools in higher education increased from about 0.4 percent to 6 percent. This number has continued to increase steadily, leading to what many have called the for-profit education "boom." For-profit schools received a total of $24 billion in federal aid to students in 2009, and Congress in March 2010 also approved $36 billion in Pell Grants for these students. A report issued in June 2010 indicated that 90 percent of the revenue produced by these schools comes from government-backed financing.

Most of the criticism of these programs has focused on the pressure that some schools have placed on prospective students to enroll and to take out student loans. The Government Accountability Office conducted a series of undercover tests to identify possible improper practices in which these schools engage. The results of the tests at 15 schools indicated that four encouraged **fraudulent** practices while all 15 "made deceptive or otherwise questionable statements to GAO's undercover applicants." For instance, a representative of a certificate program in California told and undercover applicant to alter financial aid forms to indicate the number of dependents in the household so that the applicant would qualify for grants. In another example, a representative of an admissions department told an undercover applicant that barbers can earn up to $150,000 to $200,000, even though labor statistics show that 90 percent of barbers make less than $43,000 per year.

Debate about whether and how Washington should regulate for-profit schools swirled for months. In July 2010, the Education Department issued its proposed regulations, which would require schools to prove that they prepare students to be gainfully employed in order for the school to qualify for federal financial aid. The test under the proposed regulations looks at the relationship between student loan debt and average earnings, as well as student default rates at the various institutions. After the comment period had expired, the regulations became final on October 29, 2010 and became effective on July 1, 2011.

The Education Department justified the regulations by noting that only 55 percent of recent graduates from for-profit schools were able to pay more than the accrued interest on their balances. By comparison, 88 percent of borrowers from nonprofit private institutions and 80 percent of borrowers at public institutions were able to pay down by the interest and at least some of the principal on their loans. Moreover, the median debt load carried by a student earning an associate degree a for-profit schools was $14,000, which was nearly double the median debt of a student at a non-profit private school.

Several groups, including those representing interests in education and consumer advocacy, said the regulations were a move in the right direction, yet several spokespersons said the regulations did not go far enough in regulating the industry. Senator Tom Harkin (D.-IA) has served as chair of the SENATE Health, Education, Labor, and Pensions Committee and has been a vocal critic of for-profit schools. He noted, "At first glance, the regulation appears to set a low bar. If we are allowing a school to continue to walk away with taxpayer dollars, despite the fact that less than a third of its students are able to repay their loans, that would seem to be a case of shockingly low expectations."

The Career College Association (CCA), which represents several for-profit schools, countered that the regulations are "unwise, unnecessary, [and] unproven." In January 2010, the CCA filed suit against Arne Duncan, the Secretary of the Department of Education, in the U.S. **District Court** for the District of Columbia. According to CCA, the Education Department lacked authority to implement the regulations and also engaged in a procedurally flawed process for approving the rules. More significantly, the CCA alleged that the regulations are harmful to the for-profits schools, noting that the regulations had already changed "the way schools hire, recruit, advertise and deploy their programs and shape their student bodies. In addition, they are causing schools to divert significant time and money from student education to implement policies and procedures that attempt to comply with the new regulations."

In April 2011, members of Congress engaged in negotiations to create a budget, and during these negotiations, a proposal emerged that would have blocked the Education Department from implementing the new regulation. Representative John Kline (R.-MN) argued in a letter to fellow members of Congress that the regulations "are a clear example of federal overreach into the affairs of American institutions of higher education."

According to the Education Department, the regulations will cut financial aid to about 5 percent of for-profit college programs. Moreover, about 55 percent of these schools will have to warn applicants and students that as graduates, they may have difficulty repaying any student loans.

Los Angeles School District Settlement Limits Teacher Seniority Protection

In January 2011, Los Angeles County Superior Court Judge William F. Highberger approved a groundbreaking settlement in the case of *Reed v. California*, affecting massive teacher layoffs in the greater Los Angeles Unified School District (LAUSD). The settlement allows LAUSD to lay off teachers more equitably, i.e., without strict adherence to principles of seniority and tenure. The United Teachers Los Angeles (UTLA) local teachers' union opposed the settlement. (In March and April 2011, both an intermediate state **appellate court** and the California SUPREME COURT denied UTLA's application for a stay pending appeal.)

As background, a California state **fiscal** crisis had resulted in the state's decision to reduce education funding levels. Trickling down to county and local districts, the shortage of funds resulted in a decision by LAUSD to lay off thousands of teachers. LAUSD is the nation's second largest school district, and was facing almost $400 million in fund shortages.

In 2010, the AMERICAN CIVIL LIBERTIES UNION (ACLU), on behalf of three families from schools within the LAUSD district, filed suit against the state and district in Los Angeles County Superior Court. (Eventually, several more parties joined and the case became a **class action** suit.) The plaintiffs' schools primarily served lower-income and racially diverse student populations, as well as English language learners. These schools had higher teacher turnover, resulting in newer, younger, but nonetheless often more motivated teachers on the staff. Consequently, these schools suffered more severe reductions in teaching staff than many of their affluent counterparts because the newer and younger teachers lacked employment seniority and tenure. In many of these schools, the newer, motivated teachers had made significant strides in education quality as well as student performance; in some schools, entire departments in key core subject areas had seen palpable improvement.

According to allegations contained in the complaint, LAUSD had dismissed up to two-thirds of the teachers at three of the district's historically worst-performing middle schools. Even though many of these teachers were rehired, their dismissals led to instability at the schools and the temporary hiring of substitute teachers without credentials to teach in the assigned subject areas.

In their lawsuit, plaintiffs alleged violations of the **equal protection**, education, and **privileges and immunities** clauses of the California Constitution. They asked for declaratory relief for such violations, as well as an INJUNCTION. Specifically, they requested that the court prohibit defendants from laying off teachers in certain schools, or, in the alternative, prohibit laying off more teachers in these schools than in other more affluent schools, because the plaintiffs' schools suffered disproportionately, with a greater number of their teachers lacking seniority. The plaintiffs charged that such layoffs violated students' equal access to a public education and they demanded injunctive relief to stop the infliction of "further educational harm."

In May 2010, the court granted a **preliminary injunction**, accepting many of plaintiffs' allegations as true. The court order enjoined (prohibited) LAUSD from implementing any budget-based layoffs of teachers at the three named schools that were the subject matter of the LITIGATION. It held that the LAUSD "could not bargain away students' constitutional rights."

In October 2010, the plaintiffs reached an agreement with LAUSD to settle the *Reed* case, with implications far beyond the original three schools. The settlement, approved by the Los Angeles Board of Education, was considered a landmark court settlement in that it radically limited the traditional practice of "last hired, first fired" layoff practice in most school districts nationwide. Specifically, the settlement provided that target schools, identified by LAUSD as likely to be disproportionately affected by teacher turnover, would be exempt from "last hired, first fired" practices. However, the existing layoff system (using seniority) would remain in effect at all other schools in the district. The prohibition of budget-based layoffs was expected to affect upwards of 45 schools in the district, far broader than the original three schools named in the case. The settlement further provided that the targeted schools were to develop retention incentive programs for teachers and administrators who agreed to remain on staff at those schools for a number of years and continue to contribute to the schools' academic growth. Moreover, at least some of the 45 target schools would be required to show academic achievement to remain exempt from budget-layoff status.

California Secretary of Education Bonnie Reiss, in a *Los Angeles Times* article, opined that the state needed to go even further, changing the law to allow merit-based decisions for all California schools. Indeed, in Sacramento, two competing bills on seniority reform were both killed in session. One, sponsored by Republican state senator Bob Huff would have ended seniority systems in their entirety. The other, sponsored by Democrat SENATE President **Pro Tem** Darrel Steinberg, wanted to restrict layoffs at low-performing schools to the district average.

Although the settlement affected only Los Angeles schools, the ramifications could ripple nationwide. The settlement effectively establishes that having quality teachers in high-risk or lower-income schools could be considered a constitutional right in California.

California Supreme Court Rules on Educational Aid for Unlawful Aliens

State COLLEGES AND UNIVERSITIES have historically set higher tuition rates for non-resident students. This cost differential has been generally uncontroversial. However, the state of California enacted a law that allows all persons, including unlawful ALIENS, who have attended high school in California for at least three years to qualify for in-state tuition rates. A group of plaintiffs challenged the law, alleging that it violated a federal law that prohibits states from making unlawful aliens eligible for postsecondary education benefits under certain circumstances. The California SUPREME COURT, in *Martinez v. The Regents of the University of California*, 241 P.3d 855 (2010), ruled that the California law did not violate the federal **statute** because the state law was not based on residence in California.

The plaintiffs in the lawsuit were U.S. citizens who are or were students paying nonresident tuition at a California public university or college. They claimed that they had been illegally denied exemption from nonresident tuition under California Education Code section 68130.5. This provision exempts from paying nonresident tuition all students, including unlawful aliens, who have attended

high school for at least three years in California. The plaintiffs argued that this exemption was based on residence within California, which is barred by the federal law 42 U.S.C. § 1623. The trial court dismissed the lawsuit but the California Court of Appeals reversed the ruling. The appeals court held that section 68130.5 was expressly preempted by the federal law.

The California Supreme Court reversed the appeals court in a unanimous decision. Justice Ming Chin, writing for the court, noted that the state law explicitly dealt with the issue of unlawful aliens. The statute required a "person without lawful IMMIGRATION status" to file an AFFIDAVIT with the college or university stating that the student had filed an application to legalize his or her immigration status, or would file an application "as soon as he or she is eligible to do so." The plaintiffs contended that federal immigration law preempted the state law under the U.S Constitution's **Supremacy Clause**. However, Justice Chin pointed out that **preemption** is not automatic; the state law must be shown to have sought to regulate immigration, which was defined as "a determination of who should or should not be admitted into the country, and the conditions under which a legal entrant may remain." The court had to determine whether the state law met these condition, which would trigger PREEMPTION.

Section 1623, which Congress enacted in 1996, stated that an unlawful alien "shall not be eligible on the basis of residence within a State (or a political subdivision) for any postsecondary education benefits unless a citizen or national of the United States is eligible for such a benefit (in no less an amount, duration, and scope) without regard to whether the citizen or national is such a resident." The plaintiffs maintained that the state law made unlawful aliens eligible for a benefit-in-state tuition-on the basis of residence without making a citizen eligible for the same benefit. Justice Chin stated that the "fatal flaw" in plaintiffs' argument was the contention that the state law exemption from paying out-of-state tuition was based on residence. The court concluded it was not, pointing to other criteria in the law for granting the exemption, which included a California high school degree, attendance for three years at a California high school, or in the case of unlawful aliens, the filing of an affidavit stating that they will try to legalize their immigration status. Moreover, many unlawful aliens who would qualify as California residents but for their unlawful status, would have to pay out-of-state tuition because they had not attended a California high school for at least three years.

Justice Chin noted that many nonresidents may qualify for in-state tuition, whether they are U.S citizens or unlawful aliens, by merely attending a California high school for three years. Examples included students who live in an adjoining state or country and who are permitted to attend California high schools; children of parents who live outside of California but who attend boarding schools in California; and, those students who attend three years of high school in California but then move out of state and lose their residency status. Therefore, the requirements in the state law were not "the functional equivalent of residing in California."

The court also found that Congress could have prohibited states entirely from making unlawful aliens eligible for in-state tuition, but instead included the limiting "on the basis of residence within a State" language. Though the court of appeals believed the state law's requirement of three years of California high school attendance was a "surrogate criterion" for residence, Justice Chin rejected this reasoning. The federal law's residency language could not be overcome by LEGISLATIVE HISTORY.

The plaintiffs also argued that the state law violated the Fourteenth Amendment's **Privileges and Immunities** Clause. The court of appeals agreed with this argument, finding that by making unlawful aliens, with no lawful domicile in the state of California, eligible for in-state tuition, while denying this benefit to U.S. citizens whose lawful domicile was outside California, the state had "denigrated U.S. citizenship." Moreover, the law placed the plaintiffs in a "legally disfavored position compared to that of illegal aliens." The supreme court disagreed, finding no **case law** that showed "states may never give a benefit to unlawful aliens without giving the same benefit to all American citizens." In addition, the PRIVILEGES AND IMMUNITIES Clause only applies to U.S. citizens. Justice Chin concluded that the "fact that the clause does not protect aliens does not logically lead to the conclusion that it also prohibits states from treating unlawful aliens more favorable than nonresident citizens."

ELECTION LAW

Arizona Free Enterprise Club's Freedom Club PAC v. Bennett

Controversies involving the constitutionality of campaign spending restrictions have given rise to several politically charged cases at the SUPREME COURT level during the past decade. In 2011, the Court again reviewed a campaign spending case that led a sharply divided court to conclude than an Arizona scheme designed to equalize campaign dollars available to publicly and privately financed candidates violated the FIRST AMENDMENT rights of the privately financed candidates and their financial supporters. The conservative majority's decision in *Arizona Free Enterprise Club's Freedom Club PAC v. Bennett*, Nos. 10-238, 10-239, 2011 WL 2518813 (U.S. June 27, 2011) drew a sharp rebuke in a dissenting opinion joined by each of the Court's more liberal justices.

Enacted in 1998, the Arizona Citizens Clean Elections Act, Ariz. Rev. Stat. §§ 16-940 **et seq.**, established a voluntary public financing system to fund the campaigns of candidates for state office in primary and general elections. Candidates may opt to receive public funds, though eligibility is contingent on receipt of a specified number of $5 contributions from Arizona voters. Candidates must also agree to several restrictions and obligations, including a limitation on the amount of personal funds a candidate can expend, participation in at least one public debate, adherence to an overall expenditure cap, and return of any remaining money to the state after the election.

In addition to the public funds initially allotted to a candidate, candidates may also receive equalizing, or matching, funds. The publicly financed candidate is entitled to the equalizing funds when a privately financed candidates campaign expenditures exceed the initial **allotment** of the funds given to the publicly financed candidate. The expenditures of the privately financed candidate may come from independent groups or from the candidate himself or herself. When the provision for equalizing funds is triggered, the publicly financed candidate receives roughly a dollar-for-dollar match.

A group of past and present candidates for state office, along with two independent groups that support candidates, filed suit to challenge the constitutionality of the matching-funds law. According to these plaintiffs, the law infringed on their free speech rights under the First Amendment.

The U.S. **District Court** for the District of Arizona concluded that the provision substantially burdens free speech because it would award funds to publicly financed candidates based on expenditures based on speech (i.e., the campaign expenditures) of privately funded candidates. The court also concluded that the state could not prove that the equalizing-funds provision served a compelling **state interest**. The court thus issued a permanent INJUNCTION that prevented enforcement of the provision.

The Ninth **Circuit Court** of Appeals then reviewed the case and reversed the district court. According to the Ninth Circuit, the equalizing-funds provision only imposed a minimal burden on the plaintiffs' First Amendment rights because the law "does not actually prevent anyone from speaking in the first place or cap campaign expenditures." The court concluded that the state could justify the law because the provision had a substantial relationship to the state's "important interest in reducing *quid pro quo* political corruption.

The Supreme Court agreed to review the Ninth Circuit's decision. Chief Justice JOHN ROBERTS wrote the opinion for the majority, which consisted of conservative justices ANTONIN SCALIA, ANTHONY KENNEDY, CLARENCE THOMAS, and SAMUEL ALITO. Roberts' opinion noted that several recent Supreme Court decisions have struck down various restraints on campaign expenditures. The Court has also established that laws burdening political speech are presumptively invalid and are subject to **strict scrutiny**. This meant that the State of Arizona had to prove that the equalizing-fund provision furthered a compelling STATE INTEREST and that the law was narrowly tailored to serve that interest.

The majority focused heavily on the decision in *Davis v. Federal Election Commission*, 554 U.S. 724, 128 S. Ct. 2759, 171 L. Ed. 2d 737 (2008). The Court in *Davis* struck down what was known as the "Millionaire's Amendment" to the Bipartisan Campaign Reform Act. This amendment applied when a candidate **chose** to spend more than $350,000 in personal funds on a campaign. When this occurred, the candidate's opponent was allowed to collect three times the normal contribution amount while the candidate was subject to the original contribution cap. The Court concluded that this scheme violated the rights of the candidate because the law forced the candidate "to choose between the First Amendment right to engage in unfettered political speech and subjection to discriminatory fundraising limitations." The government could not show a compelling governmental interest that justified the law, so the Court struck the law down.

The majority in *Bennett* could not distinguish the equalizing-funds provision from the one struck down in *Davis*. Under the scheme analyzed in *Davis*, if one of the candidates exceeded the personal-spending threshold, the opponent benefited from increased contribution limits, but the opponent still had to raise the funds. In Arizona's scheme, once a candidate exceeded the amount allocated to the publicly funded candidates, the publicly funded candidates would automatically receive matching funds. To the majority, this created a greater constitutional dilemma than the one presented in *Davis* because the candidate's to choice to exercise free speech by expending more than the allotment automatically triggered the increase in allotted funds to the opponents.

The Court also concluded that Arizona could not show a compelling state interest that would justify the funds provision. The State's argument that the law created a level playing field did not show a compelling governmental interest, as the Court had rejected that premise in previous cases. The Court thus reversed the Ninth Circuit's decision.

Justice Elena Kagan, joined by Justices RUTH BADER GINSBURG, STEPHEN BREYER, and Sonia Sotomayor, dissented. Kagan opened by noting the dilemmas that states face when trying to rid their election systems of corruption. Kagan stressed that "the First Amendment's core purpose is to foster a healthy, vibrant political system full of robust discussion and debate." She determined that the Arizona law was consistent with these principles.

Alaska Republican U.S. Senate Joe Miller, right, confers with his lawyer, Thomas Van Flein talk before the Alaska Supreme Court convened in Anchorage, Alaska, on December 17, 2010. Miller lost to incumbent U.S. Sen. Lisa Murkowski, R-Alaska, who ran a write-in campaign.
AP IMAGES/MARK THIESSEN

Kagan also rejected the Court's reliance on *Davis*. She recognized that *Davis* involved a "discriminatory speech restriction," whereas the Arizona law involved a "non-discriminatory speech subsidy."

Alaska Supreme Court Dismisses Challenge to Election Results

Following the midterm elections in November 2010, Joe Miller, the Republican nominee for one of two United States SENATE seats representing the State of Alaska, challenged election results that declared INCUMBENT Senator Lisa Murkowski as having won the election. Murkowski ran as a "write-in" candidate, meaning that voters had to physically write her name on the ballot, and then check the box next to her write-in name, in order to cast their vote for her.

Following Miller's challenge, a federal court judge had halted certification of election results in November pending decision by the state SUPREME COURT. However, on December 22, 2010, the Alaska Supreme Court, by a terse 4-0 unanimous decision, dismissed Miller's lawsuit and challenge to the election, allowing certification of the November results to go forward. *Miller v. Treadwell*, 245 P.3d 867 (2010). The court expressly noted in its opinion,

> that an election contest does not bar certification of an election and that there are no remaining issues raised by Miller that would prevent this election from being certified. Under [Alaska Statutes] AS

15.20.560, if an election contest ultimately changes the result of an election, judgment will be so entered and a new certification will be issued.

The Alaska Supreme Court gave Miller five days from the date of its decision to decide whether he would further pursue the claim in federal court. Five days later, on December 27, 2010, Miller conceded to Murkowski, but vowed to continue legal battle over the state's handling of the way votes were counted (see below). Meanwhile, Murkowski was sworn in, along with other members of Congress, on January 5, 2011.

Murkowski, also a Republican and incumbent Senator, had lost the Republican primary nomination to Joe Miller, who was swept into favor on the wave of Tea Party fervor backed by former Alaskan governor Sarah Palin. Believing this result to be inconsistent with the majority of Alaskan voters, Murkowski decided to run anyway as a write-in candidate.

According to the court's ultimate findings, of the 101,088 write-in ballots, 92,929 were unchallenged, and 8,139 were challenged but counted. Unofficial results appearing on the State of Alaska Division of Elections' official website showed Murkowski leading Miller by more than 9,000 votes.

However, in his challenge, Miller did not seek an official recount. Instead, he filed suit in Alaska Superior Court, challenging several vote-counting decisions made by the Alaska Division of Elections. Named as defendants in the lawsuit were the Division of Elections, Mead Treadwell (the state lieutenant governor), and Lisa Murkowski.

Miller alleged that the state violated the election and **equal protection** clauses of the U.S. Constitution in its handling of the vote count. (Murkowski intervened in the suit, challenging other vote-counting decisions.) Miller sought interpretation of election **statute** AS 15.15.360, that, according to him, would disqualify any write-in votes that misspelled the candidate's name.

The precise language of the subject statute [AS 15.15.360(a)(11)] states, in relevant part, that

> [a] vote for a write-in candidate . . . shall be counted if the oval is filled in for that candidate and if the name, as it appears on the write-in declaration of candidacy, of the

candidate or the last name of the candidate is written in the space provided.

Miller argued that the state should be held to a strict reading of that law. Specifically, Miller argued that the law required write-in ballots to be written and spelled correctly, and that the statute required disqualification of any write-in votes that misspelled the candidate's name.

Alaska Superior Court Judge William B. Carey disagreed and upheld the decisions of the Alaska Division of Elections to count all write-in votes for which the voter's intention could be ascertained. Undaunted, Miller filed for appeal with the Alaska Supreme Court. Meanwhile, a federal district judge stayed the Division of Elections' certification of the vote count results, pending decision by the state supreme court.

In its strong unanimous decision, the Alaska Supreme Court affirmed the Superior Court's ruling. First, noted the court, in resolving the parties' questions, the court was governed by long-standing Alaska election principles, including the "bedrock principle" that the right to vote was fundamental to the concept of democratic government. "Courts are reluctant to permit wholesale **disfranchisement** of qualified [voters] through no fault of their own," said the court, "where any reasonable construction of [a] statute can be found which will avoid such a result."

Even more clear, by both principle and case precedent, was that "the voter shall not be disenfranchised because of mere mistake, but [the voter's] intention shall prevail," quoting from *Edgmon v. State, Office of the Lieutenant Governor, Division of Elections*, 153 P.3d 1154 (2007). Accordingly, in the present case, the Alaska Supreme Court held,

> Our prior decisions clearly hold that a voter's intention is paramount. In light of our strong and consistently applied policy of construing statutes in order to effectuate voter intent, we hold that abbreviations, misspellings, or other minor variations in the form of the name of a candidate will be disregarded in determining the validity of the ballot, so long as the intention of the voter can be ascertained.

Miller also challenged the manual count of votes by the Division of Elections as violating **correlative** Alaska Administrative Code (AAC) § 25.085, reading it to mean that only those ballots validated by optical scanners could be counted. The court likewise dismissed this claim, stating that nothing in either the statute or the regulation required a particular procedure for manual counts.

As to Murkowski's claim that additional ballots, in which voters had clearly written in her name but failed to fill in the oval space on the ballot, the court also dismissed this, citing that the clear language of the statute required both filling in the oval and writing in the name. Notwithstanding, Murkowski had enough votes to still prevail.

EMAIL

Emails Protected by the Fourth Amendment

In a case that was celebrated by advocates for greater rights to privacy, the Sixth **Circuit Court** of Appeals ruled that federal officers had to obtain a warrant before obtaining access to emails held by an Internet service provider. The case also drew interest because the DEFENDANT had been the owner of a company that produced supplements designed for male sexual performance. *United States v. Warshak*, 631 F.3d 266 (6th Cir. 2010).

In the early 2000s, Steven Warshak owned several businesses engaged in advertising as well as sales of herbal supplements. The companies that sold these supplements were later aggregated to form Berkeley Premium Nutraceuticals, Inc. Warshak initially employed a relatively small workforce. In fact, one of his employees was his mother, who processed credit-card payments for the company. In 2001, Berkeley developed a product known as Enzyte, which was advertised as a supplement to increase the size of a man's erection. In the first three years after launching Enzyte, Warshak's company grew dramatically. He employed about 1,500 people by 2004, and the company maintained a call center that took orders 24 hours per day. By the end of 2004, Berkeley had annual sales of about $250 million, mostly due to sales of Enzyte.

Enzyte's success was largely due to Berkeley's advertising of Enzyte. In 2001, ads began to appear in a variety of magazines aimed a men. These ads stressed that according to an independent customer study that purported to show that those who took the drug experienced significant growth in the sizes of their penises.

Results from this study also appeared on radio advertisements and the company's website. About 2004, the company began to run a series of ads on network television. These television ads featured a character known as "Smilin' Bob," who wore an exaggerated smile apparently due to the success of the Enzyte product.

However, evidence surfaced that the company had fabricated the survey featured in these ads. A company employee named James Teegarden testified that Warshak had instructed him to create a spreadsheet and to make up the numbers that he inserted on the spreadsheet. Warshak later instructed Teegarden to create a list of 500 names taken from a customer database and to create a mark next to 475 of these names to indicate that they were satisfied or very satisfied. He inserted a mark noting that the remaining 25 were unsatisfied. Advertisements later cited these numbers to support its claim that Enzyte had a 96 percent customer satisfaction rating. In addition to these fabrications, company statements that two researchers from Stanford and Harvard had invented Enzyte were also false, as neither of these researchers actually existed.

Warshak and the company also engaged in other **fraudulent** acts related to the sale of Enzyte. For instance, the company had created a system through which it would take initial orders and then continue shipping the product in subsequent months and continue billing the client for additional shipments. When the Better Business Bureau received a large number of complaints, the company altered its practices, but the new practices were usually designed to mislead the customer into agreeing to the auto-shipment program. The company also engaged in fraudulent activity in its relationship with banks regarding credit card charges.

Prosecutors charged Warshak with a wide range of charges related to Berkeley's business, including the sale of Enzyte. A **grand jury** with the U.S. **District Court** for the Southern District of Ohio returned a 112-count INDICT-MENT in 2006. This indictment charged Warshak with a host of crimes, including various forms of **fraud**, **money laundering**, misbranding, and OBSTRUCTION OF JUSTICE. Steven's mother, Harriet, was also charged with several crimes. Two years later, both were tried and convicted on most counts. Warshak received a sentence of 25 years in prison along with an

order that he forfeit nearly $500 million related to revenue from his company. Harriet also received a prison sentence and became jointly and severally liable for the **forfeiture** judgment.

During the investigation beginning in 2004, the government seized about 27,000 emails from Warshak's private email account. Government investigators did not receive a warrant to seek these emails, and Warshak had no notice that the government had obtained the email messages until 2006. Warshak argued that he had a reasonable privacy interest in these emails and that the warrantless seizure of the emails violated his FOURTH AMENDMENT rights. Warshak's appeals reached the Sixth Circuit more than once. In 2007, a panel of the court ruled that Warshak indeed had a privacy interest in those emails. One year later, however, the **en banc** court held that the first decision was not ripe for **adjudication** because Warshak had argued that the government should be enjoined from future searches. *Warshak v. United States*, 532 F.3d 521 (6th Cir. 2008).

Warshak continued to argue that the government had violated his constitutional rights. A panel of the Sixth Circuit agreed with Warshak's argument, finding that "Warshak plainly manifested an expectation that his emails would be shielded from outside scrutiny." The panel noted that society in general was prepared to accept the expectation that emails were private, noting that the email had largely supplanted the letter and telephone call in terms of importance. The panel wrote, "Lovers exchange sweet nothings, and businessmen swap ambitious plans, all with the click of a mouse button." By making this comparison, the panel concluded that the government "cannot compel a commercial ISP to turn over the contents of an email without triggering the Fourth Amendment."

The government responded it was allowed to seek the emails without a warrant under the Stored Communications Act, 18 U.S.C. § 2701 **et seq**. This **statute** allows a governmental **entity** to require an Internet service provider to disclose the contents of an electronic communication. According to the government's argument, the officers had relied in **good faith** on the federal statute when it sought the emails. The court agreed with the government's argument over Warshak's objection and concluded that though the government had violated Warshak's rights, the evidence collected from the emails could have been presented at trial.

The court affirmed Warshak's conviction but remanded the case, ordering the district court to provide a more adequate explanation about the FORFEITURE portion of Warshak's sentence.

EMPLOYMENT DISCRIMINATION

Supreme Court Interprets Employment Discrimination Statute

The Uniformed Services Employment and Reemployment Rights Act of 1994 (USERRA) provides that a person who is a member of a uniformed service shall not be discriminated in employment on the basis of that membership. Such DISCRIMINATION occurs when the person's membership is a "motivating factor in the employer's actions, unless the employer can prove that the action would have been taken in the absence of this membership." The SUPREME COURT, in *Staub v.* **Proctor** *Hospital*, __U.S.__, 131 S.Ct. 1186, __L.Ed.2d__ (2011), was called on to interpret the phrase "motivating factor in the employer's action" when the company official who terminated the person has no discriminatory **animus** but is influenced by previous company action that is the product of discriminatory animus in someone else." The Court held that the company official could be held liable under the **statute**.

Vincent Staub worked as an angioplasty technician for Proctor Hospital until 2004, when he was fired. Staub was a member of the U.S. Army Reserves, which required him to attend drill one weekend per month and to train full time for two to three weeks a year. His immediate supervisor, Janice Mulally, and Michael Korenchuk, Mulally's immediate supervisor, expressed hostility towards Staub's military obligations. They scheduled him for additional shifts without notice so he would have to pay for having everyone else in the department "bend over backwards" to cover his Reserve schedule. They made disparaging comments about his service and Mulally expressed her intent to "get rid of him." In January 2004, Mulally issued Staub a disciplinary warning for allegedly violating a company rule requiring

him to stay in his work area whenever he was not working with a patient. He was told to report to Mulally or Korenchuk when he did not have a patient and his cases were completed. In April a co-worker complained to Linda Buck, Proctor's VICE PRESIDENT of human resources, about Staub's frequent unavailability and abruptness. Before Buck could implement a plan for Staub, Korenchuk informed Buck that Staub had left his desk without informing his supervisor. Staub later claimed that he had left Korenchuk a voice mail indicating that he was leaving his desk. Buck relied on Korenchuk's accusation and fired Staub after reviewing his personnel file. Staub challenged his termination through the hospital's grievance process and alleged the January disciplinary action was motivated by hostility toward his military obligations. Buck did not discuss this claim with Mulally and reaffirmed her decision.

Staub sued Proctor under the USERRA in federal **district court**, claiming his discharge with motivated by hostility to his Reserve obligations. He contended that Buck did not have any hostility but that Mulally and Korenchuk did, and that their actions influenced Buck's decision to fire him. A jury agreed with Staub, awarding him over $57,000. The Seventh **Circuit Court** of Appeals reversed the decision, finding that Staub could not succeed unless he proved that Mulally and Korenchuk exercised such "singular influence" over Buck that the decision to terminate was the product of "blind reliance." The appeals court concluded that Buck had looked past what the two supervisors had said and relied on other conversations and her review of Staub's personnel file. Because Buck was not wholly dependent on the advice of Mulally and Korenchuk, the court held that the hospital was entitled to judgment.

The Supreme Court, in an 8-0 decision (Justice Elena Kagan did not participate), overruled the Seventh Circuit. Justice ANTONIN SCALIA, writing for the Court, premised his analysis on the fact that when Congress creates a federal **tort law** it adopts the background of general TORT LAW. Staub argued that his supervisors were agents of Buck and therefore Buck and the hospital could be liable under principles of agency. Scalia disagreed, finding evidence in agency law that the "malicious mental state of one agent cannot be combined with the harmful action of another agent to hold the principal liable for a tort that requires both." On the other hand, he rejected Proctor's claim that the employer is not liable unless the decisionmaker (Buck in this case) was motivated by discriminatory animus. Proctor's approach would have "the improbable consequence" that if an employer isolates a personnel official from an employee's supervisors, gives that official the authority to terminate a person, and asks that official to review the employee's personnel file before taking adverse action, then the employer "will be effectively shielded from discriminatory acts and recommendations of supervisors that were *designed and intended* to produce the adverse action."

Justice Scalia used a different approach, holding that if a supervisor performs an act motivated by antimilitary animus "that is *intended* by the supervisor to cause an adverse employment action," and if that act is the **proximate cause** of the ultimate employment action, then the employer is liable under the USERRA. Using this analysis, the Court found that the supervisors were motivated by antimilitary animus and that this was the PROXIMATE CAUSE of Staub's termination. The Court was unsure, however, if the jury's verdict should be reinstated or whether the hospital was entitled to a new trial. The jury instructions did not follow precisely the rule that was announced in this opinion but the difference might be **harmless error**. The Court directed the Seventh Circuit to review this matter.

Thompson v. North American Stainless

Although most employment relationships fall within the "at-will" category, meaning that either the employer or the employee can terminate the relationship with or without notice or good reason, there are nonetheless prohibitions against firing at-will employees for patently illegal reasons. The most frequently litigated reason involves some form of DISCRIMINATION.

Within this subcategory are cases that allege employer retaliation against employees who file or support charges of discrimination. In *Thompson v. North American Stainless, LP*, 131 S.Ct. 863, 562 U.S. ___ (2011), the U.S. SUPREME COURT confirmed that wrongful retaliation under Title VII of the CIVIL RIGHTS Act of 1964 can extend to any employer action

effectively punishing or discouraging a reasonable employee from making or supporting a charge of discrimination. In this case, employee Miriam Regalado filed gender discrimination charges against her employer, North American Stainless (NAS). Three weeks after the EQUAL EMPLOYMENT OPPORTUNITY COMMISSION (EEOC) notified NAS of the pending charges, the company fired Regalado's fiancé, Eric Thompson, who also was an employee.

Thompson filed his own complaint with the EEOC, alleging that NAS had fired him to retaliate against Regalado for filing her charges with EEOC. After unsuccessful **conciliation** efforts, Thompson sued NAS in the U.S. **District Court** for the Eastern District of Kentucky, citing prohibited employer conduct under Title VII of the Civil Rights Act of 1964, 42 U.S.C. § 2000e et seq.

The district court dismissed the suit on the grounds that third-party retaliation claims were not cognizable under Title VII. In other words, Thompson was not engaging in protected activity that could be retaliated against. This holding was affirmed, albeit by a divided panel of the Sixth **Circuit Court** of Appeals. Upon a granted rehearing *en banc*, a full (but again divided) Sixth Circuit Court of Appeals also affirmed dismissal of Thompson's complaint, for the same reason. Therefore, Thompson "[was] not included in the class of persons for whom Congress created a retaliation cause of action," said the **appellate court**.

An unanimous U.S. Supreme Court, with short and concise explanation written by Justice Scalia, reversed. In the procedural posture of the case, the Court was required to assume that NAS fired Thompson in order to retaliate against Regalado for filing a charge of discrimination. Accordingly, the only questions before the Court, as it framed them, were first, did NAS's firing of Thompson constitute *unlawful* retaliation? Second, if it did, does Title VII grant Thompson a **cause of action**?

It was undisputed that Regalado was engaging in protected activity when she filed her EEOC claim. Assuming the facts alleged by her fiancé Thompson were true, the Court readily concluded that NAS's firing of him constituted a violation of Title VII. The **statute** permits "a person claiming to be aggrieved" to file charges with the EEOC alleging that the employer engaged in unlawful employment practices. If EEOC declines to sue the employer, it permits a **civil action** to "be brought ... by the person claiming to be aggrieved ..." § 2000e-5(b),(f)(1).

Moreover, in an earlier Court case, *Burlington N.& S. F.R. Co. v White*, 548 U.S. 53, 126 S. Ct. 2405, 165 L. Ed. 2d 345 (2006), the Court held that Title VII's anti-retaliation provision was to be construed as covering a broad range of employer conduct. In that case, the Court held that "the anti-retaliation provision, unlike the substantive provision, is not limited to discriminatory actions that affect the terms and conditions of employment." Rather, said the Court, the anti-retaliation provision was intended to prohibit any employer action that "well might have dissuaded a reasonable worker from making or supporting a charge of discrimination." It was obvious to the Court, in the present case, that a reasonable worker might be dissuaded from engaging in protected activity if she knew that her fiancé would be fired.

For its part, NAS acknowledged that its firing of Thompson met the standard outlined in *Burlington*. Instead, it argued that construing the statute and **case law** as prohibiting reprisals against third parties will create a slippery slope concerning the types of relationships entitled to protection. What about girlfriends, close friends, or trusted co-workers and confidantes?

The Court discussed the extreme parameters of interpretive scope of the term "person aggrieved." It found that Title VII's use of the term "aggrieved" best fits the regime established by the Administrative Procedure Act. The Act authorizes suit to challenge a federal agency by any "person adversely affected or aggrieved within the meaning of a relevant statute. 5 U.S.C. § 702. Such a test limits plaintiffs who sue to those who fall "within the 'zone of interests' sought to be protected by the **statutory** provision whose violation forms the legal basis for his complaint." (quoting from *Lujan v. National Wildlife Federation*, 497 U.S. 871, 110 S. Ct. 3177, 111 L. Ed. 2d 695 (1990).

Applying that test to the facts before it, Thompson fell within the "zone of interests" intended to be protected under Title VII. Accepting the facts as alleged, Thompson, an employee of NAS, was not an accidental victim of retaliation. By hurting him, NAS was

punishing Regalado. Therefore, Thompson was a person protected under Title VII and had separate standing to sue.

In a separate concurring opinion joined by Justice Stephen Breyer, Justice Ruth Bader Ginsburg noted that in its Compliance Manual, the EEOC expressly counseled that Title VII "prohibit[s] retaliation against someone so closely related to or associated with the person exercising his or her statutory rights that it would discourage or prevent the persons from pursuing those rights." Justice Elena Kagan took no part in consideration or decision of the case.

ENVIRONMENTAL LAW

An amalgam of state and federal statutes, regulations, and common-law principles covering air pollution, water pollution, hazardous waste, the wilderness, and endangered wildlife.

American Electric Power Co. v. Connecticut

In some areas of national concern, there exists a federal **common law**. One of these areas includes the law governing suits brought by one state to prevent pollution from emanating from a neighboring state. However, even where federal common law may exist, Congress may enact legislation that effectively supersedes the common law. In cases involving greenhouse emissions, Congress enacted legislation directing the Environmental Protection Agency to issue rules governing greenhouse-gas emissions emanating from fossil-fuel fired power plants. Several states and other parties had brought a lawsuit against five major power companies and sought relief based on the federal common law. In a unanimous decision, the Supreme Court held that the Congressional act displaced the federal common law. *American Electric Power Co. v. Connecticut*, No. 10-174, 2011 WL 2437011 (U.S. June 20, 2011).

In 2004, two separate groups of plaintiffs filed complaints in the U.S. **District Court** for the Southern District of New York against five large energy companies. One group of plaintiffs included eight states and New York City. The second group included three nonprofit land trusts. The plaintiffs alleged that the defendants were the "five largest emitters of carbon dioxide in the United States." The PLAINTIFF stressed that the defendants caused annual emissions of 650 million tons, representing 10 percent of emissions from all domestic human activities.

According to the plaintiffs, the defendants' activities contributed to global warming and created a "substantial and unreasonable interference with public rights." The complaints alleged that the defendants' activities created a risk for climate change and that the climate change would destroy habitats for many animals and plants. The plaintiffs asked the court to issue an INJUNCTION to cap the carbon dioxide emissions and reduce them by a certain percentage over the next decade.

The plaintiffs alleged that the defendants' activities violated the federal common-law right of interstate nuisance. This purported right stemmed from the Court's previous recognition of a specialized federal common law that applies to suits in which one state seeks to abate pollution from another state. The district court never reached the question of whether the federal common law applied, holding that the plaintiffs' allegations asserted political questions that the court could not resolve. However, the Second **Circuit Court** of Appeals reversed the district court, holding that the plaintiff had properly alleged a federal common-law claim.

The defendants had alleged that the plaintiffs could not bring a claim under the federal common law because by enacting the CLEAN AIR ACT, 42 U.S.C. §§ 7401 **et seq.**, Congress had displaced the federal common law. The Second Circuit rejected this argument, noting that the Environmental Protection Agency had not yet issued a rule regarding emission of greenhouse gases. Without such a rule in place, the Second Circuit concluded that the common law was still in place.

The Supreme Court agreed to review the case, and in an 8-0 decision reversed the Second Circuit. Justice Ruth Bader Ginsberg's majority opinion focused first on the Court's previous decision in *Massachusetts v. EPA*, 549 U.S. 497, 127 S. Ct. 1438, 167 L. Ed. 2d 248 (2007). In that case, the Court concluded that the Clean Air Act had authorized the EPA to issue rules to regulate emissions of carbon dioxide and other greenhouse gases. Before the decision, the EPA had incorrectly concluded (according to the Court) that it lacked rulemaking power. The Court held

that the EPA had thus not acted in accordance with the Clean Air Act when the EPA refused to promulgate rules on the gases and emissions.

Following the Court's decision in 2007, the EPA began the process of drafting rules related to greenhouse-gas regulation. By 2011, the EPA had issued a series of rules that apply to greenhouse gases and emissions but had not completed rules that apply to emissions from facilities, such as those operated by the defendants in *American Electric Power Co. v. Connecticut*. The EPA expects to issue a final rule by May 2012.

The Court did not believe that the lack of a final rule issued by the EPA meant that the federal common law should still control. The test for whether a federal **statute** displaces the common law is simply whether the statute "speak[s] directly to [the] question at issue," which is a much lower standard that applies when Congress decides to preempt state law through federal legislation. In this instance, the Clean Air Act "speaks directly" to emission of gases, which is precisely what the plaintiffs addressed by relying on the federal common law. The Clean Air Act also provides a number of means for enforcement, and these enforcement measures would accomplish purposes similar to those sought by the plaintiffs. Ginsburg also rejected the idea that a federal judge should be the one making a decision about levels of carbon-dioxide emissions when Congress clearly left this decision to an agency with greater expertise in this area.

Justice SAMUEL ALITO, joined by Justice CLARENCE THOMAS, filed a brief concurring opinion suggesting he only agreed with part of the majority's analysis. Justice SONIA SOTOMAYOR did not participate in the case because she previously served as a judge on the Second Circuit.

Gulf Oil Spill Costs Billions

An explosion on an oil rig in the Gulf of Mexico in April 2010 caused a massive oil spill that soiled hundreds of miles of Gulf coastline and endangered the ecosystem. By the time engineers capped the spill in July, it had become the largest marine oil spill in history. The rig was licensed to BP, and the U.S. government has named BP as the responsible party. BP established a fund to compensate Gulf residents, and the company also faces a number of claims in a large lawsuit.

BP had leased an oil rig named *Deepwater Horizon*, which was owned by a company named Transocean. On April 20, 2010, the rig was located a BP's Macondo project about 42 miles southeast of Venice, Louisiana. The rig was drilling beneath about 5,000 feet of water and about 13,000 feet under the seabed. At 10 p.m. that evening, an explosion on the rig occurred, killing 11 workers. Transocean announced the explosion in a statement the next day and said that the company had begun an investigation. On April 22, the rig sank, and a five-mile-long oil slick had become visible. The rig had an estimated value of $560 million. The well that was gushing oil had been cemented by Halliburton.

By April 25, the U.S. Coast Guard had estimated that the underwater well was leaking 1,000 barrels of crude oil per day. Three days later, the Coast Guard modified the estimate and said that 5,000 barrels were leaking each day. Louisiana declared a state of emergency because the slick posed a danger to the state's coastline and other natural resources. President BARACK OBAMA said that BP was "ultimately responsible" and that "my administration will continue to use every single available resource at our disposal, including potentially the DEPARTMENT OF DEFENSE, to address the incident."

BP chairman Tony Hayward accepted responsibility on the company's behalf and said that the company planned to pay costs for claims and for the cleanup effort. Obama visited the site on May 2. By the middle of May, though, different companies (BP, Transocean, and Halliburton) involved in the spill were blaming one another. Executives from the companies testified before the SENATE Energy Committee on May 11 and 12. Obama later criticized the executives for creating a "ridiculous spectacle" for trading blame for the disaster. Jeff Bingaman, the chair of the Senate Energy Committee, commented that the spill had been caused by "a cascade of errors, technical, human and regulatory.".

BP tried a number of different measures to control the spill. The company attempted to install a containment chamber, but the company soon discovered that the chamber would be ineffective. The company also said it would try to plug up the well by shooting materials such as shredded tires and golf balls into the well at high pressure. The company likewise tried to insert a tube into the well to capture some of the oil and gas. By the end of May, though, oil had reached the Louisiana marshlands, and BP announced that its efforts to plug the well had been unsuccessful so far. The company was also burning off a considerable amount of oil in addition to its efforts to contain and collect the oil. The company finally stopped the leak on July 15 by capping the well. Experts have estimated that about four million barrels of oil spilled into the Gulf. This is about 16 times larger than the Exxon Valdez spill in 1989.

By the middle of June, BP had spent more than a billion dollars on the spill, though U.S. officials continued to criticize BP for its efforts. Hayward appeared before Congress on June 17, where members of Congress criticized BP for cutting corners and not heeding to warnings before the disaster. By that time, BP had announced that it had agreed to set aside a $20 billion fund to handle damage claims related to the spill. However, Hayward caused a stir when he announced that he was taking a day off to engage in recreational activity. By June 22, the company had announced that company executive Bob Dudley would handle the day-to-day operations related to the spill so that Hayward could focus on other aspects of the company. A month later, the company announced that Dudley would replace Hayward as company CEO in October.

Hundreds of individuals who claimed to be harmed by the spill filed suit against BP during the summer of 2010. In August, the U.S. Judicial Panel on MULTIDISTRICT LITIGATION ruled that Judge Carl Barbier of the U.S. **District Court** for the Eastern District of Louisiana. By April 2011, more than 350 plaintiffs had filed claims against BP based on a range of theories, including those based on **tort law** and maritime law. Experts have estimated the total damages to be about $50 billion, and BP had reportedly set aside more than $30 billion during the summer of 2010 to pay the spill costs and handle the various legal claims. Under the Oil Pollution Act of 1990, Pub. L. No. 101-380, 104 Stat. 484 (1990), BP's civil liabilities would be capped at $75 million. Members of Congress in 2010 said that this cap was outdated, and the House approved a bill that would have lifted the cap. However, the measure was never approved by the Senate. BP may still own hundreds of billions in civil and criminal fines and penalties imposed by the U.S. government.

BP itself filed claims against Transocean, Halliburton, and manufacturer Cameron International, the latter of which manufactured a mechanism that was designed to prevent blowouts. BP has sought $40 billion from Transocean, arguing that the *Deepwater Horizon* was unreasonably dangerous and that the device that Cameron had installed had failed because it had a faulty design. Transocean responded by filing a COUNTERCLAIM against BP. Transocean said BP's claims were baseless, noting in a statement, "The Deepwater Horizon was a world-class drilling rig manned by a top-flight crew that was put in **jeopardy** by BP, the operator of the Macondo well, through a series of cost-saving decisions that increased risk—in some cases, severely."

As of April 2011, BP had paid less than $4 billion of the $20 billion fund it had established to pay victims of the spill. This fund is separate from the money the company set aside to pay its legal fees. About 857,000 individuals and businesses have filed claims, and the company said it had approved 300,000 of these claims. In several cases, though, the company has sought more information or simply rejected claims as baseless. According to a company statement, "Amounts requested by claimants very often bear no reasonable relationship to the damages actually proven." The company also noted that one claimant had submitted a request for the entire $20 billion fund.

California Voters Defeat Proposition 23

California voters made an historic move in November 2010 when, despite severe state budget constraints, they voted to retain the state's Global Warming Solutions Act (AB 32). They did this by defeating a ballot measure, "Proposition 23," which sought to delay implementation of the Act. Proponents of the defeated Proposition 23 claimed that continued implementation of the Global Warming Solutions Act would exacerbate the state's weak economy by raising energy prices and

increasing unemployment, but voters thought otherwise: Proposition 23 was defeated by a margin of 61 to 38 percent, representing a higher vote margin than any other proposition on the ballot.

The fight over the state's Global Warming Solutions Act had been characterized by environmentalists and some of the media as a "David and Goliath" battle. The law, which included California's Low Carbon Fuel Standard, was considered one of the nation's most ambitious and comprehensive efforts to curb greenhouse gas emissions, while the "Golden State" itself maintained its reputation as a progressive state having a larger than average population of energy and environmentally-concerned citizens. According to the *Los Angeles Times,* no environmental campaign in U.S. history could boast the level of activism as seen in California for the November 2010 vote showdown. A record 3,200 volunteers made 2.8 million telephone calls to voters and sent out 3.4 million pieces of mail urging voters to defeat Proposition 23. Additionally, opponents made 379,676 on-campus contacts with college students and operated a sophisticated outreach program by computer to identify and contact 481,000 voters with get-out-and-vote text and phone messages. It paid off.

On the other side, backers of Proposal 23 were reported to be a coalition that included two large Texas oil refineries, the California Manufacturers and Technology Association, the secretary-treasurer of the State Building and Construction Trades Council, and the Americans for Prosperity of California. However, most of California's largest corporations, such as Chevron, Pacific Gas and Electric, and Sempra Energy, remained neutral or actively opposed Proposition 23. In the end, backers raised only $10.6 million to **advance** the measure.

Conversely, more than $31 million was raised to defeat Proposition 23. Backed by the Bill Gates Foundation as well as other wealthy philanthropists such as Tom Steyer, a San Francisco HEDGE FUND manager, opponents also had the support of big-name celebrities, including Leonardo DiCaprio, Edward James Olmos, Robert Redford, and *Avatar*'s James Cameron, who all urged a "No to Proposal 23" vote. Governor Arnold Schwarzenegger also crossed the state, verbally attacking the "self-serving greed" of the two petroleum refiners that were the proposition's principal funders.

Much of the money raised by opponents was spent on television commercials urging voters to "Stop the job-killing dirty energy proposition." The funds also supported grass-roots efforts to unite dozens of entities such as unions, religious organizations, Latino community groups, green-tech trade groups, the National Wildlife FEDERATION, the Climate Works Foundation, the American Lung Association, Silicon Valley green-tech giants John Doerr and Vinod Khosla, and virtually every environmental group in the state. Fred Krupp, president of the New York-based Environmental Defense Fund, told a *Los Angeles Times* reporter, "Almost 10 million Californians got a chance to vote and sent a clear message that they want a clean energy future. And this was in an economic downturn. There has never been anything this big. It is going to send a signal to other parts of the country and beyond." As Krupp was quoted in a *BioMass* article reporting the vote results, "Voters asked their leaders to chart a future toward clean energy, less pollution, and less dependence on imported oil. Congress should pay attention."

In fact, Congress had failed to pass comprehensive climate change legislation in 2009 and 2010, mostly due to disagreement over the controversial "cap and trade" program. All eyes then turned to California to gauge whether a budget crisis would cause voters to put the environmentally-friendly law on hold. Proposition 23 was not a measure asking for a **rescission** or a re-vote on the Global Warming Solutions Act. It merely represented a measure to delay the Act's implementation until the state unemployment rate dropped to 5.5 percent or less for a full year. As of 2010, the rate was hovering near 12 percent.

But as Cathy Calfo, executive director of the Apollo Alliance, a San Francisco-based coalition of labor, business, environmental, and community leaders, said in the *BioMass* article, "We have seen firsthand what the clean energy economy can do ... As unemployment surged at the outset of the recession, jobs in California's clean energy economy actually grew by 5 percent. This state leads the nation in the number of clean energy jobs, businesses and PATENTS generated."

The Environmental Defense Fund also noted that the global green energy market was expected to increase 800 percent in the upcoming decade, from a $10 billion market in 2010 to an $80 billion market in 2020. This would make it the world's third-largest industrial sector.

The November 2010 midterm elections also brought back former California Democratic governor Jerry Brown to again serve in that capacity. Sworn into office in January 2011, he announced his objective to derive at least 33 percent of California's energy needs from renewable sources.

ERISA

CIGNA Corp. v. Amara

The EMPLOYEE RETIREMENT INCOME SECURITY ACT of 1974 (ERISA), 29 U.S.C. §§ 1001 **et seq.** establishes a number of disclosure requirements that employers must comply with regarding retirement plans. ERISA also contains provisions related to remedies available to a court when an employee seeks relief. In 2011, the U.S. SUPREME COURT reviewed a case involving some of those remedies that a court can apply. In *CIGNA Corp. v. Amara*, NO. 09-804, 2011 WL 1832824 (U.S. 2011), the Court concluded that the **district court** had applied the incorrect ERISA provision to a retirement plan administered by the health insurance company CIGNA.

Before 1998, CIGNA had provided a retirement plan for employees who had at least five years of service to the company. Under this plan, an employee at retirement would receive an **annuity**, the amount of which depended on the length of the employee's service and the employee's salary. The actual terms varied depending on when an employee had begun working at CIGNA. For some plans, the annuity would be based on two percent of the employee's average salary over the final three years of service, multiplied by the number of years the employee had worked. For other employees, the percentage was one and two-thirds for the final five years the employee worked, multiplied by the number of years worked. Under either method, a longtime company employee could earn an annuity equaling 60 percent of the employee's final salary. Thus, an longtime employee who made an average of 166,666 per year for the final three (or five) years of his employment could make $100,000 per year until death from the annuity.

CIGNA decided in 1997 to change its retirement plan. Instead of the plan that provided the annuity, the new plan would feature an account-balance plan. Under the new plan, the company would create an **individual retirement account** for each employee. The company would contribute a certain amount ranging from three to eight and a half percent to each account, with the amount depending on an employee's age, length of service, and other factors. The account earned **compound interest** of no less than four and a half percent and no more than nine percent each year. At retirement, each employee could receive the lump sum amount that was in the employee's account, or the employee could purchase an annuity from the lump sum amount. The company put the plan into place in December 1998 but applied the plan retroactively so that it made the deposits for amounts due as of January 1, 1998.

Employees were concerned about the benefits that had accrued before January 1, 1998. CIGNA promised that each employee would receive an amount equal to the value of the employee's benefit already accrued under the former plan. The method involved calculating the amount that the employee would have received as an annuity as of the employee's retirement date and then discounting the amount to the value as of January 1, 1998. The company also promised that upon retirement, employees would receive the greater of the amount of the entitled benefit as of January 1, 1998 or the amount in the retirement account created under the new plan. CIGNA told employees that the new plan would significantly enhance retirement benefits and that employees would see growth in their retirement benefits each year. Moreover, the company promised that the company would not save money from the change in retirement plans.

However, employees learned that the company actually saved about $10 million per year because of the change in plans. Moreover, some employees discovered that they were in a worse position under the new plan than they would have been had the old plan remained in force. For instance, the old plan allowed employees to retire early, beginning at age 55. Under the new plan, an employee who retired early would receive significantly less from the company's deposit that was supposed to be equal to amount of benefits accrued before January 1, 1998. The new plan also shifted risk of reduced interest rates from the company under the old plan to the employees. Under the old plan, the company had to pay the annuity amount irrespective of the rate of interest. Under the new plan, the amount in each employee's retirement account depended on the interest that had accrued, meaning that the amount depended on the interest rates.

The employees brought a **class action** suit against CIGNA, arguing that the company had failed to disclose all of the features of the new plan. In two decisions (accompanied by two long opinions and orders), Judge Mark R. Kravitz of the U.S. District Court for the District of Columbia ruled that the company had violated several of ERISA's disclosure requirements when it first implemented the plan. According to Kravitz, the company was forbidden from reducing certain benefits without providing written notice, and the company was required to provide summaries to employees of material modifications to the plans.

Under § 502(a)(1)(B) of ERISA, the employees could bring a "civil action" to "recover benefits due . . . under the terms of his plan." Kravitz relied on this section to order relief. The specific relief required the company to comply with a two-step process. The first step focused on reforming the terms of the plan. The second step focused on requiring the company to pay amounts for benefits that the company owed to employees under the reformed plan.

CIGNA appealed the decision to the Second **Circuit Court** of Appeals, which summarily affirmed the district court's decision. CIGNA then appealed the decision to the U.S. Supreme Court. In an 8-0 decision, with Justice ANTONIN SCALIA concurring and Justice SONIA SOTOMAYOR not participating, the Court vacated and remanded the case to the district court. Writing for the majority, Justice STEPHEN BREYER first considered the language contained in § 502(a)(1)(B). Breyer concluded that this section only allowed the district court to provide relief based on the terms of an existing plan. Since the district court had reformed the plan and ordered relief based on the reformed plan, the Court concluded that the district court had based its relief on the wrong law.

However, the Court acknowledged that § 502(a)(3) of ERISA could allow the relief that the district court ordered. Under § 502(a)(3), the court could order "appropriate equitable relief," which would include such typical equitable remedies as **reformation** of contract and **estoppel**. The Court remanded the case so that the district court could consider the type of equitable relief sought.

Scalia, joined by Justice CLARENCE THOMAS, did not believe that the Court had to analyze the case beyond the Court's conclusion that § 502(a)(1)(B) did not authorize the relief that the district court ordered. In his words, Scalia "would simply remand" the case without the analysis of whether § 502(a)(3) provides the underlying basis for relief.

ESTABLISHMENT CLAUSE

Latin Cross on Federal Land Violation of Establishment Clause

The placement of religious symbols and monuments on government property has spawned many constitutional battles over whether such objects violate the separation of church and state under the First Amendment's Establishment Clause. The City of San Diego has dealt with such an issue since 1989 involving a large Latin Cross that sits on a hilltop in the La Jolla community of the city. The Cross, which was first erected in the 1920s as a purely religious symbol in a La Jolla municipal park, was later surrounded with military and patriotic symbols after the 1989 lawsuit and made part of a war memorial. The controversy over the Cross led in 2006 to Congress using its **eminent domain** power to make the park a federal veterans' memorial. A lawsuit soon challenged the constitutionality of the Cross on federal land, leading to 2011 decision by the Ninth Circuit Appeals. The appeals court, in *Trunk v. City of San Diego*, 628 F.3d 1099 (9th Cir.2011), held that the Cross violated the Establishment Clause.

The history of the Cross on Mount Soledad reaches back to 1913, when it was first erected on city land. The cross was replaced in the 1920s and was blown down in 1952. The present Cross was erected in 1954. It is 29-fee high and 12 feet across. It is mounted atop a 14-foot base and weighs approximately 24 tons. It is visible from miles away and looms over the drivers who frequent Interstate 5. The Mount Soledad Memorial Association has paid for most of the Cross's upkeep, though the city has spend some public funds on it. After a lawsuit was filed in 1989 challenging the constitutionality of the Cross's location on public land, the park was updated to include an extensive war memorial. The memorial includes six concentric walls around the base of the Cross and about 2,100 black stone plaques honoring individual veterans, platoons, and groups of soldiers.

The 1989 lawsuit led to the federal **district court** applying a provision of the California state constitution to bar the display of the cross on city land. In response, the city placed on the ballot an initiative that would authorize the sale of the small parcel of land sitting directly under the Cross to the Memorial Association. Voters approved and the land was sold to the association without soliciting other offers. The district court invalidated the sale but the city remedied the situation by soliciting bids and selling it to the association again. After further LITIGATION the Ninth Circuit ruled this sale was invalid, as it structured to give an advantage to bidders who wished to preserve the Cross. This led two local U.S. congressmen to introduce in 2005 legislation that designated the site as a national veterans' memorial and authorized the federal government to accept it as a donation. The law was enacted in 2004 but was immediately challenged. Congress then enacted a law in 2006 that used its power of EMINENT DOMAIN to seize the land. The memorial was put under the control of the DEFENSE DEPARTMENT. Again there was a legal challenge. This time the district court ruled that the Cross did not violate the FIRST AMENDMENT, setting the stage for the Ninth Circuit to consider the issue.

A three-judge panel of the Ninth Circuit unanimously ruled that the location of the Cross on public land violated the Establishment Clause. Judge M. Margaret McKeown, writing for the court, acknowledged the emotions raised by the protracted litigation, noting that "Hard decisions can make good law, but they are not painless for good people and their concerns." McKeown applied the framework set out by the

U.S. Sᴜᴘʀᴇᴍᴇ Cᴏᴜʀᴛ to evaluate monuments on public land. That framework requires a fact-intensive, but flexible assessment of whether a monument is faithful to the underlying purposes of the Establishment Clause. Factors to assess include the "monument's purpose, the perception of the purpose by viewers, the extent to which the monument's physical setting suggests the sacred, and the monument's history."

The court first determined that the congressional purpose in acquiring the memorial was secular, as the legislation sought to preserve a veterans' memorial. It then explored the primary effect of the memorial to determine if it was secular or sectarian. The display of the Latin Cross was crucial to this analysis, as the court noted it was exclusively a Christian symbol. The court then looked at the history and makeup of U.S. war memorials since the Civil War. Drawing on the submission of an historical expert on war memorials, the court pointed out that the use of the cross is very rare in the nation's history. The cross "never became a default headstone in military ceremonies in the United States." Aside from crosses at Arlington and Gettysburg memorials, no crosses served as war memorials on public land.

Turning to the Mount Soledad Memorial, the appeals court found that the Cross overwhelmed the more recently added war memorial elements of the memorial. Moreover, the history of the Cross demonstrated its sectarian roots: the association regularly conducted Easter services at the memorial until at least 2000. In addition, local maps referred to it as the "Easter Cross." The court also pointed to the fact that Christian advocacy groups were behind many of the efforts to keep the Cross on Mount Soledad, including the legislation making the memorial federal property. Finally, it referenced La Jolla's anti-Semitic history as an explanation for the historical lack of complaint about the Cross. Complaints only began after the community ended discriminatory housing policies against Jews in the 1960s.

The court placed weight on the physical setting of the Cross. It dominates the memorial grounds and is the only part of the memorial visible from below. Judge McKeown concluded that a "reasonable observer would view the Cross as the primary feature of the Memorial, with the secular elements subordinated to it. It

is the cross that catches the eye at almost any angle, not the memorial plaques." The overall message conveyed by the Cross was government's endorsement of religion, which is not allowed by the Establishment Clause.

ETHICS

The branch of philosophy that defines what is good for the individual and for society and establishes the nature of obligations, or duties, that people owe themselves and one another.

Conviction and Censure of Representative Charles Rangel

Article I, Section V. of the U.S. Constitution provides that members of Congress shall discipline their own, if needed. "Each House may determine the Rules of its Proceedings, punish its Members for disorderly Behavior, and, with the Concurrence of two-thirds, expel a Member." In November 2010, House Representative and longtime congressman Charles Rangel (D-NY) became the fourth member of Congress ever to be censured by the House Ethics Committee, to date. This followed his conviction by a congressional ethics subcommittee on 11 of 13 counts of ethics violations following a condensed "trial" and six hours of deliberation.

In Congressional history, the House Ethics Committee has recommended the more severe punishment of expulsion only four times for members of Congress, although several members have resigned under threat of expulsion. At the other end of the spectrum, nine congressmen have been reprimanded, the lesser of all three punishments.

Popular "Charlie" Rangel won a 21st two-year term to Congress in the November 2010 midterm elections, even as Democrats conceded a loss of control of the House to a newly-elected Republican majority. By that time, Rangel had served 40 years in Congress, representing the Harlem district of New York and winning this latest two-year term with 80 percent of the vote.

Earlier in 2010, Rangel had resigned as chairman of the powerful House Ways and Means Committee, following admonishment for corporate/constituent-sponsored trips in violation of House "gift" rules. An initial investigation into a Caribbean trip revealed that he should have known that his aides were evading ethics rules.

The 13 charges against Rangel primarily concerned finances and **abuse of power**. The adjudicatory congressional panel, comprised of five Democrats and five Republicans, found that Rangel had used the power of his office for personal benefit. He was charged with, and convicted of, using House stationery and staff to solicit money for a school center of **public policy** named after him at the City College of New York. More seriously, he was found guilty of soliciting donors for the new center who had pending interests before the Ways and Means Committee. (Technically, members of Congress may solicit donors and funds for nonprofit entities, even those bearing their names. However, they may not use congressional staff or resources, including congressional letterhead, to do so.) Chief Counsel Blake Chisam, who led the prosecution, noted in a subsequent article in *Human Events* that "After the 2006 election, after it was clear that [Rangel] would become chair of the Ways and Means Committee, the college started to get larger contributions. The donors, they had business interests before the Congress."

The panel split on another "gift" ban charge involving the school of PUBLIC POLICY, as plans for the center included an office and the archiving of his personal and professional papers.

The panel also found Rangel guilty (two counts combined into one) of improperly using Congress's free franked-mail privileges. Rangel was additionally found guilty of improperly using a residential rent-stabilized apartment in Harlem as his campaign office; failing to report $600,000 of income on financial disclosure documents, and failing to pay taxes on rental income from REAL ESTATE he owned in the Dominican Republic.

California Democrat Zoe Lofgren, the panel's chairperson, was quoted by media reporter Reuters as saying there was "clear and convincing evidence" against Rangel. Lofgren,

noting the 9-1 vote for House censure of Rangel following his convictions, explained that reprimands were appropriate for serious ethics violations, censure for "more serious" violations, and expulsion for the most serious. Expulsion for Rangel was not considered. Ultimately, the panel's chief counsel found "no evidence of corruption" and attributed Rangel's indiscretions to being "sloppy in his personal finances."

The panel's decision came just one day after the panel rejected Rangel's emotional plea to have the trial delayed because he lacked legal counsel. In fact, he had been represented by a team of lawyers through October, at which time he parted ways with them. Rangel declared he could not afford to hire new counsel after paying nearly $2 million in legal fees over the prior two years. But according to Emily Miller, senior editor of *Human Events*, Rangel paid the $2 million with political donations to his campaign, also a House rule violation.

For his part, Rangel remained defiant, blaming the media and bad publicity for an "unfair" trial proceeding. He strongly decried continuation of the trial without his being able to obtain new legal counsel, arguing that the Constitution guaranteed him that right and that his due process rights were violated. Rangel further complained of a lack of an appeals process for House ethics panel decisions.

Several government watchdog groups called for Rangel's resignation. Fred Wertheimer of Democracy 21, in an article for *The Hill*, said that the convictions demonstrated the need for new ethics rules that prohibit members of Congress from soliciting money for their own namesake institutions or centers. He urged the House to adopt new rules barring the practice. "There are inherent conflict-of-interest and appearance problems" when members solicit funds for entities honoring them, he said. "Members of Congress should be prohibited from soliciting money to build monuments to themselves."

FEDERAL COMMUNICATIONS COMMISSION

Second Circuit Rules FCC Indecency Policy Unconstitutional

The FCC's ability to proscribe indecency over the public airwaves has been tested by the **federal courts** in a case involving the penalizing of a television network for allowing the broadcast of the F-word. The case involving the major television networks and the FCC reached the SUPREME COURT. After the Court ruled that the FCC had not acted arbitrarily and capriciously under the Administrative Procedures Act in changing its indecency policy, it remanded the case to the appeals court for further consideration. In 2010 the Second Circuit ruled that the policy was unconstitutional on FIRST AMENDMENT grounds in *Fox Television Stations, Inc. v. F.C.C ,*, 613 F.3d 317 (2010: 2nd Cir.).

The case followed a major change in the FCC's enforcement of indecency violations. It rarely sanctioned networks or local stations for the uttering of a four-letter word. However, this relaxed enforcement policy changed in 2003 when the rock star Bono uttered the F-word at the Golden Globes Award Show, broadcast by NBC. The FCC announced a new policy that any use of the F-word was indecent, no matter how fleeting or in a non-sexual context. In addition, the commission also held that the use of the word was profane. Broadcasters were put

on notice that any broadcast of the F-word would subject them to monetary penalties. In addition, the FCC suggested that broadcasters implement a delay technology that would give them the time to "bleep" out indecent and profane words from live broadcasts.

In 2006 the FCC backed up its new position by ruling that several live broadcast utterances of the F-word or the S-word violated this policy. The FCC declined to assess monetary penalties because the broadcasts occurred before the Golden Globes decision, but its shift in policy alarmed broadcasters. The FOX, CBS, NBC, and ABC television networks appealed the FCC order, contending the new policy was arbitrary and capricious and that it raised First Amendment CENSORSHIP issues.

In 2007, the Second **Circuit Court** of Appeals, in a 2-1 decision, agreed with the television networks that the policy change was arbitrary and capricious. It declined to rule on the First Amendment issue because the first ground was sufficient to settle the matter. The court reviewed the FCC's history of policing indecent speech. It noted that the FCC had not aggressively pursued isolated utterances of OBSCENITY and **profanity**. Instead, it concentrated on material that was explicitly sexual or excretory and was patently offensive as measured by contemporary community standards.

As to the FCC's 2006 ruling, the appeals court pointed out that the utterances in dispute took place on two awards shows and a morning news show. The application of the commission's new "fleeting expletive" policy had to be considered in light of its previous policy and the reasons justifying the new one. The court set aside the policy because it was arbitrary and capricious. The court acknowledged that administrative agencies should be accorded great deference in managing their responsibilities but they when they make policies there must be a "rational connection between the facts found and the choice made." The networks contended that the FCC had acted arbitrarily because it made a complete about-face on its treatment of "fleeting expletives" without providing a reasoned explanation that justified its action.

The court agreed, finding no compelling reasons to justify the change. The FCC's primary reason for the crackdown was a so-called "first blow" theory. Because the airwaves entered the privacy of the home uninvited and without warning, allowing isolated or fleeting expletives "unfairly forces viewers (including children) to take "the first blow." The court rejected this as a "reasoned basis" for overturning the prior policy for several reasons. First, the FCC did not provide a reasonable explanation for why it had changed its perception, after 30 years, that a fleeting expletive was not a harmful "first blow." Moreover, the first blow theory had no rational connection to the commission's actual policy toward fleeting expletives. The FCC had ruled that it would excuse an expletive if it occurred during a "bona fide news interview," and it had told the court during oral argument that the news exception was a broad one. For example, a broadcast of the oral argument, where the offending expletives were spoken in **open court**, would be permissible. In addition, the FCC had permitted the airing of the film "Saving Private Ryan," which had numerous expletives, because censoring the words would have detracted from the power and realism of this artistic work. These scenarios would not have prevented viewers, including children, from taking the "first blow" caused by the expletives. Therefore, this theory could not justify the change in policy.

The Supreme Court, in a 5-4 decision, overturned the appeals court decision and upheld the FCC policy in__U.S. __, 129 S.Ct. 1800, 173 L.Ed.2d 738 (2009). *Federal*

Communications Commission v. Fox Television Stations, , __U.S.__, 129 S.Ct. 1800, 173 L.Ed.2d 738 (2009). The Court concluded that there was no basis in the Administrative Procedure Act that all agency change must be subjected to more searching review. An agency must show that there are good reasons for the new policy but it "need not demonstrate to a court's satisfaction that the reasons for the new policy are better than the reasons for the old one." Based on this assumption, the Court pointed out that the FCC had announced it was breaking new ground. In addition, its reasons for expanding the scope of enforcement were "entirely rational." It was reasonable to conclude that "it made no sense to distinguish between literal and nonliteral uses of offensive words, requiring repetitive use to render only the latter indecent." Moreover, that fact that technological advances make it easier for broadcasters to bleep out offending words supported the commission's policy.

The Court remanded the case to the Second Circuit, where the broadcasters were permitted to **advance** their First Amendment challenge to the FCC policy. In its 2010 decision, the appeals court struck down the policy as unconstitutional, as it violated the First Amendment's right to **freedom of speech**.

FEDERAL PREEMPTION

Pliva v. Mensing

The U.S. FOOD AND DRUG ADMINISTRATION (FDA) is tasked with, among other things, regulating labels attached to prescription and non-prescription medications (as well as their packaging). Frequently, in products liability lawsuits, the focus is on information contained on such labels and packaging, and in particular, whether they list any warnings of side effects or adverse reactions associated with the medicine or drug.

In *Pliva, Inc. v. Mensing*, No. 09-993, 564 U.S. ___ (2011), the U.S. SUPREME COURT held that federal drug regulations applicable to generic drug manufacturers preempted any state tort laws that permitted claims for failure to provide adequate warning labels. Under the "Supremacy Clause" of the U.S. Constitution, Article IV, all laws made pursuant to the U.S. Constitution and all treaties made under the authority of the United States shall be "the supreme law of the land." The doctrine of federal **preemption** holds that, as long as a federal law is constitutional, it preempts any conflicting or divergent state laws on the same matter.

In the consolidated cases under *Pliva*, the subject medicine was generic metoclopramide. The drug is generally prescribed to speed the movement of food through the gastro-intestinal (digestive) tract. Metoclopramide is commonly used to treat problems such as diabetic gastro-paresis and gastroesophageal reflux disorder. In 1980, the FDA first approved metoclopramide tablets under the brand name Reglan. Five years later, after Reglan's patent expired, generic manufacturers began to produce and market metoclopramide.

In 2001, Gladys Mensing, a Minnesota woman, was prescribed metoclopramide (Reglan) to treat her diabetic gastroparesis. Her pharmacist filled her prescription with a generic form of Reglan, which she took for four years. She eventually developed tardive dyskinesia, a neurological disorder that manifests in uncontrollable and repetitive body movements. Another woman, Julie DeMahy, developed the same disorder after being prescribed Reglan in 2002; her pharmacist also filled her prescription with the generic metoclopramide.

In separate state-court tort actions, both women filed suit against the manufacturers of the generic metoclopramide, Pliva, Inc. and Actavis Inc., respectively. Each PLAINTIFF alleged that she had been prescribed metoclopramide, that long-term use had caused her medical disorder, and that DEFENDANT manufacturers were liable under state **tort law** for failing to provide adequate warning labels. The plaintiffs further alleged that they would not have taken the generic form of Reglan if the generic manufacturers had petitioned the FDA to strengthen the requirements of labels in order to satisfy state laws.

Plaintiffs' respective state tort laws required that manufacturers that were aware or should be aware of a drug's danger must label the drug in a way that renders it reasonably safe. The plaintiffs alleged that defendant manufacturers knew, or should have known that (1) the long-term use of metoclopramide carried a high risk of tardive dyskinesis, and (2) that their labels did not adequately warn of that risk. Taking

these allegations as true, the state laws required the manufacturers to use a different, stronger label than the one used.

But under federal law, FDA regulations, as interpreted by the FDA, prevented the defendant generic manufacturers from independently or unilaterally changing their generic drugs' safety labels. Under such federal regulation, a manufacturer wishing to market a new drug must, in the FDA approval process, prove that the new drug is safe and effective and that the proposed label is accurate and adequate. The 1984 amendments to these regulations (Hatch-Waxman Amendments) allow a generic drug manufacturer to gain FDA approval simply by showing that its drug is equivalent to an already-approved brand-name drug, and that the label proposed for it is the same as that approved for the brand-name drug.

Under FDA regulations, brand-name drug manufacturers are required to update warning labels as new facts become available. This process does not cover generics, but under FDA, generic labels must be identical to the current version of their brand-name counterparts. In other words, federal law requires generic manufactures to carry labels identical to their brand-name counterparts, but state law required manufactures to label their products in a manner that renders them "reasonable safe."

In both lawsuits, defendant manufacturers asserted affirmative defenses that FDA regulations and federal statutes pre-empted the state tort laws. Specifically, they defended that federal statutes and regulations required the same safety and effectiveness labeling for generic metoclopramide as was mandated at the time for Reglan, and their labeling met those requirements.

The Fifth and Eight Circuit Courts of Appeals, respectively, rejected these arguments and found in favor of plaintiffs. They held that plaintiffs' claims were not preempted by federal regulation or law.

The U.S. Supreme Court reversed both circuits' decisions. At the relevant time pertinent to these lawsuits, defendant manufacturers' labels were the same as that of their equivalent brand-name counterpart, Reglan. Technically, this meant that they were in a no-win situation. According to plaintiffs, they were required to strengthen their warning labels under the respective state laws, but under federal law, they were prohibited from changing their labels unless Reglan's manufacturer first changed its label. The Court held that it was impossible for them to comply with both.

As Chief Justice JOHN ROBERTS wrote separately, in this **plurality** opinion,

> If the [defendant]manufacturers had independently changed their labels to satisfy their state-law duty to attach a safer label to their generic metoclopramide, they would have violated the federal requirement that generic drug labels be the same as the corresponding brand-name drug labels … Thus, it was impossible for them to comply with both state and federal law.

The Court, thus finding the laws conflicting, turned to the question of federal PREEMPTION. It concluded that the FDA regulations preempted state TORT LAW, and that if defendants' labels were identical in warnings to that of the brand-name counterpart, they were in compliance with the law. In other words, if the plaintiffs had taken Reglan instead of the generic equivalent, they could have sued for inadequate labeling. But because generic variations only required the same label as their brand-name equivalent, plaintiffs' taking the generic form had no **cause of action**, because the generic manufacturers were in compliance with relevant federal law.

Still, the plaintiffs had argued that federal law nevertheless provided a way for the defendants to modify their labels in time to prevent the injuries here. For example, the FDA has a "changes-being-effected" process (CBE) which allows manufacturers, without prior approval, to add to or strengthen their warning labels. Alternatively, they could have sent "Dear Doctor" letters to prescribing physicians, providing additional information and warnings. However, the FDA responded that the generic manufacturers could not have employed either of these processes to unilaterally change their labels, making them different from their brand-name counterparts. The Court, deferring to the agency's interpretation of its own regulations, moved on to the question of pre-emption.

Importantly, the Court did not rule on the merits of the adequacy of the warnings contained on defendants' labels, or, for that matter, on the identical labels of their brand-name counterparts. The only question before the Court was whether state laws could hold generic manufacturers to a different labeling requirement than what was required under federal law. Where state and federal laws conflict, said the Court, federal law controls. Congress and the FDA retain the authority to change the laws, as they see fit.

The court also rejected the argument that defendants could not avail themselves of the preemption defense because they had not asked the FDA to assist them in changing the corresponding brand-name label. As the Court had found "impossibility " in requiring defendants to comply with both state and federal law, this was not a question before the Court. State law required a stronger label; it did not require communications with the FDA about the possibility of a safer label.

Justice CLARENCE THOMAS delivered the opinion of the Court, although a plurality majority prevailed. Justice SONIA SOTOMAYOR, joined by Justices RUTH BADER GINSBURG, STEPHEN BREYER, and ELENA KAGAN, dissented. The DISSENT argued that state law was not preempted unless Congress expressly declared such in federal law. They argued that public health and safety were matters entrusted to the states, and that these lawsuits concerned health and safety matters.

FIRST AMENDMENT

Ninth Circuit Strikes Down Stolen Valor Act

Although the FIRST AMENDMENT protects a person's right to free speech, the SUPREME COURT has carved out exceptions for certain types of speech. These exceptions include OBSCENITY, "fighting words," and **defamation**. If speech does not fit into one of these exceptions, courts will use the **strict scrutiny** standard of review to evaluate the government's regulation of expression. Under the STRICT SCRUTINY standard, which is the most rigorous test for constitutionality, the government must demonstrate a compelling **state interest** and show that it has used the least restrictive means possible to achieve this interest. The interplay between First Amendment exceptions and strict scrutiny was displayed by the Ninth **Circuit Court** of Appeals in *United States v. Alvarez*, 617 F.3d 1198 (9th Cir.2010). The appeals court, in a 2-1 ruling, found that a federal **criminal law** that prohibited individuals from falsely claiming they had earned military honors was unconstitutional. The majority concluded that the act failed strict scrutiny, while the dissenting judge believed the speech in question fell into one of the First Amendment exceptions to protection.

Xavier Alvarez, a newly elected California local water board official, introduced himself at a board meeting by saying he had served as a Marine for 25 years before retiring from the ARMED SERVICES and that he had been awarded the Congressional Medal of Honor in 1987. It was later revealed that Alvarez was a habitual liar, falsely claiming at different times to have played professional hockey, worked as a police officer, and to have been secretly married to a Mexican starlet. After the FBI obtained a recording of the board meeting, Alvarez was indicted on two counts of violating the Stolen Valor Act of 2005, 18 U.S.C. § 704(b)(c). The act makes it a crime for a person to falsely represent orally or in writing that he or she has been awarded any decoration or medal authorized by Congress for the U.S. armed forces. A person convicted under this law is subject to fines and up to six months imprisonment. However, if a person falsely claims the Medal of Honor, the sentence is enhanced to one year imprisonment. Alvarez conditionally pleaded guilty but reserved the right to appeal the constitutionality of the law. He was sentenced to pay a $5,000 fine, to serve three years of PROBATION, and to perform 416 hours of COMMUNITY SERVICE.

The Ninth Circuit heard Alvarez's appeal and sided with him as to the unconstitutionality of the Stolen Valor Act on a 2-1 vote. Judge Milan Smith, Jr., writing for the majority, noted that content-based restrictions of the act are ordinarily subject to strict scrutiny. However, the government argued that speech targeted by the act fell within those "well-defined" and "narrowly limited" classes of speech that are historically unprotected by the First Amendment. An erroneous statement of fact was not worthy of constitutional protection and therefore strict scrutiny was not required.

Judge Smith disagreed, stating that Supreme Court **case law** made clear that "First Amendment protection does not hinge on the truth of the matter expressed." While the government may regulate some false factual speech, not all of it is subject to restrictions. If the government

position was adopted, Smith reasoned that the speaker would have the burden of proving his false statement should be protected from criminal prosecution. Such an approach would run contrary to Supreme Court precedent. In addition, giving the government the right to regulate false factual speech would give it "license to interfere significantly with our private and public conversation." Any rule that certain speech is not protected by the First Amendment is the exception, "which may in turn be subject to other exceptions to protect against such exceptions swallowing the rule."

The majority reviewed the exceptions to First Amendment protection and concluded that none applied. It then applied strict scrutiny to the **statute**. The government argued that it had a compelling interest: the prevention of **fraudulent** claims about receipt of military honors that damages the reputation and meaning of such declaration. This interest was important to motivate the military and protect the integrity of the military honors system. Though Judge Smith acknowledged this interest, he concluded that the government had not proven that this regulation of speech was narrowly tailored to achieve this "noble interest." On the record before the court Judge Smith found it "speculative at best" whether the law was the best and only way to insure the integrity of such medals. It seemed just as likely that the meaning and reputation of the medals were unaffected by those who lie about having received them. In his view the greatest damage was done "to the reputations of the liars themselves." Moreover, the idea that battlefield heroism was motivated in any way by the desire for medals and honors defied comprehension. Therefore, the law was unconstitutional, as it made a "criminal out of a man who was proven to be nothing more than a liar."

Judge Jay Bybee dissented, arguing that the majority had misread Supreme Court cases and in the process "turned the exceptions into the rule and the rule into an exception." He contended that the general rule is that false statements of fact are not protected by the First Amendment, though there was an important exception: "where protecting a false statement is necessary 'in order to protect speech that matters.'" In this case there was no other speech that mattered-Alvarez knowingly lied about his military service and military honors.

Oklahoma state Rep. Sally Kern, R-Oklahoma City, gestures as she speaks with the media in Oklahoma City, Monday, April 11, 2011. Kern spoke in support of a bill to place into statute the provisions of a state ballot question approved by Oklahoma voters in November that bans the use of Sharia, or Islamic, law.

AP IMAGES/SUE OGROCKI

The law was not overbroad and even if there was some overbreadth it was not "substantial."

Federal Court Puts Oklahoma Ban on Sharia Law on Hold

Since the attacks of September 11, 2001, attention has been focused on international TERRORISM, especially in the Middle East. The fact that the 9-11 attackers were Muslims has placed even greater attention in the U.S. on those who believe in Islam. In Oklahoma, a question was placed on the November 2010 ballot, entitled the "Save our State Amendment," that asked the voters to approve an amendment to the state constitution. The proposed amendment prohibited Oklahoma STATE COURTS from applying INTERNATIONAL LAW or Sharia Law, which are legal precepts based on Islam. After 70 per cent of voters approved the question, state officials started the process to amend the constitution. However, a federal lawsuit was filed, challenging the constitutionality of the provision and asking the court to issue an INJUNCTION that would prevent the amendment of the constitution. The federal **district court** issued a **preliminary injunction** barring implementation of the amendment until it could conduct a full inquiry

into the merits of the case. *Awad v. Ziriax*, __F.Supp.2d__ 2010 WL4814077 (W.D. Okla.2010)

Muneer Awad, an Oklahoma resident, filed the lawsuit. Awad, a Muslim, contended that the amendment barring the use of Sharia Law violated the First Amendment's Establishment Clause and Free Exercise Clause. The state argued that Awad did not have legal standing to bring his lawsuit because he had not suffered an "injury in fact." Under the standing doctrine, **federal courts** insist that plaintiffs bringing suit must demonstrate that they have or will be injured by the law they are challenging. If they fail to prove that connection the court must dismiss the action. The state also claimed Awad lacked standing because his claim that the proposed amendment condemned his religion was personal opinion rather than a legal argument. Moreover, the state argued that Awad's claim that the amendment would invalidate his last will and **testament** was speculative.

Judge Vicki Miles-LaGrange, after reviewing the case filings and conducting a hearing, ruled that Awad did have standing to bring the lawsuit. She noted that on standing, the question was not whether there was a constitutional violation but whether there was "an injury in fact, cause by the challenged action and redressable in court." Moreover, a showing of noneconomic injury is sufficient to confer standing. The judge concluded that Awad had shown that he would suffer an invasion of his FIRST AMENDMENT rights which is "concrete, particularized and imminent." Awad had argued that the amendment would constitute an official condemnation of his religion and that this would result in "a stigma attaching to his person, relegating him to an ineffectual position within the political community." The court found that such a "psychological consequence," when produced by the government does constitute a concrete harm.

Awad also asserted that his First Amendment rights would be violated by the invalidation of his last will and testament, which incorporates various teachings of Mohammed. He argued that the amendment would prevent his last will and testament from being probated, as state courts would not be able to consider Sharia Law. For example, he would not be able to distribute certain of his assets to charity because that article in the will refers to the teaching of Mohammed. The court agreed with this argument and concluded that Awad had standing to bring the lawsuit. The state had also argued that the case was not ripe for consideration. Under the **ripeness** doctrine, courts are not to consider lawsuits which involve uncertain or contingent events. Judge Miles-LaGrange ruled that the case was ripe because all that remained for the amendment to take effect was the certification of the election results, which was a **ministerial** act. In addition, there was no need for the court to wait for an Oklahoma state court to interpret the amendment.

The district court granted Awad a PRELIMINARY INJUNCTION after applying the four-part test for such orders. The PLAINTIFF must show: a substantial likelihood of success on the merits of the case; **irreparable injury** if the injunction is not granted; the threatened injury to the plaintiff outweighs the injury to the DEFENDANT; and the injunction would not be adverse to the PUBLIC INTEREST.

The judge concluded that Awad had a substantial likelihood of succeeding with his First Amendment arguments. Under the Establishment Clause, Awad demonstrated that the amendment impermissibly inhibited religion and fostered "an excessive government entanglement with religion." The amendment reasonably could be viewed as singling out Sharia Law and conveying a "message of disapproval of plaintiff's faith." In addition, Awad had offered testimony that "Sharia Law" is not actually "law," but a set of religious traditions that provide guidance to Muslims. In addition, "Sharia Law" imposed no legal obligations and such "law" differs depending on the country in which the individual Muslim resides. Therefore, Awad's "religious traditions and faith are the only non-legal content subject to the judicial exclusion set forth in the amendment." Judge Miles-LaGrange also found that Awad would likely succeed with his Free Exercise Clause claim. The amendment could reasonably be viewed as singling out Awad's faith, so the law was not neutral on its face. Moreover, the amendment would likely prevent Awad's will from being fully probated by a state court.

As to the second part of the test, the court found that Awad would suffer IRREPARABLE INJURY because of losing his First Amendment

freedoms when the amendment became effective. The third part, involving balancing of harms, clearly favored Awad. The loss of his First Amendment freedoms outweighed "any injury that would occur from delaying the will of the voters being carried out by certifying the election results." Finally, the granting of the injunction would not be adverse to the public interest. While the public has an interest in the will of the voters being carried out, the reasons set out in the other parts of the test showed that the public "has a more profound and long-term interest in upholding an individual's constitutional rights." Therefore, the court blocked the certifying of the results while the case proceeded to a full inquiry on the merits.

Supreme Court Rules that Video Game Law Violates First Amendment

The video game industry is a multi-billion enterprise that has drawn criticism for marketing violent content to adults and children. Some states have attempted to regulate the sale and rental of violent video games to persons under the age of eighteen but they have been struck down as violating the First Amendment's guarantee of freedom of expression. The U.S. SUPREME COURT, *Brown v. Entertainment Merchants Association*, 564 U. S. _____ (2011), ruled similarly when it concluded that California's law that restricted the sale or rental of violent video games to minors violated the FIRST AMENDMENT.

In 2005, the California legislature enacted a law that prohibited the sale or rental of violent video games to minors and required that the packaging of these games be labeled "18." The law described the types of violent acts that merited this prohibition and made violations punishable by a civil fine of $1,000. The video gaming industry immediately challenged the law as unconstitutional in California federal **district court**. The district court agreed, issuing an INJUNCTION that banned the enforcement of the law. The Ninth **Circuit Court** of Appeals upheld this ruling, leading to review by the Supreme Court.

The Court, in a 7-2 decision, upheld the Ninth Circuit ruling. Justice ANTONIN SCALIA, writing for the majority, noted that the most basic principle of the First Amendment is to prevent the government from restricting expression because of its message, its ideas, its subject matter, or its content. The Court has limited restrictions to the First Amendment to a small number of areas, including OBSCENITY, incitement, and fighting words. For a law like the California video **statute**, the state had to survive the highest standard of constitutional review, **strict scrutiny**. Under this standard, the state must show a compelling **state interest** and demonstrate that it has narrowly tailored the law in the least restrictive manner. Justice Scalia concluded that California had failed to meet this standard review.

Justice Scalia cited *U.S. v. Stevens*, 559 U.S.__, 130 S. Ct. 1577, 176 L.Ed.2d 435 (2010), as the controlling precedent. In that case the Court held that new categories of unprotected speech "may not be added to the list by a legislature that concludes certain speech is too harmful to be tolerated." *Stevens* dealt with a federal statute that sought to criminalize the creation, sale, or possession of certain depictions of animal cruelty. The Court struck the law down as an impermissible content-based restriction on speech because there was no American tradition of forbidding the depiction of animal cruelty, though states have long had laws against committing it. Without "persuasive evidence that a novel restriction on content is part of a long (if heretofore unrecognized) tradition of proscription, a legislature may not restrict First Amendment rights." Justice Scalia concluded that California had tried to make violent-speech regulation look like obscenity regulation by inserting similar language into the statute but it was clear that "the obscenity exception to the First Amendment does not cover whatever a legislature finds shocking, but only depictions of "sexual conduct."

The California law sought to create a new category of content-based regulation that was permissible only for speech directed at children. Scalia called this "unprecedented and mistaken." States may protect children from harm "but that does not include a free-floating power to restrict the ideas to which children may be exposed." There was no long-standing tradition of restricting children's access to depictions of violence. Many books given to children to read, such as Grimm's Fairy Tales, contain "no shortage of gore." The consumption of violent entertainment by children has led to resistance since the 1800s. In the 1800s dime novels depicting crime were blamed for juvenile

delinquency. In the early 1900s motion pictures were attacked as corrupting youth. By the 1950s comic books were the villain. California tried to distinguish video games from other forms of entertainment by labeling them "interactive," in that the player participates in the violent action on the screen. However, Scalia concluded that all literature is interactive.

The law failed STRICT SCRUTINY because the legislature failed to identify a compelling STATE INTEREST and the law was not narrowly tailored to achieve its purpose. Scalia stated that California could not show a direct causal link between violent video games and harm to minors. Research had failed to make this causal link and could only show a possible correlation between exposure to violent entertainment and "miniscule real-world effects, such as children's feeling more aggressive or making louder noises in the few minutes after playing a violent game than after playing a non-violent game." As for the regulation itself, it failed because it was both underinclusive and overinclusive. It was underinclusive because the state failed to regulate other sources of violence, including Saturday morning cartoons, the sale of games rated for young children, or the distribution of pictures of guns. It was also underinclusive because the legislature was "perfectly willing to leave this dangerous, mind-altering material in the hands of children so long as one parent (or even an aunt or uncle) says it's OK." The law was overinclusive because not all children who are forbidden to purchase violent video games on their own have parents who care whether they buy these games. The effect of the law was imposing the state's conclusion that parents ought to restrict violent video games from their children. Finally, Scalia pointed out that the video game industry had a voluntary rating system to inform consumers about the content of games. A 2009 FEDERAL TRADE COMMISSION study found that this system was vastly superior in preventing children's access to mature content than similar systems for the movie and music industries. Scalia found there was no compelling interest in having the law fill the remaining "modest gap in concerned-parents' control."

Justices CLARENCE THOMAS and STEPHEN BREYER filed dissenting opinions. Justice Thomas argued that as originally understood by the writers of the Constitution, **freedom of speech** did not include a right to speak to minors or a right of minors to access speech "without going through the minors' parents or guardians." Justice Breyer said it made no sense to uphold bans on the sale of PORNOGRAPHY to children while protecting the sale of an interactive video game in which the player "actively, but virtually, binds and gags the woman, then tortures and kills her." Under the majority's ruling, the state could only restrict the sale of a violent video game when the bound and gagged woman was also topless. He concluded that the ruling set up an insurmountable conflict in the First Amendment.

Borough of Duryea, Pennsylvania v. Guarnieri

In addition to the more often litigated "free speech" protections of the FIRST AMENDMENT to the U.S. Constitution, the same amendment also protects "the right of the people ... to petition the Government for a **redress** of grievances." In *Borough of Duryea, Pennsylvania v. Guarnieri*, No. 09-1476, 564 U.S. ___ (2011), the U.S. SUPREME COURT was asked to determine the extent to which the First Amendment's "Petition Clause" protected public employees in routine disputes with their government employers. Under the First Amendment's "Speech Clause," an employee would generally need to show that his allegedly-protected speech regarded a matter of public concern. In this case, the issue was whether that same test (i.e., that the speech involved a matter of public concern) also applied to an employee who invoked the Petition Clause. The Supreme Court held that the same test applied.

Charles Guarnieri had been police chief for the Borough of Duryea, Pennsylvania until he was terminated from that position by the Borough Council (Duryea's legislative body) in 2003. He filed a union grievance that resulted in his reinstatement. The arbitrator in that grievance found that the Council had committed some procedural errors relating to the termination, but that Guarnieri had engaged in misconduct, including "attempting to intimidate Council members." Nonetheless, the arbitrator ordered that Guarnieri be reinstated following a disciplinary suspension.

Later, the Borough Council issued 11 directives to Guarnieri relating to his duties as police chief. The Council's attorney explained that the Council "wanted to make sure that the

chief understood what was going to be expected of him upon his return." One of the directives prohibited Guarnieri from working any overtime unless he had gotten "express permission" from the Council; another directive indicated that the "police car was to be used for official business only." Yet another one reminded him that the municipal building was a "smoke free building" and that the police department was not exempted from that.

Guarnieri then filed a second grievance under the public CIVIL RIGHTS provisions of 42 U.S.C. § 1983, alleging that the directives were issued in retaliation for his having filed the first grievance, thereby violating his First Amendment right "to petition the Government for a redress of grievances," which he considered his first union grievance to be. (He later amended his complaint to include retaliation by the Council in denying a request for $338 in overtime.)

At trial, Guarnieri's attorney told the jury that the Council, to retaliate, was "sending a message" to Guarnieri through its directives and denial of overtime pay. The jury agreed, awarding both compensatory and **punitive damages** as well as $45,000 in attorney's fees. The defendants (the Council as well as individual named defendants) appealed on the grounds that the grievances and lawsuit did not address matters of public concern.

Courts of Appeal outside of the Third Circuit have consistently held that alleged retaliatory actions by public employers against government employees do not give rise to liability under the Petition Clause unless the employee's "petition" raised a matter of public concern. In so holding, courts of appeal have drawn parallels between rights of speech and rights to petition. Guarnieri's appeal went to the Third Circuit, which, unlike the other circuits, held in his favor. The Third Circuit rejected the majority view and affirmed the award of **compensatory damages** (but found insufficient evidence for PUNITIVE DAMAGES). The **appellate** court's language that supported its opinion was that "a public employee who has petitioned the government through a formal mechanism such as the filing of a lawsuit or grievance is protected under the Petition Clause from retaliation for this activity, even if the petition concerns a matter of solely private concern."

Not so, said the U.S. Supreme Court. Justice ANTHONY KENNEDY, joined by Chief Justice Roberts and Justices Ginsburg, Breyer, Alito, Sotomayor, Kagan, and Thomas (Justice Thomas filing a separate concurring opinion) reversed. The Court expressly held that a government employer's alleged retaliatory activity against an employee did not give rise to liability under the Petition Clause of the First Amendment unless the employee's petition related to a matter of public concern.

A federal court is not the place to challenge personnel decisions taken by a public (governmental) agency against an employee, said the Court, unless that employee shows that he spoke as a citizen on a matter of public concern, and not as employee on matters relating to his personal employment relationship with his employer. Even, arguendo, if the employee did speak as a citizen on a matter of public concern, the employee' speech is not automatically protected. It is subjected to a court's balancing test, weighing the employee's right to engage in speech with the government's interest in promoting its mission and the efficiency of the public services it performs. This same framework, used to govern public employees' Speech Clause claims, will protect both employees' First Amendment rights as well as protect government interests, when applied to the Petition Clause as well. The same governmental interests that justify caution and restraint in protecting public employees' speech are just as relevant in Petition Clause cases, said the Court.

Finally, Guarnieri had raised the argument that applying the "public concern" test to the Petition Clause would be inappropriate because many petitions were private in nature. The Court found no merit in this argument, pointing out that petitions are frequently used to address a wide range of political, social, and other matters of PUBLIC INTEREST.

The lone dissenter, Justice Scalia, concurred in the judgment in part, but expressed the opinion that lawsuits should not even be covered by the Petition Clause because they were not a form of petitioning.

Nevada Commission on Ethics v. Carrigan

Nevada state law requires public officials to recuse themselves from voting on issues which may represent a CONFLICT OF INTEREST. Relevant language of Nev. Rev. Stat. § 281A.420 and subparagraphs (the Ethics in Government Law) requires recusal where "a matter with respect to which the independence of judgment of a **reasonable person** in his situation would be materially affected by … [among other things] his commitment in a private capacity to the interests of others." This includes a "commitment to a [specified] person," such as a member of the officer's household, a personal relative, employee, business associate, along with "any other commitment or relationship that is substantially similar" to the ones specifically enumerated in the preceding paragraphs (subsequently referred to as the "catchall provision"). In *Nevada Commission on Ethics v. Carrigan*, No. 10-568, 564 U.S. ___ (2011), the U.S. SUPREME COURT held that such a law did not violate a legislator's FIRST AMENDMENT free speech rights.

The above Ethics in Government Law is administered and enforced by the Nevada Commission on Ethics. In 2005, the Commission began an investigation after receiving complaints that Michael Carrigan, an elected member of the City Council of Sparks, Nevada, had violated the Law by voting to approve an application for a hotel/casino project known as "the Lazy 8." The complaints asserted that Carrigan should have recused himself from voting, because the Lazy 8 project was proposed by the Red Hawk Land Company. Carrigan's longtime friend and campaign manager, Carlos Vasquez, was a paid consultant for Red Hawk Land Company, which would benefit substantially from approval of the project.

Following investigation, the Commission concluded that Carrigan had a disqualifying conflict of interest under the "catchall provision" because his relationship to Vasquez was "substantially similar" to the prohibited relationships specifically enumerated in the law. For his part, Carrigan had consulted the Sparks City attorney, who advised that if Carrigan disclosed his relationship with Vasquez before voting on the Lazy 8 project (which he did), this would satisfy the Ethics in Government Law. Notwithstanding, the Commission censured Carrigan for failing to abstain from voting, but did not impose a civil penalty because his violation was not willful.

Carrigan filed for **judicial review** in the First Judicial **District Court** of the State of

Nevada, alleging that the "catchall" provision in the Ethics in Government Laws was unconstitutionally overbroad and violated his First Amendment free speech rights. The District Court denied his petition, but a divided Nevada Supreme Court reversed. After taking note that voting was protected by the First Amendment, the state high court applied **strict scrutiny** and found that the catchall definition was overbroad. The U.S. Supreme Court granted **certiorari**.

Justice ANTONIN SCALIA delivered the opinion for the Court, joined by Chief Justice Roberts and Justices Kennedy, Thomas, Ginsburg, Breyer, Sotomayor, and Kagan. The Court first noted that the First Amendment prohibits restriction on speech because of its message, its ideas, its subject matter, or its content. But the Amendment does not apply to unprotected speech, e.g., OBSCENITY or libel. In this case, the Nevada Supreme Court found that a legislator's vote was protected speech because voting was "a core legislative function." The U.S. Supreme Court disagreed. It distinguished between votes cast in a representative capacity by a legislator and his own free speech.

The Court then summarized a history of legislative rules. Legislative conflict-of-interest recusal rules have been around for 200 years, said the Court; within 15 year of the founding of our nation, both the HOUSE OF REPRESENTATIVES (in 1789) and the SENATE (in 1801) had adopted recusal rules, in itself creating a presumption that such rules are constitutional. Federal conflict of rules relating to judges and the judiciary also date back to the founding. But it is the reason behind such rules, and not their longstanding history, that explains their validity.

After noting that Nevada's recusal rule restricted not only the voting, but also "advocating the passage or failure" of a legislative matter, the Court explained that

> . . . a legislator's vote is the commitment of his apportioned share of the legislature's power to the passage or defeat of a particular proposal. The legislative power thus committed is not personal to the legislator, but belongs to the people; the legislator has no personal right to it.

Therefore, said the Court, requiring recusal upon a legislator when voting or debating an issue, for the purpose of avoiding conflicts of interest, is not a restriction on the legislator's protected speech. Since there is no personal right, there can be no First Amendment violation.

Justice ANTHONY KENNEDY wrote a separate concurring opinion, based on the facts of this case. Justice SAMUEL ALITO, while concurring in part and concurring in the judgment but disagreed with the Court's "suggestion that restrictions upon legislators' voting are not restrictions upon legislators' speech."

Albert Snyder talks about his son, Matthew, a Marine who was killed in Iraq, and about his Supreme Court case that will focus on a lawsuit he filed against Rev. Fred Phelps and the Westboro Baptist Church for protesting his son's funeral.
AP IMAGES/ANN FOSTER, FILE

Snyder v. Phelps

In a case that prompted a public outcry but which did not surprise legal experts, the U.S. SUPREME COURT ruled that the FIRST AMENDMENT protected the right of the Westboro Baptist Church to picket at military funerals and other high-profile events. The father of a fallen marine, Albert Snyder, had obtained a $4 million verdict against the church after the church protested at the son's funeral in 2006. However, the Fourth **Circuit Court** of Appeals in 2009 reversed the verdict, and the Supreme Court affirmed the Fourth Circuit's decision in an 8-1 vote. Only Justice SAMUEL ALITO dissented.

A minister named Fred Phelps founded the Westboro Baptist Church in Topeka, Kansas in 1955. The church developed the belief that God hates and punishes the United States for tolerating homosexuality. The church expresses its views by holding protests, often choosing to picket at funerals of fallen soldiers. During the two decades before the Supreme Court's decision, the church had picketed at nearly 600 funerals.

In 2006, the church decided to hold a protest at the funeral of Marine Lance Corporal Matthew Snyder, who had died in the line of duty in Iraq. Snyder's father decided to hold Matthew's funeral at a Catholic church in Westminster, Maryland. Phelps and six other members of his family (also members of the church) traveled to Maryland. Phelps notified the authorities that the group would picket during the funeral, and the church had to limit it activities to certain locations on public land. The protest took place about 1,000 feet away from the church. Consistent with its practices at other funerals, the church members held signs with such messages as "Thank God for Dead Soldiers" and "God Hates Fags." Albert Snyder said he saw the signs as he drove to the funeral, but he could not see what the signs said. He did not see the signs until he watched a news broadcast later that evening.

Phelps sued the church the U.S. **District Court** for the District of Maryland. He alleged several causes of action, including **defamation**, publicity given to private life, intentional infliction of emotional distress, intrusion upon seclusion, and civil CONSPIRACY. The court dismissed two of the claims when the court concluded that Phelps could not prove defamation or publicity given to private life. However, the court allowed the claims to proceed against Westboro's argument that the First Amendment shielded the church from liability. At trial, Snyder produced evidence that he suffered extreme emotional distress resulting from Westboro's protesting. A jury initially awarded Snyder more than $10 million in compensatory and **punitive damages**, though the court later reduced the total award to $5 million.

Westboro appealed the decision to the Fourth Circuit Court of Appeals. A three-judge panel for the court reviewed the church's First Amendment arguments and concluded that the church's speech was constitutionally protected. In reviewing Snyder's claims, the court determined that the church had not stated actual and objectively verifiable facts about Matthew or Albert Snyder. Instead, the court concluded that the signs merely contained "imaginative and hyperbolic rhetoric intended to spark debate about issues with which the Defendants are concerned." Therefore, the court reversed the district court's decision and set aside the judgment. *Snyder v. Phelps*, 580 F.3d 206 (4th Cir. 2009).

The U.S. Supreme Court agreed to review the case in 2010. Snyder argued that the Court should take the context of Westboro's speech into account. More specifically, Snyder argued that the church members had mounted a personal attack on Snyder and his family. Snyder further argued that the church had merely tried to "immunize their conduct by claiming they were actually protesting the United States' tolerance of homosexuality or the supposed evils of the Catholic Church." Snyder further argued that Westboro's speech should not be afforded full First Amendment protection because the church **chose** to spread its message by exploiting the funeral.

Chief Justice JOHN ROBERTS, writing for an 8-1 majority, disagreed with Snyder, however. According to the majority, the church's speech involved matters of public concern, which are entitled to the "highest rung" of First Amendment protection. The fact that the speech contained such messages as "God Hates You", the messages as a whole highlight such issues as "the political and moral conduct of the United States and its citizens, the fate of our Nation, homosexuality in the military, and scandals involving the Catholic clergy." These matters of public import were worthy of constitutional protection according to Roberts' opinion. Roberts further noted that the church members "had the right to be where they were." The church members had notified authorities before the fact and remained in the area where authorities had said the members could hold their protest. Roberts concluded, "As a Nation we have chosen ... to protect even hurtful speech on public issues to ensure that we do not stifle public debate. That choice requires that we shield Westboro from tort liability for its PICKETING in this case." *Snyder v. Phelps*, 131 S. Ct. 1207 (2011).

Alito opened his DISSENT by stressing, "Our profound national commitment to free and open debate is not a license for the vicious verbal ASSAULT that occurred in this case." Alito argued that the tort of intentional infliction of emotional distress is already very narrow, and Alito argued that the First Amendment should not shield the church from liability for speech used at a private funeral causing emotional distress to a private figure.

To add to his injuries, Albert Snyder was ordered to pay more than $100,000 in court costs to the church. Snyder publicly stated he would refuse to pay. The church, on the other hand, acted emboldened by the Court's decision, with church members saying they would step up their protesting efforts.

Sorrell v. IMS Health

The circle of commerce surrounding pharmaceutical drugs starts with manufacturers, who market their drugs to doctors through a process called "detailing." When pharmacies fill prescriptions, they necessarily receive "prescriber-identifying information." They then sell that information to "data miners" who produce market analyses and reports about prescriber (market) behavior, and sell these reports/analyses back to the pharmaceutical manufacturers. The "detailers" employed by the manufacturers refine this raw data to assist with marketing tactics and increase sales to doctors.

In *Sorrel v. IMS Health Inc.*, No. 10-779, 564 U.S. ___ (2011), the U.S. SUPREME COURT held that a Vermont **statute** which restricted access to prescriber information without the prescriber's consent (with enumerated exceptions) was unconstitutional under the Free Speech Clause of the FIRST AMENDMENT to the U.S. Constitution. In affirming the decision of the **Circuit Court** of Appeals for the Second Circuit, the Supreme Court agreed that the state law imposed both content and speaker-based burdens on protected expression (speech) of pharmaceutical marketers and data miners, without adequate justification (i.e., a compelling **state interest**).

Passed in 2007, the Vermont Prescription Confidentiality Law [Vt. Stat. Ann. Tit.18 § 4631(d)] provided, in relevant part, that, absent the prescriber's consent, prescriber-identifying information may not be sold by pharmacies and similar entities, disclosed by those entities for marketing purposes, or used for marketing by pharmaceutical manufacturers. Some exceptions were allowed under the statute, e.g., for "health care research."

Plaintiffs IMS Health Inc. and Verispan, LLC, Vermont data miners and an association of brand-name pharmaceutical manufacturers (Pharmaceutical Research and Manufacturers of America, PhRMA) joined forces and filed suit against state officials, alleging that § 4631(d) violated their rights under the Free Speech Clause. They sought declaratory and injunctive relief. Although the **district court** denied relief, the Second Circuit reversed. It found the Vermont statute unconstitutionally burdened the speech of the plaintiffs, without adequate justification.

The U.S. Supreme Court agreed. The statute, on its face, enacted a content and speaker-based restriction on the sale, disclosure, and use of prescriber-identifying information. But the statute clearly targeted pharmaceutical marketers and detailers, since it allowed prescriber-identifying information to be bought, sold, and acquired for other types of speech and by other speakers. A review of the legislative record and legislative findings of purpose confirmed that the law was aimed at detailers, particularly those who promoted brand-named drugs. This meant that Vermont's law went even beyond mere content DISCRIMINATION, actually reaching viewpoint discrimination, said the Court. Accordingly, the statute warranted HEIGHTENED SCRUTINY under the First Amendment.

For its part, the state and its officials argued that heightened scrutiny was unwarranted for regulation of what amounted to "commercial speech." But the Court found that the law had more than a mere incidental effect on speech, as it actually imposed a burden based on the content of the speech and the identity of the speaker. The state next argued that, because prescriber-identifying information was actually generated in order to comply with a legal mandate, the law was more like a restriction on access to government-held information. To this argument, the Court acknowledged some basis in case precedent. However, the Court distinguished **case law** (*Los Angeles Police Dept. v. United Reporting Publishing Corp.*, 528 U.S. 32, 120 S. Ct. 483, 145 L. Ed. 2d 451 (1999). Unlike the parties in that case, Vermont had imposed a restriction on access to information in private hands. Moreover, the PLAINTIFF in the other case was presumed to have suffered no First Amendment injury, whereas in this case, plaintiffs alleged burden on their speech. Finally, Vermont argued that the sale, transfer, and use of the prescriber-identifying information constituted conduct, not speech. However, the Court reiterated that, for First Amendment purposes, the creation and dissemination of information were speech.

Next, the Court looked to Vermont's stated justifications. To sustain the statute's targeted, content-based burden on protected speech, the state needed to show, at a minimum, that the statute directly advanced a substantial government interest and that the statute was drawn (tailored) to achieve that interest. Vermont argued that the statute was needed to protect medical privacy, including physician confidentiality and the integrity of the doctor-patient relationship. The Court did not find that the statute was drawn to serve that interest. Pharmacies may share prescriber-identifying information with anyone, for any reason, except for marketing. If the statute had been drawn more narrowly to allow sale or disclosure in only a few well-justified circumstances, it may have fared better.

As to the argument that the statute prevents the undermining of the doctor-patient relationship (presumably by allowing detailers to influence doctor's treatment decisions), such a result is possible only because the information may be persuasive. The fear that speech might persuade obviously provides no lawful basis for prohibiting it.

Finally, Vermont expressed the objective of lowering costs of medical services and promoting public health. But attempting to achieve this through the indirect means of restraining certain selected speech or viewpoints, by certain speakers, cannot justify content-based burdens on that speech. In this case, the "audience" is comprised of prescribing physicians, i.e., well-educated, sophisticated, and experienced consumers. While the state may be displeased that market detailers with prescriber-identifying information are effective in promoting their brand-name drugs, the state may not burden or interfere with protected expression in order to sway public debate in a preferred direction, said the Court.

Justice ANTHONY KENNEDY delivered the opinion of the majority, in which he was joined by Chief Justice Roberts and Justices Scalia, Thomas, Alito, and Sotomayor. Justice STEPHEN BREYER filed a dissenting opinion, joined by Justices Ginsburg and Kagan, in which he opined that the First Amendment did not require such a heightened scrutiny test for a lawful governmental effort to regulate a commercial enterprise. Further, the statute would meet the standard this Court has previously applied when the government sought to regulate commercial speech.

Sixth Circuit Removes Ten Commandments from Ohio Courtroom

In February 2011, the U.S. Court of Appeals for the Sixth Circuit upheld a lower court ruling that barred display of the Ten Commandments in an Ohio courthouse. *ACLU of Ohio v. DeWeese*, 633 F.3d 424 (6th Cir. 2011). Over the years, courts have seemingly taken differing views regarding the display of the Ten Commandments on government or public properties (as violating the Establishment Clause of the FIRST AMENDMENT to the U.S. Constitution). Even the U.S. SUPREME COURT, in the 2005 case of *McCreary County v. ACLU of Kentucky*, 545 U.S. 844, 125 S. Ct. 2722, 162 L. Ed. 2d 729, prohibited a Ten Commandments display in a Kentucky courthouse, while, on the same day, issued another opinion upholding the six-foot-tall display of the Ten Commandments on the grounds of the Texas State Capitol. *Van Orden v. Perry*, 545 U.S. 677, 125 S. Ct. 2854, 162 L. Ed. 2d 607 (2005).

Specifically, the Supreme Court carefully explained those two dichotomous opinions. In *McCreary*, the Court had found a predominantly religious (and therefore improper) purpose behind the display, whereas, in *Perry*, the Court found the six-foot monument on the Capitol grounds to have a "valid secular purpose," having existed at that site, alongside other historical documents, for nearly 40 years. A **reasonable person** touring the grounds, said the Court, would not conclude that the state was endorsing the Commandments' religious message. The Court expressly ruled that religious materials could be allowed as part of an educational or historical display.

That ruling triggered numerous displays and monuments depicting the Ten Commandments in Alabama, Georgia, Indiana, Maryland, Nebraska, Ohio, Tennessee, and West Virginia to be challenged and taken down. But within the Sixth Circuit, which governs Kentucky,

Ohio, Tennessee, and Michigan, a December 2005 decision upheld a Ten Commandments display in a Mercer County, Kentucky courthouse, using the Supreme Court's *Perry* guidelines, because it was originally accompanied by other historical documents, including the BILL OF RIGHTS and the DECLARATION OF INDEPENDENCE. Similarly, in 2010, the Sixth Circuit denied a rehearing *en banc* of its panel decision that a display of the Ten Commandments in a Grayson County, Kentucky courthouse was constitutional, because, from the outset, it had presented a valid secular purpose.

However, at the same time (June 2010), the Sixth Circuit disallowed an amended display in the above *McCreary* case (that had been remanded from the U.S. Supreme Court and involved both McCreary and Pulaski County Courthouses, Kentucky), finding that their amended and modified displays, "in a long line of attempts to comply with the Constitution for LITIGATION purposes," represented just another strategy that "did not minimize the residue of religious purpose." The 2010 Sixth Circuit decision upheld a permanent INJUNCTION of the displays. The opinion and decision expressly distinguished the reasons why displays were allowed in Grayson and Mercer counties, but not in McCreary and Pulaski counties (among others): the original displays, existing for years, had not expressed an "avowedly religious purpose." Conversely, following the U.S. Supreme Court decision, McCreary and Pulaski counties had amended their displays to now include multiple religious and secular documents. The new, amended displays were entitled, "Foundations of American Law and Government," but, according to the **appellate court**, did not successfully "purge" the original religious intent by merely substituting the documents that surrounded the commandments on the display from religious texts to more historical writings.

Likewise, the 2011 Sixth Circuit's decision involving the Ohio courthouse represented years of back-and-forth litigation as well as amended displays in Judge James Deweese's Richland County **Common Pleas** Court. The controversy began in 2000, when Judge DeWeese hung two posters in his courtroom, one of the Bill of Rights and one of the Ten Commandments. The AMERICAN CIVIL LIBERTIES UNION (ACLU) brought an action in the U.S.

District Court for the Northern District of Ohio, seeking an injunction and declaration that the Ten Commandments poster violated the Establishment Clause. The district court granted the injunction, which was upheld on appeal *ACLU of Ohio Found., Inc. v. Ashbrook*, 375 F.3d 484 (6th Cir. 2004).

Two years after the **appellate** decision, in 2006, Judge DeWeese hung a new poster in his courtroom, entitled "Philosophies of Law in Conflict." Immediately under the title were the following three comments:

> 1. There is a conflict of legal and moral philosophies raging in the United States. That conflict is between MORAL RELATIVISM and moral absolutism. We are moving towards moral relativism. 2. All law is legislated morality. The only question is whose morality. Because morality is based on faith, there is no such thing as religious neutrality in law or morality. 3. Ultimately, there are only two views: Either God is the final authority, and we acknowledge His unchanging standards of behavior. Or man is the final authority, and standards of behavior change at the whim of individuals or societies. Here are examples. (Below this appeared two columns, one entitled, "Moral Absolutes: The Ten Commandments," [which listed them underneath] and the other, entitled "Moral Relatives: Humanist Precepts" [listing seven examples from various sources].)

At the bottom of the poster was another comment by Judge DeWeese, lamenting that society was paying a high price for moving from moral absolutism to moral relativism. The comment went on to note that "Our Constitution was made for a moral and religious people." The comment also noted that both the Declaration of Independence and the Ohio Constitution acknowledged God as the One who providently superintended the affairs of man.

The procedural history of the 2011 case continued with a 2008 motion filed by PLAINTIFF ACLU of Ohio, arguing that DeWeese had violated the district court's previous order enjoining the display of the commandments. The district court, however, disagreed, finding that the modified display was different from the original poster and therefore, its display did not violate the previous order. Plaintiff ACLU then filed a new lawsuit in the U.S. District Court for the Northern District of Ohio, arguing that the new poster violated the First and Fourteenth

Amendments to the U.S. Constitution, and requesting a new injunction preventing display of the new poster. The district court agreed, granting ACLU **summary judgment**.

The Sixth Circuit, finding that challenges under the Establishment Clause fell under the U.S. Supreme Court's 1971 decision in *Lemon v. Kurtzman*, 403 U.S. 602, 91 S. Ct. 2105, 29 L. Ed. 2d 745 (1971) and subsequent cases that slightly modified the three-prong test set out therein. Essentially, the test asks (1) whether the challenged action has a secular purpose; (2) whether the action's primary effect neither advances nor inhibits religion; and (3) whether the action fosters an excessive entanglement with religion.

In determining a government's purpose (in this case, for displaying the Ten Commandments), the *Lemon* test gives deference to a government actor's stated reasons. However, in this particular case, the Sixth Circuit noted Judge DeWeese's defiant past violations of the Establishment Clause in considering present conduct, casting doubt on the now-purportedly secular purpose for hanging the poster in his courtroom. The Sixth Circuit concluded that Judge DeWeese was merely attempting "to veil his religious purpose by casting his religious advocacy in philosophical terms." The APPELLATE court also found that the textual content of the new poster violated the endorsement test because it acted in a manner that a reasonable person would view as an endorsement of religion. Accordingly, the Sixth Circuit affirmed the district court's decision.

FORECLOSURE

Massachusetts Supreme Judicial Court Rules Against Banks in Critical Foreclosure Case

The Massachusetts Supreme Judicial Court in 2011 issued a ruling against two major U.S. banks that had sought to validate titles on property the banks had obtained in **foreclosure** actions. The result was that the court invalidated two foreclosures, and commentators said the decision could have a wide-reaching impact on thousands of others in Massachusetts. However, representatives for the banks said that the decision's effect would be limited to Massachusetts because the decision was based on a peculiar state law. The two banks involved were Wells Fargo & Co. and U.S. Bank National Association, subsidiary of U.S. Bancorp.

The U.S. Bank matter focused on property owned by Antonio Ibanez. He had taken out a $103,500 loan on a home in Springfield and secured the loan with a mortgage to his lender, Rose Mortgage. As is customary, the mortgage was assigned to several other entities, including Option One Mortgage Company; Lehman Brothers Bank, FSB; Lehman Brothers Holdings, Inc.; and Structured Asset SECURITIES Corporation. The assignment to Structured Asset Securities Corporation resulted in the Ibanez mortgage being pooled into a trust. The mortgages in this trust that were pooled together were converted into mortgage-backed securities. The complicated transaction is part of a process known as securitization.

At the time of these transactions, U.S. Bank was the **trustee** for the Structured Asset Securities Corporation. However, none of the paperwork showed that proper transactions to the Lehman Brothers entities or to the Structured Asset Securities Corporation. Instead, Option One Mortgage remained the record holder of the Ibanez mortgage throughout this process.

Nevertheless, U.S. Bank proceeded with the FORECLOSURE of the Ibanez property as if U.S. Bank were the record holder of the mortgage. Massachusetts law requires a mortgage holder to file a complaint under the SERVICEMEMBERS CIVIL RELIEF ACT, which prohibits foreclosures against active service members. The complaint asks a court to certify that the mortgagee is not entitled to benefit from the Servicemembers Act. U.S. Bank filed this action and represented itself as present holder of the Ibanez mortgage. U.S. Bank then forced a foreclosure sale, at which U.S. Bank bought the Ibanez property for an amount significantly less than the outstanding debt and estimated **fair market value** of the property. More than a year after the sale, the successor to Option One Mortgage assigned the Ibanez mortgage to U.S. Bank.

A similar transaction occurred with regard to the matter involving Wells Fargo. Mark and Tammy LaRace had given a mortgage on their property in Springfield to Option One. Option One then assigned the mortgage to Bank of America, which later assigned the mortgage to the Asset Backed Funding Corporation. Wells Fargo served as trustee for the Asset Backed

Funding Corporation. Wells Fargo filed an action to foreclose on the LaRace property under the Servicemembers Act, and once approved, Wells Fargo held a foreclosure sale. As was the case with the Ibanez property, Option One remained the record holder of the LaRace mortgage and did not formally assign the mortgage (through Option One's successor) to Wells Fargo until ten months after the foreclosure sale.

Under Massachusetts law, a mortgage holder generally does not have to seek court approval to foreclose on mortgaged property. The only exception to this is a limited procedure under the Servicemembers Act, under which a court certifies that a mortgage holder is not a BENEFICIARY under Act. Once the court certifies that the mortgagor is not entitled to relief, the mortgage holder may proceed with a foreclosure sale. However, because the mortgage holder has such substantial power without judicial oversight, Massachusetts courts have followed a principle that "one who sells under a power [of sale] must follow strictly its terms. If he fails to do so there is no valid execution of the power, and the sale is wholly void."

Both U.S. Bank and Wells Fargo brought actions in 2008 in the Massachusetts Land Court seeking to establish that they had proper title to the Ibanez and LaRace properties, respectively. The Land Court had to consider whether the banks were legally entitled to foreclose on the property, since in both cases Option One's successor had not assigned the properties to the banks until long after the foreclosure sale. The banks produced evidence showing that the mortgages had been pooled together, but neither bank could provide evidence that the record holders had assigned the properties to the banks before the foreclosure sales. Accordingly, the Land Court in both cases invalidated the foreclosure sales.

Both banks appealed the Land Court's decisions to the Supreme Judicial Court of Massachusetts. In a unanimous decision, the court affirmed the Land Court's decision. The court agreed that parties must adhere to the foreclosure law strictly and that the **statutory power of sale** only extends to "the mortgagee or his executors, administrators, successors or assigns." Moreover, an assignment of a mortgage requires a writing signed by the party granting the assignment. Neither U.S. Bank nor Wells Fargo was able to provide any writing showing an assignment before the sale. The court also concluded that the banks had failed to post a proper notice by publishing the notice in the *Boston Globe* instead of a local Springfield paper. *U.S. Bank Nat'l Ass'n v. Ibanez*, 941 N.E.2d 40 (Mass. 2011).

The decision invalidated the foreclosure sales on both properties. The LaRaces had been able to move back into their home after the Land Court had ruled against Wells Fargo in 2009, and the high court's decision allowed them to seek permanent recovery of their home. Ibanez's attorney also expressed satisfaction with the decision, though Ibanez had not returned to his home at the time of the decision.

Stock for both Wells Fargo and U.S. Bancorp fell a day after the decision, though both banks said the decision would not affect their day-to-day operations because the decision was based on a specific Massachusetts law. Massachusetts is one of 27 states that do not require judicial approval for a mortgage holder to foreclose.

FOURTH AMENDMENT

Davis v. United States

The FOURTH AMENDMENT to the U.S. Constitution prohibits police officers from engaging in unreasonable searches or seizures. The text of the amendment does not, however, establish a remedy that applies when an officer finds evidence through an unreasonable search or seizure. The SUPREME COURT developed the **exclusionary rule** to deter officers from engaging in Fourth Amendment violations. On the other hand, the Court has acknowledged circumstances in which the EXCLUSIONARY RULE does not apply. In *Davis v. United States*, No. 09-11328, 2011 WL 2369583 (U.S. June 16, 2011), the Court determined that when police conduct a search based on reasonable reliance on binding **appellate** precedent, the exclusionary rule does not require suppression of evidence found pursuant to the search.

In 2007, police in Alabama conducted a routine traffic stop. The officers asked a passenger what his name was, and he responded that he was "Ernest Harris." The officer later determined that the man's name was Willie

Gene Davis. The officer could smell alcohol on Davis' breath and noticed that Davis was fidgeting with the pockets of his jacket. The car's driver failed a field sobriety test, and the officer then asked Davis to step away from the car.

Davis removed his jacket when he exited the car, even though the officer said for Davis to leave the jacket on. Davis left the jacket in the car seat. The officer took Davis to the rear of the vehicle, which is where the officer discovered Davis' actual identity. After verifying Davis' identity and birth date with a police dispatcher, the officer arrested Davis for giving a false name. The officer placed Davis in the back of a patrol car, while the driver was placed in a separate car. Both Davis and the driver were handcuffed. The officer thereafter searched the vehicle and found a revolver in Davis' jacket pocket.

Davis was indicted for possessing a firearm in violation of 18 U.S.C. § 922(g)(1), which prohibits possession of a firearm by a person who has previously been convicted of a crime. At the time, precedent the Eleventh **Circuit Court** of Appeals established that the officer's search was constitutional under the Fourth Amendment. Davis acknowledged as much when he filed a motion to suppress the evidence. The **district court** denied Davis' motion, and Davis was convicted. He received a sentence of 220 months in prison.

When Davis filed his motion to suppress the gun as evidence, the Supreme Court had granted **certiorari** in the case of *Arizona v. Gant* (No. 07-542). The Court later ruled that officers cannot conduct a warrantless search of a vehicle once the arrestee has been secured and is no longer within reaching distance of the passenger compartment at the time of the search. The Court's ruling in Arizona v. Gant, 129 S. Ct. 1710, 173 L. Ed. 2d 485 (2009), conflicted with the existing Eleventh Circuit precedent. Thus, what would have been a legal search before *Gant* became unconstitutional.

Davis appealed to the Eleventh Circuit, where he argued that evidence of the gun should be suppressed because the officer found the gun pursuant to a search determined to be illegal in *Gant*. The question before the **appellate court** was thus whether the exclusionary rule should apply when officers rely on existing APPELLATE precedent to conduct a search

but the precedent is later overruled. The circuit courts of appeals were split on the question, with the Ninth and Tenth Circuits reaching opposition conclusions on the question.

A panel of the Eleventh Circuit determined that the exclusionary rule did not apply. The court determined that the officer did not deliberately violate Davis' rights, given that the search was legal under Eleventh Circuit **case law** at the time. The court concluded, "Because the exclusionary rule is justified solely by its potential to deter police misconduct, suppressing evidence obtained from an unlawful search is inappropriate when the offending officer reasonably relied on well-settled precedent." *Davis v. United States*, 598 F.3d 1259 (11th Cir. 2010).

Given the split among circuit courts, the Supreme Court agreed to review the case. In a 7-2 vote, the Court affirmed the Eleventh Circuit. Justice SAMUEL ALITO, writing for the majority, stressed that the exclusionary rule is limited to circumstances in which the deterrence benefits of suppressing evidence outweigh the heavy costs of the exclusionary rule. Thus, whether the rule applies generally depends on the flagrancy of the police action in question. When police deliberately or recklessly disregard constitutional rights, then the exclusionary rule should apply. However, Alito wrote, the same logic does not apply when the officer acts on a good-faith belief that the officer's conduct is legal.

Alito also noted that the Court's decisions are often retroactive in effect. Thus, when the Court decided *Gant* before Davis' conviction had become final, *Gant* applied to Davis' case. However, the retroactive effect of the rule does not mean that the remedy of exclusion should also apply. Thus, in this instance, Alito concluded that exclusionary rule should not require suppression of the gun, and the Court affirmed Davis' conviction.

Justice SONIA SOTOMAYOR concurred in the judgment. She agreed with the Court's conclusion but noted that the Court did not answer the question of how the exclusionary rule should apply when the former law is unsettled.

Justice STEPHEN BREYER, joined by Justice RUTH BADER GINSBURG, dissented. Breyer criticized the Court's "new 'good faith'" exception to the exclusionary rule and noted that the decision left Davis with a right but without a remedy. Breyer stressed that he believed the decision would undermine the exclusionary rule and could lead to more acts of police misconduct.

California Supreme Court Allows Warrantless Search of Cell Phone Messages

The FOURTH AMENDMENT to the U.S. Constitution provides that "[t]he right of the people to be secure in their persons, houses, papers, and effects, against unreasonable searches and seizures, shall not be violated, and no warrants shall issue, but upon **probable cause**, supported by oath or affirmation, and particularly describing the place to be searched, and the persons or things to be seized."

Over the years, the U.S. SUPREME COURT has construed this constitutional protection as it applies to various facts and circumstances. In one of its oft-cited cases, *Katz v. United States,* 389 U.S. 347, 88 S. Ct. 507, 19 L. Ed. 2d 576 (1967), the Court held that searches *without* a warrant, i.e., searches conducted outside the judicial process, without prior approval by a judge or **magistrate**, "are *per se* unreasonable ... subject only to a few specifically established and well-delineated exceptions." One of those specific and well-established exceptions (permitting warrantless searches) is a "search incident to a lawful arrest." *United States v. Robinson,* 414 U.S. 218, 94 S. Ct. 467, 38 L. Ed. 2d 427 (1973).

In January 2011, the Supreme Court of California, affirming a lower **appellate court** decision, agreed that a warrantless search of an arrested person's cell phone text message folder constituted a valid search "incident to a lawful custodial arrest." The quintessential issue in the case involved more than the cell phone (which more readily could be considered property incidental or connected to the person) but rather, involved the personal data stored in messages, which could be considered as triggering greater Fourth Amendment protection.

Facts surrounding the legal issue stem from the arrest of DEFENDANT Gregory Diaz on April 25, 2007. At that time (around 2:50 p.m.), Senior Deputy Victor Fazio of the Ventura County Sheriff's Department witnessed Diaz selling Ecstasy to a police informant posing as a drug purchaser in the back seat of a car Diaz was driving. The informant was wearing a wireless transmitter. Immediately after the sale, Fazio closed in and arrested Diaz. Six tablets of Ecstasy were seized in connection with the arrest, and an immediate pat-down and search of Diaz's person revealed a small amount of marijuana in his pocket along with a cell phone. These items were placed into evidence at the police station, where Fazio then conducted an interview of Diaz (4:18 p.m.). Diaz denied any knowledge of the drug transaction. Following the interview, at approximately 4:23 p.m., Fazio reviewed the text message folder of Diaz's cell phone, discovering a message that read "6 4 80." Based on his specialized training and experience, Fazio interpreted this to mean "six Ecstasy pills for $80." Within minutes of finding this message, Fazio confronted Diaz with it, and Diaz then admitted participating in the illegal drug sale.

Charged with selling a controlled substance, Diaz pleaded not guilty and moved to suppress information gained from the search (the text messages) as well as his confession that followed his being confronted with the text messages. He argued that they were the fruits of an illegal Fourth Amendment search. His main argument was that the search of cell phone messages was "too remote in time" to be considered as "incident" to his arrest.

The trial court denied the motion, stating for the record,

> "The defendant was under arrest for a **felony** charge involving the sale of drugs. His property was seized from him. Evidence was seized from him ... Incident to the arrest[,] search of his person and everything that turned up is really fair game in terms of being evidence of a crime or instrumentality of a crime or whatever the theory might be. And under these circumstances I don't believe there's authority that a warrant was required."

Defendant Diaz then withdrew his not guilty plea, pleaded guilty to a lesser crime of transportation of a controlled substance (accepted by the trial court) and received a **suspended sentence** in conjunction with a three-year PROBATION. Still, he appealed.

The California **Court of Appeal** affirmed the trial court. Its decision noted that, under governing precedent, because the cell phone "was immediately associated with [defendant]'s person at the time of his arrest," it was properly subjected to a delayed warrantless search.

So also held the California Supreme Court. In affirming both lower court decisions, the state high court relied on U.S. Supreme Court precedent [the *Robinson* and *Robinson* case (above) as well as *United States v. Edwards*, 415 U.S. 800, 94 S. Ct. 1234, 39 L. Ed. 2d 771 (1974) and *United States v. Chadwick*, 433 U.S. 1, 97 S. Ct. 2476, 53 L. Ed. 2d 538 (1977)]. First, it addressed Defendant's strongest argument, that the search of the cell phone was "too remote" in time to qualify as a valid search incident to his arrest.

The state high court found that resolution of this issue rested squarely within the three above-cited U.S. Supreme Court cases. In *Robinson,* the police officer conducted a pat-down search following arrest for a revoked operator's driving license. He removed a crumpled cigarette package from the breast pocket of defendant's search, determined it contained objects other than cigarettes, and upon opening the crumpled package, found 14 heroin capsules. The Supreme Court held this to be a lawful warrantless search, as police may conduct a full search of the arrestee's person incident to a lawful arrest.

Further, under *Edwards,* although this exception has been traditionally justified by the reasonableness of searching for weapons, instruments of escape, or evidence of a crime that may be destroyed, the authority exists whether or not the police have reason to believe the arrestee had on his or her person, or in his or her "immediate control," any evidence to destroy or weapons. (In the *Edwards* case, police lawfully arrested the defendant for attempting to break into a post office. Ten hours later, police made the defendant change clothes, then tested his old clothes for evidence of paint chips matching samples from the post office window. The Supreme Court said, importantly, "[O]nce the accused is lawfully arrested and is in CUSTODY, the effects in his possession at the place of detention that were subject to search at the time and place of his arrest may lawfully be searched and seized without a warrant, even though a substantial period of time has elapsed."

But in *Chadwick,* the Supreme Court found that a warrantless search of a footlocker seized at time of arrest was not justified, as the arrestee's privacy interest in the contents was not eliminated simply because he was under arrest.

Using this precedent as guidance, the California Supreme Court had to decide whether the cell phone was like the cigarette package in *Robinson* or the footlocker in *Chadwick.* Finding it akin to the cigarette package, the high court also dismissed, as contrary to the above precedents, defense arguments that the validity of the search hinged on the amount of personal information a particular item might contain. The court noted that case precedents held that the loss of privacy upon arrest extended beyond the arrestee's body to include "personal property . . . immediately associated with the person of the arrestee" at the time of arrest. (*Chadwick,* 433 U.S. at 15).

Kentucky v. King

The U.S. SUPREME COURT has recognized that the FOURTH AMENDMENT to the U.S. Constitution does not require police officers to obtain a warrant to search a home in every instance. One exception to the warrant requirement applies when exigent circumstances justify the warrantless search. Several lower courts had established specific standards regarding when the exigent-circumstances rule applied and when it did not apply. The U.S. Supreme Court in *Kentucky v. King*, No. 09-1272, 2011 WL 1832821 (U.S. 2011) clarified the rule, holding that a warrantless entry of an apartment while police chased a drug suspect was constitutional under the Fourth Amendment.

On October 13, 2005, police in Lexington, Kentucky arranged for a confidential informant to buy crack cocaine from a drug dealer. Several officers stood nearby waiting to make an arrest when the sale took place. After the sale, an undercover officer gave a signal to the other officers to make the arrest. The officer later gave a description of the suspect on the radio and told other officers that the suspect had entered the breezeway of an apartment complex. The undercover officer stressed that officers needed to arrive at the scene quickly so that the suspect would not enter an apartment.

The officers entered the breezeway. The undercover officer in pursuit radioed other officers that the suspect had entered the back right apartment at the apartment complex.

However, the other officers did not hear this instruction because they were no longer near the radio. The officers approached the back of the apartment complex when they heard a door slam shut. The officers also smelled the odor of burnt marijuana, and it was clear to the officers that the smell was coming from the back left apartment. A detective approached a door of the back left apartment and knocked on the door. When the detective knocked and announced that the police were present, the officers heard movement inside the apartment.

The officers later testified that they believed that a crime was occurring because of the smell of marijuana and because it appeared from the noise that evidence was being destroyed. One of the officers kicked down the door, and the officers entered the apartment. Though the officers found drugs and drug paraphernalia, the officers never found the original suspect in that apartment (though they later found him when they searched the back right apartment).

Among the individuals in the left apartment was Hollis King, who later pleaded guilty to trafficking of a controlled substance, possession of marijuana, and persistent **felony** offender. King received a sentence of 11 years in prison. King had reserved his right to appeal, and he appealed his conviction to the Kentucky Court of Appeals. The **appellate court** disagreed with some of the trial court's conclusions of law. However, the **appellate** court ruled that the entry into the apartment was permissible under the circumstances.

The Kentucky Supreme Court agreed to review the case. The question before the court was whether the police had proper exigent circumstances to enter the left apartment without a warrant. Assuming that police have **probable cause** to believe that a crime has been committed, two instances, among others, justify a warrantless entry. First, police may enter a home without a warrant when the police are in "hot pursuit" of a fleeing suspect. And second, police may make such an entry when police believe that destruction of evidence is imminent. In this case, the Kentucky high court concluded that the **hot pursuit** rule could not apply because King did not know that he was being pursued. Instead, the officers were pursuing a completely different suspect.

The court's analysis of the second justification was more complicated. The court first concluded that the smell of burning marijuana alone was not enough to create an exigent circumstance. Thus, the only other exigency could have been the result of the police knocking on the door and announcing their presence. Several lower courts have established ruled about whether the police created the exigent circumstances, which generally precludes application of the exigent-circumstances rule. The court announced a test that it applied to the present case: when police have not acted in **bad faith**, the court must determine "[w]hether, regardless of **good faith**, it was reasonably foreseeable that the investigative tactics employed by the police would create the exigent circumstances relied upon to justify a warrantless entry." In King's case, the court concluded that by knocking on the door and announcing their presence, the police created the exigent circumstance. Thus, the court concluded that the warrantless search violated King's Fourth Amendment rights. *King v. Commonwealth*, 302 S.W. 3d 649 (Ky. 2010).

The U.S. Supreme Court agreed to review the case, and in an 8-1 vote, reversed the Kentucky Supreme Court. Writing for the majority, Justice SAMUEL ALITO noted that the lower **federal courts** and various STATE COURTS had created different tests regarding exigent circumstances that support a warrantless search. According to Alito, several of these tests were unnecessary because the basis for any Fourth Amendment test should relate to the reasonableness of the search. Accordingly, Alito stated, "Where, as here, the police did not create the exigency by engaging or threatening to engage in conduct that violates the Fourth Amendment, warrantless entry to prevent the destruction of evidence is reasonable an thus allowed."

In the present case, the officers' act of banging on the apartment door and announcing their presence was proper under the Fourth Amendment. Thus, the officers neither engaged in nor threatened the engage in conduct that would violate the Fourth Amendment before the officers entered the apartment without a warrant. The Court left open the question of whether other circumstances may have been present to render the entry unreasonable, but as for the facts on the record, the Court concluded that the entry was permissible.

Justice RUTH BADER GINSBURG dissented. She argued that the Court had given police a way to "routinely . . . dishonor the Fourth Amendment" in drug cases by simply knocking, listening, and entering, even though police had time to obtain a warrant. Accordingly, Ginsburg would have required the police to obtain the warrant before entering.

Placing GPS Device on Automobile is a Search under the Fourth Amendment

The popularity of global positioning system (GPS) devices in AUTOMOBILES is due to the device's ability to guide a driver to a location. Law enforcement has recognized the surveillance possibilities of attaching a GPS device to a vehicle and then recording all the movements of the vehicle. Defendants have argued that evidence obtained using a GPS device that was attached without a warrant should not be admissible at trial, as the use of GPS constitutes an unreasonable **search and seizure** under the FOURTH AMENDMENT. **Federal courts** had been hostile to this argument until the District of Columbia **Circuit Court** of Appeals ruled in *U.S. v. Maynard*, 615 F.3d 544 (D.C. Cir.2010) that police needed a warrant to attach a GPS device on a vehicle. The appeals court noted that the police had tracked the DEFENDANT 24 hours a day for four weeks without a valid warrant.

In 2004 the FBI and the District of Columbia police department began investigating Antoine Jones and Lawrence Maynard for narcotics violations. Jones owned and Maynard managed a nightclub in the District of Columbia. The pair was eventually charged with a single count of CONSPIRACY to distribute and possess with intent to distribute five or more kilograms of cocaine and 50 or more grams of cocaine base. A joint trial of Jones and Maynard in 2008 culminated in a jury finding them both guilty. The men filed appeals with the D.C. Circuit Court of Appeals, contending that a number of actions taken by police violated their constitutional rights. The appeals court rejected these joint issues and upheld Maynard's conviction. However, the court examined Jones' claim that the evidence collected by police using an GPS device attached to his automobile was an illegal, warrantless search that required suppression of the evidence obtained by the device.

Judge DOUGLAS GINSBURG, writing for a unanimous three-judge panel, agreed with Jones. The court looked at three issues: was the use of the device a search; if it was a search, whether it was reasonable; and, whether any error was harmless. As to the threshold issue, Jones argued that under long-standing SUPREME COURT Fourth Amendment precedent the use of the GPS device violated his "reasonable expectation of privacy." The government countered that a 1983 Supreme Court decision in which the Court held the use of a beeper device to aid tracking a suspect to his drub lab was applicable and governed this case. Judge Ginsburg examined the 1983 case and concluded that it did not control the case, noting that the Court "explicitly distinguished between the limited information discovered by use of the beeper-movements during a discrete journey and more comprehensive or sustained monitoring of the sort at issue in this case."

The court then looked at whether Jones's locations were exposed to the public, as his reasonable expectation of privacy would be judged as to the public nature of his actions. Judge Ginsburg held that the "totality" of Jones' movements over the course of a month was not exposed to the public for two reasons. First, unlike one's movements during a single journey, the whole of one's movements over the course of a month is not actually exposed to the public "because the likelihood anyone will observe all those movements is effectively nil." Second, "the whole of one's movements is not exposed constructively even though each individual movement is exposed, because that whole reveals more" than does the sum of its parts.

The government claimed that Jones's movements during the month of GPS surveillance were actually exposed to the public because the police lawfully could have followed him everywhere on public roads. Judge Ginsburg rejected this argument, stating that the critical task is to determine "not what another person can physically and may lawfully do but rather what a **reasonable person** expects another might actually do." In this case Jones could not reasonably expect that police would follow his every movement for four weeks. Prolonged surveillance reveals types of information not revealed by short-term surveillance. Moreover, "the sequence of a person's movements can reveal still more." The court concluded "Society recognizes Jones's expectation of privacy in his movements over the course of a month as reasonable." Ginsburg also noted that several states have enacted laws that ban private citizens from using electronic trafficking devices to track the movement and location of persons. These states have justified this prohibition because such tracking would violate a person's "reasonable expectation of privacy."

Having established that the use of the GPS device was a search, the appeals examined whether it could be justified as reasonable under the Fourth Amendment. Judge Ginsburg rejected the government's claim that the warrantless search was reasonable under the automobile exception to the warrant requirement. That exception permits police to search a car without a warrant if they "have reason to believe it contains contraband." The exception did not authorize them to install a tracking device without a warrant. Finally, the court reviewed whether, despite the infirmities of the search, the government's error was harmless and did not affect Jones's conviction. The government claimed the evidence against Jones was overwhelming, even if the GPS evidence was excluded. The court disagreed, finding that the evidence linking Jones to the conspiracy "was not strong, let alone overwhelming." There was no evidence of a drug transaction in which Jones was involved, nor any evidence that Jones possessed any drugs. Judge Ginsburg concluded that the GPS evidence was essential to the government's case, for the prosecution had linked this information with Jones's cellphone records "to paint a picture" of Jones' movements "that made credible the ALLEGATION that he was involved in drug trafficking." Moreover, in the government's opening remarks and its closing statement to the jury, the GPS evidence played a central part in making the case against Jones. Therefore, the court reversed Jones's conviction.

Pennsylvania Appellate Court Allows GPS Tracking into Evidence

In December 2010, a Pennsylvania appeals court (Superior Court) overturned the decision of a Chester County Court of **Common Pleas** court that had banned the use of evidence obtained by global satellite positioning (GPS). The underlying case involved criminal **burglary**, and the local police had obtained a SEARCH WARRANT requesting the use of GPS, which had been granted. The Court of COMMON PLEAS

opined in its decision that, weighing privacy interests against such technology, along with a lack of case history for guidance, the evidence should be suppressed. The **appellate** Superior COURT OPINION remained unpublished, pending remand to the trial court and any new appeals filed after judgment was entered.

Police in West Chester, Pennsylvania were attempting to solve a string of burglaries that appeared to be related. The burglars involved in the crimes were characterized as "smash and grab" small-time thieves desperate for any money they could get, most likely for drugs, police had alleged. They suspected that Edward Heinzman and his brothers were involved. They petitioned for and received a local search warrant allowing them to track, by GPS technology, the whereabouts of a certain white SUV registered to Heinzman's mother. According to the Common Pleas Court, the only information the police had provided in the AFFIDAVIT for the warrant was that the brothers had been charged with similar offenses in the past, and that a similar SUV (as the one they wanted to track) had been seen near some of the burglaries. Police believed the white SUV was being used as the getaway vehicle in the commercial burglaries that had started in the summer of 2007.

In January 2008, the police installed a GPS mobile tracking device in a white 1994 Ford Explorer registered to the Heinzmans' mother. On at least four occasions in April 2008, police, by using global positioning coordinates through the GPS tracker, were able to place the Ford Explorer at or near the "smash and grab" burglaries of businesses in Downingtown, Easttown, Newtown Square, and Gap, Lancaster County.

Although Edward Heinzman gave the Ford to his sister later in April 2008 (he reportedly told an ACCOMPLICE that he believed the SUV was "hot" and had been spotted by police), he and his brothers, John Heinzman and Chester Heinzman were charged with four of the burglaries.

Edward Heinzman moved to suppress the GPS tracking evidence in the Chester County Court of Common Pleas (the trial court). After reviewing the motion to suppress, Judge Thomas Gavin noted on the record that there was virtually no **case law** to guide judges in determining whether police were within their constitutional authority to track criminal suspects with GPS.

He then granted the motion to suppress the evidence (March 2010), leaving police with little to go forward on. The judge noted that he believed that the information provided by police to secure permission to attach the GPS to the car was insufficient (short of the requisite "reasonable suspicion"). He ordered that all evidence about the vehicle's location during the burglaries be suppressed (not admissible). Moreover, the judge opined that the use of such technology by police was an intrusion upon privacy. "I accept that an organized society has the right to be aware of the movements of a person who has been tried and convicted of a crime," he wrote in his opinion. "However, even in that circumstance, the ability to track a person's whereabouts 24/7 exists only where the person is incarcerated." (The GPS necessarily stayed attached to the vehicle 24/7.) "Just because [the] DEFENDANT was arrested for these types of crimes in the past and has access to a SUV is no indication that he was continuing to commit them," continued the judge. He concluded that the justifications proffered by the police amounted to no more than "vague assertions."

In December 2010, a three-member panel of the Pennsylvania Superior Court, a state **appellate court**, reversed. In overturning the judge's decision, the Superior Court ruled that prosecutors could use the GPS evidence at trial. The court agreed with the prosecutors' argument that the trial judge had "improperly reviewed the [search warrant affidavit] by analyzing individual facts instead of looking to the totality of the circumstances." For example, the similarities between the recent burglaries and ones committed by Heinzman in the past included the use of a pry bar to smash windows or force doors open to gain entry to locked buildings. A similar white van had been used, and there were multiple suspects at the scene. Most of the burglaries involved sums of less than $500, sometimes as little as what would be left in a cash register to make change when the businesses would reopen in the morning. The most ever taken during these robberies, according to records, was $800 and six cartons of cigarettes from the Kennett Beverage Company in Kennett (April 2008). The burglaries (about 30 in all)

occurred across Chester, Lancaster, and Delaware counties. The five co-defendants were arrested after a high speed chase on May 1, 2008.

The opinion quoted approvingly from what the prosecutors had argued, that "reasonable suspicion existed that criminality was afoot, and this use of a mobile tracking device was justified."

As of 2011, the use of GPS technology by police remained controversial and had produced different results in different jurisdictions. In November 2010, the U.S. **Circuit Court** of Appeals for the D.C. Circuit declined to hear *en banc* a petition by the U.S. DEPARTMENT OF JUSTICE to overturn an earlier ruling preventing the government from using GPS to track suspects without a warrant {No. 08-3034). With respect to electronic privacy, the U.S. SUPREME COURT had ruled, in *City of Ontario, California v. Quon*, No. 08-1332, 560 U.S. ___ (2010), that even where there may be a reasonable expectation of privacy (in work-issued electronic devices), an employer's search of private text messages did not violate the FOURTH AMENDMENT as long as the search was not excessive in its reach and was pursuant to a legitimate work-related purpose.

Tolentino v. New York

In the law of **search and seizure** under the FOURTH AMENDMENT to the U.S. Constitution, it is well established that incriminating or inculpating evidence that is seized during an otherwise illegal search is not admissible as evidence against the person in any subsequent criminal proceeding (the "exclusionary rule"). This evidentiary principle is often referred to as the "tainted fruit from the poisonous tree" exclusionary doctrine.

One week after hearing oral arguments regarding the suppression of certain evidence seized during an ostensibly illegal police search, the U.S. SUPREME COURT announced, without comment, that it was dismissing the **writ** of **certiorari** it had previously granted in the matter of *Tolentino V. New York,* No. 09-11556, 131 S. Ct. 595, 563 U.S. ___ (2011). The dismissal of the case before the Court effectively preserved the decision of the next lower court, in this case, the Court of Appeals of New York, which is the state's highest court. Notwithstanding, there remained a split of authority on this specific issue among the nation's circuit courts of appeals. The precise issue questioned whether pre-existing identity-related governmental documents, such as motor vehicle records, could be suppressed (i.e., not allowed into evidence) if they were obtained during an illegal (unconstitutional) police search?

Looking, then, to the preserved opinion of the Court of Appeals of New York, in *The People v. Tolentino*, 14 N.Y. 3d 382, 962 N.E. 2d 1212 (2010), the state high court held that driver/motor vehicle (DMV) records were not suppressible as "tainted fruit" of an alleged illegal police stop because such records were public records, already in the possession of government authorities. (The court's opinion included other reasons/rationale, discussed below.)

On New Year's Day in 2005, Jose Tolentino was stopped by police while driving his car in Manhattan, New York City, ostensibly for playing music too loudly. After learning his name, police ran a computer check of DMV files to look up his driving record. His record revealed that he had at least ten driving license suspensions imposed on at least ten different dates. Tolentino was then arrested and charged with one count of aggravated unlicensed operation of a motor vehicle in the first degree.

At a subsequent motion hearing, Tolentino sought to suppress both his driving record and any statements made after his arrest, on the grounds that the police had unlawfully stopped his vehicle and illegally obtained his driving record, making this evidence "tainted fruit." In response, the state argued that first, the stop was legal, and in the alternative, even if unlawful, a defendant's identity is never a suppressible fruit, and further, a public agency already possessed these records.

The trial judge held that Tolentino (or anyone else, for that matter) did not possess a legitimate expectation of privacy in DMV files maintained by the government. Such records, held the court, did not constitute evidence subject to suppression "under a **fruit of the poisonous tree** analysis." Subsequently, Tolentino pleaded guilty to the crime in exchange for five years' PROBATION.

Thereafter, Tolentino appealed, on the same argument that his driving record was

suppressible and that he was entitled to a remand for a hearing. The state **Appellate Division** denied the request and unanimously affirmed the trial court's decision (59 AD3d 298, 1st Dept 2009). The APPELLATE Division relied on previous precedent from the U.S. Supreme Court for the proposition that the identity of a DEFENDANT is never suppressible as the fruit of an unlawful arrest. *INS v. Lopez-Mendoza*, 468 U.S. 1032, 104 S. Ct. 3479, 82 L. Ed. 2d 778 (1984). Further, because Tolentino's identity led to the discovery of his DMV records, those records were likewise not suppressible. (The court also noted that the DMV records had been compiled independently of Tolentino's arrest.) Tolentino again appealed to the state's highest court.

The Court of Appeals for New York, in affirming the lower courts' decisions, acknowledged that under *Lopez-Mendoza*, a defendant's "body or identity" is never itself suppressible in a civil or criminal proceeding, even if an unlawful arrest, search, or interrogation is conceded. A contrary holding would permit defendants to hide their identity and undermine the administration of the entire criminal justice system. Tolentino did not dispute this, but rather claimed that the pre-existing DMV records could be suppressed because, without the alleged illegal stop, police would not have learned his name and would not have been able to access those records.

The court went on to cite several federal circuits which have addressed this issue and collectively held that, when police stop or seize a defendant, learn his or her name, and use that name to check pre-existing government IMMIGRATION files, the records are not subject to suppression/exclusion. Here, the facts were analogous, said the court.

The fact that DMV files were pre-existing public records further supported the rationale in the present case, said the court, noting Note 22 in a **plurality** opinion by the U.S. Supreme Court in *United States v. Crews*, 445 U.S. 463, 100 S. Ct. 1244, 63 L. Ed. 2d 537 (1980), "[t]he **exclusionary rule** enjoins the Government from benefiting from evidence it has unlawfully obtained; it does not reach backward to taint information that was in official hands prior to any illegality." Accordingly, the order of the New York Appellate Division was upheld by the state high court.

FRAUD

A false representation of a matter of fact–whether by words or by conduct, by false or misleading allegations, or by concealment of what should have been disclosed–that deceives and is intended to deceive another so that the individual will act upon it to her or his legal injury.

High Salaries in Small California City Lead to Resignations, a Recall Election, and Corruption Charges

Bell, California, located in Los Angeles County, is barely more than a blip on a map, especially given its proximity to the more prominent L.A. suburbs. With a population of about 38,000, Bell is also one of the poorest cities in L.A. county, with more than a quarter of the city living below the poverty line and the city's median household income standing at less than $30,000 per year. Citizens of Bell were shocked during the summer of 2010 to learn that the city paid its city manager nearly $800,000 per year and paid most of the other public officials salaries that far exceeded the salaries of individuals in much larger cities in the L.A. area. The controversy led to several resignations as well as a special election to remove the mayor and city council members, and prosecutors charged the city manager and his assistant with multiple counts of corruption.

Part of the controversy began quietly in 2005, when the city held a special election to change its status from a "general law" city to a charter city. During the same year, the State of California passed a law limiting the salaries of city council members for general law cities. The change in status meant that salaries of Bell city council members were exempt from the limitation. The city supported the move by informing citizens that the city would retain more local control, but citizens were not informed that the move would render the city exempt from the salary limitations. With only 400 individuals voting, including a large number of absentee votes, the measure passed with little fanfare.

During most of the next five years, nobody apparently questioned the effect of the election, which cost the city between $40,000 and $60,000. The effect on how much city council members were paid, however, was substantial, as salaries jumped more than 50 percent during a five-year period between 2005 and 2010.

Council members are part-time employees, yet Bell paid them $96,996 a year by the time the scandal broke in 2010. Ordinarily, city council members in a city the size of Bell would be paid about $400 per month.

In 2010, the neighboring City of Maywood had been dropped by its insurance company, and without the ability to provide liability or worker's compensation insurance, the city decided to lay off all of its city employees. This included police officers and city administrators. Maywood decided to outsource all of its city functions, and officials in Bell stepped in to help. Bell's Assistant City Manager, Angela Spaccia, took over as acting city manager in Maywood, with Bell paying her salary.

Two reporters with the *Los Angeles Times*—Jeff Gottlieb and Ruben Vives—began an investigation to determine whether officials in Maywood had committed any **malfeasance**. During their investigation, the reporters discovered that officials in Bell were paid relatively enormous amounts of money. Documents revealed that Bell City Manager Robert Rizzo received an income of just under $800,000, which was more than double what the chief executive of Los Angeles County made, and more than triple what city managers in nearby Long Beach and Manhattan Beach made.

The documents further revealed that most public officials in Bell made more than their counterparts elsewhere. Bell Police Chief Randy Adams made $457,000, which was more than the police chiefs in Los Angeles and New York and more than the Los Angeles County sheriff. The city council members were paid large sums for sitting on a variety of boards, though investigations showed that these boards did very little. Spaccia's salary of $376,288 also raised eyebrows as she was paid more than most city managers. Both Rizzo and Spaccia had contracts that called for 12 percent annual increases to their salaries, and each was guaranteed a large **pension** upon retirement.

Rizzo, Spaccia, and Bell Mayor Oscar Hernandez defended the salaries. Rizzo commented that he could make that amount of money in the private sector and that Bell was simply paying him **market value**. Hernandez added, "Our city is one of the best in the area. That is the result of the city manager. It's not because I say it. It's because my community says it."

The community did not respond positively to the news, however. Citizens immediately began to protest, and many attended the Bell City Council meeting on July 19. Many of the demonstrators shouted "fuera," or "get out" in Spanish. County officials had already begun to investigate the salaries to determine whether they were legal. However, a spokeswoman with the L.A. County district attorney's office said that much of what happened in Bell was legal because the citizens approved the ballot measure in 2005 and the city council approved Rizzo's salary, salary increases, and pension. Further investigation showed that Rizzo had devised a plan to give himself and 40 other city employees very large retirement packages. Rizzo would receive about $1 million per year from his pension, while Spaccia and other public officials would receive several hundred thousand dollars.

In September 2010, prosecutors charged Rizzo, Spaccia, Hernandez, and several city council members on several counts of corruption. Rizzo faced the most serious charges, as prosecutors brought more than 50 counts against him. He was accused of stealing public funds, writing his own employment contracts, and illegally influencing a contract between the city and a private company. Los Angeles County Superior Judge Mary Lou Villar ordered Rizzo to wear an electronic monitoring device 24 hours per day.

Prosecutors later alleged that Rizzo loaned city money to other city officials as part of his effort to keep them from objecting to his large salary. According to one of the prosecutors, "Money is power, and Mr. Rizzo used the city's money to gain power for himself." The PROSECUTOR made the statement in March 2011 during a **preliminary hearing** to determine whether Rizzo should stand trial for the allegations. Two weeks later, a **grand jury** in L.A. indicted Rizzo, Spaccia, and six other officials.

Spaccia has denied any wrongdoing, telling reporters that she was betrayed and that she felt naive. However, an email that she wrote while still in her former position put her in a negative light in the public eye. She wrote in the email, "We will all get fat together . . . Bob [Rizzo] has an expression he likes to use on occasion . . . Pigs get Fat . . . Hogs get slaughtered! So long as we're not hogs . . . All is well!?"

Hassan Nemazee, left, leaves federal court after pleading guilty to a $292 million bank-fraud scheme in New York, Thursday, March 18, 2010.
AP IMAGES/DAVID GOLDMAN

Clinton and Obama Financial Backer Sentenced to 12 Years for Running Ponzi Scheme

At one time, Hassan Nemazee was one of the leading fundraisers for the DEMOCRATIC PARTY. During the 2008 presidential race, he served as a national finance chairman for Hillary Clinton's campaign, and he was often quoted in the press based on his financing role. However, by 2009, authorities had found evidence that he had stolen hundreds of millions of dollars in the form of a **Ponzi scheme**. He pleaded guilty to **fraud** charges, and in July 2010, he was sentenced to 12 years in prison.

Nemazee's family was originally from Iran, but Nemazee himself was born and raised in Washington, D.C. His father was a shipping magnate and later became an Iranian diplomat in Washington. The family lost most of its property during the Iranian revolution in the late 1970s. Nemazee graduated with honors from Harvard University in 1972 before entering into the financial services industry in the 1970s and 1980s. He established Nemazee Capital in 1987. He has served as a member of a number of advisory boards and committees, including various committees at Harvard University.

He first gained national attention in 1999 when President BILL CLINTON nominated him to serve as ambassador to Argentina. However, *Forbes* magazine published an article that year that called Nemazee's business dealings into question. The article noted, "The White House press release [about Nemazee's nomination] . . . says that Hassan Nemazee is a 'New York investor' True enough, but there is quite a story that goes with his investing, and it is not a happy one. People who have done business with this man have come to regret it." The article detailed several instances in which Nemazee had taken advantage of friends and relatives in business transactions. One former classmate called him "the Iranian equivalent of J.R. Ewing." Nemazee claimed at the time that the article's facts were baseless. However, Republicans also questioned Nemazee's experience, and the SENATE Foreign Relations Committee eventually rejected his appointment.

Despite the negative press, Nemazee remained as a prominent figure in the Democratic Party. He had been a significant donor to the campaign of Clinton and AL GORE, and he supported Gore's candidacy for president in 2000. In 2002, Nemazee joined the finance team of John Kerry, who ran for president as the Democratic nominee in 2004. Nemazee is known to have entertained both Clinton and Kerry at his home. Nemazee later became the national finance chair for the Democratic Senatorial Campaign Committee, and during his time as chair, the committee reportedly raised $115 million.

Nemazee then became a major supporter for Hillary Clinton's run for the Democratic nomination for president in 2008. He served as a national finance chairman for her campaign, but when she withdrew from the race, he focused his support on the Barack Obama's campaign. After the Democratic National Convention in August 2008, Nemazee helped to raise more than $500,000 for Obama's campaign. Nemazee was also a donor to Obama's inauguration in 2009. Nemazee has reportedly donated more than $450,000 of his own funds to support Democratic candidates for office.

His legal problems began when he tried to obtain a $74.9 million loan from Citibank in 2009. He provided documents that purported to show that he had accounts with **collateral** worth hundreds of millions of dollars. He also provided contact information at various financial institutions, which would purportedly back his statement about his financial strength.

However, officials at Citibank discovered that the documents he provided had been forged and that he had the accounts he listed were either nonexistent or had been closed years earlier. Moreover, the contact information he provided were to phone numbers that he controlled.

Officials with the FEDERAL BUREAU OF INVESTIGATION interviewed him in August 2009, and he was arrested on August 25. He was released on $25 million bond, pending further investigation. He immediately paid the $75 million loan to Citibank by fraudulently obtaining a loan in the same amount from HSBC Bank USA. The FRAUD also extended to Bank of America, to which Nemazee owed $142 million as of August 2009. Prosecutors alleged that Nemazee had established a large PONZI SCHEME whereby he would borrow money from one bank through **fraudulent** means to pay another. His motive, said prosecutors, was to maintain a lavish lifestyle. His lawyers said that he had other motives, noting that his business had suffered severe financial setbacks. He wanted to maintain a successful appearance, so he began borrowing the money even though he lacked the means to repay the large loans.

He pleaded guilty to charges of bank fraud and wire fraud. As part of a plea deal, he agreed to forfeit property worth an estimated $292 million and repay the three banks he had defrauded. At his sentencing, U.S. District Judge Sidney H. Stein of Manhattan said, "You've done a great deal of good in your life. On the other side of the **ledger**, the crime is breathtaking in its brazenness and scope." Nemazee had previously told Stein that he was "deeply ashamed" of his conduct and that he would accept full responsibility for his actions, which were caused by "several financial difficulties."

Though prosecutors had recommended a sentence of between 15 and 19 years, Stein sentenced Nemazee to 12 years. Stein indicated that a longer sentence would have been severe given the circumstances.

Fallout from Madoff Fraud Scheme Continues

Former investor Bernie Madoff, who ran a massive **Ponzi scheme** that cost his investors billions, has been in prison since 2009. However, family members and others involved with the scheme have been the subject of several probes as officials attempt to recover money for victims. The investigation has included major banks as well as the owners of the New York Mets.

Madoff was originally arrested on December 11, 2008 and was later charged with SECURITIES **fraud**. He also faced a **civil action** brought by the SECURITIES AND EXCHANGE COMMISSION. The charges related to Madoff's investment business, which had been one of the most successful in the United States. Madoff admitted to investigators that the business was nothing more than a $65 billion PONZI SCHEME, under which investors believe they are receiving legitimate returns but which are actually being paid through funds received from new investors. Madoff pleaded guilty to 11 charges in March 2009, and in June 2009, he was sentenced to 150 years in prison. He was assigned to the Butner Federal Correctional Complex outside of Raleigh, North Carolina. He is not scheduled for release until 2139.

Judge Louis L. Stanton appointed New York lawyer Irving H. Picard to serve as **trustee** for the **liquidation** of Madoff's business, Bernard L. Madoff Investment Securities, LLC. One of Picard's first targets was Bernie's wife, Ruth Madoff. Picard sued Ruth for $44.8 million in July 2009, asserting that Ruth had benefited from her husband's FRAUD with a "life of splendor." Picard's efforts led to the seizure of many of Madoff's assets, including multiple homes, yachts, and so forth. Several other items, including Bernie's expensive watches and some of his wife's jewelry, were also auctioned off.

Madoff's sons, Mark and Andrew, were also the subject of investigation. Madoff first admitted to the fraud to his sons, and they had turned in their father to the authorities. Although most reports indicated that the sons had fully cooperated with investigators, federal prosecutors in February 2010 announced that they were seeking criminal charges related to tax fraud. The criminal investigation continued throughout 2010, with authorities seeking subpoenas to search the sons' personal files. On December 10, 2010, the two-year anniversary of the date that Bernie Madoff confessed to his sons, Mark committed SUICIDE at his New York apartment. According to reports, Mark wrote to one of his lawyers that "No one wants to hear the truth." Mark Madoff was 46 at the time of his death.

New York Mets owner Fred Wilpon watches a Mets baseball game May 29, 2011, in New York. Wilpon's ownership of the team was imperiled due to his ties to the Bernard Madoff case.
AP IMAGES/KATHY KMONICEK

Mark Madoff's death came just weeks after an INDICTMENT was filed against five of Bernie Madoff's former employees. The group, known as the Madoff Five, include secretary Annette Bongiorno; office worker JoAnn Crupi; chief operations officer Daniel Bonventre; and computer programmers Jerome O'Hara and George Perez. According to the indictment, Bongiorno and Crupi both "'executed'" trades in the accounts of (wealthy clients) only on paper … and that achieved annual rates of return that had been predetermined by Madoff." According to prosecutors, Bongiorno deposited about $920,000 into her own account but withdrew more than $14 million. The five either posted bond or were released on HOUSE ARREST in January 2011.

Picard had filed a total of 19 suits by the end of September 2010. In these suits, he sought recovery of $15.5 million from family members as well as major investors and those who ran funds related to Madoff's business. In December 2010, Picard announced that he had filed additional lawsuit seeking more than $17 billion from more of Madoff's family along with former directors of Madoff's investment branch in London as well as seven global banks. The total amount sought in these lawsuits came to more than $32 billion. Picard also announced that he had reached a $7.2 billion settlement with the estate of Jeffry M. Picower, who had amassed a fortune through legitimate trading before becoming involved in Madoff's scheme.

In an additional action, Picard filed suit in federal BANKRUPTCY court against J.P. Morgan Chase & Co. Picard first filed the suit in December 2010 under seal, but the suit became public in February 2011. According to the filing, bankers at J.P. Morgan had internally questioned whether Madoff was running a Ponzi scheme. According to the suit, "While numerous financial institutions enabled Madoff's fraud, [J.P. Morgan] was at the very center of that fraud, and thoroughly complicity in it." The suit alleged that J.P. Morgan and Madoff had a relationship that lasted for more than two decades. Bankers had encountered numerous discrepancies related to Madoff's account, especially during the mid-2000s, but nobody at J.P. Morgan made an inquiry. The suit against J.P. Morgan seeks $1 billion in profits and fees along with $5.4 billion in damages.

In yet another suit filed in federal bankruptcy court, Picard has sought about $1 billion from brothers-in-law Fred Wilpon and Saul Katz, owners of the New York Mets baseball franchise. Unlike most others involved in the various lawsuits, Picard has not charged that Wilpon and Katz actively participated in Madoff's fraud. Instead, Picard has alleged that the two earned significant profits from Madoff's firm despite red flags that should have warned them that Madoff's scheme was a fraud.

FREEDOM OF INFORMATION ACT

A federal law (5 U.S.C.A. § 552 et seq.) providing for the disclosure of information held by administrative agencies to the public, unless the documents requested fall into one of the specific exemptions set forth in the statute.

FCC v. AT&T Inc.

In the recent past, the U.S. SUPREME COURT has extended certain rights to apply to corporations in the same way those rights apply to individuals. The most significant example of this was the Court's decision in *Citizens United v. FEC*, 130 S. Ct. 876 (2010), where the Court determined that corporations possessed free-speech rights that allowed them to support political causes in the same way that an individual person could. However, in the case of FCC v. AT&T Inc., 131 S. Ct. 1177 (2011), a unanimous Court agreed that a corporation does not have a personal privacy right that exempts the corporation from requests under the FREEDOM OF INFORMATION ACT.

In 2004, the FEDERAL COMMUNICATIONS COMMISSION investigated allegations that AT&T had overcharged the government for services related to a program for enhancing access to TELECOMMUNICATIONS and information services for schools and libraries. During the investigation, AT&T provided numerous documents in the form of invoices, emails, employee information, and responses to **interrogatories**. The company eventually resolved the matter by agreeing to pay $500,000 to the government and to execute a plan that would ensure compliance with the FCC's program.

Several months after the investigation ended, a trade association that represents some of AT&T's competitors submitted a request under the Freedom of Information Act (FOIA), 5 U.S.C. § 552. This request asked for "all pleadings and correspondence" from provided by AT&T to the FCC. AT&T contested the request, arguing that several exemptions applied.

Under 5 U.S.C. § 552(b)(7)(C), the FOIA exempts "records or information compiled for law enforcement purposes . . . [that could] could reasonably be expected to constitute an unwarranted invasion of personal privacy. . . ." The FCC's Enforcement Bureau agreed with AT&T that this exemption applied, as the Bureau concluded that "businesses do not possess 'personal privacy' interests" that the exemption requires. The FCC as a whole agreed with the Bureau, noting that the conclusion was consistent with FCC and judicial precedent.

AT&T appealed the decision to the U.S. Court of Appeals for the Third Circuit. The Third Circuit disagreed with the FCC's arguments focusing on the text of the FOIA. In reading the **statute**, the Third Circuit determined that the text was unambiguous in establishing that a corporation can have a personal privacy interest to which the exemption would apply. Accordingly, the court remanded the case to the FCC for further proceedings. *AT&T Inc. v. FCC*, 582 F.3d 490 (3d Cir. 2009).

The U.S. Supreme Court agreed to hear the FCC's appeal. AT&T stressed that the Administrative Procedure Act, 5 U.S.C. § 551(2) defines the word "person" to include "an individual, partnership, corporation, association, or public or private organization other than an agency." Accordingly, AT&T argued, the word "personal" must also include corporations and partnerships as well as individuals.

Writing for the unanimous Court, Chief Justice JOHN ROBERTS disagreed with AT&T's textual argument. Roberts stressed that although adjectives usually reflect the meaning of corresponding nouns, this is not always the case. For instance, the adjective crabbed refers to handwriting that is difficult to read, whereas the noun crab refers either to a crustacean or a type of apple. Likewise, the adjective "cranky" refers more to "fretful fussiness" than to the noun "crank," which refers to "a part of an axis bent at right angles."

Roberts then turned his attention to the words person and personal, noting that the FOIA defines person but not personal. Since the statute does not define personal, the Court had to give the word is ordinary meaning. Roberts concluded that the word personal is ordinarily used to refer to individuals. He noted, "We do not usually speak of personal characteristics, personal effects, personal correspondence, personal influence, or personal tragedy as referring to corporations or other artificial entities."

The Court also rejected AT&T's argument that "personal privacy" simply means "privacy of a person." Roberts' opinion noted that two words together "may assume a more particular meaning than words in isolation." For instance, the meaning of the term golden cup may mean cup of gold, but the term golden boy does not mean boy of gold. Instead, golden boy means a boy who is "charming, lucky,and talented," according to the Court. Similarly, personal privacy "suggests a type of privacy evocative of human concerns—not the sort usually associated with an **entity** like, say, AT&T."

Having rejected AT&T's argument, the Court ruled that the FOIA exemption did not apply to the corporation. Therefore, the ruling opened the door for AT&T's competitors to receive the emails and other information submitted during the FCC's investigation. Roberts' final statement: "We trust that AT&T will not take it personally."

Commentators noted that while the decision did not expand on the Court's conclusion in *Citizens United*, corporations would have little reason to worry that many corporate files would become available to the public. This is because several other exemptions would continue to apply that would allow corporations to prevent access to corporate records.

Supreme Court Strikes Down FOIA Exemption Interpretation

The FREEDOM OF INFORMATION ACT (FOIA) gives citizens the ability to secure federal government records, subject to a limited number of exemptions. Enacted in 1964, the FOIA provides nine exemptions for specific categories of material. Exemption 2 protects from disclosure material that is "related solely to the internal personnel rules and practices of an agency." A 1981 D.C. **Circuit Court** of Appeals expanded this exemption by including any "predominantly internal materials" whose disclosure would "significantly risk circumvention of agency regulations or statutes." Other circuit courts of appeal adopted this interpretation of Exemption 2, while some circuits limited it to personnel rules and practices. The SUPREME COURT, in *Milner v. Department of the Navy*, __U.S.__, __S.Ct. __, __L.Ed.2d__ 2011 WL 767699 (2011), overturned the more expansive reading of Exemption 2, finding that the appeals courts had no **statutory** basis to expand the scope of the provision.

The FOIA request that led to the Court decision involved the Navy's operations at Naval Magazine Indian Island, a base in Puget Sound, Washington. The Navy keeps ammunition and explosives on the island and organizes its storage and transport using data known as the Explosives Safety Quantity Distance (ESQD) information. This information prescribes minimum separation distances between explosives and aids the Navy in designing and constructing storage facilities to help prevent chain reactions in case of detonation. In 2003 and 2004, Glen Milner, a Puget Sound resident, submitted FOIA requests for all ESQD information relating to Indian Island. The Navy refused to release the data, stating that release of the information would threaten the security of the base and surrounding community. To justify its refusal, the Navy cited Exemption 2. Milner filed suit in Washington federal **district court**, challenging the denial of his FOIA requests. The district court dismissed his lawsuit and the Ninth Circuit Court of Appeals upheld the ruling, citing the D.C. Circuit's interpretation of Exemption 2 first announced in *Crooker v. Bureau of Alcohol, Tobacco & Firearms*, 670 F.2d 1051 (1981). *Crooker* expanded Exemption 2 to include predominantly internal materials whose disclosure would "significantly risk circumvention of agency regulations or statutes. This interpretation was adopted by three other circuit courts, leading to a new terminology. Courts using *Crooker* referred to materials involving human resources and employee relations as a "Low 2" exemption and materials whose disclosure risked circumvention of the law as a "High 2" exemption. Because other circuit courts of appeals rejected the *Crooker* approach, the Supreme Court agreed to hear Milner's appeal and attempt to settle the issue.

The Court, in an 8-1 decision, overturned the Ninth Circuit ruling and rejected the *Crooker* interpretation of Exemption 2. Justice Elena Kagan, writing for the Court, noted that the appeals courts had failed to read closely the pertinent part of Exemption 2: "related solely to the internal personnel rules and practices of an agency." The key word was "personnel," which as used in the sentence as an adjective referred to human resources matters. The common meaning of personnel confirmed that personnel meant the selection, placement, and training of employees and the formulation of policies, procedures, and relations with or involving employees or their representatives. Exemption 2 used "personnel" in the "exact same way," meaning that the exemption only dealt with the conditions of employment in federal agencies. Justice Kagan pointed out that circuit courts that used *Crooker* had no problem identifying that human resource records were Low 2 exemptions. However, the statutory language went no further than human resource materials. The Court stated that its construction of the language "simply makes clear that Low 2 is all of 2 (and that High 2 is not 2 at all)."

The Court concluded that the underlying purpose of the FOIA confirmed this understanding of the exemption. The goal of the FOIA is to provide broad disclosure and therefore any exemption must be read narrowly. The Navy contended that LEGISLATIVE HISTORY supported the High 2 exemption but Justice Kagan found it ambiguous. Exemption 2

could not support the withholding of ESQD information because it had nothing to do with personnel rules and practices. The plain meaning of Exemption 2 made this clear. The Navy tried to convince the Court to adopt the High 2 exemption but got nowhere. High 2's circumvention requirement had no basis in Exemption 2's language. The only way to "arrive at High 2 is by taking a red pen to the statute-'cutting out some' words and 'pasting in others' until little of the actual provision remains." Because this was so, "High 2 is better labeled 'Non 2' (and Low 2 . . . just 2)." This "text-light" approach could not be saved by legislative history.

The Navy also claimed that a 1986 amendment to the FOIA codified the *Crooker* interpretation. Justice Kagan rejected this approach as well, finding that the amendment dealt with Exemption 7(E), not Exemption 2. The *Crooker* construction of Exemption 2 rendered Exemption 7(E), which deals with internal law enforcement materials, superfluous, as any document eligible for withholding under Exemption 7(E) would also be withheld using the High 2 reading. If Congress had agreed with *Crooker*, it would have had no reason to alter Exemption 7(E). It could have left the **statute** alone or it would have amended Exemption 2 specifically to ratify *Crooker*. The Court also rejected the claim of dissenting Justice STEPHEN BREYER that the Low-High exemption scheme should remain because it had been followed for 30 years. The Court noted that just a handful of cases had relied on *Crooker* in that time period and that the circuits who had considered the issue had been split.

FREEDOM OF SPEECH

Ninth Circuit Rules that Tattoos and Tattoo Parlors are Protected by the First Amendment

The growing popularity of tattoos in the United States has led to the growth in the number of tattooists and tattoo parlors. Some municipalities have sought to ban tattoo parlors, arguing that unsanitary procedures at such establishments can result in the transmission of diseases such as hepatitis, syphilis, tuberculosis, leprosy, and HIV. It is also likely that city governments have traditionally viewed tattoo parlors as unsavory establishments, catering to customers who do not

Lawsuit plaintiff, Johnny Anderson poses in front of a tattoo display at his Yer Cheat'n Heart Tattoo parlor in Gardena Calif., Thursday, Sept 9, 2010. A federal appeals court ruled Thursday that tattoos are artistic expressions entitled to full free speech protections in striking down a city's tattoo studio ban.

AP IMAGES/NICK UT

embrace middle-class values. Times have changed, however, and tattooists have sought to claim constitutional protection under the FIRST AMENDMENT, arguing that they should be treated like painters and other visual artists. The Ninth **Circuit Court** of Appeals became the first court to adopt this position, ruling in *Anderson v. City of Hermosa Beach*, 621 F.3d 1051 (9th Cir.2010) that tattoos are a purely expressive activity that are protected by the First Amendment. Therefore, a total ban on tattoo establishments is not a reasonable "time, place or manner" restriction.

Johnny Anderson co-owned a tattoo parlor in the City of Los Angeles and sought to open another one in the City of Hermosa Beach, which is also in the County of Los Angeles. Hermosa Beach did not have any tattoo parlors and had enacted an **ordinance** barring them because of public health concerns. The city pointed out that there were 300 tattoo establishments in the county and over 859 tattooists. The county employed only one person to inspect these establishments and that person admitted many had never been inspected, leaving it up to the owners to make sure that their equipment was properly sterilized and that safety procedures were followed. After the city turned down Anderson's application to open a

tattoo parlor, he filed a federal lawsuit alleging that the prohibition by the city violated the First Amendment.

The **district court** dismissed Anderson's lawsuit, concluding that the act of tattooing was not protected expression under the First Amendment. The court acknowledged that the tattoo process was "non-verbal conduct expressive of an idea," but it was not "sufficiently imbued with the elements of communication" to receive First Amendment protection. It reasoned that because the customer "had ultimate control over which design she wants tattooed on her skin," the tattoo artist did not "convey an idea or message discernible to an identifiable audience." Having established that no First Amendment rights were at issue, the court applied the rational basis standard of constitutional review to find that Hermosa Beach's public health concerns were a reasonable basis for banning tattoo parlors.

The Ninth Circuit overturned the district court ruling. Judge Jay Bybee, writing for a unanimous three-judge panel, admitted that all other **federal courts** had followed the district court reasoning, but concluded that the reasoning was flawed. The appeals court set out to determine if tattooing was a purely expressive activity entitled to First Amendment protection rather than conduct expressive of an idea, which may not be protected. Bybee concluded that tattooing was a purely expressive activity. First, there was not disagreement that the tattoo itself is pure First Amendment speech, as they are generally composed of "words, realistic or abstract images, symbols, or a combination of these" elements. Tattoos can express a variety of messages and serve many functions including decorative, religious, magical, and punitive. They can also indicate identity, status, occupation, or ownership. Though the court admitted it did not have an extensive understanding of tattoos as compares to classical paintings, it took "judicial notice of the skill artistry, and care that modern tattooists have demonstrated."

The court then examined the tattooing process to determine if the process itself was purely expressive activity. Judge Bybee stated that tattooing "is a process like writing words down or drawing a picture except that it is performed on a person's skin." Just as in writing or painting, the process of tattooing was not intended to "symbolize" anything; the purpose of the process was to produce the tattoo. All of these processes were "inextricably intertwined with the purely expressive product."

As to the business of tattooing, the fact the city's ban related to tattooing businesses had no effect on whether the activity regulated was protected by the First Amendment. Prior cases in which cities had tried to regulate the sale of paintings and visual artwork had led to the conclusion that the sale as well as the creation of artwork deserves First Amendment protection. Having established that the First Amendment protects tattoo parlors, the appeals court applied the **strict scrutiny** standard of constitutional review to the Hermosa Beach ordinance.

Under this standard the government must show that it has a compelling interest and that the law is narrowly drawn to achieve this end. As to First Amendment cases, the government must show that the law is a reasonable "time, place, or manner" restriction. The city's complete ban on tattoo parlors was based on health and safety concerns. Anderson did not dispute that the city had a significant interest in protecting health and safety, but he argued that the ordinance was broader than it needed to be. The regulations could permit tattooing but

insist upon sanitary conditions. The city disagreed, noting the county had only one tattoo parlor inspector and that there were no state laws governing the sterilization, sanitation, and standards for tattooists.

The appeals court agreed that a total ban might be more convenient for addressing the city's health concerns but concluded that city "has given us no reason to conclude that these concerns cannot be adequately addressed through regulation of tattooing rather than a total ban on tattoo parlors." Therefore, the court struck down the ordinance as a violation of the First Amendment.

Arizona Joins Other States Restricting Funeral Protesters

In January 2011, Arizona legislators passed an emergency measure, SENATE Bill 888, targeting publicity-seeking protesters in an effort to stop them from PICKETING and demonstrating at funerals and burial services throughout the state. The state made no secret about its main target, Topeka-Kansas-based Westboro Baptist Church, which had been disrupting funerals since at least 1999. The church's self-described "Fundamentalist Protestant" congregation, comprised primarily of extended family members of the church's founder, Fred Phelps, had gained considerable national infamy by demonstrating and picketing at the funerals of U.S. soldiers, gay persons, AIDS victims, and even Coretta Scott King. However, when the church contacted CNN News to announce its plans to demonstrate at the funeral of a nine-year-old girl killed in the January 2011 Tucson, Arizona gun attack that wounded U.S. Representative Gabrielle Giffords, Arizona lawmakers sprang into action to block the demonstration.

The notoriety of Westboro Baptist Church became more widespread after members traveled to Westminster, Maryland in 1999 to protest outside the funeral of Matthew Shepard, a young gay man who was beaten and left hanging on a fence to die in Laramie, Wyoming. In subsequent years, the church continued to appear at dozens of funerals with its mostly anti-gay, anti-war, and anti-divorce messages. The church protesters spoke, sang, and demonstrated with signs bearing messages such as, "God Hates You," "Thank God for Dead Soldiers," "God Hates Fags," or "You're Going to Hell." Following casualties from the wars in

Afghanistan and Iraq, the church seized an opportunity to demonstrate at several funerals of deceased soldiers, claiming their deaths represented punishment from God for America's (and the military's) tolerance of homosexuality.

Responding to an angry and shocked public, legislators in many states began to enact laws prohibiting or restricting any form of protesting or picketing at funerals or funeral services. The issue came to a head in 2006, when $5 million in damages was awarded in a civil lawsuit against DEFENDANT Westboro Baptist Church to the family of a Marine killed in Irag, after church members picketed the Marine's funeral. The monetary award to the family of Matthew Snyder was grounded in a state tort action for intentional infliction of emotional distress and intrusion upon seclusion. Westboro Church appealed the verdict on FIRST AMENDMENT (free speech) grounds, and the U.S. SUPREME COURT eventually granted **certiorari**. *Snyder v. Phelps*, No. 09-751, 562 U.S. ___ (2011).

While the Supreme Court decision was still pending, in January 2011, a lone gunman who appeared at a Tucson, Arizona political rally featuring U.S. Representative Gabrielle Gifford, shot and killed several innocent bystanders and attendees, including a little girl, Christina Green, in his attempt to kill the congress-woman. When Westboro Baptist Church made its announcement through media outlets that it intended to stage a protest at nine-year-old Christina Green's funeral (because Green's family "was Catholic"), local residents started to organize an effort to stop it.

Chelsea Cohen and Trevor Hill, University of Arizona students, along with Tuscon resident Janna Zankich, were instrumental in organizing and coordinating large groups of volunteers who wanted to help block protesters from the mourners. Cohen organized an "angel action," a large group of volunteers willing to wear 8-by-10-foot "angel wings" to shield funeral mourners from picketers. A Facebook request by Christin Gilmer resulted in hundreds of responses with pledges to volunteer. Soon, the local Democratic and REPUBLICAN PARTY organizations publicly asked persons to come out and

line the funeral routes to form a human barricade, if Westboro Church members followed through with its announced plans. Finally, Arizona lawmakers put aside their political differences to stand united against the church's intrusion.

Knowing that the *Snyder* case was still pending before the U.S. Supreme Court, Arizona's Senate Bill 888 was fashioned after those in other states, which generally do not restrict the *content* of protest speech, but rather restrict the time and place where such protests may take place. Arizona's measure, passed unanimously in both chambers, barred protests within 300 feet of any residence, cemetery, funeral home, church, synagogue, or other establishment, within one hour before or after a funeral or burial service. Violators would face a Class 1 **misdemeanor** charge. Arizona Governor Jan Brewer signed the bill into law on January 11, 2011.

On that day, the Associated Press reported that Westboro Baptist Church would not be at the little girl's funeral, but would picket the subsequent funeral (a few days later) of U.S. **District Court** Judge John Roll, who was also killed in the same Tucson gun tragedy. They also announced that they would picket at the road intersection at which Congresswoman Giffords was shot.

On March 2, 2011, the U.S. Supreme Court decided the *Snyder* case, holding in its 8-1 opinion that the First Amendment did protect Westboro from state tort liability for intentional infliction of emotional distress (for its picketing of the Snyder funeral in 2006). The Court stated that, while Westboro's members were engaging in protected speech about "matters of public import [while] on public property," still, "[e]ven protected speech is not equally permissible in all places at all times." The Court noted that Maryland now has a law restricting such picketing, but the law was not in effect in 2006. (As to the tort claim of intrusion upon seclusion in the *Snyder* case, the Court said that this also must fail, as Westboro members were more than 1,000 feet from Snyder's funeral, their demonstration was peaceful, and they did not disrupt the funeral.)

GAMBLING

Washington Supreme Court Upholds State Ban on Internet Gambling

The popularity of Internet gambling has lead states to ban the activity. States have taken this approach in large part because of the harmful societal effects of gambling. Though proponents of Internet gambling argue that states should regulate rather than prohibit this new way of gambling, opponents say it would be impossible to regulate the actions of companies that operate outside the state and often outside the United States. The Washington Supreme Court, in *Rousso v. State of Washington*, 239 P.3d 1084 (2010), upheld the state law that banned Internet gambling, finding that it did not violate the dormant **Commerce Clause** of the U.S. Constitution.

Lee Rousso, a Washington resident, enjoyed Internet gambling but could not play because state law banned the activity. He filed a lawsuit in state court asking that the court issue a **declaratory judgment** stating that the law violated the dormant Commerce Clause. He contended that the law impermissibly burdened interstate and international commerce. The dormant Commerce Clause is a construction created by the U.S. Supreme Court. Since Congress has the power to regulate interstate commerce under the Constitution's Commerce Clause, the Court reasoned that states are precluded from doing so by enacting laws or regulations that excessively burden interstate commerce. The state trial court dismissed Rousso's lawsuit, ruling that the law was constitutional. The Washington Court of Appeals upheld this decision.

The Washington Supreme Court, in a unanimous ruling, agreed with the lower courts. Justice Richard Sanders, writing for the court, noted that analyzing a dormant Commerce Clause required a number of steps. The first step was to determine whether Congress had expressly authorized the state regulation of Internet gambling. The court found that two federal laws that dealt with Internet GAMING only authorized a state to criminalize some or all gambling activities within the state's borders. Therefore, the Commerce Clause itself was not in issue, setting up the dormant Commerce Clause analysis.

The court next looked at whether the state law banning Internet gambling by its language or effect discriminated against interstate commerce in favor of in-state economic interests. Justice Sanders concluded that the language of the law was not discriminatory, as it "equally prohibits Internet gambling regardless of whether the person or **entity** hosting the game is located in Washington, another state, or another country." Similarly, the law did not have a discriminatory effect on interstate commerce because it prohibited Internet gambling "evenhandedly, regardless of whether the company running the web site is located in or outside the state of Washington."

Rousso had argued that the law discriminated against Internet gambling sites, all of which were located outside Washington, in favor of in-state "brick and mortar" gambling businesses. The court rejected this argument, finding that Rousso has mistakenly identified a direct discriminatory effect on interstate commerce. The question was how the effects of the ban were imposed on in-state and out-of-state businesses, not what the effect is on the business's revenues. The court also found no merit in Rousso's claim that the law directly discriminated against Internet gambling because the ban had the secondary effect of promoting in-state, brick and mortar gambling. Justice Sanders found that Internet gambling and brick and mortar gambling were two different activities, "presenting risks and concerns of a different nature, and creating different regulatory challenges." The dormant Commerce Clause only prevents a state from discriminating based on whether the business is in-state or out-of-state. The state law in question treated all entities engaging in Internet gambling equally, regardless of origin.

The court also noted that the discriminatory effect under the dormant Commerce Clause analysis must be direct. The ban on Internet gambling in Washington had a direct effect on those operations by preventing them from **doing business** in the state. However, even if the ban increased business for in-state, brick and mortar gambling, this increase was not a direct effect of the ban. The law did not deal with in-state brick and mortar gambling, just online gaming. The alleged secondary effect could just as easily occur for any goods or services purchased by a person who might have gambled online if it was legal in Washington. Justice Sanders concluded that "Purchasing substitute goods and services does not constitute *direct*discriminatory effects.

The next step in the analysis required the court to determine if the burden on interstate commerce was clearly excessive in relation to a legitimate **state interest**. The STATE INTEREST in regulating gambling was clearly legitimate. The effects of gambling included ties to ORGANIZED CRIME, **money laundering**, gambling addiction,

and underage gambling." Internet gambling introduced "new ways to exacerbate these same threats to health, WELFARE, safety and morals." Gambling online allowed gambling addicts and underage gamblers to easily gamble "from their homes immediately and on demand, at any time, on any day, unhindered by in-person regulatory measures." The state had ample and legitimate interests in addressing the effects of Internet gambling.

The analysis then turned to whether the burden on interstate commerce was clearly excessive. The supreme court rejected Rousso's claim that there were less restrictive means of regulating Internet gambling. The court noted that a regulatory system designed to monitor and address problems with Internet gambling would take significant time and resources to design and implement. In addition, there would likely be loopholes that would allow some concerns to slip through the cracks. The legislature avoided these shortcomings by banning Internet gambling; the courts had no authority to second-guess that decision. If the legislature had sought to regulate Internet gambling the burdening on interstate commerce would have been a "nightmare." The state would have had to impose "intrusive vigilance" on foreign Internet gambling sites, which would have forced these operations to tailor their operations to the laws of one state.

GAY AND LESBIAN RIGHTS

9th Circuit Sends California Initiative Banning Same-Sex Marriage Case to California Supreme Court

The battle over same-sex marriage in California moved to the **federal courts** after the citizens of the state adopted Proposition 8 in 2008, an initiative that amended the state constitution limiting marriage to those between a man and a woman. The federal **district court** struck down the amendment in 2010 but the leaders of the Proposition 8 initiative filed an appeal with the Ninth **Circuit Court** of Appeals after the governor and attorney general declined to defend the amendment. The Ninth Circuit, in *Perry v. Schwarzenegger*, 528 F.3d 1191 (9th Cir.2011), declined to review the merits of the appeal, focusing on whether the Proposition 8

Stuart Gaffney, center, holds up a sign while celebrating the decision in the United States District Court proceedings challenging Proposition 8 outside of the Phillip Burton Federal Building in San Francisco, Wednesday, Aug. 4, 2010.

AP IMAGES/ERIC RISBERG

leaders had legal standing to bring the appeal. The federal appeals court, which is required to apply state law on such questions, concluded that there was no definitive ruling to apply. Therefore, it certified the question to the California SUPREME COURT, requesting that the court supply an answer.

In May 2008, the California Supreme Court struck down state laws limiting marriage to those between a man and a woman, concluding that these laws violated the **equal protection** clause of the state constitution. In the months after the ruling 18,000 marriage license were issued to same-sex couples. Five Californians drafted Proposition 8, filed it and worked to have it enacted by California voters in November 2008. After it was enacted, opponents of the provision filed an action with the California Supreme Court, arguing that the initiative improperly sought to revise, rather than amend, the constitution. The attorney general and two other state officials were named in the suit but they declined to participate. The Supreme Court upheld Proposition 8 but ruled that the 18,000 marriages by same-sex couples would remain valid. A few days later a federal lawsuit was filed by a group of Californians challenging

the federal constitutionality of the initiative. The governor and attorney general were named as defendants but they declined to defend Proposition 8. The five leaders of Proposition 8 were allowed to intervene in the lawsuit to defend the initiative. After a 12-day **bench trial** (no jury was involved) the district court judge struck down Proposition 8, ruling that the initiative violated the Due Process Clause and the EQUAL PROTECTION Clause of the FOURTEENTH AMENDMENT.

The proponents of the initiative filed an appeal with the Ninth Circuit but the public officials did not. The appeals court stayed the district court's INJUNCTION that would have allowed same-sex couples to obtain marriage licenses again until the appeal was concluded. The opponents of Proposition 8 argued that the Ninth Circuit did not have jurisdiction to hear the appeal because the proponents did not have legal standing to bring the appeal. The court agreed that this was a threshold issue and asked both sides to file briefs on the matter. If the proponents did not have standing, then the appeal would be dismissed and the district court's injunction would go into effect.

The three-judge appeals panel concluded that it could not decide the issue at this stage in the proceedings. Under a 1997 U.S. Supreme Court ruling, persons seeking to appeal a lower court ruling must satisfy standing requirements at the **appellate** level just as they do at the district court level. The Proposition 8 proponents had been granted standing to intervene at the district court level but that was not enough to establish standing to appeal. To meet the standing requirements, the proponents had to establish "a concrete injury relating to the judgment" they sought to appeal. However, states have the power to create new interests, the invasion of which may confer standing. The question therefore became whether California law afforded the proponents, acting as private citizens, the interest or authority to appeal the case.

The Ninth Circuit noted that the citizen initiative has always enjoyed "a highly protected status in California." The legislature may not amend or appeal an initiative **statute** unless the voters have first approved it, and the governor has no VETO power over initiatives. However, in this case the governor's refusal to defend the proposition or appeal the district court ruling could be viewed as similar to a veto. The court stated that the voters of California "would appear to be ill-served by allowing elected officials to nullify" propositions in this way.

Proposition 8 proponents pointed to the fact the California Supreme Court allowed them to intervene in the 2008 state lawsuit after the initiative was enacted, even when the attorney general declined to participate. However, the appeals court found this unpersuasive because the supreme court had not explained why it allowed the proponents to intervene. The court could not "simply infer" that the proponents had "either the particularized state-created interest or the authority under the state constitution or other state law to act as agents of the People" to grant them standing to participate as the sole appellants on the appeal.

Because the California Supreme Court had not issued an authoritative ruling on the question of standing for proposition proponents, the appeals court was required to certify a question to that court, asking for an answer on

this topic. It did so in its opinion. Once the California Supreme Court issues a decision that answers the question, the Ninth Circuit will apply that precedent and make a ruling on standing. If the proponents do not have standing, the appeal will be dismissed and the initiative will become invalid. If the proponents do have standing, the court will consider the substantive issues argued by both sides and then issue a decision.

Repeal of Don't Ask, Don't Tell Military Policy

On December 22, 2010, after months of debate and years of political controversy, President BARACK OBAMA signed into law the Don't Ask, Don't Tell **Repeal** Act of 2010, Pub. L. No. 111-321, 124 Stat. 3515 (2010), ending the military's 17-year policy banning openly-gay and lesbian persons from serving in the armed forces. In comments before a cheering crowd gathered for the signing at the U.S. DEPARTMENT OF INTERIOR, Obama said that "it [was] the right thing to do," noting that "tens of thousands of Americans in uniform" will no longer be asked to live a lie. "We are a nation that believes all men and women are created equal," said the president. Passage of the bill was a major victory for Obama, who promised to repeal the ban in his 2008 presidential campaign.

The repeal was not immediately effective, but was to take place 60 days after certain conditions were fulfilled. These conditions included the receipt, by the Secretary of Defense, of a report he had requested earlier in the year, *Report of the Comprehensive Review of the Issues Associated with a Repeal of "Don't Ask, Don't Tell,"* (already received by the time President Obama signed the bill), as well as subsequent completion of the Pentagon's implementation plan (based on recommendations found in the Report). The 87-page completed plan generally instructed military officials to examine and rewrite a series of policies, regulations, and directives related to current law. A third condition was the receipt, by Congress, of written certification from the President, Secretary of Defense, and Chairman of the Joint Chiefs of Staff, that repeal was consistent with the Armed Forces' standards of military readiness and effectiveness, unit cohesion, and recruiting and retention. As of early

A Marine asks a question during a training session to familiarize Marines with the military's new position on gay and lesbian service members and the repeal of the "don't ask, don't tell" policy at Camp Pendleton, Calif.
AP IMAGES/LENNY IGNELZI

June 2011, such certification was still pending but expected.

The controversial "Don't Ask, Don't Tell" policy was developed during the Clinton administration to address longstanding DEPARTMENT OF DEFENSE regulations making homosexuals ineligible from serving openly in the military. However, in 1993, Congress overwhelmingly passed legislation (P.L. 103-160, statutorily codified at 10 U.S.C. § 654) which incorporated the existing regulations clearly stating that homosexuality was "incompatible with military service." Clinton, whose presidential campaign had included a promise to lift the ban on homosexuals, had failed to deliver. In compromise, the Clinton administration continued its interim policy of not asking "the question" regarding homosexuality. This informal policy was used by recruiters and military personnel, who often refrained from asking prospective recruits about their sexual orientation. If asked, only those recruits denying such orientation were accepted. Once accepted into service, the recruits were expected to conceal their orientation or risk separation from service. Hence, the adopted name for the policy, "don't ask, don't tell." (In 1996, the U.S. Court of Appeals for the Fourth Circuit upheld the 1993 *law* [10 U.S.C. § 654] and

denied the appeal of Navy Lt. Paul G. Thomasson, who was discharged from the service for professed homosexuality.)

More correctly, then, the new law signed by President Obama effectively ends the "Don't Ask, Don't Tell" *policy* by rendering it unnecessary and obsolete: the new law authorized repeal of the codified law, 10 U.S.C. § 654, that banned homosexuals from serving in the armed forces. Specific language in the new law mandated that until all of the enumerated conditions were met, the "Don't Ask, Don't Tell" policy would remain in effect.

The new legislation was originally introduced (H.R. 2965) as part of the National Defense Authorization Act (NDAA) of 2011. In early December 2010, Senator Joe Lieberman (D-CT) introduced a stand-alone version of the relevant provisions under S. 4023, which had 49 co-sponsors. Representative Patrick Murphy (D-PA) then introduced H.R. 6520, the House companion bill. The House then substituted the language of H.R. 2965 with that of H.R. 6520 and then passed H.R. 2965, as amended, by a vote of 250-175.

The new 2010 law expressly stated that nothing contained therein "shall be construed to require the furnishing of benefits in violation of Section 7 of Title 1, United States Code (relating to the definitions of 'marriage' and 'spouse' and referred to as the Defense of Marriage Act)." Further, nothing in this section or amendments thereto "shall be construed to create a private cause of action."

In early 2011, despite not yet being officially certified to do so, the Department of Defense ordered the Armed Forces to begin preparing and training personnel on the policy change. This included chaplains, medical personnel, and combat troops preparing for deployment to Afghanistan. One example was a Marine Corps class that included a video highlighting the Corps placing value on diversity, and a 19-page PowerPoint presentation depicting 14 scenarios (of potential homosexually-oriented conduct that might be witnessed or observed by others), along with expected and/or appropriate responsive conduct by the observer/witness.

HABEAS CORPUS

[Latin, You have the body.] A writ (court order) that commands an individual or a government official who has restrained another to produce the prisoner at a designated time and place so that the court can determine the legality of custody and decide whether to order the prisoner's release.

Wilson v. Corcoran

In the case of *Wilson v. Corcoran*, No. 10-91, 131 S. Ct. 13, 562 U.S. ___ (2010) involving convicted Corcoran's petition for a **writ** of **habeas corpus** in federal **district court**, the U.S. SUPREME COURT issued a *per curiam*) ruling (an opinion from the entire court, not authored by any particular justice). It vacated the judgment of the Court of Appeals for the Seventh Circuit, and remanded the matter for reconsideration on the merits. The Court expressed no opinion on the merits of the habeas petition. However, the OPENING STATEMENT of the Court in its*per curiam*) opinion clearly stated the reasons for its action:

> **Federal courts** may not issue writs of habeas **corpus** to state prisoners whose confinement does not violate federal law. Because the Court of Appeals granted the writ to **respondent** [Corcoran] without finding such a violation, we vacate its judgment and remand.

In 1997, an Indiana jury convicted Joseph Corcoran of murdering four men, including his brother and his sister's fiancé. The jury was instructed on **statutory** aggravating factors, and found that Corcoran's crimes met the aggravating circumstance of multiple murders. The jury then unanimously recommended the death sentence; the trial judge agreed and sentenced Corcoran to death. At sentencing, the trial judge addressed Corcoran by remarking,

> "[T]he knowing and intentional murders of four innocent people is an extremely heinous and aggravated crime ... It makes you, Mr. Corcoran, a very dangerous, evil mass MURDER. And I am convinced in my heart of hearts ... if given the opportunity, you will murder again."

On appeal, the Indiana Supreme Court, while holding that the state trial court's reference to the innocence of the victims and the heinous nature of the crimes was permissible to provide "an appropriate context" for consideration of alleged aggravating and **mitigating circumstances**, nonetheless vacated the sentence and remanded for resentencing. It did so out of concern that the trial court might have meant that it weighed these factors as aggravating circumstances.

The trial court, on remand, issued a revised sentencing order, stating,

> The trial Court, in balancing the proved aggravators and mitigators, emphasizes to the Supreme Court that it only relied upon those proven statutory aggravators. The trial Court's remarks at the sentencing hearing, and the language in the original sentencing

order, explain why such high weight was given to the statutory aggravator of multiple murder, and further support the trial Court's personal conclusion that the sentence is appropriate punishment for this offender and these crimes.

At that point, the Supreme Court accepted this explanation, back on appeal from Corcoran, and it affirmed the sentence from the trial court.

Next, Corcoran petitioned the U.S. District Court for the Northern District of Indiana for a writ of HABEAS CORPUS. Corcoran asserted several grounds for relief, including a claim that the trial court relied on non-statutory aggravating factors when it sentenced him (notwithstanding the trial court's previous clarification, accepted by the Indiana Supreme Court). This, claimed Corcoran, violated the prohibition against **cruel and unusual punishment** under the EIGHTH AMENDMENT to the U.S. Constitution, applicable to states under the Fourteenth. Of course, the State specifically rejected this contention in its response.

The district court, however, granted habeas relief on a wholly different ground: that the PROSECUTOR offered to take the death penalty off the table in exchange for a waiver of a jury trial, in violation of the SIXTH AMENDMENT to the U.S. Constitution. It did not address the sentencing challenges, considering them moot because it granted habeas relief on other grounds.

Now, on the state's appeal, the Seventh Circuit reversed the district court's Sixth Amendment ruling. It, too, did not address the remaining sentencing claims. It remanded the matter with instructions to the district court "to deny the writ." This, in turn, was vacated by the U.S. Supreme Court, on **certiorari**. *Corcoran v. Levenhagen*, 558 U.S. 1 (2009). The Court explained that the Seventh Circuit "should have permitted the District Court to consider Corcoran's unresolved challenges to his death sentence on remand, or should have itself explained why such consideration was unnecessary."

Without briefing from the parties, the Seventh Circuit simply changed course and granted habeas relief. First it concluded that Corcoran's challenge to his sentence had been waived by his failure to include it in his original cross-appeal. However, the Seventh Circuit found that the claim satisfied plain-error

review. It then considered the trial court's representation that it relied only on aggravating factors authorized under Indiana law. The Seventh Circuit concluded that the Indiana Supreme Court had made an "unreasonable determination of the facts" when it accepted the trial court's explanation. Then it remanded to the Indiana trial court to reconsider the sentence determination in order "to prevent non-compliance with Indiana law."

In response to this latest turn of decisions, the state filed a petition for rehearing *en banc* (before the entire Seventh Circuit). It argued that the Seventh Circuit panel had erred in granting relief in the absence of a federal violation. It also argued that the panel erred by second-guessing the Indiana Supreme Court's factual determination that its own trial court complied with Indiana law (citing *Wainwright v. Goode*, 464 U.S. 78, 104 S. ct. 378, 78 L. Ed. 2d 187 (1983) (per curiam).

The Seventh Circuit denied rehearing. But it did go back and amend the language to its opinion to reflect that Corcoran "contended that, under the circumstances of this case, noncompliance with state law also violates the federal Constitution and thus warrants him relief under 28 U.S.C. § 22254(d)(2). [The state] has not advanced any contrary argument based on *Wainwright v. Goode* ... "

The Supreme Court, in rejecting this, noted that the amended language of the Seventh Circuit's opinion "did not cure the defect." First, it was insufficient that a habeas petitioner merely assert a constitutional violation. The federal court cannot grant relief unless it agrees with the assertion. Here, the opinion reflected no such agreement or even discussion, nor did it even articulate what federal right had been ostensibly violated. Second, the state had indeed, explicitly disputed that any constitutional violation occurred in its arguments before the federal district court. This was the last forum where the subject had been raised.

Accordingly, without expressing any view as to the merits of the habeas petition, the Supreme Court vacated the judgment of the Seventh **Circuit Court** of Appeals and remanded for the above considerations.

Wall v. Kholi

Under the Antiterrorism and Effective Death Penalty Act of 1996 (AEDPA), a state inmate must file a petition for **writ** of **habeas corpus** within one year of the date in which a state court's judgment has been final. However, another provision in the federal **statute** tolls this limitations period when the inmate has sought **collateral** review in state court. In *Wall v. Kholi*, 131 S. Ct. 1278 (2011), the SUPREME COURT determined that an inmate who had sought a reduced sentence in Rhode Island STATE COURTS had sought a collateral review, thus tolling the time in which the inmate could seek the petition for writ of habeas **corpus**.

In 1993, Khalil Kholi was convicted on ten counts of first-degree sexual ASSAULT related to charges that he sexually molested his two stepdaughters. He received two consecutive life sentences, which he appealed to the Rhode Island state courts. In 1996, the Rhode Island Supreme Court affirmed his convictions. *State v. Kholi*, 672 A.2d 429 (R.I. 1996). Kholi later filed a **pro se** application for postconviction relief, arguing that he had received in effective assistance **of counsel**. The trial court did not resolve the application for relief for nearly six years before the court finally denied the petition in 2003. The Rhode Island Supreme Court affirmed the denial of his application for relief in 2006. *Kholi v. Wall*, 911 A.2d 262 (R.I. 2006).

Kholi also filed a motion with a state superior court to reduce his sentence, but the judge denied his motion. The Rhode Island Supreme Court also affirmed that decision. He filed his motion to reduce his sentence pursuant to Rule 35 of the Rhode Island Superior Court Rules of **Criminal Procedure**, which gives the trial court discretion to "correct" or "reduce" a sentence.

The AEDPA required Kholi to file a petition for writ of HABEAS CORPUS within one year of the date on which his judgment had been final after the conclusion of direct review by the Rhode Island courts. However, the AEDPA also contains a provision that tolls the one-year limitations period while "a properly filed application for State post-conviction or other collateral review with respect to the pertinent judgment or claimâ is still pending. Kholi did not file his federal habeas petition until September 2007. Kholi's direct appeal had tolled more than nine years from date of the final review of his direct appeal. Nevertheless, Kholi argued that his Rule 35 motion had further tolled the limitations period.

Kholi raised his argument in the U.S. **District Court** for the District of Rhode Island. The district judge referred Kholi's motion to a **magistrate** judge. On December 12, 2007, the magistrate judge issued an opinion concluding that Kholi's motion was more of a plea for leniency than a true review. Accordingly, the judge concluded that the Rule 35 motion should toll the limitations period under the AEDPA. The district judge then adopted the magistrate judge's report and recommendation and entered judgment against Kholi's petition. *Kholi v. Wall*, No. 07-346, 2008 WL 60194 (D.R.I. Jan. 3, 2008).

Kholi appealed the district court's decision to the First **Circuit Court** of Appeals. A three-judge panel of the **appellate court** acknowledged that the district court's position "has impressive support in the case law" but that the **federal courts** were not unanimous in their conclusion that plea for leniency of the sort sought by Kholi was not subject to the tolling provision. The First Circuit had never decided whether a sentence-reduction motion could give rise to tolling, so the panel treated the matter as one of **first impression**. According to the panel, the plain meaning of the AEDPA supported Kholi's argument, with the panel noting that the sentence reduction indeed involved a review of the sentence. The panel likewise looked at the purpose behind the AEDPA. Although part of the purpose was to safeguard state-court judgments, the panel determined that Congress had designed the AEDPA to encourage state prisoners to exhaust state remedies before bringing claims in federal court. Based on its reading of the statute, the panel concluded that the Rule 35 had tolled the limitations period. *Kholi v. Wall*, 582 F.3d 147 (1st Cir. 2009).

The Supreme Court agreed to review the case, and in a unanimous vote, affirmed the First Circuit panel's decision. Justice SAMUEL ALITO wrote the majority opinion, joined by each of the other justices other than Justice ANTONIN SCALIA, who dissented to a single footnote in the majority opinion. Alito addressed the meaning of "collateral review," noting that the Court had never comprehensively defined the phrase. Looking at dictionary definitions as well as usage in previous cases, the majority determined that the term "collateral" referred to something that stands "apart from the process of direct review" and that "review" referred to a "judicial reexamination." Accordingly, the Court focused on a collateral review as a judicial examination that is apart from the process of direct **judicial review**.

In view of these definitions, the majority had little trouble concluding that the Rule 35 motion to reduce the sentence was a collateral review. The process was something separate from the direct review process. Moreover, the process requires a judicial reexamination of the sentence by reviewing a number of different factors. The majority was unpersuaded by Rhode Island's argument calling for a more strict definition of collateral review.

Justice Scalia wrote a short one-paragraph DISSENT noting that he disagreed with a footnote in the majority opinion in which the majority declined to determine whether a Rule 35 motion seeks direct review of a conviction.

Supreme Court Reaffirms Habeas Denial if No Federal Law is Violated

The **federal courts** deal regularly with petitions for **habeas corpus** filed by inmates in state prisons. Under the federal habeas statute, inmates and federal courts are required to conform to certain legal standards. The U.S. SUPREME COURT reviews a number of habeas cases each term, defining the parameters of the habeas **statute**. In *Wilson v. Corcoran*, __U.S.__, 131 S.Ct. 13, 178 L.Ed.2d 276 (2010), the Court chastised a federal **circuit court** of appeals for violating a basic premise: federal courts may not issue writs of habeas **corpus** to state prisoners whose confinement does not violate federal law. The Court made clear that a federal court's disagreement with a state court's interpretation of state law could not support a **writ** of HABEAS CORPUS.

In 1997, Joseph Corcoran shot and killed four men, including his brother and his sister's fiancé. An Indiana jury found him guilty of four counts of MURDER, found the **statutory** aggravating circumstances of multiple murders, and recommended CAPITAL PUNISHMENT. The trial judge told Corcoran at his sentencing that his crime was "an extremely heinous and aggravated crime," that the county had never experienced "a mass murderer such as yourself," that the DEFENDANT was a "very dangerous, evil mass murderer," and that given the

opportunity Corcoran would murder again. The Indiana Supreme Court vacated Corcoran's death sentence, concluding that the trial judge might have violated state law by relying on nonstatutory aggravating factors when imposing the death penalty. The U.S. Supreme Court requires states to write death penalty laws that list specific aggravating factors that can trigger capital punishment. These objective factors are to be used so as to avoid subjective and emotional factors to enter into the death penalty decision.

On remand to the trial court the judge issued a revised sentencing order. In the order the judge stated that he had "only relied upon those proven statutory aggravators." His remarks at the sentencing hearing and the language in the original sentencing order "explain why such high weight was given to the statutory aggravator of multiple murder." Corcoran again appealed, but this time the Indiana Supreme Court accepted the trial judge's explanation and affirmed the death sentence. The court explained that it was "now satisfied" that the trial court had relied only on the statutory aggravators. There was "no lack of clarity [in the trial court's] statement and no plausible reason to believe it untrue."

Corcoran filed a petition for a writ of habeas CORPUS with an Indiana federal **district court**, asserting that despite the trial court's assurances, it had improperly relied on nonstatutory aggravating factors when it resentenced him. The federal district court did not address this claim, granting Corcoran habeas relief on a wholly different ground: the offer by the PROSECUTOR to take the death penalty table off the table in exchange for a waiver of a jury trial violated the SIXTH AMENDMENT. The Seventh Circuit Court of Appeals vacated this writ and directed the district court to dismiss the writ. Corcoran appealed to the U.S. Supreme Court, arguing that his remaining sentencing claims had not been heard by the district court. The Supreme Court agreed and directed the Seventh Circuit to remand to the district court to deal with the unresolved challenges. The Seventh Circuit ignored this instruction and issued an order granting Corcoran habeas relief based on the trial judge's sentencing statement. The appeals court applied a plain-error analysis, concluding that unlike the Indiana Supreme Court it was not satisfied with the trial court's representation that it relied only on statutory aggravating factors. Because the revised sentencing order said that it had used the "nonstatutory factors of heinousness, victims' innocence, and future dangerousness to determine the weight given to the aggravator of multiple murders," the Indiana Supreme Court had made an "unreasonable determination of the facts" when it accepted the trial court's explanation. The Seventh Circuit directed the state trial court to reconsider its sentencing determination in order to "prevent non-compliance with Indiana law."

The U.S. Supreme Court, in a unanimous *per curiam* decision (no justice signed the opinion), overturned the Seventh Circuit decision. The Court stated that only noncompliance with federal law renders a state criminal judgment subject to attack through habeas relief. The federal habeas statutes provides that a federal court may only grant a habeas writ to a state prisoner if he is in CUSTODY "in violation of the Constitution or laws or treaties of the United States." It is not the province of federal courts to examine "state-court determinations on state-law questions." In this case the appeals court found "no hint" that a federal right was infringed. The fact the federal habeas statute gave the Seventh Circuit the right to overturn unreasonable determinations by STATE COURTS did not remove the threshold requirement that a federal right or law must be infringed by the state court.

HEALTH CARE

Lower Courts Divided in Challenges to Health Care Reform Law

When President BARACK OBAMA signed the Patient Protection and Affordable Care Act, Pub. L. No. 111-148, 124 Stat. 119 on March 23, 2010, opponents of the measure immediately promised to challenge the law in the courts. Two of these challenges failed in late 2010, as federal district courts in Michigan and Virginia upheld the law. However, a federal judge in Florida in January 2011 struck down the law as unconstitutional. As of May 2011, appeals of these decisions were still pending.

Health care reform was a major point of contention during the 2008 presidential election and corresponding debates. Both Obama and Republican candidate JOHN McCAIN put forth proposals to extend health care insurance to more Americans and to bring down health-care costs. With Obama's victory in the election, one of his main priorities was to push a health-care reform measure through Congress. Throughout 2009, Obama worked with Democratic lawmakers to construct a health care reform bill that would satisfy both liberals who supported the reforms and conservatives who most opposed the entire reform effort. Even without Republican support, the bill passed in March 2010.

The act contains several controversial features. Many of the provisions restricted practices used by insurance companies, such as dropping a patient's coverage for making an error on an insurance application or denying coverage to children with preexisting conditions. A more controversial provision requires all Americans to maintain health insurance or pay a penalty. The requirement is contained in Section 1501 of the Act and is known as the "Minimum Essential Coverage Provision." Critics charged that the mandatory insurance requirement violated the Constitution. Twenty-six states joined in one of the suits, as did the NATIONAL FEDERATION OF INDEPENDENT BUSINESSES (NFIB).

The State of Virginia was one of the first to challenge the law, bringing a suit in the U.S. **District Court** for the Eastern District of Virginia in Richmond. Virginia argued that Minimum Essential Coverage Provision violated the **Commerce Clause** of the U.S. Constitution. The state also argued that the penalty imposed on those who do not obtain insurance is not a tax, and so the state argued that Congress did not have authority under the **General Welfare** Clause of the Constitution to impose this requirement. Parties challenging in the law in other cases made similar arguments.

Also filing suit in a Virginia federal court was Liberty University, a religious institution of higher education, which sued several officials in the federal government and sought to enjoin enforcement of the new law. In addition to the COMMERCE CLAUSE arguments also raised by the State of Virginia, Liberty argued that the new law violated both the Establishment Clause and the Free Exercise Clause of the FIRST AMENDMENT. Part of the basis for Liberty's argument was that the new law required the university to violate sincere religious beliefs regarding abortions. Liberty brought its case in the Lynchburg Division of the U.S. District Court for the Western District of Virginia.

Two judges in the Virginia cases came to completely different conclusions. On November 30, 2010, Judge Norman Moon ruled that Congress had proper authority under the Commerce Clause to impose the mandatory-insurance requirement. Moon concluded that Congress had a rational basis for asserting that health care affected interstate commerce such that Congress could regulate health care in the manner it did pursuant to the Commerce Clause. Moon likewise rejected Liberty's arguments based on religious grounds, finding no plausible claim that the act burdened Liberty's religious practices. Accordingly, Moon dismissed the case. *Liberty University, Inc. v. Gaithner*, 753 F. Supp. 2d 611 (W.D. Va. 2010). Moon's decision regarding the Commerce Clause was consistent with a federal judge's decision in Michigan two months earlier.

Just days later, Judge Henry Hudson of the Eastern District of Virginia struck down the law. According to Hudson's opinion, the issue regarding congressional power focused on whether Congress was regulating activities that substantially affected interstate commerce. If so, then Congress could regulate health care in the manner that it did under the Commerce Clause. Virginia argued that the Minimum Essential Coverage Provision did not involve an economic activity that could be the subject of congressional regulation under the Commerce Clause. Hudson agreed, concluding that "an individual's personal decision to purchase—or decline to purchase—health insurance from a private provider is beyond the historical reach of the Commerce Clause." *Virginia v. Sebelius*, 728 F. Supp. 2d 758 (E.D. Va. 2010).

The Fourth **Circuit Court** of Appeals will resolve the two cases. As of May 2011, a panel of the **appellate court** had heard oral arguments in the appeals for both of the district court cases.

In January, another federal judge reached the same conclusion that Hudson had. Judge Roger Vinson of the U.S. District Court for the Northern District of Florida reviewed a case brought by 26 states and the NFIB. Vinson concluded that the Congress had exceeded its bounds by including the Minimum Essential Coverage Provision. According to Vinson: "Congress is [not] without power to address the problems and inequities in our health care system. The health care market is more than one sixth of the national economy, and without doubt Congress has the power to reform and regulate the market. That has not been debated in this case. The principal dispute has been about how Congress **chose** to exercise that power here."

The Obama administration filed an appeal of Vinson's decision with the Eleventh Circuit Court of Appeals. Oral arguments were scheduled to take place on June 8.

Actions against the health-care law have not been limited to the courts. In April 2011, Idaho Governor CL "Butch" Otter (R.) issued an EXECUTIVE ORDER to prohibit the state from implementing the act. According to the order, the law violates the TENTH AMENDMENT and that the federal government overstepped its bounds by approving the new law.

IMMIGRATION

The entrance into a country of foreigners for purposes of permanent residence. The correlative term emigration denotes the act of such persons in leaving their former country.

Federal Courts Halt Enforcement of Arizona Immigration Law Provisions

The state of Arizona drew national and international attention in 2010 when the legislature enacted and the governor signed the Support Our Law Enforcement and Safe Neighborhoods Act. 2010 Arizona Session Laws, Chapter 113. The state, frustrated by continuing large-scale illegal IMMIGRATION, drug and human trafficking crimes, and serious public safety concerns, enacted a serious of provisions that, among other things, required officers to check a person's immigration status under certain circumstances, and authorized officers to make warrantless arrest of a person where there was **probable cause** to believe that the person committed an offense that would make them removable from the United States. The act also made it a crime for ALIENS not to apply for or carry registration papers. The United States government filed a federal lawsuit, asking that the court issue a **preliminary injunction** that would order the state not to enforce any provisions of the act until the court made a final determination as to the act's constitutionality. The **district court**, in *U.S. v. Arizona*, 703

F.Supp.2d 980 (2010), declined to enjoin the entire act but did bar enforcement of the most controversial provisions. In 2011, the Ninth **Circuit Court** of Appeals upheld the district court's PRELIMINARY INJUNCTION in *U.S. v. Arizona*, __F.3d__ 2011 WL 1346945 (9th. Cir.2011).

The federal government argued in its lawsuit that the U.S. Constitution and federal law preempted Arizona from enacting the immigration provisions. District Court Judge Susan Bolton acknowledged that the federal Immigration and Nationality Act (INA) empowers a number of federal agencies, including the Departments of Justice, Homeland Security, and State, to administer and enforce immigration laws. The INA mandated an alien registration system and established a procedure for removing aliens from the United States under certain conditions. Federal alien SMUGGLING laws make it a crime to knowingly bring an unauthorized alien into the country, while the Immigration Reform and Control Act (IRCA) created sanctions against employers who knowingly employ illegal aliens. In 1996, the passage of the Illegal Immigration Reform and Immigrant Responsibility Act (IIRIRA) created several employment eligibility verification programs.

Judge Bolton noted that for the U.S. government to obtain a preliminary INJUNCTION, it had to establish four things: a substantial likelihood of success on the merits of the case;

irreparable injury if the injunction is not granted; the threatened injury to the United States outweighs the injury to the DEFENDANT; and the injunction would not be adverse to the PUBLIC INTEREST. The U.S. argued that the law was unconstitutional because it violated the U.S. Constitution's **Supremacy Clause**, which makes federal law "the supreme law of the land." The SUPREME COURT has consistently ruled that the federal government has broad and exclusive authority to regulate immigration, yet Bolton also stated that the Court had concluded that not every state law which deals with aliens "is a regulation of immigration and thus per se preempted by this constitutional power." Applying the latter precedent, the court concluded that some provisions of the act did not appear unconstitutional. Therefore, she refused to grant a blanket injunction.

The court did find the U.S. government would likely prevail in its attack on the law's provision that "Any person who is arrested shall have the person's immigration status determined before the person is released." The U.S. government argued that the mandatory determination of immigration status for all arrestees conflicted with federal law because it imposed substantial burdens on lawful immigrants by frustrating nationally-uniform rules governing the treatment of aliens throughout the country. The judge concluded that these immigration checks would extend the time people who are

never technically "arrested" would be held by authorities. In addition, these requests for immigration status would shift the **allocation** of federal resources away from federal priorities, which were currently dedicated in large part to national security concerns. Therefore, the state provision was preempted by federal law.

The court also found that the U.S. government would prevail in its **preemption** claim on the law's provision that required police to make an immigration check on persons they stopped or detained. The judge agreed that the impact on lawfully-present aliens was enhanced because "this requirement applies to stops for even minor, non-criminal violations of state law, including jaywalking, failing to have a dog on a leash, or riding a bicycle on the sidewalk." The impact on federal resources under the arrest provision applied as well to the stop provision, thereby leading to the conclusion of federal PREEMPTION.

Section 3 of the Arizona law made it a crime to violate federal registration laws and applied state criminal penalties for violations of the federal law. Judge Bolton found that the current federal alien registration requirements created "an integrated and comprehensive system." Section 3's attempt to supplement this system was preempted by the federal law because it "stood as an obstacle to the uniform, federal registration scheme." Section 5's provision making it a crime for working without proper authorization was preempted for similar reasons." Finally, Section 6's requirement that police arrest a person without a warrant if the officer believes the person has committed "any public offense that makes the person removable from the United States" was preempted by federal law. Judge Bolton concluded that this provision targeted only aliens-legal and illegal-because "only aliens are removable." There was "substantial complexity" for an officer to make such a determination. Moreover, because removal is determined ultimately by a federal judge, there was a "substantial likelihood that officers will wrongfully arrest legal resident aliens under this new provision. Therefore, it was likely that the U.S. government could prove preemption. The court also found that the U.S. had proved the other three elements need for obtaining a preliminary injunction.

The state appealed the preliminary injunction to the Ninth Circuit. In a 2-1 decision, the appeals court ruled that Bolton had not abused her discretion in issuing the injunction. Though the appeals court did not rule on the constitutional arguments, it did indicate it was sympathetic to the preemption arguments raised by the U.S. government. The case continued in Bolton's court, as the judge hears evidence as to whether provisions of the law will be permanently enjoined.

Chamber of Commerce of the United States of America v. Whiting

Arizona lawmakers have been vocal about their displeasure with Congress about its unwillingness to move forward with comprehensive IMMIGRATION reform. In 2007, Arizona approved a law requiring employers to verify that their employees are legal or not. An employer that employs illegal immigrations faces revocation of its license to do business in the state. Several businesses and CIVIL RIGHTS groups challenged the law in court. However, the U.S. SUPREME COURT in *Chamber of Commerce of the United States of America v. Whiting*, No. 09-115, 2011 WL 2039365 (U.S. May 26, 2011) ruled that the law was not preempted by federal law.

Congress established sanctions for hiring unauthorized ALIENS by passing the Immigration Reform and Control Act of 1986 (IRCA), Pub. L. No. 99-603, 100 Stat. 3359. This **statute** defines an alien to include someone not lawfully admitted to the United States for permanent residence or not authorized to be employed under the Act or by the Attorney General of the United States. The IRCA also established a paper-based method for verifying whether an employee was eligible to work. This method, known as the I-9 system, requires employees to submit proper identification to their employers. The Act also requires employers to examine the identification documents and establishes sanctions for employers who fail to do so. The Attorney General is responsible for enforcing the IRCA.

The IRCA expressly preempts state law. A section of the IRCA states: "The provisions of this section preempt any State or local law imposing civil or criminal sanctions (other than through licensing and similar laws) upon those who employ, or recruit or refer for a fee for employment, unauthorized aliens." The part of the provision in parentheses is known as the savings clause.

Salvador Reza speaking in July 2010 outside Phoenix City Hall in Phoenix. Community members from the Puente Movement were petitioning the city to not enforce Arizona's immigration bill, SB 1070.

AP IMAGES/MATT YORK

Congress subsequently approved later acts designed to improve the efficiency and accuracy of an employer's verification of a new employee's eligibility to be employed. Congress eventually set up a system known as E-Verify, which is based on the Internet and serves as an alternative to the older I-9 system. The system either confirms or does not confirm whether an employee is authorized to work. If the system does not confirm, the employee has eight days to challenge the system's findings. If an employer employs someone who is not confirmed, or who has challenged a nonconfirmation finding but has failed, the employer must notify the HOMELAND SECURITY DEPARTMENT. If an employer continues to employ the person after receiving notice from the system that the employee is not confirmed, the employer is subject to civil penalties.

In 2007, the Arizona Legislature approved the Legal Arizona Workers Act, Ariz. Rev. Stat. §§ 23-212 **et seq.** This statute provides that when an employer continues to employ an alien who has not been confirmed, the state can revoke the employer's license to do business in the state. The law also requires employers to use the E-Verify system, even though the federal law does not require this system's use. The Arizona statute incorporates several provisions, including definitions, that are very similar to provisions in the IRCA.

Almost immediately after the statute's enactment, a group of business and civil rights organizations brought suit challenging the new law. The plaintiffs' main argument was that the IRCA preempted the Arizona law because the Arizona law was not a licensing or similar law as those terms are used in the IRCA. Moreover, the plaintiffs asserted that the new law's requirement that employers use the E-Verify system conflicted with federal law because the federal law does not require this system's use by all employers.

Judge Neil Vincent Wake of U.S. **District Court** for the District of Arizona upheld the statute. The plaintiffs then appealed to the Ninth **Circuit Court** of Appeals. A three-judge panel in 2008 affirmed the district court's judgment. According to the opinion written by Judge Mary M. Schroeder, federal law did not preempt any of the Arizona statute's provisions. The court also concluded that the statute did not violate the due process rights of the employers. *Chicanos Por La Causa, Inc. v. Napolitano*, 558 F.3d 856 (9th Cir. 2008).

The U.S. Supreme Court agreed to review the case, and in a 5-3 decision, affirmed the Ninth Circuit. Justice Elena Kagan recused herself because of her previous role as **solicitor general**, and the remaining eight judges were divided in their opinions. Chief Justice JOHN ROBERTS wrote the opinion of the Court, but Justice CLARENCE THOMAS only joined part of Roberts' opinion, and so other parts of the opinion were only supported by a **plurality**.

According to Roberts, the Arizona law was clearly a licensing law that fell under the savings clause of the IRCA. Roberts pointed out that the Arizona law defined "license" by using terms found in the federal Administrative Procedure Act, 5 U.S.C. § 551(8). Moreover, Roberts pointed out that the term "licensing" in 5 U. S.C. § 551(9) included terms such as revocation, suspension, ANNULMENT, and withdrawal. Roberts thus rejected the plaintiffs' argument that the law was not a licensing statute because it merely suspended or revoked licenses rather than granting them.

Roberts also concluded that the Arizona law was not impliedly preempted by federal law based on the Congress' broad reach in enacting the immigration statutes. According to Roberts, Congress reserved some power for the states in the area of licensing, so the implied **preemption** argument failed. However, because Justice Clarence Thomas did not join the part of Roberts' opinion addressing implied PREEMPTION, so Roberts failed to garner a majority for that section of his opinion.

Justice STEPHEN BREYER wrote a lengthy DISSENT, as did Justice SONIA SOTOMAYOR. Breyer argued that the Arizona law "strays beyond the bounds of the federal licensing exception." Roberts also argued that the majority had misconstrued the language of the preemption provision in the IRCA. Sotomayor argued that Congress intended to create a comprehensive scheme related to employment of illegal aliens and Congress could not have intended for the preemption provision to apply that way that the majority held.

Supreme Court Deadlocks on Immigration Case

Children born outside the United States who have one U.S.-citizen parent can claim U.S. citizenship if the citizen parent had been physically present in the United States for a certain amount of time before the child's birth. The time periods differ for mothers and fathers; the mother must have been physically present for one year, while the father must have resided in the U.S. for at least five years. The SUPREME COURT, in *Flores-Villar v. United States*, __U.S.__, S.Ct. , __L.Ed.2d__ 2011 WL 2297764 (2011), attempted to review whether these different time periods constituted gender DISCRIMINATION. However, Justice Elena Kagan did not participate in the case because she had been **Solicitor General** when the Supreme Court accepted review. The eight remaining justices deadlocked 4-4, thereby affirming the decision of the Ninth **Circuit Court** of Appeals.

Ruben Flores-Villar was born in Tijuana, Mexico in 1984 to Ruben Trinidad Floresvillar-Sandez, his U.S. citizen biological father who was sixteen at the time , and Maria Mercedes Negrete, his non-U.S. citizen mother. The father was issued a Certificate of Citizenship in 1999, based on the fact that his mother, who was Flores-Villar's paternal grandparent, is a U.S. citizen by birth. His father and grandmother brought Flores-Villar to the U.S. for medical treatment when he was two years old and the three ended up residing in San Diego permanently. Floresvillar-Sandez was not listed on Flores-Villar's birth certificate but he filed an acknowledgment of PATERNITY with the Civil Registry in Mexico in 1985.

In 1997, Flores-Villar was convicted in U.S. **district court** of importing marijuana. In 2003 he was convicted of two counts of illegal entry into the United States and was removed from the United States. He reentered the U.S. numerous times and was sent back to Mexico. In 2006 he was arrested and charged with being a deported alien in the United States after DEPORTATION. Flores-Villar argued in his defense that he believed he was a U.S. citizen through his father. He also filed an application seeking a Certificate of Citizenship. The application was denied on the ground that it was physically impossible for his father, who was sixteen when he was born, to have been present in the United States for five years after his fourteenth birthday, as required by U.S. IMMIGRATION law. The district court found Flores-Villar guilty. He then appealed to the Ninth Circuit Court of Appeals.

The Ninth Circuit affirmed the district court ruling. *U.S. v. Flores-Villar*, 536 F.3d 990 (2008). Judge Pamela Rymer, writing for the three-judge panel, noted that if a U.S. citizen father had a child out of wedlock, with a non-U.S. citizen mother, the father must have resided in the U.S. for at least five years after his fourteenth birthday to confer citizenship on his child. However, a U.S. citizen mother had to reside in the U.S. for a continuous period of only one year prior to the child's birth to confer citizenship. Flores-Villar contended that this disparity amounted to illegal gender and AGE DISCRIMINATION. However, Judge Rymer found instructive a Supreme Court case, *Nguyen v. INS*, 533 U.S. 53, 121 S.Ct. 2053, 150 L.Ed.2d 115 (2001), that dealt with different rules for obtaining citizenship that depended upon whether the one parent with U.S. citizenship was the mother or the father. The U.S. citizen father in that case objected to the number of affirmative steps a citizen father, but not a citizen mother, must take to obtain citizenship for the child. The Supreme Court identified two important government interests that were substantially furthered by this distinction. The first was "assuring that a biological parent-child

relationship exists." This relation is easier to verify in the case of the mother, while a father's relationship is not so easily established. The second interest was ensuring "that the child and the citizen parent have some demonstrated opportunity or potential to develop not just a relationship that is recognized, as a formal matter, by the law, but one that consists of the real, everyday ties that provide a connection between child and citizen parent, and, in turn, the United States." Unlike an unwed mother, there is no assurance that the child and his biological father will ever meet.

Judge Rymer admitted that although the means at issue were different in this case, the two interests given in *Nguyen* still applied. The shorter residency requirement for mothers furthered the objective of avoiding stateless children, for many countries confer citizenship based on bloodline rather than, as the United States does, on place of birth. If a U.S. citizen mother is not a dual national and the illegitimate child is born in a country that does not recognize citizenship by place of birth alone, "the child can acquire no citizenship other than the mother's at birth." The more lenient policy for mothers clearly demonstrated to the appeals court a rational basis for the **statute**. Flores-Villar agreed that avoiding stateless children was a legitimate goal but fathers should not be penalized to realize this goal. He contended the real purpose of the laws was to "perpetuate the stereotypical notion that women should have CUSTODY of illegitimate children." Judge Rymer rejected this argument, finding that the one-year residency for mothers was directly related to statelessness.

As to the claim of age discrimination, Flores-Villar noted that under the law it was physically and legally impossible for U.S. citizen fathers under age nineteen to confer citizenship on their foreign-born, illegitimate children even if they had resided in the U.S. for ten years. Therefore, it treated men over the age of nineteen more favorably. The court found no merit in this argument, concluding that "it is not irrational to believe that a United States citizen father who has spent at least five years in residence during his teenage years would have more of a connection with this country to pass on that, say, a father who lived in the United States between the ages of one and ten."

Third Circuit Strikes Down Municipal Immigration Laws

National concerns about the effects of illegal IMMIGRATION have led Congress to enact laws that seek to stem the tide of illegal ALIENS into the United States. Despite these efforts, state and local governments have in recent years begun to enact laws that attempt to prevent illegal aliens from being employed or renting housing. These efforts have been challenged in **federal courts**, as private plaintiffs and the U.S. government argued that the federal government has exclusive authority to regulate immigration. The Third **Circuit Court** of Appeals, in *Lozano v. City of Hazelton*, 620 F.3d 170 (3rd.Cir 2010), agreed with private plaintiffs that municipal ordinances imposing requirements on employers and landlords not to hire or rent to illegal aliens were preempted by federal law.

The city of Hazelton, Pennsylvania is located in the northeastern part of the state, near New York and New Jersey. Its population grew from 23,000 in 2000 to almost 33,000 by 2009, largely due to an influx of Latino families from the two neighboring states. The newcomers included U.S. citizens, lawful permanent residents, and illegal aliens. City officials concluded that illegal aliens were causing certain social problems in the city and that the federal government could not be relied upon to prevent such aliens from moving into the city or to remove them. In 2006 the city council enacted a series of ordinances designed to tackle these concerns. The Illegal Immigration Relief Act **Ordinance** (IIRAO) attempted to regulate the employment of illegal aliens and the rental of housing to illegal aliens. The Rental Registration Ordinance (RO) required any prospective occupant of rental housing to apply for and receive an occupancy permit.

The IIRAO stated that it was unlawful for any business to hire an illegal alien. Businesses that applied for a city business permit had to sign an AFFIDAVIT affirming that they did not knowingly use the services or hire illegal aliens. Citizens could file a complaint with the city if they believed a business was employing illegal aliens. The business then had three days to provide information to the city or face suspension of its business license. If the city inspector determined that illegal aliens were employed, the license was suspended until the business informed the city it had fired the illegal workers.

A second offense would lead to the suspension of the license for a minimum of 20 days. As for housing, the IIRAO made it illegal for person or business to let, least, or rent a dwelling to an illegal alien. The enforcement mechanisms were similar to those for employment. The RO required that a person seeking an occupancy permit had to pay a $10 application fee and show proper identification that proved legal citizenship and residency.

Before the laws went into effect a group of individuals and local Hispanic business association filed a federal lawsuit, arguing that the laws were unconstitutional. The **district court** conducted a nine-day **bench trial** before issuing an opinion and an order than permanently enjoined the city from enforcing the ordinances. The court concluded that the IIRAO and the RO violated the Supremacy and Due Process Clauses of the U.S. Constitution. The city then appealed to the Third Circuit.

A three-judge panel unanimously found that the provisions in question were preempted by the federal government. Chief Judge Theodore McKee, writing for the appeals court, noted that Congress had enacted a series of laws that regulate immigration. Under these laws an alien who is in the U.S. unlawfully faces the prospect of a removal proceeding being initiated against her. However, actually being ordered removed "is never a certainty until all **legal proceedings** have concluded." The Immigration Reform and Control Act (IRCA) regulates the employment of illegal aliens and creates a employment verification system. The Illegal Immigration Reform and Immigrant Responsibility Act of 1996 directed the implementation of three pilot projects for confirmation of employment eligibility. One of these programs, E-Verify, was expanded to all 50 states in 2003. Under E-Verify, an employer enters information from an employee's documents into an online system and that information is transmitted to the SOCIAL SECURITY Administration and the DEPARTMENT OF HOMELAND SECURITY for authentication. Employers, however, are not required to use E-Verify.

The court acknowledged that states and municipalities may legislate in some areas involving immigration. However, a state law is preempted by federal law if it is "essentially a determination of who should or should not be admitted into the country, and the conditions under which a legal entrant may remain." The employment provisions of the IIRAO were not expressly preempted by federal law. However, they were invalid because they were "conflict pre-empted." This type of **preemption** occurs when it is impossible for a person to comply with both the federal law and the state law provisions, or if the state provisions "stand as an obstacle to the objectives underlying" the federal law. Judge McKee concluded that the IIRAO substantially undermined the careful balance in IRCA of the goals of preventing the hiring of illegal aliens, lessening the disruption of U.S. business, and minimizing the possibility of employment DISCRIMINATION.

As to the housing provisions, the appeals court agreed with the district court that they were preempted by federal law. Though localities may regulate rental housing to ensure public health and safety, Judge McKee stated that "we cannot bury our heads in the sand ostrich-like ignoring the reality of what these ordinances accomplish." The city had attempted to use these provisions to regulate residence based only on immigration status. This was impermissible because the federal government had always been the sole authority as to which aliens may live in the United States. The attempt by the city to "usurp authority that the Constitution has placed beyond the vicissitudes of local governments" could not stand.

Second Circuits Upholds Statutory Due Process for Noncitizens Fighting Deportation

Under federal law, the government must provide **due process of law** to noncitizens the government wants to remove from the United States. The law surrounding removals of noncitizens began to change in the 1990s, when Congressional provisions sought to limit the ways they could fight their removal. Specifically, Congress has tried to prevent noncitizens from using various legal procedures to delay removal. However, under the U.S. Constitution's Suspension Clause, Article I, § 9, cl. 2, "[t]he Privilege of the **Writ** of **Habeas Corpus** shall not be suspended, unless when in Cases of Rebellion or Invasion the public Safety may require it." When Congress enacted the REAL ID Act of 2005, Pub.L. 109-13, 119 Stat. 302, (May 11, 2005), which deals with national standards for issuing drivers licenses and identification (ID) cards, it included provisions

dealing with IMMIGRATION as related to TERRORISM. The law imposed stronger requirements to qualify for ASYLUM and it made it easier to deport noncitizens for terrorist activities. Section 106 of the act explicitly precludes habeas **corpus** review by the **federal courts**. A noncitizen may only file a petition for review with the court of appeals to challenge removal from the United States. The Second **Circuit Court** of Appeals addressed in *Luna v. Holder*, __F.3d__, 2011 WL 722607 (2nd.Cir. 2011), whether that section could bar habeas review. The appeals court concluded that it could because there was a **statutory** procedure in place that gave noncitizens the ability to challenge their removal even if they missed a filing deadline.

Worklis Luna and Tasmann Thompson were noncitizens that the Immigration and NATURALIZATION Service (INS) sought to deport to respectively the Dominican Republic and Haiti. The INS based these removal actions on the fact that both men had been convicted of felonies in the U.S. Thompson asked unsuccessfully for an attorney to represent him in the removal action. After he was ordered removed, he appealed to the Board of Immigration Appeals (BIA), which upheld his removal. He had 30 days to file a petition to review with the Second Circuit Court of Appeals but he failed to do so. He later filed a motion with the appeals court seeking review, arguing that he was prevented from filing a timely petition because he was incarcerated in a detention facility and was unable to obtain legal documents. Thompson was returned to Haiti but he continued to press his case with the Second Circuit.

Luna challenged his removal unsuccessfully through the INS and BIA. Although he had an attorney, he later discovered that this lawyer had failed to inform him that he would not file a petition for review with the appeals court because there were no good arguments he could make on behalf of his client. By the time Luna found out the 30-day filing period had expired.

The Second Circuit ruled that although the two men could not challenge their removals in the appeals court using HABEAS CORPUS, there was a statutory scheme that gave them essentially the same relief. The Court had initially ruled months earlier that the motion to reopen the removal process was an inadequate and ineffective substitute for habeas, concluding that the process set up by the Attorney General in regulations gave too much discretion to the government. After the government filed a motion to withdraw the opinion, the court granted it and asked for briefing on the statutory motion to reopen process that the court ignored in its initial decision.

Under the statutory process, a noncitizen would first file a statutory motion to reopen with the BIA requesting that the BIA reissue the final order of removal in light of the alleged ineffective assistance **of counsel** or governmental interference. If the BIA does so, the noncitizen has a new 30 days to file in the court of appeals a petition for review of the merits of the removal order. If the BIA does not reissue the removal order, the noncitizen has 30 days to petition the appeals court for review of that decision but not the merits of the removal order. If the appeals court finds no meritorious claim on review, which will include at least review of "constitutional claims and questions of law," it will affirm the BIA. If the court concludes that the BIA has erred, the court may remand or, if appropriate, order the BIA to reissue the final order of removal. After the removal order is reissued, the noncitizen will have 30 days to petition the appeals court for review of the merits of the removal order.

The appeals court concluded that this process protected the due process rights of noncitizens sufficiently so as not to implicate the Suspension Clause. However, it acknowledged the concerns of the plaintiffs and immigrant rights groups, who argued that the BIA could subvert the statutory process. The court warned the BIA that it could not contract the jurisdiction that Congress gave it by applying its own rules as to motions to reopen. The appeals court stated that it had "the authority to direct the BIA to reissue a final order of removal," surmising that Congress would not have granted it the "authority to review denied motions to reopen but denied us the power to effectuate that review." In addition, this process was the "most streamlined and efficient" remedy in the context of the REAL ID Act. Therefore, the court dismissed the petitions for review, but directed Luna and Thompson to file motions to reopen with the BIA requesting that it ignore the filing deadlines and reissue the final orders of removal.

IMMUNITY

Exemption from performing duties that the law generally requires other citizens to perform, or from a penalty or burden that the law generally places on other citizens.

Ashcroft v. Al-Kidd

Following the SEPTEMBER 11TH ATTACKS in 2001, the administration under President GEORGE W. BUSH engaged in a number of tactics designed to detain terrorist suspects. One such tactic was to use a federal material witness **statute** to take those suspected of having ties to TERRORISM into CUSTODY. Federal authorities could then hold these suspects indefinitely for the reason that the authorities could later call the suspects as witnesses in federal trial. Once such suspect was arrested and detained in 2003 as a material witness in a trial of a suspected terrorist. However, he was never called as a witness, and he later sued former Attorney General JOHN ASHCROFT for violating his constitutional rights. The SUPREME COURT reviewed the case in 2011 and concluded that Ashcroft was entitled to qualified IMMUNITY.

The PLAINTIFF in the case was Abdullah al-Kidd, a U.S. citizen who was born Lavoni T. Kidd and who changed his name after converting to become a Muslim. He had played football at the University of Idaho and was married to a U.S. citizen. The couple had two children. Federal authorities had investigated al-Kidd in 2002, but no evidence ever linked al-Kidd to criminal activity.

In 2003, al-Kidd planned to fly to Saudi Arabia to study Arabic and Islamic law. However, a **grand jury** in Idaho indicted Sami Omar Al-Hussayen on charges of visa **fraud** and making false statements to U.S. officials. Federal officers told a U.S. **magistrate** that al-Kidd was a material witness in the Al-Hussayen trial and that if al-Kidd were allowed to fly to Saudi Arabia, crucial information would be lost. The magistrate issued a warrant that allowed federal authorities to arrest al-Kidd, and he was taken into custody as he prepared to board his flight at Dulles International Airport.

While in custody, al-Kidd was handcuffed frequently. Federal authorities detained him for 16 days at various locations in Virginia, Oklahoma, and Idaho. Authorities confined him a high-security units of these facilities, and he was strip-searched. Moreover, he was allowed out of his cell for only one or two hours per day, and authorities kept his cell lit 24 hours per day. He was finally released but had to live under a number of restrictions, such as reporting to a PROBATION officer and consenting to home visits. He was finally released from the conditions at the conclusion of Al-Hussayen's trial. Al-Hussayen was not convicted, and prosecutors never called al-Kidd as a witness.

Al-Kidd brought an action under the Supreme Court case of *Bivens v. Six Unknown Federal Narcotics Agents*, 403 U.S. 388, 91 S. Ct. 1999, 29 L. Ed. 2d 619. In this action, al-Kidd challenged the constitutionality of the federal government's policy, as directed by Ashcroft, the former attorney general. Al-Kidd brought the action against Ashcroft, the United States, and two FBI agents.

Ashcroft filed a motion to dismiss the claims against him, asserting defenses based on absolute and qualified immunity. For al-Kidd to maintain his claim against Ashcroft, he had to prove two elements: (1) that Ashcroft had violated al-Kidd's constitutional or **statutory** rights; and (2) that the right had been clearly established at the time of the challenged conduct.

The U.S. **District Court** for the District of Idaho denied Ashcroft's motion to dismiss the claims against him. He appealed the case to the Ninth **Circuit Court** of Appeals, which affirmed the district court's ruling. The Ninth Circuit concluded that Ashcroft had used the material witness tactic as a pretext for detaining al-Kidd. The court concluded that this action violated the FOURTH AMENDMENT and that Ashcroft could not assert immunity because of this conclusion. *Al-Kidd v. Ashcroft*, 580 F.3d 949 (9th Cir. 2009).

By a vote of 8-0, the Supreme Court reversed the Ninth Circuit. However, the justices were split about the reason for the judgment. Justice ANTONIN SCALIA wrote for the majority and was joined by Chief Justice JOHN ROBERTS and Justices SAMUEL ALITO, ANTHONY KENNEDY, and CLARENCE THOMAS. Kennedy also wrote a separate concurrence, as did Justices RUTH BADER GINSBURG and SONIA SOTOMAYOR. Justice Elena Kagan did not take part in the case.

Justice Scalia concluded that the federal officers had not violated al-Kidd's constitutional

Former Attorney General John Ashcroft.
AP IMAGES/CLIFF OWEN, FILE

rights even if the officers subjectively intended to use the material-witness statute to detain al-Kidd. Moreover, Scalia concluded that the Fourth Amendment cases had not clearly established that the government's actions in detaining material witnesses violated the constitution. Scalia rejected al-Kidd's argument that Ashcroft had violated a clearly established right by using the material-witness statute as a pretext for detaining al-Kidd. Without such a clearly established right, Ashcroft was entitled to qualified immunity.

Justice Kennedy stressed in his concurrence that the Court only decided the case according to the arguments put before it. However, his opinion suggested that use of the material-witness statute for detention would violate the Fourth Amendment. Justices Ginsburg and Sotomayor disagreed with Justice Scalia regarding whether the federal officials had violated al-Kidd's rights. However, both justices agreed that the law was not clearly established, so they agreed that Ashcroft was entitled to immunity.

Winning Parties May Appeal to Supreme Court on Immunity Issues

The U.S. SUPREME COURT picks and chooses the cases it wished to hear. Though federal law permits a winning party to appeal to the

Supreme Court, the Court has had a blanket policy of not accepting these cases for review. However, in *Camreta v. Greene*, __ U.S. 131, S. Ct. 2020, __L.Ed.2d__ 2011 WL 2039369 (2011), the Court reversed course and carved out an exception for cases involving qualified IMMUNITY for state and federal officials who have been sued for damages under 42 U.S.C. § 1983. Despite this decision, the winning parties in this case were denied a ruling on the merits of their constitutional argument because the losing party no longer had a stake in the outcome of the case.

In 2003, police in Oregon arrested Nimrod Greene for suspected SEXUAL ABUSE of a boy unrelated to him. The parents of the boy told police they suspected Green has molested his 9-year-old daughter, S.G. The police reported this information to the Oregon Department of Human Services, which assigned child protective services caseworker Bob Camreta to the case. Camreta and Deschutes County deputy sheriff James Alford went to S.G.'s elementary school and interviewed her about the allegations. Camreta and Alford did not have a warrant to interview S.G. nor did they have the consent of her mother. S.G. admitted she had been abused but Greene's jury deadlocked and the charges were later dismissed. S.G's mother sued Camreta and Alford under § 1983, alleging that their in-school interview violated the Fourth Amendment's ban against unreasonable seizures. The Oregon federal **district court** granted **summary judgment** to the government officials and dismissed the case. S.G.'s mother appealed the decision to the Ninth **Circuit Court** of Appeals, which first ruled that the interview did violate S.G.'s FOURTH AMENDMENT rights. However, the appeals court further held that the two men were entitled to qualified immunity because no clearly established law had warned them of the illegality of their conduct. The Ninth Circuit explained that it ruled on the merits of the constitutional claim rather than holding the officials immune from suit because it wanted to provide guidance to child WELFARE workers on the scope of the Fourth Amendment in their work. The court stated that government officials investigating allegations of CHILD ABUSE "should cease operating on the assumption that a 'special need' automatically justifies dispensing with traditional Fourth Amendment protections in this context."

Although Camreta and Alford received a judgment in their favor, they elected to petition the Supreme Court to review the Ninth Circuit's ruling that their conduct violated the Fourth Amendment. Suprisingly, the Supreme Court agreed to hear their appeal.

The Court, in a 7-2 decision, concluded that it could not render a ruling on the Fourth Amendment violation because the case was moot. However, the Court did announce that it was proper for prevailing parties to petition for review when the issue at stake involved qualified immunity. Justice Elena Kagan, writing for the majority, noted that the federal law setting the jurisdictional standards for the Supreme Court states that the Court can grant review "upon the petition of any party." That language includes petitions brought by litigants who have prevailed, as well as those who have lost, in the court below. Justice Kagan found constitutional grounds for Camreta and Alford's petition to be adjudicated by the Court. The Court may hear legal disputes only in the context of Article III's cases or controversy section. The Court has interpreted this to mean that a party has a stake in the outcome of the lawsuit, based on three conditions: the petitioner must show that he has "suffered an injury in fact that is caused by the "conduct complained of" and that "will be redressed by a favorable decision." In the case of immunized officials such as Camreta and Greene, they have a stake in the outcome on the constitutional ruling because the judgment of the Ninth Circuit may have prospective effect on the parties. If either of them conducted an interview in the future that lacked a warrant or parental consent, they could be subject to a damages award because the Ninth Circuit had "clearly established" the law and put child welfare workers on notice. Therefore, only by overturning the Fourth Amendment ruling would they be able to constitutionally engage in the same conduct in the future.

As to the practice of the Supreme Court of generally declining to hear cases at the request of the **prevailing party**, Justice Kagan acknowledged that the Court's resources "are not well spent superintending each word a lower court utters en route to a final judgment in the petitioning party's favor." However, the Court concluded that where a policy reason is sufficiently important, it should allow an appeal. Qualified immunity cases were sufficiently important to make such an exception. When courts dismiss § 1983 on qualified immunity grounds because the law was not established, it "threatens to leave standards of conduct permanently in limbo."Because the court did not resolve the claim of official immunity, the official persists in the challenged practice because he knows he cannot be held liable monetarily because the law still is not clearly established. When courts like the Ninth Circuit announce a rule for interviewing children in sexual abuse cases, that decision should be reviewable in the Supreme Court "at the behest of an immunized official." In announcing this review policy, Justice Kagan pointed out that it only concerns what the Court may do, for "what we actually will choose to review is a different matter." The decision did no more than "exempt one special category of cases from our usual rule against considering prevailing parties' petitions. Going forward, we will consider these petitions one by one in accord with our usual standards."

Despite this ruling, the Court refused to rule on the constitutional issue. The Court ruled that the case was moot because S.G. was almost 18, did not live in Oregon or intend to return, and was about to graduate from high school. S.G. no longer had a plaintiff's stake in the outcome of the case because she was not affected by the Ninth Circuit ruling. However, the Court did not merely dismiss the appeal. It vacated the Ninth Circuits' Fourth Amendment ruling, again putting the question of what a child protection worker must do to constitutionally interview a child in legal limbo.

IMPEACHMENT

To accuse; to charge a liability upon; to sue. To dispute, disparage, deny, or contradict; as in to impeach a judgment or decree, or impeach a witness; or as used in the rule that a jury cannot impeach its verdict. To proceed against a public officer for crime or misfeasance, before a proper court, by the presentation of a written accusation called articles of impeachment.

Senate Removes Federal Judge Following Impeachment

The United States SENATE in December 2010 voted to remove U.S. District Judge G. Thomas Porteous, Jr. from office. The vote came nine months after the HOUSE OF REPRESENTATIVES voted to IMPEACH Porteous based on several

incidents that occurred when he was both a state court and a federal court judge. The trial in the Senate was the first since 1999, when the Senate declined to remove President BILL CLINTON. Porteous was the first federal judge removed from office since 1989.

Section 4 of Article II to the United States Constitution provides, " The President, VICE PRESIDENT and all civil officers of the United States, shall be removed from office on IMPEACHMENT for, and conviction of, TREASON, BRIBERY, or other high crimes and misdemeanors." This provision applies not only to executive branch officers but also to federal judges. Article I of the Constitution, in turn, provides that the House of Representative serves to impeach an officer, meaning that the House approves a legal statement of the various charges brought against an official. A House impeachment is followed by a trial in the Senate. Both votes require a two-thirds majority. A total of 15 judges, including Porteous, have been impeached. Most have chosen to resign in lieu of facing removal by the Senate.

Porteous served as a judge with the 24th Judicial **District Court** of Louisiana based in Gretna from 1984 to 1994. He had previously served in a variety of other capacities, including city attorney of Harahan, Louisiana. After ten years on the bench of the state court, President Clinton nominated Porteous for a seat on the U.S. District Court for the Eastern District of Louisiana. He presided over several noteworthy cases, including a decision in 1999 to strike down a ban on partial-birth abortions.

Some details of Porteous' personal life began to become public in 2001, though, when he filed for BANKRUPTCY. He had close ties with bail bondsman Louis Marcotte III, who was the focus of a corruption investigation centered on activities at the state courthouse in Gretna. Marcotte was accused of bribing several judges in exchange for lucrative bonds. During the investigation, known as Operation Wrinkled Robe, allegations arose that Marcotte had arranged favors for Porteous, including car repairs. Because of this investigation, Porteous recused himself in 2003 from all cases involving the federal government, including criminal cases. Marcotte was later sentenced to 38 months in prison, and Operation Wrinkled Robe eventually led to the prosecution of two state judges.

Personal tragedy followed. Porteous lost his home to Hurricane Katrina in 2005, and his wife died several months later. At that point, Porteous was under investigation by a federal **grand jury**. In 2006, the district court gave Porteous a one-year furlough from his **docket** for medical reasons. After one year, Porteous returned to the bench and picked up both his civil and criminal dockets. In 2007, the Justice Department decided to drop its case against Porteous, reportedly because investigators did not believe they could obtain a unanimous conviction against him.

However, he remained the subject of a probe into judicial misconduct. On December 20, 2007, the Judicial Council of the Fifth **Circuit Court** of Appeals completed a report of its findings regarding Porteous' conduct. According to the report, Porteous had made numerous false statements, including several made while he was in the middle of his personal bankruptcy. The report also stated that he received gifts and other valuable items from attorneys who had cases on Porteous' docket. Moreover, the report accused Porteous of "fraudulent and deceptive conduct" regarding a private debt he owed and of making false and misleading financial disclosure statements. The Fifth Circuit barred Porteous from hearing certain cases and referred the case to the Judicial Conference of the United States.

Commentators expected Porteous to be impeached, but the House turned its attention to Judge Samuel Kent of Texas, who had been charged with sexual assault along with several other crimes. The House of Representatives convened a task force to review the accusations brought against Porteous. The chair of the task force, Representative Adam Schiff (D-Cal.), later said, "Our investigation found that Porteous participated in a pattern of corrupt conduct for years."

Representative John Conyers, Jr. (D-Mich.) introduced four **articles of impeachment** against Porteous on January 21, 2010. In addition to the allegations raised by the council of the Fifth Circuit, the resolution alleged that Porteous had engaged in a corrupt financial relationship with the law firm of Amato & Creely, P.C. and that Porteous had received substantial sums of money from the firm in exchange for certain favors. For instance, Porteous had named the firm as curator of

hundreds of cases. In return, the firm paid Porteous roughly half the fees earned from its curatorship. Another article specified accusations related to Porteous' relationship with Marcotte, including setting, reducing, and splitting bonds with Marcotte while Porteous was still a state-court judge. The final article stated that Porteous had knowingly made false statements when he was nominated in 1994 to serve as federal judge.

The House met for five days in March 2010. Porteous attended some of the proceedings, but he did not speak. His attorney, however, questioned a few of the witnesses. Nevertheless, the House approved each of the four **articles** of impeachment by unanimous votes. Representative Jim Sensenbrenner (R-Wisc.) said that he had never seen the "overwhelming and blatant corruption we have before us today. Judge Porteous is one of a kind and it is time for him to receive his comeuppance."

Porteous refused to resign, arguing that he did nothing to justify his removal from office. The Senate thus had to prepare for its first trial in 11 years. Legal experts raised some concerns about the charges because several allegations related to activities that occurred before Porteous was appointed to the federal bench. Defense lawyers argued that the FBI and the Senate actually knew about some of the allegations against Porteous before his confirmation in 1994 but nevertheless approved his candidacy.

The Senate convened a 12-member committee in September 2010 to hear the evidence. The committee held more than 40 hours of hearings before referring the matter to the full Senate. On December 8, 2010, the Senate voted to remove Porteous on each of the four counts, though the Senate members voted unanimously on only one of the four counts.

Porteous became the eighth judge removed from office by the Senate.

INTERNATIONAL LAW

The body of law governing the legal relations between states or nations.

Nuclear Weapons Treaty With Russia

In February 2011, the New Strategic Arms Reduction Treaty (New START) went into effect, after Secretary of State Hilary Clinton

and Russian FEDERATION Foreign Minister Sergey Lavrov exchanged instruments of **ratification** in Munich, Germany. President BARACK OBAMA had signed the Treaty on behalf of the United States a few days earlier, after Congress ratified its language on December 22, 2010, the last day of session of the 111th Congress. The treaty was considered the broadest pact between the former COLD WAR foes in nearly two decades. While the new treaty did not represent a major step forward in disarmament, it would reduce deployed long-range nuclear warheads by up to 30 percent on each side. As of 2010, the two super powers held more than 90 percent of the world's NUCLEAR WEAPONS, with Russia's arsenal inventoried at 12,000 and the United States at 9,600. The third largest holder of nuclear arms was France, with 300, according to the Federation of American Scientists (FAS).

The New START limits the number of deployed nuclear warheads at 1,500 for each country, according to the U.S. DEPARTMENT OF STATE. It also reduces the number of deployed nuclear-capable submarines, long-range missiles, and heavy bombers to 700, with an additional 100 in reserve. (The treaty does not address stockpiled, or non-deployed, nuclear weapons, which each country is believed to have in the thousands.) First inspection rights and exhibition of offensive arms were scheduled for no later than 60 days from the enactment of the treaty, February 5. Moreover, within the first 45 days, the two nations agreed to exchange full data on their respective weapons and facilities. Other important provisions included the exchange of lists of inspectors and aircrew members dealing with nuclear arms, mutual demonstrations and continued updates regarding databases and inspections.

The original START was signed in 1991, then replaced in 2002 by former leaders President GEORGE W. BUSH and Prime Minister Vladimir Putin. The treaties were effective for ten years. The New START is also good for ten years, at which time it may be extended or allowed to expire.

The New START Treaty is between the two most powerful nations of Russia and the United States, who hold between 90 and 95 percent of all nuclear weapons in the world. The U.S. SENATE had struggled to have the treaty ratified before the session ended, and in the end, a political power play threatened to delay RATIFICATION. Republicans attempted to push the vote

Former Boston University medical student Philip Markoff stands during his arraignment in Suffolk Superior Court in Boston, on charges he killed a masseuse at a Boston hotel that he met through Craigslist.

AP IMAGES/BIZUAYEHU TESFAYE, POOL, FILE

over to 2012, when they would have six more senators and more bargaining power. But in the end, several Republicans joined Senate Democrats, all voting 67 to 28 to invoke "cloture" to close debate and move on to the ratification vote. It passed with a resounding 71 to 26 vote, easily clearing the threshold of two-thirds of senators present as required by the Constitution for treaty ratification.

Senator John F. Kerry (D-MA), the Senate Foreign Relations Committee chairman, said after the vote, "The winners are not defined by party or ideology. The winners are the American people, who are safer with fewer Russian missiles aimed at them." Kerry said the treaty's impact would "echo around the world" as an example of superpowers working together to reduce the global threat of nuclear weapons. "With this treaty, we send a message to Iran and North Korea that the international community remains united to restrain the nuclear ambitions of countries that operate outside the law," he said.

There are other nuclear non-proliferation agreements and treaties between nations. The international treaty known as the NPT (Non-proliferation of Nuclear Weapons) entered into force in 1970. NPT has the widest adherence of

any arms control agreement; a total of 187 parties have joined the treaty. Signatories to this treaty are divided into two categories: the nuclear weapon states (NWS) (United States, Russia, China, France, and the United Kingdom) and non-nuclear-weapon states (NNWS). The Article VIII, paragraph 3 of the NPT calls for review and revision as needed, every five years; the May 2010 NPT Review Conference included agreement on a process leading to the establishment of a Middle East zone free of WEAPONS OF MASS DESTRUCTION and their means of delivery.

India, Pakistan, and Israel are known to possess or are suspected of having nuclear weapons, but they are not members and remain outside the treaty. On January 10, 2003, North Korea announced that it was withdrawing from the treaty, effective the following day, although Article X of the NPT requires three months' notice. North Korea has argued that it satisfied that requirement by first giving notice in 1993, then suspending the decision one day before it became legally binding. There has been no formal legal opinion as to whether North Korea remains a party and still bound.

INTERNET

A worldwide telecommunications network of business, government, and personal computers.

Internet Site Craigslist Removes Adult Section Amid Pressure

The popular online site for classified advertisements, Craigslist, came under fire in 2010 for its adult services section. Attorneys general for 18 states signed a letter condemning the section, which the letter said was used to promote PROSTITUTION and PORNOGRAPHY. Though the company said that it was being unfairly targeted, the company removed the section just weeks after it received the letter.

Craigslist began as an email distribution list in the San Francisco area in 1995, one year before it became a web-based company. It has expanded continuously since then, becoming incorporated as a for-profit company in 1999. It was founded by Internet entrepreneur Craig Newmark, and its current chief executive officer is Jim Buckmaster. As of 2011, it serves a total of 570 cities in 50 countries, allowing users to place free classified advertisements. The company makes money by charging for certain ads in larger cities. For instance, paid job advertisements in the San Francisco area cost $75. The company employs about 32 people. The site is the largest classified service in the world and ranks as one of the tenth largest sites in the United States.

The site's most popular sections relate to job postings, housing, sales, and services. Several parts of the site are more adult-oriented, though. The site contains a popular personals section, which allows individuals to connect with one another for dating and the like. The fact that the site is free and generally uncensored has bolstered its popularity. The site relies on a system of flagging, whereby users can identify inappropriate or illegal postings, which can lead the site to remove an certain ad.

The site's erotic services section became the subject of scandal in 2009. A former medical student named Philip Markoff allegedly met two women through Craislist, including a stripper and an escort. Police alleged that Markoff robbed one of the women and killed the other at a hotel in Boston. The crimes happened within a four-day span during April 2009. The press dubbed Markoff the "Craigslist Killer," and he remained in CUSTODY for more than a year. He later committed SUICIDE while awaiting trial.

Attorneys general in several states, including Andrew M. Cuomo of New York, called on Craigslist to shut down its erotic services section altogether, arguing that the section had led to Markoff's crimes as well as similar acts in other states. Craigslist in May 2009 announced that it would close its erotic services section and instead replace it with an adult services section, which the company would monitor closely. Cuomo said that the move was insufficient. He added, "Rather than work with [the New York Attorney General's] office to prevent further abuses, in the middle of the night, Craigslist took unilateral action which we suspect will prove to be half-baked." Buckmaster responded, "In striking this new balance we have sought to incorporate important feedback from all the groups that have expressed strongly held views on this subject, including some of the state A.G.'s, free speech advocates and legal businesses who are accustomed to being entitled to advertise." Buckmaster also said that he thought advertisements run in traditional newspapers created a risk of violence many times greater than the ads run on Craigslist.

The move hardly satisfied state authorities and the public in general. In July 2010, two girls who said they had been the subject of human sex trafficking through Craigslist ads sent a letter to company officials asking the company to shut down the adult services section. One month later, a group of 18 attorneys general in August 2010 signed a letter demanding the same. The letter stressed that Craigslist lacked the ability to effectively combat the number of ads for prostitution on the site, noting that "[p]rostitution is a booming business on Craigslist, perhaps more than ever before.". The letter continued, "We understand that prostitution is profitable—but its human toll is intolerable, and Craigslist should cease being an enabler. Despite its much-touted 'manual review' of Adult Services, Craigslist has failed to block blatant prostitution ads." The state attorneys general who signed the letter included those from Connecticut, Arkansas, Idaho, Illinois, Iowa, Kansas, Maryland, Michigan, Mississippi, Missouri, Montana, New Hampshire, Ohio, Rhode Island, South Carolina, Tennessee, Texas, and Virginia.

Craigslist initially resisted shutting the section down. A company spokesperson noted, "We strongly support the attorneys general desire to end trafficking in children and women, through the Internet or by any other means. We hope to work closely with them, as we are with experts at nonprofits and in law enforcement, to prevent misuse of our site in facilitation of trafficking, and to combat such crimes wherever they appear, online or offline." However, on September 4, 2010, the company unilaterally removed the section, replacing the link with the word "censored." Less than a week later, the company removed the reference altogether. The company never released a statement regarding its decision, but as of April 2011, the section remains down. Craiglist also removed its adult services section from its Canadian sites in December 2010.

Commentators have viewed the debate over the adult services section as one of free speech versus public safety. Though some have spoken in the site's defense, most suggest it would be nearly impossible for the site to reopen its adult services section without serious backlash from authorities and much of the public.

Kentucky Appeals Court Allows Unauthorized Facebook Photographs in Evidence

In February 2011, the Kentucky Court of Appeals, in an unpublished decision, ruled that photographs appearing on the social network site Facebook, posted without the knowledge or permission of the person "tagged" (identified) in the photographs, were nonetheless admissible evidence in this appealed DIVORCE and CUSTODY matter. *LaLonde v. LaLonde,* No. 2009-CA-02279 (CA Ky 2011). (Such proffered evidence still needed to meet other evidentiary rules relating to **demonstrative evidence**, in particular, authentication.) The **appellate court** was simply addressing the prevailing party's argument that nothing within the law required a party's permission when another person took a photograph and posted it on a Facebook page.

Jessica and Adam LaLonde were married in Michigan in 2005 and had one child, a son born in 2006. In 2007, Jessica was diagnosed with bipolar II disorder and stopped working outside of the home, on the recommendation of her physician. In 2008, the family moved to Kentucky. While Adam worked, Jessica stayed home and cared for their child.

Later in 2008, Jessica moved back to Michigan, agreeing with her husband that they would alternate time with their son approximately every three weeks. Notwithstanding, Jessica also filed for divorce in Michigan, alleging her son was a Michigan resident. After Adam filed a motion for temporary relief, a Michigan court determined that their child was a resident of Kentucky and that Kentucky was the appropriate **venue** for a divorce proceeding.

On the custody matter of the divorce agreement, a final hearing was held before a domestic relations commissioner in February 2009. At the hearing, testimony of mental health providers who treated Jessica in Michigan was submitted. This consisted of a telephonic DEPOSITION of Jessica's psychiatric nurse practitioner, who described Jessica's medications and treatment for her Bipolar II Disorder, and a deposition of Jessica's psychologist. During that second deposition, her psychologist confirmed that the use of alcohol would have an effect on Jessica's medications. Following these evidentiary submissions, Adam was allowed time to submit rebuttal evidence in response to testimony from Jessica's mental health care providers.

Ultimately, the domestic relations commissioner filed a report in October 2009 recommending joint custody but with Adam, the father, having physical custody of their son, and Jessica being awarded parenting time according to county guidelines. Jessica filed exceptions to the report, but the trial court overruled them and granted a divorce decree adopting the domestic commissioner's report and recommendations.

On appeal, Jessica argued that the commissioner's decision was based, at least in part, on improperly admitted evidence, to wit, photographs of Jessica introduced by Adam in his rebuttal, that had been taken from the Facebook site. The pictures generally depicted Jessica at parties and apparently consuming alcoholic beverages against the advice of her mental health care providers. Adam had offered these photographs to rebut Jessica's truthfulness with her treatment providers when she indicated that she had stopped or at least significantly lessened her alcohol consumption.

Jessica had objected to the introduction of these photographs but was overruled. On appeal, she argued that Adam had failed to properly authenticate the photographs. Kentucky Rule of Evidence (KRE) 901(a), similar to other state and federal rules, provides that DEMONSTRATIVE EVIDENCE such as photographs must be accompanied by sufficient evidence to support a finding that the photographs are an accurate representation of what is claimed. Generally, such supporting evidence consists of testimony from the person who took the photographs. But, said the Kentucky Court of Appeals, this was not the only way to authenticate a photograph. Under KRE 901(b)(1), authentication only requires "[t]estimony that a matter is what it is claimed to be." In this case, Jessica conceded that she had been drinking alcohol and that the pictures accurately reflected that conduct. Therefore, the court found that her own testimony was sufficient to authenticate the photographs and they were thus properly admitted into evidence.

Jessica raised a second objection that she never gave permission for her photographs to be published on Facebook, which allows anyone to post pictures and "tag" or identify the persons in the photographs. In conjunction with that argument, she argued that with modern digital photography and techniques, photograph images may be altered, as well as time and date stamps. Although the court acknowledged such a possibility, it noted that Jessica did not suggest that such techniques had been used on the subject photographs in her case, thereby offering no more than speculative argument. Indeed, she had acknowledged with her own testimony that the photographs were accurate, leading to the conclusion that they were not altered.

Further, noted the **appellate** court, nothing in the law required her permission when another person takes a photograph and posts it on a Facebook page, nor is her permission required if she is "tagged" or identified as a person in those posted photographs.

Other arguments raised by Jessica on appeal, and contained in the unpublished opinion and decision, did not relate to the Facebook photographs and are therefore not discussed herein. The APPELLATE court concluded that substantial evidence existed to support the findings of the trial court and its decision would not be disturbed.

Adjunct law professor Omer Tene of Stanford University's Center for Internet and Society found looming issues in the Kentucky decision that permeated well beyond the immediate divorce and custody consequences. In an article on the general subject, he noted that many European policymakers were contemplating the viability of a "right to oblivion" that could tie into unwanted Internet exposure. Article 5(3) of the European e-Privacy Detective, requiring opt-in consent for **third party** tracking cookies, remained pending as of early 2011. Within the United States, the FEDERAL TRADE COMMISSION (FTC) was still working on a "Do Not Track (DNT)" proposal, involving a one-time, universal opt-out from online behavioral ads (OBA).

FCC Issues Net Neutrality Rules

The regulation of Internet Service Providers (ISPs) by the FEDERAL COMMUNICATIONS COMMISSION (FCC) has become know by the phrase "Net Neutrality. The FCC has attempted to impose a set of regulation on ISPs for several years, generating objections and lawsuits from corporations with a commercial stake in the

FCC Chairman Julius Genachowski is interviewed at his office in Washington. New rules aimed at prohibiting broadband providers from becoming gatekeepers of Internet traffic had just enough votes to pass the Federal Communications Commission in December 2010.
AP IMAGES/JACQUELYN MARTIN, FILE

Internet and from consumer and FIRST AMENDMENT advocates. The courts and Congress have also played a part in developing a framework for regulating Internet communications and business relationships. In December 2010, the FCC, on a 3-2 vote, issued a report and order (FCC 10-201) that sets out rules that it contends preserve the Internet as an open network enabling consumer choice, freedom of expression, user control, competition and the freedom to innovate.

In its report the FCC expressed concern that broadband providers have acted in ways that endanger the Internet's openness by blocking or degrading disfavored content and applications without disclosing their practices to consumers. For example, in 2007, Comcast was accused of blocking access to peer-to-peer networks such as BitTorrent because these users were slowing down Comcast's network. Comcast denied that it cut off these services completely but it did restrict access during peak times. In addition, broadband providers may have financial interests in services that may compete with online content and services.

The FCC relied on several **statutory** provisions to justify its rulemaking. These include

Section 706 of the TELECOMMUNICATIONS Act of 1996. This provision directs the FCC to "encourage the deployment on a reasonable and timely basis" of "advanced telecommunications capability" to all persons. If the Commission finds that such capability is not being deployed in a reasonable and timely fashion, it "shall take immediate action to accelerate deployment of such capability by removing barriers to infrastructure investment and by promoting competition in the telecommunications market," under Section 706(b). The FCC concluded in July 2010 that broadband deployment to all Americans was not reasonably and timely, thereby triggering Section 7096(b).

The FCC also cited Title 1 of the Communications Act, which deals with protecting competition, and consumers of telecommunication services. The advent of Internet voice services like VoIP now serves as competition to traditional phone services. Title III of the Communications Act authorizes the commission to license spectrum used to provide fixed and mobile wireless services. Title IV of the Communications Act protects competition in video services. With the growth of Internet video distribution, cable or telephone company interference with the online transmission of programming would frustrate the law's intent to promote competition and diversity in this area.

There are three major Net Neutrality Rules: (1) Transparency; (2) No Blocking; and (3) No Unreasonable Blocking. The Transparency Rule states that "A person engaged in the provision of broadband Internet access service shall publicly disclose accurate information regarding the network management practices, performance, and commercial terms of its broadband Internet access services sufficient for consumers to make informed choices regarding use of such services and for content, application, service, and device providers to develop, market, and maintain Internet offerings." This means that ISPs must disclose to their users whether they slow down their networks at peak times of the day, whether it imposes caps on how much data a user may download in a month, and in the case of wireless and phone providers, whether there are roaming fees.

The No Blocking Rule states that "A person engaged in the provision of fixed broadband Internet access service, insofar as such person is so engaged, shall not block lawful content,

applications, services, or non-harmful devices, subject to reasonable network management. A person engaged in the provision of mobile broadband Internet access service, insofar as such person is so engaged, shall not block consumers from accessing lawful websites, subject to reasonable network management; nor shall such person block applications that compete with the provider's voice or video telephony services, subject to reasonable network."

This rule addresses the peer-to-peer network issues surrounding Comcast's actions in 2007. Under this rule an ISP cannot select certain applications or services to block in order to improve network performance. An ISP, for example, could not block a streaming movie service such as Netflix because some users were slowing down the network by downloading a large amount of content. However, there are differences in the rule for fixed and wireless ISPs. Fixed providers cannot block lawful content, applications, services, or "non-harmful" devices, or charge providers of these services for using their networks. Wireless providers cannot block access to lawful web sites or block applications that compete with their own voice or video telephone services.

The No Unreasonable DISCRIMINATION Rule states that "A person engaged in the provision of fixed broadband Internet access service, insofar as such person is so engaged, shall not unreasonably discriminate in transmitting lawful network traffic over a consumer's broadband Internet access service. Reasonable network management shall not constitute unreasonable discrimination." This rule allows ISPs to manage their networks but they cannot cutoff selected services that soak up bandwidth, such as Netflix. However, ISPs can block spam, viruses, malware, CHILD PORNOGRAPHY, etc. In addition, ISPs may not be able to impose "paid prioritization" schemes that would allow a commercial site such as Amazon to load faster than smaller e-commerce sites.

The FCC included in the report and rules many definitions, including broadband Internet access service, reasonable network management, and pay for priority unlikely to satisfy "No Unreasonable Discrimination Rule.

Republicans in Congress have objected to the regulations, arguing that the FCC should not intrude on free market competition and hurt job growth in the communications industry. A bill was introduced in the HOUSE OF REPRESENTATIVES in 2011 that seeks to overturn the regulations. The House also stripped out funding for the FCC to implement the rules. It is unclear whether this legislative effort will succeed.

WikiLeaks Continues to Cause Controversy

The whistle-blowing website WikiLeaks in 2010 was at the center of a controversy regarding the release of thousands of documents related to the wars in Afghanistan and Iraq. The site's founder and editor, Julian Assange, has steadfastly refused to back down, insisting that the site will continue to reveal secret government information. The information leaks have led to the prosecution of an army private who allegedly downloaded classified information and shared the information with WikiLeaks.

WikiLeaks opened in 2006, and at the time of its launch, the site claimed that it had more than one million documents. The site's founders were reportedly from a number of countries, including the United States, China, Australia, South Africa, and various European nations. Assange has served as the site's editor since its launch, and he is generally considered to be the site's founder. The site originally allowed users to add information, much like users on Wikipedia, but as of 2011 the site no longer allows users to edit information.

Between 2006 and 2009, the site released a variety of documents. In 2007, the site published a document containing the protocols followed by the U.S. Army at the detention camp at the Guantanamo Bay naval base. A year later, the site revealed the contents of the private email account of Sarah Palin, the 2008 Republican candidate for VICE PRESIDENT. Palin had used a private Yahoo! account to send work-related messages, and a 20-year-old student from Tennessee named David Kernell (also the son of a state representative) hacked into Palin's account. Other notable documents released by WikiLeaks have related to toxic dumping in Africa and pager messages sent after the SEPTEMBER 11TH ATTACKS in 2001. In 2010, the site also released a counterintelligence report produced for the U.S. DEFENSE DEPARTMENT as well as classified footage of a U.S. airstrike in Baghdad in 2007.

Wikileaks founder Julian Assange.
LEWIS WHYLD/
PA WIRE URN:10301896
(PRESS ASSOCIATION VIA
AP IMAGES)

Much of the backlash against WikiLeaks occurred because of the site's release of a large number of documents related to the wars in Iraq and Afghanistan. On July 25, 2010, the site released to three major newspapers more than 92,000 documents related to the war in Afghanistan, though the site would not release about 15,000 of those documents so that the site could remove information about sources. The press dubbed the release the "Afghan War Diaries."The newspapers that received the information included *The New York Times*, *The Guardian*, and *Der Spiegel*. According to the *New York Times*, "These reports are used by desk officers in the Pentagon and troops in the field when they make operational plans and prepare briefings on the situation in the war zone. Most of the reports are routine, even mundane, but many add insights, texture and context to a war that has been waged for nearly nine years." Though most of the documents were classified as low-level in terms of secrets, the documents revealed previously unavailable details about civilian and friendly-fire casualties.

The U.S. Army decried the release of the documents and demanded that WikiLeaks not released the remaining 15,000 documents. WikiLeaks responded that the would not comply with the Army's demand and that the site would continue to release secret information. Assange likened the release of the Afghan War Diaries to the release of the Pentagon Papers in the 1970s. He noted, "There doesn't seem to be an equivalent disclosure made during the course of the war when it might have some effect. The nearest equivalent is perhaps the Pentagon Papers released by Daniel Ellsberg in the 1970s which was about 10,000 papers - but that was already four years old when it was released." Some commentators later said Assange's claims regarding the Pentagon Papers were exaggerated.

Within weeks of the release, the JUSTICE DEPARTMENT announced that it was weighing whether to seek criminal charges against WikiLeaks or Assange. However, because Assange is an Australian national who spends much of his time in Iceland, Sweden, and Belgium, prosecuting him would be difficult. Reports in October 2010 indicated that Assange was constantly on the run and was losing support of some of his loyal followers. Assange nevertheless responded by announcing the release of nearly 400,000 documents related to the IRAQ WAR. The Pentagon reportedly said that the release of what have been dubbed the "Iraq War Logs" is the "largest leak of classified documents" in U.S. history.

About a month later, WikiLeaks announced it would release another massive amount of classified documents. This leak related to a series of diplomatic cables sent from U.S. officials to diplomats abroad. U.S. SECRETARY OF STATE HILLARY CLINTON called the release an "attack" on the United States as well as the international community, and reports indicated that the STATE DEPARTMENT was warning several hundred individuals identified in the cables that their safety was at risk. However, some officials later said that while the cables contained embarrassing information, the leak was not damaging.

The WikiLeaks controversy has led to one significant prosecution. Private Bradley Manning, an Army intelligence analyst, allegedly downloaded thousands of documents from Army computers, including diplomatic cables and intelligence reports. Manning reportedly admitted on an online discussion that he had downloaded the documents and provided them to WikiLeaks. Manning was arrested in May 2010 on charges that he had downloaded classified information and illegally communicating national defense information. In 2011, the military brought additional charges against Manning for aiding the enemy, which is a capital offense. Prosecutors have said that they would not seek the death penalty, however.

Assange has also been the subject of a criminal investigation that he committed RAPE in Sweden. A court in England in 2011 agreed to extradite him to Sweden for questioning. However, Assange appealed the English court's decision and has remained free on bond as of April 2011.

JURISDICTION

Supreme Court Limits Jurisdiction Over Foreign Corporations

Businesses that do not regularly operate in a state often contest the jurisdiction of that state's courts to hear lawsuits filed against them by state residents. The U.S. SUPREME COURT has issued decisions that have sought to clarify when a foreign business may be sued in a state where it has a minimal presence. Such was the case in *Goodyear Dunlop Tires Operation, S.A. v. Brown*, __U.S.131, S. Ct. 63, __L.Ed.2d__ 2011 WL2518815 (2011), where North Carolina residents sought to sue the European subsidiaries of a U.S. corporation for an accident that happened in France. The Court ruled that the foreign subsidiaries did not have enough of a presence in the state to give the courts jurisdiction to hear the **wrongful death** lawsuit.

In 2004 a bus that was headed for the Paris airport overturned. The bus passengers were teenage soccer players from North Carolina. Two boys, Julian Brown and Matthew Helms, were killed in the accident. The boys' parents filed a WRONGFUL DEATH lawsuit in a North Carolina court, alleging that the accident was caused by defective tires manufactured by three European subsidiaries of Goodyear USA. The lawsuit claimed that the plies of the tires separated, causing the accident and that the companies were negligent in making and testing the tires. Though Goodyear USA, with

corporate headquarters in Ohio, was registered to do business in North Carolina, none of the subsidiaries were registered. The subsidiaries challenged the jurisdiction of the North Carolina courts, arguing that they had no place of business in the state, or any employees or bank accounts in the state. They did not design, manufacture, or advertise their products in North Carolina. Moreover, the companies did not solicit business in the state or sell or ship tires to North Carolina customers. A small percentage of their tires were distributed in North Carolina by other Goodyear USA affiliates, but they were typically custom ordered to equip specialized vehicles such as cement mixers, waste haulers, and boat and horse trailers. Finally, the subsidiaries noted that the particular tire involved in the accident had never been distributed in North Carolina.

The trial court denied the motion of the three companies to dismiss the case for lack of jurisdiction. The North Carolina Court of Appeals upheld this ruling, finding that there was **general jurisdiction** to hear the case. The appeals court found that the subsidiaries had placed their tires "in the stream of interstate commerce without any limitation on the extent to which those tires could be sold in North Carolina." Though the companies had not taken any affirmative steps to ship tires to North Carolina, the court concluded that the tires had made their way to the state as a consequence of the distribution process of other

Goodyear USA subsidiaries. The tires involved in the accident conformed to U.S. government tire standards and bore markings required for sale in the U.S. The appeals court also believed it was in the best interest of the plaintiffs to seek justice in North Carolina than in France. The North Carolina Supreme Court denied discretionary review, which allowed the companies to successfully obtain review by the U.S. Supreme Court.

The Court, in a unanimous opinion, overturned the North Carolina Court of Appeals decision. Justice RUTH BADER GINSBURG, writing for the Court, noted that in its prior decisions the Court had identified two types of jurisdiction: specific and general. A state court will have special jurisdiction where the corporation's instate activity is "continuous and systematic" and that activity gave rise to the action that lead to the lawsuit. Special jurisdiction also attaches through the commission of certain "single or occasional acts" in a state. In contrast, GENERAL JURISDICTION is present when continuous corporate operations within a state are "so substantial and of such a nature arising from dealings entirely distinct from those activities."

Justice Ginsburg concluded that there was no specific jurisdiction in this case, as there was no act by which the defendants purposefully availed themselves of the "privilege of conducting activities" within North Carolina, thereby "invoking the benefits and protections of its laws." Lacking even a single act that occurred in North Carolina, specific jurisdiction was unavailable. As for general jurisdiction, Ginsburg emphasized that only two decisions by the Court since 1945 had considered whether an out-of-state corporations' in-state contacts were sufficiently "continuous and systematic" to justify the exercise of general jurisdiction. One decision found general jurisdiction, while the other one denied it. The North Carolina courts had justified general jurisdiction by relying on the foreign subsidiaries' placement of tires in the "stream of commerce." In such cases, a nonresident DEFENDANT, acting outside the state, places in the stream of commerce a product that ultimately causes harm inside the state. In fact, many states, including North Carolina, have enacted long-arm statutes that authorize specific jurisdiction in such circumstances. However, the problem in this case was that the North Carolina courts' "sprawling view of general jurisdiction" would make any manufacturer or seller of goods amenable to suit "wherever its products are distributed." The foreign subsidiaries of Goodyear were "in no sense home in North Carolina." Their "attenuated connections" to the state "fell far short of the contact needed to sustain general jurisdiction. Therefore, the lawsuit against the subsidiaries should be dismissed.

J. McIntyre Machinery, Ltd. v. Nicastro

In order for any court to hear and decide a pending case, it must have jurisdiction (proper authority) over both the subject matter and the parties involved. In *J. McIntyre Machinery, LTD v. Nicastro*, No. 09-1343, 564 U.S. ___ (2011), the U.S. SUPREME COURT better clarified the reaches of jurisdiction over DEFENDANT companies who neither do direct business in a particular state nor engage in any other activities in the state that indicate an intent to invoke or benefit from the protection of that state's laws. The Court, in its **plurality** opinion, found no **personal jurisdiction** over such parties under the Due Process Clause of the FOURTEENTH AMENDMENT, as they have had insufficient contacts with the state to warrant the state's jurisdictional authority over them. (The concept of "due process" prohibits a state from depriving one of life, liberty, or property without "due," i.e., just and fair, process.)

The case arose from a products liability lawsuit filed in a New Jersey state court. Robert Nicastro severely injured his hand while using a metal-shearing machine manufactured by J. McIntyre Machinery, Ltd. (J. McIntyre). The subject machine was made in England by J. McIntyre, which is incorporated and operates from England, but which used an Ohio company to sell and distribute its machinery in the United States. For purposes of "jurisdiction," J. McIntyre was a "foreign corporation."

In his products liability lawsuit, Nicastro sued for his injuries in a New Jersey state court, as the accident occurred in New Jersey. In order to show that J. McIntyre could be compelled to appear and face **adjudication** in a New Jersey state court, Nicastro needed to show that J. McIntyre had "sufficient contacts" with that state to purposely avail itself of the privilege of conducting activities in that state. Due Process protects defendants from being coerced except by lawful judicial authority (jurisdiction) over them.

At oral arguments on the matter, Nicastro's attorney premised jurisdiction on the fact that J. McIntyre had negotiated with a U.S. company to sell its machines, had attended several trade shows in the United States, and had sold other machines that ended up in New Jersey. For its part, defendant McIntyre argued that the company itself did not sell its machines in this country and there was no ALLEGATION that the distributor was under J. McInyre's control. Further, argued the company, the annual conventions took place in various states, but not in New Jersey, and finally, no more than four machines (the record indicated only one) ended up in New Jersey.

There was little discussion about what happened at the lower court level, but the New Jersey Supreme Court eventually ruled that New Jersey's courts could exercise jurisdiction over a foreign manufacturer, without violating the Fourteenth Amendment's Due Process Clause, if the manufacturer knew or reasonably should have known that its products were distributed throughout a nationwide distribution system that might lead to sales in other states. (This doctrine of jurisdiction, to establish necessary "minimum contacts" with a state, stems from language in Supreme Court precedent, including, *Asahi Metal Industry Co. v. Superior Court of Cal., Solano Cty.*, 480 U.S. 102, 107 S. Ct. 1026, 94 L. Ed. 2d 92 (1987), wherein the Court found jurisdiction if a foreign manufacture knowingly entered its products into the "stream of commerce," anticipating that they will ultimately be purchased by consumers in the forum state.)

The New Jersey Supreme Court, relying in part on the test established in *Asahi*, found sufficient minimum contacts on the part of J. McIntyre, even though it had never advertised in, sent goods to, or in any relevant sense targeted the state of New Jersey. In the court's view, jurisdiction was proper because, among other things, the injury occurred in New Jersey; J. McIntyre knew or reasonably should have known that its machines would be marketed and sold, through its U.S. distributor, to anyone in any state that wanted one; at least one machine was sold to a New Jersey customer, namely, Nicastro's employer; the company's representatives attended trade shows in the

states (not New Jersey); the company held both U.S. and European PATENTS on its technology; and its distributor structured its advertising and sales efforts according to J. McIntyre's direction and guidance.

However, the U.S. Supreme Court reversed in its plurality opinion, with six justices joining to reverse the decision of New Jersey's high court, but only four joining in the lead opinion. The Court started by summarizing the long-held rule of PERSONAL JURISDICTION, that a state may not exercise jurisdiction over a defendant unless the defendant "personally avails itself of the privilege of conducting activities within the forum state, thus invoking the benefits and protections of its laws." *Hanson v. Denckla*, 357 U.S. 235, 78 S. Ct. 1228, 2 L. Ed. 2d 1283 (1958).

The Court next noted that the New Jersey Supreme Court had issued an extensive opinion with careful attention to case precedent in reaching its conclusion. But, said the Court, the state high court's use of the "stream of commerce" metaphor carried its decision "far afield," and could not be sustained. Reverting back to *Hanson*'s language that made jurisdiction consistent with "fair play and substantial justice," no "streamline of commerce" can displace that general rule for products liability cases, said the Court.

Justice ANTHONY KENNEDY wrote the opinion of the Court, joined by Chief Justice John Roberts and Justices Antonin Scalia and Clarence Thomas. Justice Stephen Breyer, joined by Justice Samuel Alito, concurred in the judgment. Justice RUTH BADER GINSBURG dissented, joined by Justices Sonia Sotomayor and Elena Kagan. The DISSENT was critical of the outcome, essentially characterizing it as laying out a road map for a foreign company, whose only objectives are to expand its sales and profits, to avoid liability by "engaging a U.S. distributor to ship its machines stateside."

Supreme Court Clarifies Court of Federal Claims Lawsuits

Persons who wish to sue the United States for damages for non-tort actions must file lawsuits with the Court of Federal Claims (CFC). Since 1868, Congress has restricted the jurisdiction of the CFC when related actions are pending elsewhere. This restriction had been thought to be based on situations where, for example, a lawsuit filed in federal **district court** and a lawsuit filed by the same party in the CFC alleged similar facts and there is overlap in the relief requested in both courts. The SUPREME COURT, in *U.S. v. Tohono O'Odham Nation*, __U.S.__, 131 S.Ct. 1723, __L.Ed.2d__ (2011), limited jurisdiction even further, barring a lawsuit in the CFC if the two suits merely allege the same operative facts.

The Tohono O'Odham Nation is a federally-recognized Indian Tribe whose main reservation is in the Sonoran Desert of southern Arizona. This land and other parcels that the Nation holds amount to approximately 3 million acres. The Nation filed lawsuits in the District of Columbia federal district court and in the CFC, alleging violations by the federal government of its **fiduciary** duty to managing the Nation's land and other assets. The Nation filed first in the district court and the next day in the CFC. In its complaints to the two courts the Nation alleged the government had failed to provide an accurate accounting of trust property, had benefited from **self-dealing**, and had not used reasonable skill in investing trust assets. In the district court the Nation asked for equitable relief, including an accounting of assets. In the CFC complaint the Nation asked for money damages. The CFC case was dismissed for lacking jurisdiction. Under 28 U.S.C. § 1500, the CFC lacks jurisdiction over an action "for or in respect to" a claim that is also the subject of an action pending in another court. On appeal, the Court of Appeals for the Federal Circuit reversed the dismissal, ruling that two lawsuits are for or in respect to the same claim only if they share operative facts and also seek overlapping relief. Because the two lawsuits sought completely different relief, the Tohono suits were not for or in respect the same claim.

The Supreme Court, in a 7-1 decision (Justice Elena Kagan did not participate in the case), overruled the Federal Circuit ruling. Justice ANTHONY KENNEDY, writing for the majority, noted Congress had added § 1500 in 1868 to curb duplicate lawsuits brought by residents of the CONFEDERACY following the Civil War. These "cotton claimants" sought to recover for cotton taken by the federal government by suing in the CFC and in other courts. The text of § 1500 reflected "a robust response to the problem first presented by the cotton claimants." The CFC has no jurisdiction over a claim if the PLAINTIFF has another suit for or in respect to that claim pending against the United States or its agents. In a 1993 decision, the Court had ruled that two suits are for or in respect to the same claim when they are "based on substantially the same operative facts ..., at least if there [is] some overlap in the relief requested." However, that case did not decide whether the jurisdictional bar also operated if the suits are based on the same operative facts but do not seek overlapping relief. Justice Kennedy concluded that the more reasonable interpretation of § 1500 was that it barred jurisdiction on facts alone. This reading made sense "in light of the unique remedial powers of the CFC." It is the only court for most non-tort requests for significant monetary relief against the United States. Unlike federal district courts, the CFC has not general power to provide equitable relief against the government or its officers. It can only issue judgments for money. This "distinct" jurisdiction made overlapping relief the exception and distinct relief the norm. Therefore, a law that sought to preclude suits in the CFC that "duplicate suits elsewhere would be unlikely to require remedial overlap."

The Federal Circuit concluded that there was no purpose for § 1500 today. The Supreme Court disagreed, finding that it saved the government from "burdens of redundant litigation." Developing a factual record through discovery is a major cost of LITIGATION, as is the preparation and examination of witnesses at trial. An interpretation of § 1500 that is focused on the facts rather than the relief a party seeks preserves the function it was meant to serve and "keeps the provision from becoming a mere PLEADING rule, to be circumvented by carving up a single transaction into overlapping pieces seeking different relief." Justice Kennedy also found that concentrating on operative facts was consistent with the doctrine of claim preclusion, or **res judicata**, which prohibits "repetitious suits involving the same cause of action" once "a court of competent jurisdiction has entered a final judgment on the merits." Lawsuits are precluded when there is factual overlap, with "claims arising from the same transaction." Therefore, basing § 1500 on the underlying facts harmonized with the principles of preclusion law.

The Nation argued that it would be unjust to adopt the "same operative facts" interpretation because it would force plaintiffs to choose between partial remedies available in different courts. Justice Kennedy did not see hardship, for the Nation could have filed in the CFC alone and if successful the tribe would be compensated for its losses caused by the government's breach of duty. The Nation could also have started with the district court lawsuit. Congress has provided every year since 1990 that the **statute of limitations** on Indian trust mismanagement claims shall not run until the affected tribe had been given an appropriate accounting. In addition, if the Nation still believed there were hardships, it was "free to direct their complaints to Congress." The Nation now had the option of dismissing the district court lawsuit and refiling in the CFC if the **statute** of limitations was no bar. Otherwise, it could proceed with the district court action and then proceed with a CFC claim.

JUVENILE LAW

An area of the law that deals with the actions and well-being of persons who are not yet adults.

J.D.B. v. North Carolina

In *Miranda v. Arizona,* 384 U.S. 436, 86 S. Ct. 1602, 16 L. Ed. 2d 694 (1966), the SUPREME COURT established that police officers must give suspects warnings about the suspects' constitutional rights before continuing with interrogations. These safeguards only apply, however, when the suspect is in CUSTODY. In 2011, the Court reviewed a case in which a 13-year-old boy was questioned at a school without receiving *Miranda* warnings. Courts in North Carolina held that J.D.B. was not in custody at the time of questioning, but a divided Supreme Court disagreed, holding the police interrogator should have considered the child's age when determining whether the child was "in custody." *J.D.B. v. North Carolina*, No. 09-11121, 2011 WL 2369508 (U.S. June 16, 2011).

The case involved a boy known by the initials J.D.B. He was a seventh-grade student at a middle school in Chapel Hill, North Carolina. Two home break-ins occurred in Chapel Hill, and after one of them, J.D.B. was seen behind a residence in the neighborhood where the break-ins had occurred. Police questioned him at that time and also spoke to J.D.B.'s grandmother, who was his legal **guardian**.

Police discovered days later that a digital camera that had been stolen from one of the houses was found in J.D.B.'s possession at the middle school. A uniformed police officer removed J.D.B. from the classroom and took J.D.B. to a closed-door conference room. A juvenile investigator named DiCostanzo went to the school and informed the uniformed police officer, the assistant principal, and the administrative intern that he would question J.D.B. The school administrators verified for DiCostanzo the boy's birth date, address, and contact information, but nobody contacted the boy's grandmother.

DiCostanzo and the other officer were present in the conference room along with the assistant principal and the intern. With the conference door closed, the officers and others questioned J.D.B. for 30 to 45 minutes. J.D.B. never received *Miranda* warnings during the meeting, nor was he allowed to speak to his grandmother or told he could leave. During the meeting, the conversation turned from the topics of sports and family life to the accusations about the break-ins. During the conversation, the assistant principal warned J.D.B. to "do the right thing" and that "the truth always comes out in the end."

J.D.B. finally asked DiCostanzo if he would be in trouble if he returned the items. DiCostanzo responded that it would help, but then explained that J.D.B. would be charged either way. DiCostanzo further explained that he might have to obtain a secure custody order if he thought that J.D.B. might break into other homes. When J.D.B. asked what this meant, DiCostanzo said that he would have to send J.D.B. to juvenile detention before J.D.B. would appear before a court. After learning of this, J.D.B. confessed to the crimes. DiCostanzo then told J.D.B. that he could refuse to answer the questions and that he was free to leave. Upon nodding that he understood these rights, J.D.B. offered more detail about the break-ins and the location of the stolen items. J.D.B. was then allowed to take the bus home.

A PUBLIC DEFENDER represented J.D.B., who faced a count of breaking and entering and another count of **larceny**. The public defender moved to suppress the statements and any evidence discovered because of the statements. According to the motion, the investigators had interrogated J.D.B. without affording the boy his *Miranda*, rights. The motion further argued that J.D.B.'s statements had been involuntary. The trial court held a suppression hearing at which both DiCostanzo and J.D.B. testified. The court concluded that J.D.B. was not in custody at the time of his questioning and that the statements were voluntary. J.D.B. then admitted to the counts, and the court ruled that J.D.B. was delinquent.

Both the North Carolina Court of Appeals and the North Carolina Supreme Court affirmed the trial court's decision. The North Carolina Supreme Court specifically declined "to extent the test for custody to include consideration of the age . . . of an individual subjected to questioning by the police."

The U.S. Supreme Court agreed to review the case. In 5-4 decision, the Court reversed the North Carolina Supreme Court. The majority opinion, written by Justice SONIA SOTOMAYOR, noted that custodial police interrogation typically entails inherently compelling pressures. These pressures can lead innocent adults to admit to crimes that they did not commit. The principal reason that underlies the *Miranda* warnings is that the coercive nature of **custodial interrogation** can blur the line between a voluntary and an involuntary statement. The Court only requires these warnings when the suspect is "in custody."

The pressures inherent in custodial police interrogations are even more pronounced when the suspect is a juvenile. Sotomayor and the majority concluded that courts and police had to take a juvenile's age into consideration when determining whether the circumstances were such that the boy should have received the warnings. Thus, in a situation where an officer knew or should have known about a child's age at the time of questioning, the officer should consider the child in custody and give the warnings.

The Court did not decide whether J.D.B. was actually in custody at the time of the interrogation, and the Court remanded the case to the North Carolina STATE COURTS to make this decision.

Justice SAMUEL ALITO disagreed with the majority, arguing that the Court's decision was unnecessary and conflicted with the underlying rationale behind the *Miranda* warnings. Alito asserted that the Court did not have to give a "complete makeover" to *Miranda* to tailor a rule that applies to juvenile suspects. Chief Justice JOHN ROBERTS and Justice ANTONIN SCALIA and CLARENCE THOMAS joined Alito's DISSENT.

LABOR LAW

Kasten v. Saint-Gobain Performance Plastics

The FAIR LABOR STANDARDS ACT of 1938 (FLSA), 29 U.S.C. § 201 *et seq.*, controls many aspects of employer-employee relations regarding common employment issues such as minimum wages, maximum work hours, and overtime pay rules. It also contains an anti-retaliation provision forbidding employers from discharging any employee "because such employee has filed any complaint" alleging a violation of the Act (FLSA). 29 U.S.C. § 215(a)(3). In *Kasten v. Saint-Gobain Performance Plastic Corporation,* No. 09-834, 563 U.S. ___ (2011), the U.S. SUPREME COURT held that "filing any complaint" included oral, as well as formal written, complaints.

Kevin Kasten was employed at Saint-Gobain's Portage, Wisconsin manufacturing facility. Employees at that facility "punched in" and "punched out" on a Kronos timeclock at the beginning and end of each work shift (and for lunch). The timeclock was located in an area where Kasten and other employees changed in and out of their protective gear for the shift. This resulted in the employees not getting credit for, i.e., being paid for, the time spent getting in and out of protective gear.

According to Kasten, he carefully followed the company's internal grievance resolution procedures and the company's "Code of Ethics and Business Conduct" (which **imputed** employees with "the responsibility to report ... suspected violations of ... any applicable law of which he or she is aware") when he initially raised his concern about the location of the timeclock with his immediate supervisor. Again following internal procedures, he next spoke with a human resources employee, then the human relations manager, followed by the operations manager. Each of these communications was in the form of an oral complaint that the location of the timeclock was illegal because it excluded "the time you come in and start doing stuff." He also alleged that he repeatedly told company representatives that, if challenged legally on this issue, they "would lose." Shortly thereafter, Kasten was fired.

The employer denied that Kasten made any significant complaints and responded that Kasten was discharged from employment after he repeatedly failed to record his comings and goings on the timeclock, even after several warnings.

In any event, in a separate but related civil suit, the federal **district court** agreed with Kasten, finding that the company's failure to compensate "for time spent donning and doffing certain required protective gear and walking to work areas" did indeed violate the Act. In the present lawsuit, Kasten alleged unlawful retaliation under FLSA for having complained to company officials about the timeclocks.

But this time, the federal district court disagreed, finding that the FLSA's anti-retaliatory clause did not cover oral complaints. The Seventh **Circuit Court** of Appeals affirmed, holding that oral complaints were not "protected activity" under the FLSA. To resolve a conflict among the circuits courts of appeals, the U.S. Supreme Court granted **certiorari**.

Justice STEPHEN BREYER, writing for the majority, reversed the lower courts. He was joined by Chief Justice Roberts and Justices Kennedy, Ginsburg, Alito, and Sotomayor. (Justice Kagan did not take part in consideration or decision.) First looking to the express language of the FLSA provision, the Court considered the phrase, " ... has filed any complaint." Some dictionary (as well as legislative and regulatory) definitions of "filed" contemplated only a writing, while others contemplated a broader meaning, leaving resolution inconclusive. On the other hand, the FLSA language referring to the filing of "*any* complaint" seemed to suggest a broader understanding to include both oral and written complaints. But suggestion is insufficient for conclusive law. Because the text, taken alone, was therefore inconclusive, the Court looked further.

Looking to functional considerations, i.e., practical effect, the Court concluded that a narrow interpretation of the language (only to include written complaints) would undermine the FLSA's basic objective, which is to prohibit labor conditions that were detrimental to maintaining a minimum standard of living for health and well-being of workers. Moreover, limiting complaints to written ones would reduce the flexibility of federal agencies, which often rely on "information and complaints received from employees" to enforce substantive standards (quoting from *Mitchell*

v. Robert DeMario Jewelry, Inc., 361 U.S. 288, 80 S. Ct. 332, 4 L. Ed. 2d 323 (1960). Such feedback from employees often comes in the form of hotlines, interviews, or questionnaires. Finally, the National Labor Relations Act (NLRA) has a similar anti-retaliatory provision, which has been broadly interpreted to protect workers who were simply "participating" in a NLRB investigation. *NLRB v. Scrivener*, 405 U.S. 117, 123, 92 S. Ct. 798, 31 L. Ed. 2d 79 (1972).

Clearly, the focus on the complaint process is to put an employer on notice. The Court acknowledged that "filing a complaint" contemplated, at a minimum, a complaint that contained a degree of formality, clarity, and sufficiency of detail for "a reasonable employer to understand [it] ... in light of both content and context, as an assertion of rights protected by the **statute** and a call for their protection." Therefore, an objective standard would permit a complaint either in written or oral form, as long as it sufficed to place an employer on such notice. This objective standard is also consistent with the views of administrative agencies responsible for enforcing the FLSA, the Court finding that they shared such a broader understanding of the complaint process.

The Court did not consider the alternative claim raised by Saint-Gobain that the anti-retaliation provision only applied to complaints filed with the Government, not those filed internally with employers. This claim had not been previously raised in the CERTIORARI briefs, and its resolution was not a predicate to the resolution of the oral vs. written issue before the court.

Justice Scalia filed a dissenting opinion, joined by Justice Thomas. The DISSENT opined that "the plain meaning" of the text contemplated only an official grievance filed with a court or an agency, not oral complaints from an employee to an employer.

MEDICINE

Appeals Court Reinstates Stem Cell Research Funding

In April 2011, the U.S. Court of Appeals for the District of Columbia Circuit overturned a 2010 federal district judge's ruling that placed a **preliminary injunction** on federal funding for human embryonic stem cell research. (A PRELIMINARY INJUNCTION grants temporary relief to a party in a pending law suit until the full case can be heard and decided on the merits.) The 2010 preliminary INJUNCTION, issued by District Judge Royce Lamberth, followed his ruling in which he opined that all embryonic stem cell (ESC) research conducted at the National Institutes of Health (NIH) constituted destruction of human embryos, in violation of federal law. However, on appeal, the D.C. **Circuit Court** of Appeals found ambiguity in the subject federal law and concluded that the original plaintiffs were unlikely to prevail on the merits. Importantly, the only question before the **appellate court** in the 2011 decision was the propriety of the preliminary injunction; the court did not address other constitutional issues still being litigated at the **district court** level.

The suit was brought by two scientists (Drs. James Sherley and Theresa Deisher) who asked the court to enjoin the NIH from funding research using human embryonic stem cells (ESCs). *Sherley v. Sebelius,* No. 10-5287 (D.C. Circuit).

Specifically, the case involved only embryonic stem cells (ESCs). Adult stem cells, found in various tissues and organs of the body, are programmed to reproduce and often replace aging or damaged cells for that tissue or organ. Conversely, ESCs are "blank," i.e., not yet developed to a stage where they will grow into specialized tissue. They are considered "pluripotent" at this embryonic stage, capable of developing into any of nearly 200 different types of human cells. By removing the inner cell mass of an embryo (which contains about 30 different cells, only some of which are stem cells), scientists can isolate and separate the stem cells (ESCs) so that they divide continuously without differentiating, and form a "stem cell line" of identical cells. Thereafter, any of these stem cells in the line can then be extracted and caused to develop into the type of cell pertinent to the specific research, e.g., growing new skin, a new kidney, or infection-fighting blood cells.

In 1996, during the Bush administration, Congress passed the Dickey-Wicker Amendment, Pub. L. No. 111-117, 123 Stat. 3034 (as an appropriations **rider** attached to another law) that barred federal funding for research in which human embryos are either created or destroyed "for research purposes." At that time, scientists had not yet been able to stabilize ESCs in a laboratory setting (let alone grow stem cell lines from them), and the **congressional record** seemed to indicate that the primary objective of

Dickey-Wicker was to stop funding of research using embryos that had been created for the purpose of *in vitro* fertilization.

Three years later, in 1999, general counsel for the U.S. DEPARTMENT OF HEALTH AND HUMAN SERVICES (HHS) issued a legal memorandum addressing whether the Dickey-Wicker Amendment permitted federal funding of research using ESCs that had been derived before the funded project began. The memorandum concluded that such funding was possible because ESCs were not "embryos." Thereafter, in 2001, President GEORGE W. BUSH announced a policy wherein federal funding would be limited to projects using the already-existing cell lines derived from "embryos that ha[d] already been destroyed." In other words, a technical distinction was made between the creation or destruction of *embryos* for human research (still prohibited under federal funding) and the use of continually-propagating ESCs derived from a stem cell line, the original embryo for which had been long destroyed prior to the law. (At that time, there were approximately 60 existing stem cell lines.) After notice and comment, NIH published funding guidelines ethically consistent with this legal guidance.

Each year since 2001, Congress continued to reenact Dickey-Wicker. Meanwhile, private funding kept research alive in ESCs. In 2009, President Obama lifted the restriction imposed by President Bush and permitted MIH to support and conduct such research "to the extent permitted by law." (EXECUTIVE ORDER 13,505). After notice and **solicitation** of comments, NIH then issued 2009 Guidelines, which were still in effect as of 2011.

Importantly, in the 2009 Guidelines, the NIH expressly noted that funding of the derivation of stem cells from human embryos remained prohibited. It further addressed Dickey=Wickers as follows,

> Since 1999, [HHS] has consistently interpreted [Dickey-Wicker] as not applicable to research using [ESCs], because [ESCs] are not embryos as defined by Section 509. This longstanding interpretation has been left unchanged by Congress, which has annually reenacted the Dickey [sic] Amendment with full knowledge that HHS has been funding [ESC] research since 2001. These guidelines therefore recognize the distinction, accepted by Congress, between the derivation of stem

cells from an embryo that results in the embryo's destruction, for which Federal funding is prohibited, and research involving [ESCs] that does not involve an embryo nor result in an embryo's destruction, for which Federal funding is permitted.

After the 2009 NIH Guidelines were published, Congress again reenacted Dickey-Wicker as part of the **fiscal** 2010 appropriations bill. Meanwhile, Drs. Sherley and Deisher filed their lawsuit, alleging that the NIH 2009 Guidelines violated Dickey-Wicker. Originally fighting dismissal for lack of standing, they won an appeal on that issue and were found to have standing based on the fact that they were competing with ESC researchers for NIH funding. Following the 2010 district court's ruling in their favor, the government moved to stay the court's injunction until it could appeal; the D.C. Court of Appeals granted a temporary stay until its decision.

The D.C. **appellate** court reviewed, through precedent **case law**, whether plaintiffs had shown a requisite hardship that warranted relief in the form of preliminary injunction. True, the plaintiffs were competing with ESC researchers for funding, but, the court noted, they had been competing since 2001. Further, noted the court, invalidating the Guidelines (as being in violation of Dickey Wicker, the ultimate relief sought by plaintiffs) would not necessarily result in plaintiffs getting more grant money. The court found that it could not conclude that if plaintiffs litigated their case on the merits, without the benefit of interim relief (the preliminary injunction), they would suffer a significant additional burden on their ability to secure research funding. On the other hand, the hardship placed on the ESC researchers by a preliminary injunction would be certain and substantial.

Second, said the APPELLATE court, the NIH, in its 2009 Guidelines, unequivocally noted that Congress had continually reenacted Dickey Wicker, unchanged, year after year, "with full knowledge that HHS has been funding [ESC] research since 2001." If the appellate court were to read the NIH Guidelines as plaintiffs proposed, such ESC research policy would have been prohibited under Dickey Wicker. This did not make legal sense. Therefore, the agency's interpretation, rather than plaintiffs, was more indicative of Congress's intent. As it did not appear, then, that plaintiffs would prevail on the merits, the preliminary injunction was not warranted.

MILITARY LAW

The body of laws, rules, and regulations developed to meet the needs of the military. It encompasses service in the military, the constitutional rights of service members, the military criminal justice system, and the international law of armed conflict.

9th Circuit Strikes Down Municipal Ban on Military Recruiting of Minors

The federal government's right to recruit individuals to serve in the U.S. armed forces is based on Article I of the U.S. Constitution's provision that gives Congress the power to "raise and support Armies" and to "make Rules for the Government and Regulation of the land and naval Forces." Though COLLEGES AND UNIVERSITIES have prevented military recruiters from using campus facilities because of the "Don't Ask, Don't Tell" policy on gay and lesbians in the military, two California cities took the unprecedented step of enacting ordinances that barred recruiters from targeting minors in their cities. The U.S. government challenged the constitutionality of these ordinances and prevailed upon the **federal courts** to strike them down in *City of Arcata v. United States*, 629 F.3d 986(9th Cir:2010).The Ninth **Circuit Court** of Appeals ruled that federal law preempted local governments from regulating the activities of military recruiters. Moreover, the ordinances discriminated against recruiters because private citizens could discuss the same issues with teenagers without fear of prosecution.

The voters in the cities of Arcata and Eureka, California approved ballot measures in November 2008 which enacted the Arcata and Eureka Youth Protection Acts respectively. The ordinances were proposed in response to alleged violations of law governing military recruitment. The findings contained in each **ordinance** stated that military recruiters targeted teenagers using ad campaigns, mailings, phone calls, email, and direct personal contact. The findings also alleged that recruiters promoted enlistment by "glorifying military service and exaggerating the educational and career benefits, while ignoring the dangers." The ordinance sought to prohibit the federal government from recruiting teenagers under the age of 18, as well as initiating contact or promoting the future enlistment of minors under 18. A recruiter who violated the ordinance would be subject to civil penalties for each infraction. However, the ordinance specifically exempted non-government employees or agents from these restrictions.

The federal government filed a suit in federal court in December 2008, asking the court to declare the ordinances invalid under the Constitution's **Supremacy Clause**. The government argued that the ordinances violated the doctrine of intergovernmental IMMUNITY because they directly regulated and discriminated against the federal government. It also contended that the ordinances were preempted by federal law. The **district court** declared the ordinances invalid and issued an INJUNCTION that barred the cities from enforcing them. The cities then appealed to the Ninth Circuit.

The appeals court upheld the district court's rulings. Judge Matthew Kennelly, writing for a unanimous three-judge panel, first swept away the cities' jurisdictional challenges. The cities claimed the government had not show an injury in fact, so as to qualify standing to bring the lawsuit. The cities alleged that the government had only claimed a "hypothetical negative impact on federal recruiting objectives." Judge Kennelly found that the government had standing because the government was the sole target of the ordinances and that its recruiters faced civil penalties for recruiting minors under the age of 18. He noted that the cities were ready to enforce the ordinances if upheld by the courts. These two facts conferred standing on the government to seek legal **redress** from an "imminent adverse impact. The appeals court also found that the government had standing to ask for a **declaratory judgment** that the ordinances were invalid. Congress had given federal district courts jurisdiction over "all civil actions, suits, or proceedings commenced by the United States."

As to the merits of the appeal, the court first looked at the Constitution's SUPREMACY CLAUSE. The doctrine of intergovernmental immunity, first announced in the landmark case of McCulloch v. Maryland, 17 U.S. (4 Wheat.) 316, 4 L.Ed. 579 (1819), makes state and local laws invalid if they regulate the United States directly or discriminate against the federal government. Judge Kennelly found that the district court had properly applied this doctrine because the ordinances sought to directly regulate the conduct of agents of the federal government. By "constraining the conduct of federal agents and employees," the ordinances seek to regulate the government directly. Unlike other state and local laws that may affect the federal government incidentally as the consequence of a "broad, neutrally applicable rule," the ordinances in question targeted the federal government directly.

The cities also claimed that they had authority under the Constitution's TENTH AMENDMENT to enact the ordinances. Judge Kennelly pointed out that the Tenth Amendment reserves powers to the states that are not delegated to the federal government, yet Article I empowers Congress to "raise and support Armies." In addition, the SUPREME COURT has ruled that the federal government can determine, without question from any state authority, how the armies shall be raised. Therefore, the Tenth Amendment could not be invoked to save the ordinances.

The appeals court also dismissed the cities' contention that they would enforce the ordinances only to the extent they are consistent with federal law. This declaration could not "cure the ordinances' infirmity because there is no exception to the doctrine of intergovernmental immunity for state statutes consistent with federal law."

MURDER

The unlawful killing of another human being without justification or excuse.

"Dateline" TV Episode Casts Doubts on Prosecutor's Case

In July 2010, a "Dateline" television news story profiled the nearly decade-old MURDER of a little girl in Rock Hill, South Carolina, and the subsequent RAPE and murder charges against her own father in the case. Later tests from DNA found on the 12-year-old girl's body showed that the DNA matched that of another man, who, at the time, lived a block away. Notwithstanding, as the father had since confessed to sexually assaulting and strangling his daughter, both men were tried together, and both were convicted of the rape and murder. Prosecutors and police believed that

the two men conspired to rape and kill little Amanda Cope, but argued that her father, Billy Cope, had masterminded it.

The "Dateline" special cast new doubts on that CONSPIRACY, showing that the two men had never met each other, and that the other man, James Sanders, a convicted burglar, was the real killer. Both men have been serving life sentences since the 2004 convictions. Although at the time of Amanda's murder, Cope and Sanders lived near each other, both maintained that they had never met each other. Complicating the case further, Sanders was subsequently convicted of sexual ASSAULT during a **burglary** that occurred months after the Cope murder.

Amanda Cope was murdered in her bedroom between 2:00 and 4:00 a.m. on November 29, 2001. Police who later checked the exterior and interior of the house found no signs of forced entry, and all doors and windows were secure and intact. Amanda's younger sister testified at trial that she and Amanda had locked both doors before they went to bed that evening.

Billy Cope, the girl's father, told police that he had awakened at 6:00 a.m. and called out to awaken Amanda. When she did not respond, he went to her room, where he found her lying on her bed. He called 911. (Later, at trial, evidence was introduced that Cope was detached and matter-of-fact in his call, telling the dispatcher, "She's dead . . . cold as a cucumber.") Cope told police that he had not heard any sounds that night because he slept with a sleep apnea machine that made a loud noise.

When Jason Dillon, an emergency medical technician (EMT) arrived, Cope was standing outside. He told Dillon that Amanda had been dead "four hours" or "for hours," (Dillon did not ask Cope which one he meant to say). Cope further told Dillon that his daughter had choked herself with her blanket. Cope told Dillon that he found his daughter naked and he dressed her.

When the **forensic** pathologist arrived, he found Amanda lying on her back in her bed, with her shirt pulled up and her left breast exposed. He testified that it appeared she had not dressed herself because her brassiere was unattached and her pants had been pulled up unevenly. He also testified that he had determined, following his examination, that Amanda had been beaten, strangled, severely sexually assaulted, and sodomized with a blunt object such as a broom handle. He further testified that he believed Amanda had been sexually abused and sodomized over a period of time. Moreover, he testified, it did not appear that Amanda was strangled by her blanket. Some of her injuries were consistent with a 300-pound man jumping on her (at the time of Cope's arrest, he weighed 333 pounds). The pathologist also took DNA swabs of her right breast, which had a bite mark on it, and semen found on her pants. Both DNA samples matched co-defendant James Sanders.

On November 30, 2001, after being told he failed a voluntary POLYGRAPH test, Cope gave his first (of three) confessions, both to acts of **sodomy** and sexual assault and to strangulation. On December 2, while in CUSTODY, he told police he wanted to talk to them again, and on December 3, he rescinded his earlier confession as incorrect, substituting it with another, in which he had been dreaming that he was attacking an ex-girlfriend who had aborted his child, only to awaken and find that it was his own daughter he had assaulted. He cleaned up all incriminating evidence, then went back to bed, he told police, hoping the whole thing would prove to be a bad dream when he awoke in the morning.

After this second confession, Cope agreed to accompany police back to the residence to reenact the crime on videotape. During this third (videotaped) confession, Cope further admitted to sexually abusing his daughter since October.

Since there was no inculpatory DNA EVIDENCE matching Cope with the crimes (saliva, semen, etc.), his defense attorneys appealed, arguing that his was a classic case of a "false confession." According to Cope's attorney, Jim Morton, Cope had denied any connection with the rape and murder several hundred times before finally confessing. According to Martin, a distraught Cope thought, "Well, I'll just make something up. I'll tell them what they'll want to hear, but it won't pan out, because the evidence won't show this."

As to the conspiracy conviction, Morton argued that this was the result of prosecutors suddenly realizing that the DNA did not match the man they had obtained a false confession from. To save face, he argued, they accused both men of conspiring to rape and murder Amanda.

Both men lost their appeals in 2009 before the South Carolina Court of Appeals. The **appellate court** expressly noted in its opinion,

> Nevertheless, in the present case, the DNA evidence on Child's body, along with Cope's admissions about his interactions with Child shortly before she died, place Cope and Sanders together at the time of the assault on Child and her resulting death. Likewise, the testimony regarding lack of forced entry and the cluttered condition of the home constitute evidence that Sanders, who had no known connection with Cope's family, received assistance to navigate his way to Child's bedroom. Finally, Cope's staging of the crime scene after Child died is evidence that a cover-up had begun before Cope called police to his home on the pretext that Child had accidentally strangled herself, notwithstanding compelling forensic evidence that Sanders was present and actively participating during the same time period in which her death was determined to have occurred. Although each of these factors alone may have supported only a mere suspicion of a conspiracy between Cope and Sanders, it is our view that when considered together, they yield the requisite level of proof of "acts, declarations, or specific conduct" by the alleged conspirators to withstand a **directed verdict** motion on this charge.

Following the 2010 "Dateline" airing of the story, Kevin Brackett, the 16th Circuit solicitor, faced reporters and defended the conviction of Cope. He complained that the "Dateline" episode intentionally slanted the facts to create a one-sided story making prosecutors "look bad." For example, he said, "Dateline" reported that he had refused their request to talk to him, but in reality, he had been advised to do so by a deputy attorney general, because the case was still pending at the state SUPREME COURT level.

Arizona Gunman Kills Six and Wounds 12 Others at Political Gathering

On January 8, 2011, an Arizona man burst forward from a small gathering of constituents at a "Congress on Your Corner" rally outside a local grocery market, shot State Representative Gabrielle ("Gabby") Giffords (D-AZ) in the forehead at near pointblank range, then released a spray of bullets that killed six and wounded 12 others. A bystander reported to authorities that he had seen a young man wearing sneakers and

possibly navy blue sweats approach Giffords with a raised semiautomatic pistol. He then shot her in the face, while people near her tried to flee but were trapped by a table and a concrete post. The gunman then fired into the crowd, reported the bystander.

After firing a round of at least 30 bullets from a 9mm Glock handgun, the gunman was overtaken and subdued only after he stopped to reload his gun with another magazine, at which time other bystanders and attendees tackled and held him until police arrived. The 40-year-old congresswoman Giffords, who received a bullet to the brain, was rushed to University Medical Center, where she underwent brain surgery and was listed in critical condition. Five others died at the scene, and a sixth, little 9-year-old Christina Taylor-Greene, died at a nearby hospital.

Also killed that morning were 63-year-old U.S. **District Court** Judge John Roll, 30-year-old Gabriel Zimmerman (Giffords' community outreach director), 76-year-old Dorthy Murray, 76-year-old Dorwin Stoddard, and 79-year-old Phyllis Scheck, according to the Pima County Sheriff's Department. It was

later revealed that Judge Roll had been shot while kneeling to shield another victim, Ronald Barber, a Giffords employee, who survived two gunshot wounds. The remaining 12 persons who were shot were expected to survive their wounds as well. One of Giffords' congressional interns was credited with cradling her and keeping her alive until help arrived. Following her surgeries, Giffords ultimately survived, spending several days in a coma followed by several months in intensive rehabilitation and physical therapy. An additional surgery in May 2011 was to fit her skull with a ceramic prosthesis to replace part of her cranium, and to install a permanent tube to drain fluid from her skull.

At first, authorities did not believe the gunman in CUSTODY, 22-year-old Jared Lee Loughner, had acted alone, and actively pursued identification of another middle-aged man seen on video fleeing the scene. The second man, who was later identified and questioned by police, was released after authorities determined that he had no involvement and that Loughner had acted alone. Loughner was described by Pima County Sheriff Clarence

Dupnik at a press conference later that evening as being "mentally unstable."

It was not immediately clear what had motivated the suspect Loughner, who was seen shooting the victims in "gory" video clips filmed on nearby security cameras near the grocery market. However, it was immediately known that a person using the same name had posted several convoluted videos on YouTube with vague anti-government messages. Investigators learned days later that Loughner had been conducting Internet Web searches about "famous assassins" and "lethal injection" just hours before he took a taxi to the event where Giffords was scheduled to be.

Even though questions of Loughner's mental health surfaced almost immediately, the Pima County Sheriff's Department was quick to denounce the nation's vitriolic political climate, noting Arizona's part in fueling such rhetoric, especially after its crackdown on illegal IMMIGRATION. As Sheriff Dupnik told media reporters, fiery rhetoric "may be free speech, but it's not without consequences."

On the day following the shootings, January 9, 2011, Loughner was charged with five federal counts, including the attempt to assassinate a member of Congress, the killing of two federal employees, and the attempted killing of two more federal employees, in violation of 18 U.S.C. §§ 3511(c), 1111, 1113, and 1114, among others. In March 2011, 49 new federal charges against him were filed in the U.S. District Court for the District of Arizona; at a hearing on March 10, Loughner pleaded not guilty to all of them. Arizona judges had recused themselves, and Judge Larry A. Burns of the U.S. District Court in San Diego was appointed to the case.

In May 2011, Judge Burns ruled that Loughner was not mentally competent to stand trial. The ruling came after it had been determined by two experts who had examined him at a federal psychiatric facility in Missouri, that he appeared to suffer from schizophrenia and also experienced delusional and irrational thoughts. Prosecutors had requested that the court order psychological tests, sooner rather than later, to determine whether Loughner understood the charges against him. In support of their request, they had submitted evidence including postings by Loughner on the Internet. Defense counsel, Judy Clarke, had opposed such testing, arguing that it could interfere with her ability to establish a rapport with Loughner. During the hearing, the judge stated that he had received two letters from Loughner, complaining about his LEGAL REPRESENTATION, but the judge did not intend to address their substance as he determined that they were consequential to his mental illness.

In June 2011, Judge Burns ruled that prison officials could forcibly give antipsychotic drugs to Loughner in a bid to make him mentally fit for trial. Defense counsel had filed a motion to prevent any forced medication without court approval. The judge noted that he did not wish to second-guess physicians at the federal prison, who determined that Loughner was a danger.

NATIVE AMERICAN RIGHTS

United States v. Jicarilla Apache Nation

In the 2011 case of *United States v. Jicarilla Apache Nation,* No. 10-382, 564 U.S. ___ (2011), the U.S. SUPREME COURT considered the extent to which a **common law** exception to an evidentiary **attorney-client privilege** (prohibiting disclosure of confidential communications) might apply to the United States in its monetary trust relationship with Native American Indian tribes.

The Jicarilla Apache Nation (the Tribe) has, on its 900,000-acre reservation lands in Northern New Mexico, certain natural resources (timber, gravel, oil and gas) that are developed pursuant to federal statutes. These statutes are administered by the U.S. Department of the Interior. Proceeds from the development of the natural resources are held by the United States, in trust, for the Tribe.

The Tribe had filed, in the Court of Federal Claims, a breach-of-trust action alleging mismanagement of its trust funds by the U.S. Government, in violation of 25 U.S.C. § 161-162(a) and other laws. The Tribe sought monetary damages. During the discovery stage of the pending LITIGATION, the Tribe moved to compel production of certain documents. The government produced thousands of documents, but withheld approximately 226 of them under the doctrine of ATTORNEY-CLIENT PRIVILEGE. Although it later released 71 of those

documents, it continued to hold 155 of them, constituting communications with its attorneys regarding management of the trust.

But the Tribe wanted to see all of the documents. To support its motion to compel production, it asserted that under COMMON LAW, there is an exception to the attorney-client privilege when a **trustee** obtains legal advice related to the exercise of **fiduciary** duties relating to that trust. In such cases, the exception means that trustees cannot withhold attorney-client communications from the BENEFICIARY of the trust.

The Claims Court granted the motion in part, specifically holding that departmental communications relating to the management of trust funds fell within a "fiduciary exception" to the attorney-client privilege. In other words, trustees who obtained legal advice related to trust administration could not assert the attorney-client privilege as against trust beneficiaries seeking to review those communications. The government then appealed for a **writ** of **mandamus** (an order from a higher court directing a lower court to do something) for the Claims Court to vacate its order compelling production of the withheld documents.

But the U.S. Court of Appeals for the Federal Circuit, in December 2009, agreed with the Claims Court. It, too, likened the trust relationship between the United States and the Indian tribes to a private trust, thereby triggering the FIDUCIARY exception. The **appellate court** found that the government had failed to claim or prove that it had "considered a specific competing interest in those communications."

In its reversal of the lower courts, the Supreme Court held that, although parallels may be drawn between the government's responsibilities to a tribe (with respect to management of the funds) and the duties of a private trustee, the analogy does not reach the point of creating a fiduciary exception (to the attorney-client privilege) that would apply to the relationship between the United States and the Indian tribes. This is primarily so because the government's responsibilities and obligations to the tribes are expressly created by **statute**, and are so governed by statute, not by common law. In fulfilling its **statutory** duties, said the Court, the government acts not as a private trustee, but instead acts pursuant to its sovereign interest in the execution of federal statutory law.

The fiduciary exception, explained the Court, is based on consideration of two criteria. First, courts identify the "real client" by considering whether the legal advice sought was paid for by the trust (ultimately the beneficiaries), whether the trustee had reason to seek advice in a personal capacity rather than fiduciary capacity, and whether the advice could have been intended for any purpose other than

to benefit the trust (and its beneficiaries). Applying those factors to the present case, the Court concluded that the United States did not obtain the legal advice as a "mere representative" of the Tribe, nor was the Tribe the "real client" for whom the advice was intended. The government also sought (and seeks) legal advice in its capacity as a sovereign, with a sovereign interest distinct from the Tribe beneficiaries' private interests. Further, the Government's attorneys are paid by congressional appropriations, not by the Tribe or its trust fund.

In summary, the U.S. government does not have the same common-law disclosure obligations as a private trustee. In the present case, statute, to wit, 25 U.S.C. § 161-162(a), outlines and governs the government's "trust responsibilities," not common law.

Justice SAMUEL ALITO delivered the majority opinion, in which he was joined by Chief Justice Roberts, as well as Justices Scalia, Kennedy, and Thomas. Justice RUTH BADER GINSBURG filed a separate opinion concurring in the judgment, and she was joined by Justice Breyer. Newly-appointed Justice Kagan took no part in the consideration or decision. The lone dissenter, Justice SONIA SOTOMAYOR, delivered a 21-page opinion in which she expressed her conclusion that the rationale behind the common law exception fully supported its application in this case; she would have denied the government's reliance on an attorney-client privilege.

OBSTRUCTION OF JUSTICE

A criminal offense that involves interference, through words or actions, with the proper operations of a court or officers of the court.

Fowler v. United States

A criminal DEFENDANT who kills a person with the intent to prevent the person from communicating about the possible commission of a federal offense can be convicted on a specific type of MURDER under federal law. Lower **federal courts** have struggled with how the **statute** should apply, however. In 2011, the U.S. SUPREME COURT ruled that federal prosecutors must prove that there was a reasonable likelihood that the murder victim would have made at least one communication to a federal law enforcement officer. The Court's decision in *Fowler v. United States*, No. 10-5443, 2011 WL 2039370 (U.S. 2011) vacated the conviction of a Florida man who had been charged under the federal statute.

In March 1998, a group of men robbed a Holiday Inn in Dunbee, Florida and then planned to rob a bank the next day. The men recruited two others, including Charles Andrew Fowler, to participate in the bank **robbery**. The men loaded a stolen vehicle with guns, masks, and gloves, and they went to a local cemetery to prepare for the ROBBERY. While at the cemetery, the men wore dark clothes and gloves. They took drugs and drank alcohol. At one point, Fowler left the group so that he could use cocaine on his own.

While Fowler was separated from the others, an officer named Todd Horner drove up behind the stolen car. The cemetery was a high-crime area, with suspects often leaving stolen cars there. Horner reported to a city dispatcher that he was going to investigate the suspicious vehicle that Fowler and the others brought to the cemetery. Horner pulled a gun on the group and told them to give their names. Fowler then snuck up on Horner from behind. Another of the men, Christopher Gamble, talked to Horner to keep the officer distracted. Fowler was able to grab Horner's gun, and with the help of the others, Fowler took control of the gun. Horner was able to identify Gamble even though the men had not revealed their names. The men lost control of themselves, and Fowler told Horner to get on his knees. At the urging of another man, Fowler shot Horner in the head, killing him It took several years before anyone was charged with Horner's murder.

In 1999, Gamble was later convicted on charges stemming from the robbery of a liquor store. He was sentenced to 20 years in prison. Some three years after his conviction, he informed law enforcement officials about his involvement in the Horner murder. His admission led to his own conviction for which he received a life sentence. His admission also led to the INDICTMENT of Fowler.

Prosecutors charged Fowler with murder based on a federal statute contained in 18 U.S.C. § 1512(a)(1)(C). This statute provides that it is a federal offense to "kill ... another person, with intent to ... prevent the communication by any person to a law enforcement officer or judge of the United States of information relating to the commission or possible commission of a Federal offense.... " Fowler was convicted on the charge when prosecutors proved that he murdered Horner to prevent the officer from informing a federal law enforcement officer or judge about one of several possible federal offenses that Fowler had committed. Fowler received a life sentence for his conviction.

Fowler appealed his conviction, arguing that the **district court** had applied the statute incorrectly. According to Fowler, the prosecution failed to prove that Horner would have communicated anything about a federal offense when the officer approached the stolen car at the cemetery. Moreover, Fowler asserted that the prosecution had not proven that any federal investigation of any sort would have resulted from Horner's reporting.

According to the majority of federal circuit courts of appeals, the government was not required to prove that a federal investigation was underway or imminent. Instead, these courts had ruled that prosecutors only needed to show that the defendant intended to prevent a murder victim from potentially communicating with federal law enforcement officials. The Eleventh **Circuit Court** of Appeals, which heard Fowler's appeal, agreed with the majority of lower federal courts and held that the government only needed to prove that Fowler might

have possibly communicated with federal authorities about a possible federal crime. *United States v. Fowler*, 603 F.3d 883 (11th Cir. 2010).

In a 7-2 decision, the Supreme Court disagreed with the Eleventh Circuit's opinion. Writing for the majority, Justice Stephen Breyer reviewed the **statutory** text in question and concluded that the government had to prove something more than the possible communication between the victim and federal authorities. The Court agreed with Fowler's argument that the proper standard should be whether there was a reasonable likelihood that had the victim communicated with law enforcement officers that at least one relevant communication would have reached a federal law enforcement officer. Since the lower courts had not considered this standard in Fowler's case, the Court remanded the case for a new trial.

Justice Scalia filed a concurring opinion. According to Scalia, the government should have to prove that "the defendant intended to prevent a communication which, had it been made, would **beyond a reasonable doubt** have been made to a federal law enforcement officer" (emphasis in original). Scalia also argued that the prosecution had provided insufficient evidence to support Fowler's conviction.

On the other hand, Justice Samuel Alito, joined by Justice Ruth Bader Ginsburg, dissented. Alito argued that the majority had effectively amended the statute by adding a new element. He also argued that the Court's new test "makes little sense" and that it "will create confusion for trial judges and juries."

PAROLE

The conditional release of a person convicted of a crime prior to the expiration of that person's term of imprisonment, subject to both the supervision of the correctional authorities during the remainder of the term and a resumption of the imprisonment upon violation of the conditions imposed.

Federal Courts Cannot Review California Parole System

Each state has its own PAROLE system. Once created, a state creates a liberty interest for each prisoner eligible for parole. This means that if the prisoner is denied parole, the prisoner must have the right to seek **judicial review** in state court. If the STATE COURTS deny the prisoner's claims, the prisoner may seek federal **habeas corpus** review. However, the prisoner must identify a federal right or law that gives the federal jurisdiction to consider the petition for habeas **corpus**. The U.S. SUPREME COURT, in *Swarthout v. Cooke*, __U.S.__, 131 S.Ct. 859, 178 L.Ed.2d 732 (2011), ruled that a federal **circuit court** of appeals had overstepped it jurisdiction when it granted habeas relieve to a California state prisoner who contested his parole decision. The Court made clear that **federal courts** must let states manage their parole system.

Damon Cooke was convicted of attempted first-degree MURDER in 1991 by a California state court. He was sentenced to an indeterminate term of seven years to life in prison with the possibility of parole. In November 2002 the California Parole Board determined that Cooke was not yet suitable for parole based on the "especially cruel and callous manner" of his crime. The board also said Cooke was unsuitable for parole because he had not participated fully in rehabilitative programs, he had failed to develop marketable skills, and he has committee three incidents of misconduct while in prison. The board dismissed as not credible a favorable psychological report because it contained several inconsistent and erroneous statements.

Cooke filed for a **writ** of HABEAS CORPUS in a state trial court, seeking a reversal of the board's decision. The court rejected his claim, finding that the board had some evidence to support the denial His appeals to the California Court of Appeals and the California Supreme Court were unsuccessful. In 2004 Cooke filed a habeas petition in California federal **district court**. The court denied his petition but the Ninth Circuit Court of Appeals reversed. The appeals court ruled that California's parole law created a liberty interest protected by the Due Process Clause. In addition, it found that the state parole law's standard of review for denial of parole was a "component" of that federally protected liberty interest. The standard of review, as established by the California Supreme Court, is characterized as whether "some evidence" supports the conclusion that the inmate is unsuitable for parole because "he or she currently is dangerous." The Ninth Circuit concluded that the state court had made an "unreasonable determination of the facts in light of the evidence" under the federal habeas **statute** by finding any evidence at all that Cooke posed a threat to public safety if paroled.

Another inmate, Elijah Clay, was involved with this Supreme Court appeal. Clay was convicted of first-degree murder in 1978 and in 2003 was found suitable for parole by the California Parole Board. However, the governor exercised his authority to review the case and denied Clay parole based on gravity of his crime, his past criminal record, and other factors. Clay unsuccessfully challenged his denial in state court but both the federal district court and the Ninth Circuit granted him habeas relief. Both federal courts found the governor's decision was an unreasonable application of the "some evidence" rule and was an unreasonable determination of the facts in light of the evidence presented. The state appealed both decisions to the U.S. Supreme Court.

The U.S. Supreme Court, in a unanimous *per curium* decision (no justice signed the opinion), overturned the Ninth Circuit rulings. The Court presumed the Ninth Circuit had believed it could grant habeas relief because of an error of state law or that the correct application of the state's "some evidence" rule was required by the U.S. Constitution's Due Process Clause. Both presumptions were incorrect. As to the first, the federal habeas statute "unambiguously provides" that federal habeas relief can be granted to a state prisoner only if he is in CUSTODY in violation of the Constitution, laws, or treaties of the United States. Habeas cannot be granted for errors of state law.

As for the Due Process Clause, the Court noted that a two-part analysis governs reviews. The Court first examines whether there is a liberty or property interest of which a person has been deprived. If so, the Court then inquires whether the procedures followed by the state were constitutionally sufficient. The Court agreed that the Ninth Circuit's conclusion that California law creates a liberty interest in parole was a reasonable application of the Court's prior cases. However, the Court stated that whatever liberty interested existed was a **state interest** created by California law. There is no right under the U.S. Constitution to be paroled from prison and the states "are

under no duty to offer parole to their prisoners." When a state does create a parole system and hence a liberty interest, it must provide fair procedures. In a prior case the Court had held that states must only provide minimal procedures. An inmate has a right to be heard and to be provided with a statement of the reasons why parole was denied. California's system provided these two components and the Court stated it did not have to provide anything more.

The Ninth Circuit erred in thinking the "some evidence" rule was a component of the liberty interest. The Supreme Court found that such reasoning would subject the federal courts to merits reviews of all state-prescribed procedures in cases involving liberty or property interests, including criminal prosecutions. This was wrong, for the Court had long recognized that a "mere error of state law" is not a denial of due process. The only federal right at issue was procedural. Therefore, the only "relevant inquiry" was the process Cooke and Clay received, "not whether the state court decided the case correctly."

PATENTS

Rights, granted to inventors by the federal government, pursuant to its power under Article I, Section 8, Clause 8, of the U.S. Constitution, that permit them to exclude others from making, using, or selling an invention for a definite, or restricted, period of time.

Costco v. Omega

There are times when the U.S. SUPREME COURT just cannot agree, resulting in a **split decision** (if only eight justices are considering the case). Such was the case in *Costco Wholesale Corporation v. Omega*, No. 08-1423, 131 S. Ct. 565, 562 U.S. ___ (2010), where a newly-appointed Justice ELENA KAGAN took no part in consideration or decision. This resulted in a split 4-4 decision, without published opinion, effectively affirming the decision of the lower **Circuit Court** of Appeals for the Ninth Circuit. Unfortunately, the case involved an important patent law issue; because of the SPLIT DECISION, the issue was left in a less-than-precedent-setting status.

The "first sale doctrine" in patent law, codified as Section § 109(a) of the COPYRIGHT Act, essentially provides that after the first authorized sale/distribution of a copy of a copyrighted work, the copyright owner's right to control further distribution of that copy is "exhausted" (lost) (also known as copyright exhaustion). For example, the purchase of a new book or DVD from a retail **entity** (that is authorized by the publisher or copyright owner) triggers the doctrine. Thereafter, the original purchaser can resell the book to a used book dealer or resell the DVD to someone else, and there is no copyright INFRINGEMENT. The actual **statutory** language, in pertinent part, reads:

> [T]he owner of a particular copy or phonorecord lawfully made under this title, or any person authorized by such owner, is entitled, without the authority of the copyright owner, to sell or otherwise dispose of the possession of that copy or phonorecord. 17 U.S.C. § 109(a).

In *Costco,* the Supreme Court was requested to interpret the first sale doctrine within the context of international sales. Specifically, Omega manufactures watches in Switzerland. It sells them through a global network of authorized distributors and retailers. The warehouse club retailer Costco began purchasing authentic, branded Omega watches (not "bootlegged" look-alikes) from foreign markets and reselling them in Costco's California stores. These "gray market" transactions started with unidentified third parties purchasing genuine Omega watches from the foreign markets and selling them to ENE Limited, a New York Company, which in turn sold them to Costco.

Omega's authorized retailers began to complain that they could not compete with Costco, which sold the watches for about $700 less than Omega's suggested retail price. This created a major headache for Omega because it did not have a contractual relationship with Costco; therefore, there was no breach. Further, Costco's "gray market" purchases were not illegal, so Omega was unable to stop the resale of its watches.

In 2003, Omega started engraving the backside of its watches with a small design, the "Omega Globe" containing the Omega logo, and registered the design with the U.S. Copyright Office. Following Costco's sale of approximately 43 watches in 2004, Omega filed suit in a California federal **district court** for copyright infringement, alleging unauthorized

sale of copyrighted goods under sections § 106 (3) and § 602(a). Costco argued that Omega's control over the watches was exhausted by the first sale doctrine under § 109(a) (see above).

At issue was the interrelationship between three provisions of the Copyright Act: § 109(a), § 106(3), and § 602(a), which provides that importation into the United States "without the authority of the owner of copyright under this title, of copies ... of a work that have been acquired outside the United States" is a copyright infringement.

In previous U.S. Supreme Court precedent, *Quality King Distributors Inc. v. L'anza Research International Inc.,* 523 U.S. 135, 118 S. Ct. 1125, 140 L. Ed. 2d 254 (1998), the Court held that, for purposes of the "first sale doctrine," copies made in the United States and initially sold overseas were "lawfully made under" the Copyright Act. Therefore, the first sale, albeit overseas, "exhausted" the copyright owner's right to control further distribution.

But *Quality King* differed in that the protected goods were manufactured in the United States. Here, in *Costco,* the goods were both manufactured and sold overseas, then imported to the United States for resale.

The district court ruled in favor of Costco, granting **summary judgment** on the basis of the first sale doctrine under § 109(a). On appeal, the Ninth Circuit looked to its own precedent to determine whether it must now OVERRULE such precedent in light of *Quality King.* It found that its own precedent did not conflict with the Supreme Court's decision in *Quality King,* which did not address foreign-manufactured goods.

Accordingly, the Ninth Circuit summarized its general rule that § 109(a) refers only to copies legally made in the United States. Therefore, the first sale doctrine under § 109 (a) is not available as a defense to infringement claims under § 106(3) and § 602(a). Omega neither manufactured nor authorized sale of its watches in the United States.

The Ninth Circuit then reversed the decision of the district court and ruled in favor of Omega, finding that Costco was not authorized to sell its watches in the United States, constituting copyright infringement. The equally divided U.S. Supreme Court affirmed without opinion.

Global-Tech Appliances v. SEB

Under patent law, liability for patent INFRINGE-
MENT generally attaches directly to the infring-
ing actor. However, Section § 271(b) of the
COPYRIGHT Act of 1952 (35 U.S.C. § 271 *et seq.*)
addresses the concept of induced infringement, stating that "[w]hoever actively induces
infringement of a patent shall be liable as an
infringer." In *Global-Tech Appliances v. SEB*,
No. 10-6, 131 S. Ct. 458, 563 U.S. ___ (2011),
the U.S. SUPREME COURT held that under § 271
(b), induced infringement requires knowledge
that the induced acts constitute patent
infringement, and described what constitutes
"knowledge."

SEB, a French maker of consumer appliances, had, in the 1980s, invented a "cool-
touch" deep fryer for home cooking use,
having external surfaces that remained cool
during the deep-frying process. In 1991, SEB
obtained a U.S. patent for its design and
eventually began selling the cool-touch fryer
in the United States under its well-known
"T-Fal" brand. The SEB fryer was considered
superior to other products on the market and
was a commercial success.

In 1997, an American competitor of SEB,
Sunbeam Products Inc., negotiated with Pentalpha Enterprises, Ltd., a Hong Kong subsidiary of Global-Tech Appliances, Inc., to supply
Sunbeam with deep fryers. In order to develop
a deep fryer for Sunbeam, Pentalpha purchased an SEB fryer in Hong Kong and copied
all of its designed components except its
cosmetic features. (Because the purchased
SEB fryer was made for sale in a foreign
market, it bore no U.S. patent markings on it.)
After copying the design, Pentalpha retained
an attorney to conduct a right-to-use study.
Pentalpha refrained from telling the attorney
that it had copied the design directly from
SEB's product.

Because SEB's Hong Kong product did not
have a U.S. patent number on it, the attorney
failed to locate SEB's patent. In August 1997,
the attorney issued an opinion letter that
Pentalpha's deep fryer did not infringe any
PATENTS that he had found. Within days,
Pentalpha commenced selling deep fryers to
Sunbeam, resold in the United States under the
Sunbeam brand name. By using a manufacturer
with lower manufacturing costs, Sunbeam was
able to offer its deep fryer at a lower price to
consumers, undercutting SEB in the market.

As SEB's customers began defecting to
Sunbeam, SEB filed suit against Sunbeam for
patent infringement. Sunbeam notified Pentalpha, but undeterred, Pentalpha continued to
market its deep fryer to Fingerhut and Mon-
tgomery Ward, each selling the product under
their respective brand names.

Sunbeam settled the lawsuit with SEB, then
sued Pentalpha directly. It asserted two theories
of recovery, both direct infringement under
§ 271(a) and indirect (induced) infringement
under § 271(b) of the Copyright Act. The gist of
the complaint was that Pentalpha had "actively
induced" Sunbeam and other purchasers of
Pentalpha's deep fryer to sell or offer to sell
them (under their own TRADEMARKS) in violation
of SEB's patent rights.

The federal jury found in favor for PLAINTIFF
SEB on the induced infringement theory. The
U.S. **Circuit Court** of Appeals for the Federal
Circuit affirmed.

The issue on appeal related to what kind or
level of knowledge on the part of Pentalpha
did plaintiffs need to show (that the deep fryer
product whose design was copied by Pentalpha
was protected by registered patent), in order to
prove that Pentalpha "actively induced"
infringement under § 271(b). The actual
statutory language is devoid of any mention
of intent as a criterion for imposing liability.

The Federal Circuit **appellate court** held
that induced infringement under § 271(b)
required a showing that the alleged infringer
knew or should have known that his actions
would induce actual infringements. This, therefore, required proof that the alleged infringer
knew of the patent. In this case, held the federal
circuit court of appeals, although there was no
direct proof that Pentalpha knew of SEB's
patent, there was sufficient proof that it
deliberately disregarded a known risk that such
protected patent rights existed, in light of the
notice it received from Sunbeam over SEB's
lawsuit. According to the federal **appellate**
court, such "deliberate indifference" (flagrant
disregard) was no different than, but was rather
a form of, actual knowledge.

Delivering the U.S. Supreme Court's 8-1
opinion affirming the Federal Circuit, Justice
SAMUEL ALITO agreed that induced infringement

under § 271(b) requires knowledge that the induced acts constitute patent infringement. The Court noted that pre-1952 **case law** did not treat induced infringement as a separate theory for indirect liability, but treated it as contributory infringement, i.e., the aiding and **abetting** of direct infringement by another party. When Congress enacted § 271, it expressly separated contributory infringement into two distinct offenses: induced infringement under § 271(b) and the sale of a component of a patented invention under § 271(c).

However, the Court failed to adopt (and agreed with Petalpha) that "deliberate indifference to a known risk that a patent exists is not an appropriate standard under § 271(b)." Instead, the Court adopted the "willful blindness" standard derived from **criminal law** as the appropriate standard. The Court went on to explain that a finding of willful blindness under § 271(b) requires a showing that (1)defendant must subjectively believe that there is a high probability that a patent exists; and (2)defendant must take deliberate actions to avoid learning of that fact. These requirements serve to separate willful blindness from mere recklessness or NEGLIGENCE.

Applying these requirements to the facts at hand, the Court noted that Pentalpha believed that SEB's deep fryer represented advanced technology that would be valuable in a U.S. market, as evidenced by the fact that Pentalpha copied the entire design and left out only the cosmetic details of SEB's fryer. The Court also found, as revealing, that Petalpha **chose** to copy an overseas model of SEB's deep fryer, aware that it would not bear any U.S. patent markings. But even more telling, said the Court, was Pentalpha's decision not to inform its attorney that the product he was specifically evaluating for a right-to-use (without patent infringement) had been copied from SEB's deep fryer. The totality of these facts clearly showed Pentalpha's conduct as having reached far beyond mere recklessness.

Although alone in his DISSENT, Justice ANTHONY KENNEDY proffered a strong one, opining that the majority was incorrect in the definition it now adopted. He contended that the majority should have remanded to the Federal Circuit for consideration of whether there was sufficient evidence of knowledge to support the jury's finding of inducement.

Microsoft Corp. v. i4i Limited Partnership

The Patent Act of 1952 establishes that courts should presume that PATENTS are valid, and party challenging a patent bears the burden of proving that the patent is invalid. The U.S. Court of Appeals for the Federal Circuit, which has jurisdiction to review patent appeals, has long required a party challenging a patent's validity to prove invalidity by clear and convincing evidence. Software giant Microsoft Corporation challenged this standard before both the Federal Circuit and the SUPREME COURT. However, in a unanimous decision in 2011, the Supreme Court ruled that the clear-and-convincing standard was correct. The result of the decision was that the Court upheld a record $290 million verdict against Microsoft awarded to a small Canadian company.

The party that sued Microsoft was i4i Limited Partnership. The company began as a software consulting company during the late 1980s. The company developed and maintained customized software for its clients. The company also created, marketed, and sold software on the open market. The company developed a method for processing and storing information about the structure of an electronic document. In 1994, i4i applied for a patent for this method, and four years later, the U.S. PATENT AND TRADEMARK OFFICE approved the patent.

The i4i patent focuses more specifically on a method that improves the method for editing electronic documents containing certain markup languages, including XML (eXtensible Markup Language). The method specifically allows a user to create custom XML by storing a document's content separately from data known as metacodes.

In 2003, Microsoft added the ability for a user of Microsoft Word to edit XML. Four years later, i4i brought its patent-infringement suit against Microsoft, arguing that the feature in Microsoft Word to process or edit custom XML infringed on the i4i patent. According to the suit, Microsoft's INFRINGEMENT was willful. Microsoft then filed a COUNTERCLAIM in which it sought a **declaratory judgment** that the i4i patent was invalid and unenforceable. The case was tried in the U.S. **District Court** for the Eastern District of Texas.

The district court denied Microsoft's motion for judgment as a MATTER OF LAW, allowing the case to proceed to the jury. The jury determined that Microsoft had infringed on i4i's patent with regard to each of the company's claims. Moreover, the jury ruled against Microsoft in its assertion that the patent was invalid. The jury then awarded $290 million in damages to i4i. After the trial, Microsoft moved for a new trial, but the district court denied Microsoft's motion.

Among the issues that Microsoft raised at the district court and on appeal was one focusing on the standard that Microsoft had to satisfy to show that the patent was invalid. The district court instructed the jury that Microsoft had the burden to prove that the patent was invalid by showing clear and convincing evidence of invalidity. The basis for this instruction was on the Federal Circuit's construction of § 282 of the Patent Act. Under that section, "[a] patent shall be presumed valid." Moreover, the **statute** provides, "[t]he burden of establishing invalidity of a patent or any claim thereof shall rest on the party asserting such invalidity." The Federal Circuit since deciding *American Hoist & Derrick Co. v. Sowa & Sons, Inc.*, 725 F.2d 1350 (Fed. Cir. 1984) has required clear-and-convincing evidence to prove invalidity, and the court rejected Microsoft's argument that the courts should apply a lower standard. *i4i Limited Partnership v. Microsoft Corporation*,, 598 F.3d 831, 848 (Fed. Cir. 2010).

The U.S. Supreme Court agreed to review the decision, focusing principally on the question of whether clear-and-convincing evidence was the proper standard. Writing for the Court, Justice SONIA SOTOMAYOR acknowledged that Congress had not expressly established the standard of proof in § 282. However, when a statute or rule established a presumption of validity in more general contexts, the **common law** required a party challenging the validity to show clear-and-convincing (or "clear and cogent evidence" according to some standards). When Congress **chose** to create a presumption of validity, Sotomayor wrote, the Congress used a term with "settled meaning in the common law."

Microsoft made several arguments about why a lower standard should apply. The company argued that before Congress had passed the Patent Act, the Court had applied the clear-and-convincing evidence standard

only in limited circumstances. However, the Court found this argument to be unpersuasive given the Court's reading of those cases. Microsoft also argued that the Federal Circuit's reading of the statute was flawed, but the Court did not find Microsoft's alternative theories to be persuasive. Microsoft also argued unsuccessfully that a lower standard should apply where evidence before the jury had not been considered by the Patent and Trademark Office. According to the Court, the language Congress used in the Act contradicts this argument.

Justice STEPHEN BREYER filed a separate concurrence in which he emphasized that the clear-and-convincing evidence applied only to questions of fact and not to questions of law. Justice CLARENCE THOMAS also concurred, arguing that he was not convinced that Congress had codified the clear-and-convincing evidence standard.

The $290 verdict is reportedly the largest patent infringement verdict ever affirmed on appeal. Loudon Owen, the chairman of i4i, said, "This is one of the most significant business cases the court has decided in decades."

Supreme Court Rules University Does Not Own Patent Outright

The U.S. Constitution gives Congress the authority to enact laws regarding inventions. Though federal patent law has grown more complex since the 1790s, the basic idea that inventors have the right to patent their inventions has remained the same. However, when an employee of a company or a university invents something, the employee may assign the rights to the organization by contract. The issue become even more complicated when the federal government provides funding to an organization that uses the money for an invention. The SUPREME COURT, in *Board of Trustees of the Leland Stanford Junior University v. Roche Molecular Systems, Inc.*, __U.S.__, S.Ct. , __L.Ed.2d__ 20011 WL 2175210(2011), ruled that a federal law does not automatically negate an inventor's right in a government-funded invention.

In 1985, Cetus, a California research company, began to develop methods of measuring the levels of human immunodeficiency virus (HIV), the virus that causes AIDS. The company developed a Nobel Prize winning technique, polymerase chain reaction, or

PCR, that was central to its efforts to quantify the amount of HIV in a blood sample. In 1988 the company began to collaborate with Stanford University's Department of Infectious Diseases to test new AIDS drugs. Mark Holodniy, a research fellow in the university department, was unfamiliar with using PCR. His supervisor allowed him to conduct research at Cetus. As a condition for gaining access to Cetus, Holodniy signed a visitor's confidentiality agreement that stated he "will assign and do[es] hereby assign" to Cetus his "right, title and interest in each of the ideas, inventions and improvements" made "as a consequence of [his] access." Holodniy worked at Cetus for nine months, in that time devising a PCR-based procedure for calculating the amount of HIV in a patient's blood. The technique gave doctors a tool to determine whether a patient would benefit from HIV therapy. He returned to Stanford and refined this method over the next few years. He also signed an agreement with Stanford, agreeing to assign his patent rights to the university. The university secured three PATENTS to the process. Meanwhile, Roche Molecular Systems acquired Cetus, including the rights Holodniy had assigned, and marketed HIV test kits that are used in hospitals and AIDS clinics worldwide. Stanford responded in 2005 by filing suit against Roche, alleging that the kits infringed on its three patents.

Stanford argued that Holodniy had no rights to assign to Roche because the university's HIV research was federally funded, giving it superior rights in the invention under the federal Bayh-Dole Act. This law gives the federal government a license to the subject invention, which Stanford did provide. The law also provides that the contractor may "elect to retain title to any subject invention." Stanford made this election. The **district court** concluded that the Bayh-Dole Act provisions meant that Holodniy had no interest to assign to Roche. It further concluded the law meant an individual inventor may obtain title to the federally funded invention only after the government and the contractor declined to do so. The Court of Appeals for the Federal Circuit overturned the district court ruling. It first found that Holodniy's initial agreement with Stanford was merely a promise to assign rights in the future, whereas his agreement with Cetus

actually assigned rights in the invention to the company. Second, the appeals court ruled that the Bayh-Dole Act did not automatically void the inventor's right in a federally-funded project or void the rights Cetus obtained from Holodniy. It ordered the district court to dismiss the suit because Roche's ownership interest in the patent deprived Stanford of standing to sue for INFRINGEMENT.

The Supreme Court, in a 7-2 decision, upheld the **circuit court** of appeals. Chief Justice JOHN ROBERTS, writing for the majority, rejected the university's argument, and that of the federal government as a **friend of the court**, that the Bayh-Dole Act reordered "the normal priority of rights in an invention when the invention is conceived or first reduced to practice with the support of federal funds." Roberts acknowledged that other federal laws have divested inventors of their patent rights pursuant to federal contracts involving nuclear material, atomic energy, and inventions involving the National Aeronautics and Space Administration (NASA). However, such language was "notably absent" from the Bayh-Dole Act. There were no provisions in the law that expressly deprived inventors of their interest in federally funded inventions. All the law stated was that contractors may "elect to retain title to any subject invention." A "subject invention" was defined as "any invention of the contractor conceived or first actually reduced to practice in the performance of work under a funding agreement."

Robert's rejected Stanford's reading of this definition to mean all inventions made by the contractor's employees with the aid of federal funding, concluding that this reading "assumes Congress subtly set aside two centuries of patent law in a **statutory** definition." The Court in prior cases had rejected the idea that "mere employment is sufficient to vest title to an employee's invention in the employer." The Bayh-Dole act gave Stanford the right to elect to retain tile but it did not vest title in the university. The law "simply assures contractors that they may keep title to whatever it is they already have," and serves to clarify the order of priority of rights between the federal government and the federal contractor that already belongs to the contractor.

The Court noted that its construction of the Bayh-Dole Act was reflected in the common practice among parties operating under the law.

Contractors generally establish policies to obtain assignments from their employees. The National Institute of Health, which provided federal funds to Stanford for this research, issued guidance documents that stated an inventor has initial ownership of an invention and that contracts should have in place agreements that require the inventor to assign or give up ownership of an invention. If Stanford had drafted an "effective assignment" it would have had the protection that it sought through its interpretation of the Bayh-Dole Act.

PREEMPTION

Federal Vaccine Act Preempts Design-Defect Claims

Vaccines have proved highly effective in eliminating many infectious diseases. They became so effective that in the 1970s and 1980s that the focus shifted to those individuals who were injured by the vaccine itself. Faced with lawsuits from these plaintiffs, drug companies stopped manufacturing vaccines. Congress responded by enacting the National Childhood Vaccine Injury Act (NCVIA) in 1986. The act set up a no-fault compensation program which allowed claimants to receive compensation quickly through a fund created by an **excise** tax on each vaccine dose. The vaccine manufacturers were given significant tort-liability protections in return. The U.S. SUPREME COURT, in *Bruesewitz v. Wyeth LLC*, __U.S.__, 131 S.Ct. 1068, __L.Ed.2d__ (2011), ruled that the act preempted state tort lawsuits against vaccine manufacturers based on design-defect claims.

Hannah Bruesewitz was born in October 1991. In April 1992 she was given a DTP vaccine (diphtheria, tetanus, and pertussis) made by Lederle Laboratories, which was later purchased by Wyeth. Within 24 hours she started to experience seizures. She suffered over 100 seizures during the next month and her doctors eventually diagnosed her with a seizure disorder and developmental delay. Now a teenager, Hannah is still diagnosed with these conditions. In 1995 her parents filed a vaccine injury petition under the NCVIA with the Federal **Court of Claims**, alleging she suffered from injuries that were listed by the act as related to DTP vaccines. The act's Vaccine Injury Table lists the vaccines covered by the law, lists the compensable, adverse side effects,

and indicates how soon after vaccination those side effects should first manifest themselves. If claimants can show that they qualify under these conditions they do not have show causation. If the side effect is unlisted, the claimant bears the burden of proving that the vaccine causes the side effect. The court denied the Bruesewitzes' claims, which led them to file a state tort lawsuit against Wyeth in 2005. They alleged that defective design of the DTP vaccine was subject to **strict liability** and liability for negligent design under Pennsylvania **common law**. Wyeth moved the case to federal **district court**, which dismissed the lawsuit, finding that the two theories of liability were preempted by the NCVIA. The Third **Circuit Court** of Appeals upheld the ruling and the Supreme Court agreed to hear the case.

The Court, in a 6-2 decision (Justice Elena Kagan did not participate), upheld the Third Circuit decision. Justice ANTONIN SCALIA, writing for the majority, looked to the provision of the NCVIA that dealt with liability for vaccine manufacturers. The law stated that no vaccine manufacturer was liable for civil liability "if the injury or death resulted from side effects that were unavoidable even though the vaccine was properly prepared and was accompanied by proper directions and warnings." The term "unavoidable" meant in this context that "any remaining side effects, including those resulting from design defects, are deemed to have been unavoidable." Therefore, state tort actions based on design-defect claims are preempted. If a manufacturer could be held liable for failure to use a different design, the word "unavailable" would have no impact. A side effect of a vaccine could always have been avoidable by using a different vaccine that did not contain the harmful element. Justice Scalia concluded the language of the provision suggests that the design of a vaccine is a given, not subject to state tort claims. The NCVIA established as a complete defense unavoidability *"with respect to the particular design."*

The Bruesewitzes contended that the term "unavoidable" was a **term of art** that incorporated a comment found in the *Restatement (Second) of Torts*. They argued this comment had, by 1986, been adopted by a majority of courts to require that an "unavoidably unsafe product" "was quite incapable of being made safer for [its] intended . . . use." Justice Scalia rejected this argument, concluding that the drafters of the NCVIA did not have this comment in mind when drafting the liability provision.

The Court found that the structure of the NCVIA and of vaccine regulation in general reinforced what the liability provision stated. Manufacturers obtain a license from the FOOD AND DRUG ADMINISTRATION (FDA) that sets out the manufacturing method that must be followed and the directions and warnings that must accompany the vaccine. If a vaccine maker deviated from these terms there would be objective evidence of manufacturing defects or inadequate warnings. In addition, there are over 90 FDA regulations that regulate the manufacturing process. Design defects, on the other hand, are not mentioned in the NCVIA or FDA regulations. Justice Scalia noted that the safest design is not always the best one, for "Striking the right balance between safety and efficacy is especially difficult with respect to vaccines." While the NCVIA "micromanages" manufacturers, it is "silent on how to evaluate competing designs." This silence strongly suggested that design defects were not mentioned because they are not a basis for liability. Taxing manufacturers under the NCVIA to fund the compensation program, "while leaving their liability for design defect virtually unaltered, would hardly coax manufacturers back into the market."

Justice SONIA SOTOMAYOR, in a dissenting opinion joined by Justice RUTH BADER GINSBURG, contended that vaccine manufacturers have been subject to a legal duty to improve the designs of their vaccines "in light of advances in science and technology." The majority's decision misread the NCVIA and its LEGISLATIVE HISTORY.

PRISONERS' RIGHTS

The nature and extent of the privileges afforded to individuals kept in custody or confinement against their will because they were convicted of performing an unlawful act.

Federal Courts May Order California to Reduce Prison Population

Federal courts intervened in the 1970s and 1980s to improve conditions for inmates in state prisons, who suffered from overcrowding and poor medical care and mental health treatment. Courts issued far-ranging orders, which have come to be known as structural injunctions. Using these orders, federal district judges oversaw the implementation of changes for many years, usually with the assistance of aides known as special masters. States objected to this oversight, which meant paying for the construction of more facilities and hiring more employees. Congress responded with the Prison LITIGATION Reform Act of 1995 (PLRA), Pub. L. No. 104-134. One provision, 18 U.S.C. § 3626, requires a three-judge panel to be convened to determine whether a state can be ordered to reduce its prison population. Such a panel was convened to deal with the state of California's prison system, which holds twice as many inmates than for which the facilities were designed. The panel ordered a reduction, which triggered an appeal to the SUPREME COURT. The Court, in *Brown v. Plata*, 131 S.Ct. 1910 (2011), ruled that the panel had ruled correctly and did not violate the terms of the PLRA.

In 1990, a federal lawsuit was filed by inmates alleging that California failed to provide prisoners with minimal, adequate care for serious mental illness. The court issued an order that appointed a SPECIAL MASTER to oversee efforts to improve mental health care, but in 2002 the special master reported that care was deteriorating due to increased overcrowding. In 2001, a federal lawsuit was filed by inmates, alleging deficient medical care. The state admitted that deficiencies in medical care violated the Eighth Amendment's prohibition against **cruel and unusual punishment**, and agreed to a remedial INJUNCTION. When the state failed to comply with the terms of the order, the court in 2005 appointed a **receiver** to oversee remedial efforts. In 2008, the receiver reported continuing problems caused by overcrowding. The plaintiffs in both the mental health care and medical care cases asked the district courts to convene a three-judge court that could order the state to reductions in prison population, believing that overcrowding was the primary cause for the problems in these areas. The judges in both cased granted the requests and the cases were consolidated before a single three-judge court. The two **district court** judges were appointed to the panel by the Chief Judge of the Ninth **Circuit Court** of Appeals, along with a Ninth Circuit judge. After taking testimony and making detailed findings of fact, the court ordered California to reduce its prison population to 137.5 percent of design capacity within two years. The court found that California would not be able to reduce capacity through new construction. Therefore, it ordered the state to design a compliance plan and submit it for approval. California appealed the injunction to the Supreme Court. At the time the appeal was heard, the state needed to reduce its prison population by 37,000 persons to comply with the order. The state argued that the panel had violated the PRLA and had committed errors in determining the amount of reduction the state needed to make.

The Supreme Court, in a 5-4 decision, upheld the court order. Justice ANTHONY KENNEDY, writing for the majority, pointed to the long-standing problems in the California prison system. He agreed with the three-judge panel that overcrowding "has overtaken the limited resources of prison staff; imposed demands well beyond the capacity of medical and mental health facilities and created unsanitary and unsafe conditions that make progress in the provision of care difficult or impossible to achieve." The reduction in prison population was needed to remedy the violation of prisoners' constitutional rights. Kennedy devoted many pages of his opinion to describing the harsh conditions in California prisons. The lack of mental health care had lead to a SUICIDE rate of almost one per week, while prisoners with serious medical conditions died for lack of prompt treatment. Overcrowding in prison facilities meant placing 200 prisoners in a gymnasium monitored by as few as two or three correctional officers.

The Court found no reason to doubt the facts contained in the 184-page opinion of the three-judge panel. The issues at hand concerned the application of the PRLA provision by the three-judge panel. California argued that it was error to convene the three-judge court without giving it more time to comply with prior orders in both cases. Justice Kennedy concluded that the state had been given sufficient time, as the PRLA stated that the court may be convened if a district court had "previously entered an order for less intrusive relief that has failed to remedy" the problem. The first order in the mental health case was entered in 1995, while the court in the medical care case entered its

first order in 2002. Clearly, the courts had given California sufficient time.

Justice Kennedy also found that the panel had met the PRLA's requirement in finding that "crowding is the primary cause of the violation." He recited the many findings concerning crowding, including increased risk of unsafe and unsanitary living conditions and increased violence among prisoners and against correctional officers. California sought to undermine this argument by showing that other factors contributed to these conditions. However, the Court ruled that the three-judge panel only had to show that overcrowding was the "primary" cause of the problems. The Court also agreed that the panel had met the PRLA requirement that it find by clear and convincing evidence that "no other relief will remedy the violation of the Federal right." Justice Kennedy pointed out that the order did not mandate that prisoners be released. The order gave the state discretion to comply with the population limit by transferring inmates to county jails or facilities in other state and by constructing new facilities. However, the panel and the Court noted that California's **fiscal** crisis meant that the building of new facilities was unlikely. The order was not overbroad and the state had the opportunity to ask the three-judge panel for modifications. Justice Kennedy devoted the closing pages of his opinion to describing things the state could ask the panel to change, including an extension from two to five years.

Justices ANTONIN SCALIA and SAMUEL ALITO issued dissenting opinions, and both were joined by a justice. Justice Scalia ridiculed the panel findings and the Court's reasoning, arguing that the Court had granted the plaintiffs precisely what the PRLA sought to deny them.

PRIVACY

Federal Contract Employees Background Checks Legal

Since the early 1950s, individuals seeking to be hired as federal employees have been required to submit to government background checks. In the wake of the terrorist attacks on September 11, 2001, President GEORGE W. BUSH issued an order requiring all current and future federal contract employees to submit to the same background check. A group of current contract employees working for the National Aeronautics and Space Administration (NASA) objected to a question dealing with drug use and counseling, as well as open-ended questions on a questionnaire sent to persons used as references by the employee. The SUPREME COURT, in *National Aeronautics and Space Administration v. Nelso*, __U.S.__, 131 S.Ct. 746, 178 L.Ed.2d 667 (2011), ruled that the two inquiries did not violate the employees' right to privacy.

The case involved contractors who worked at the Jet Propulsion Laboratory (JPL) in Pasadena, California. JPL, a NASA facility, is staffed completely by contract employees. Though NASA owns JPL, the California Institute of Technology (Cal Tech) operates it under government contract. JPL has developed most of the U.S. unmanned space mission technology, including the Mars Rovers. Though JPL is charged with practical endeavors, many scientists at the facility engage in pure research topics. After NASA directed all employees at the JPL to complete the background check process by October 27, a group of 28 contract employees filed suit in federal **district court**. The group challenged a question on drug use, which asked if the employee had "used, possessed, supplied, or manufactured illegal drugs" in the last year. If the answer is yes, the employee is to provide details, including information about "any treatment or counseling received. " The form instructs the employee that a truthful response could not be used as evidence against the person in a criminal proceeding. The group also challenged open-ended questions on a form sent to former employers, schools, landlords, and other references. The form asks if the reference has "any reason to question" the employee's "honesty or trustworthiness." If also asks if the reference knows of any "adverse information" concerning the employee's "violations of the law," "financial integrity," "abuse of alcohol and/or drugs," mental or emotional stability," "general behavior or conduct," or any other matters. If the reference answers yes for any of these categories, the form calls for an explanation in the space below. That space is also available for providing additional information, whether good or bad, that may bear on "suitability for government employment or a security clearance."

The district court dismissed the lawsuit but the Ninth **Circuit Court** of Appeals reversed this decision and granted a **preliminary injunction** pending a full hearing. The appeals court found that these two issues in the background check process were likely unconstitutional. As for the employee questionnaire, the court noted that the employees found most of the questions acceptable. As to the questions concerning illegal drugs, the court believed the inquiries into recent drug involvement were needed to further the government's legitimate interest in combating illegal-drug use. However, requiring disclosure of drug treatment and counseling furthered no legitimate interest and therefore were likely unconstitutional. As to the open-ended questions asked of references, the court found these even "more problematic." The "open-ended and highly private" questions were not "narrowly tailored" to meet the government's interest in verifying contractors' identities and "ensuring the security of the JPL." These questions, like the drug questions, likely violated the employees' informational privacy rights.

The Supreme Court, in an 8-0 decision (Justice Elena Kagan did not participate), overruled the Ninth Circuit. Justice SAMUEL ALITO, writing for the Court, noted that **judicial review** of the government's challenged inquiries "must take into account the context in which they arise." When the government asks employees and their references to fill out the background check forms, it does not exercise its sovereign power "to regulate or license." Instead, the government acts in its capacity "as proprietor" and manager of its "internal operation." The Court has long given the government more leeway in dealing with citizen employees that when it brings its sovereign power to "bear on citizens at large."

Justice Alito noted that the two forms in question are part of a standard employment background check that is used by millions of private employers. In addition, the government began using similar background checks for all federal service employees in 1953. Reasonable investigations of applicants and employees help the government to ensure the security of its facilities and in employing "a competent, reliable workforce." The JPL employees argued that because they were contract employees and not civil servants that the government's authority to manage its affairs was diminished. The Court disagreed, concluding that the government's interest as a proprietor was not subject to such formalities. There were no relevant distinctions as a practical matter between NASA civil servants and contract employees; the two classes of employees performed "functionally equivalent duties." The multibillion dollar work at the JPL was of critical importance to NASA's mission, giving the government a strong interest in conducting "basic background checks into the contract employees minding the store."

As to the particular issues raised by the employees, Justice Alito found that the drug questions and the open-ended reference questions were reasonable, employment-related inquiries that furthered the government's "interests in managing its internal operations. The follow-up drug use question was used as a "mitigating factor in determining whether to grant employees long-term access to federal facilities. The open-ended reference questions were "reasonably aimed at identifying capable employees who will faithfully conduct the Government's business." Moreover, requiring a reference to answer a long list of reasons as to why a person might not be suitable for a particular would be a "daunting job." Alito noted that "references do not have all day to answer a laundry list of specific questions. " Finally, the Court pointed out that the information provided in the background checks was confidential and protected by the federal Privacy Act. Concerns about informational privacy were addressed through this law and other administrative procedures.

RELIGION

Arizona Christian School Tuition Organization v. Winn

The FIRST AMENDMENT to the U.S. Constitution provides that "Congress shall make no law respecting an establishment of religion." This provision also applies to state governments through the Due Process Clause of the FOURTEENTH AMENDMENT. In previous cases, the SUPREME COURT has recognized that in some limited circumstances, a taxpayer may have standing to challenge a government program that aids religious organizations. However, in 2011, the Court narrowed this exception by deciding that taxpayers in Arizona did have standing to challenge an Arizona tax-credit program. The case of *Arizona Christian School Tuition Organization v. Winn*, Nos. 09-987, 09-991, 2011 WL 1225707 (U.S. April 4, 2011) marked the first time that Justice Elena Kagan filed a DISSENT.

In 1997, the Arizona legislature approved a **statute** permitting taxpayers to claim dollar-for-dollar tax credits for contributions to school tuition organizations, known as STOs. The statute defines an STO as a private nonprofit organization that allocates a minimum of 90 percent of its funds for tuition grants and scholarships for qualifying private schools in the state. The statute does not prohibit STOs from proving scholarships and funding for religious-based private schools. The maximum credit per year is $500 for individuals and $1,000 for married couples filing jointly. Any taxpayer in Arizona may claim the credit, irrespective of whether the taxpayer has children or otherwise pays private school tuition.

A group of citizens challenged the legislation before it became operative. In 1999, the Arizona Supreme Court held that the statute violated neither the Establishment Clause of the U.S. Constitution nor the comparable provision of the Arizona Constitution. *Kotterman v. Killian*, 972 P.2d 626 (Ariz. 1999). A group of different plaintiffs then sued the director of Arizona's Department of Revenue in the U.S. **District Court** for the District of Arizona. The district court determined that the Tax INJUNCTION Act, 28 U.S.C. § 1341 barred the suit, but the Ninth **Circuit Court** of Appeals reversed the district court and the U.S. Supreme Court affirmed the Ninth Circuit's opinion. *Winn v. Killian*, 307 F.3d 1011 (9th Cir. 2002), *aff'd*, 542 U.S. 88 (2004).

After the case was remanded, the district court allowed two STOs and two parents of scholarship recipients to intervene as defendants in the case. One of the STOs that intervened, Arizona Christian School Tuition Organization, only gives scholarships to religious schools. The defendants moved for the court dismiss the suit, raising among other arguments that the taxpayers lacked standing to bring the suit. The district court ruled that the program did not violate the Establishment Clause, but the Ninth Circuit reversed. According to the Ninth Circuit, the taxpayers who brought suit had standing to sue, and the plaintiffs had stated a valid claim for a violation of the Establishment Clause. *Winn v. Arizona Christian School Tuition Organization*, 562 F.3d 1002 (9th Cir. 2009).

The Ninth Circuit based much of its opinion on the Supreme Court's decision in *Flast v. Cohen*, 392 U.S. 83, 88 S. Ct. 1942, 20 L. Ed. 2d 947 (1968). The Court in *Flast* recognized the taxpayers effectively suffer an injury when government spending provides aid to religion. Accordingly, the principle established in *Flast* and its progeny has been that the challenged program involves "a sufficient nexus between the taxpayer's standing as a taxpayer and the ... [legislative] exercise of taxing and spending power." *Bowen v. Kendrick*, 487 U.S. 589, 108 S. Ct. 2562, 101 L. Ed. 2d 520 (1988).

The Supreme Court reviewed the decision, and with a vote of 5-4, reversed the Ninth Circuit. Justice ANTHONY KENNEDY delivered the opinion for the majority. Kennedy reviewed the much of the Court's doctrine regarding taxpayer standing before turning to the issue of standing under *Flast*. Kennedy stressed that *Flast* established a "narrow exception" to the general rule that a taxpayer lacks standing. The Court's focus in *Flast* was on government spending. However, in the case of the Arizona statute, the issue was not about government expenditures but instead about tax credits. Kennedy found the distinction to be meaningful. He wrote, "A dissenter whose tax dollars are 'extracted and spent' knows that he has in some small measure been made to contribute to an establishment in violation of conscience." By comparison, when the government decides to give a tax credit, the decision essentially means that the government has declined to impose the tax. According to Kennedy, the dissenting taxpayer has not spent or contributed anything. Accordingly, Kennedy determined that the rule in *Flast* did not provide a basis for taxpayer standing and, accordingly, the taxpayers in the case lacked such standing.

Kagan's dissent strongly stated that the majority's opinion "ravag[ed] *Flast*" and "devastates taxpayer standing in Establishment Clause cases." Kagan saw no meaningful difference between a government expenditure and a tax credit. According to her dissent, "The Court's opinion thus offers a roadmap—more truly, just a one-step instruction—to any government that wishes to insulate its financing of religious activity from legal challenge. Structure the funding as a tax expenditure, and *Flast* will not stand in the way. No taxpayer will have standing to object."

While liberal groups, including the AMERICAN CIVIL LIBERTIES UNION, decried the decision, others celebrated it. According to some commentators, the decision could open the door for programs providing for school vouchers. According to this argument, the case's main principle is that because the donations (i.e., vouchers) can be made with pre-tax dollars, the government never has the money, and the program does not violate the Establishment Clause.

9th Circuit Rules Pretrial Detention Facilities Covered by Religious Freedom Law

Congress passed the Religious Land Use and Institutionalized Persons Act of 2000 (RLUIPA), 42 U.S.C. § 2000cc-1 et seq., to protect the religious freedoms of institutionalized persons who are dependent on the government's permission and accommodation for exercise of their religion. The act prohibits state and local governments from imposing "a substantial burden on the religious exercise of a person residing in or confined to an institution" unless the government shows that imposing that burden "is the least restrictive means" of furthering a "compelling governmental interest." The term "institution" includes a jail, prison, other correctional facilities, and "a pretrial detention facility." The Ninth **Circuit Court** of Appeals was called upon to decide whether a courthouse holding facility was an "institution" as defined by RLUIPA in *Khatib v. County of Orange*, __F.3d__ 2011 WL 873301 (2011).

Souhair Khatib, a practicing Muslim, wore a hijab or headscarf when she appeared in Orange County , California County Superior Court with her husband to ask for an extension to complete their 30 days of COMMUNITY SERVICE for WELFARE **fraud**. The court revoked her PROBATION and ordered her taken into CUSTODY. Khatib was handcuffed and taken to the Santa Clara Courthouse's holding facility. During booking a male officer ordered her to remove the headscarf. Having her head uncovered in public, especially in front of men outside her immediate family, was a serious breach of Khatib's faith. Khatib explained her religious beliefs, the fact this would be a humiliating experience, and asked that she be allowed to wear it. She was warned that the headscarf would be removed by male officers if she did not do it voluntarily. Khatib complied. She spent most of the day in the holding cell in view of mail officers and inmates, which caused her great discomfort and distress. At a hearing in the afternoon the court reinstated Khatib's probation and gave her extra time to complete her community service.

Khatib filed a complaint against the county, the sheriff, and the courthouse officers, alleging that the removal of the hijab violated RLUIPA. The federal **district court** dismissed her claims on the grounds that the courthouse holding facility was not an institution as defined by RLUIPA. The court noted the differences between longer-term facilities and courthouse holding facilities, concluding that RLUIPA did not apply to "temporary and transitory" facilities.

Khatib appealed to the Ninth Circuit, which overturned the district court decision. Judge M. Margaret McKeown, writing for the three-judge panel, applied the plain meaning rule to the interpretation of the RLUIPA provision. Section 3 of the act provided that an individual must have been "residing in or confined to "a covered "institution" to invoke the law's protections. RLUIPA incorporated by reference the definition of "institution" from the CIVIL RIGHTS of Institutionalized Persons Act of 1980, (CRIPA) 42 U.S.C. §1997 *et seq*, which defines the term to include "any facility or institution" that is "a jail, prison, or other correctional facility [or] pretrial detention facility." The appeals court found that under "the ordinary, common meaning of these terms, the Santa Ana Courthouse holding facility falls with the definitions of 'pretrial detention facility" and of "jail."

Judge McKeown found that the **best evidence** for this conclusion came from an annual report issued by the Orange County courts. The report listed the courthouse facility as one of the county's adult jail facilities and stated that it was used to confine persons "solely for the purpose of a court appearance for a period not exceeding 12 hours." Though RLUIPA and CRIPA did not define "pretrial detention facility," dictionary definitions and court cases revealed that the most common definition of a "pretrial detainee" is "an individual who is held in custody pending **adjudication** of guilt or innocence." Therefore, a pretrial detention facility is one "where individuals who are not yet convicted are held pending court proceedings." The Orange County report noted that the facility was a secure detention facility and was used for confinement of persons. Therefore, the appeals court's conclusion "could hardly be clearer" that the plain meaning of a pretrial detention facility described the Orange County holding facility. In addition, it was not contested by the county that Khatib had been confined to the facility.

The court rejected the county's argument that RLUIPA was limited to protecting inmates at long-term facilities with residential capabilities. Judge McKeown noted that RLUIPA did not include "any temporal restriction on the term 'institution.'" She also pointed to language in the act that the law should be construed liberally in favor of religious freedom. The appeals court applied a similar analysis to the term "jail," as a pretrial detention facility could also be classified as one. Jail was not defined in RLUIPA or CRIPA, but the common dictionary meaning of jail is a building for the confinement of persons held in lawful custody. Judge McKeown concluded that the courthouse facility could be considered a jail and that it "would not be surprising to find functionally identical facilities labeled as a jail in one jurisdiction and a pretrial detention facility in another."

The court's reversal allowed Khatib to press her case but Judge McKeown stated that under RLUIPA the county would be allowed to argue that the accommodation asked by Khatib was excessive, imposed unjustified burdens on other institutionalized persons, or jeopardized the "the effective functioning of an institution."

Federal Courts Uphold Use of "Under Gods" in Pledges of Allegiance

Three different circuit courts of appeals in 2010 considered whether the phrase "under God" violates the Establishment Clause of the FIRST

AMENDMENT to the U.S. Constitution. In each of the three cases, the courts voted that the phrase was not unconstitutional. The challenges were addressed by the courts in the First, Fifth, and Ninth Circuits.

Congress has approved several iterations of the Pledge of ALLEGIANCE. The original version was approved in 1892, and it read as follows: "I pledge allegiance to my flag and the republic for which it stands: one nation indivisible with liberty and justice for all." The Pledge underwent four revisions between 1892 and 1954, with the final version inserting the phrase "under God" so that the Pledge now reads as: "I pledge allegiance to the flag of the United States of America, and to the republic for which it stands, one nation under God, indivisible, with liberty and justice for all." 4 U.S.C. § 4.

The First Amendment to the Constitution provides, "Congress shall make no law respecting an establishment of religion … " Several individuals have challenged the Pledge in the past, arguing that laws mandating students to recite it violate the Establishment Clause. Courts have historically upheld the Pledge's constitutionality.

The first federal **appellate court** to address a challenge to the Pledge in 2010 was the Ninth Circuit. In 2002, a panel of the Ninth Circuit considered a challenge brought by Michael Newdow, an atheist who said that a school district's policy of requiring his daughter to recite the Pledge violated his right to direct his child's religious upbringing. The panel agreed with Newdow, but he lost the case on further appeal when the U.S. SUPREME COURT ruled that he did not have standing to assert his claim. The basis of his loss of standing was that he had lost CUSTODY of his daughter.

Newdow was again a PLAINTIFF in an action first considered by the U.S. **District Court** for the Eastern District of California. He and other plaintiffs, including at least one with full custody of a child, challenged the practice in California of having school children recite the Pledge. The district court agreed with Newdow and the other plaintiffs on the basis of previous cases in the Ninth Circuit. Thus, the district court entered a RESTRAINING ORDER preventing California schools from requiring students to recite the Pledge. *Newdow v. United States Congress*, 383 F. Supp. 2d 1229 (E.D. Cal. 2005).

A panel of the Ninth Circuit reviewed other historical documents that contained religious references. This included the DECLARATION OF INDEPENDENCE, which states, "We hold these truths to be self-evident, that all men are created equal, *that they are endowed by their Creator* with certain unalienable Rights, that among these are Life, Liberty, and the Pursuit of Happiness" (emphasis added). In other contexts, mere references to God or religion by the government have not violated the Establishment Clause. After reviewing the history and purpose of the Pledge, the Ninth Circuit concluded that "the Pledge is one of allegiance to our Republic, not of allegiance to God or to any religion. Furthermore, Congress' ostensible and predominant purpose when it enacted and amended the Pledge over time was patriotic, not religious." Accordingly, the Ninth Circuit reversed the district court's decision. *Newdow v. Rio Linda Union School Dist.*, 597 F.3d 1007 (9th Cir. 2010).

The First Circuit considered a similar challenge brought by a group known as the Freedom from Religion Foundation and several groups of parent. New Hampshire state law requires school children to recite the pledge each day. The law allows students to stand or sit in silence if they do not wish to participate. Like the Ninth Circuit, the First Circuit determined that the Pledge had a secular purpose, that New Hampshire law does not coerce children into participating in religion, and that the law did not impair parents' abilities to instruct their children regarding religion. *Freedom from Religion Foundation v. Hanover School District*, 626 F.3d 1 (1st Cir. 2010).

The Fifth Circuit considered a somewhat different matter. The Texas Legislature in 2007 approved an amendment to a **statute** establishing a state pledge of allegiance. The statute requires students to state the following: "Honor the Texas flag; I pledge allegiance to thee, Texas, one state under God, one and indivisible." Parents may excuse their children from reciting this pledge. According to the history surrounding the change, which added the phrase "under God," the sponsor of the legislation wanted the state pledge to mirror the national Pledge.

Several parents challenged the new law, arguing that the law violated the Establishment Clause. The Fifth Circuit noted that though the Supreme Court had not finally resolved the question of whether the national Pledge is constitutional, the Court in **dicta** had suggested several times that it was. The court likewise reviewed holdings from other federal **appellate** courts, including the Ninth Circuit's 2010 opinion in *Newdow*. Like the other **federal courts**, the Fifth Circuit panel reviewed whether the state pledge had a secular purpose, whether its principal or primary effect was to **advance** religion, and whether the law created an excessive government entanglement with religion. After determining that the Texas law did none of these, the court ruled that the state pledge did not violate the Establishment Clause. *Croft v. Perry*, 624 F.3d 157 (5th Cir. 2010).

With these opinions, the First, Fifth, and Ninth Circuits joined the Fourth and Seventh Circuits in upholding the Pledge as constitutional.

Sossamon v. Texas

In 2000, Congress passed the Religious Land Use and Institutionalized Persons Act (RLUIPA), 42 U.S.C. §§ 2000cc **et seq.** to prevent governments from placing burdens on inmates and other institutionalized persons on their religious worship. Under the act, a PLAINTIFF may assert a **statutory** violation against a state actor and "obtain appropriate relief against a government." Questions arose about whether this law waived state **sovereign immunity**, allowing plaintiffs to recover monetary damages against a state when the plaintiffs' religious rights were violated. In *Sossamon v. Texas*, No. 08-1438 (April 20, 2011), the U.S. SUPREME COURT ruled that the **statute** did not waive SOVEREIGN IMMUNITY, thus denying a claim brought by an inmate who alleged that the State of Texas deprived him of his free exercise of his religious beliefs.

The origins of the RLUIPA date back to the Court's decision in *Employment Division, Department of Human Resources of Oregon v. Smith*, 494 U.S. 872, 110 S. Ct. 1595, 108 L. Ed. 2d 876 (1990), in which the Court rejected the application of a heightened level of scrutiny for state acts that allegedly infringed in a person's free exercise of religion. In response to the decision, Congress enacted the Religious

Freedom Restoration Act of 1993 (RFRA), 42 U.S.C. §§ 2000bb et seq., which stated that it would restore a compelling interest test to cases in which the "free exercise of religion was substantially burdened." However, the Court responded in 1997 by declaring that Congress had exceeded its constitutional power under the FOURTEENTH AMENDMENT and struck down the law in *City of Boerne v. Flores*, 521 U.S. 507, 117 S. Ct. 2157, 138 L. Ed. 2d 624 (1997).

Three years later, Congress approved the RLUIPA pursuant to Congress' power under the Spending Clause and **Commerce Clause**. The new statute only applied to land-use regulation and restrictions on the exercise of religion by institutionalized persons. The RLUIPA borrowed language from the RFRA, including ADOPTION of the compelling interest test when a government imposes a substantial burden on an institutionalized person's free exercise of religion. The RLUIPA also borrowed another provision regarding private causes of action. The provision states: "A person may assert a violation of [RLUIPA] as a claim or defense in a judicial proceeding and obtain appropriate relief against a government."

Henry Leroy Sossamon is an inmate at the Robertson Prison Unit near Abiline, Texas. He claimed that he was denied access to the prison chapel to engage in Christian worship and that the alternative offered by the prison were insufficient. More specifically, the alternative venues to conduct worship lack Christian symbols or furnishings, such as an altar and cross, and do not allow prisoners to receive holy communion. Moreover, Sossamon complained that religious services were constantly interrupted by security personnel. If a prisoner refuses to return to work in order to complete his **prayer** or devotion, the prisoner could be subjected to harassment and a strip search. He presented evidence that a inmate who has been placed on cell restriction for disciplinary reasons is refused the right to attend religious services.

Sossamon brought a **pro se** suit against the State of Texas and several defendants, arguing that prison officials violated his constitutional rights as well as rights guaranteed under RLUIPA. Other claims were based on a Texas statute that is similar to the RLUIPA. The U.S. **District Court** for the Western District of Texas ruled against Sossamon on each of claims. In particular, the district court held that the prison had not substantially burdened his religious freedom by refusing to allow him to use the chapel for religious services, noting that the prison's policy of requiring inmates to use a classroom facility was sufficient. *Sossamon v. Lone Star State of Texas*, 713 F. Supp. 2d 657 (W.D. Tex. 2007). On appeal, the Fifth **Circuit Court** of Appeals affirmed the district court's opinion on most points but reversed the lower court with regard to the prison's policy of the prisoner using the prison chapel. (By the time the case reached the Supreme Court, however, the prison had changed its policy and allowed inmates to use the chapel subject to some safety precautions.) In particular, the Fifth Circuit ruled that the RLUIPA did not waive state sovereign IMMUNITY, and this immunity prevented Sossamon from recovering money damages from the state. *Sossamon v. Lone Star State of Texas*, 560 F.3d 316 (5th Cir. 2009).

In a 6-2 decision, the Supreme Court affirmed the Fifth Circuit. Writing for the majority, Justice CLARENCE THOMAS acknowledged that both the State of Texas and Sossamon had made plausible arguments about the meaning of "appropriate relief" as stated in the statute. However, Thomas reiterated a general standard the Court had established in prior cases: "[W]here a statute is susceptible of multiple plausible interpretations, including one preserving immunity, we will not consider a State to have waived its sovereign immunity." With regard to the RLUIPA, Thomas concluded that the statute was "not so free from ambiguity" that the Court would conclude that Texas had agreed to waive its immunity by accepting federal funds. The Court likewise rejected other similar arguments and affirmed the Fifth Circuit's decision.

Justice SONIA SOTOMAYOR, joined by Justice STEPHEN BREYER, dissented. Sotomayor found it "difficult to understand" the majority's basis for concluding that the statute did not provide clear notice that the phrase "appropriate relief" would include monetary damages against the state. The majority concluded that the statute provided clear notice that a plaintiff may receive equitable relief under the statute, but the same was not true of damages. She noted that "sovereign immunity is not simply a defense against certain classes of remedies—it is a defense against being sued at all." In sum, she believed that "the majority's decision significantly undermines Congress' ability to provided needed **redress** for violations of individuals' rights under federal law. . . ."

RIGHT TO COUNSEL

Turner v. Rogers

The SIXTH AMENDMENT to the U.S. Constitution guarantees to criminal defendants the right to legal counsel (among other rights). In *Turner v. Rogers*, No. 10-10, 564 U.S. ___ (2011), which was not a criminal proceeding, but rather, a civil matter in a South Carolina family court, a judge sentenced Michael Turner to one year in prison for "contempt of court" in failing to pay court-ordered CHILD SUPPORT. Turner could not afford legal counsel, let alone the child support. The question before the U.S. SUPREME COURT was whether the 14th Amendment's Due Process Clause requires states to provide counsel to indigent persons potentially facing such INCARCERATION in a civil CONTEMPT proceeding, parallel to the Sixth Amendment's requirement in criminal proceedings. (The 14th Amendment to the U.S. Constitution prohibits states from depriving a person of life, liberty, or property, without due process of law.)

In a fact-specific decision, a narrow majority of the Court held that it did not, where the custodial parent entitled to receive child support is also not represented by counsel (as in this case). But, with further regard to due process, the Court issued a cautionary statement that states must nonetheless have alternative procedures in place to assure a fundamentally fair determination regarding potential incarceration for willful contempt of court: whether the supporting parent is even able to comply with the child support order.

Starting with relevant South Carolina law, the state family courts enforce their child support orders through civil contempt proceedings. On a monthly basis, family court clerks review outstanding child support orders, identify parents who have fallen behind more than five days in their payments, and then issue "show cause" orders to them (an order to appear before the court to "show cause" why he or she should not be held in contempt of court). S.C. Rule Family Ct. 24 (2011). The "show cause" order cites the relevant support order, the amount in **arrears**, and a date for a court hearing. At the hearing, a parent may show his or her inability to pay, to demonstrate that he or she is not in willful contempt. However, if the parent fails to make the required showing, the court may hold him or her in civil contempt, punishable by up to one year in prison. S.C. Code Ann. § 63-3-620.

In June 2003, a South Carolina family court entered an order requiring Turner to pay $51.73 in child support on a weekly basis to Rebecca Rogers, to help support their child. In the ensuing months and years, Turner frequently missed payments or paid them late. On four different occasions, he had been sentenced to 90 days' imprisonment, but usually came up with the money just before or during the first few days of serving in jail. A fifth time, he could not pay and spent six months in jail. After his release, he remained in ARREARS with his payments. In March 2006, he received a new "show cause" order from the family court. Turner failed to appear and the action was postponed until a civil contempt hearing was scheduled in January 2008. Both parents appeared without counsel.

At the hearing, during which Turner was advised that his arrearage amounted to $5,728.76, the judge asked Turner if there was anything he wanted to say. Turner replied that after release from the last jail sentence, he got "back on dope," although he paid "a little bit here and there" (to Rogers) after he got back to work. He then told the court that "in September" he had broken his back and was "laid up for two months," which served to break his drug habit. He then pleaded with the judge, "And, now I'm off the dope and everything. I just hope that you give me a chance. I don't know what else to say. I mean, I know I done wrong, and I should have been paying and helping her, and I'm sorry. I mean, dope had a hold to me."

After asking Rogers if she had anything to say, the judge found Turner "in willful contempt" and sentenced him to 12 months imprisonment. He also placed a **lien** on any SOCIAL SECURITY disability benefits Turner might receive. The judge further added that he would not allow Turner any good time or work credits, but would allow daily work-release if Turner got a job, and the only way Turner's sentence could be relieved would be if Turner paid the $5,728.76 in full. When Turner asked

why he would not be eligible for good-time or work credits, the judge said, "Because that's my ruling."

The judge made no express finding concerning Turner's ability to pay, nor did he ask any follow-up questions or otherwise address the ability-to-pay issue. Importantly, the family court judge, after the hearing, filled out a prewritten form, entitled, "Order for Contempt of Court," which included the following printed statement:

> Defendant (was) (was not) gainfully employed and/or (had) (did not have) the ability to make these support payments when due. The judge did not circle any of the choices indicated on the statement, i.e., signed the form without indicating whether Turner was even able to make the payments.

While serving his sentence, Turner gained the assistance of pro bono counsel. An appeal was filed on his behalf claiming that the U.S. Constitution entitled him to legal counsel at his contempt hearing. Although the South Carolina Supreme Court did not hear his case until after he had completed his sentence, it rejected his "right to counsel" claim, noting that such right only attached to criminal proceedings because those proceedings involved significantly different "constitutional safeguards" than Turner's situation. And the right to government-paid counsel, said the court, was not one of those safeguards.

In its narrow decision, the U.S. Supreme Court agreed, but vacated and remanded on general Due Process concerns. The Court noted that it is well established that a court may not impose punishment for civil contempt when it is clearly established that the person held in contempt is unable to comply with the underlying order. *Hicks v. Feiock,* 485 U.S. 624, 108 S. Ct. 1423, 99 L. Ed. 2d 721 (1988). Citing other Supreme Court precedent, the Court also noted that previous cases have found a presumption of a RIGHT TO COUNSEL in civil cases *only* where incarceration is threatened, and even then, not in all cases. Civil contempt proceedings to compel support payments invoke "specific dictates of due process," that require the examination of distinct factors to determine if a right to counsel attaches, said the Court.

To reduce the risk of a constitutional deprivation of liberty, said the Court, due process requires (1) notice to a civil contempt

DEFENDANT that his "ability to pay" is a critical issue in the contempt proceeding; (2) the use of a form that elicits relevant financial information from him; (3) an opportunity for him to respond to questions and statements regarding his financial status; and (4) an express finding by the court that he has the ability to pay. Finally, if the opposing party/parent appears without counsel, such asymmetry in representation would also warrant no need to provide counsel for the person considered in contempt.

Justice STEPHEN BREYER was joined by Justices Kennedy, Ginsburg, Sotomayor, and Kagan. Justice CLARENCE THOMAS filed a dissenting opinion, joined in part by Chief Justice Roberts and Justice Alito, essentially saying that the Due Process Clause of the FOURTEENTH AMENDMENT did not provide such a right to counsel in civil contempt proceedings, and that this was the only question before the Court, period.

RIPARIAN RIGHTS

The rights, which belong to landowners through whose property a natural watercourse runs, to the benefit of such stream for all purposes to which it can be applied.

Montana v. Wyoming

When legal controversies exist between two states, the U.S. SUPREME COURT has **original jurisdiction** over the matter, pursuant to Article III, Section 2 of the U.S. Constitution. (It also has exclusive jurisdiction under 28 U.S.C. 1251.) Accordingly, the high court sits as trial court and considers the dispute on the merits, rather than on an **appellate** review basis. In *Montana v. Wyoming and North Dakota*, No. 137, Orig., 563 U.S. ___ (2011), two states disagreed over respective rights to water coming from the Tongue and Powder rivers, both tributaries to the massive Yellowstone River. The controversy stemmed from disagreement over the meaning and scope of terms in the 1950 Yellowstone River Compact, to which the states of Montana, Wyoming, and North Dakota were signatories.

Specifically, Article V of the Compact provides:

> Appropriative rights to the beneficial uses of the water of the Yellowstone River System existing in each signatory State as of January 1, 1950, shall continue to be enjoyed in accordance with the laws governing the acquisition and use of water under the doctrine of appropriation.

In apparent reliance on the above language, Montana filed a bill of complaint in 2007, alleging that Wyoming had violated Article V by allowing its upstream, existing (pre-1950) water users to switch from flood irrigation to sprinkler irrigation systems. This, Montana argued, increased crop consumption of water as well as decreased the volume of wastewater runoff that returned to the river system. In turn, the decreased wastewater runoff left less water for downstream (pre-1950) users, who were equally entitled to the water under the Compact. Essentially, the argument was that Wyoming was using more than its share of the precious water, and that Montana's users could therefore not "continue to enjoy" their "appropriative rights" under the language of the Compact.

Importantly, Montana conceded that Wyoming's users were existing pre-1950 users. Rather, Montana complained that Wyoming had incorporated a number of new, post-1950 *uses* that threatened water availability downstream. This included the irrigation of new acreage, the construction of new storage facilities and groundwater pumping, and the increased consumption of water on existing agricultural acreage through the employment of sprinkler rather that flood irrigation. As a result, even if Wyoming's pre-1950 water users diverted (appropriated) the same amount of water as before, less water was reaching Montana downstream (less flood runoff back into the river system). Montana argued that Wyoming was prohibited from employing these new uses, to the extent that they deprived pre-1950 Montana users from their respective WATER RIGHTS.

Wyoming filed a motion to dismiss for FAILURE TO STATE A CLAIM. In 2008, the Court appointed a SPECIAL MASTER to oversee the suit and investigate arguments made in the motion. Following briefing and argument, Special Master Barton Thompson recommended denying the motion to dismiss, finding that at least some of Montana's substantive allegations did state claims for relief. To the point, the Special Master found that "Article V of the Compact protects pre-1950 appropriations in Montana from new surface and groundwater diversions in Wyoming, whether for direct use or for storage, that prevent adequate water from reaching Montana to satisfy those pre-1950 appropriations."

However, the Special Master agreed with Wyoming about "efficiency improvements" (e.g., converting from flood to sprinkler irrigation systems) by pre-1950 users ("appropriators"). In that regard, the Special Master found that Montana did not state a **claim for relief**, i.e., did not articulate a **cause of action** for which the Court could grant relief. The states did not object to most of the Special Master's findings. However, Montana filed an exception to the rejection of its "increased efficiency" claim. This was the only claim before the Supreme Court.

Key to resolving the conflict was an understanding of water "appropriation" rights in Article V of the Compact (see above). The question before the Court, articulated by Justice Thomas in his majority opinion, was therefore "whether Article V(A) allows Wyoming's pre-1950 water users-diverting the same quantity of water for the same irrigation purpose and acreage as before 1950-to increase their consumption of water by improving their irrigation systems even if it reduces the flow of water to Montana's pre-1950 users." The Special Master had concluded that Montana's arguments failed in this regard, and the Court's majority agreed with the Special Master.

Both Special Master and Supreme Court majority found that the relevant language of Article V of the Compact incorporated the ordinary doctrine of APPROPRIATION, without significant deviation. That doctrine allows appropriators to improve their irrigation systems, even to the detriment of downstream appropriators/users. Moreover, the doctrine of appropriation provides that rights to water for irrigation are perfected and enforced according to seniority, starting with the first party to divert water from a natural stream and apply it to a "beneficial use."

Accordingly, held the majority,

We conclude that the plain terms of the Compact protect ordinary '[a]ppropriative rights to the beneficial uses of [water] ... existing in each signatory State as of January 1, 1950.' Art. V(A), *ibid*. And the **best evidence** we have shows that the doctrine of appropriation in Wyoming and Montana allows appropriators to improve the efficiency of their irrigation systems, even to the detriment of downstream appropriators.

Justice CLARENCE THOMAS was joined in the majority opinion by Chief Justice Roberts and Justices Kennedy, Ginsburg, Breyer, Alito, and Sotomayor. Justice ANTONIN SCALIA was the lone dissenter. He disagreed with the majority's substitution of what he referred to as its own "none-too-confident" reading of the **common law** of appropriation for the Compact's definition of "beneficial use."

SECOND AMENDMENT

Court of Appeals Shoots Down Chicago's New Gun Law

For nearly three decades, the City of Chicago, Illinois, had ordinances in place that effectively banned handgun possession by private citizens. In 2008, the U.S. Supreme Court struck down a handgun ban in the District of Columbia, holding that the Second Amendment to the U.S. Constitution secures to individuals the right to keep and bear arms for self-defense, including, and most notably, in their homes. *District of Columbia v. Heller,* 554 U.S. 570. Following that decision, Chicago's ban on handguns was challenged. In 2010, the Supreme Court held, in *McDonald v. City of Chicago,* 130 S. Ct. 3020,that the Second Amendment right to possess operable firearms (including handguns) applied to the states and subsidiary local governments as well. This rendered Chicago's law "unenforceable."

Within hours of the decision, Chicago Mayor Richard Daley spoke to the media, stating that the Chicago City Council, upon reviewing the Court decision, would be revamping a new ordinance that would protect not only Second Amendment rights for its citizens but would also protect them. Pursuant to that objective, the City Council convened hearings, took testimony, consulted with the City's legal counsel, and met with gun-control advocates, law-enforcement officers, and academic experts. Just four days after the Supreme Court's ruling, the Council lifted its previous ban on handgun possession and unanimously adopted its new Responsible Gun Owners Ordinance.

The Responsible Gun Owners Ordinance, effective July 12, 2010, contained several new provisions restricting, but not banning, handguns within the city. For example, in addition to restricting handgun possession to inside the home (residence), it restricted long guns outside the home or the owner's place of business (CHI.MUN.CODE § 8-20-030). A person may have "no more than one firearm in his home assembled and operable," (CHI. MUN.CODE § 8-20-040), and "unsafe handguns" as well as assault weapons and certain firearm accessories and types of ammunition were banned in their entirety (CHI.MUN. CODE §§ 8-20-060, 8-20-085, 8-20-170). The sale or transfer of firearms was prohibited, excepting through inheritance or between peace officers, (CHI.MUN.CODE § 8-20-120). Further, the possession of any or all firearms was prohibited without a Chicago Firearm Permit and registration certificate. Permits were valid for three years. Registration certificates required annual reporting, failure to file for which could result in revocation of permit, registration certificate, or both. The ordinance provided a 90-day "grandfather" clause after its effective date for previously-acquired firearms to be registered.

Chicago Mayor Richard M. Daley speaks during a news conference, Monday, June 28, 2010, in Chicago, after the U.S Supreme Court overturned Chicago's handgun regulations.

AP IMAGES/M. SPENCER GREEN

As pertinent here, the ordinance further mandated one hour of range training (firing range) as a prerequisite to gun ownership (CHI. MUN.CODE § 8-20-120), and it also barred firing ranges from operating within city borders (CHI.MUN.CODE § 8-20-080.

In August 2010, the new law was challenged as unconstitutional under the Second Amendment. Specifically, plaintiffs challenged the law's treatment of firing ranges. The lawsuit was filed by the Illinois State Rifle Association, the Second Amendment Foundation (a gun ownership advocacy group), Action Target, Inc. (a Utah-based business that designs and builds firing ranges), and three private citizens. They argued that the Second Amendment also protected their right to maintain proficiency in the use of firearms, including the right to practice marksmanship at a firing range. The new law banning ranges within Chicago, they argued, was unconstitutional. On the one hand, the City severely burdened Second Amendment rights to possess firearms for self-defense because it conditioned possession on range training, while at the same time, it banned range training anywhere in the city. The plaintiffs asked for an injunction preventing the new provisions from going into effect.

In October 2010, the U.S. District Court for the Northern District of Illinois denied their motion, but in July 2011, the U.S. Court of Appeals for the Seventh Circuit, reversed and granted a preliminary injunction. *Rhonda Ezell, et al., v. City of Chicago,* No. 10-3525 (7th Cir. 2011). To be sure, noted the appellate court, standards for evaluating Second Amendment claims were just emerging, and this type of litigation was quite new. Nonetheless, said the court, the district court's decision "reflects misunderstandings about the nature of the plaintiffs' harm, the structure of this kind of constitutional claim, and the proper decision method for evaluating alleged infringements of Second Amendment rights." The appellate court concluded that plaintiffs were entitled to a preliminary injunction against the ban on firing ranges.As Justice Diane Sykes said in the opinion, "The harm to their Second Amendment Rights cannot be remedied by damages, their challenge has a strong likelihood of success on the merits, and the city's claimed harm to the public interest is based entirely on speculation."

Chicago aldermen, anticipating the possibility of such an appellate result, immediately passed a new measure permitting ranges, but restricting them to enclosed spaces within districts zoned only for manufacturing, and at least 1,000 feet from schools, residential dwellings, houses of worship, or other ranges.

Third Circuit Rules That Felons Do Not Have Second Amendment Rights

The SECOND AMENDMENT to the U.S. Constitution provides, "A well regulated MILITIA being necessary to the security of a free State, the right of the People to keep and bear arms shall not be infringed." Since the U.S. Supreme Court's decision in *District of Columbia v. Heller*, 554 U.S. 570, 128 S. Ct. 2783, 171 L. Ed. 2d 637 (2008), several parties in LITIGATION have argued that the government had infringed on their right to bear arms. The Court in *McDonald v. City of Chicago*, 130 S. Ct. 3020 (2010) ruled that the Second Amendment applies to the states through the Due Process Clause of the FOURTEENTH AMENDMENT. However, several lower courts have ruled against Second Amendment protections, noting that the right to bear arms in a limited right.

One such lower court was the Third Circuit, which in 2011 ruled that the Second Amendment did not render unconstitutional a federal **statute** prohibiting a convicted felon of carrying a weapon. The court's decision in *United States v. Barton*, 633 F.3d 168 (3d Cir. 2011) was consistent with holdings in other lower **federal courts** that under some circumstances, restrictions against gun possession and ownership are presumptively lawful.

The case involved James Barton, who in 2007 received $300 from a confidential police informant in exchange for a 32-caliber revolver along with ammunition. The serial number of the gun had been drilled out, making the gun untraceable. Information from the informant allowed police to obtain a warrant to search Barton's residence. During that search, officers discovered a number of pistols, rifles, and shotguns, along with various types of ammunition.

A federal statute contained in 18 U.S.C. § 922(g)(1) states: "It shall be unlawful for any person . . . who has been convicted in any court of, a crime punishable by imprisonment for a term exceeding one year . . . to ship or transport in interstate orforeign commerce, or possess in or affecting commerce, any firearm or ammunition; or to receive any firearm or ammunition which has been shipped or transported in interstate or foreign commerce." Barton had two prior **felony** convictions for possession of cocaine with intent to distribute and for receipt of a stolen firearm. Because of these two convictions, he was charged with violating 18 U.S.C. § 922(g)(1).

Barton argued that his conviction should be thrown out because of a principle announced in *Heller*. The Court in that case had announced that the Second Amendment protects a FUNDAMENTAL RIGHT to "use arms in defense of hearth and home." However, the **district court** rejected this argument, relying instead on other language contained in *Heller*.

In deciding *Heller*, the Court stated that a number of restrictions on firearms were presumptively lawful, including: "prohibitions on the possession of firearms by felons and the mentally ill, laws forbidding the carrying of firearms in sensitive places such as schools and government buildings, [and] laws imposing conditions and qualifications on the commercial sale of . . . arms." In *McDonald*, the Court noted that this list was not exhaustive and reflected the historical understanding of the protections offered by the Second Amendment.

Barton argued that the list of presumptively lawful restrictions was only **dicta**, meaning that it was not of central importance to the decision and thus should not bind lower courts. In some of the lower court decisions following *Heller* courts have concluded that the language was indeed DICTA. However, other circuits have disagreed, stating that the language was designed to limit the Court's holding and that the language was not dicta.

The Third Circuit concluded that the list of presumptively lawful restrictions was not dicta. Accordingly, the court determined that it was bound to follow the list established in *Heller*. The court then turned its attention to Barton's specific challenges. He argued first that the statute was unconstitutional on its face, meaning that the law could not be valid under any set of circumstances. However, given that the SUPREME COURT had determined that restrictions on possession of firearms by felons was presumptively lawful, the Third Circuit rejected the facial challenge.

GUN CONTROL AND MENTAL ILLNESS DISQUALIFICATION IN THE AFTERMATH OF THE 2011 TUCSON SHOOTINGS

On the morning of January 8, 2011, a 22-year-old Tucson, Arizona man burst forward from a small gathering of constituents at a meet-and-greet-your-congressman event outside a local grocery market. He then shot State Representative Gabrielle ("Gabby") Giffords (D-AZ) in the forehead at near pointblank range, then released a spray of gunfire that killed six people and wounded 12 others. After firing a round of at least 30 bullets from a 9mm Glock handgun, the gunman was overtaken and subdued only after he stopped to reload his gun with another magazine, at which time bystanders and attendees tackled and held him until police arrived. Congresswoman Giffords, who received a bullet to the brain, miraculously survived after multiple surgeries and months of rehabilitation. Five others died at the scene, and a sixth, little 9-year-old Christina Taylor-Greene, died at a nearby hospital. (The other 12 victims who were shot eventually recovered from their wounds). The suspect, Jared Lee Loughner, was deemed mentally incompetent to stand trial in May 2011. In the days preceding the shootings, Loughner, a troubled college expellee whose conduct had raised several previous concerns about his mental health, had videotaped messages and diatribes demonizing school, politicians, and the government at large.

Prior to this horrific crime, the nation had suffered when another mentally deranged young man went berserk on the campus of Virginia Polytechnic Institute (Virginia Tech)in April 2007, killing 27 students and five faculty members before taking his own life. In that tragedy, Seung-Hui Cho, a disgruntled student with prior mental health problems, had spent the two hours before the shootings video-taping himself in violent messages for the media.

Each time a mass shooting occurs in the United States, Congress and state legislators, jolted into immediate legislative responsiveness, vow that it will never happen again. But it does.

Not that Congress or state legislatures are ineffectual or to blame. Rather, it is argued, it is just not that easy to identify, and track, in advance, a person who may go berserk and commit such heinous crimes. Too many educated and knowledgeable professionals have argued that strict gun control will not eliminate such terrible acts.

Since 1968, federal law has banned certain mentally ill persons from purchasing guns, to wit, those who have been deemed a danger to themselves or others, involuntarily committed, or adjudicated as not guilty by reasons of insanity or incompetent to stand trial. However, in the 2007 Virginia Tech rampage, Seung-Hui Cho was able to purchase two guns, even though he had been ruled a danger to himself during a 2005 court hearing and was ordered to undergo outpatient mental health treatment.

Likewise, in the 2011 Tucson tragedy, suspect Jared Loughner had legally purchased his semiautomatic weapon from a local shop two months before the shooting. Yet Loughner was considered so mentally unstable that he was expelled from community college following complaints by several students of his bizarre behavior and violent talk, not allowed to re-enroll until cleared by a mental health professional. Because he was never deemed mentally ill by a judge, or committed to an institution, he was able to purchase his gun.

How was this possible? Where did these two, and others, fall through the cracks? Could these tragedies have been prevented with better disqualifying rules for mental health issues?

Congressional Efforts to Prevent Guns in the Hands of the Mentally Ill Under the 1993 Brady Bill (named after James Brady, who was also shot but not killed by a lone deranged gunman, John Hinckley, during an attempted assassination of former President Ronald Reagan) established the nationwide background check system (NICS) still in effect today. The system also tracks convicted felons and ostensibly prevents them from purchasing guns. As of December 31, 2010, the NICS Index included more than 1.2 million records on individuals who had been adjudicated as mentally defective. A few states voluntarily shared mental health records, but were not required to do so.

Following the Virginia Tech massacre, a reactive Congress passed the NICS Improvement Amendments Act of 2007, Pub. L. No. 110-180, 121 Stat. 2559. The law, effective in 2008, established financial incentives to prompt state, local, and tribal governments to transfer "mental defective" files to the FBI for inclusion in the NICS Index. Moreover, states were now required to either submit records or risk losing up to five percent of federal funds that states receive to fight crime. But such penalties, although potentially substantial, do not become mandatory until 2018.

In February 2011, Associated Press (AP) journalist Greg Bluestein reported that more than half the states failed to comply with the file-sharing law by the deadline of January 2011. In states with no or low compliance, gun dealers were potentially checking names of prospective applicants against woefully inadequate lists, thereby compromising the entire system.

Nine states failed to supply any names to the database: Alaska, Delaware, Idaho, Massachusetts, Minnesota, New Mexico, Pennsylvania, Rhode Island, and

South Dakota). Another 17 states submitted very few records (fewer than 25): Hawaii, Illinois, Kentucky, Louisiana, Maine, Mississippi, Montana, Nebraska, New Hampshire, Jew Jersey, North Dakota, Oklahoma, Oregon, South Carolina, Vermont, Wisconsin, and Wyoming. Eleven states had provided more than 1,000 records each. According to records AP obtained in late 2010 through a public Freedom of Information Act request (FOIA), California had forwarded records of more than 250,000 persons, while Virginia did so for more than 100,000.

But the federal government also fell back on its end of responsibility. According to the U.S. Department of Justice, in fiscal year 2009, the government dispensed only about $10 million to the states to assist with compliance, not close to the $187.5 million it had pledged. In 2010, it provided $20 million. All in all, Congress had promised $1.3 billion between 2009 and 2013 to bring states into compliance.

Officials have blamed privacy laws and antiquated record-keeping systems for some of the failures; for others, it is a severe lack of funding. In some states, the amount of federal incentive money they could lose for not complying was less than what it would have cost them to update their record-sharing systems.

States Try to Close the Loopholes
In the Virginia Tech tragedy, federal officials later said that the killer, Cho, should have been barred from purchasing his guns, but for the failure of state officials to forward records for inclusion in the NICS national database. Virginia officials countered that state law only required forwarding the records of persons who had been committed to mental hospitals; Cho was not. That loophole has since been changed by state law. Virginia now forwards records of those who have even undergone outpatient mental health treatment.

In Pennsylvania, Loughner would have been able to purchase his gun as easily as he did in Arizona. Although many state officials consider the law

adequate and working as it was designed to, others have called for Pennsylvania to amend its law to reflect provisions found in nearby New Jersey. The application for a New Jersey handgun purchase requires applicants to answer questions about whether they have ever been voluntarily seen and/or treated by a doctor for any mental or psychiatric condition, on either an inpatient or outpatient basis. They must also provide the doctor's names and other details. Moreover, and importantly, the background check includes not only investigation of records, but also interviews with applicants' family members, neighbors, and others who may have information about the individual applicant's mental state.

Advocating for the Mentally Ill
Many professionals have acknowledged that stricter mental health disqualifications, like those in the New Jersey law, will not solve all the problems. As Phil Goldsmith, president of CeaseFirePA and an advocate for New Jersey's law, told *The Philadelphia Weekly*, "Are people gonna get their hands on guns no matter what? Of course they are. But should we make it so easy for them? Of course not."

Others are more vehemently opposed to stricter mental health laws. Debbie Plotnick, director of advocacy at the Philadelphia-based Mental Health Association of Southeastern Pennsylvania, opined that people with mental health problems were being "singled-out," scapegoated, and stigmatized. "They're going to try to take more people's rights away based on no history of violence but based on assumption, without any proof, that people with mental-health conditions are violent," she argued. "There's no evidence that just because you've had an involuntary hospitalization that you are violent or you will ever be violent. There's nothing whatsoever to back that up. A lot of people have had suicidal depression as teenagers and they're involuntarily sent to treatment, and then they get better, and then they're banned from buying a gun."

There are some statistics to back up her argument. A 2009 study published by Oxford University concluded that one's chance of being killed by a stranger with schizophrenia was one in 14.3 million. To put this in perspective, a person would be three times more likely to be hit by lightning and killed. Plotnick also pointed to data that suggested only three to five percent of violent acts committed annually in the United States could be attributed to persons with mental illness.

Looking to the Future The 111th Congress and its gun control debates were overshadowed by the 2010 U.S. Supreme Court case of *McDonald v. City of Chicago*, 561 U.S. ___, 130 S. Ct. 3020, 177 L. Ed. 2d 894 (2010), which affirmed that state and local, not just federal, bans on gun ownership may violate Second Amendment rights to own guns for self protection. (The Court only addressed bans, not limitations, on gun ownership.) Notwithstanding, in 2010 and 2011, Congress reconsidered or newly considered other provisions. They addressed, e.g., veterans adjudicated as mentally incompetent and loss of gun rights (S. 669 and H.R. 6132) and screening firearms background check applicants against terror watch lists. Although not enacted, they could re-emerge in the 112th Congress.

Much of the hesitation to enact new legislation revolves around the difficulty in defining mental health problems. In May 2011, Representative Carolyn McCarthy (D-NY) and Senator Chuck Schumer (D-NY) introduced, in their respective chambers, versions of the Fix Gun Checks Act of 2011. Both versions include a section dedicated to codifying into federal law a more precise understanding of what it means to be "adjudicated as a mental defective." The proposed language would include any person who appears to "lack the mental capacity or contract or manage his own affairs," or is "compelled" to receive counseling or medication, in addition to the more obvious definitions mentioned earlier.

Barton also argued that 18 U.S.C. § 922(g)(1) was unconstitutional as applied to Barton. The Supreme Court's presumption did not entirely resolve this issue because a party can rebut the presumption. The Third Circuit briefly reviewed the history of the Second Amendment along with the history of laws restriction possession of firearms by felons. The court noted that for him to prevail, "Barton must present facts about himself and his background that distinguish his circumstances from those of persons historically barred from Second Amendment protections." According to the court, Barton failed to do so. The fact that officers confiscated weapons at Barton's home did not help his case. The court stressed that in a number of instances, felons forfeit civil liberties, and restricting a felon from possessing a weapon, even in his home, was consistent with other restrictions.

SECTION 1983

Fox v. Vice

When a PLAINTIFF brings a CIVIL RIGHTS lawsuit under 28 U.S.C. § 1983 (called a "Section 1983 action") but makes frivolous claims, the **district court** may award attorney's fees to the DEFENDANT. However, a case may involve both frivolous and non-frivolous claims, and lower **federal courts** have struggled with the question of whether and to what extent the defendant should receive attorney's fees when such a case arises. The U.S. SUPREME COURT in 2011 resolved this issue by ruling that the court can award attorney's fees for those costs that a defendant would not have incurred but for the plaintiff's frivolous claims.

The facts in *Fox v. Vice*, No. 10-114, 2011 WL 2175211 (U.S. 2011) arose in the Town of Vinton, Louisiana in 2005, when Ricky Fox challenged INCUMBENT police chief Billy Ray Vice in an election. Two events occurred before the election that led Fox to bring a lawsuit against Vice. First, Vice attempted to convince Fox to withdraw from the race by sending Fox a letter in which Vice anonymously threatened to BLACKMAIL Fox. Second, a **third party** accused Fox of uttering a racial slur, and Vice persuaded the THIRD PARTY to file a false police report about the alleged utterance.

Fox thus alleged that Vice had engaged in "dirty tricks" during the campaign. Fox

nevertheless won the election. Moreover, Vice was convicted in 2007 of criminal EXTORTION for his actions during the campaign. Still, Fox filed a lawsuit against Vice and the Town of Vinton, alleging claims based both on state law claims and on federal civil rights violations.

Because the suit involved federal questions, Vice removed the case to federal court in 2006. Following the discovery pretrial phase, Vice and the Town moved for **summary judgment**. They argued that Fox had not alleged a claim based on federal law. Fox responded to the motion by admitting that he had not presented a valid federal **cause of action**. Specifically, Fox acknowledged that Vice had not acted under the "color of law" when he wrote the extortion letter and that Vice and the Town had not deprived Fox of a right, privilege, or IMMUNITY based on federal law.

U.S. **Magistrate** Judge Kathleen Kay of the U.S. District Court for the Western District of Louisiana dismissed Fox's claims in light of these admissions. Kay then remanded the case to state court, noting that the work that Vice's attorneys had done—trial preparation, legal research, and discovery—could help with regard to Fox's state-law claims. Vice then requested that the court award him attorney's fees, arguing that Fox had brought claims that were frivolous, unreasonable, and without foundation.

When a plaintiff brings a claim under SECTION 1983, a court has the discretion to "allow the **prevailing party**, other than the United States, a reasonable attorney's free as part of the costs." Rule 54(d)(1) of the Federal Rules of **Civil Procedure** further allows a court to award costs to a PREVAILING PARTY.

Vice argued that his lawyers had engaged in five long depositions during the discovery phase. Moreover, his lawyers had to review a number of records to defend against Fox's claims. Vice supported his argument by submitting billing records that showed the time his attorneys spent on the entire suit. The billing record differentiated between the claims based on federal law and the claims based on state law.

Kay granted Vice's motion and awarded the attorney's fees. She concluded that Fox's federal claims were indeed frivolous. Moreover, she did not require Vice to separate the time spent on the frivolous federal claims and the non-frivolous state-law claims to determine which costs related to which claims. Instead, the court concluded that the claims had arisen from "the same transaction and were so interrelated that their prosecution or defense entailed proof or denial of essentially the same facts." The court thus awarded to Vice all of the attorney's fees he incurred in defending the suit.

Fox appealed the decision to the Fifth **Circuit Court** of Appeals. In a 2-1 decision, the court agreed with the district court. Fox argued that all of his claims had to be frivolous to justify an award to the defendant. However, the court rejected the argument, noting that such a rule would allow a plaintiff to prosecute any frivolous claims so long as the plaintiff also added at least one non-frivolous claim. The court agreed with the district court's decision and upheld the award. *Fox v. Vice*, 594 F.3d 423 (5th Cir. 2010).

Because lower federal courts had reached different conclusions about how to treat awards for frivolous and non-frivolous claims under Section 1983, the Supreme Court agreed to review the case. In a unanimous decision, the Court vacated the Fifth Circuit's opinion. Justice Elena Kagan, writing for the Court, noted that "if life were like the movies," it would be easy to award fees based on winners and losers because a fictional case often only has clear winners and clear losers. In the "messy" world of real-life LITIGATION, some claims succeed while others fail. In the end, "courts must deal with this untidiness in awarding fees."

The Court concluded that the real question in the matter came down to allocating which part of the work that the attorney did related to the frivolous claims versus the non-frivolous claims. The Court rejected Vice's argument that the district court should award fees for work "fairly attributable" to the frivolous claims. Instead, the Court adopted a so-called but-for test: "Section 1988 permits the defendant to receive only the portion of his fees that he would not have paid but for the frivolous claim."

Since the district court had not allocated the award based on the but-for standard, the Court remanded the case to the lower courts for further proceedings.

SECURITIES

Evidence of a corporation's debts or property.

Erica P. John Fund v. Halliburton

Section § 10(b) of the SECURITIES Exchange Act of 1934, 15 U.S.C. § 78j(b), as well as **correlative** SECURITIES AND EXCHANGE COMMISSION (SEC) Rule 10b-5,17 CFR § 240.10b-5 (2010) compel the disclosure of certain information to prospective investors, the withholding of which may constitute actionable securities **fraud**, inuring to the benefit of investors allegedly harmed (financially) by the non-disclosures. Moreover, the Act punishes **fraudulent** mis-representations or misinformation provided to prospective investors, usually intended to induce investors to purchase stock.

As in any lawsuit alleging FRAUD, plaintiffs in such SEC securities fraud cases must prove certain elements, including reliance on the material misrepresentations or omissions; sub-sequent purchases or sales of securities in connection with the alleged misrepresentations or omissions; economic loss; and loss causation. In *Erica P. John Fund v. Halliburton,* No. 09-1403, 131 S. Ct 856, 563 U.S. ___ (2011), an unanimous U.S. SUPREME COURT held that plaintiffs in a securities fraud case do *not* have to prove loss causation in order to obtain class certification (to be joined as plaintiffs in a **class action** lawsuit).

The lead PLAINTIFF in this case was the Erica P. John Fund, Inc. (the EPJ Fund). It and other investors, including the Archdiocese of Milwaukee Supporting Fund, Inc., were shareholders who filed a securities fraud lawsuit against Halliburton and one of its executives (collectively referred to herein as Halliburton). The complaint alleged, among other things, that Houston-based Halliburton had falsified earnings reports, downplayed asbestos liability, and overstated the benefits of a merger, all mis-representations designed to inflate the company's stock price. The complaint further alleged that later, Halliburton made several corrective disclosures to shareholders, causing the stock price to drop and shareholders to lose their money. The lawsuit was brought on behalf of all investors who purchased Halliburton **common stock** between June 1999 and December 2001.

Pursuant to Federal Rule of **Civil Procedure** 23, the EPJ Fund sought to be named representative plaintiffs of a proposed class of plaintiff investors requesting to be certified as such by the court. The federal **district court** found that the lawsuit could proceed as a CLASS ACTION under Rule 23, but found that plaintiff EPJ Fund had failed to satisfy Fifth Circuit precedent that required securities fraud plaintiffs to prove "loss causation" in order to obtain class certification. (Proving loss causation essentially requires plaintiffs to show that defendants' deceptive conduct caused the investors' economic loss.) On appeal to the Fifth Circuit, the denial of class certification was affirmed, for the stated reason.

At the U.S. Supreme Court level, Chief Justice JOHN ROBERTS, JR. wrote for an unanimous Court. In sum, the succinct, 10-page opinion held that while securities fraud plaintiffs ultimately must prove their case on the merits, (including causation between their losses and the alleged misrepresentations or omissions they relied upon), this need not be proved at the early stage of petition for class certification. The Court, quoting Rule 23(b)(3), noted that, in order to certify a class under this rule, a court must find

> that the questions of law or fact common to class members predominate over any questions affecting only individual members and that a class action is superior to other available methods for fairly and efficiently adjudicating the controversy.

Whether common questions of law or fact predominate in such an action often turns on the element of reliance, noted the Court. Traditionally, plaintiffs demonstrate reliance by showing that they were aware of a company's statement and then engaged in a relevant transaction (e.g., stock purchase) based on that specific company statement (MISREPRESENTATION). In the previous case of *Basic Inc. v. Levinson,* 485 U.S. 224, 108 S. Ct. 978, 99 L. Ed. 2d 194, the Court simplified the process by allowing plaintiffs to invoke a **rebuttable presumption** or reliance based on what is known as the "fraud on the market" theory. The theory reflects a presumption that "the market price of shares traded on well-developed markets reflects all publicly available information, and, hence, any material representations."

Further, the Court has previously referred to this element of reliance, in relation to private

Rule 10b(5) securities fraud actions, as "transaction causation," not loss causation. Showing transaction causation means showing facts surrounding an investor's decision to engage in a financial transaction, whereas loss causation requires a plaintiff to show that the misrepresentation caused a subsequent economic loss. This has nothing to do with whether an investor relied on the misrepresentation in the first place, either directly or through the fraud-on-the-markets theory, said the Court. Therefore, loss causation was an inappropriate element for plaintiffs to show, simply to be certified as a class.

Although Halliburton urged that the Fifth Circuit did not actually require the EPJ Fund to prove loss causation, but rather used that term to imply the needed proof of "price impact," i. e., whether the alleged misrepresentations affected the market price in the first place. The Court rejected this argument, saying that whatever Halliburton thought the Court of Appeals was saying or meant to say, what it did say was "loss causation. Taking the Court of Appeals at its word, the Supreme Court vacated and remanded.

Matrixx Initiatives v. Siracusano

A great deal of the SECURITIES and Exchange Act of 1934, 48 Stat. 891, followed the spiraling STOCK MARKET crash and "Great Depression" of 1929-1931. Congress intended to protect investors and members of the public from **fraudulent** financial transactions in the stock market. Section 10(b) of the Act [15 U.S.C. § 78j(b)], as well as SECURITIES AND EXCHANGE COMMISSION (SEC) Rule 10b-5 [17 CFR § 240.10b-5 (2010)] compel the disclosure of certain information to prospective investors, the withholding of which may constitute actionable securities **fraud**, inuring to the benefit of investors allegedly harmed (financially) by the non-disclosures.

In *Matrixx Initiatives Inc. v. Siracusano,* No. 09-1156, 562 U.S. ___ (2011), the U.S. SUPREME COURT was asked whether an investor can state a claim for securities FRAUD under the above provisions, based on a pharmaceutical company's failure to disclose to investors reports of adverse medical side effects associated with one of its drug products, if the reports do not reflect a statistically significant number of adverse events. An unanimous Court, in an opinion written by Justice Sotomayor, said yes. In so holding, the Court declined to adopt a "statistical significance" threshold for requiring disclosures of drug adverse event reports, as proposed by the pharmaceutical manufacturer, Matrixx Initiatives, Inc. (Matrixx). The Court's decision unanimously affirmed the opinion of the Ninth **Circuit Court** of Appeals, holding the same.

Matrixx, a manufacturer of over-the-counter pharmaceutical products, relied on its Zicam Cold Remedy product ("Zicam") forabout 70 percent of its total sales. Zicam is generally administered via nasal spray. Assuming facts contained in the subject complaint as true (as the Supreme Court was postured to do, on appeal), by as early as 1999, Matrixx had received medical information reporting incidents of "anosmia" in a cluster of patients who had used Zicam. The medical term anosmia refers to the loss of the sense of smell. Other incidences of anosmia occurred in additional patients during the next several years, and Matrixx received reports of same. Matrixx also received reports from both doctors and researchers who indicated a plausible causal link between the intranasal application of Zicam (i.e., its key ingredient, zinc gluconate) and patient reports of anosmia. When Matrixx later became aware that a doctor and colleague would be presenting such findings at a medical seminar, linking ten cases of anosmia to Zicam, Matrixx successfully prevented the physicians from referring to Zicam by name during the presentation. During the same time that nine plaintiffs filed four **product liability** lawsuits against Matrixx, alleging that Zicam had damaged their sense(s) of smell, Matrixx was making positive statements about the company and projected results for Zicam in its SEC filings. It neither expressly identified the lawsuits as liability risks, nor made any disclosure about information it had received suggesting a link to anosmia.

Following some media blitz in 2004 (a "Good Morning America" television broadcast; a Dow Jones news report that the U.S. Food and Drug Administration [FDA] was investigating complaints of Zicam-related anosmia), Matrixx filed a Form 8-K Current Report with the SEC, indicating that a two-day meeting of physicians and scientists, convened by Matrixx, resulted in the panel's opinion that there was insufficient evidence to either confirm or refute such a causal link.

A group of investors subsequently filed the present **class action** suit for securities fraud. They alleged that Matrixx and three of its executives (hereinafter collectively as Matrixx) failed to disclose reports of a suggested link between Zicam and anosmia and failed to disclose the pending products liability complaints. The plaintiffs further alleged that such failures constituted violations of § 10(b) of the Act and SEC Rule 10b-5, and resulted in misleading statements by Matrixx about the company's financial health and product safety record, and projected results for Zicam in particular. They further alleged that these disclosures and misleading statements represented an effort to maintain artificially inflated prices for Matrixx's securities.

Matrixx defended by asserting that plaintiffs failed to plead the requisite "material misstatement or omission" and "scienter" elements of a securities fraud claim. ("Scienter" refers to a mental state indicating an intent to deceive, manipulate, or defraud.)The federal **district court** in Arizona agreed and dismissed the case. However, the Ninth Circuit Court of Appeals reversed, finding that plaintiffs had met their burden and had articulated a viable claim.

The Ninth Circuit found particular error in the district court having adopted Matrixx's argument that plaintiffs were required to make an ALLEGATION of "statistical significance" (of the alleged medical findings and reports) to establish the requisite "materiality" element for a viable claim. It further held that Matrixx's withholding of information about reports of adverse effects and about the pending lawsuits created a strong inference of "scienter" sufficient to state a viable **cause of action** (assuming plaintiffs' allegations as true).

In summary, the U.S. Supreme Court agreed, citing relevant Supreme Court precedent. First, it is true that, to prevail on such a claim, plaintiffs needed to prove a material MISREPRESENTATION or omission, as well as **scienter**. *Stoneridge Investment Partners, LLC* *v. Scientific-Atlanta,* 552 U.S. 148, 157, 128 S. Ct. 761, 169 L. Ed. 2d 627 (2008). Importantly, Matrixx had argued that plaintiffs did not allege that the withheld medical reports reflected statistically significant evidence that Zicam caused anosmia. Matrixx urged the Court to adopt a "bright-line rule" for determining whether the withheld information in the medical reports was "material" by determining whether there was a sufficient number of such reports to establish a statistical significance.

But the Court has previously held, in *Basic Inc. v. Levinson,* 485 U.S. 224, 108 S. Ct. 978, 99 L. Ed. 2d 194 (1988), that § 10(b)'s "materiality" requirement was satisfied where there was a "substantial likelihood that the disclosure of the omitted fact would have been viewed by the reasonable investor as having significantly altered the 'total mix' of information made available." In other words, statistical significance is not the only reliable indicator of causation, nor should a single fact or occurrence always be deemed determinative to find materiality. Instead, it should be one of many factors in the "total mix" of information available to prospective investors to facilitate their informed decisions (whether to invest). Accordingly, the Court applied *Basic*'s "total mix" standard in the present case, to conclude that plaintiffs had alleged facts suggesting a significant risk to the commercial viability of Zicam, which in turn would make it substantially likely that a reasonable investor would have viewed this information as having significantly altered the "total mix" of information made available.

As to SCIENTER, the Court quoted from *Tellabs, Inc. v. Makor Issues & Rights, Ltd.,* 551 U.S. 308, 319, 127 S. Ct. 2499, 168 L. Ed. 2d 179 (2007), that, under the Private Securities LITIGATION Reform Act of 1995, scienter is adequately pleaded "only if a **reasonable person** would deem the inference of scienter cogent and at least as compelling as any opposing inference one could draw from the facts alleged." The facts alleged in this case give rise to "a cogent and compelling" inference that Matrixx **chose** not to disclose the adverse information, not because it believed it was statistically insignificant, but because it understood their likely effect on the market. Accordingly, plaintiffs had adequately pleaded the element of scienter as well.

Janus Capital Group, Inc. v. First Derivative Traders

The U.S. SUPREME COURT has long recognized that an investor may bring a private **cause of action** when a person makes an untrue statement of material fact with regard to the purchase or sale of a security. However, Court has narrowed the scope of this CAUSE OF ACTION, noting that Congress never explicitly authorized such a suit when Congress first created the **statute** or at later times when Congress reviewed the statute. In 2011, the Court determined that a group of investors could not bring an action against a **mutual fund** advisor, even though the MUTUAL FUND and the advisor were closely related. *Janus Capital Group, Inc. v. First Derivative Traders,* No. 09-525, 2011 WL 2297762 (U.S. June 13, 2011).

Janus Capital Group created a family of mutual funds, including the Janus Investment Fund ("Fund"), which exists as a Massachusetts **business trust**. The Fund retained Janus Capital Management, L.L.C. to serve as the Fund's investment advisor and administrator. Janus Capital Management is a wholly owned subsidiary of Janus Capital Group. The Fund is a separate legal **entity** that is owned entirely by its investors. The Fund also owns no assets other than those owned by its investors. Each of the Fund's officers were also the officers of Janus Capital Management, but only one member of the Fund's board of trustees was affiliated with Janus Capital Management.

Much of the dispute between the investors and the Janus parties arose because of a prospectus issued about a trading strategy known as "market timing," which is a practice that involves delays in fund valuations. During the early 2000s, the Fund stated in several prospectuses that various funds were not suitable for market timing and suggested that Janus Capital Management would adopt policies that would curb use of the strategy. Market timing is not an illegal practice, but it can harm some of the mutual fund investors.

The New York Attorney General in 2003 filed a complaint against Janus Capital Group and Janus Capital Management. The complaint charged that the companies had secretly allowed market timing in several of the funds run by Janus Capital Management. When the complaint became public, investors withdrew substantial amounts from several mutual funds.

the state at that time. One of the law's most controversial measure prohibited any sex offender from living within 2,000 feet (about two-fifths of a mile) of a park or a school. The prior law prohibited certain sex offenders from living within one-quarter to one-half mile from a school. Some members of the legislature expressed concern that this provision would be unenforceable or would result in some sex offenders moving from urban areas to rural areas. Nevertheless, the measure was approved by 70.5 percent of the vote in November 2006.

Registered sex offenders were indeed affected by the new law. Many argued that they had no place to live in many of the urban areas because residential areas are typically located within 2,000 feet of a school, park, or both. Some of these offenders argued that the law was an unconstitutional ex post facto law that inflicted a greater punishment on them after they had been convicted and even after they had completed their sentences. The California Division of Adult PAROLE Operations (DAPO) later issued established a policy requiring registered sex offenders who were paroled after November 8, 2006 to prove they complied with the new law.

Four individuals who had registered as sex offenders before the new law passed challenged the law through a **habeas corpus** petition. Three of the four had been convicted of RAPE, while the fourth had been convicted of indecent exposure. Each of the four had committed subsequent crimes or parole violations that were not based on sex offenses. However, when each was paroled, the individual had to comply with the new residency requirement. Each of the four was unable to find compliant housing.

The four filed a petition for habeas **corpus** relief in 2007 and raised several arguments. The first argument was that the new law was an unconstitutional retroactive application of several sections of the California Penal Code. The petitioners likewise argued that the law constituted an ex post facto law and that the law infringed on their federal constitutional rights. In 2007, the California SUPREME COURT issued an order staying enforcement of the new law pending further analysis by the court.

On February 1, 2010, the court issued an opinion that rejected most of the petitioner's arguments. The court determined that Proposition 83 was not unconstitutionally retroactive

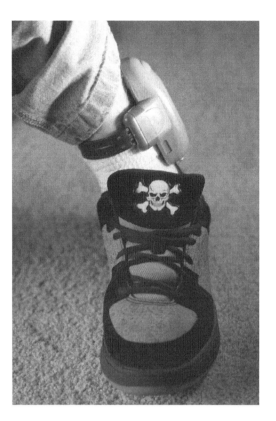

Sex offender parolee Jason Beasley, 28, shows his Corrections Department-issued GPS tracking devices on his ankle at his temporary apartment in San Leandro, California. "Jessica's Law," approved by 70 percent of California voters nearly a year ago, bars registered sex offenders from living within 2,000 feet of a school or park where children regularly gather.
AP IMAGES/JEFF CHIU

because each was released from prison on parole after the law had gone into effect, even if they were in prison for crimes that were not based on sex offenses. For a similar reason, the court concluded that Proposition 83 was not an ex post facto law because it was not being applied retroactively to the particular defendants in the case.

The petitioners were more persuasive with regard to arguments that the law is unconstitutional as applied. The petitioners provided maps purporting to show that nearly all of the cities of San Diego, Los Angeles, and San Francisco were off-limits to registered sex offenders on parole. The petitioners also alleged that the DAPO had failed in its duty to assist the parolees with finding compliant housing under the act. However, the court determined that the petitioners had not provided sufficient evidence on which to based the ruling. The court decided to remand the case to the various trial courts in which each case originated for further evidentiary proceedings. *In re E.J.*, 223 P.3d 31 (Cal. 2010).

In one of the trials in Los Angeles, petitioners produced evidence that because of the law, the number of sex offenders who were

Former football star Lawrence Taylor, center, leaves Rockland County Courthouse in New City, N.Y., Tuesday, March 22, 2011. The 52-year-old ex-linebacker pleaded guilty in January to sexual misconduct and patronizing a 16-year-old prostitute.

AP IMAGES/SETH WENIG

homeless skyrocketed. More specifically, this number rose from 30 in 2007 to 259 in 2010. Superior Court Judge Peter Espinoza also noted that his court had received about 650 HABEAS CORPUS petitions raising concerns about the new law, and hundreds more were being prepared. Based on this evidence, Espinoza ruled that the law was unconstitutional. He wrote, "Rather than protecting public safety, it appears that the sharp rise in homelessness rates in sex offenders on active parole in Los Angeles County actually undermines public safety. The evidence presented suggests that despite lay belief, a sex offender parolee's residential proximity to a school or park where children regularly gather does not bear on the parolee's likelihood to commit a sexual offense against a child." Based on his conclusion, Espinoza placed a temporary ban in enforcement of the residency requirement in Los Angeles County despite protests from the Los Angeles Police Department.

In February 2011, Superior Court Judge Michael Wellington reached a similar conclusion.

Wellington decided that the law infringed upon parolees' constitutional rights because the law is overly broad. He specifically noted that the 2,000-foot restriction applies to any sex offender, including those who have not committed crimes against children. Since the residency restriction was designed to protect children from sexual predators, the law's application was overly broad, according to the opinion.

Lawrence Taylor Pleads Guilty to Sex Offenses

Hall of Fame football player Lawrence Taylor ran into legal problems in 2010 when he was charged and indicted with third-degree RAPE for paying to have sex with a 16-year-old prostitute. Taylor admitted to having sex with the girl, but he denied that he knew she was only 16 years old. He finally pleaded guilty to two **misdemeanor** charges based on a plea bargain agreement. Although Taylor only received PROBATION, he must register as a sex offender.

Taylor was an All-American at the University of North Carolina, and the New York Giants made him the second overall selection in the 1981 NFL Draft. He developed the reputation as a ferocious defender and quickly became the most dominant defensive player in the league. He was named to ten Pro Bowls and helped to lead the Giants to two Super Bowl appearances. He also earned a slew of additional awards during his playing days, including the league's most valuable player award. He was likewise named a member of the leagues All-Decade Team for the 1980s and the NFL 75th Anniversary Team. He was finally elected to the Pro Football Hall of Fame in 1999.

Taylor has become nearly as well-known for his indiscretions off the field as he was for his success on the field. He failed multiple drug tests during his playing days, leading to his suspension in 1988. He reportedly used drugs heavily after his playing days ended, and though he went into rehab during the mid-1990s, he was arrested on two different occasions for attempting to purchase cocaine from undercover police officers. He had started a company that sold sporting goods, but the company failed in the middle of the 1990s. He also had financial problems, and in 1997, he pleaded guilty to charges of filing a false TAX RETURN. He was sentenced to three months of HOUSE ARREST in 2000.

Taylor remained in the public eye after his playing days. He appeared in several movies, including Oliver Stone's *Any Given Sunday* in 1999. Taylor emerged by 2003 as an apparently changed man, telling reporters that his reckless days were behind him. In 2009, though, he started having problems again. He was arrested in November 2009 for leaving the scene of an accident. It marked the second time he was charged with this type of offense, as he had been arrested in 1996 for leaving the scene of a one-car accident.

The most serious charges Taylor has faced related to an incident that occurred at a Holiday Inn hotel in Ramapo, New York. On May 6, 2010, Taylor paid for a 16-year-old runaway to have sex with him at the hotel room. He paid the girl $300. The girl, later identified as Christina Fierro, claimed that she had been physically assaulted and verbally threatened as her pimp drove more than 25 miles to the hotel. The pimp was 37-year-old Rasheed Davis.

On June 23, 2010, a **grand jury** in Rockland County, New York returned a six-count INDICT-MENT against Taylor. The indictment included charges of rape, criminal sexual act in the THIRD DEGREE, endangering the WELFARE of a child, patronizing a prostitute, and two counts of SEXUAL ABUSE. Rockford County District Attorney commented, "One of the most effective ways to target PROSTITUTION is to go after the johns. This indictment underscores our serious commitment to prosecuting those defendants who create a market for the region's growing sex trade."

Taylor's attorneys did not present any evidence before the GRAND JURY. Taylor's attorney, Arthur Aidala, said that the decision not to present evidence before the grand jury, but he told reporters that Taylor would defend himself when the case finally went to trial. Aidald noted, " I am saying that he did not have sexual intercourse as defined by the penal code." Aidala also said he did not expect a plea bargain in the case. Several report contained various denials by Taylor, including statements that he did not know how old the girl was or that he actually had sexual intercourse with her.

In January 2011, Taylor finally agreed to plead guilty to two misdemeanor charges. The charges included counts for soliciting a prostitute and for sexual misconduct in having sex with a woman without her consent. The basis of the second charge was that the girl was only 16 at the time of the incident and by law could not consent to having sex. Taylor had admitted to having sex with the girl, and he also acknowledged that DNA tests proved that he indeed had intercourse with her. According to one PROSECU-TOR, the district attorney's office found the plea bargain acceptable because Taylor had assisted in investigations in human sex trafficking.

Taylor was formally sentenced on March 22, 2011. Fierro appeared at the sentencing and was reportedly prepared to make a statement that she thought he should serve a prison sentence. However, she was not allowed to speak before the court. Her appearance prompted speculation that she would bring a civil lawsuit against Taylor. Fierro was represented by GLORIA ALLRED, who described Fierro as a "sex-trafficking victim."

At the hearing, Taylor received six years of probation and was required to register as a sex offender. In April 2011, Rockland County Court Judge William Kelly determined that Taylor was a low-risk sex offender, meaning that although he would have to register, his photo would not appear on public online registries. Prosecutors had argued that Taylor should receive what is known as Level 2 status, but Taylor's attorney argued that Taylor was only seeking female companionship and was not targeting children. Kelly agreed with the defense, noting, "My God, there's been so much publicity already."

SEXUAL HARASSMENT

Unwelcome sexual advances, requests for sexual favors, and other verbal or physical conduct of a sexual nature that tends to create a hostile or offensive work environment.

Former Banker Claims Citigroup Fired Her for Being Too Sexy

Debrahlee Lorenzana caused a stir in the New York office of Citygroup, based mostly on her habit of wearing sexy clothing to work. Citigroup fired her after reportedly instructing her to wear less attractive clothing. Lorenzana responded by filing a lawsuit and a complaint with the New York Division of HUMAN RIGHTS, alleging that Citigroup had committed SEX DISCRIMINATION and then retaliated against Lorenzana for speaking out against the company.

Debrahlee Lorenzana, left, and her attorney Gloria Allred, walk to a curbside news conference in New York's Financial District, Monday, June 28, 2010.

AP IMAGES/RICHARD DREW

Lorenzana had sought publicity before she joined Citigroup. In 2003, she was the focus of a Discovery Health Channel series chronicling her preparation for her fourth plastic surgery to increase her breast size. The four-part series was entitled "Plastic Surgery New York Style." Then 26, Lorenzana had already had surgery on her breasts along with a tummy tuck and liposuction. She commented on the show that she loved plastic surgery and that she wanted to look like a Playboy Playmate.

Lorenzana, who is of Puerto Rican and Italian descent, moved to Queens after the birth of her son. Her first job in finance was with the Municipal CREDIT UNION, where she earned an award as sales representative of the month. However, she resigned in 2003 after claiming that a male supervisor had sexually harassed her. She had a variety of other jobs before Citibank (one of the Citigroup brands) hired her to work at its new office in the Chrysler Building. She was hired as a business banking officer in September 2008. She was the only woman hired as a business banker in the office.

She allegedly wore clothes that revealed her figure, which caught the attention of her male supervisors. According to Lorenzana's allegations, two managers began to make offhanded comments regarding her appearance. Her wardrobe consisted of form-fitting clothing and high heels. Although she claimed that she never dress provocatively, her managers informed her that her appearance tended to distract her male colleagues. The managers told her that she could no longer wear form-fitting business suits or certain skirts that were too tight. She also alleged that a manager told her she must come to work with straightened hair instead of allowing it to remain curly, which is its natural state. Lorenzara told a reporter with "The Early Show" on CBS, "(I was told) my body type was very different than my other colleagues and because of that, they were able to wear a list of clothing items, but I wasn't." Citigroup has a dress-code policy forbidding provocative clothing, though the policy does not specify items of clothing that are forbidden.

Lorenzana said she did not receive sufficient training to complete tasks essentially to her job, including opening a checking account or take out a loan application for a client. She alleged that she had to forward those accounts to male colleagues with more authority and that those male colleagues would then keep the accounts.

She complained to the company's human resources department, and after several months, an HR representative finally visited the branch. Lorenzana said she presented the representative of pictures of clothing that other women were allowed to wear, stressing that the other women wore clothing more provocative than what Lorenzana was forbidden to wear. However, after the HR representative's visit, she said that the managers became worse. She told a reporter with the *Village Voice* that the managers "picked on (her) every single day." She continue to ask for more training sessions, but she was refused. Meanwhile, her performance had suffered, a quarterly report indicated that she was not performing at a level comparable to her peers. A letter she received in June 2009 said that she was being placed on PROBATION.

Lorenzana then sent letters to vice presidents with the company's human resources department, stressing that she was having to endure a hostile work environment. However, the vice presidents never responded to her messages. In July 2009, the company transferred her to the company's Rockefeller Center branch. However, she was apparently demoted provided further federal protection against sale of tribal lands. However, the State of New York continued to acquire OIN reservation property. Although the federal government objected to early efforts by the state to acquire property, the state was able to acquire land more freely in the years that followed, usually through treaties signed by the State and OIN without objections from the federal government. During the first half of the nineteenth century, many of the members of the OIN tribe had moved out of New York, with many relocating to Wisconsin. By 1838, only 5,000 acres of the reservation remained, and only 620 members remained in New York while another 600 lived in Wisconsin. The acreage continually decreased, and by 1920, the OIN only held 32 acres.

Beginning in 1951, the OIN began to challenge the **cession** of lands from the tribe to the State of New York. In 1971, the Indian Claims Commission determined that the federal government had a **fiduciary** duty under the Nonintercourse Act and other statutes to make sure that the OIN had received "conscionable consideration" for the OIN lands. Later decisions determined that the federal government had actual or constructive knowledge of the transactions and that the federal government would be liable to OIN for any instance in which OIN did not receive proper consideration. OIN **chose** a different route, however, arguing because of the application of the Nonintercourse Act, the tribe's right of possession had not been terminated. LITIGATION about ownership of this property continued into the 1990s. Although these efforts were largely unsuccessful for the tribe, members of OIN were able to acquire, on the open market, land that had once been part of the reservation.

Questions arose about whether local entities could tax the properties that the tribe had reacquired. The tribe argued that because the land had been part of the reservation that the land remained in Indian country established through the early treaties. Because this land was part of the reservation, the tribe argued, it should not be subject to state or local taxation based on the tribe's SOVEREIGN IMMUNITY. Although the tribe prevailed in the Second Circuit Court of Appeals, the U.S. Supreme Court ruled against OIN. In *City of Sherrill,*

N.Y. v. Oneida Indian Nation of N.Y., 544 U.S. 197, 125 S. Ct. 1478, 161 L. Ed. 2d 386 (2005), the Court concluded that the tribe's purchasing of the old lands could not rekindle "embers of sovereignty that long ago grew cold."

Taxation of the tribal property caused further problems. Two counties—Madison and Oneida—had instituted **foreclosure** actions against OIN for the tribe's failure to pay taxes on the tribe property in question. In both instances, courts prevented the counties from FORECLOSURE on the properties. In separate actions, the U.S. **District Court** for the Northern District of New York concluded that the counties could not foreclose on the properties for a variety of reasons, including the application of the tribe's sovereign IMMUNITY.

The counties appealed the decision to the Second Circuit, which affirmed the district court's decisions. The court reviewed a series of Supreme Court cases that addressed whether a tribe could be immune from suit. In the case of *Kiowa Tribe of Okla. v. Mfg. Tech., Inc.,* 523 U.S. 751, 118 S. Ct. 1700, 140 L. Ed. 2d 981 (1998), the Court concluded that a tribe's immunity from suit is independent of the tribe's land. Applying the principle to OIN's case, the Second Circuit concluded that the tribe was immune from the foreclosure suit even though the county could properly tax the land. *Oneida Indian Nation of N.Y. v. Madison County,* 605 F.3d 149 (2d Cir. 2010). Two of the three judges that reviewed the case also agreed that the "decision defies common sense," yet the court was bound by precedent to rule as it did.

The counties appealed the case to the Supreme Court, which agreed to review the decision. However, in November 2010, the tribe had waived "its sovereign immunity to enforcement of real property taxation through foreclosure by state, county and local governments within and throughout the United States." Commentators suggested that the tribe was concerned that the Supreme Court would carve out an exception to the doctrine of tribal immunity, so OIN decided to avoid the issue by waiving its immunity. The Court remanded the case to the Second Circuit, where the OIN planned to challenge the foreclosures as violations of New York state law. *Madison County, N.Y. v. Onedia Indian Nation of N.Y.,,* 131 S. Ct. 704, 178 L. Ed. 2d 587 (2011).

SPEEDY TRIAL

California Supreme Court Dismisses Criminal Cases Due to Court Backlog

Criminal defendants have constitutional and **statutory** rights to a SPEEDY TRIAL. In California's Riverside County, chronic problems with judicial staffing and court budgets made it virtually impossible to comply with a state law that requires bringing a **felony** case to trial within 60 days from the date a DEFENDANT is arraigned or indicted. The California SUPREME COURT created a task force to solve the problem and sent retired judges and active judges from other counties into Riverside County to try criminal cases. Despite these efforts, criminal defendants waited long periods of time before having trials or having their cases dismissed for the lack of a speedy trial. The California Supreme Court revisited these issues in *People v. Engram*, 240 P.3d 237 (2010). In this case the court ruled that a trial judge acted properly in dismissing a defendant's case for delay. The judge refused to assign judicial resources from the civil department to the criminal department. In addition, the unavailability of a judge or courtroom within the speedy trial period was not **good cause** for continuing the case.

The problem with delays in criminal trials in Riverside County did not subside after the state court system attempted to reduce the backlog. The district attorney for the county insisted that a California **statute** required the Riverside court to extend its efforts even further by making every trial court judge and courtroom available to handle criminal trials where the speedy trial statute required dismissal. This would have meant that judges assigned to FAMILY LAW, **probate**, and juvenile matters would have been forced to put aside their cases. The California Supreme Court rejected the district attorney's contention in two appeals but the district attorney continued to press the argument in *Engram*.

Terrion Engram was initially charged with attempted premeditated MURDER and first degree **burglary**. A jury acquitted him of the attempted murder charge but found him guilty on the BURGLARY charge. In 2007, the court of appeals reversed the burglary conviction and ordered a new trial. The new trial was scheduled for May 2008, which resulted in a MISTRIAL. A third trial was scheduled for July 2008 but the district attorney requested the court to move the trial to late August, citing a lack of preparation time. The court granted the request but on the day of trial the district attorney asked the court to postpone the trial for two weeks. Again the trial court agreed but further postponements were requested and granted, pushing the trial date to September 29. When the case was called for trial that day the defendant's lawyer told the court he was ready for trial and that Engram objected to any further delays. This case and 17 others called that day in court were "last-day" cases under the speedy trial statute. When the trial judge announced that there were no available courtrooms to which the case could be assigned for trial, Engram's lawyer told the court that he would file for dismissal of the charge.

The district attorney advanced two arguments for not dismissing the case. First, although there were no courtrooms available for criminal cases, the court could use a courtroom that handled juvenile, probate, or family matters. Second, the district attorney contended that if the court did not have sufficient resources to try the case, then this would amount to good cause to continue the case until a courtroom was available. The trial court refused to commandeer a civil courtroom, citing the important issues involving families and children that are handled by these courts. Under state law, the court had to determine how to allocate its business in light of the social values that were at play in the administration of the courts. As to the second argument, the court determined the circumstances in Engram's case did not constitute good cause. Therefore, the court dismissed Engram's case due to the lack of a judge and a courtroom to try the case in a timely manner. The court of appeals upheld these rulings and the California Supreme Court accepted the district attorney's petition for review.

The supreme court, in a unanimous decision, upheld the lower courts. Chief Justice Ronald George, writing for the court, addressed both of the arguments made by the district attorney in the lower courts. He first noted that a court "has both the inherent authority and responsibility to fairly and efficiently administer all of the judicial proceedings that are pending before it." Although a California statute stated that criminal cases must be given precedence over civil matters, the court pointed out that the statute also stated that this policy should be carried out to the "greatest degree that is consistent with the ends of justice." Chief Justice George concluded that, in accord with its past decisions, the policy could not be interpreted as "an absolute or inflexible rule mandating such precedence under all circumstances." A trial court must always maintain "ultimate control" over the order in which cases should be considered. The important and pressing matters in family, probate, and juvenile proceedings could not be pushed aside when time was of the essence in many of these cases. The statute could not be read to remove a court's case-by-case comparison of each pending criminal and civil case.

The court also rejected the district attorney's claim that the lack of court resources provided good cause for continuing, rather than dismissing, Engram's case. In prior cases the court had made clear that a defendant's right to a speedy trial could not be denied by "simply asserting that the public resources provided by the State's criminal-justice system are limited and that each case must await its turn." The criminal calendar congestion that led to the dismissal of Engram's case, as well as 17 others that day was a "chronic condition," rather than an "exceptional circumstance." Therefore, there was no good cause to continue the cases.

United States v. Tinklenberg

The SIXTH AMENDMENT to the U.S. Constitution guarantees, among other things, a "speedy trial" for criminal defendants. Pursuant thereto, the SPEEDY TRIAL Act of 1974, 18 U.S.C. § 3161 *et seq.*, states that in any case where a plea of not guilty is entered, "the trial . . . shall commence within seventy days" from the later of either (1) the "filing date" of the information or INDICTMENT, or (2) the defendant's initial appearance before a judicial officer (i.e., an ARRAIGNMENT). There are several exclusions from the 70-day period that are listed in the text of the law, including "delay resulting from any pretrial motion, from the filing of the motion through the conclusion of the hearing on, or other prompt **disposition** of, such motion."

In *United States v. Tinklenberg*, No. 09-1498, 131 S. Ct. 62, 563 U.S. ___ (2011) the U.S. SUPREME COURT held that, under the Act, the time between the filing of such a pretrial motion and its actual disposition is excluded from the 70-day period, regardless of whether it actually causes, or is expected to cause, delay in starting the trial. In so holding, the Court reversed the decision of the U.S. Court of Appeals for the Sixth Circuit, which held that such a pretrial motion fell within the exclusion only if it actually caused delay, or the expectation of delay, of trial. 579 F.3d 589 (6th Cir. 2009).

In 2005, Jason Tinklenberg was indicted for various violations of federal gun and drug laws. He made his initial appearance for the charges before a judicial officer on October 31, 2005. His trial began on August 14, 2006, which was 287 days later. However, just prior to the commencement of trial, defense counsel requested the court to dismiss the indictment on the grounds that the trial was way beyond the 70-day limit found in the Speedy Trial Act. The **district court**, examining the delay, found that 218 of the 287 days fell within various exclusions under the Act, leaving 69 nonexcludable days. The district court then denied Tinklenberg's motion and trial proceeded. He was convicted and sentenced. He appealed.

The Sixth **Circuit Court** of Appeals agreed with the district court on many of the excludable days. There were, however, three pretrial motions, the excludability of time for which the **appellate court** disagreed with the district court about. The government had filed the first motion (unopposed) on August 1, 2006 (14 days before trial started) to conduct a video DEPOSITION of a witness. The trial court disposed of the motion on August 3. The government also filed the second motion (also unopposed) on August 8, to bring seized firearms into the courtroom as evidence at trial. This motion was disposed of by the court on August 10. The third motion was filed by DEFENDANT Tinklenberg, a motion to dismiss the indictment under the Speedy Trial Act. This motion was filed on August 11, 2006, and disposed of (denied) on August 14, 2006, at which time trial commenced.

According to the decision of the Sixth Circuit, the nine days during which the three motions were pending were not excludable (from the 70-day period under the Act) because the motions did not actually cause a delay, or the expectation of delay, of trial. These nine days, if not excluded, would put the number of days above 70. Therefore, the Sixth Circuit found a violation of the Act. Further, since, by the time of the **appellate** decision, Tinklenberg had served his prison sentence, the Sixth Circuit ordered the district court to dismiss the indictment with prejudice.

The U.S. Supreme Court, in a majority opinion delivered by Justice STEPHEN BREYER, disagreed with the Sixth Circuit's interpretation of the relevant provisions of the Act. Specifically, Subparagraph (D), listing some of the exclusions relevant in this case, repeats the word "delay" in its enumerated textual exclusions, e.g., "any period of delay resulting from . . ." or "the following periods of delay shall be excluded . . ." The Sixth Circuit had reasoned that, read most naturally, that subparagraph excluded only enumerated exceptions that actually caused a delay (in trial commencement).

But the Supreme Court found the language alone as not dispositive in resolving the basic question presented. The Court found several other considerations which, taken together, "compel[led]" the conclusion that Congress intended subparagraph (D) to apply automatically, irrespective of whether such enumerated exclusions actually caused delay. Accordingly, the Court concluded that nothing in the Act required that the filing of a pretrial motion must actually cause, or be expected to cause, a delay of trial.

Next, the Court went on to discuss the Sixth Circuit's interpretation of Subparagraph (F), which excludes from the 70-day limit any "delay resulting from transportation of any defendant . . . to and from places of examination . . . , except that any time consumed in excess of ten days shall be presumed to be unreasonable." The lower courts agreed that a total of 20 days had been consumed by transporting Tinklenberg for competency evaluations. Because the government offered no justification, all days in excess of ten (the additional ten of 20) were therefore 'unreasonable" and excluded. But the Sixth Circuit only found two days to be excessive (unreasonable), and exempted the other eight weekend and holidays from the count, incorporating Federal Rule of **Criminal Procedure** 45(a) as parallel guidance. The Supreme Court found this also to be in error, holding that nothing in the Act required incorporation of such Rule.

In an ironic conclusion, The Court noted that although the interpretations made by the Sixth Circuit in both subparagraphs (D) and (F) were mistaken, they served to cancel each other out. Therefore, the Sixth Circuit's ultimate conclusion that Tinklenberg's trial failed to comply with the Act's deadline was correct. The Supreme Court affirmed the APPELLATE court's holding that the indictment be dismissed with prejudice, in favor of Tinklenberg.

Justice Breyer was joined in the majority opinion by Justices Anthony Kennedy, Ruth Bader Ginsburg, Samuel Alito, and Sonia Sotomayor, and joined in Parts I and III by Chief Justice John Roberts as well as Justices Antonin Scalia and Clarence Thomas. Justice Scalia filed an opinion concurring in part and concurring in the judgment, joined by Chief Justice Roberts and Justice Thomas. As to Part II of the majority's opinion, he agreed that a pretrial motion need not actually postpone a trial, or create an expectation of postponement, but he would have derived such a conclusion from the text of the Act alone, and saw no need to look beyond the text.

Newly-appointed Justice Elena Kagan took no part in consideration or decision of the case.

SPORTS LAW

NFL Labor Dispute

In February 2011, the National Football League (NFL) was riding a good wave. Super Bowl XLV had been watched by an average of 111 million viewers. The average national telecast for the season brought in roughly 17.9 million viewers, up about 1.3 million viewers per game from the 2009 Season. The industry was now worth about $9 billion, bringing unprecedented wealth to its owners and players during 24 years of labor peace.

But all that ended just one month later, when talks broke down between players and the League's 32 owners over how to divvy up that wealth. Despite two extensions to the **collective bargaining agreement** (CBA) between League owners and the players' union and 16 days of talks overseen by a federal mediator (which followed months of off-and-on negotiating), the two sides could not agree to a deal.

Just hours before the CBA was to expire on March 4, 2011, the players' union called off labor negotiations and decertified itself. Ten players, including quarterbacks Tom Brady, Peyton Manning and Drew Brees, as well as Chargers wide receiver Vincent Jackson, filed an anti-trust suit in federal court, asking for an INJUNCTION that would force the league to continue operating fully and not lock them out. Anti-trust laws prohibit the union from filing suit against the owners. However, once the union dissolved, or decertified, players were free to file suit. Commentators anticipated a protracted battle.

As background, following players' strikes in 1982 and 1987, the sport established a system of FREE AGENCY and a salary cap as part of a settlement for a 1993 anti-trust class-action lawsuit filed by the players (lead PLAINTIFF Reggie White of the Eagles). Years of peace ensued, with former NFL Commissioner Paul Tagliabue and late union chief Gene Upshaw working together to negotiate repeat extensions of the labor deal (CBA), roughly every two years. In 2006, prior to his retirement, Tagliabue negotiated another CBA extension, with just Buffalo and Cincinnati voting against it. Both sides could opt out in 2008. Roger Goodell then took over as commissioner.

In 2008, the NFL, exercising its option, backed out of the CBA, citing high costs and the need for "givebacks" from the players, i.e., the owners wanted back what they perceived was given away under Tagliabue. The 2010 season was left open without salary caps. Later that year, union chief Upshaw passed away. After six months without leadership, the players elected Washington attorney DeMaurice Smith to replace him. Now Goodell and Smith were left to pick up the pieces.

Prior to the 2010 season without a salary cap, league owners were credited with about $1.3 billion for expenses and the players received 60 percent of the remaining revenue. According to the union, that represented about half the sport's total income at that time.

The issues separating the parties in 2011 began with league owners wanting to take another $1 billion off the top, before the players' share was calculated. The union filed a collusion claim with the NFL's SPECIAL MASTER, University of Pennsylvania law professor Stephen B. Burbank, alleging that the teams conspired to restrict players' salaries, interfering with the movement of free agents. When the

New York Giants quarterback Eli Manning, right, throws as wide receiver Victor Cruz looks on during an unofficial football June 10, 2011. The workout gave the players an opportunity to practice together during the NFL labor lockout.
AP IMAGES/JULIO CORTEZ

CBA expired, similar charges went to federal **district court**.

The NFL responded by filing its own charges with the National Labor Relations Board (NLRB), accusing the union of not bargaining in **good faith** after the union announced its plans to stop negotiations and decertify. The NFL argued that its need to take more off the top of the now $9 billion annual revenue was justified because player salaries were increasing at a rate faster than the League's revenues, creating an unsustainable business model.

As it stood in mid-2011, the players remained free agents bound only as a trade association. The decertified union could no longer bargain on behalf of the players, and the only option for the parties was to settle their respective LITIGATION claims. The League projected that if work stoppage continued into August and September, it would lose $400 million in lost revenue for each canceled week of the regular season, estimated to be up to $1 billion by September. The NFL Players Association disputed this claim.

The League earlier had proposed lengthening the regular season to 18 games per team, imposing a wage scale for rookies, and testing players for human growth hormone. But the money remained the key issue separating the parties.

In June 2011, ESPN.com reported that NFL owners were ready to offer a plan giving players 48 percent of all revenues. Previously, players were getting close to 60 percent, but not before the League recouped the first $1 billion off the top (see above). In reality, the players wound up with closer to 50 percent of all revenues after such a reduction. So it appeared that they might be closer to a deal. The two sides finally came to an agreement on a new, 10-year labor contract in late July 2011, leading the owners to lift the lockout, allowing league business to begin. Fans were able to breathe sighs of relief as only one preseason game was lost.

STATUTE OF LIMITATIONS

A type of federal or state law that restricts the time within which legal proceedings may be brought.

California Timeliness Requirement Bars Habeas Relief in Federal Court

Most states set firm statutes of limitations for prisoners who seek post-conviction relief. California courts are an exception, applying a general reasonableness standard to determine whether a **habeas corpus** petition is timely filed. The U.S. SUPREME COURT was faced with the question whether this timeliness requirement, when applied by a California state court, is an independent state ground adequate to bar habeas **corpus** relief in federal court. The Court, in *Walker v. Martin*, __U.S.__, 131 S. Ct. 1120, __L.Ed.2d__ (2011), ruled that the California requirement was sufficient to bar federal court habeas relief.

Under California law a prisoner must file a habeas petition "as promptly as the circumstances allow." Petitioners must state when they first learned of the asserted claims and explain why they did not seek postconviction relief sooner. When claims have been substantially denied without justification, the court may deny the petition as untimely. California courts signal that a habeas petition is denied by citing the titles of the two controlling cases issued by the California Supreme Court. When a denial order is issued without these citations or any explanation the ruling usually is on the merits of the petition. In addition, California habeas petitioners may file a petition in a trial court, court of appeals, or the supreme court. There is no appeal of these petitions. Instead, the petitioner must file a new petition in a higher court.

Charles W. Martin participated in a 1986 **robbery** and MURDER in California. He fled the state but eight years later was extradited to California to stand trial. He was convicted of murder and ROBBERY and sentenced to life in prison without the possibility of PAROLE. The California **appellate** courts affirmed his convictions in 1997. In 1998, Martin filed his first habeas petition in state court, which was denied the following year. He then filed a federal habeas petition in U.S. **district court**, claiming for the first time that he had received ineffective assistance **of counsel**. The federal court stayed the proceedings and directed Martin to exhaust his state remedies by raising this issue in state court. In March 2002 he filed a habeas petition with the California Supreme Court on the ineffective counsel matter. He did not explain why he omitted this claim on his first state habeas petition, which had bee filed five years before. Sixth months later the California Supreme Court denied his petition using the two cases that deal with untimely petitions.

Martin then returned to federal court and filed an amended petition. The federal district court denied his petition based upon the untimeliness ruling of the supreme court. The Ninth **Circuit Court** of Appeals vacated this dismissal order and directed the district court to determine the adequacy of the state's time bar. The district court rejected the petition again, finding that the state's time bar was clearly defined, well established, and consistently applied. The Ninth Circuit again disagreed with the lower court, concluding that time bar had not been shown to be firmly defined or consistently applied. The U.S. Supreme Court agreed to hear California's appeal.

The Court, in a unanimous decision, overruled the Ninth Circuit ruling. Justice RUTH BADER GINSBURG, writing for the Court, noted that a recent Court decision had made clear that a state procedural bar may count as an adequate and independent ground for denying a federal habeas petition. This was important because a federal habeas court will not review a claim rejected by a state court if the state court's decision rests on a state law ground that is independent of the **federal question** and adequate to support the judgment. To be an adequate procedural ground a state rule must be "firmly established and regularly followed." In this case, Martin alleged that the discretionary time requirement failed on this ground. Justice Ginsburg disagreed, pointing to prior decisions in which the Court stated that discretionary requirements could be firmly established and regularly followed. The California time rule was based on three cases in which the state supreme court had instructed habeas petitioners to allege with specificity the absence of substantial delay, a **good cause** for delay, or eligibility for one of four exceptions to the time bar. This **case law** made it plain that Martin's five-year delay was substantial. Contrary to Martin's assertion, the time rule was not too vague to be firmly established.

Justice Ginsburg also found that the time rule was regularly followed. The California Supreme Court summarily denies hundreds of habeas petitions each year by citing the two controlling cases and nothing more. On the same day Martin's petition was denied, 21 other petitions were denied using the summary details. Moreover, other California courts regularly cite the same two cases when denying a habeas petition. Martin argued that the use of summary decisions made it impossible to tell why the California Supreme Court decides some delayed petitions on the merits and rejects others as untimely. Ginsburg saw no reason to reject the time bar simply because the court opted not to use the time-barred citations in favor of dismissing a petition on the merits "if that is the easiest path."

The Ninth Circuit found that the time bar was not consistently applied because outcomes varied from case to case. In one case a one year delay was too long, while in another case 14 months was determined not to be a substantial delay. Justice Ginsburg rejected this approach because discretion "enables a court to home in on case-specific considerations and to avoid the harsh results that sometimes attend consistent application of an unyielding rule." There was no reason to discourage standards that allowed courts to exercise discretion.

TAXATION

The process whereby charges are imposed on individuals or property by the legislative branch of the federal government and by many state governments to raise funds for public purposes.

Railroad May Sue State Over Alleged Discriminatory Taxes

A 1976 federal law restricts the ability of state and local governments to levy discriminatory taxes on rail **carriers**. Under the Railroad Revitalization and Regulatory Reform Act (the 4-R Act), a state or its subdivisions may not "Impose another tax that discriminates against a rail carrier." In *CSX Transportation, Inc.*, __U.S. __, 131 S.Ct. 1101, __L.Ed.2d__ (2011), the U.S. SUPREME COURT ruled that a rail carrier may sue a state because it exempts interstate trucking and water carriers from sales and use taxes on diesel fuel while requiring railroads to pay these taxes on fuel.

CSX Transportation, Inc. is an interstate rail carrier that operates in the state of Alabama. Alabama imposes a 4% sales tax on the gross receipts of retail businesses and a **use tax** of 4% on the storage, use, or consumption of tangible PERSONAL PROPERTY. CSX paid these taxes when it purchased or consumed diesel fuel. However, the state exempted its main competitors-interstate motor and water carriers-from paying sales and use taxes on their fuel. CSX filed suit in federal **district court**, alleging that the state's taxing scheme violated the 4-R Act. The district

court dismissed the lawsuit and the Eleventh **Circuit Court** of Appeals upheld this decision. The appeals court relied on a 2008 circuit decision involving the 4-R Act, which involved a similar challenge to the application of Alabama sales and use taxes. The 2008 opinion in turn relied on a 1994 Supreme Court decision. In that case the Court held that a railroad could not invoke the 4-R Act to challenge a generally applicable property tax on the basis that certain non-railroad property was exempt from the tax. Though the CSX case involved sales and use taxes and not property taxes, the appeals court concluded that the difference was immaterial. Therefore, CSX could not object to the sales and use taxes simply because the state provided exemptions from them. The Supreme Court agreed to hear CSX's appeal because other circuit courts of appeals did allow railroads to bring challenges under the 4-R Act to non-property taxes from which their competitors were exempt.

The Supreme Court, in a 7-2 decision, overturned the Eleventh Circuit ruling. Justice Elena Kagan, writing for the majority, started with the language of the 4-R Act provision: A state may not "Impose another tax that discriminates against a rail carrier." The Court had to answer two questions: Was CSX challenging "another tax" within the meaning of the **statute**? If so, might that tax "discriminate" against rail carriers by exempting their competitors? The first question was relatively easy to answer. An **excise** tax, like the state's sales and use taxes, was "another tax."Although the 4-R Act did not define "tax," the word's ordinary definition sufficed to show that its meaning was expansive. A state seeks to raise revenue using various types of taxes. Therefore, "another tax" was best understood to encompass any form of tax not otherwise listed in the 4-R Act provisions. In other words, "another tax" was a catch-all.

Justice Kagan rejected the state's contention that "another tax" was limited to gross-receipts taxes that some states imposed instead of property taxes at the time the 4-R Act was passed in 1976. Moreover, CSX was not challenging the imposition of taxes on its fuel. Instead, it was challenging the exemptions the state had given to other modes of commercial freight transportation. The key question then became whether the tax was discriminatory because of these exemptions. Again, the 4-R Act did not define "discriminate" and again the Court looked at the ordinary meaning of this word, which is to fail to treat all persons equally when no reasonable distinction can be found between those favored and those disfavored. If one group of taxpayers is taxed at a 2% rate and another group at a 4% rate, the tax is discriminatory against the second group if both groups are the same. This DISCRIMINATION would continue if the first group's rate was reduced to 0%, which amounts to an exemption from the tax. To argue as Alabama did that such a tax did not "discriminate" would be to adopt a definition "at odd with the word's natural meaning." Justice Kagan pointed to prior Court decisions in which the Court had found tax schemes with exemptions discriminatory.

Alabama sought to limit the 4-R Act to state tax schemes that unjustifiably exempt local actors, as opposed to interstate entities. Justice Kagan rejected this claim, finding that the act did not make such a distinction. The act referred to rail carriers, not interstate rail carriers. The real distinction was between railroads and other actors, whether interstate or local. The state also contended that the Court's prior decision on the 4-R Act ·was directly applicable to this case. The Court disagreed, finding that its holding that a rail carrier could not challenge exemptions to property was based on a different provision of the act. The provision before the Court did not allow the state to grant non-property tax exemptions; therefore, the Court could not read in the language from the other provision into this one. Alabama also argued that even if the prior Court decision was limited to property tax exemptions, the Court should extend it to non-property tax exemptions in order to prevent inconsistent or anomalous results. The Court found this argument unavailing as well.

TELECOMMUNICATIONS

The transmission of words, sounds, images, or data in the form of electronic or electromagnetic signals or impulses.

Talk America v. Mich. Bell Telephone Co.

Until Congress enacted the TELECOMMUNICATIONS Act of 1996, Pub. L. No. 104-104, 110 Stat. 56, newer local exchange **carriers** (LEC) had a difficult time breaking into a local market because INCUMBENT LECs owned the local exchange networks. If a new LEC wanted to compete in an area, the LEC would basically have to replicate the incumbent LEC's existing network, which would be cost-prohibitive. The Act opened the doors to competition by requiring incumbent LEC's to share parts of existing networks through leases. An issue arose about whether an incumbent LEC had to provide access to a transmission facility. In *Talk America, Inc. v. Mich. Bell Telephone Co.*, Nos. 10-313, 10-329, 2011 WL 2224429 (U.S. June 9, 2011), the SUPREME COURT resolved this issue by deferring to the FEDERAL COMMUNICATIONS COMMISSION (FCC), which concluded that the incumbent had to provide access to the facility for purposes of interconnection between networks.

The Telecommunications Act broke up what was practically a **monopoly** held by the incumbent LECs. Congress allowed new LECs to enter the market by requiring the incumbents either to connect to the incumbents' existing equipment or to purchase or lease existing elements or services of the incumbents' networks. LECs establish rates, terms, and conditions by signing interconnections agreements. Although state public-utility commissions oversee the interconnection agreements, the FCC has authority to promulgate regulations implementing provisions of the Act.

Two sections of the Act gave rise to the dispute before the Supreme Court. First, the Act in § 251(c)(3) requires an incumbent LEC to lease certain network elements as required by the FEC. The competitive LEC may lease these elements on an "unbundled basis" meaning that the competitive LEC can choose which elements it wants to lease. The purpose of this section is to make it easier for the competitive LEC to create its own network without having to build all of the elements from the ground up. The FCC has issued regulations identifying the network elements that an incumbent LEC must make available for lease. In identifying which elements an incumbent must make available, the FCC must consider the access is necessary and whether denying access would impair a competitor's ability to provide service.

A second provision contained in § 251(c)(2) requires incumbent LECs to provide "interconnection" between the incumbents' networks and the competitive LEC's facility. This section is designed to allow users on a competitive LEC's network to call users on the incumbent's network, and vice versa. Like the leasing of network elements, the incumbents provide interconnection on a cost-based rate. The duty on the incumbents to provide interconnection is independent of other rules, and the impairment requirement does not apply to interconnection.

Until it changed its position in 2003, the FCC had determined that incumbents had to provide cost-based access to entrance facilities, which are the locations where the various transmission cables enter a building and run into wiring rooms. The FCC changed this position in 2003, deciding that incumbents did not have to provide unbundled access to entrance facilities because the FCC concluded that these facilities were not network elements. In making its decision, the FCC noted that the entrance facilities were both for interconnection and for what is called "backhauling" traffic, which relates to part of the connections within a telecommunications network. In issuing its order, the FCC noted that incumbents still had to provide access to entrance facilities for the purpose of interconnection. The order only affected the need to provide unbundled access to the facilities for the purpose of backhauling traffic.

The FCC issued its order amid a series of reviews by the D.C. **Circuit Court** of Appeals. In 2004, the D.C. Circuit vacated the FCC's order because the FCC did not engage in an analysis of whether restricting access to the entrance facilities would impair the ability of the competitors to provide service. The FCC issued a new order in 2005, concluding that unbundled access to the entrance facilities was not necessary because requiring competitive LECs to pay competitive rates for use of the entrance fees did not impair these LECs from competing.

In light of this order, an incumbent LEC, Michigan Bell Telephone Company, notified several competitive LECs that Michigan Bell would start charging competitive rates for use of the entrance facilities. The competitive LECs complained to the state public service commission, which ordered Michigan Bell to continue providing access to the entrance facilities at cost-based rates. Michigan Bell brought suit to challenge the commission's ruling, and the **district court** held that Michigan Bell did not have to provide these services at cost-based rates. The competitive LECs then appealed to the Sixth Circuit Court of Appeals, which also considered an amicus brief filed by the FCC. The FCC argued that Michigan Bell had to provide access to the entrance facilities for purposes of interconnection. However, the Sixth Circuit refused to defer to the FCC's position and held that Michigan Bell did not have to provide access to the entrance facilities at the regulated rates. *Michigan Bell Telephone Co. v. Covad Communications Co.*, 597 F.3d 370 (6th Cir. 2010).

The Sixth Circuit's decision also differed from conclusions made by the Seventh and Eighth Circuits, and the Supreme Court agreed to review the decision. In a unanimous vote (with Justice Elena Kagan not participating), the Court reversed the Sixth Circuit. Writing for the majority, Justice CLARENCE THOMAS determined that the **statute** in question contained ambiguities about what the terms focusing on interconnection mean. With the absence of an unambiguous statute, Thomas turned to the FCC's explanation given in the commission's amicus brief.

The commission asserted that incumbent LECs must provide cost-based access to entrance facilities for three main reasons. First, the commission concluded that the incumbent must lease "technically feasible" facilities for interconnection purposes. Second, the FCC determined that entrance facilities are part of an incumbent network, so the incumbent must lease the facility for interconnection purposes if it is technically feasible. Third, it is technically feasible for an incumbent to provide access to the entrance facilities, and this was especially true in Michigan Bell's case.

Thomas then concluded that the FCC's interpretation was neither plainly erroneous nor inconsistent with the agency's regulations. Accordingly, the Court deferred to the FCC's interpretation and concluded that Michigan Bell had to provide cost-based access to the entrance facilities.

Justice ANTONIN SCALIA concurred, noting that he doubted whether the rule requiring deference to an agency's interpretation of its own rule. However, Scalia said he would have reached the same conclusion even without deferring to the FCC.

TENTH AMENDMENT

An amendment to the United States Constitution and part of the Bill of Rights, stating: "The powers not delegated to the United States by the Constitution, nor prohibited by it to the States, are reserved to the States respectively, or to the people."

Bond v. United States

The TENTH AMENDMENT to the U.S. Constitution provides, "The powers not delegated to the United States by the Constitution, nor prohibited by it to the States, are reserved to the States respectively, or to the people." Several lower **federal courts** have struggled to decide whether a private party unassociated with a state or a state actor has standing to challenge a federal government action on Tenth Amendment grounds. In 2011, the U.S. SUPREME COURT ruled that a criminal DEFENDANT convicted of using a chemical weapon in violation of a federal **statute** had standing to challenge the conviction based on the Tenth Amendment. *Bond v. United States*, No. 09-1227, 2011 WL 2369334 (U.S. June 16, 2011).

The facts of the case were rather unusual. The case involved a microbiologist named Carol Anne Bond. She was first excited to learn that her best friend, Myrlinda Haynes, had become pregnant. However, Bond became enraged after learning that the father of Haynes' baby was Bond's husband. Bond decided to take revenge by poisoning Haynes. Bond worked for chemical manufacturer Rohm and Haas, and Bond stole an amount of 10-chloro10H-phenoxarsine from her employer. She also ordered a vial of potassium dichromate over the Internet. Each of these chemicals can cause toxic harm even with minimal contact to human skin. The chemicals can also be fatal if swallowed in small amounts.

Bond harassed Haynes by calling and threatening her. During the next several months, Bond additionally made at least 24 attempts to poison Haynes. Bond spread the chemicals over a variety of objects, including Haynes' doorknob, car door handles, and mailbox. Haynes noticed the chemicals and was able to avoid contact in most instances. However, Haynes sustained a chemical burn on her thumb on one occasion.

After reporting the incident to the local police (who did not respond to Haynes' satisfaction), Haynes complained to her local postal carrier about the chemicals on the mailbox. The United States Postal Inspection Service placed surveillance cameras at Haynes' home. The cameras caught Bond putting chemicals inside the muffler of Haynes' car and opening Haynes' mailbox to take out a business envelope. The film also showed Bond going back and forth from her car to Haynes' car with the chemicals. The inspectors later found that several pounds of potassium dichromate were missing from Rohm and Haas.

A **grand jury** in the U.S. **District Court** for the Eastern District of Pennsylvania changed Bond with two counts of possessing and using a chemical weapon in violation of a criminal statute contained in 18 U.S.C. § 229(a)(1). Bond was also charged with two counts of mail theft. The district court rejected several of Bond's arguments about the charges, including an argument that 18 U.S.C. § 229 is unconstitutional because it violates principles contained in the Tenth Amendment. After the court denied her motions, Bond pleaded guilty but reserved the right to appeal. Bond received a six-year prison sentence, along with five-years supervised release and monetary penalties.

Congress enacted 18 U.S.C. § 229 as part of the United States' implementation of the Chemical Weapons Convention, which the United States ratified in 1993. The statute prohibits any person "to develop, produce, otherwise acquire, transfer directly or indirectly, receive, stockpile, retain, own, possess, or use, or threaten to use, any chemical weapon...." The statute defines "chemical weapon" in terms of the weapon containing a toxic chemical, and the statute defines "toxic chemical" to include "any chemical which through its chemical action on life processes can cause death, temporary incapacitation or permanent harm to humans or animals."

Bond argued that the statute violates principles of FEDERALISM because the statute is not "based on a valid exercise of constitutional authority" and does not "require proof of a federal interest." The district court rejected her argument, but the Third **Circuit Court** of Appeals went a step further, concluding that Bond did not have standing as an individual to challenge the law based on the Tenth Amendment.

With lower circuit courts of appeals split on the question of whether a private figure can challenge a federal law based on Tenth Amendment grounds, the Supreme Court agreed to review the case. In a unanimous decision, the Court reversed the Third Circuit. Justice ANTHONY KENNEDY, writing for the Court, noted that the Third Circuit had misplaced its reliance on the Supreme Court's decision in *Tennessee Electric Power Co. v. TVA*, 306 U.S. 118, 59 S. Ct. 366, 83 L. Ed. 543 (1939). The Court in that **case stated** that certain utility companies did not have standing to sue a federally chartered **entity** under the Tenth Amendment. However, Kennedy noted that the Court used "standing" and "cause of action" interchangeably, which is not consistent with modern usage of the term standing. Kennedy finally concluded that the statement in *Tennessee Electric* was inconsistent with later precedents.

Kennedy also reviewed other instances in which the Court has allowed individuals to challenge federal statutes based on constitutional grounds. Kennedy could not find a basis to deny an individual such as Bond the right to challenge the federal law, so the Court reversed the Third Circuit.

Justice RUTH BADER GINSBURG, joined by Justice STEPHEN BREYER, concurred. Ginsburg argued that Bond had the personal right not to be convicted under a constitutionally invalid law, and this right should have given Bond standing to challenge the law.

Federal Courts Rules DOMA Unconstitutional

When the Supreme Judicial Court of Massachusetts held in 2003 that excluding same-sex couples from marriage violated provisions of the state constitution, it set in motion other legal challenges relating to the definition of marriage. The Commonwealth of Massachusetts soon was faced with federal issues relating to the 1996 Defense of Marriage Act (DOMA), Pub.L. No. 104-199, 110 Stat. 2419 (1996). DOMA denies federal recognition of same-sex marriages and authorizes states to refuse to recognize same-sex marriages licensed in other states. The commonwealth sued the federal government, claiming that DOMA violated the TENTH AMENDMENT, which reserves to the states all powers not expressly delegated to the federal government. It claimed that Congress did not have the authority to intrude on an area of law that has historically been the province of the states. A federal **district court** agreed with this argument in *Massachusetts v. U.S. DEPARTMENT OF HEALTH AND HUMAN SERVICES*, 698 F. Supp.2nd 234 (2010).

Massachusetts sought to gain federal approval for granting same-sex couples the same rights as heterosexual couples in three areas. First, the state constructed and maintains two cemeteries that are used for the burial of eligible military veterans. It received federal funding for these cemeteries and the Department of Veterans Affairs (VA) reimburses the state $300 for the costs associated with the burial of each veteran. The state is bound by VA regulations, which require that only veterans, their spouses, and certain children may be buried in these cemeteries. When the state asked whether a same-sex spouse qualified for burial, the VA replied that it would not be entitled to recapture the federal grant funds used to construct and maintain the cemeteries if a same-sex spouse who was not independently eligible was buried there. A branch of the VA later published a directive that confirmed this policy.

The Massachusetts **Medicaid** program, called MassHealth, also was effected by DOMA. MassHealth receives federal funding to provide medical services to low-income individuals. To qualify for federal funding the Department of Health and Human Services (HHS) must approve a state plan describing the scope and nature of the MassHealth program. Marital status is an important factor in determining whether an individual is eligible for coverage by the program. Because of DOMA, federal law requires Massachusetts to assess eligibility for same-sex spouses as though each were single. This has had severe financial consequences, as there is no federal funding for covering same-sex spouses who do not qualify for MEDICAID when assessed as single, even thought they would qualify if assessed as married. The recognition of same-sex marriages makes some individuals eligible for benefits for which they otherwise would not be. HHS informed Mass Health officials that DOMA did not give it the discretion to recognize same-sex marriage for the purposes of federal funding of Medicaid.

Following these federal decisions the commonwealth filed a lawsuit in federal court, challenging DOMA. Judge Joseph Tauro ruled in favor of Massachusetts, finding that DOMA violated both the Spending Clause and the Tenth Amendment of the U.S. Constitution. Tauro stated that the powers invested with Congress are "defined and limited," and pointed out that in the First **Circuit Court** of Appeals federal regulations of FAMILY LAW have only been upheld where they were "firmly rooted in an enumerated federal power." The U.S. government contended that the Spending Clause, Article 1, § 8, gave Congress the authority to enact DOMA. This clause gave Congress the power to raise and spend money to promote the "general welfare" of the public. Judge Tauro noted that much of DOMA's reach was not limited to provisions relating to federal spending; there were 1,138 federal laws in which marital status was a factor, including laws on COPYRIGHT, the Family and Medical Leave Act, and testimonial privileges in court.

Though Congress has broad powers to define how money is disbursed to the states, it was not, in Tauro's view, unlimited. He examined two restrictions on congressional power: legislation must not be barred by other constitutional provisions and the conditions set by Congress must not be unrelated to the federal interest in particular projects or programs funded under the challenged law. As to the first, the court ruled that DOMA impermissibly conditioned the receipt of federal funds on the state's violation of the **Equal Protection** Clause of the FOURTEENTH AMENDMENT by requiring that the state deny certain marriage-based benefits to same-sex married couples. Therefore, the court ruled that the Spending Clause could not justify the constitutionality of DOMA.

Judge Tauro also ruled that DOMA impermissibly interfered with Massachusetts's laws on domestic relations. He first noted that DOMA directly imposed "significant additional healthcare costs" on the state. More important was the fact that marital status determinations have always been an attribute of state sovereignty. Laws on marriage and DIVORCE had always been purely local in nature; state control over marital status determinations predated the American Revolution. Therefore, DOMA could not regulate such issues. Finally, compliance with DOMA impaired Massachusetts's ability to structure its operations in areas that states have traditionally managed. The restrictions DOMA placed on state government and the additional financial burdens and inequalities demonstrated that DOMA "plainly encroaches upon the firmly entrenched province of the state, and, in doing so, offends the Tenth Amendment. For that reason, the **statute** is invalid."

TERRORISM

The unlawful use of force or violence against persons or property in order to coerce or intimate a government or the civilian population in furtherance of political or social objectives.

Four Convicted in New York Bomb Plot

In May 2011, a federal judge upheld the convictions of four "home-grown terrorists," all working-class Muslims from the city of Newburgh, east of New York City, who had plotted to blow up several New York synagogues and shoot down military airplanes from the sky with heat-seeking missiles. The men were convicted by a federal jury in October 2010, following several weeks of trial and eight days of deliberation. Two of the four were convicted on all eight charges against them, including CONSPIRACY to use WEAPONS OF MASS DESTRUCTION and attempting to kill officers and employees of the U.S. government; the other two were each convicted of seven of the eight charges.

Defense counsel had petitioned to have the verdicts set aside and the INDICTMENT dismissed, based on a defense (as presented at trial) of **entrapment**. But neither the jury nor the judge agreed. Notwithstanding, U.S. **District Court** Judge Colleen McMahon, in her ruling, did agree that the government had built a "troubling" case that focused on the work of an FBI-paid informer whose methods, she suggested, bordered on ENTRAPMENT. (Defense counsel planned to appeal her ruling.)

The convictions stem from a nighttime raid and arrests of the four men in May 2009 after leaving vehicles they believed were loaded with explosives outside a synagogue and a Jewish center in the Bronx. (The entire scenario was under heavy surveillance.) At the time, they did not know that their car bombs were non-explosive "duds" secretly provided by the Federal Bureau of Investigations (FBI), as were the Stinger missiles they purchased.

The trial included 13 days of testimony from the FBI undercover informant, 53-year-old Pakistani-born Shahed Hussain. Originally assigned to infiltrate a mosque in Newburgh, he befriended one of the four defendants there, 44-year-old James Cromitie. Hussain told Cromitie he was a representative of a Pakistani terror organization eager to finance a holy war on U.S. soil. Secretly recording their conversations, Hussain caught on tape several statements from Cromitie, avowing his hatred for Americans and Jews in particular. In a December 2008 meeting, a laughing Cromitie was video-taped telling Hussain how he fantasized about doing something big, "like blowing up a football stadium," and then joked that he should get a Purple Heart for such a major attack. In the tape, Hussain mostly remained quiet except for an occasional "hmmm."

Cromitie allegedly recruited the three additional defendants from the Muslim mosque: Onta Williams, 34; David Williams IV, 29 (the two were not related); and Laguerre Payen, 28 years old. Hussain continued to record their meetings over several months, as they discussed getting revenge for perceived U.S. aggression in the Middle East, potential targets, planting bombs in synagogues in nearby Riverdale, and firing Stinger missiles at military transport planes at Stewart International Airport.

Several videos were presented to the jury at trial, along with Hussain's testimony, some

David Williams, center, is led by police officers from a federal building in New York after being arrested for plotting to bomb New York synagogues and shoot down military aircraft.
AP IMAGES/ROBERT MECEA, FILE

showing the men inspecting shoulder missile launchers in a bugged warehouse in Connecticut two weeks before the planned attack. At the end of this video, Cromitie and two others (along with the informant) bow their heads in **prayer**.

Notwithstanding, in an April 2009 video, Cromitie appeared less enthusiastic, expressing concern for "anyone to get hurt." Hussain then warned him that his handlers in Pakistan were becoming impatient. After they agreed that women and children should be spared, Cromitie's demeanor visibly changed as he avowed that U.S. soldiers and men were targets. "I don't care if it's a whole synagogue of men, I will take them down," he said on the video tape. "I'm not worried about nothing. What I'm worried about is my safety."

At trial, defense painted a picture of four working-class men egged on by promises of money and other rewards, who would never have been involved in such a plot were it not for the pressure put on them by Hussain. Characterizing the four defendants as aimless nobodies, the defense sought to portray Hussain as a master manipulator who entrapped them in order to win favorable treatment with the U.S. government regarding his own pending punishment in a separate **fraud** case. Labeling Hussain a "liar," defense counsel implored that, without the help of the FBI, Cromitie would not have done anything.

But prosecutors countered that the FBI did exactly what it was supposed to do: it caught four men before they could do any real harm, even though the four believed they had planted bombs that would do real harm. During closing arguments, Assistant U.S. Attorney David Raskin told the jury, "Ordinary people wouldn't even dream of what these defendants did."

In her ruling affirming the verdicts, Judge McMahon agreed that Hussain was the prime mover and shaker of all the criminal activity that occurred, "right up until the last moments of the conspiracy, when he had to stop the car he was driving and 'arm' the 'explosive device' because the utterly inept Cromitie could not figure out how to do it." Added the judge, "This court is not familiar with a case in which so many different tactics were used on a single individual." Nonetheless, the judge continued, "Cromitie is not a particularly intelligent man, but it defies reason to think that he was unaware [that he was getting involved in terrorism]." In conclusion, the court found that, while the government's conduct was questionable (i.e., borderline entrapment), it did not rise to the level of "outrageous misconduct." Ultimately, said the judge, Cromitie justified Hussain's persistence when he proved "ready and willing to commit terrorist acts."

Guantanamo Bay Status as of 2011

The U.S. Naval Station at Guantanamo Bay, Cuba dates from 1903, when the American government leased a 45-square-mile site for use as a coal supply station in the wake of the SPANISH-AMERICAN WAR. Many years later, when the United States broke off diplomatic relations with Cuba following the rise in power of Fidel Castro, the base continued to exist as "one foreign power's self-enclosed outpost in a hostile land," according to a 2011 article in *The New York Times*.

Following the terrorist attacks on the United States on September 11, 2001, and the subsequent invasion of Afghanistan, then-President GEORGE W. BUSH made Guantanamo the central prison for suspects considered to be "unlawful enemy combatants" in the new "war on terror." As of 2011, of the 779 persons detained at Guantanamo prison, 600 have been transferred and 172 remain. Seven detainees died while in CUSTODY.

Two days after his inauguration, in January 2009, President BARACK OBAMA, attempting to make good on campaign promises, signed executives orders that directed the closing of Guantanamo prison within one year, and also ending the Central Intelligence Agency's controversial secret interrogation program. However, over the next two years, his efforts would be thwarted by a variety of factors, including: Republican resistance in Congress; reluctance on the part of other nations to accept Guantanamo prisoners or detainees; the 2010 highly-publicized "leak" of thousands of classified documents by the anti-secrecy website WikiLeaks; the escape of hundreds of terrorists held in other nations' prisons; and the capture and death of terrorist leader, Osama bin Laden, the location of his whereabouts reportedly gained through earlier interrogations of Guantanamo detainees.

Backpedaling in the face of such opposition, in January 2010, the Obama administration released new guidelines for the handling and **disposition** of Guantanamo detainees. According to a report published by National Public Radio (NPR)(see below),the guidelines "put less emphasis on abstract risk categories and more on individualized decisions about whether detainees could be feasibly prosecuted or safely transferred to other countries, or whether their potential threat to the [United States] was such that they would need to be detained indefinitely under the laws of war." The new guidelines require a twice-yearly review of all detainee files, along with recommended action, to be conducted by a 60-person Task Force consisting of members from the U.S. DEPARTMENT OF JUSTICE, DEPARTMENT OF DEFENSE, DEPARTMENT OF HOMELAND SECURITY, the STATE DEPARTMENT, the CIA, the FBI, and other intelligence agencies.

Again in early 2011, President Obama revisited his earlier halt on military trials for detainees (in favor of civilian trials in federal **district court**), following the disastrous media and public outcry over the intended civilian trials in New York City of five suspected terrorists (and Guantanamo detainees), including Khalid Shaikh Mohammed, the self-professed chief plotter of the September 11 attacks. Consulting with military and intelligence experts, Obama signed an EXECUTIVE ORDER setting forth new rules requiring a review of Guantanamo detainees' status within a year, followed by a new review every three years to determine whether (1)they still remained a threat, (2)should be scheduled for a military trial, or (3)should be released. The executive order also mandated compliance with the Geneva Conventions and the international treaty banning inhumane treatment and torture. Obama stated for the record that he remained committed to closing Guantanamo in the future and to charging several suspected terrorists in civilian criminal courts.

In April 2011, the *New York Times* along with National Public Radio (NPR) published lengthy reports on the contents of many of the thousands of classified documents that were leaked. According to these reports and assessments, the documents involving Guantanamo showed detainee evaluations that invited challenge. Some were subjectively vague, repeating words such as "possibly" or "unknown;" others quoted witnesses who were other detainees, the mental state of which could be highly unreliable. Moreover, one of the detainees slated for military trial was Abd al-Rahim al-Nashiri, a Saudi charged with planning the bombing of the American destroyer *USS Cole,* in Yemen in 2000. But other documents show that he may have been subjected to the controversial interrogation technique known as "waterboarding," which could provide defense assertions that he had been tortured, thereby jeopardizing and complicating a trial outcome.

Still other documents evidenced the struggle to identify suitable potential placement of some of the detainees in other friendly countries. For example, as of 2011, nearly 60 of the remaining Guantanamo detainees were from Yemen, which had such an unstable government at the time (fighting civilian overthrow and demands for a change in power) that it was deemed impossible to return them there. No other country came forward to offer acceptance.

In an April 2011 statement, the Obama administration expressed disappointment in the fact that the NPR, *New York Times,* and others were publishing the classified Guantanamo documents, "strongly condemn[ing] the leaking of this sensitive information." The statement continued,

> Both the previous and the current administrations have made every effort to act with the utmost care and diligence in transferring detainees from Guantanamo … Both administrations have made the protection of American citizens the top priority, and we

are concerned that the disclosure of these documents could be damaging to these efforts. The statement was signed by Pentagon Press Secretary Geoff Morrell and Ambassador Dan Fried, special envoy from the State Department in charge of negotiating the closure of the Guantanamo facility.

High Seas Pirate Convicted and Sentenced

In April 2011, a Somali man accused of high seas PIRACY was sentenced in U.S. **District Court**, Washington, D.C., to serve 25 years in prison for attacking a merchant vessel in the Gulf of Aden and holding its crew for ransom for 71 days. Jama Idle Ibrahim, a/k/a Jaamac Ciidle, was previously sentenced in November 2010 to 30 years' imprisonment in Virginia, after PLEADING guilty there to charges connected with the April 2010 pirate attack on Navy vessel *USS Ashland*, also in the Gulf of Aden. Ibrahim's D.C. sentence was to run concurrently with his Virginia sentence.

According to court documents, in the April 2010 attack, 39-year-old Ibrahim and five other Somalis sailed the high seas in search of merchant ships to attack and seize, intending to plunder the vessels and hold the crews for ransom. The six men sighted a ship, which turned out to be the *USS Ashland,* chased it until they were alongside, and began firing (with AK-47s) at the Navy vessel and people onboard. In the statement of facts accompanying the entry of his plea, Ibrahim admitted that all six men were willing participants in the planned piracy and that their purpose for firing upon the vessel was to cause the vessel to surrender to them, at which point they would board, seize the ship, crew, and contents.

Investigations in both cases were conducted by the Federal Bureau of Investigations (FBI), members of the Joint TERRORISM Task Force, and the Naval Criminal Investigative Service. Prosecution was conducted by the U.S. Attorney's Office and the U.S. Department of Justice's National Security Division. In a November 2010 press release from the U.S. Attorney's Office in Norfolk, U.S. Attorney Neil H. MacBride stated,

> Today marks the first sentencing in Norfolk for acts of piracy in more than 150 years … Piracy is a growing threat throughout the world, and today's sentence, along with last week's convictions, demonstrates that the

United States will hold modern-day pirates accountable in U.S. courtrooms.

Likewise, the conviction and April 2011 sentencing of Ibrahim for the 2008-2009 attack on a merchant vessel represented the first D.C.-based prosecution of piracy. In that case, Ibrahim and other Somalis, on/about November 7, 2008, approached the *M/V CEC Future* in the Gulf of Aden and began firing upon the vessel with AK-47s, rocket-propelled grenades, and other hand guns. The ship was owned by Clipper Group, a Danish company, and it contained cargo belonging to Texas-based McDermott International, Inc.

After overtaking the vessel, Ibrahim and accomplices boarded the ship and forced the 13-member crew to anchor in waters off the Somali coast. During the takeover, additional pirates boarded the vessel and controlled the crew movements with their weapons. After stealing money, food and supplies from the ship, the pirates continued to hold the vessel for ransom for 71 days. The vessel was finally released on January 16, 2009, after the Clipper Group paid $1.7 million in ransom to the pirates.

Ibrahim pleaded guilty on September 8, 2010 to CONSPIRACY to commit piracy under the **law of nations** and conspiracy to use a firearm during and in relation to a crime of violence. For his guilty pleas, Ibrahim received the maximum penalty of five years in prison for the piracy conspiracy charge, and the maximum penalty of 20 years in prison for the firearm conspiracy charge.

The CEO of the Clipper Group attended the sentencing hearing and told the court of his gratitude that Ibrahim was pursued via the U.S. legal system, in light of the importance of bringing pirates to justice. James McJunkin, Assistant FBI Director for the Washington Field Office, announced the sentence after Ibrahim's appearance in the U.S. District Court for the District of Columbia. Said McJunkin, "The FBI is charged with investigating attacks against U.S. citizens and U.S. interests, wherever in the world they occur." U.S. Attorney Ronald Machen, Jr. added, "Modern-day pirates are nothing like the swashbuckling heroes in Hollywood movies. Today's pirates are ruthless criminals who hold ships and their crews hostage with AK-47s and rocket propelled grenades. Twenty-five years in prison is a just

punishment for this attack that threatened international commerce and human life."

The Hague Justice Portal publishes information about pending international piracy suits. At the time it announced the sentencing of Ibrahim (November 2010) in the matter of *United States of America v. Jama Idle Ibrahim,* it listed other piracy cases still pending: *United States of America v. Saciid et al, United States of America v. Salad et al,* and *United States of America v. Muse.*

TORT LAW

A body of rights, obligations, and remedies that is applied by courts in civil proceedings to provide relief for persons who have suffered harm from the wrongful acts of others. The person who sustains injury or suffers pecuniary damage as the result of tortious conduct is known as the plaintiff, and the person who is responsible for inflicting the injury and incurs liability for the damage is known as the defendant or tortfeasor.

Federal Appeals Courts Finds No Link Between Vaccines and Autism

Public awareness of childhood autism in the past 20 years has lead to increased efforts to determine what causes this disability. One theory that gained worldwide recognition contended that there was a causative link between the administration of childhood vaccines and the onset of autism. Under a federal law governing childhood vaccine injuries, about 5,000 cases have been filed with the Court of Federal Claims alleging a link between vaccines and autism. Seemingly strong evidence supporting this theory from a laboratory in the United Kingdom was later questioned by researchers who believed the testing was at best unreliable and at worst **fraudulent**. The Federal **Circuit Court** of Appeals, in *Cedillo v. Secretary of Health and Human Services,* 617 F.3d 1328 (Fed. Cir.2010), upheld a special master's rulings that there was no evidence a vaccine caused the autism of a young child.

Under the National Childhood Vaccine Injury Act of 1986, 42 U.S.C. §§ 300aa-1 to 34, the Court of Federal Claims created the **Omnibus** Autism Proceeding (OAP) to determine the relationship, if any, between vaccines and autistic spectral disorders. The petitioners, who are parents of children with autism, proposed a "test case" approach to present general causation evidence. Three test cases were selected, including one filed by the parents of Michelle Cedillo. Her parents alleged that measles-mumps-rubella (MMR) vaccine, together with vaccines containing a mercury-based preservative called thimerosal (TCVs) caused their daughter to suffer from a number of medical conditions, including autism. Michelle, who was born in 1994, seemed a healthy child during her first 15 months of life. At 15 months she received an MMR vaccination. Soon after, she experienced a high fever. Her doctor concluded Michelle had the flu and prescribed antibiotics. At her 18-month well-child visit no significant medical concerns were noted but the doctor wrote that Michelle seemed to be talking less than at her prior visit. A year later her doctor suspected she was developmentally delayed. Michelle was diagnosed a few months later with severe autism and severe mental retardation. In 1998 her parents filed for compensation under the Vaccine Act. In order to win compensation, a petitioner must show by a preponderance of the evidence that the child received a listed vaccine and suffered a corresponding listed injury. A vaccine is presumed or in fact, to have caused the injury. However, in Michelle's case, the injury was not listed, which required her parents to prove that the vaccine caused her autism. The 5,000 petitioners argued that ethyl mercury in thimerosal in various childhood vaccines caused autism. In Michelle's case the parents claimed the thimerosal damaged her immune system, which prevented the measles virus in the MMR vaccine to replicate in her body and ultimately entered her brain, causing inflammation and autism.

A SPECIAL MASTER conducted a three-week evidentiary hearing in 2007, in which general causation and evidence specific to the Cedillo case was presented. Michelle's parents presented the testimony of six expert witnesses. The experts relied on testing by Unigenetics Ltd. Laboratory in Dublin, Ireland. Unigenetics claimed that a technique was successfully used to identify and amplify measles virus genetic material from the blood and tissue of autistic children, including Michelle, who had received an MMR vaccine. This research formed the basis for a 2002 article that announced the link between vaccines and autism. The for-profit laboratory, which was no longer in business,

had been established to support civil LITIGATION against manufacturers of vaccine in the United Kingdom. Though the Cedillos' experts testified that Unigenetics had reliably detected persistent vaccine-strain measles in the bodies of children with autism, including Michelle, the government offered evidence to the contrary. Its experts contended the Unigenetics testing was unreliable and could not prove the causation needed to link the MMR vaccine with Michelle's autism. One expert, after analyzing the lab's equipment and notebooks, concluded that procedures used by Unigenetics rendered the testing unreliable. He also questioned the veracity of the information contained in the lab notebooks, finding signs of alteration of data.

The special master issued a decision in 2009, denying compensation for Michelle. He concluded that the evidence did not demonstrate either that TCVs could harm infant immune systems, or that they harmed Michelle's immune system. The special master also concluded that there was no evidence that the MMR vaccine alone or in combination with TCVs could cause autism in general, or in Michelle's case. He also found that the evidence that came from the Unigenetics testing suffered from significant flaws and was not reliable. Michelle's parents appealed this ruling to the Federal Circuit Court of Appeals.

The appeals court upheld all the findings and conclusions of the special master. The court noted that it was required not to "second guess" the special masters' factual findings, particularly in cases "in which the medical evidence of causation is in dispute." For the Cedillos to prevail they had to prove that the vaccine was "not only a but-for cause of the injury but also a substantial factor in bringing about the injury. The court concluded that they had failed, by a preponderance of the evidence, to show this level of causation. The Cedillos' raised a host of issues that all centered on the misapplication of law and procedure by the special master. The appeals court found no merit in these arguments, especially those that contended the special master had unfairly given the government's experts access to documents that were not available to them. The court pointed out that the special master sought to help the petitioners obtain documents from the United Kingdom and that the Cedillos did not make requests when they were given the opportunity.

CSX Transportation, Inc. v. McBride

The Federal Employers' Liability Act (FELA), 45 U.S.C. § 51 provides, "Every **common carrier** by railroad ... shall be liable for any person suffering injury while he is employed by such carrier ... for such injury or death resulting in whole or in part from the NEGLIGENCE of any of the officers, agents, or employees of such carrier...." Questions have arisen about whether a PLAINTIFF bringing a FELA case is required to prove **proximate cause**, which is an element in a common-law negligence claim. A transportation company involved in FELA LITIGATION argued that the proximate-cause standard was the appropriate standard, but a divided SUPREME COURT held that a lower standard should apply. *CSX Transportation, Inc. v. McBride*, No. 10-235, 2011 WL 2472795 (U.S. June 23, 2011).

The DEFENDANT in the case was CSX Transportation, Inc., which operates an interstate system of railroads. The railroad transports freight over long distances and also makes local runs, which involve picking up smaller cars for transportation. The process for adding and removing cars during local runs is known as "switching," which requires engineers to start and stop more frequently than when the railroad is moving freight over the long distances.

The engineer slows down the train by using a system of multiple brakes. Automatic brakes slow down the individual cars to a train, while a separate independent brake slows down the locomotives. The process of slowing a train down requires timing by the person applying the brake, for if the locomotive brakes too quickly, the cars in the rear may run into cars in front of them. The process of slowing a long train is called "actuating" or "bailing off" and involves application of the automatic brake while releasing the independent brake. Heavier, wide-bodied locomotives required a slightly different actuating maneuver compared with what is required for smaller locomotives.

CSX employed Robert McBride as an engineer. He became a locomotive engineer in 1999, and for about five years he transported trains from Evansville, Indiana to Nashville, Tennessee and back again. McBride eventually transferred to a division that involved more local runs. To qualify for these local runs, he was paired with a supervising engineer, who explained the route, the methods for switching cars, and so forth. McBride was accustomed to standard-body cars, but when he went on his qualifying run in April 2004, the locomotive cars were wide-bodied.

McBride's qualifying run involved several stops, which required him to switch cars for several hours at a time. The process of performing the switching operations required McBride to push a button to actuate the automatic brake and then to grab a lever to release the independent brakes. After about seven or eight constant hours of engaging in this process, McBride's hand grew numb. His hand struck the independent brake, making his hand feel as if it had caught fire. The injury he suffered required two surgeries, and he never regained full use of his hand.

McBride brought a suit against CSX under FELA, alleging that CSX was negligent. He specifically alleged that because of the way in which CSX had configured the trains, McBride had to constantly use the actuator button, which eventually caused his hand to fatigue, which led to his hand hitting the independent brake. Regarding the causation element that he had to prove, McBride submitted the following jury charge based on the Seventh Circuit's pattern instruction: "Defendant 'caused or contributed to' Plaintiff's injury if Defendant's negligence played a part—no matter how small—in bringing about the injury. The mere fact that an injury occurred does not necessarily mean that the injury was caused by negligence."

CSX proposed its own jury charge, which required the jury to find that CSX's negligence was the PROXIMATE CAUSE of McBride's injury. Counsel for CSX described the use of proximate cause as follows: "When I use the expression 'proximate cause,' I mean any cause which, in natural or probable sequence, produced the injury complained of. It need not be the only cause, nor the last or nearest cause. It is sufficient if it concurs with some other cause acting at the same time, which in combination with it causes the injury."

The **district court** rejected CSX's instruction and used McBride's. The jury then rendered a verdict in McBride's favor. CSX appealed the district court's decision to the Seventh **Circuit Court** of Appeals, which affirmed the district court's judgment. The

Seventh Circuit analyzed the case under the Supreme Court's decision in *Rogers v. Missouri Pacific Railroad Co.*, 352 U.S. 500, 77 S. Ct. 443, 1 L. Ed. 2d 493 (1957). The *Rogers* case has stood for the proposition that FELA requires a lower causation standard than the common-law proximate cause standard, but the Court had never exactly what the standard should be.

The Court granted **certiorari** to review the Seventh Circuit's opinion. In a 5-4 decision, the Court affirmed. In writing for the majority, Justice RUTH BADER GINSBURG looked at the broad language of FELA along with a statement in *Rogers* about the causation standard: "[W]hether the proofs justify with reason the conclusion that employer negligence played any part, even the slightest, in producing the injury or death for which damages are sought." Ginsburg noted that the district court had relied on *Rogers*, so if that **case stated** the law correctly, then the district court and the Seventh Circuit must have applied the law properly.

Ginsburg reviewed the decision in *Rogers* and concluded that it indeed stated the law correctly, noting that "*Rogers* is most sensibly read as a comprehensive statement of the FELA causation standard." Not only had lower courts followed the *Rogers* standard for years, but also "every Court of Appeals that reviews judgments of FELA cases has approved jury instructions on causation identical or substantively equivalent to the Seventh Circuit's instruction" in the CSX case. The majority opinion then rejected CSX's remaining arguments and affirmed the lower court's decision.

Chief Justice JOHN ROBERTS, joined by Justices ANTONIN SCALIA, ANTHONY KENNEDY, and SAMUEL ALITO, dissented. According to Roberts, the Court had never dispensed with the proximate cause requirement. Instead, FELA had abrogated four specific common-law tort principles, though proximate cause was not one of this principles. According to Roberts, the Court in *Rogers* addressed a particular application of proximate cause, but the Court never repudiated proximate cause altogether. Roberts asserts that the majority's approach will support a "boundless theory of liability."

U.S. SUPREME COURT

Elena Kagan Becomes Fourth Woman to Serve as Supreme Court Justice

For the first time in its history, the U.S. SUPREME COURT consists of three female justices. This occurred when the SENATE confirmed President Barack Obama's nomination of former Harvard Law School Dean Elena Kagan to replace the retired JOHN PAUL STEVENS. Although Kagan had no prior judicial experience, her confirmation in the Senate went relatively smoothly. She wrote her first opinion in January 2011.

Kagan was born in New York City on April 28, 1960. She grew up in a Jewish family and continues to identify herself with Conservative Judaism. Her father was an attorney while her mother was a school teacher. Both of her brothers also became school teachers. She attended Hunter College High School, and in her graduation picture, she appears in a judge's robe holding a gavel. The quote next to her picture was from former Supreme Court Justice FELIX FRANKFURTER: "Government is itself an art ... one of the subtlest of arts." Reports have indicated that one of Kagan's childhood goals was to become a Supreme Court justice. However, Kagan has been less open about her childhood than Justice SONIA SOTOMAYOR, who was also raised in New York. Several reports noted that Kagan was very interested in

literature and each year re-read Jane Austen's *Pride and Prejudice.*

Also like Sotomayor, Kagan attended Princeton University, where she studied history. She also served as the editor of the campus newspaper, *The Daily Princetonian.* She also interned at the office of a Democratic congressman from New York and served as assistant press secretary for another member of Congress. She completed a senior honors thesis focusing on the socialist movement in the 1960s, and she graduated *summa cum laude* in 1981. She also earned the prestigious Daniel M. Sachs Class of 1960 Graduating Scholarship, which allowed her to earn a master of philosophy degree from Oxford University in 1983.

She continued her education by attending Harvard Law School. She stood out among her classmates and became an editor of the *Harvard Law Review.* Numerous philosophical debates arose during her time on the law review, but she showed an ability to work with those on both sides of a debate. According to one classmate, "She was someone who could always navigate easily between and among factions. And I think that has remained a touchstone throughout her career."

Following her graduation from Harvard in 1986, she clerked for Judge Abner Mikva for the U.S. Court of Appeals for the District of

U.S. solicitor general Elena Kagan smiles in the East Room of the White House in Washington, August 6, 2010, during a ceremony with President Barack Obama , after her confirmation as Supreme Court justice by the Senate the previous day.

AP IMAGES/PABLO MARTINEZ MONSIVAIS

Columbia Circuit. One year later, she served as clerk for Justice THURGOOD MARSHALL of the Supreme Court. She took a position as a litigator with the law firm of Williams & Connolly in Washington. However, that position only lasted two years; friends told reporters that Kagan never seemed to be motivated by money, which in part led her to find other work that would challenge and interest her.

In 1991, she accepted a faculty position with the University of Chicago Law School. During the same year, an Illinois state senator named BARACK OBAMA also began teaching **constitutional law** as a lecturer. She experienced immediate success in the classroom and impressed her colleagues. She wrote about narrow topics that did not involve significant ideological positions.

She earned tenure at Chicago in 1995, but she did not stay long after that. She accepted a position as associate counsel in the White House in 1995, and she later served as a deputy to Bill Clinton's Domestic Policy Council. She so impressed Clinton that he later nominated her to fill a vacancy on the D.C. **Circuit Court** of Appeals. However, the Republican chair of the SENATE JUDICIARY COMMITTEE, Orrin Hatch, refused to schedule a hearing, which caused her nomination to fall through.

Kagan tried to return to Chicago, but she was rebuffed by the faculty. She accepted a visiting professorship at Harvard, and her performance there led the school to promote

her to full professor in 2001. Two years later, then-Harvard President Lawrence Summers appointed her as dean. At the time, Harvard was experiencing a sharp divide among its faculty due to competing ideologies. She immediately earned a reputation as a consensus-builder, and because of her ability to bridge the gap between the two sides of the faculty divide, the school was able to hire 43 full-time permanent faculty during less than six years while she was dean. Students also noted that Kagan made the school more student-friendly.

In 2009, Obama lured her away from academia once again. He appointed her to serve a **solicitor general**, even though she had never argued a case before the U.S. Supreme Court. Her first argument was in the case of *Citizens United v. FEC*, which involved the important question of whether Congress could limit corporate campaign spending for elections. Kagan argued in favor of the limits on the government's behalf, but her argument eventually lost.

Obama and liberal members of Congress were especially upset over the decision, and several thought that Obama's selection of Kagan as a nominee to replace Stevens directly resulted from the decision. Kagan had expressed strong views on a few issues, such as her belief that gays and lesbians should be able to serve openly in the military. However, she had written little compared with most academics, and many of the briefs and memos she had written revealed little about her personal beliefs. Most expected her to be a more moderate liberal on the Court, much like Stevens was.

The biggest point of contention in her nomination was that she had never before served as a judge at any level. Senator Scott Brown (R.-Mass.) noted that she was a "brilliant woman," but he refused to vote for her because of her lack of judicial experience. Nevertheless, she earned 63 votes from the Senate as a whole, including votes from five Republicans.

Kagan official assumed office in August 2010. During her first year on the bench, she had to RECUSE herself from 26 cases because of her former role as solicitor general. However, as of May 2011, only one of the cases in which she recused herself resulted in a 4-4 tie. She authored her first opinion in the BANKRUPTCY case of *Ransom v. FIA Card Services, N.A.*, 131 S. Ct. 716, 178 L. Ed. 2d 603 (2011). She filed her first DISSENT in the case of *Arizona Christian School Tuition Organization v. Winn*,, 131 S. Ct. 1436 (2011), which involved the question of whether a taxpayer had standing to challenge a state tax credit on the grounds that the credit violated the Establishment Clause of the FIRST AMENDMENT. The other three liberal justices on the Court—Sotomayor, RUTH BADER GINSBURG, and Stephen Breyer—joined Kagan's dissent.

VETERANS' RIGHTS

Henderson v. Shinseki

Congress established the Court of Appeals for Veterans Claims to review claims decided by the Board of Veterans' Appeals. Under the system established by Congress, a party that wishes to file a notice of appeal must do so within 120 days of date in which the Board's **final decision** is mailed. A party who failed to file a notice of appeal within the 120 days argued that he should have been allowed more time. Both the Court of Appeals for Veterans Claims and the Federal **Circuit Court** of Appeals ruled that the courts lacked jurisdiction to review the appeal because he had not met the deadline. However, the U.S. SUPREME COURT in *Henderson v. Shinseki*, 131 S. Ct. 1197 (2011) decided that the 120-day deadline is not jurisdictional.

The case focused on claims made by David Henderson, who served in the military during the KOREAN WAR from 1950 to 1952. However, he was diagnosed with paranoid schizophrenia and was discharged. Based on his condition, he received a 100% disability rating. He developed a need for in-home care many years later, and in August 2001, he filed a claim for monthly compensation with a regional office of the Department of Veterans Affairs. The regional office denied the claim, and Henderson appealed to the Board. The Board, in turn, also denied the claim on August 30, 2004.

Before 1988, a veteran whose claim was denied could not obtain any further review. However, Congress that year passed the Veterans' **Judicial Review** Act, Pub. L. No. 100-687, 102 Stat. 4105 (1988), creating the Court of Appeals for Veterans Claims as an Article I court. Under 38 U.S.C. § 7266(a): "In order to obtain review by the Court of Appeals for Veterans Claims of a final decision of the Board of Veterans' Appeals, a person adversely affected by such decision shall file a notice of appeal with the Court within 120 days after the date on which notice of the decision is mailed pursuant to section 7104(e) of this title." Section 7104(e) in turn provides that the Board must promptly mail a copy of its written decision to the last known address of the claimant.

Henderson filed his notice of appeal with the Court of Appeals for Veterans Claims on January 12, 2005. The court did not receive the notice until 15 days after the expiration of the 120-day period to file the appeal. The court asked Henderson to explain why the court should not dismiss his appeal as untimely. He told the court that his failure to respond was a direct result of his mental illness, and he asked the court to allow his appeal based on equitable tolling principles.

In March 2006, a judge with the Court of Appeals for Veterans Claims ruled that Henderson could not rely on equitable tolling, so the judge dismissed the case because Henderson had not filed his appeal in a timely manner. The court then revoked its initial order and assigned counsel to represent Henderson. While Henderson's subsequent appeal was pending, though, the Supreme Court decided the case of *Bowles v. Russell*, 551 U.S. 205, 127 S. Ct. 2360, 168 L. Ed. 2d 96 (2007). In that case, the Court determined that a **statutory** limit on the length of time to file an appeal in an ordinary civil case presented a jurisdictional issue. Thus, failure to file a notice of appeal in a timely manner in such a civil case means that the **appellate court** lacks jurisdiction to review the lower court's decision.

In light of the Court's decision in *Bowles*, a three-judge panel of the Court of Veterans Appeals ruled that equitable tolling was inapplicable because when Henderson failed to file a notice of appeal in a timely manner, the court could not review the case because the court lacked jurisdiction. Without jurisdiction, the court could not rule whether equitable tolling was available to Henderson.

Henderson appealed the decision to the Federal Circuit, which agreed to review the case **en banc**. The Federal Circuit had decided in two previous cases that equitable tolling could be available when a party failed to meet the 120-day deadline to file an appeal when the Court of Veterans Appeals. A divided en **banc** court agreed, though, that the court lacked jurisdiction following the decision in *Bowles*.

The Supreme Court agreed to review the case, and in a 8-0 vote, reversed the Federal Circuit. Justice SAMUEL ALITO wrote for the Court and focused much of his attention on the meaning of the Court's decision in *Bowles*. Alito noted that the Court is somewhat reluctant to conclude that the **federal courts** lack jurisdiction to review certain issues. However, Alito also acknowledged that Congress is entitled to render a rule jurisdictional in nature. The question, then, was whether Congress had intended for the 120-day notice requirement to affect the jurisdiction of the courts to review claims.

The rule reviewed in *Bowles* clearly involved an instance where Congress had labeled a filing period to involve a jurisdictional question. However, the rule that applies to veterans appeals is distinctive for several reasons. Unlike the deadline that applies to ordinary civil claims, the 120-day deadline is part of a unique administrative scheme in which parties appeal a claim first to an Article I court before filing further appeals with an Article III court. Alito also stressed a number of other significant differences between veterans cases and ordinary civil cases, including the application of a limitations period in civil LITIGATION, the adversarial nature of civil litigation compared with veterans claims, burdens of proof that apply to civil claims that do not apply to veterans claims, and other contrasting points.

Without a clear indication that Congress intended for the 120-day deadline to raise a jurisdictional question, the Court concluded that the lower courts had jurisdiction to consider Henderson's equitable tolling argument. Accordingly, the Court remanded the case for further proceedings to determine whether any exception to the deadline, including equitable tolling, may apply.

Justice Elena Kagan recused herself from participating in the case.

VOTING RIGHTS ACT

An enactment by Congress in 1965 (42 U.S.C.A. § 1973 et seq.) that prohibits the states and their political subdivisions from imposing voting qualifications or prerequisites to voting, or standards, practices, or procedures that deny or curtail the right of a U.S. citizen to vote because of race, color, or membership in a language minority group.

Ninth Circuit Upholds Washington Felony Disenfranchisement Law

All but two states have laws that bar or temporarily restrict persons convicted of felonies from voting. Only two states permit felons to vote: Maine and Vermont.Felons have litigated whether such laws deprive violate Section 2 of the Voting Rights Act (VRA). Most recently, the Ninth **Circuit Court** of Appeals reviewed the issue twice in 2010. A three-judge panel of the appeals court ruled that the Voting Rights Act barred a State of Washington constitutional provision that disenfranchised felons. However, the Ninth Circuit, meeting *en banc*(the entire court), reversed the panel decision.

The three-judge panel, in *Farrakhan v. Gregoire*, 590 F.3d 989 (9th Cir.2010), became the first court to rule that because of racial DISCRIMINATION in the state's criminal justice system, the **felony** disenfranchisement provision results in the denial of the right to vote on account of race. The panel overturned a 2006 **district court** ruling that acknowledged it had "no doubt that members of racial minorities have experienced discrimination in Washington's criminal justice system," but concluded that "Washington's history, or lack thereof, of racial bias in its electoral process and in its decision to enact the felon disenfranchisement provisions, counterbalance the contemporary discriminatory effects that result from the day-to-day functioning of Washington's criminal justice system." The state had failed to refute these facts, concentrating instead on attacking the credibility of the plaintiffs' experts as to the ultimate effect of Washington's felon disenfranchisement law.

In addition, the court concluded that under Section 2 of the Voting Rights Act, the "totality of the circumstances" did not support a finding that the state's felon disenfranchisement law results in racial discrimination. Therefore, the court concluded, "Section 2 of the VRA demands that such racial discrimination not spread to the ballot box."

The dissenting member of the panel pointed out that Washington had enacted an amendment in 2009 that provides that the State will provisionally restore voting rights to felons convicted in Washington STATE COURTS so long as the individual is no longer under the authority of the Department of Corrections, and to those convicted of federal felonies or felonies in other states as long as the person is no longer incarcerated. The judge noted that as a result, "we are left to consider the Voting Rights Act challenge of only those felons still serving their prison terms. Both the parties and the courts have seemingly considered felons generally, as a single group; the bifurcation of classes of felons came about as a consequence of this new legislation. Thus, within this LITIGATION, no court has addressed whether these two sets of individuals present meaningful analytical differences."

In a *per curiam* decision, (a decision issued by the court rather than by an individual judge), *Farrakhan v. Gregoire*, 623 F.3d 990 (9th Cir. 2010), overturned the panel decision. The full Ninth Circuit noted that Washington had disenfranchised felons since 1866, four years before the FIFTEENTH AMENDMENT was ratified. Moreover, the plaintiffs had not alleged the law was enacted for the purpose of disenfranchising minorities or that their convictions and subsequent disenfranchisement "resulted from intentional racial discrimination in the operation of the state's criminal justice system." The introduction of statistical evidence of racial disparities in the criminal justice system was permitted but this evidence had to be considered under Section 2's "totality of the circumstances" balancing. The appeals court agreed with the district court that other factors counterbalanced this statistical evidence.

The court also found compelling the fact that three other circuit courts of appeals had found that "felon disenfranchisement laws are categorically exempt from challenges" brought under Section 2 of the Voting Rights Act. Based on these opinions the court concluded that the three-judge panel decision "sweeps too broadly." The history of felony disenfranchisement laws predated the Jim Crow era; the laws were for the most part not enacted based on racial considerations. Moreover, Congress was aware of these laws when the law was enacted in 1965 and amended in 1982 yet it did not address the issue.

The appeals court therefore held that: "plaintiffs bringing a section 2 VRA challenge to a felon disenfranchisement law based on the operation of a state's criminal justice system must at least show that the criminal justice system is infected by intentional discrimination or that the felon disenfranchisement law was enacted with such intent. Our ruling is limited to this narrow issue, and we express no view as to any of the other issues raised by the parties and amici. We also leave for another day the question of whether a PLAINTIFF who has made the required showing would necessarily establish that a felon disenfranchisement law violates section 2."

WHISTLEBLOWER

The disclosure by a person, usually an employee, in a government agency or private enterprise; to the public or to those in authority, of mismanagement, corruption, illegality, or some other wrongdoing.

Schindler v. Kirk

Employees or former employees who disclose information to authorities/officials regarding illegal conduct on the part of their employers are often referred to as "whistleblowers." Most states protect whistleblowers who disclose such information from retaliation by their employers. In some cases where **statutory** illegal conduct exists but the state has taken no action, whistleblowers and informers can file a "qui tam" **civil action** (literally, "Who as well _____"), meaning that the PLAINTIFF states that he sues on behalf of himself as well as the state. In such actions, any monetary fines, penalties, or fees that are awarded and recovered generally are shared between the person who brings the action and the state or other institution.

In the case of *Schindler Elevator Corp. v. Kirk,* No. 10-188, 563 U.S. ___ (2011)Daniel Kirk brought such a suit. In it, he alleged that his former employer, Schindler Elevator Corporation, had submitted hundreds of false claims for payment under federal contracts regarding employment of veterans under the Vietnam Era Veterans Readjustment Assistance Act (VEVRAA) 38 U.S.C. § 4212. The VEVRAA requires federal contractors to certify, each year, the number of "qualified covered veterans" they employ, train, and promote, in return for federal monetary incentives.

Kirk, an Army VIETNAM WAR veteran, was employed by Schindler and its predecessor, Millar Elevator Industries, from 1978 to 2003. In August 2003, he was demoted to a non-managerial position, but resigned from the company instead. After the U.S. DEPARTMENT OF LABOR denied his claim that his demotion was in violation of VEVRAA, Kirk filed his *qui tam* suit in the U.S. **District Court** for the Southern District of New York.

Kirk filed his suit in 2005 under the False Claims Act, 31 U.S.C. §§ 3729-3733, which prohibits submitting to the United States false or **fraudulent** claims for payment. The Act expressly authorizes *qui tam* suits. In his suit, Kirk alleged that Schindler had failed to file the requisite annual reports from 1998 to 2004, and that the 2004, 2005, and 2006 contained false information. Kirk based his allegations on information obtained by his wife through three FREEDOM OF INFORMATION ACT (FOIA) requests to the Department of Labor. Kirk challenged that each claim for payment on the hundreds of government contracts submitted by Schindler was a separate violation of the False Claims Act.

The problem with Kirk's claim was that the Federal Claims Act contains what is known as a public disclosure bar. The actual language in the Act prohibits private parties from bringing *qui tam* suits to recover falsely or fraudulently obtained federal payments, where those suits are "based upon the public disclosure of allegations or transactions in a criminal, civil, or administrative hearing, in a congressional, administrative, or Government Accounting Office report, hearing, audit, or investigation, or from the news media." 31 U.S.C. § 3730(e)(4)(A).

The federal district court granted Schindler's motion to dismiss, agreeing that, among other things, the Act's public disclosure bar deprived the court of jurisdiction, as Kirk's allegations were based on information disclosed in a government "report" or "investigation." Relatedly, Kirk's complaint, therefore, failed to state a claim upon which relief could be granted.

The Second **Circuit Court** of Appeals vacated that decision and remanded the case, essentially holding that an agency's response to an FOIA request was not a "report" or "investigation" under the Act (and therefore not subject to the bar).

The U.S. SUPREME COURT disagreed. Writing for the five-justice majority, Justice CLARENCE THOMAS found that a federal agency's written response to a FOIA request for records constituted a "report" within the meaning of the Federal Claims Act's public disclosure bar. Because the Act itself does not define "report," the Court looked to the word's ordinary meaning, defined generally as something that provides information. The Court also found no textual basis for adopting a more narrow meaning. Therefore, the Department of Labor's three written FOIA responses, along with accompanying documents and records, were "reports" within the public disclosure bar's ordinary meaning.

The Court briefly discussed its holding as being consistent with the public disclosure bar's drafting history. It found that the bar was designed to discourage the "opportunistic" LITIGATION that could occur if anyone, such as Kirk, could simply identify any regulatory filing or certification requirement, submit FOIA requests until one of them reveals a federal contractor who is out of compliance, and reap a potential windfall in a *qui tam* action.

Justice Ruth Bader Ginsburg filed a dissenting opinion, joined by Justices Stephen Breyer and Sonia Sotomayor. The DISSENT opined that Kirk, a Vietnam War veteran and former employee, had cause to believe that Schindler failed to meet VEVRAA's annual requirements, confirmed by the information he received pursuant to the FOIA requests. To rank the Department of Labor's FOIA response an "administrative ... report" akin to a Government Accounting Office report (subject to the bar) weakened the force of the False Claims Act as a weapon against fraudulent claims from government contractors.

WHITE COLLAR CRIME

Tom DeLay Received Three-Year Sentence for Money Laundering and Conspiracy

Tom DeLay spent more than two decades as a member of the House of Representative and became of the chamber's most valuable members. However, he was charged in 2005 with **money laundering** after an investigation into campaign finances revealed his crime. In November 2010, a Texas jury convicted DeLay, and a judge in January 2011 sentenced him to three years in prison. DeLay vowed to fight the convictions.

DeLay was elected to the Texas HOUSE OF REPRESENTATIVES in 1978, just six years before he was elected to the U.S. House. In 1988, he became deputy minority whip at a time when the DEMOCRATIC PARTY dominated both chambers of Congress. DeLay was heavily involved in helping to lead Republicans to wins during the 1994 midterm elections, giving Republicans control of both the House and SENATE for the first time since 1952. He was elected as House majority whip in 1995. In 2002, he became House majority leader, a position he held until his resignation. DeLay earned the nickname "The Hammer" during his political career.

In September 2001, DeLay founded the POLITICAL ACTION COMMITTEE Texans for a Republican Majoirty (TRMPAC). The goal of this committee was to promote the Republic Party. DeLay and political activist Jim Ellis selected John Colyandro to serve as the committee's executive director. Colyandro in 2004 was indicated on a charge that he had accepted illegal corporate donations. Moreover, he was and risks." Moreover, the amount of information available to defense counsel at this point in the case is limited. If the Court were to allow liberal application of postconviction ineffective counsel claims, prosecutors would become wary of plea bargains. Therefore, measuring competence of legal counsel must be measured differently at different stages of the case. In the case of early pleas like Moore's, the Court needed to consider what effect the suppression of Moore's confession to police would have had on the case. The PROSECUTOR faced the cost of LITIGATION and the risk of trying the case without this confession. Moore's lawyer could reasonably believe that a quick plea bargain would allow his client to take advantage of these concerns. Moreover, the case involved multiple defendants, which could lead to one of them agreeing to testify against Moore at trial in exchange for a better deal. Delaying the case could have led to enhanced charges and punishments. Finally, Moore's confession to the two individuals would have placed his case in **jeopardy** at trial. In light of these factors, Justice Kennedy concluded that Moore's lawyer made a reasonable choice to seek a quick plea bargain. The state court did not violate clearly established law when it found the lawyer's representation effective.

Justice Kennedy reinforced this decision by pointing out the difference between inadequate assistance of counsel claims based on a full trial on the merits and pleas made before the prosecution has finalized all the charges. In his view, "Hindsight and second guesses" are inappropriate when plea bargains are involved. Because there is "no extended, formal record," there is "a most substantial burden on the claimant to show ineffective counsel." To find otherwise would undermine the stability brought to the criminal justice system by the plea bargain process.

Harrington v. Richter

In enacting the Antiterrorism and Effective Death Penalty Act of 1996 (AEDPA), amending 28 U.S.C. § 2254 et seq., Congress clearly intended "to prevent defendants (and **federal courts**) from using **habeas corpus** review as a vehicle to second guess the reasonable decisions of state courts," noted Chief Justice Roberts, Jr. in the earlier case of Renico v. Letts, 559 U.S. ___ (2010). Under AEDPA, federal courts are prohibited from granting habeas relief unless the state court's **adjudication** "resulted in a decision that was contrary to, or involved an unreasonable application of, clearly established Federal law, as determined by the SUPREME COURT of the United States," 28 U.S.C. § 2254 (d)(1), or resulted in a decision that was based on an unreasonable determination of the facts in light of the evidence presented in the state court proceeding, 28 U.S.C. § 2254(d)(2).

In the subsequent 2011 "ineffective counsel" case of Harrington v. Richter, No. 09-587, 131 S. Ct. 770, 562 U.S. ___, the Court issued three important rulings. First, it ruled that 28 U.S.C. § 2254(d)'s restriction on re-litigating habeas claims applies even where a state high court's (here, the California Supreme Court) denial of habeas relief is not accompanied by explanation or reason. Second, the Court ruled that the Ninth Circuit failed to accord the required deference to state decisions, thereby showing an "improper" understanding of § 2254(d)'s unreasonableness standard. And third, the Court reversed the Ninth Circuit's substantive holding that Richter had demonstrated an unreasonable application of federal law, to wit, Strickland v. Washington, 466 U.S. 668, 104 S. Ct. 2052, 80 L. Ed. 2d 674 (1984).

The Court's rulings effectively reversed the Ninth Circuit, affirmed the lower state and federal court decisions, and reinstated the conviction and sentence (life without PAROLE) of Jason Richter.

Sometime after midnight on December 20,1994, police were called to the California residence of a drug dealer, Joshua Johnson, where they found him wounded and his friend, Patrick Klein, lying on a couch, bleeding and unconscious. Both had been shot twice. Johnson was hysterical and covered with blood, He told police that hours earlier, he and Klein had been smoking marijuana with two other men, Richter and Branscombe. After falling asleep, he awakened to find Richter and Branscombe in his bedroom. Branscombe then shot Johnson. Hearing more gunfire and sounds of the assailants fleeing, the wounded Johnson exited the bedroom and found Klein bleeding on the couch. He called 911. A gun safe, a pistol, and $6,000 in cash were all missing from his bedroom. Johnson recovered from his wounds but Klein died. AUTOPSY findings revealed that one bullet removed from Klein's body was .22-caliber, and the other was .32-caliber.

Investigators searching Richter's residence found Johnson's gun safe, two boxes of .22-caliber ammunition, and a gun magazine loaded with the same brand and type ammunition. Both Richter and Branscombe were arrested. Richter first denied involvement, but later admitted taking Johnson's pistol and disposing of it as well as the .32-caliber gun that Branscombe had used. Richter's counsel produced Johnson's missing gun, but neither of the guns used to shoot Johnson or Klein were recovered. A ballistics expert later concluded that the .22-caliber bullet that struck Klein as well as the shell casing found in the living room matched the ammunition found in Richter's home, and also bore markings consistent with the model of gun fitting for which the magazine found in his home was designed.

Richter and Branscombe were tried together on charges of MURDER, attempted murder, **burglary**, and **robbery**. At trial, Johnson's account of events was corroborated by evidence found at the scene, including shell casings from both .22-caliber and .32-caliber guns, blood splatters, and pooled blood in the bedroom doorway. A blood sample had been taken at the time from the wall, but not the doorway.

Building its case around Johnson's testimony, the prosecution later adjusted its approach after Richter's counsel, in OPENING STATEMENT, outlined the theory that Branscombe shot Johnson in SELF-DEFENSE and that Klein was killed in the crossfire in the bedroom doorway (where a blood sample had not been taken from the pooled blood). In response, prosecution called a blood pattern/spatter expert who concluded that it was unlikely that Klein had been shot outside the living room and then moved to the couch. A serologist expert also testified that the blood sample taken near the blood pool (near the bedroom doorway) was not Klein's. However, under CROSS-EXAMINATION, the expert conceded that she had not tested the blood sample for cross-contamination, and that a degraded sample would make it more difficult to tell if it contained blood of Klein's type. Although defense counsel called Richter to testify as to his version of events, the jury convicted him and he was sentenced to life without parole, affirmed on appeal.

After exhausting state **appellate** reviews, Richter sought state habeas relief from the California Supreme Court. The gist of his appeal was couched in claims of ineffective counsel. Specifically, Richter argued that his counsel failed to present EXPERT TESTIMONY on blood evidence, and he backed up his appeal with affidavits from forensics experts. Notwithstanding, the California Supreme Court denied his petition in a one-sentence summary order. Moving to federal **district court**, Richter again filed for habeas relief, reasserting the same claims. The district court denied his petition, as did the subsequent three-judge panel of the Ninth Circuit. However, the Ninth Circuit granted rehearing *en banc* (before all judges) and this time, Richter succeeded in convincing the **appellate court** that he was entitled to habeas relief. As a preliminary matter, the APPELLATE court questioned whether § 2254(d) was even applicable, since the California Supreme Court had only issued a summary denial, without explaining why. However, the appellate court proceeded to review on the merits of Richter's claims, holding, by a 5-4 decision, that his trial counsel was ineffective for failing to consult experts on blood evidence and pursuing a trial strategy based on cross-examination. The U.S. Supreme Court then granted review.

Justice ANTHONY KENNEDY, writing for the Court, first noted that by its very terms, § 2254 (d) barred relitigation of a claim "adjudicated on the merits" in state court (notwithstanding the "unreasonableness" exceptions). Nothing in the **statutory** text required a statement of reasons for the denial. The Court also stated that when a state court denies relief, an ADJUDICATION on the merits can be presumed, absent contrary indications.

Second, the Court wholly rejected the habeas relief ordered by the Ninth Circuit, finding that Richter was not entitled to any such relief. The Court admonished the Ninth Circuit's failure to accord the required deference to state decisions as required by *Strickland*. The (*Strickland* decision held that, to succeed on an ineffective counsel claim, a DEFENDANT must show both substandard performance by counsel and prejudice.) Here, the Ninth Circuit should have been asking whether the state court's application of *Strickland* was unreasonable, not whether defense counsel's performance fell below that standard. Said the Court,

The Court of Appeals gave § 2254(d) no operation or function in its reasoning. Its analysis illustrates a lack of deference to the state court's determination and an improper intervention in state criminal processes, contrary to the purpose and mandate of AEDPA and to the now well-settled meaning and function of habeas **corpus** in the federal system.

Finally, as to the Ninth Circuit's improper *de novo* review (on the merits), the Court also found error in the Ninth Circuit's finding of prejudice. To show prejudice, there must be a substantial likelihood of a different outcome at trial. The California Supreme Court could have reasonably concluded that Richter's proffered evidence (limited to just one aspect of the evidence offered against him regarding the blood) fell short of the standard. A competent attorney may just as readily adopt a trial strategy that did not require using blood evidence experts.

Justice Elena Kagan took no part in consideration or decision. All others joined, excepting Justice Ruth Bader Ginsburg, who filed a separate opinion concurring in the judgment.

SOCIAL SECURITY ACT

Legislation (42 U.S.C.A. § 301 et seq.) designed to assist in the maintenance of the financial well-being of eligible persons, enacted in 1935 as part of President Franklin D. Roosevelt's New Deal.

Supreme Court Rules that Medical Residents Must Pay Social Security

Most Americans who work for wages must pay taxes under the Federal Insurance Contributions Act (FICA), which collects funds for SOCIAL SECURITY. A question has long lingered as to whether doctors who serve as medical residents should be viewed as "students" whose service is exempted from FICA taxes. A group of medical education organizations challenged a TREASURY DEPARTMENT regulation that limited the student exemption to situations where the educational aspect of the relationship between the employer and employee predominated over the service aspect. Because medical residents work between 50 and 80 hours a week, the government concluded that their service predominated over the education component. Therefore the residents must have FICA taxes deducted from their paychecks. The SUPREME COURT, in *Mayo Foundation for Medical Educ. And Research v. U.S.*,

__U.S.__, 131 S.Ct. 704, 178 L.Ed.2d 588 (2011), ruled that the regulation was proper and was due deference from the Court.

The Mayo Foundation for Medical Education and Research, the Mayo Clinic, and the Regents of the University of Minnesota (collectively Mayo), offer medical residency programs that provided additional education to medical school graduates. Newly minted doctors use residency programs to specialize in a field of medicine and to become board certified to practice in that specialty. Mayo's residency program lasts from three to five years and trains doctors primarily through hands-on experience. Residents typically work between 50 to 80 hours per week caring for patients under the supervision of resident supervisors and by faculty members known as attending physicians. In 2005, Mayo paid its residents annual "stipends" that ranged between $41,000 and $56,000. Mayo also provided health insurance, MALPRACTICE insurance, and paid vacation time. Mayo residents were also required to take part in structured educational programs. They were assigned readings in textbooks and medical journals and were expected to attend weekly lectures. However, most of their time was spent treating patients.

The legal dispute over collecting FICA taxes from medical residents had simmered for over 50 years. Congress had excluded from FICA taxation services performed by employees of schools, colleges, and universities who were students enrolled and attending such educational institutions. The Treasury Department had applied the student exception as long as students worked for their schools "as an incident to and for the purpose of pursuing a course of study." Until 2005 the department determined whether an individual's work was incident to his studies on a case-by-case basis. The prime factors were the numbers of hours worked and the course load taken. The Social Security Administration (SSA) also issued regulations and looked at the student exception on a case-by-case basis. However, the SSA had always held that resident physicians were not students.

After a 1998 federal **circuit court** of appeals ruled that the SSA could not categorically deny medical residents student status, the INTERNAL REVENUE SERVICE (IRS) received more than 7,000 claims seeking FICA refunds on the grounds that medical residents qualified as students. This led the Treasury Department to issue a new rule in 2005 that categorically provided that working 40 hours or more a week disqualified the employee from the FICA exception. Mayo filed suit in federal court, arguing that the 40-hour, full-time employee rule was invalid. The **district court** agreed with Mayo but the Eighth Circuit Court of Appeals reversed this ruling. The appeals court concluded that the department's regulation was a permissible interpretation of the **statute**.

The Supreme Court, in a unanimous decision with Justice Elena Kagan not participating, upheld the Eighth Circuit ruling. Chief Justice JOHN ROBERTS, writing for the Court, applied a two-part analysis that governs the review of federal administrative regulations. The first step requires a court to determine whether Congress has "directly addressed the precise question at issue." Roberts agreed with the Eighth Circuit that Congress had not done so, as the statute did not define the term "student" and did not address whether medical residents were subject to FICA. Mayo argued that the dictionary definition of "student" clearly encompassed residents, as residents studied and applied the mind to acquiring learning using books, observation, or experiment. The Court found no merit in this claim, as it did not eliminate "the statute's ambiguity as applied to working professionals."

If Congress has not directly addressed the precise question, then the Court will proceed to the second part of the analysis to determine if the regulation is proper. A court may not disturb an agency rule unless it is "arbitrary or capricious in substance, or manifestly contrary to the statute." However, in this case Mayo argued that this was not the proper framework to contest an IRS regulation. Mayo contended that the Court should apply a multi-factor analysis that was announced by the Court many years prior to its use of the two-part analysis. Chief Justice Roberts declined to use the multi-factor analysis, as Mayo had failed to show "any justification for applying a less deferential standard of review to Treasury Department regulations than we apply to the rules of any other agency." Because of this the Court was "not inclined to carve out an approach to administrative review good for tax law only."

The Court concluded that the second part of the analysis of the regulation demonstrated that the department had the authority to make "interpretive choices for **statutory** implementation" that were as complex as other agencies. The full-time employee rule was a "reasonable interpretation" of the statute. Mayo contended that the IRS should make a case-by-case review of each resident's student status, but the Court found that this categorical rule was a reasonable way to "distinguish between workers who study and students who work." Moreover, the rule was more administratively efficient and it furthered the purpose of the Social Security Act by taxing residents. Therefore, the regulation was reasonable.

SOVEREIGN IMMUNITY

The legal protection that prevents a sovereign state or person from being sued without consent.

Madison County, N.Y. v. Oneida Indian Nation of N.Y.

In a somewhat surprising case before the U.S. SUPREME COURT, the Court vacated a lower court's judgment in favor of Oneida Indian Nation of New York (OIN) after the tribe waived its **sovereign immunity**, thus rendering the issues before the Court irrelevant. The Court remanded the case back to the Second **Circuit Court** of Appeals. The decision was the latest in a long line of cases involving the Oneida tribe.

At the time of the American Revolution, OIN was among the most powerful Indian tribes in the northeast. OIN's homeland in central New York consisted of about six million acres. However, after the Revolution, the State of New York came under pressure to allow settlement on OIN's land. In 1788, the State of New York and OIN entered into the Treaty of Fort Schuyler, under which OIN ceded all of its land to the state in exchange for payments of money and kind. The treaty allowed OIN to retain about 300,000 acres as a reservation for its own cultivation and use.

The federal government in 1790 passed the Indian Trade and Intercourse Act, also known as the Nonintercourse Act. Ch. 33, 1 Stat. 137. This Act forbids sales of tribal land without approval by the federal government. Later acts charged with laundering $190,000 in corporate funds through the Republican National State Elections Committee (RNSEC). The funds eventually went to Texas Republican candidates for the House, which contravened Texas election laws.

About a year and a half after Colyandro's INDICTMENT, a Texas **grand jury** indicted the TRMPAC on charges that the committee accepted $120,000 in illegal corporate campaign contributions. The committee allegedly received most of these contributions around the time of the 2002 Texas legislative elections that allowed Republicans to take control of the Texas House for the first time in more than a century. Under Texas law, corporations cannot make political contributions for election purposes. Instead, use of these donations is limited to administrative costs. However, evidence showed that the TRMPAC had spent at least $523,000 in corporate funds. The committee did not report most of this money to state election officials.

A DeLay spokesperson said after the committee's indictment that it would not affect DeLay himself. However, on September 28, 2005, the same GRAND JURY indicted both DeLay and Ellis. The two men, along with Colyandro, faced charges MONEY LAUNDERING (a first-degree **felony**) and criminal CONSPIRACY (a second-degree felony). Ellis and Colyandro also faced additional charges related to illegally accepting political contributions in violation of the Texas election laws.

The indictment against the men was filed in the Travis County **District Court** in Austin. The grand jury focused much of its attention on a check for $190,000 to the (RNSEC) and signed by Colyandro. The indictment also found that Ellis had delivered the check to the RNSEC, along with the names of several Republican candidates for the Texas House of Representatives. Seven of these candidates received funds in amounts ranging from $20,000 to $40,000. Other charges in the indictment focused on various amounts that TRMPAC illegally received from different corporations. DeLay turned himself in to the Harris County Sheriff's Office in Houston on October 20, 2005, and he was released on $10,000 bond. DeLay's trial would not take place until 2010, however.

The indictment was not the only controversy in which DeLay had become embroiled. A federal investigation revealed that DeLay had

Former House Majority Leader Tom DeLay arrives at the Travis County courthouse in Austin, Texas, for jury selection in his corruption trial.
AP IMAGES/JACK PLUNKETT, FILE

received money from Russian oil executives through an advocacy group funded by clients of disgraced former lobbyist Jack Abramoff. Though the investigation into his ties with Abramoff never resulted in charges filed, the criminal charges and the federal investigation led to DeLay's resignation from Congress in 2005. For five years, he remained out of the public spotlight except for an appearance on televisions "Dancing with the Stars" in 2009.

The trial took place over the course of three weeks, during which prosecutors presented more than 30 witnesses and many emails and other documents. DeLay's lawyer, Dick DeGuerin, argued that what the TRMPAC did was nothing more than a money swap that the attorney alleged was common practice among political campaigns and political action committees. He said that no funds from corporations ever went into the hands of a Texas political candidate. The jury deliberated for 19 hours before reaching a guilty verdict on both charges. He faced a possible life sentence for the convictions.

Before state district judge Pat Priest in January, DeLay sought to receive PROBATION. DeGuerin noted to reporters that nobody in the case was actually injured or suffered any economic loss. DeGuerin called nine witnesses to testify on DeLay's behalf, including former U.S. House Speaker Dennis Hastert. The defense also produced letters and other correspondence supporting DeLay. DeLay's attorney further argued that the Democratic district attorney who tried the case had done so only with political motives driving him.

Nevertheless, Priest sentenced DeLay to three years in prison on the conspiracy count and ten years of probation on the money laundering count. At the sentencing, Priest said, "Before there were Republicans and Democrats, there was America, and what America is about is the rule of law." Priest also said he did not believe that the Travis County District Attorney's Office had "picked on" DeLay based on political motives.

As of May 1, 2011, DeLay remained free on bond, pending his appeal. His attorney has stated that the money laundering charge should not stand under Texas law because the money did not come from any illegal activity. DeLay's appeal could take years before it is resolved.

Discrimination

SUNSHINE IN THE COURTROOM ACT OF 2009

A BILL

To provide for media coverage of Federal court proceedings.

Be it enacted by the Senate and House of Representatives of the United States of America in Congress assembled,

SECTION 1. SHORT TITLE.

This Act may be cited as the 'Sunshine in the Courtroom Act of 2009'.

SEC. 2. FEDERAL APPELLATE AND DISTRICT COURTS.

(a) Definitions- In this section:

(1) PRESIDING JUDGE- The term 'presiding judge' means the judge presiding over the court proceeding concerned. In proceedings in which more than 1 judge participates, the presiding judge shall be the senior active judge so participating or, in the case of a circuit court of appeals, the senior active circuit judge so participating, except that–

(A) in en banc sittings of any United States circuit court of appeals, the presiding judge shall be the chief judge of the circuit whenever the chief judge participates; and

(B) in en banc sittings of the Supreme Court of the United States, the presiding judge shall be the Chief Justice whenever the Chief Justice participates.

(2) APPELLATE COURT OF THE UNITED STATES- The term 'appellate court of the United States' means any United States circuit court of appeals and the Supreme Court of the United States.

(b) Authority of Presiding Judge To Allow Media Coverage of Court Proceedings-

(1) AUTHORITY OF APPELLATE COURTS-

(A) IN GENERAL- Except as provided under subparagraph (B), the presiding judge of an appellate court of the United States may, at the discretion of that judge, permit the photographing, electronic recording, broadcasting, or televising to the public of any court proceeding over which that judge presides.

(B) EXCEPTION- The presiding judge shall not permit any action under subparagraph (A), if–

(i) in the case of a proceeding involving only the presiding judge, that judge determines the action would constitute a violation of the due process rights of any party; or

(ii) in the case of a proceeding involving the participation of more than 1 judge, a majority of the judges participating determine that the action would constitute a violation of the due process rights of any party.

(2) AUTHORITY OF DISTRICT COURTS-

(A) IN GENERAL-

(i) AUTHORITY- Notwithstanding any other provision of law, except as provided under clause (iii), the presiding judge of a district court of the United States may, at the discretion of that judge, permit the photographing, electronic recording, broadcasting, or televising to the public of any court proceeding over which that judge presides.

(ii) OBSCURING OF WITNESSES- Except as provided under clause (iii)–

(I) upon the request of any witness (other than a party) in a trial proceeding, the court shall order the face and voice of the witness to be disguised or otherwise obscured in such manner as to render the witness unrecognizable to the broadcast audience of the trial proceeding; and

(II) the presiding judge in a trial proceeding shall inform each witness who is not a party that the witness has the right to request the image and voice of that witness to be obscured during the witness' testimony.

(iii) EXCEPTION- The presiding judge shall not permit any action under this subparagraph–

(I) if that judge determines the action would constitute a violation of the due process rights of any party; and

(II) until the Judicial Conference of the United States promulgates mandatory guidelines under paragraph (5).

(B) NO MEDIA COVERAGE OF JURORS- The presiding judge shall not permit the photographing, electronic recording, broadcasting, or televising of any juror in a trial proceeding, or of the jury selection process.

(C) DISCRETION OF THE JUDGE- The presiding judge shall have the discretion to obscure the face and voice of an individual, if good cause is shown that the photographing, electronic recording, broadcasting, or televising of the individual would threaten–

(i) the safety of the individual;

(ii) the security of the court;

(iii) the integrity of future or ongoing law enforcement operations; or

(iv) the interest of justice.

(D) SUNSET OF DISTRICT COURT AUTHORITY- The authority under this paragraph shall terminate 3 years after the date of the enactment of this Act.

(3) INTERLOCUTORY APPEALS BARRED- The decision of the presiding judge under this subsection of whether or not to permit, deny, or terminate the photographing, electronic recording, broadcasting, or televising of a court proceeding may not be challenged through an interlocutory appeal.

(4) ADVISORY GUIDELINES- The Judicial Conference of the United States may promulgate advisory guidelines to which a presiding judge, at the discretion of that judge, may refer in making decisions with respect to the management and administration of photographing, recording, broadcasting, or televising described under paragraphs (1) and (2).

(5) MANDATORY GUIDELINES- Not later than 6 months after the date of enactment of this Act, the Judicial Conference of the United States shall promulgate mandatory guidelines which a presiding judge is required to follow for obscuring of certain vulnerable witnesses, including crime victims, minor victims, families of victims, cooperating witnesses, undercover law enforcement officers or agents, witnesses subject to section 3521 of title 18, United States Code, relating to witness relocation and protection, or minors under the age of 18 years. The guidelines shall include procedures for determining, at the earliest practicable time in any investigation or case, which witnesses should be considered vulnerable under this section.

(6) PROCEDURES- In the interests of justice and fairness, the presiding judge of the court in which media use is desired has discretion to promulgate rules and disciplinary measures for the courtroom use of any form of media or media equipment and the acquisition or distribution of any of the images or sounds obtained in the courtroom. The presiding judge shall also have discretion to require written acknowledgment of the rules by anyone individually or on behalf of any entity before being allowed to acquire any images or sounds from the courtroom.

(7) NO BROADCAST OF CONFERENCES BETWEEN ATTORNEYS AND CLIENTS- There shall be no audio pickup or broadcast of conferences which occur in a court proceeding between attorneys and their clients, between co-counsel of a client, between adverse counsel, or between counsel and the presiding judge, if the conferences are not part of the official record of the proceedings.

(8) EXPENSES- A court may require that any accommodations to effectuate this Act be made without public expense.

to the position of telemarketer, and in August 2009, the manager at the Rockefeller branch—a female—fired Lorenzana.

She hired attorney Jack Tuckner to file a lawsuit against Citigroup, which he did in November 2009. The case did not become a significant news items for several months, but in June 2010, the press started to focus on the story. Several newspapers in the New York area ran stories about the alleged harassment and her lawsuit, with some media outlets noting that Lorenzana was essentially saying she was "fired for being too sexy." Tuckner had reportedly asked Lorenzana to pose for several pictures at his office so that she would have pictures to reveal how conservative her attire was. However, the media outlets then received copies of many of these photos to include with their stories about her case. Reports indicated that her case would have to go to ARBITRATION because of a clause in her contract.

Later in June 2010, Lorenzana hired celebrity lawyer GLORIA ALLRED. On June 28, 2010, Lorenzana held a makeshift press conference in which she announced that she had asked the New York Division on Human Rights to investigate her claim. Lorenzana claimed that she was not pursuing the case for fame, but Citigroup responded that the suit and complaint was just another attempt to gain personal publicity. Reports noted that the public had a divided view of the case, with some showing sympathy for an alleged SEXUAL HARASSMENT victim and others viewing her as a someone seeking attention. By the time she filed her complaint, she was working at a branch of JP Morgan Chase.

SIXTH AMENDMENT

Bullcoming v. New Mexico

The Confrontation Clause of the SIXTH AMENDMENT provides that an accused in a criminal prosecution has the right "to be confronted with the witnesses against him." Recent decisions by the U.S. SUPREME COURT have established that a trial court can admit evidence of testimonial statements of witnesses who are absent from trial only in narrow circumstances. However, the New Mexico Supreme Court in 2010 ruled that a trial court could admit testimonial evidence regarding a blood-alcohol report even though the analyst who prepared the report was unavailable for trial. The U.S. Supreme Court in *Bullcoming v. New Mexico*, No. 09-10876, 2011 WL 2472799 (U.S. June 23, 2011) reversed the New Mexico decision, ruling that the DEFENDANT had the right under the Sixth Amendment to confront the analyst.

The case involved Donald Bullcoming, who in August 2005 rear-ended a pick-up truck. The driver of the truck noticed that Bullcoming's eyes were bloodshot. The driver also noticed that Bullcoming's breath smelled like alcohol, so the driver told his girlfriend to call the police. Bullcoming attempted to leave the scene, but he was soon apprehended. The officer who stopped Bullcoming asked him to perform field sobriety tests, which Bullcoming failed. The officer then arrested Bullcoming for driving under the influence of an intoxicating liquor (**DWI**).

Bullcoming refused to take a breathalyzer test, so officers had to obtain a warrant to obtain blood for a blood-alcohol analysis. Upon receiving the warrant, the officers took Bullcoming to a local hospital. The officers then sent the blood sample to the New Mexico Department of Health, Scientific Laboratory Division for testing. Police officers and staff members at the laboratory filled out a standard form that contained the laboratory's report.

The **forensic** analyst who conducted the blood testing was Curtis Caylor, who recorded his findings on this form. According to Caylor's report, Bullcoming's blood sample showed 0.21 grams of alcohol per hundred milliliters, which is an extraordinarily high number. Caylor affirmed in the report that he had received the blood with the seal intact, and he stated the procedures that the laboratory followed in testing the blood sample. In another part of the report, an examiner certified that Caylor was qualified to conduct the report and that Caylor had followed the correct procedures in testing the blood. The blood-testing process requires specialized knowledge, and human error by the forensic analyst can distort the findings. Thus, the identity of the analyst who conducted the test was important. Based on Caylor's report, prosecutors charged Bullcoming with aggravated DWI.

At the time of Bullcoming's trial in November 2005, the Supreme Court had decided *Crawford v. Washington*, 541 U.S. 36, 124 S. Ct. 1354, 158 L. Ed. 2d 177 (2004). In that case, the Court established that the testimonial statements of a witness who is absent from trial is admissible only when two conditions are met: (1) the declarant is unavailable; and (2) the defendant had a prior opportunity to cross-examine the declarant. The prosecution in Bullcoming's trial announced that Caylor had been placed on unpaid leave and that the state would not call Caylor as a witness. Instead, the state called a different analyst, who confirmed the contents of Caylor's report. Bullcoming's attorney objected, arguing that Bullcoming had the right to confront Caylor. However, the judge overruled the objection, and based in part on the report, the jury convicted Bullcoming of aggravated DWI.

A New Mexico **appellate court** affirmed Bullcoming's conviction. After this, the U.S. Supreme Court decided in *Melendez-Diaz v. Massachusetts*, 129 S. Ct. 2527 (2009) that a defendant had the right to confront a witnesses about the contents of a forensic laboratory report. In so ruling, the Court rejected an argument that the report should be admissible as an exception to *Crawford*.

Bullcoming appealed his conviction again to the New Mexico Supreme Court, arguing that the decision in *Melendez-Diaz* proved that he was entitled to confront Caylor about the contents of the report. However, the New Mexico Supreme Court determined that Caylor was nothing more than a "mere scrivener" who transcribed the results that appeared on the machine that tested the blood. Moreover, the court determined that the other analyst had sufficient expertise in the machine and that the defense's opportunity to cross-examine the expert about how the machine functioned.

The U.S. Supreme Court granted **certiorari**, and in a 5-4 decision, reversed the New Mexico Supreme Court. Justice Ruth Bader Ginsberg wrote for the majority, which included liberal justices SONIA SOTOMAYOR and Elena Kagan along with conservative Justices ANTONIN SCALIA and CLARENCE THOMAS. Ginsburg examined the Court's decisions in *Crawford* and *Melendez-Diaz* and found that the STATE COURTS had tried to create an exception that did not comply with the U.S. Supreme Court's precedent.

The Court specifically rejected both grounds on which the New Mexico Supreme Court had based its decision. First, use of the machine that tested the blood required expertise to operate. Caylor could have made any of a number of mistakes during the testing process, and the defense was entitled to confront Caylor to question the analyst about any of these possible mistakes. Second, the testimony of the other analyst was not adequate to protect Bullcoming's rights under the Confrontation Clause because the analyst could only provide surrogate testimony. The other analyst had not actually witnessed Caylor's procedures and could only testify as to the contents of Caylor's final report.

Justice ANTHONY KENNEDY dissented along with three other justices. According to Kennedy, the majority took a "new and serious misstep" by extending the holding of *Melendez-Diaz*. According to Kennedy, the difference in *Melendez-Diaz* and Bullcoming's case was that nobody was available to testify in the former, while another analyst was available to testify in the latter. Kennedy concluded that Caylor himself was not a necessary witness for purposes of the Confrontation Clause.

During police investigations, officers almost always hear statements that may be inculpatory towards a potential criminal DEFENDANT. In some instances, these statements might be made to enable the officer to address an ongoing emergency. However, in other circumstances, the emergency may have ended, and officers take statements intending to gather evidence for later use in a criminal trial. In 2011, the U.S. SUPREME COURT considered a case where a victim's statements to officers implicated a man later convicted of MURDER. In an 6-2 decision, the Court determined that the statements were admissible because the statements were made with the primary purpose of enabling the police to handle the emergency. The decision prompted a scathing DISSENT by Justice ANTONIN SCALIA.

The victim in the case was Anthony Covington, who lived with his brother a few houses away from the defendant, Richard Bryant. In April 2001, Covington decided to redeem a coat that he had given to Bryant in exchange for cocaine. Covington's brother later heard gunfire, and police responded. The officers found Covington lying on the ground at a gas station about six blocks from Bryant's house. Officers questioned Covington about the shooting, and Covington said that Bryant had shot him after the two had a short conversation through a closed door at Bryant's home. Covington said he recognized Bryant as the shooter based on Bryant's voice. The officers' questioning continued for five to ten minutes until emergency medical personnel arrived. Covington died hours later.

The officers proceeded to Bryant's house, where they discovered blood, a bullet, and what appeared to be a bullet hole in the back door. The officers also found Covington's wallet at the scene. Bryant's girlfriend said that Bryant had not been home at the time of the shooting, but a MEDICAL EXAMINER later concluded that the bullet that killed Covington had passed through some intermediate target, such as a door. One year after the incident, Bryant was arrested in California and extradited to Michigan. Although his first trial resulted in a HUNG JURY, he was later convicted of second-degree murder along with other counts related to the shooting.

Bryant appealed his conviction to a Michigan **appellate court** and to the Michigan Supreme Court. Bryant's trial occurred before the U.S. Supreme Court had decided the cases of *Crawford v. Washington*, 541 U.S. 36, 124 S.Ct. 1354, 158 L. Ed. 2d 177 (2004) and *Davis v. Washington*, 547 U.S. 813, 126 S. Ct. 2266, 165 L. Ed. 2d 224 (2006). Both of these cases had construed the Confrontation Clause of the SIXTH AMENDMENT. In light of these decisions, the Michigan Supreme Court reversed the conviction, ruling that the statements were testimonial in nature and thus inadmissible. The U.S. Supreme Court in 2010 agreed to review the case.

In *Crawford*, the Court held that if a statement is testimonial in nature, the Sixth Amendment requires that the person making the statement is unavailable and that the opposing party had a prior opportunity to cross-examine the person making the state-ment. In that case, a victim of spousal abuse made statements at a police station, but she later refused to testify based on spousal privilege. The Court held that her statements were testimonial in nature and inadmissible in a trial against her husband because her husband did not have the opportunity to cross-examine her before trial. In *Davis*, however, a victim made statements to a 911 operator, and the statements described an ongoing domestic disturbance. The Court concluded that these statements were nontestimonial in nature, and thus admissible, because the statements were necessary to resolve the ongoing emergency.

The Michigan Supreme Court concluded that police had taken Covington's statements to establish facts about the crime, making these statements testimonial. However, the U.S. Supreme Court disagreed. An opinion by Justice SONIA SOTOMAYOR reviewed both *Craw-ford* and Davis extensively, noting that the Court was required to conduct an objective analysis of the circumstances to determine the primary purpose of the interrogation. Soto-mayor disagreed with the Michigan Supreme Court's conclusion about what amounted to an ongoing emergency. Sotomayor noted that "there was an ongoing emergency ... where an armed shooter, whose motive for and location after the shooting were unknown, had mortally wounded Covington within a few blocks and a few minutes of the location where the police found Covington." The officers' line of question was, Sotomayor wrote, consist with questions necessary to resolve the ongoing emergency. Accordingly, the majority concluded that Covington's statements were non-testimonial in nature and admissible at trial.

Much of the discussion about this opinion centered on Justice Scalia's dissent, which attacked the majority opinion with such WORDS AND PHRASES as "gross distortion of the facts," "utter nonsense," and "unprincipled." Scalia only recognizes a few narrow exceptions to the Sixth Amendment's Confrontation Clause, and to him, this case did not fit within one of those exceptions. In fact, had the majority applied the correct standing, according to Scalia, this would have been "an absurdly easy case" because there was little doubt to Scalia that the officers were gathering evidence when they asked Covington the questions.

Scalia's decision to use such strong language in his dissent prompted several questions among legal commentators. Long-time Supreme COURT REPORTER Linda Greenhouse of the *New York Times* said it is a puzzle as to what Scalia hopes to accomplish with his dissents. She noted, "Antonin Scalia, approaching his 25th anniversary as a Supreme Court justice, has cast a long shadow but has accomplished surprisingly little. Nearly every time he has come close to achieving one of his jurisprudential goals, his colleagues have either hung back at the last minute or, feeling buyer's remorse, retreated at the next opportunity."

Supreme Court Rules Plea Bargain Did Not Violate Sixth Amendment

The SIXTH AMENDMENT provides that criminal defendants have the right to effective LEGAL REPRESENTATION. The U.S. SUPREME COURT has established a standard for determining inadequate assistance **of counsel** that relies on whether a lawyer's representation fell below an objective standard of reasonableness. Though most claims of ineffective legal counsel deal with trial issues, plea bargains are also open to review. The Court, in *Premo v. Moore*, __ U.S.__, 131 S.Ct. 733, 178 L.Ed.2d 649 (2011) ruled that a defendant's lawyer acting reasonably in negotiating a plea bargain at an early stage of the case. The fact that the lawyer did not challenge the admissibility of his client's confession did not mean representation was ineffective; two witnesses were ready to testify to the defendant's admission of the crime and the state could have increased the severity of the charges the longer the criminal investigation continued.

In 1995, Randy Moore and two confederates attacked Kenneth Rogers at his home. They tied him up with duct tape and threw him in the trunk of a car. They drove into rural Oregon, where Moore shot and killed Rogers. Following the crime, Moore and one of his accomplices told Moore's brother and the accomplice's girlfriend that they were trying to scare Rogers. The plan was to leave him in the countryside and make him walk home. However, the gun Moore was carrying accidentally discharged, killing Rogers. Moore and the ACCOMPLICE told the same story to police. Moore's lawyer convinced him to plead NO CONTEST to **felony** MURDER in exchange for a sentence of 300 months, the minimum sentence allowed by law for the offense. Moore later filed for postconviction relief in Oregon state court, arguing that he had been denied his right to effective assistance OF COUNSEL. He contended his lawyer should have filed a motion challenging the admissibility of his confession before advising him to take the plea bargain. The **district court** found that such a motion would have been fruitless because of the admissible confession

Moore had made to the two individuals. The court also noted the testimony of Moore's lawyer, who said he had discussed the suppression motion with his client and had advised him it would not solve the admission at trial of the testimony of the two witnesses. In addition, the lawyer had advised Moore that he could be charged with aggravated murder, which carried a potential death sentence or life imprisonment without PAROLE. The prosecution could raise the charge based on the beating and abuse meted out to Rogers before the shooting.

Moore filed a petition for **habeas corpus** in Oregon federal district court, again claiming ineffective assistance of counsel. The district court dismissed the petition but the Ninth **Circuit Court** of Appeals ruled that the state court's conclusion that there was effective legal counsel was an unreasonable application of the U.S Supreme Court's clearly established law. The state challenged this decision and the Supreme Court agreed to hear its petition for relief.

In a unanimous decision (Justice Elena Kagan did not participate), the Court overruled the Ninth Circuit. Justice ANTHONY KENNEDY, writing for the Court, noted that federal habeas review of state court decisions is guided by 28 U.S.C.A. § 2254, which states that habeas should not be granted unless the state court's decision resulted from an "unreasonable application of clearly established federal law." To establish ineffective assistance of counsel a DEFENDANT must show both deficient performance by the lawyer and prejudice. A deficient performance is established by showing that the lawyer's representation "fell below an objective standard of reasonableness." In addition, a court must apply a "strong presumption" that the lawyer's representation was within the "wide range" of reasonable professional assistance. As to prejudice, the person challenging the conviction must demonstrate a "reasonable probability that, but for counsel's unprofessional errors, the result of the proceeding would have been different."

Justice Kennedy applied these rules to Moore's case. He concluded the Oregon courts had not unreasonably applied the ineffective counsel law established by the Court. Kennedy pointed out that plea bargains "are the result of complex negotiations suffused with uncertainty, and defense attorneys must make careful strategic choices in balancing opportunities need for rehabilitation in setting the length of the sentence. *United States v. Duran,* 37 F.3d 557 (1994).

To resolve a split among the nation's circuit courts of appeal, the U.S. Supreme Court granted **certiorari** (review) of the case. In June 2011, it reversed the Ninth Circuit, holding instead that 8 U.S.C. § 3582(a) did not permit sentencing courts to impose *or* lengthen a term of imprisonment for the purpose of fostering a defendant's rehabilitation.

Newly-appointed Justice ELENA KAGAN wrote the opinion for an unanimous Court. The opinion first reviewed the history behind the Sentencing Reform Act of 1984. Prior to that enactment, said the Court, the federal government had employed a system of "indeterminate sentencing," leaving courts to their own discretion in meting what they deemed to be a correct punishment and/or rehabilitation. Over the years, that system produced "serious disparities" in the sentences imposed on similarly-situated defendants who had committed essentially similar crimes. Moreover, the system failed to achieve the intended "rehabilitation" of most criminals.

Under the SRA, however, at a minimum, a court must impose at least imprisonment, PROBATION, or a fine § 3551(b). Under § 3582 (a), as relevant here, a court ordering imprisonment must "recogniz[e] that imprisonment is not an appropriate means of promoting correction and rehabilitation." A similar provision instructed the Sentencing Commission (the Sentencing Guideline's author) to insure that the guidelines reflect the inappropriateness of imposing a sentence to a term of imprisonment for the purpose of rehabilitating the defendant." 28 U.S.C. § 994(k).

Looking to the plain text, the Court found that the Ninth Circuit's reasoning, that § 3582 (a)'s term "imprisonment" relates to the decision whether to incarcerate, but not the determination of length of sentence, was flawed. Because "imprisonment" naturally refers to a state or period of confinement, the term does not distinguish between a defendant's initial placement into prison and his continued stay there. In fact, by repeating § 3582(a)'s message to the Sentencing Commission, Congress made sure that sentencing officials would work together with judges to implement the **statutory** directive to reject imprisonment as a

means of promoting rehabilitation. Although a sentencing court may recommend that a defendant be placed in a particular prison program or facility, the decision and authority ultimately rests with the Bureau of Prisons.

In this case, noted the Court, the sentencing transcript suggested that Tapia's sentence may have been lengthened for the purpose of her rehabilitative needs, which is inappropriate. In reversing, the Court said that the Ninth Circuit, on remand, needed to consider the effect of Tapia's failure to object to the sentence at the time it was imposed.

Justice SONIA SOTOMAYOR wrote a separate concurring opinion, in which she was joined by Justice Alito. While agreeing that § 3582(a) precluded **federal courts** "from imposing or lengthening a prison term in order to promote a criminal defendant's rehabilitation," she expressed "skepticism" that the district judge had actually violated that prohibition in this case. She noted that the judge had made a careful record of his consideration and review of the sentencing factors separately and the factual seriousness of Tapia's offenses, warranting lengthy imprisonment.

SEX OFFENSES

California's Version of Jessica's Law Faces Legal Challenges

In 2006, California voters approved Proposition 83 as the state's version of Jessica's Law. Among its provisions, the law made a number of revisions to the California Penal Code, as it strengthened penalties for SEX OFFENSES, broadened the definitions of these offenses, established lifetime GPS monitoring for certain offenders, and prohibited offenders from living within 2,000 feet of schools and parks. Several individuals challenged some of Proposition 83's provisions, and in 2010 and 2011, two state court judges ruled that parts of the law were unconstitutional.

California state senator George Runner and State Assemblywoman Sharon Runner proposed Proposition 83, known as the Sexual Predator and Control Act: Jessica's Law. The name Jessica's Law came from a similar law passed in Florida to punish sex offenders and make it more difficult for these offenders to commit new crimes. The California law would apply to the 90,000 registered sex offenders in initial sentencing and a subsequent resentencing after a prior sentence has been set aside on appeal." In addition, postsentencing rehabilitation may be relevant to the statutory factors Congress has instructed district courts to use, such as "the history and characteristics of the defendant."

In Pepper's case, Judge Bennett recognized that Pepper's extensive rehabilitation was clearly relevant to the selection of an appropriate sentence. Evidence of Pepper's conduct since his release from prison in 2005 was, in Sotomayor's view, "the most up-to-date picture of Pepper's 'history and characteristics.'" His postsentencing conduct also shed light on the likelihood that he would engage in future criminal acts. This is a central factor "that district courts must assess when imposing sentence." Justice Sotomayor rejected the claim that another federal **statute** that restricts the discretion of a **district court** when a sentence is set aside on appeal prevented post-sentencing rehabilitation evidence. The *Booker* decision invalidated this law when it made the Sentencing Guidelines advisory.

The Court also found the Eighth Circuit's categorical ban on postsentencing rehabilitation illogical, as it would also bar consideration of any postsentencing information, such as the defendant's committing of any postsentencing offenses. Justice Sotomayor noted that the appeals court did not accept the logical consequence of this approach, "as it permits district courts to consider postsentencing conduct that would support a higher sentence." There was no evidence that Congress intended to allow only postsentencing evidence "detrimental to a defendant while turning a blind eye to favorable evidence of a defendant's postsentencing rehabilitation." The Court remanded the case to the district court to apply all postsentencing evidence since Pepper's last sentencing in 2009.

Tapia v. United States

In *Tapia v. United States*, No. 10-5400, 564 U.S. ___ (2011) the U.S. SUPREME COURT held that judges were not empowered to impose or lengthen prison terms in order to facilitate defendants' acceptance into drug rehabilitation programs. More specifically, the Court held that the Sentencing Reform Act of 1984 precluded such sentencing considerations. The unanimous

decision by the high court reversed the decision of the Ninth **Circuit Court** of Appeals.

DEFENDANT Alejandra Tapia had been convicted of SMUGGLING unauthorized ALIENS into the United States, in violation of federal law, specifically, 8 U.S.C. § 1324(a)(2)(B), as well as possession of a firearm and jumping bail. At sentencing, the **district court** determined that under the applicable sentencing guidelines, 41 to 51 months were recommended for her offenses. The court then decided to impose a 51-month sentence, followed by three years of supervised release. At the hearing, the court explained its decision to impose a longer sentence, referring to Tapia's need for drug treatment, and cited the Bureau of Prison's Residential Drug Abuse Program (RDAP), also referred to as the 500 hour Drug Program). The court wanted Tapia to serve a prison term long enough to qualify for and complete this program, stating on record:

> The sentence has to be sufficient to provide needed correctional treatment, and here I think the needed correctional treatment is the 500 hour Drug Program ... Here I have to say that one of the factors that-I am going to impose a 51-month sentence, ... and one of the factors that affects this is the need to provide treatment. In other words, so she is in long enough to get the 500 Hour Drug Program, number one.

At the sentence hearing, Tapia did not object to the sentence imposed. However, later on appeal, Tapia argued that the sentence was improper because her prison term had been lengthened in order to make her eligible for the 500 Hour Drug Program (the RDAP). Specifically, Tapia argued that the court's sentencing violated § 3582(a) of the Sentencing Reform Act, [8 U.S.C. § 3582(a)], which instructs courts to "recogniz[e] that imprisonment is not an appropriate means of promoting correction and rehabilitation."

The U.S. Court of Appeals for the Ninth Circuit disagreed. Relying on Ninth Circuit precedent, the **appellate court** ruled that8 U.S.C. § 3582(a) distinguishes between a court's *deciding to impose* a sentence of imprisonment, and a court's *determination as to the length* of a prison term. According to Ninth Circuit precedent, a court could not impose a prison term to assist a defendant with rehabilitation, but "[o]nce imprisonment is chosen as a punishment," a court could consider the defendant's

Defendant's Post-Sentencing Rehabilitation May be Used in Resentencing

In cases where a defendant's sentence has been set aside, the question has arisen whether the court, when resentencing the DEFENDANT, may use post-sentencing rehabilitation evidence to reduce the severity of the sentence. The Sentencing Reform Act of 1984 created the Federal Sentencing Commission, which created uniform sentencing formulas and removed most judicial discretion in fashioning a sentence. However, one provision of the act stated that a court "may consider, without limitation, any information concerning the background, character, and conduct of the defendant, unless otherwise prohibited by law." 18 U.S.C. § 3661. The SUPREME COURT, in *Pepper v. United States*, __U.S.__, 131 S.Ct. 1229, __L.Ed.2d__ (2011), ruled that this language gave courts the authority to use post-sentencing rehabilitation evidence to reduce the criminal sentence of a defendant.

In 2003, Jason Pepper was arrested and charged with CONSPIRACY to distribute 500 grams or more of methamphetamine. He pleaded guilty and appeared before Iowa Federal District Judge Mark Bennett for sentencing. Under the sentencing guidelines, Pepper's sentencing range was 97 to 121 months. The government asked for a downward departure of 15 percent because Pepper had assisted law enforcement. Instead, Bennett sentenced Pepper to a 24-month prison term, which was a 75 percent downward departure, followed by five years of supervised release. The government appealed the sentence and in 2005 the Eighth **Circuit Court** of Appeals reversed and remanded in light of the Supreme Court's decision in *United States v. Booker*, 543 U.S. 220, 125 S.Ct. 738, 160 L.Ed.2d 621 (2005). The Court ruled in that case that the sentencing guidelines were unconstitutional and instructed district courts to read the sentencing guidelines as "effectively advisory." Pepper completed his 24-month prison term three days after the Eighth Circuit decision and began his term of supervised release.

In May 2006, Judge Bennett conducted a resentencing hearing and heard from Pepper and two other witnesses. Pepper told the court that he had been a drug addict but had successfully completed a 500-hour drug treatment program while in prison and that he no

longer used drugs. He informed the court that he had enrolled at a local community college and was doing very well academically. Moreover, he had found employment and was following all the terms of his release. Pepper's father recounted how his son had turned his life around and Pepper's PROBATION officer testified that a 24-month prison term was reasonable in light of his post-sentencing rehabilitation and his low risk of **recidivism**. Judge Bennett agreed, first granting a 40 percent downward departure based on his substantial assistance to law enforcement. He then granted a further 59 percent downward departure based on Pepper's rehabilitation since the initial sentencing. The government again appealed and the Eighth Circuit again reversed and remanded for resentencing. It concluded that Bennett had abused his discretion by impermissibly using the post-sentence rehabilitation evidence. It also ordered the case reassigned to a different judge. The new judge, Linda Reade, convened another sentencing hearing in 2008 and in 2008 sentenced Pepper to 65 months imprisonment followed by 12 months of supervised release. The Eighth Circuit upheld this sentence.

The Supreme Court, in a 6-2 decision (Justice Elena Kagan did not participate), overruled the Eighth Circuit, finding that post-sentence evidence of a defendant's rehabilitation could be used to support a downward departure on resentencing. Justice SONIA SOTOMAYOR, writing for the majority, noted that it has been a federal judicial tradition for the sentencing judge to consider every convicted person as an individual and to treat each case as unique. In 1970, Congress codified this principle, which was later renumbered as § 3661 in the Sentencing Reform Act of 1984. That provision stated clearly that a court "may consider, without limitation, any information concerning the background, character, and conduct of the defendant, unless otherwise prohibited by law." The 1984 law did constrain the discretion of sentencing courts and the Court in *Booker*, directed courts to "give respectful consideration to the Guidelines." However, the Court had made clear in later decisions that courts were permitted to tailor sentences "in light of other **statutory** concerns as well." Such a statutory concern was expressed in § 3661. The plain language of this provision "makes no distinction between a defendant's

McNeill. Police then conducted a search of McNeill's body, and the officers found 3.1 grams of crack cocaine that was packaged to be distributed. McNeill was also carrying a large sum of money in cash.

The Armed Career Criminal Act (ACCA), 18 U.S.C. § 924(e) establishes an enhanced sentence for a DEFENDANT who has "three previous convictions . . . for a violent **felony** or a serious drug offense." The **statute** further defines a serious drug offense as "an offense under State law, involving the manufacturing, distributing, and possessing with intent to manufacture or distribute, a controlled substance . . ., for which the maximum term of imprisonment of ten years or more is prescribed by law."

McNeill had previously been convicted of six offenses for drug trafficking under North Carolina law. He also had convictions for ASSAULT with a deadly weapon and **common law robbery**. However, his six prior convictions stemmed from crimes that he committed in 1991, 1992, and 1994. In 1994, the North Carolina Legislature revised its sentencing scheme and reduced the maximum sentences for the crimes for which McNeill had been committed. Thus, at the time of his arrest in 2007, his previous individual drug offenses would not carry 10-year maximum sentences.

McNeill was indicted on counts for possession of a firearm, possession of crack cocaine with intent to distribute, and possession of a firearm during and in relation to a drug trafficking crime. He pleaded guilty on the first two counts, and the third was dismissed. The trial court reviewed his previous drug offenses and determined that the ACCA sentencing provision applied. Thus, the court sentenced McNeill to a total of 540 months (45 years) in prison.

McNeill appealed his sentence, arguing that the mandatory minimum 15-year sentence should not apply. He argued that because North Carolina had reduced the maximum sentence of drug trafficking charges to less than 10 years, his convictions should not qualify as serious drug offenses. The **district court** disagreed, concluding that the court should determine whether the offense is a serious drug offense by considering the crime's maximum sentence at the time of conviction. In other words, since the maximum sentence for McNeill's crimes was 10 years at

the time of his conviction, the crime was a serious drug offense. McNeill appealed his decision to the Fourth **Circuit Court** of Appeals, which affirmed the district court's conclusion. *United States v. McNeill*, 598 F.3d 161 (4th Cir. 2010).

McNeill relied on opinions from two federal circuit courts of appeals to support his position. In 1994, the Sixth Circuit ruled that the district court should consider the severity of the state crime at the time of the federal sentencing rather than at the time of the original conviction. The Second Circuit in 2008 reached the same conclusion, noting that the ACCA's definition of serious drug offense uses the present tense when referring to the applicable state law.

On the other hand, the Fifth Circuit in 2003 concluded that the district court should consider the severity of a sentence under Texas law based on the time of the original conviction and not according to the time of federal sentencing.

The U.S. SUPREME COURT agreed to review McNeill's case. In a unanimous decision, the Court affirmed the Fourth Circuit's conclusion. Writing for the Court, Justice CLARENCE THOMAS reviewed the plain meaning of the ACCA's text. According to Thomas, the text was unambiguous. He wrote, "The statute requires the court to determine whether a 'previous conviction' was for a serious drug offense. The only way to answer this backward-looking question is to consult the law that applied at the time of that conviction."

Thomas rejected McNeill's argument that because the ACCA uses the present tense to describe the serious drug offense that the court should consider the severity of the law at the present time. Thomas responded that McNeill's argument distorted the plain meaning of the statute. Thomas further noted that requiring a court to consider the current penalty of a crime would lead to absurd results. More specifically, Thomas rejected the premise that a former crime would simply disappear for purposes of the ACCA because state decided to reduce a sentence for a drug offense long after a defendant had been sentenced.

By concluding that McNeill's crimes were serious drug offenses, the Court determined that the district court had properly applied the ACCA. Therefore, the Court affirmed the Fourth Circuit's opinion.

This led not only to a loss in the value of the Fund but also in the overall value of Janus Capital Group. During September 2003, Janus Capital Group's stock fell 25%.

A group of plaintiffs who owned stock in Janus Capital Group as of September 3, 2003 formed a class (First Derivative Traders) that brought suit against Janus Capital Group and Janus Capital Management. First Derivative alleged that these companies violated both § 10(b) of the Securities Exchange Act of 1934, 15 U.S.C. § 78j(b) and Rule 10b-5 as issued by the Securities and Exchange Commission. According to the complaint, Janus Capital Group and Janus Capital Management "caused mutual fund prospectuses to be issued for Janus mutual funds and made them available to the investing public, which created the misleading impression that [the Janus companies] would implement measures to curb market timing in the [mutual funds]." The complaint further alleged that had investors known the truth about the market timing strategy, the funds would have been less attractive to investors, which meant that Janus Capital Group's stock would have been traded at a lower price.

Rule 10b-5 makes it illegal for a person to "make any untrue statement of material fact or to omit to state a material fact in order to make the statements made, in the light of the circumstances under which they were made, not misleading. . . . " The question in this dispute between First Derivative and the Janus companies was whether the companies "made" the statements in the prospectuses, given that the Fund itself issued the prospectus.

The U.S. **District Court** for the District of Maryland ruled against First Derivative, holding that these plaintiffs had failed to state a claim. First Derivative then appealed the case to the Fourth **Circuit Court** of Appeals. The **appellate court** reversed the district court's decision, finding that First Derivative had indeed pleaded a valid claim. The Fourth Circuit ruled that Janus Capital Group and Janus Capital Management had both made the statements in the prospectuses because they had both participated in writing and disseminating these prospectuses. However, the Fourth Circuit concluded that the plaintiffs could only maintain a claim against Janus Capital Management because the PLAINTIFF could not prove that they had relied on any statement attributed to Janus Capital Group.

The Supreme Court agreed to review the case to resolve whether First Derivative could sustain its claim against Janus Capital Management. Writing for the majority, Justice CLARENCE THOMAS focused on the dictionary definition of the word "make." According to the majority's definition of the terms, the only person who could make a statement was the one who uttered it and not just anyone who helped prepare the statement. Thomas noted, "Even when a speechwriter drafts a speech, the content is entirely within the control of the person who delivers it. And it is the speaker who takes credit—or blame— for what is ultimately said."

The Court was sharply divided along ideological lines, with four conservative justices joining Thomas and three liberal justices siding with Justice STEPHEN BREYER, who dissented. Breyer disagreed with the majority's limited definition of the word "make," noting that common usage and use of the word in previous cases supported a broader reading of the term. Breyer further argued that the majority left a gap in the law, stressing that in some instances nobody would make a statement under the Court's limited definition.

Commentators noted that the case represented a hit to the plaintiff's bar because it narrowed the range of defendants who might be liable false statements related to securities. This was thus called a huge victory for the $12 trillion mutual-fund industry. On the other hand, other commentators noted that because the Court was so sharply divided, the matter may not be closed for good.

SENTENCING

The postconviction stage of the criminal justice process, in which the defendant is brought before the court for the imposition of a penalty.

Abbott v. United States

As part of the GUN CONTROL Act of 1968, 18 U.S.C. 924(c) expressly proscribes, as a discrete offense, the use, carrying, or possession of a deadly weapon in connection with "any crime of violence or drug trafficking crime." Violation of this **statutory** provision carries a minimum prison term of five years, in addition to "any other term of imprisonment imposed on the [offender.]" § 924(c)(1)(D). In two separate cases consolidated under *Abbott v. United States,* No. 09-479, 131 S. Ct. 18, 562 U.S. ___ (2010), the U.S. SUPREME COURT interpreted this statutory provision in light of Congress' 1998 amendment imposing the five-year minimum prison sentence "[e]xcept to the extent that a greater minimum sentence is otherwise provided by [§ 924(c) itself] or by any other provision of law."

The Court held that a DEFENDANT is subject to a separate, mandatory, consecutive sentence for a § 924(c) conviction, not subsumed by, or served concurrently with, any other higher mandatory minimum sentence on a different count of conviction. The unanimous 8-0 decision (with Justice ELENA KAGAN taking no part in deliberations or decision) affirmed opinions of the lower courts as well as agreed with the government's proffered interpretation of the **statute**.

As background, following a jury trial in the U.S. **District Court** for the Eastern District of Pennsylvania, Kevin Abbott was convicted on several counts related to possessing a firearm in furtherance of drug-trafficking crime, including a count under § 924(c). Already having an extensive criminal history, Abbott, for his felon-in-possession conviction, was given a 15-year mandatory minimum sentence under the Armed Career Criminal Act, and the district court added an additional five years for the § 924(c) violation, yielding a total prison term of 20 years. (In the unrelated companion case, *Gould v. United States,* No. 09-7073, Carlos Rashad Gould was likewise convicted of a drug-trafficking crime carrying a mandatory minimum sentence of ten years, and the U.S. District Court for the Northern District of Texas likewise added five years for a § 924(c) violation.)

In separate appeals before different circuits, Abbott and Gould both advanced similar arguments that, under the statute's "except ..." clause, their § 924(c) sentence should run concurrently with their other sentences, because they had already received greater mandatory minimum sentences for their convictions on other counts. Specifically, since § 924(c)'s statutory language imposed a minimum term of five years as a consecutive sentence "[e]xcept to the extent that a greater minimum sentence is otherwise provided by

[§ 924(c) itself] or by any other provision of law," they qualified to have their [§ 924(c) mandatory minimum sentences merged (served concurrently) with any greater mandatory minimum sentence imposed for other counts, because the Armed Career Criminal Act qualified as "any other provision of law" that "provided" a "greater minimum sentence."

Their separate arguments were rejected by the Third and Fifth Circuit Courts of Appeals, respectively. The **appellate** courts agreed with the government's construction of the statute, reading it to require a sentence of at least five years tacked onto any other sentence received. The government had argued that the subject "except" clause (referring to "a greater minimum sentence ... otherwise provided") meant a greater minimum sentence provided elsewhere for a § 924(c)violation. In other words, the "except" clause applied only when another provision, whether contained within or outside of § 924(c), mandated a longer minimum sentence for violation of § 924(c). For example, within § 924(c) itself, a mandatory minimum sentence of five years for a § 924(c) violation is increased to seven years if a firearm is brandished and to ten years if the firearm is discharged. (§ 924(c)(1)(A)(i) (ii), and (iii). Therefore, argued the government, the 1998 amendments, adding the "except" clause, were intended to enhance sentences involving firearms, not to create opportunities for merging mandatory minimum sentences.

The APPELLATE courts concluded that the "otherwise provided" language in the "except" clause begged the question, "otherwise provided *for what?*" Asking themselves that question, the courts had responded, in their opinions, "for conduct offending § 924(c), i.e., possessing a firearm in connection with a crime of violence or drug trafficking crime." Therefore, the courts concluded in their analyses, a defendant was not spared from a separate, consecutive sentence for a § 924(c) violation simply because he faced a higher mandatory minimum sentence for a different count of conviction.

The Supreme Court agreed. Writing for the unanimous Court, Justice RUTH BADER GINSBURG noted,

> We hold, in accord with the courts below, and in line with the majority of the Courts of Appeals, that a defendant is subject to a mandatory, consecutive sentence for a § 924(c)

President Barack Obama signs the Fair Sentencing Act, Tuesday, Aug. 3, 2010, in the Oval Office of the White House in Washington. Joining him, from left are, Attorney General Eric Holder, Sen. Patrick Leahy, D-Vt., Rep. Bobby Scott, D-Va., Senate Majority Whip Richard Durbin, of Ill., Sen. Jeff Sessions, R-Ala., Sen. Orrin Hatch, R-Utah, and Rep. Sheila Jackson Lee, D-Texas.
AP IMAGES/PABLO MARTINEZ MONSIVAIS

conviction, and is not spared from that sentence by virtue of receiving a higher mandatory minimum on a different count of conviction. Under the "except" clause as we comprehend it, a § 924(c) offender is not subject to stacked sentences for violating § 924(c). If he possessed, brandished, and discharged a gun, the mandatory penalty would be 10 years, not 22. He is, however, subject to the highest mandatory minimum specified for his conduct in § 924(c), unless another provision of law directed to conduct proscribed by § 924(c) imposes an even greater mandatory minimum.

Congress Reduces Sentencing Disparity Between Crack and Powder Cocaine

Since Congress enacted in 1986 a crack cocaine criminal **statute** that sentenced dealers of crack cocaine to longer prison terms than powder cocaine dealers, critics have argued that the law was unfair, misguided, and racially discriminatory, for most crack cocaine dealers were African American, while most powder cocaine dealers were white. The U.S. Sentencing Guidelines Commission enforced the law's requirements but by the mid-1990s had appealed to Congress to modify the sentencing formula. The SUPREME COURT made the sentencing guidelines in 2005 and in 2007 issued a decision that upheld a district court's ruling that ignored the sentencing formula. Congress finally responded by enacting the Fair Sentencing Act of 2010 (Pub. L. 111-220), which reduced the sentencing disparity between the two forms of cocaine

from a 100-to-1 ratio to an 18-to-1 ratio and eliminated the five-year mandatory minimum sentence for simple possession of crack cocaine.

The 1986 crack cocaine criminal statute was enacted at a time when public opinion viewed this new drug as a problem of overwhelming dimensions. Congress justified tougher penalties on the general ground that physical and societal effects of crack were much worse than powder cocaine. The Sentencing Guidelines Commission applied the 100-to-1 ratio as embodied by statute. Congress had selected this ratio because it believed one gram of crack is equivalent to one hundred grams of powder cocaine. Congress justified tougher penalties on the general ground that physical and societal effects of crack were much worse than powder cocaine. Within 5 years the commission began to have second thoughts about this disparity. It was concerned because: (1) studies had shown no support for the conclusion that crack was more harmful than powder cocaine; (2) retail crack dealers got longer sentences than the wholesale distributors of powder cocaine; and, (3) the disparity fostered disrespect for and lack of confidence in the criminal justice system. Though the commission produced reports in 1997 and 2002 recommending that Congress lower the ratio, neither proposal was adopted.

When Congress created the Sentencing Guidelines Commission in 1984 it sought to reduce the discretion of federal judges when sentencing defendants. The commission was charged with developing point schemes based on the crime committed and the criminal history of the defendants. Judges were directed to impose mandatory minimum sentences. Judges could impose harsher sentences with little trouble but "downward departures" were discouraged. In its landmark 2005 decision, *United States v. Booker* , 543 U.S. 220, 125 S.Ct. 738, 160 L.Ed.2d 621 (2005), the Supreme Court ruled that the sentencing guidelines were unconstitutional and instructed district courts to read the sentencing guidelines as "effectively advisory." The guidelines now served as one factor among several that courts must consider in determining an appropriate sentence. The *Booker* decision also instructed the courts that "reasonableness" is the standard controlling **appellate** review of **district court** sentences. Seen in this light, a judge may consider the disparity between crack and powder cocaine sentencing formulas.

The Court addressed the crack cocaine sentencing guidelines in *Kimbrough v. United States*, 552 U.S. 85, 128 S.Ct. 558, 169 L.Ed.2d 481 (2007). The Court concluded that a district court had the freedom to deviate from the 100-to-1 ratio when the disparity between crack cocaine and powder cocaine yielded a sentence greater than necessary. As long as the sentence met the reasonableness standard, a court could ignore the 100-to-1 ratio. In 2007 the commission again asked Congress to lower the ratio but this time made an ameliorating change by reducing the base offense level for crack and powder cocaine offenses by two levels. This amendment produced sentences for crack cocaine between two and five times longer than sentences for equal amounts of powder cocaine.

Congress took up the issue in 2009 and passed the Fair Sentencing Act of 2010 in August, 2010. The law increased the amount of crack cocaine that would result in a mandatory minimum prison term for trafficking (from 5 grams to 28 grams for a five-year minimum and from 50 grams to 280 grams for a ten-year minimum sentence) and increased the fines for drug trafficking and for importing and exporting controlled substances. The law eliminated a mandatory minimum of five years imprisonment for first-time possession of crack cocaine. The act directed the Sentencing Guidelines Commission to amend its guidelines to increase

sentences for those convicted of committing violent acts in the course of drug trafficking, incorporate aggravating and mitigating factors in drug trafficking offenses guidelines, issue the changes within 90 days of the law's enactment, and report to Congress on the impact of the changes in these sentencing changes. The law reduced **statutory** penalties.

The commission enacted changes in a temporary, emergency amendment that became effective November 1, 2010. It estimated that the new average sentence for trafficking in crack cocaine would be 101 months, a 13.7 percent decrease (27 months) in average sentence length. More than 1,500 prison beds would be saved after five years and more than 3,800 beds would be saved after ten years. The new law would impact 3,000 crack offenders each year and it would save $42 million in the first five years. However, the reforms in mandatory minimum sentences were not applied retroactively to those already serving time in federal prison.

McNeill v. United States

Under federal law, a defendant who unlawfully possesses a firearm must receive a 15-year sentence if the defendant also has three prior serious drug offenses. The law defines a serious drug offense as one carrying a maximum of 10 years imprisonment or more. The serious drug offenses are based on state laws. In some instances, defendants have been convicted of drug offenses that carried a maximum of at least 10 years' imprisonment, but states have subsequently reduced the maximum penalty after the defendants' convictions. The lower federal courts have been split about whether an offense qualifies as a serious drug offense if the maximum sentence is reduced after the defendant's conviction. In *McNeill v. United States*, No. 10-5258, 2011 WL 2175212 (U.S. 2011), the Supreme Court unanimously ruled that courts should consider the sentence at the time of the original conviction.

In February 2007, Clifton Terelle McNeill ran through a red light. Police tried to stop him in a routine traffic stop, but McNeill made police chase him for several miles. He then fled from police after exiting his car. One of the pursuing officers finally caught up to McNeill and tackled him. The officer found a .38-caliber revolver lying on the ground underneath

(9) INHERENT AUTHORITY- Nothing in this Act shall limit the inherent authority of a court to protect witnesses or clear the courtroom to preserve the decorum and integrity of the legal process or protect the safety of an individual.

First Amendment

STOLEN VALOR ACT OF 2005

An Act

To amend title 18, United States Code, to enhance protections relating to the reputation and meaning of the Medal of Honor and other military decorations and awards, and for other purposes.

Be it enacted by the Senate and House of Representatives of the United States of America in Congress assembled,

SECTION 1. SHORT TITLE.

This Act may be cited as the 'Stolen Valor Act of 2005'.

SEC. 2. FINDINGS.

Congress makes the following findings:

(1) Fraudulent claims surrounding the receipt of the Medal of Honor, the distinguished-service cross, the Navy cross, the Air Force cross, the Purple Heart, and other decorations and medals awarded by the President or the Armed Forces of the United States damage the reputation and meaning of such decorations and medals.

(2) Federal law enforcement officers have limited ability to prosecute fraudulent claims of receipt of military decorations and medals.

(3) Legislative action is necessary to permit law enforcement officers to protect the reputation and meaning of military decorations and medals.

SEC. 3. ENHANCED PROTECTION OF MEANING OF MILITARY DECORATIONS AND MEDALS.

(a) Expansion of General Criminal Offense- Subsection (a) of section 704 of title 18, United States Code, is amended by striking 'manufactures, or sells' and inserting 'purchases, attempts to purchase, solicits for purchase, mails, ships, imports, exports, produces blank certificates of receipt for, manufactures, sells, attempts to sell, advertises for sale, trades, barters, or exchanges for anything of value'.

(b) Establishment of Criminal Offense Relating to False Claims About Receipt of Decorations and Medals- Such section 704 is further amended–

(1) by redesignating subsection (b) as subsection (c);

(2) by inserting after subsection (a) the following:

(b) False Claims About Receipt of Military Decorations or Medals- Whoever falsely represents himself or herself, verbally or in writing, to have been awarded any decoration or medal authorized by Congress for the Armed Forces of the United States, any of the service medals or badges awarded to the members of such forces, the ribbon, button, or rosette of any such badge, decoration, or medal, or any colorable imitation of such item shall be fined under this title, imprisoned not more than six months, or both; and

(3) in paragraph (1) of subsection (c), as redesignated by paragraph (1) of this subsection, by inserting 'or (b)' after 'subsection (a)'.

(c) Enhanced Penalty for Offenses Involving Certain Other Medals- Such section 704 is further amended by adding at the end the following:

(d) Enhanced Penalty for Offenses Involving Certain Other Medals- If a decoration or medal involved in an offense described in subsection (a) or (b) is a distinguished-service cross awarded under section 3742 of title 10, a Navy cross awarded under section 6242 of title 10, an Air Force cross awarded under section 8742 of section 10, a silver star awarded under section 3746, 6244, or 8746 of title 10, a Purple Heart awarded under section 1129 of title 10, or any replacement or duplicate medal for such medal as authorized by law, in lieu of the punishment provided in the applicable subsection, the offender shall be fined under this title, imprisoned not more than 1 year, or both.

Sentencing

FAIR SENTENCING ACT OF 2010

SECTION 1. SHORT TITLE.

This Act may be cited as the 'Fair Sentencing Act of 2010'.

SEC. 2. COCAINE SENTENCING DISPARITY REDUCTION.

(a) CSA- Section 401(b)(1) of the Controlled Substances Act (21 U.S.C. 841(b)(1)) is amended–

(1) in subparagraph (A)(iii), by striking '50 grams' and inserting '280 grams'; and

(2) in subparagraph (B)(iii), by striking '5 grams' and inserting '28 grams'.

(b) Import and Export Act- Section 1010(b) of the Controlled Substances Import and Export Act (21 U.S.C. 960(b)) is amended–

(1) in paragraph (1)(C), by striking '50 grams' and inserting '280 grams'; and

(2) in paragraph (2)(C), by striking '5 grams' and inserting '28 grams'.

SEC. 3. ELIMINATION OF MANDATORY MINIMUM SENTENCE FOR SIMPLE POSSESSION.

Section 404(a) of the Controlled Substances Act (21 U.S.C. 844(a)) is amended by striking the sentence beginning 'Notwithstanding the preceding sentence,'.

SEC. 4. INCREASED PENALTIES FOR MAJOR DRUG TRAFFICKERS.

(a) Increased Penalties for Manufacture, Distribution, Dispensation, or Possession With Intent To Manufacture, Distribute, or Dispense- Section 401(b)(1) of the Controlled Substances Act (21 U.S.C. 841(b)) is amended–

(1) in subparagraph (A), by striking '$4,000,000', '$10,000,000', '$8,000,000', and '$20,000,000' and inserting '$10,000,000', '$50,000,000', '$20,000,000', and '$75,000,000', respectively; and

(2) in subparagraph (B), by striking '$2,000,000', '$5,000,000', '$4,000,000', and '$10,000,000' and inserting '$5,000,000', '$25,000,000', '$8,000,000', and '$50,000,000', respectively.

(b) Increased Penalties for Importation and Exportation- Section 1010(b) of the Controlled Substances Import and Export Act (21 U.S.C. 960(b)) is amended–

(1) in paragraph (1), by striking '$4,000,000', '$10,000,000', '$8,000,000', and '$20,000,000' and inserting '$10,000,000', '$50,000,000', '$20,000,000', and '$75,000,000', respectively; and

(2) in paragraph (2), by striking '$2,000,000', '$5,000,000', '$4,000,000', and '$10,000,000' and inserting '$5,000,000',

'$25,000,000', '$8,000,000', and '$50,000,000', respectively.

SEC. 5. ENHANCEMENTS FOR ACTS OF VIOLENCE DURING THE COURSE OF A DRUG TRAFFICKING OFFENSE.

Pursuant to its authority under section 994 of title 28, United States Code, the United States Sentencing Commission shall review and amend the Federal sentencing guidelines to ensure that the guidelines provide an additional penalty increase of at least 2 offense levels if the defendant used violence, made a credible threat to use violence, or directed the use of violence during a drug trafficking offense.

SEC. 6. INCREASED EMPHASIS ON DEFENDANT'S ROLE AND CERTAIN AGGRAVATING FACTORS.

Pursuant to its authority under section 994 of title 28, United States Code, the United States Sentencing Commission shall review and amend the Federal sentencing guidelines to ensure an additional increase of at least 2 offense levels if–

(1) the defendant bribed, or attempted to bribe, a Federal, State, or local law enforcement official in connection with a drug trafficking offense;

(2) the defendant maintained an establishment for the manufacture or distribution of a controlled substance, as generally described in section 416 of the Controlled Substances Act (21 U.S.C. 856); or

(3)(A) the defendant is an organizer, leader, manager, or supervisor of drug trafficking activity subject to an aggravating role enhancement under the guidelines; and

(B) the offense involved 1 or more of the following super-aggravating factors:

(i) The defendant–

(I) used another person to purchase, sell, transport, or store controlled substances;

(II) used impulse, fear, friendship, affection, or some combination thereof to involve such person in the offense; and

(III) such person had a minimum knowledge of the illegal enterprise and was to receive little or no compensation from the illegal transaction.

(ii) The defendant–

(I) knowingly distributed a controlled substance to a person under the age of 18 years, a person over the age of 64 years, or a pregnant individual;

(II) knowingly involved a person under the age of 18 years, a person over the age of 64 years, or a pregnant individual in drug trafficking;

(III) knowingly distributed a controlled substance to an individual who was unusually vulnerable due to physical or mental condition, or who was particularly susceptible to criminal conduct; or

(IV) knowingly involved an individual who was unusually vulnerable due to physical or mental condition, or who was particularly susceptible to criminal conduct, in the offense.

(iii) The defendant was involved in the importation into the United States of a controlled substance.

(iv) The defendant engaged in witness intimidation, tampered with or destroyed evidence, or otherwise obstructed justice in connection with the investigation or prosecution of the offense.

(v) The defendant committed the drug trafficking offense as part of a pattern of criminal conduct engaged in as a livelihood.

SEC. 7. INCREASED EMPHASIS ON DEFENDANT'S ROLE AND CERTAIN MITI-GATING FACTORS.

Pursuant to its authority under section 994 of title 28, United States Code, the United States Sentencing Commission shall review and amend the Federal sentencing guidelines and policy statements to ensure that—

(1) if the defendant is subject to a minimal role adjustment under the guidelines, the base offense level for the defendant based solely on drug quantity shall not exceed level 32; and

(2) there is an additional reduction of 2 offense levels if the defendant—

(A) otherwise qualifies for a minimal role adjustment under the guidelines and had a minimum knowledge of the illegal enterprise;

(B) was to receive no monetary compensation from the illegal transaction; and

(C) was motivated by an intimate or familial relationship or by threats or fear when the defendant was otherwise unlikely to commit such an offense.

SEC. 8. EMERGENCY AUTHORITY FOR UNITED STATES SENTENCING COMMISSION.

The United States Sentencing Commission shall—

(1) promulgate the guidelines, policy statements, or amendments provided for in this Act as soon as practicable, and in any event not later than 90 days after the date of enactment of this Act, in accordance with the procedure set forth in section 21(a) of the Sentencing Act of 1987 (28 U.S.C. 994 note), as though the authority under that Act had not expired; and

(2) pursuant to the emergency authority provided under paragraph (1), make such conforming amendments to the Federal sentencing guidelines as the Commission determines necessary to achieve consistency with other guideline provisions and applicable law.

SEC. 9. REPORT ON EFFECTIVENESS OF DRUG COURTS.

(a) In General- Not later than 1 year after the date of enactment of this Act, the Comptroller General of the United States shall submit to Congress a report analyzing the effectiveness of drug court programs receiving funds under the drug court grant program under part EE of title I of the Omnibus Crime Control and Safe Streets Act of 1968 (42 U.S.C. 3797-u et seq.).

(b) Contents- The report submitted under subsection (a) shall—

(1) assess the efforts of the Department of Justice to collect data on the performance of federally funded drug courts;

(2) address the effect of drug courts on recidivism and substance abuse rates;

(3) address any cost benefits resulting from the use of drug courts as alternatives to incarceration;

(4) assess the response of the Department of Justice to previous recommendations made by the Comptroller General regarding drug court programs; and

(5) make recommendations concerning the performance, impact, and cost-effectiveness of federally funded drug court programs.

SEC. 10. UNITED STATES SENTENCING COMMISSION REPORT ON IMPACT OF CHANGES TO FEDERAL COCAINE SENTENCING LAW.

Not later than 5 years after the date of enactment of this Act, the United States Sentencing Commission, pursuant to the authority under sections 994 and 995 of title 28, United States Code, and the responsibility of the United States Sentencing Commission to advise Congress on sentencing policy under section 995(a)(20) of title 28, United States Code, shall study and submit to Congress a report regarding the impact of the changes in Federal sentencing law under this Act and the amendments made by this Act.

ADOPTION

FLORIDA COURT OF APPEALS STRIKES DOWN BAN ON GAY ADOPTION

Alsenas, Linda. *Gay America: Struggle for Equality.* Amulet Press, 2008.

Pinello, Daniel. *Gay Rights and American Law.* Cambridge University Press, 2003.

CALIFORNIA SUPREME COURT UPHOLDS BAN ON AFFIRMATIVE ACTION

Covington, Robert and Decker, Kurt. *Employment Law in a Nutshell.* Saint Paul, MN: West Group. 2002. Second Edition.

Lewis, Jr., Harold and Norman, Elizabeth. *Civil Rights Law and Practice.* Saint Paul, MN: West Group. 2004.

Vieira, Norman. *Constitutional Civil Rights in a Nutshell.* Saint Paul, MN.: West Group. 1998.

ARBITRATION

SUPREME COURT STRIKES DOWN STATE CLASS ACTION ARBITRATION RULE

Barett, Jerome. *A History of Alternative Dispute Resolution: The Story of a Political, Social, and Cultural Movement.* Hoboken, N.J.: Jossey-Bass. 2004.

Nolan-Haley, Jaqueline. *Alternative Dispute Resolution In A Nutshell.* Saint Paul, MN: Westgroup. Second Edition. 2001.

Ware, Stephen. *Alternative Dispute Resolution.* Saint Paul, MN: Westgroup. 2001.

STATE TORT LAWS NOT PREEMPTED BY FEDERAL SEATBELT LAW

Epstein, Richard. *Federal Preemption.* AEI Press, 2007.

O'Reilly, James. *Federal Preemption of State and Local Law.* American Bar Association, 2006.

Zimmerman, Joseph. *Congressional Preemption.* State University of New York Press, 2006.

BANKRUPTCY

RANSOM V. FIA CARD SERVICES

Ransom v. FIA Card Services, No. 09-907, Available at www.supremecourt.gov/opinions/09-907.htm

"Ransom v. FIA Card Services." Accessed 4 April 2011 at http://www.oyez.org/cases/2010-2019/2010_09_907

STERN V. MARSHALL

Stern v. Marshall, No. 10-179, Available at www.supremecourt.gov/opinions/10pdf/10-179.pdf

Wade, Michael. "Anna Nicole Smith and the Art of 'Forum-Shopping'." *Washington Examiner,* 7 January 2011.

Wisconsin Law Journal. "10-179 Stern v. Marshall." Accessed on 24 June 2011 at http://wislawjournal.com/2011/06/23/10-179-stern-v-marshall/

BANKS AND BANKING

CONGRESS PASSES MASSIVE FINANCIAL REFORM LEGISLATION

Attkisson, Sharyl. "Financial Reform Law: What's In, and What's Out." CBS News. July 21, 2010.

Lamoreaux, Matthew G. "Financial Regulatory Reform: What You Need to Know." *Journal of Accountancy.* Sept. 2010.

Wiseman, Paul. "Financial Reform Bill Passes Senate, Heads to White House." *USA Today.* July 16, 2010.

CAPITAL PUNISHMENT

WASHINGTON SUPREME COURT UPHOLDS INDEFINITE SOLITARY CONFINEMENT FOR DEATH ROW INMATE

In re Pers. Restraint Petition of Gentry, No. 84039-3. Accessed 4 June 2011 at http://courts.wa.gov/opinions/pdf/840393.no1

Putney, John Paul. "Washington Supreme Court Upholds Indefinite Solitary Confinement for Death Row Prisoners." *Jurist PaperChase,* January 2011. Available at http://jurist.org/paperchase/2011/01/washington-supreme-court-upholds-indefinite-solitary...

Sullivan, Jennifer. "Court Upholds Solitude for State's Death-row Inmates." *The Seattle Times,* 30 December 2010.

CIVIL RIGHTS

PROSECUTOR NOT LIABLE FOR WITHHOLDING EVIDENCE FROM DEFENDANT

Lewis, Jr., Harold and Norman, Elizabeth. *Civil Rights Law and Practice.* Saint Paul, MN: West Gropu. 2004.

Vieira, Norman. *Constitutional Civil Rights in a Nutshell.* Saint Paul, MN.: West Group. 1998.

SUPREME COURT LIMITS APPEALS OF DENIALS OF OFFICIAL IMMUNITY

Covington, Robert and Decker, Kurt. *Employment Law in a Nutshell.* Saint Paul, MN: West Group. 2002. Second Edition.

Lewis, Jr., Harold and Norman, Elizabeth. *Civil Rights Law and Practice.* Saint Paul, MN: West Group. 2004.

Vieira, Norman. *Constitutional Civil Rights in a Nutshell.* Saint Paul, MN.: West Group. 1998.

CLASS ACTION

SETTLEMENT IN USDA v. NATIVE AMERICAN FARMERS CASE

Chappell, Bill. "U.S. Reaches $680M Deal With Native American Farmers." NPR News, 19 October 2010. Available at http://www.npr.org

Hagstrom, Jerry. "Settlement Reached in Native American Farmer Case." *AG Week,* 26 October 2010. Available at http://www.agweek.com/event/article/id/17370

Horowitz, Carl. "USDA Capitulates to Native American Farmers; Settles for $760 Million." National Legal and Policy Center publication, 2 November 2010. Available at http://nlpc.org/stories/2010/11/02/usda-capitulates-native-american-farmers-settles-760-million

SMITH v. BAYER CORPORATION

Greer, Marcy Hogan. *A Practitioner's Guide to Class Action.* Chicago: American Bar Association, 2010.

Klonoff, Robert H. *Class Action and Other Multi-Party Litigation in a Nutshell,* 3d Ed. St. Paul, Minn.: Thomson/West, 2007.

WAL-MART STORES v. DUKES

Elwood, John. "Too Many Claims." *The New York Times,* 21 June 2011

Wal-Mart Stores, Inc.v. Dukes, No. 10-277, Available at www.supremecourt.gov/opinions/10pdf/10-277.pdf

"Wal-Mart v. Dukes." *Corporate Law Report,* 21 June 2011, Available at http://corporatelaw.jdsupra.com

CONSUMER PROTECTION

CHASE BANK USA v. McCOY

Chase Bank USA v. McCoy. No. 09-329, Available at www.supremecourt.gov/opinions/10pdf/09-329.pdf

Conery, Ben. "Supreme Court Rules on Credit Card Rate Hikes, Retaliation Litigation." *Washington Times,* 24 January 2011. AAvailable at http://www.employerlawreport.com/2011/01/articles/workforce-strategies

The Oyez Project. "Chase Bank USA v. McCoy." Accessed 4 April 2011 at http://www.oyez.org/cases/2010-2019/2010_09_329

CONTRACT

LOCAL GOVERNMENT CANNOT SUE DRUG MANUFACTURERS FOR OVERCHARGING

Rohwer, Claude, and Skrocki, Anthony *Contracts in a Nutshell, 7th Ed.,* West: 2010.

GENERAL DYNAMICS CORP. v. UNITED STATES

Holland, Jesse J. "Court Won't Help Either Side Fight Over Plane." *Business Week.* May 23, 2011.

Kendall, Brent. "US High Court Rules for Boeing, General Dynamics in Fighter Jet Case." *Wall Street Journal.* May 23, 2011.

COURTS

FEDERAL JUDICIARY APPROVE CAMERAS IN THE COURTROOM PILOT PROGRAM

Biskupic, Joan. "Judicial Panel Weighs Courtroom Cameras." *USA Today,* September 15, 2010.

Barnes, Robert. "Supreme Court Bars Broadcast of Prop 8 Trial in California. *Washington Post,* January 14, 2010.

TELEVISED TRIALS GAIN IN POPULARITY AND VIEWING

Brown, Donal. "Supreme Court Scuttles Plan for Televising Prop 8 Trial." 14 January 2010. Accessed 30 June 2011 at http://www.firstamendmentcoalition.org/tag/televising-trials/

"Court TV for James Arthur Ray Sweat Lodge Trial." *Phoenix New Times,* 8 March 2011.

Fine, David R. "Televising Trials." *The National Law Journal,* 25 June 2010.

"Judge to Hear Debate Over Televising Trial of Dr. Conrad Murray." Associated Press Release, 7 February 2011. Available at http://www.lawmedconsultant.com

Stelter, Brian. "Casey Anthony Coverage Gives HLN an Identity." *The New York TImes,* 12 June 2011.

Tilley, M. Kelly. "Canceled: The End of Televised Federal Trials." 11 June 2011. Accessed 30 June 2011 at http://www.osbar.org/publications/bulletin/11june/cancelled

CRIMINAL LAW

FEDERAL HABEAS REVIEW LIMITED TO STATE COURT RECORD

Palmer, John. 2006. *Constitutional Rights of Prisoners.* 8th ed. New York: Anderson Pub. Co.

Tomkovicz, James J. 2002. *The Right to the Assistance of Counsel: A Reference Guide to the United States Constitution.* Westport, Conn.: Greenwood.

DEPARTMENT OF THE TREASURY

CONGRESS CREATES THE FINANCIAL STABILITY OVERSIGHT COUNCIL

Holzer, Jessica and Jamila Trindle. "Financial Oversight Council Comes Under Fire." *Wall Street Journal.* April 14, 2011.

Kashkari, Neel. "The Financial Stability Oversight Council: A Deficit Killer?" *Washington Post.* April 7, 2011

DNA EVIDENCE

SKINNER V. SWITZER

Turner, Allan. "Justice Clear Way for Killer's DNA Request." *Houston Chronicle.* March 7, 2011.

Weiss, Debra Cassens. "Supreme Court Allows State Prisoners to Seek DNA Evidence Through US Civil Rights Law." *ABA Journal.* March 7, 2011.

DRUGS AND NARCOTICS

DEPIERRE V. UNITED STATES

Beaver, Alyssa L. "Getting a Fix on Cocaine Sentencing Policy: Reforming the Sentencing Scheme of the Anti-Drug Abuse Act of 1986." *Fordham Law Review.* April 2010.

King, Andrew. "The Meaning of the Term 'Cocaine Base' in 21 U.S.C. § 841(b)(1): A Circuit Split Over Statutory Interpretation." *Duquesne Law Review.* Winter 2010.

MICHIGAN LAW DOES NOT PREVENT EMPLOYMENT DISCHARGE OF MEDICAL MARIJUANA USER

Agar, John. "Judge Upholds Walmart's Firing of Michigan Medical Marijuana User." *The Grand Rapids Press,* 11 February 2011.

Casias v. Wal-Mart, No. 1:10-CV-781. Accessed 4 June 2011 at http://www.justia.org/opinions

Dubault, Robert A."Michigan Medical marijuana Act Does Not Override Employment Policies." Publications, Warner, Norcross, & Judd, 14 February 2011. Accessed on 10 June 2011 at http://www.wnj.com/michigan-medical-marijuana-act-does-not-prohibit-termination-for-p...

Jackson Lewis, LLP. "Federal Court in Michigan Dismisses Medical Marijuana User's Claims Arising from Positive Drug Test." 16 February 2011. Available at http://www.jacksonlewis.com/resources.php?NewsID=3539.

DUE PROCESS

LOS ANGELES COUNTY V. HUMPHRIES

Los Angeles County, California v. Humphries, No. 09-350, Available at www.supremecourt.gov/opinions/09-350.htm

Los Angeles County, California v. Humphries, No. 09-350, Available at www.supremecourt.gov/opinions/10pdf/09-350.pdf

"Los Angeles County, CA v. Humphries." Accessed 4 April 2011 at http://www.oyez.org/cases/2010-2019/2010_09_350

EDUCATION LAW

THE HEALTHY, HUNGER-FREE KIDS ACT OF 2010

Jalonich, Mary Clare. "Congress Sends Child Nutrition Bill to Obama." 2 December 2010. Accessed 20 April 2011 at http://www.msnbc.com/id/40479069

Starr, Penny. "Michele Obama on Deciding What Kids Eat: 'We Can't Just Leave it Up to the Parents.'" 13 December 2010. Accessed on 20 April 2011 at http://www.cns.news.com/news/articles

U.S. Department of Agriculture. "USDA Upgrades Nutritional Standards for School Meals." Press, Release, 14 January 2011. Available at http://www.iscnewsroom.com/2011/01/14/usda-upgrades-nutritional-standards-for-school-meals

White House Press Office. "Child Nutrition Reauthorization: Healthy, Hunger-Free Kids Act of 2010." Press Release, 10 December 2010. Available at http://www.whitehouse.gov/sites/files/

Dias, Elizabeth. "For-Profit Colleges: Educators or Predators?" *Time.* June 29, 2010.

Government Accountability Office. *For-Profit Colleges: Undercover Testing Finds Colleges Encouraged Fraud and Engaged in Deceptive Marketing Practices.* Aug. 4, 2010.

Lauerman, John. "For-Profit Colleges Lose Effort to Block Proposed Regulations." *Bloomberg.* April 12, 2011.

LOS ANGELES SCHOOL DISTRICT SETTLEMENT LIMITS TEACHER SENIORITY PROTECTION

Hoag, Christina. "California Court Approves Settlement Limiting Seniority-based Layoffs in Los Angeles Schools." *Washington Post,* 21 January 2011.

Felch, Jason and Jason Song. "Judge OKs Settlement That Limits Use of Seniority in L.A. Teacher Layoffs." *Los Angeles Times,* 21 January 2011.

National Access Network. "Access Quality Education: California Ltigation." Accessed on 20 April 2011 at http://www.schoolfunding.info/states/ca/lit_ca.php3

Song, Jason, et al. "Settlement Limits L.A. Teacher's Seniority Protection." *Los Angeles Times,* 6 October 2010.

CALIFORNIA SUPREME COURT RULES ON EDUCATIONAL AID FOR UNLAWFUL ALIENS

Phelan, Margaret and Gillespie, James. *Immigration Law Handbook.* Oxford University Press, 2007.

Scaros, Constantinos. *Learning About Immigration Law.* Thomson Delmaer Learning, 2006.

Weissbrodt, David and Danielson, Laura. *Immigration Law and Procedure in a Nutshell, 5th Edition.* West Group, 2005.

ELECTION LAW

ARIZONA FREE ENTERPRISE CLUB'S FREEDOM CLUB PAC V. BENNETT

"Another Political Speech Victory." *Wall St. Journal.* June 28, 2011.

Dionne, E.J., Jr. "The Supreme Court's Continuing Defense of the Powerful." *Washington Post.* June 29, 2011.

ALASKA SUPREME COURT DISMISSES CHALLENGE TO ELECTION RESULTS

Miller v. Treadwell, et al, Accessed 4 June 2011 at http://www.courts.alaska.gov/ops/sp-6532.pdf

"Miller Won't Block Murkowski." Associated Press Release, 27 December 2010. Available at http://politico.com/news/stories/1210/456821

Posner, Sarah. "Alaska Supreme Court Dismisses Challenge to Midterm Election Results." *Jurist PaperChase,* 24 December 2010. Available at http://jurist.org/paperchase/2010/12/alaka-supreme-court-dismisses-challenge- ...

EMAIL

EMAILS PROTECTED BY THE FOURTH AMENDMENT

McCullagh, Declan. "Justice Department Opposes Digital Privacy Reforms." CNET.com. April 6, 2011.

"Sixth Circuit Rules That Email Protected from Warrantless Searches." *Wall St. Journal.* Dec. 15, 2010.

EMPLOYMENT DISCRIMINATION

SUPREME COURT INTERPRETS EMPLOYMENT DISCRIMINATION STATUTE

Covington, Robert and Decker, Kurt. *Employment Law in a Nutshell.* Saint Paul, MN: West Group. 2002. Second Edition.

Lewis, Jr., Harold and Norman, Elizabeth. *Civil Rights Law and Practice.* Saint Paul, MN: West Group. 2004.

Vieira, Norman. *Constitutional Civil Rights in a Nutshell.* Saint Paul, MN.: West Group. 1998.

THOMPSON V. NORTH AMERICAN STAINLESS

LaPlante, Jamie. "Supreme Court Holds Third Party Retaliation is an Actionable Claim- Reversing Sixth Circuit." *Employer Law Report,* 25 January 2011. Available at http://www.employerlawreport.com/2011/01/articles/workforce-strategies

ENVIRONMENTAL LAW

AMERICAN ELECTRIC POWER CO. V. CONNECTICUT

Ferrey, Steven. *Environmental Law: Examples and Explanations,* 5th Ed. New York: Aspen Publishers, 2010.

Salzman, James and Barton H. Thompson Jr. *Environmental Law and Policy,* 3d Ed. New York: Foundation Press, 2010.

GULF OIL SPILL COSTS BILLIONS

Feeley, Jef and Margaret Cronin Fisk. "BP Gulf-Spill Lawsuits Consolidated in New Orleans." Bloomberg. Aug. 10, 2010.

Robertson, Campbell and John Schwartz. "Many Hit by Spill Now Feel Caught in Claim Process." *New York Times.* April 18, 2011.

Schwartz, John. "Man with $20 Billion to Disburse Finds No Shortage of Claims or Critics." *New York Times.* April 18, 2011.

CALIFORNIA VOTERS DEFEAT PROPOSITION 23

Liggett, Brit. "California Climate Law Survives, Proposition 23 Defeated." *Inhabitat,* 4 November 2010.

Roosevelt, Margot. "Proposition 23: Backers Were Outspent, Out-organized." *Los Angeles Times,* 2 November 2010.

Voegele, Eric. "California Voters Defeat Proposition 23." *BioMass,* 4 November 2010.

ERISA

CIGNA CORP. V. AMARA

Wiedenbeck, Peter J. *ERISA: Principles of Employee Benefit Law.* New York: Oxford University Press, 2010.

Zanglein, Jayne E. and Susan J. Stabile. *ERISA Litigation.* Arlington, VA: BNA Books, 2008.

ESTABLISHMENT CLAUSE

LATIN CROSS ON FEDERAL LAND VIOLATION OF ESTABLISHMENT CLAUSE

Barron, Jerome, Dienes, Thomas. *First Amendment Law in a Nutshell, 3rd ed.* West Group, 2004.

Farber, Daniel. *The First Amendment: Concepts and Insights.* Foundation Press, 2002.

ETHICS

CONVICTION AND CENSURE OF REPRESENTATIVE CHARLES RANGEL

"Charlie Rangel Convicted of Ethics Violations." Reuters Press Release, 16 November 2010. Available at http://www.reuters.com

"Charlie Rangel Found Guilty of Ethics Violations, Says He Was 'Deprived of Due Process.'" *New York Post,* 16 November 2010.

Crabtree, Susan and Jordan Fabian. "House Ethics Panel Convicts Rep. Rangel on 11 of 13 Counts of Rule Violations." *The Hill,* 16 November 2010.

Miller, Emily. "Charles Rangel Sentenced to Censure By the House." *Human Events,* 18 November 2010. Accessed on 20 April 2011 at http://www.humanevents.com.article.php?=40082

"Rangel Sentencing Set for Thursday." *The Washington Times,* 17 November 2010.

FEDERAL COMMUNICATIONS COMMISSION DNA EVIDENCE

SECOND CIRCUIT RULES FCC INDECENCY POLICY UNCONSTITUTIONAL

Carter, T. Barton. *Mass Communications Law in a Nutshell. 6th ed.* West Group, 2006.

Tomlinson, Richard. *Tele-Revolution.* Penobscot Press, 2000.

Zarkin, Kimberly and Zarkin, Michael. *The Federal Communications Commission.* Greenwood Press, 2006.

FEDERAL PREEMPTION

PLIVA V. MENSING

Klukowski, Kenneth "Supreme Court's Pliva Decision Is Another Blow Against Trial Attorneys." *The Washington Examiner,* 26 June 2011.

Pliva v. Mensing. No. 09-993. Available at www.supremecourt.gov/opinions/10pdf/09-993.pdf

The Oyez Project. "Pliva v. Mensing." Accessed 27 June 2011 at http://www.oyez.org/cases/2010-2019/2010_09-993

Walker, Emily P. "Medical News: Supreme Court Rules for Generic Drugmakers on Labeling Issue." 24 June 2011. Accessed on 28 June 2011 at http://www.medpagetoday.com/Washington-WATCH/27256

FIRST AMENDMENT

NINTH CIRCUIT STRIKES DOWN STOLEN VALOR ACT

Barron, Jerome, Dienes, Thomas. *First Amendment Law in a Nutshell, 3rd ed.* West Group, 2004.

Farber, Daniel. *The First Amendment: Concepts and Insights.* Foundation Press, 2002.

FEDERAL COURT PUTS OKLAHOMA BAN ON SHARIA LAW ON HOLD

Barron, Jerome, Dienes, Thomas. *First Amendment Law in a Nutshell, 3rd ed.* West Group, 2004.

Farber, Daniel. *The First Amendment: Concepts and Insights.* Foundation Press, 2002.

SUPREME COURT RULES THAT VIDEO GAME LAW VIOLATES FIRST AMENDMENT

Barron, Jerome, Dienes, Thomas. *First Amendment Law in a Nutshell, 3rd ed.* West Group, 2004.

Farber, Daniel. *The First Amendment: Concepts and Insights.* Foundation Press, 2002.

BOROUGH OF DURYEA, PENNSYLVANIA V. GUARNIERI

Borough of Duryea v. Guarnieri, No. 09-1476, Available at www.supremecourt.gov/opinions/10pdf/09-1476.pdf

Illinois Municipal League. "Public Employment-First Amendment: Borough of Duryea v. Guarnieri." 20 June 2011. Available at http://www.iml.prg/page.cfm?key=6354

"Supreme Court Rulees for Clinic in Borough of Duryea v. Guarnieri." University of Virginia School of Law Press Release, 20 June 2011. Accessed on 24 June at http://www.law.virginia.edu/html/news/2011_sum/cllinic_duryea.html

NEVADA COMMISSION ON ETHICS V. CARRIGAN

Illinois Municipal League. "Nevada Commission on Ethics v. Carrigan, No-10-568 (U.S. June 13, 2011)." Accessed on 24 June 2011 at http://www.iml/org/page.cfm?key=6356

Nevada Commission on Ethics v. Carrigan, No. 10-568, Available at www.supremecourt.gov/opinions/10pdf/10-568.pdf

"Nevada Commission on Ethics v. Carrigan." *New Jersey Law Journal,* 15 June 2011.

The Oyez Project. "Nevada Commission on Ethics v. Carrigan." Accessed 24 June 2011 at http://www.oyez.org/cases/2010-2019/2010_10_568

SNYDER V. PHELPS

Frank, Steve. "Westboro and the Trouble with Certainty." *Philadelphia Inquirer.* March 10, 2011.

Gregory, Sean. "Why the Supreme Court Ruled for Westboro." *Time.* March 3, 2011.

Liptak, Adam. "Justice Rule for Protesters at Military Funerals." *New York Times.* March 2, 2011.

SORRELL V. IMS HEALTH

Electronic Privacy Information Center. "IMS Health v. Sorrell." Accessed 24 June at http://epic.org/privacy/ims_sorrell/

Sorrell v. IMS Health Inc. No. 10-779. Available at www.supremecourt.gov/opinions/10pdf/10-779.pdf

The Oyez Project. "Sorrell v. IMS Health, Inc." Accessed 24 June 2011 at http://www.oyez.org/cases/2010-2019/2010_10_779

Wisconsin Law Journal. "10-779 Sorrell v. IMS Health Inc." Accessed on 24 June 2011 at http://wislawjournal.com/2011/06/23/10-779-stern-v-marshall/

SIXTH CIRCUIT REMOVES TEN COMMANDMENTS FROM OHIO COURTROOM

"6th Circuit Declines Appeal for Ten Commandments." *The McCreary County Record,* 16 June 2010.

ACLU of Ohio v. DeWeese, Accessed 4 May 2011 at http://www.ca6.uscourts.gov/opinions-pdf/11a0029p.06.pdf

Makowsky, Daniel. "Sixth Circuit Rules Against Ten Commandments in Ohio Courthouse." *Jurist,* February 2011. Available at http://jurist.org/paperchase/2011/02/sixth-circuit-rules-againsst-ten-commandments...

Weiss, Debra Cassens. "6th Circuit Rules Against Ohio Judge's Modified Ten Commandments Poster." *American Bar Journal,* 3 February 2011. Available at http://www.abajournal.com/news/article/6th_circuit_rules_against_ohio_judges_modified...

FORECLOSURE

MASSACHUSETTS SUPREME JUDICIAL COURT RULES AGAINST BANKS IN CRITICAL FORECLOSURE CASE

Associated Press. "Court Rules Against Banks in Foreclosure Case." *Salt Lake Tribune.* Jan. 7, 2011.

Weidlich, Thom. "Banks Lose Pivotal Foreclosure Case in Massachusetts High Court." Bloomberg. Jan. 7, 2011.

FOURTH AMENDMENT

DAVIS V. UNITED STATES

Bloom, Robert M. and Mark S. Brodin. *Criminal Procedure: The Constitution and the Police.* New York: Aspen Publishers, 6th ed., 2010.

Dressler, Joshua and Alan C. Michaels. *Understanding Criminal Procedure.* New Providence, N.J.: LexisNexis, 5th ed., 2010.

CALIFORNIA SUPREME COURT ALLOWS WARRANTLESS SEARCH OF CELL PHONE MESSAGES

Minkevitch, Hannah. "People v. Diaz." *Berkeley Technology Law Journal,* 23 February 2011.

Lombardo, Domenic J. "The California Supreme Court Authorizes Warrantless Searches of Cell Phones." 2 May 2011. Available at http://www.sandiegocriminallawyer.com/recent-criminal-law-developments/

People v. Diaz, Accessed 4 June 2011 at http://www.courtinfo.ca.gov/opinions/documents/5166600.pdf

KENTUCKY V. KING

Bloom, Robert M. and Mark S. Brodin. *Criminal Procedure: The Constitution and the Police.* New York: Aspen Publishers, 6th ed., 2010.

Dressler, Joshua and Alan C. Michaels. *Understanding Criminal Procedure.* New Providence, N.J.: LexisNexis, 5th ed., 2010.

PLACING GPS DEVICE ON AUTOMOBILE IS A SEARCH UNDER THE FOURTH AMENDMENT

Dash, Samuel. *The Intruders: Unreasonable Searches and Seizures from King John to John Ashcroft.* Rutgers University Press. 2004.

Cammack, Mark and Garland, Norman. *Advanced Criminal Procedure in a Nutshell.* West Publishing Co. 2001.

Long, Carolyn. *Mapp V. Ohio: Guarding Against Unreasonable Searches And Seizures.* University Press of Kansas. 2006.

PENNSYLVANIA APPELLATE COURT ALLOWS GPS TRACKING INTO EVIDENCE

"Appeals Panel in Pa. Says GPS Evidence Can Be Used." ABC Local Daily News, West Chester, PA, 25 December 2010. Accessed 28 June 2011 at http://abclocal.go.com/wpvi/story?section=news/local&id=7863707

Correa, Eryn. "Pennsylvania Appeals Court Allows Evidence Obtained with GPS Technology." *Jurist PaperChase*, 26 December 2010. Available at http://jurist.org/paperchase/2010/12/pennsylvaniea-appeals-court-allows-evidence-obtained-...

Rellahan, Michael. "Pa. Court Ruling Favors GPS Tracking Evidence." *The Daily Local*, (Chester County, PA), 25 December 2010.

TOLENTINO V. NEW YORK

People v. Tolentino, No. 37. 14 N.Y.3d 382; 962 NE 2d 1212 (2010). Available at http://caselaw.findlaw.com

Tolentino v. New York. Available at www.supremecourt.gov/opinions/10pdf/10-1156.pdf

The Wisconsin State Public Defender. "Tolentino v. New York." *On Point*, 15 November 2010. Accessed on 20 April at http://www.wisconsinappeals.net/?p=3161

FRAUD

HIGH SALARIES IN SMALL CALIFORNIA CITY LEAD TO RESIGNATIONS, A RECALL ELECTION, AND CORRUPTION CHARGES

Gottlieb, Jeff and Ruben Vives. "Is a City Manager Worth $800, 000?" *Los Angeles Times*. July 15, 2010.

Knoll, Corina. "Robert Rizzo Steered Bell Contracts to Business Partner, Prosecutor Says." *Los Angeles Times*. March 16, 2011.

CLINTON AND OBAMA FINANCIAL BACKER SENTENCED TO 12 YEARS FOR RUNNING PONZI SCHEME

Glovin, David. "Fundraiser Namazee Gets 12 Years for City, HSBC Fraud." *Washington Post*. July 15, 2010.

Moynihan, Colin. "Financier Gets 12 Years for Stealing $292 Million." *New York Times*. July 15, 2010

FALLOUT FROM MADOFF FRAUD SCHEME CONTINUES

Rothfield, Michael. "Madoff Kin, Global Banks Sued for Funds." *Wall St. Journal*. Dec. 8, 2010.

Rothfield, Micahel. "Trustee: J.P. Morgan Abetted Madoff." *Wall St. Journal*. Feb. 4, 2011.

FREEDOM OF INFORMATION ACT

FCC V. AT&T INC.

Biskupic, Joan. "Supreme Court: No Privacy Exemption for Businesses in FOIA." *USA Today*. March 1, 2011.

Kendall, Brent. "AT&T Loses Privacy Ruling." *Wall Street Journal*. March 2, 2011

SUPREME COURT STRIKES DOWN FOIA EXEMPTION INTERPRETATION

Smith, Kelvin. *Freedom Of Information: A Practical Guide To Implementing The Act*, Library Association Publisher Ltd, 2004.

FREEDOM OF SPEECH

NINTH CIRCUIT RULES THAT TATTOOS AND TATTOO PARLORS ARE PROTECTED BY THE FIRST AMENDMENT

Barron, Jerome, Dienes, Thomas. *First Amendment Law in a Nutshell, 3rd ed.* West Group, 2004.

Farber, Daniel. *The First Amendment: Concepts and Insights.* Foundation Press, 2002.

ARIZONA JOINS OTHER STATES RESTRICTING FUNERAL PROTESTERS

Chappell, Bill. "Supreme Court Sides With Westboro Church on Funeral Protests." 2 March 2011. Accessed June 4, 2011 at http://www.npr.org/blogs/thetwo-way/2011/03/02/134194791/supreme-court-sides-with-westboro-church-on-funeral-protests

CNN News. "Arizona Enacts Funeral Protest Legislation." 11 January 2011. Accessed June 4, 2011 at http://www.npr.org/blogs/thetwo-way/2011/03/02/134194791/supreme-court-sides-with-westboro-church-on-funeral-protests

delPuerto, Luige. "Legislature Swiftly Passes, Brewer Signs Bill to Restrict Funeral Protests." *Arizona Capitol Times*, 11 January 2011.

Mehta, Seema and Nicone Santa Cruz. "Tucson Rallies to Protect Girl's Family From Protesters." *Los Angeles Times*, 11 January 2011.

Snyder v. Phelps, No. 09-751, Available at www.supremecourt.gov/opinions/10pdf/09-751.pdf

GAMBLING

WASHINGTON SUPREME COURT UPHOLDS STATE BAN ON INTERNET GAMBLING

Schwartz, David. *Cutting The Wire: Gaming Prohibition And The Internet*, University of Nevada Press, 2005.

Burbank, Jeff. *License To Steal: Nevada's Gaming Control System In The Megaresort Age.*, University of Nevada Press, 2005.

GAY AND LESBIAN RIGHTS

9TH CIRCUIT SENDS CALIFORNIA INITIATIVE BANNING SAME-SEX MARRIAGE CASE TO CALIFORNIA SUPREME COURT

Pinello, Daniel. *Gay Rights and American Law.* Cambridge University Press, 2003.

Alsenas, Linda. *Gay America: Struggle for Equality.* Amulet Press, 2008.

REPEAL OF DON'T ASK, DON'T TELL MILITARY POLICY

Center for Military Readiness. "Legislative History of the Law Regarding Homosexuals in the Military." 22 August 2008. Accessed 4 May 2011 at http://www.cmrlink.org/HMilitary.asp?docID=336

"H.R. 2965, Don't Ask, Don't Tell Repeal Act of 2010." *DPC Reports,* 17 December 2010. Available at http://dpc.senate.gov/dpcdoc.cfm?doc_name=1b-111-2-191

Levine, Britany. "Marines' 'Don't Ask, Don't Tell' Repeal Training Revealed." *Orange County Register,* 22 April 2010.

"Obama Signs Repeal of 'Don't Ask, Don't Tell' Policy." CNN News article, 22 December 2010. Available at http://articles.cnn.com/2010-12-22/politics

HABEAS CORPUS

WILSON V. CORCORAN

Conery, Ben. "Supreme Court Rules on Credit Card Rate Hikes, Retaliation Litigation." *Washington Times,* 24 January 2011. Available at http://www.employerlawreport.com/2011/01/articles/workforce-strategies

Wilson v. Corcoran. No. 10-91. Available at www.supremecourt.gov/opinions/10pdf/10-91.pdf

The Oyez Project. "Chase Bank USA v. McCoy." Accessed 4 April 2011 at http://www.oyez.org/cases/2010-2019/2010_10_91

WALL V. KHOLI

Bizzaro, Amelia. "On Appeal: Motion for Sentence Modification Tolls AEDPA." *Wisconsin Law Journal.* Aprli 6, 2011.

Cole, David and James X. Dempsey. *Terrorism and the Constitution: Sacrificing Civil Liberties in the Name of National Security.* 2006.

SUPREME COURT REAFFIRMS HABEAS DENIAL IF NO FEDERAL LAW IS VIOLATED

Tomkovicz, James J. 2002. *The Right to the Assistance of Counsel: A Reference Guide to the United States Constitution.* Westport, Conn.: Greenwood.

Palmer, John. 2006. *Constitutional Rights of Prisoners.* 8th ed. New York: Anderson Pub. Co.

HEALTH CARE

LOWER COURTS DIVIDED IN CHALLENGES TO HEALTH CARE REFORM LAW

Biskupic, Joan. "Judges Hear Arguments on Obama Health Care Law." *USA Today.* May 11, 2011.

Kendall, Brent. "Meaning of Ruling Is Sought." *Wall St. Journal.* February 18, 2011.

Sack, Kevin. "Administration Seeks Clarity from Judge on Health Ruling." *New York Times.* February 17, 2011.

IMMIGRATION

FEDERAL COURTS HALT ENFORCEMENT OF ARIZONA IMMIGRATION LAW PROVISIONS

Phelan, Margaret and Gillespie, James. *Immigration Law Handbook.* Oxford University Press, 2007.

Scaros, Constantinos. *Learning About Immigration Law.* Thomson Delmaer Learning, 2006.

Weissbrodt, David and Danielson, Laura. *Immigration Law and Procedure in a Nutshell, 5th Edition.* West Group, 2005.

CHAMBER OF COMMERCE OF THE UNITED STATES OF AMERICA V. WHITING

Associated Press. "Supreme Court Upholds Ariz. Law Punishing Employers Who Knowingly Hire Illegal Immigrants." *Washington Post.* May 26, 2011.

Kim, Mallie Jane. "Is Supreme Court Right to OK Arizona's 'Business Death Penalty'?" *U.S News and World Report.* May 26, 2011.

SUPREME COURT DEADLOCKS ON IMMIGRATION CASE

Phelan, Margaret and Gillespie, James. *Immigration Law Handbook.* Oxford University Press, 2007.

Scaros, Constantinos. *Learning About Immigration Law.* Thomson Delmaer Learning, 2006.

Weissbrodt, David and Danielson, Laura. *Immigration Law and Procedure in a Nutshell, 5th Edition.* West Group, 2005.

THIRD CIRCUIT STRIKES DOWN MUNICIPAL IMMIGRATION LAWS

Phelan, Margaret and Gillespie, James. *Immigration Law Handbook.* Oxford University Press, 2007.

Scaros, Constantinos. *Learning About Immigration Law.* Thomson Delmaer Learning, 2006.

Weissbrodt, David and Danielson, Laura. *Immigration Law and Procedure in a Nutshell, 5th Edition.* West Group, 2005.

SECOND CIRCUITS UPHOLDS STATUTORY DUE PROCESS FOR NONCITIZENS FIGHTING DEPORTATION

Phelan, Margaret and Gillespie, James. *Immigration Law Handbook.* Oxford University Press, 2007.

Scaros, Constantinos. *Learning About Immigration Law.* Thomson Delmar Learning, 2006.

Weissbrodt, David and Danielson, Laura. *Immigration Law and Procedure in a Nutshell, 5th Edition.* West Group, 2005.

IMMUNITY

ASHCROFT V. AL-KIDD

Brown, Mark R. "Qualified Immunity and Interlocatory Fact-Finding in the Courts of Appeals." *Penn State Law Review.* Spring 2010.

Jeffries, John C., Jr. "What's Wrong with Qualified Immunity?" *Florida Law Review.* Sept. 2010.

WINNING PARTIES MAY APPEAL TO SUPREME COURT ON IMMUNITY ISSUES

Dash, Samuel. *The Intruders: Unreasonable Searches and Seizures from King John to John Ashcroft.* Rutgers University Press. 2004.

Cammack, Mark and Garland, Norman. *Advanced Criminal Procedure in a Nutshell.* West Publishing Co. 2001.

Long, Carolyn. *Mapp V. Ohio: Guarding Against Unreasonable Searches And Seizures.* University Press of Kansas. 2006.

IMPEACHMENT

SENATE REMOVES FEDERAL JUDGE FOLLOWING IMPEACHMENT

Ingram, David. "Senate Preps for Trial of Federal Judge." *National Law Journal.* Sept. 6, 2010.

O'Keefe, Ed. "First Senate Impeachment Trial Since Clinton Starts." *Washington Post.* Sept. 13, 2010.

INTERNATIONAL LAW

NUCLEAR WEAPONS TREATY WITH RUSSIA

"2010 Review Conference of the Parties to the Treaty on the Non-Proliferation of Nuclear Weapons." Accesssed on 29 June 2011 at http://www.un.org/en/conf/npt/2010/

Bennett, Rachel. "Nuclear Weapons Treaty With Russia Limits Armed Warheads to 1, 550." WTOL Local News, Toledo, Ohio 5 February 2011. Accessed June 30, 2011 at http://www.wtol.com/story/13977480/nuclear-weapons-treaty-with-russia...

Sheridan, Mary Beth and William Branigin. "Senate Ratifies New U.S.-Russia Nuclear Weapons Treaty." *Washington Post,* 22 December 2010.

"Treaty on the Non-Proliferation of Nuclear Weapons." Accesssed on 29 June 2011 at http://www.un.org/Depts/dda/WMD/treaty/

INTERNET

INTERNET SITE CRAIGSLIST REMOVES ADULT SECTION AMID PRESSURE

"Craigslist.com Blocks Access to Adult Services Ads." Reuters. Sept. 4, 2010.

Miler, Claire Cain. "Craigslist Pulls 'Censored' Label from Sex Ads Area." *New York Times.* Sept. 9, 2010.

Shiels, Maggie. "Craigslist Dumps 'Adult Service' Adverts." BBC News. Sept. 4, 2010.

KENTUCKY APPEALS COURT ALLOWS UNAUTHORIZED FACEBOOK PHOTOGRAPHS IN EVIDENCE

Florida Law Commentary. "Is There a Law Against Posting Photos and Tagging People on Facebook?" 31 March 2011. Available at http://www.floridalawcommentary.com/2011/03/31/internet-marketing-for-young-lawyers

LaLonde v. LaLonde, Accessed 4 May 2011 at http://www.opinions.kycourts.net/coa/2009-CA-002279.pdf

Tene, Omer. "You've Been Tagged." 21 March 2011. Available at http://cyberlaw.stanford.edu/node/6642

FCC ISSUES NET NEUTRALITY RULES

Rustad, Michael L. *Internet Law in a Nutshell,* West: St. Paul, MN. 2009.

Stelter, Brian. "FCC Faces Challenges to Net Rules." *New York Times,* December 10, 2010.

WIKILEAKS CONTINUES TO CAUSE CONTROVERSY

Burns, John F. and Ravi Somaiya. "WikiLeaks Founder on the Run, Trailed by Notoriety." *New York Times.* Oct. 23, 2010.

Entous, Adam and Evan Perez. "Prosecutors Eye WikiLeaks Charges." *Wall Street Journal.* Aug. 21, 2010.

JURISDICTION

SUPREME COURT LIMITS JURISDICTION OVER FOREIGN CORPORATIONS

Chemerinsky, Erwin. 2007. *Federal Jurisdiction.* 5th ed. Boston: Aspen.

Little, Laura. 2007. *Federal Courts Examples & Explanations.* Boston: Aspen.

Wright, Charles Alan. 2002. *Law of Federal Courts.* 6th ed. St. Paul, Minn.: West Group.

J. MCINTYRE MACHINERY, LTD. V. NICASTRO

J. NcIntyre Machinery, Ltd. V. Nicastro, No. 09-1343. Available at www.supremecourt.gov/opinions/10pdf/09-1343.pdf

The Oyez Project. "J. McIntyre Machinery, Ltd. V. Nicastro." Accessed 29 June 2011 at http://www.oyez.org/cases/2010-2019/2010_09_1343

Wisconsin Law Journal. "09-1343 J. McIntyre Machinery, Ltd., v. Nicastro." Accessed on 29 June 2011 at http://wislawjournal.com/2011/06/27/09-1343-j-mcintyre-machinery-ltd-v-nicastro/

SUPREME COURT CLARIFIES COURT OF FEDERAL CLAIMS LAWSUITS

Chemerinsky, Erwin. 2007. *Federal Jurisdiction.* 5th ed. Boston: Aspen.

Little, Laura. 2007. *Federal Courts Examples & Explanations.* Boston: Aspen.

Wright, Charles Alan. 2002. *Law of Federal Courts.* 6th ed. St. Paul, Minn.: West Group.

JUVENILE LAW

J.D.B. v. NORTH CAROLINA

Gardner, Martin R. *Understanding Juvenile Law,* 3d Ed. Newark, N.J.: LexisNexis, 2009.

Morgan, Thomas S. and Harold C. Gaither, Jr. *Juvenile Law and Practice,* 3d Ed. Eagan, Minn.: Thomson/West, 2008

LABOR LAW

KASTEN V. SAINT-GOBAIN PERFORMANCE PLASTICS

American Bar Association. "Kasten v. Saint-GObain Performance Plastics Corporation." *Hot Topic* Labor and Employment Law News. Available at http://www.americanbar.org/content/newsletter/groups/labor_law/ll_hottopics/2011

Kasten v. Saint-Gobain Performance Plastics Corporation, No. 09-834, Available at www.supremecourt.gov/opinions/10pdf/09-834.pdf

The Oyez Project. "Kasten v. Saint-GobainAbbott v. United States." U.S. Supreme Court Media Report, accessed on 23 March 2011. Available at http://www.oyez.org/cases/2010-2019/2010/2010_09_834

MEDICINE

APPEALS COURT REINSTATES STEM CELL RESEARCH FUNDING

"Appeals Court Lifts Ban on Federal Funding for Stem Cell Research." Associated Press News Release, 29 April 2011. Available at http://www.npr.org/2011/04/29/135840798/appeals-court-overturns-stem-cell-resesarch-ban

"Appeals Court Overturns Stem Cell Research Ban." 29 April 2011. Available at http://www.articles.cnn.com/2011.../stem.cells_1_stem-cell-research-cell-types-ban-research?/

"Judge Stops Federal Funding of Embryonic Stem Cell Research." 29 April 2011. Available at http://www.articles.cnn.com/.../stem.cell.funding_1_cell-types-cell-research-dickey-wicker-amendment?

Meckler, Laura, et al. "Judge Roils Stem-Cell Research." *Wall Street Journal,* 24 August 2010.

Sherley v. Sebelius, Accessed 4 May 2011 at http://www.cadc.uscourts.gov/intent/opinions.nsf/

MILITARY LAW

9TH CIRCUIT STRIKES DOWN MUNICIPAL BAN ON MILITARY RECRUITING OF MINORS

Epstein, Richard. *Federal Preemption.* AEI Press, 2007.

O'Reilly, James. *Federal Preemption of State and Local Law.* American Bar Association, 2006.

Zimmerman, Joseph. *Congressional Preemption.* State University of New York Press, 2006.

MURDER

"DATELINE" TV EPISODE CASTS DOUBTS ON PROSECUTOR'S CASE

Dys, Andrew. "Dad of Slain Girl Wants New Trial." *The Herald,* (Rock Hill, SC) 14 April 2006.

"Prosecutor Fires Back After 'Dateline' Story Profiles Rock Hill Murder." Local News Story, WSOC-TV, 19 July 2010. Available at http://www.wscotctv.com/news/24288588/detail.html

State v. Cope, No. 4526 (04-GS-46-2614-2618, et seq.) Accessed 10 June at http://www.sccourts.org/opinions/advsheets/no432009

Wagner, Dave. "Innocent Man Behind Bars?" Local News Story, News Channel 36, 7 May 2010. Available at http://www.wcnc.news/local/innocent/behind-bars-93143179.html

ARIZONA GUNMAN KILLS SIX AND WOUNDS 12 OTHERS AT POLITICAL GATHERING

"Arizona Shooting." *the New York Times,* 29 June 2011.

"California: Forced Drugs Approved for Loughner." *the New York Times,* 29 June 2011.

"Criminal Complaint Against Jared Lee Loughner Document." *The New York Times,* Accessed 30 June 2011 at http://documents/nytimes.com/criminal-complaint-against-jared-lee-loughner/

Dwyer, Devin, et al. "Cops Hunt Second Man Believed to Be Involved in Congresswoman Giffords Shooting." ABC News, 8 January 2011. Accessed 30 June 2011 at http://abcnews.go.com/Politics/rep-gabrielle-giffords-shot-grocery-store-event/

Murray, Shailagh and Sari Horwitz. "Rep. Gabrielle Giffords Shot in Tucson Rampage; federal Judge Killed." *the Washington Post,* 9 January 2011.

NATIVE AMERICAN RIGHTS

UNITED STATES V. JICARILLA APACHE NATION

The Oyez Project. "United States v. Jicarilla Apache Nation." U.S. Supreme Court Media Report, accessed on 23 June 2011. Available at http://www.oyez.org/cases/2010-2019/2010/2010_10_382

Bloom, Robert M. and Mark S. Brodin. *Criminal Procedure: The Constitution and hte Police.* New York: Aspen, 2010.

Kasprisin, Justin Alexander. "Obstruction of Justice." *American Criminal Law Review.* Spring 2010.

Zagger, Zack. "Supreme Court Rules No Fiduciary Exception in Trust Between US, Native American Tribe." *Jurist PaperChase,* 13 June 2011. Available at http://jurist.org/paperchase/2011/06/supreme-court-rules-no-fiduciary-exception-in-trust...

OBSTRUCTION OF JUSTICE

FOWLER V. UNITED STATES

Bloom, Robert M. and Mark S. Brodin. *Criminal Procedure: The Constitution and hte Police.* New York: Aspen, 2010.

Kasprisin, Justin Alexander. "Obstruction of Justice." *American Criminal Law Review.* Spring 2010.

PAROLE

FEDERAL COURTS CANNOT REVIEW CALIFORNIA PAROLE SYSTEM

Palmer, John. 2006. *Constitutional Rights of Prisoners.* 8th ed. New York: Anderson Pub. Co.

Tomkovicz, James J. 2002. *The Right to the Assistance of Counsel: A Reference Guide to the United States Constitution.* Westport, Conn.: Greenwood.

PATENTS

COSTCO V.OMEGA

Costco Wholesale Corporation v. Omega, No. 08-1423, Available at www.supremecourt.gov/orders/courtorders/110810zor.pdf

Costco Wholesale Corporation v. Omega, No. 01423, Available at www.supremecourt.gov/opinions/08-1423.htm

Costco Wholesale Corporation v. Omega, Nos. 07-55368 and 07-56206. 541 F.3d 982 Available at www.ca9.uscourts.gov/datastore/opinions/2008/09/03/0755368.pdf

McGill, Matt. "Costco v. Omega- The Patent Angle." *Patent Litigation Weekly,* 13 September 2010

GLOBAL-TECH APPLIANCES V. SEB

Global-Tech Appliances, Inc. v. SEB, No. 10-06. Available at www.supremecourt.gov/opinions/10pdf/10-06.pdf

"Global-Tech Appliances v. SEB." Accessed 31 May 2011 at http://www.oyez.org/cases/2010-2019/2010_10_06

Noonan, Kevin E. "Global-Tech Appliances v. SEB S. A. (2011)." *Patent Docs,* 31 May 2011. Available at http://www.patentdocs.org

MICROSOFT CORP. V. I4I LIMITED PARTNERSHIP

Landers, Amy L. *Understanding Patent Law.* Newark, N.J.: LexisNexis, 2008.

Mueller, Janice M. *Patent Law.* New York: Aspen Publishers, 2009.

Vicini, James. "Microsoft Loses U.S. Supreme Court Case on Patent." Reuters, June 10, 2011

SUPREME COURT RULES UNIVERSITY DOES NOT OWN PATENT OUTRIGHT

Klien, Sheldon. 2009. "Introduction to Trademarks: Patents, Copyrights, Trademarks and Literary Property Course Handbook Series." *Practicing Law Institute*Pat 123.

Miller, Arthur, and Davis, Michael. 2007. *Intellectual Property-Patents, Trademarks And Copyright in a Nutshell.* St. Paul, Minn.: Thomson West.

PREEMPTION

FEDERAL VACCINE ACT PREEMPTS DESIGN-DEFECT CLAIMS

Epstein, Richard. *Federal Preemption.* AEI Press, 2007.

O'Reilly, James. *Federal Preemption of State and Local Law.* American Bar Association, 2006.

Zimmerman, Joseph. *Congressional Preemption.* State University of New York Press, 2006.

PRISONERS' RIGHTS

FEDERAL COURTS MAY ORDER CALIFORNIA TO REDUCE PRISON POPULATION

Lewis, Jr., Harold and Norman, Elizabeth. *Civil Rights Law and Practice.* West Gropu. 2004.

Palmer, John. *Constitutional Rights of Prisoners. 8th Edition.* Anderson Pub. Co. 2006

Vieira, Norman. *Constitutional Civil Rights in a Nutshell.* West Group. 1998.

PRIVACY

FEDERAL CONTRACT EMPLOYEES BACKGROUND CHECKS LEGAL

Covington, Robert and Decker, Kurt. *Employment Law in a Nutshell.* Saint Paul, MN: West Group. 2002. Second Edition.

Lewis, Jr., Harold and Norman, Elizabeth. *Civil Rights Law and Practice.* Saint Paul, MN: West Group. 2004.

Vieira, Norman. *Constitutional Civil Rights in a Nutshell.* Saint Paul, MN.: West Group. 1998.

RELIGION

Arizona Christian School Tuition Organization v. Winn

Barnes, Robert. "Supreme Court Tosses Private-School Tax-Credit Challenge." *Washington Post.* April 11, 2011.

"Justice Kagan Dissents." *New York Times.* April 9, 2011.

Federal Courts Uphold Use of "Under Gods" in Pledges of Allegiance

Associated Press. "Court OKs 'under God' in Pledge of Allegiance." MSNBC.com. March 11, 2010.

"'God' in Pledge, National Motto Ruled Constitutional." *Christian Post.* March 12, 2010.

Sossamon v. Texas

Lindell, Chuck. "U.S. Supreme Court Backs Texas in Prison Lawsuit." *Austin American-Statesman.* April 20, 2011.

Robbins, Mary Alice. "High Court to Hear Case Involving Damages Under Religious Freedom Law." *Texas Lawyer.* Nov. 1, 2010.

Weiss, Debra Cassens. "Texas Immune from Prisoner Damages Suit Under Religious Rights Law, Supreme Court Rules." *ABA Journal.* April 20, 2011.

9th Circuit Rules Pretrial Detention Facilities Covered by Religious Freedom Law

Barron, Jerome, Dienes, Thomas. *First Amendment Law in a Nutshell, 3rd ed.* West Group, 2004.

Farber, Daniel. *The First Amendment: Concepts and Insights.* Foundation Press, 2002.

RIGHT TO COUNSEL

Turner v. Rogers

Cohen, Andrew. "Turner's Trumpet: Child Support and the Right to Counsel." *The Atlantic,* June 2011.

Diller, Rebecca. "Turner v. Rogers: What the Court Did and Didn't Say." Brennan Center for Justice, 21 June 2011. Available at http://www.acslaw.org

The Oyez Project. "Turner v. Rogers." Accessed 24 June 2011 at http://www.oyez.org/cases/2010-2019/2010_10_10

Turner v. Rogers, No. 10-10, Available at www.supremecourt.gov/opinions/10pdf/09-1476.pdf

RIPARIAN RIGHTS

Montana v. Wyoming

Belczyk, Jaclyn. "Supreme Court Rules for Wyoming in Water Dispute." *Jurist: Paper Chase,* 02 May 2011. Available at http://jurist.org/paperchase/2011/05/supreme-court-rules-for-wyoming-in-water-dispute.php

"Court Sides with Wyoming in Dispute with Montana." *Kansas City Star,* 02 May 2011.

Montana v. Wyoming, No. 137, Orig., available at www.supremecourt.gov/opinions/

"Montana V. Wyoming." Accessed 30 April 2011 at http://www.oyez.org/cases/2000-2009/2006/2006-137%20.orig

SECOND AMENDMENT

Court of Appeals Shoots Down Chicago's New Gun Law

Ezell v. City of Chicago, No. 10-3525. Accessed 6 July 2011 at http://www.ca7.uscourts.gov/tmp/9COR60TS

Harris, Andrew. "Chicago Firing-Range Ban Teetering; City Revamps Ordinance." Bloomberg News, 9 July 2011. Accessed 6 July 2011 at http://www.bloomberg.com/news/2011-07-06/chicago-ban-on-firing-ranges-blocked

Rose, Veronica. "OLR Backgrounder: State Gun Laws After Heller and McDonald." Accessed 6 July 2011 at http://www.cga.ct.gov/2010/rpt/2010-R-0455.htm .

Savage, David. "Daley: City Will Revise Gun Law Afer Supreme Court Ruling." 28 June 2010. Accessed 6 July 2011 at http://archive.chicagobreakingnews.com/2010/06/united-states-supreme-court-scotus-gun-control...

Third Circuit Rules That Felons Do Not Have Second Amendment Rights

Cook, Philip J., Jens Ludwig, and Adam M. Samaha. "Gun Control After Heller: Threats and Sideshows from a Social Welfar Perspective." *UCLA Law Review.* June 2009.

Kopel, David B. and Clayton Cramer. "State Court Standards of Review for the Right to Keep and Bear Arms." *Santa Clara Law Review.* 2010.

SECTION 1983

Fox v. Vice

Collins, Michael G. *Section 1983 Litigation in a Nutshell.* 4th ed. St. Paul, Minn.: West, 2011.

Schwartz, Martin A. and Kathryn R. Urbonya. *Section 1983 Litigation.* 2d ed. Washington, D.c.: Federal Judicial Center.

Gun Control and Mental Illness Disqualification in the Aftermath of the 2011 Tucson Shootings

Bluestein, Greg. "Few States Follow Mental Health Gun Law." *Salon,* 17 February 2011. Available at

http://www.salon.com/news/feature/2011/02/17/mental_health_gun_law

Graff, Corey. "Federal Gun Control Legislation to Expand Scope of Mental Health Disqualification." *Gun Digest,* 16 May 2011.

Harris, Elizabeth A. "Bloomberg and Relatives of Shooting Victims Push for Stricter Gun Control." *The New York Times,* 24 January 2011.

"Keeping Guns from the Dangerously Mentally Ill: State and Territorial Records of Disqualifying Mental Illness in the NICS Index and in State Agencies." Accessed on 30 July 2011 at http://www.bradycampaign.org/facts//2011_01_05

Krouse, William J. "Gun Control Legislation." Congressional Recodrd Service (CRS) Report for Congress, 3 February 2011. Accessed on 30 July 2011 at http://www.crs.gov

Lacey, Marc. "Family of Slain Giffords Aide Pushing Restrictions on Ammunition." *The New York Times,* 12 April 2011.

SECURITIES

ERICA P. JOHN FUND V. HALLIBURTON

Erica P. John Fund v. Halliburton, Available at www.supremecourt.gov/opinions/10pdf/09-1403.pdf

"Erica P. John Fund v. Hallliburton." Accessed 8 June 2011 at http://www.oyez.org/cases/2010-2019/2010_09_1403

"Erica P. John Fund, Inc. v. Halliburton Co." *The Recorder,* California Legal Report, 6 June 2011.

MATRIXX INITIATIVES V. SIRACUSANO

Kaye Scholler LLP. "Matrixx Initiatives, Inc. v. Siracusano: U.S. Supreme Court Rejects 'Statistical Significance' as Threshold for Required Disclosure of Drug Adverse Event Reports." Client Report, 31 March 2011.

Matrixx Initiatives Inc. v. Siracusano, No. 09-1156, Available at www.supremecourt.gov/opinions/10pdf/09-1156.pdf

"Matrixx Initiatives, Inc. v. Siracusano." Accessed 4 April 2011 at http://www.oyez.org/cases/2010-2019/2010_09_1156

Washington Legal Foundation. "Matrixx Initiatives, Inc. v. Siracusano." Accessed 20 April 2011 at http://www.wlf.org/litigating/case_detail.asp?id=634

JANUS CAPITAL GROUP, INC. V. FIRST DERIVATIVE TRADERS

Liptak, Adam. "In a 5-4 Vote, Supreme Court Limits Securities Fraud Suits." *New York Times.* June 13, 2011.

"A Thwarted Liability Scheme." *Wall Street Journal.* June 14, 2011.

SENTENCING

ABBOTT V. UNITED STATES

Abbott v. United States, Accessed 23 March 2011 at http://supreme.justia.com/us/562/09-479/

Abbott v. United States, Available at www.supreme-court.gov/opinions/09-479.htm

The Oyez Project. "Abbott v. United States." U.S. Supreme Court Media Report, accessed on 23 March 2011. Available at http://www.oyez.org/cases/2010-2019/2010/2010_09_479

CONGRESS REDUCES SENTENCING DISPARITY BETWEEN CRACK AND POWDER COCAINE

Branham, Lynm. *The Law of Sentencing and Corrections in a Nutshell.* West Group, 2005.

Stith, Kate. *Fear of Judging: Sentencing Guidelines in the Federal Courts.* University of Chicago Press, 1998.

Tonry, Michael. *Sentencing Matters.* Oxford University Press, 2004.

McNEILL V. UNITED STATES

Debold, David, Phylis Skloot Bamberger, and David Gottlieb. *Practice Under the Federal Sentencing Guidelines.* New York: Aspen Publishers, 5th ed. 2010.

Shepard's Editorial Staff. *Federal Sentencing Guidelines Handbook.* Colorado Springs, Colo.: Shepard's/McGraw-Hill.

DEFENDANT'S POST-SENTENCING REHABILITATION MAY BE USED IN RESENTENCING

Branham, Lynm. *The Law of Sentencing and Corrections in a Nutshell.* West Group, 2005.

Stith, Kate. *Fear of Judging: Sentencing Guidelines in the Federal Courts.* University of Chicago Press, 1998.

Tonry, Michael. *Sentencing Matters.* Oxford University Press, 2004.

TAPIA V. UNITED STATES

Associated Press. "Court Says Judges Can't Give Extra Time for Rehab." News Release, 16 June 2011. Accessed 20 June 2011 at http://www.hosted.ap.org/.../US_Supreme_Court_Rehabilitation?

Doyle, Michael. "Sentences Can't Be Lengthened for Rehab, Supreme Court Rules." *Kansas City Star,* 16 June 2011. Accessed 4 June 2011 at http://www.martindale.com/criminal-law/article_Faegre-Benson-LLP_1290644.htm

Tapia v. United States, No. 10-5400, Available at www.supremecourt.gov/opinions/10pdf/10-5400.pdf

SEX OFFENSES

CALIFORNIA'S VERSION OF JESSICA'S LAW FACES LEGAL CHALLENGES

Blankstein, Andrew. "Part of Jessica's Law Ruled Unconstitutional." *Los Angeles Times.* Nov. 5, 2010.

Littlefield, Dana. "Judge Rules Parts of Jessica's Law May Not Be Enforceable." *San Diego Union-Tribune.* Feb. 18, 2011

LAWRENCE TAYLOR PLEADS GUILTY TO SEX OFFENSES

"Grand Jury Indicts Taylor on Rape Charge." ESPN.com. June 23, 2010.

"Lawrence Taylor Is Given Probation in Sex Case." *L.A. Times.* March 22, 2011

SEXUAL HARASSMENT

FORMER BANKER CLAIMS CITIGROUP FIRED HER FOR BEING TOO SEXY

Martinez, Jose. "Debrahlee Lorenzana Sues Citigroup, Claims Bank Fired Her for Being Too Sexy." *N.Y. Daily News.* June 3, 2010.

Peltz, Jennifer. "Fired NY Banker's Suit, and Suits, Raise Eyebrows." ABCNews.com. June 28, 2010

SIXTH AMENDMENT

BULLCOMING V. NEW MEXICO

Dressler, Joshua and Alan C. Michaels. *Understanding Criminal Procedure,* 5th Ed. New Providence, N.J.: LexisNexis, 2010.

Marcus, Paul and Jack Zimmerman. *Criminal Procedure in Practice,* 3d Ed. Louisville, Colo.: National Institute for Trial Advocacy, 2009.

Greenhouse, Linda. "Justice Scalia Dissents." *New Times.* March 9, 2011.

Moallem, Lily. "Case Brief: Scalia Dissents in *Michigan v. Bryant,*" *Hastings Law Journal.* March 29, 2011.

SUPREME COURT RULES PLEA BARGAIN DID NOT VIOLATE SIXTH AMENDMENT

Branham, Lynm. *The Law of Sentencing and Corrections in a Nutshell.* West Group, 2005.

Stith, Kate. *Fear of Judging: Sentencing Guidelines in the Federal Courts.* University of Chicago Press, 1998.

Tonry, Michael. *Sentencing Matters.* Oxford University Press, 2004.

HARRINGTON V. RICHTER

Criminal Justice Legal Foundation. "Supreme Court Rebukes Ninth Circuit in Unanimous Decision." Press release, 19 January 2011. Available at http://www.clf.org/releases/11-02.htm

Harrington v. Richter, No. 09-587350, Available at www.supremecourt.gov/opinions/10pdf/09-587.pdf

"Harrington v. Richter." Accessed 4 April 2011 at http://www.oyez.org/cases/2010-2019/2009_09_587

"Justices Take 6th Amendment Case." *On the Docket,* U.S. Supreme Court Media Report, 22 February 2010. Available at http://onthedocket.org/cases/2009/harrington-v-richter

SOCIAL SECURITY ACT

SUPREME COURT RULES THAT MEDICAL RESIDENTS MUST PAY SOCIAL SECURITY

Covington, Robert and Decker, Kurt. *Employment Law in a Nutshell. Second Edition.* Saint Paul, MN: West Group. 2002.

SOVEREIGN IMMUNITY

MADISON COUNTY, N.Y. V. ONEIDA INDIAN NATION OF N.Y.

Associated Press. "High Court Dismisses Oneida Foreclosure Case." *Bloomberg Business Week.* Jan. 10, 2011.

Traynor, Caitlin. "Oneida Indian Nation Files Foreclosure Brief." *Oneida Daily Dispatch.* Feb. 4, 2011.

SPEEDY TRIAL

CALIFORNIA SUPREME COURT DISMISSES CRIMINAL CASES DUE TO COURT BACKLOG

Cammack, Mark. 2006 *Advanced Criminal Procedure in a Nutshell.* 2d ed. St. Paul, Minn.: Thomson West.

Garcia, Alfredo. 2002. *The Fifth Amendment: A Comprehensive Approach.* Westport, Conn.: Greenwood Press.

Stuart, Gary L. 2008 *Miranda: The Story of America's Right to Remain Silent.* Tucson, Ariz.: Univ. of Arizona Press.

UNITED STATES V. TINKLENBERG

Van Oort, Aaron D. "Supreme Court Decides 'United States v. Tinklenberg.'" 31 May 2011. Accessed 4 June 2011 at http://www.martindale.com/criminal-law/article_Faegre-Benson-LLP_1290644.htm

United States v. Tinklenberg, No. 09-1498, Available at www.supremecourt.gov/opinions/10pdf/09-1498.pdf

"United States v. Tinklenberg." Accessed 4 April 2011 at http://www.oyez.org/cases/2010-2019/2010/2010_09_1498

SPORTS LAW

NFL LABOR DISPUTE

Gregory, Sean. "Sports Labor Strife: Progress in NFL, Pain in NBA." 24 June 2011. Accessed 30 June 2011 at http://newsfeed.time.com/2011/06/24/sports-labor-strife-progress-in-nfl-pain-in-nba/

Maske, Mark. "NFL labor Dispute Has Prosperous League on the Brink of Shutting Down." *the Washington Post,* 3 March 2011.

"NFL Labor Strife: A Primer (What You Should Know)." 4 March 2011. Accessed 30 June 2011 at http://www.rep-am.com/time_out

"What Are the Issues in NFL Labor Dispute?" *San Diego Union-Tribune,* 11 March 2011.

STATUTE OF LIMITATIONS

CALIFORNIA TIMELINESS REQUIREMENT BARS HABEAS RELIEF IN FEDERAL COURT

Tomkovicz, James J. 2002. *The Right to the Assistance of Counsel: A Reference Guide to the United States Constitution.* Westport, Conn.: Greenwood.

Palmer, John. 2006. *Constitutional Rights of Prisoners.* 8th ed. New York: Anderson Pub. Co.

TAXATION

RAILROAD MAY SUE STATE OVER ALLEGED DISCRIMINATORY TAXES

Chemerinsky, Erwin. 2007. *Federal Jurisdiction.* 5th ed. Boston: Aspen.

Goldfarb, Charles B. *Telecommunications Act: Competition, Innovation, and Reform.* New York: Nova Science Publishers, 2006.

Temple, Riley K. and Halprin Temple. "Recent Developments in Wireline Competition." *Practising Law Institute: Patents, Copyrights, Trademarks, and Literary Property Course Handbook Series.* December 2002.

TENTH AMENDMENT

BOND V. UNITED STATES

Connolly, Katherine A. "Who's Left Standing for State Sovereignty? Private Party Standing to Raise Tenth Amendment Claims." *Boston College Law Review.* November 2010.

Gershengorn, Ara B. "Private Party Standing to Raise Tenth Amendment Commandeering Challenges." *Columbia Law Review.* May 2000.

FEDERAL COURTS RULES DOMA UNCONSTITUTIONAL

Gerstmann, Evan. 2008. *Same-Sex Marriage and the Constitution.* 2nd ed. New York: Cambridge Univ. Press.

Goldberg-Hiller, Jonathan. 2002. *The Limits to Union: Same-Sex Marriage and the Politics of Civil Rights.* Ann Arbor: Univ. of Michigan Press.

Strasser, Mark. "Same-Sex Marriages and Civil Unions: On Meaning, Free Exercise, and Constitutional Guarantees." 2002. *Loyola Law Journal* 33.

TERRORISM

FOUR CONVICTED IN NEW YORK BOMB PLOT

Hays, Tom. "Jury Rejects Entrapment Defense in NYC Bomb Plot." ABC Nesm 18 October 2010. Accessed June 4, 2011 at http://abcnews.go.com

O'Connor, Anahad. "Judge upholds Verdicts in Synagogue Bomb Plot." *New York Times,* 3 May 2011.

Susman, Tina. Four Convicted in New York Synagogue Bomb Plot." *Los Angeles Times,* 19 October 2010.

GUANTANAMO BAY STATUS AS OF 2011

"Guantanamo Bay Naval Base." *The New York Times,* 25 April 2011.

"Guantanamo Detainee Had Worked as Qaeda Courier." *The New York Times,* 19 May 2011.

Rosenberg, Carol, and Tom Lassiter. "WikiLeaks Reveal Prison Secrets." *The Miami Herald,* 24 April 2011.

Temple-Raston, Dina, et al. "Military Documents Detail Life at Guantanamo." NPR Report, 25 April 2011. Accessed 20 June 2011 at http://www.npr.org/2011/04/25/135690218

HIGH SEAS PIRATE CONVICTED AND SENTENCED

"Jama Idle Ibrahim Sentenced in D.C. for Piracy." *TBD,* 7 April 2011. Accessed 20 June 2011 at http://www.tbd.com/articles/2011/04/jama-idle-ibrahim...

"Somali Sentenced to 25 Year Prison Term for Armed Piracy in Attack on Merchant Ship." *Newsroom Magazine,* 7 April 2011. Accessed 20 June 2011 at http://newsroom-magazine.com/2011/executive-branch/justice-department/fbi/jama-idle-ibrahim

The Hague Justice Portal. "United States of America v. Jama Idle Ibrahim." 29 November 2010. Accessed 20 June 2011 at http://www.haguejusticeportal.net/eCache/DEF/12/448.html

U.S. Attorney's Office, Eastern District of Virginia. "Somali Sentenced for Acts of Piracy Against the USS Ashland." FBI Press Release, 29 November 2010. Accessed 20 June 2011 at http://www.fbi.gov/norfolk/press-releases/2010/nf112910.htm

TORT LAW

FEDERAL APPEALS COURTS FINDS NO LINK BETWEEN VACCINES AND AUTISM

Mnookin, Seth. 2011. *The Panic Virus: A True Story of Medicine, Science, and Fear*, Simon and Schuster.

Offit, Paul A. 2010 *Autism's False Prophets: Bad Science, Risky Medicine, and the Search for a Cure.*, Columbia University Press.

CSX TRANSPORTATION, INC. V. MCBRIDE

Kriewaldt, David. "The Effect of FELA/Jones Act's Substantive Standard fo Causation on the *Daubert* Standard for Admissibility of Expert Testimony." *University of San Francisco Maritime Law Journal.* 2010.

Loumiet, James R. and William G. Jungbauer. *Train Accident Reconstruction and FELA and Railroad Litigation*, 4th Ed. Tuscon, Ariz.: Lawywers & Judges Pub. Co, 2005.

U.S. SUPREME COURT

ELENA KAGAN BECOMES FOURTH WOMAN TO SERVE AS SUPREME COURT JUSTICE

Arsenault, Mark. "Senate Confirms Kagan as 112th Justice to Supreme Court." *Boston Globe.* August 5, 2010.

Foderaro, Lisa W. "Growing Up, Kagan Tested Boundaries of Her Faith." *New York Times.* May 12, 2010.

Stolberg, Sheryl, Katharine Q. Seelye, and Lisa W. Foderaro. "A Climb Marked by Confidence and Canniness." *New York Times.* May 10, 2010.

VETERANS' RIGHTS

HENDERSON V. SHINSEKI

Liptak, Adam. "Unanimously, Supreme Court Backs Veterans in 2 Cases." *New York Times.* March 1, 2011.

Totenberg, Nina. "Troops, Vets Find Vindication on the Supreme Court." NPR. March 1, 2011.

VOTING RIGHTS ACT

NINTH CIRCUIT UPHOLDS WASHINGTON FELONY DISENFRANCHISEMENT LAW

Lewis, Jr., Harold and Norman, Elizabeth. *Civil Rights Law and Practice.* West Group, 2004.

Vieira, Norman. *Constitutional Civil Rights in a Nutshell.* West Group, 1998.

WHISTLEBLOWER

SCHINDLER V. KIRK

American Bar Association (ABA). "Schindler v. Kirk." U.S. Sup. Ct. 10-188. Accessed 20 May 2011 at http://www.aba.org.

Schindler v. Kirk, No. 10-188. Available at www.supremecourt.gov/opinions/10pdf/10-188.pdf

The Oyez Project. "Schindler v. Kirk." Accessed 20 May 2011 at http://www.oyez.org/cases/2010-2019/2010_10_188

WHITE COLLAR CRIME

TOM DELAY RECEIVED THREE-YEAR SENTENCE FOR MONEY LAUNDERING AND CONSPIRACY

McKinley, James C. Jr. "DeLay Sentenced to 3 Years in Conspiracy and Money-Laundering Case." *New York Times.* Jan. 10, 2011.

Ratcliffe, R.G. "DeLay Flunked Attitude Test." *Houston Chronicle.* Jan. 11, 2011.

Abandonment: The surrender, relinquishment, disclaimer, or cession of property or of rights. Voluntary relinquishment of all right, title, claim, and possession, with the intention of not reclaiming it.

Abet: To encourage or incite another to commit a crime. This word is usually applied to aiding in the commission of a crime. To abet another to commit a murder is to command, procure, counsel, encourage, induce, or assist. To facilitate the commission of a crime, promote its accomplishment, or help in advancing or bringing it about.

Abuse of discretion: A failure to take into proper consideration the facts and law relating to a particular matter; an ARBITRARY or unreasonable departure from precedent and settled judicial custom.

Abuse of power: Improper use of authority by someone who has that authority because he or she holds a public office.

Accretion: The act of adding portions of soil to the soil already in possession of the owner by gradual deposition through the operation of natural causes.

Actual notice: Conveying facts to a person with the intention to apprise that person of a proceeding in which his or her interests are involved, or informing a person of some fact that he or she has a right to know and which the informer has a legal duty to communicate.

Adjudication: The legal process of resolving a dispute. The formal giving or pronouncing of a judgment or decree in a court proceeding; also the judgment or decision given. The entry of a decree by a court in respect to the parties in a case. It implies a hearing by a court, after notice, of legal evidence on the factual issue(s) involved. The equivalent of a determination. It indicates that the claims of all the parties thereto have been considered and set at rest.

Administrative agency: An official governmental body empowered with the authority to direct and supervise the implementation of particular legislative acts. In addition to *agency*, such governmental bodies may be called commissions, corporations (e.g., FEDERAL DEPOSIT INSURANCE CORPORATION), boards, departments, or divisions.

Advance: To pay money or give something of value before the date designated to do so; to provide capital to help a planned enterprise, expecting a return from it; to give someone an item before payment has been made for it.

Advancement: A gift of money or property made by a person while alive to his or her child or other legally recognized heir, the value of which the person intends to be deducted from the child's or heir's eventual share in the estate after the giver's death.

Adversary proceeding: Any action, hearing, investigation, inquest, or inquiry brought by one party against another in which the party seeking relief has given legal notice to and provided the other party with an opportunity to contest the claims that have been made against him or her. A court trial is a typical example of an adversary proceeding.

Advisory opinion: An opinion by a court as to the legality of proposed legislation or conduct, given in response to a request by the government, legislature, or some other interested party.

Affirmative action: Employment programs required by federal statutes and regulations designed to remedy discriminatory practices in hiring minority group members; i.e. positive steps designed to eliminate existing and continuing discrimination, to remedy lingering effects of past discrimination, and to create systems and procedures to prevent future discrimination; commonly based on population percentages of minority groups in a particular area. Factors considered are race, color, sex, creed, and age.

Affirmative defense: A new fact or set of facts that operates to defeat a claim even if the facts supporting that claim are true.

Allocation: The apportionment or designation of an item for a specific purpose or to a particular place.

Allotment: A portion, share, or division. The proportionate distribution of shares of stock in a corporation. The partition and distribution of land.

Animus: *[Latin, Mind, soul, or intention.]* A tendency or an inclination toward a definite, sometimes unavoidable, goal; an aim, objective, or purpose.

Annuity: A right to receive periodic payments, usually fixed in size, for life or a term of years that is created by a contract or other legal document.

Antitrust law: Legislation enacted by the federal and various state governments to regulate trade and commerce by preventing unlawful restraints, price-fixing, and monopolies; to promote competition; and to encourage the production of quality goods and services at the lowest prices, with the primary goal of safeguarding public welfare by ensuring that consumer demands will be met by the manufacture and sale of goods at reasonable prices.

Appellant: A person who, dissatisfied with the judgment rendered in a lawsuit decided in a lower court or the findings from a proceeding before an ADMINISTRATIVE AGENCY, asks a superior court to review the decision.

Appellate: Relating to appeals; reviews by superior courts of decisions of inferior courts or administrative agencies and other proceedings.

Appellate court: A court having jurisdiction to review decisions of a trial-level or other lower court.

Apportionment: The process by which legislative seats are distributed among units entitled to representation; determination of the number of representatives that a state, county, or other subdivision may send to a legislative body. The U.S. Constitution provides for a census every ten years, on the basis of which Congress apportions representatives according to population; each state, however, must have at least one representative. Districting is the establishment of the precise geographical boundaries of each such unit or constituency. Apportionment by state statute that denies the rule of ONE-PERSON, ONE-VOTE is violative of EQUAL PROTECTION OF LAWS.

Array: The entire group of jurors selected for a trial from which a smaller group is subsequently chosen to form a petit jury or a GRAND JURY; the list of potential jurors.

Arrears: A sum of money that has not been paid or has only been paid in part at the time it is due.

Articles: Series or subdivisions of individual and distinct sections of a document, statute, or other writing, such as the ARTICLES OF CONFEDERATION. Codes or systems of rules created by written agreements of parties or by statute that establish standards of legally acceptable behavior in a business relationship, such as articles of incorporation or articles of partnership. Writings that embody contractual terms of agreements between parties.

Articles of impeachment: Formal written allegations of the causes that warrant the criminal trial of a public official before a quasi-political court.

Assigns: Individuals to whom property is, will, or may be transferred by conveyance, will, DESCENT AND DISTRIBUTION, or statute; assignees.

Attorney-client privilege: In the law of evidence, a client's privilege to refuse to disclose, and to prevent any other person from disclosing, confidential communications between the client and his or her attorney. Such privilege protects communications between attorney and client that are made for the purpose of furnishing or obtaining professional legal advice or assistance. That privilege that permits an attorney to refuse to testify as to communications from the client. It belongs to the client, not the attorney, and hence only the client may waive it. In federal courts, state law is applied with respect to such privilege.

Avulsion: The immediate and noticeable addition to land caused by its removal from the property of another, by a sudden change in a water bed or in the course of a stream.

Bad faith: The fraudulent deception of another person; the intentional or malicious refusal to perform some duty or contractual obligation.

Banc: *[French, Bench.]* The location where a court customarily or permanently sits.

Battery: At common law, an intentional unpermitted act causing harmful or offensive contact with the "person" of another.

Bench trial: A trial conducted before a judge presiding without a jury.

Beneficial interest: Profits or advantages from property derived from the terms of a trust agreement.

Bequest: A gift of PERSONAL PROPERTY, such as money, stock, bonds, or jewelry, owned by a decedent at the time of death which is directed by the provisions of the decedent's will; a legacy.

Best evidence: An original document or object offered as proof of a fact in a lawsuit as opposed to a photocopy of, or other substitute for, the item or the testimony of a witness describing it.

Beyond a reasonable doubt: The standard that must be met by the prosecution's evidence in a criminal prosecution

Bilateral contract: An agreement formed by an exchange of a promise in which the promise of one party is consideration supporting the promise of the other party.

Bill of lading: A document signed by a carrier (a transporter of goods) or the carrier's representative and issued to a consignor (the shipper of goods) that evidences the receipt of goods for shipment to a specified designation and person.

Bona fide: *[Latin, In good faith.]* Honest; genuine; actual; authentic; acting without the intention of defrauding.

Burglary: The criminal offense of breaking and entering a building illegally for the purpose of committing a crime.

Business trust: An unincorporated business organization created by a legal document, a declaration of trust, and used in place of a corporation or partnership for the transaction of various kinds of business with limited liability.

Bylaws: The rules and regulations enacted by an association or a corporation to provide a framework for its operation and management.

Carriers: Individuals or businesses that are employed to deliver people or property to an agreed destination.

Case law: Legal principles enunciated and embodied in judicial decisions that are derived from the application of particular areas of law to the facts of individual cases.

Cause of action: The fact or combination of facts that gives a person the right to seek judicial redress or relief against another. Also, the legal theory forming the basis of a lawsuit.

Certiorari: *[Latin, To be informed of.]* At COMMON LAW, an original writ or order issued by the Chancery or King's Bench, commanding officers of inferior courts to submit the record of a cause pending before them to give the party more certain and speedy justice.

Cession: The act of relinquishing one's right.

Chose: *[French, Thing.]* Chattel; item of PERSONAL PROPERTY.

Circuit court: A specific tribunal that possesses the legal authority to hear cases within its own geographical territory.

Civil action: A lawsuit brought to enforce, redress, or protect rights of private litigants—the plaintiffs and the defendants—not a criminal proceeding.

Civil procedure: The methods, procedures, and practices used in civil cases.

Claim for relief: The section of a modern complaint that states the redress sought from a court by a person who initiates a lawsuit.

Class action: A lawsuit that allows a large number of people with a common interest in a matter to sue or be sued as a group.

Closing argument: The final factual and legal argument made by each attorney on all sides of a case in a trial prior to a verdict or judgment.

Codicil: A document that is executed by a person who had previously made his or her will, to modify, delete, qualify, or revoke provisions contained in it.

Collateral: Related; indirect; not bearing immediately upon an issue. The property pledged or given as a security interest, or a guarantee for payment of a debt, that will be taken or kept by the creditor in case of a default on the original debt.

Collateral estoppel: A doctrine by which an earlier decision rendered by a court in a lawsuit between parties is conclusive as to the issues or controverted points so that they cannot be relitigated in subsequent proceedings involving the same parties.

Collective bargaining agreement: The contractual agreement between an employer and a LABOR UNION that governs wages, hours, and working conditions for employees and which can be enforced against both the employer and the union for failure to comply with its terms. Such an agreement is ordinarily reached following the process of COLLECTIVE BARGAINING. A high profile example of such bargaining happens in the world of professional BASEBALL.

Comity: Courtesy; respect; a disposition to perform some official act out of goodwill and tradition rather than obligation or law. The acceptance or ADOPTION of decisions or laws by a court of another jurisdiction, either foreign or domestic, based on public policy rather than legal mandate.

Commerce clause: The provision of the U.S. Constitution that gives Congress exclusive power over trade activities among the states and with foreign countries and Indian tribes.

Common carrier: An individual or business that advertises to the public that it is available for hire to transport people or property in exchange for a fee.

Common law: The ancient law of England based upon societal customs and recognized and enforced by the judgments and decrees of the courts. The general body of statutes and case law that governed England and the American colonies prior to the American Revolution.

Common pleas: Trial-level courts of general jurisdiction. One of the royal common-law courts in England existing since the beginning of the thirteenth century and developing from the Curia Regis, or the King's Court.

Common stock: Evidence of participation in the ownership of a corporation that takes the form of printed certificates.

Compensatory damages: A sum of money awarded in a civil action by a court to indemnify a person for the particular loss, detriment, or injury suffered as a result of the unlawful conduct of another.

Compound interest: Interest generated by the sum of the principal and any accrued interest.

Court administrator: An officer of the judicial system who performs administrative and clerical duties essential to the proper operation of the business of a court, such as tracking trial dates, keeping records, entering judgments, and issuing process.

Court of appeal: An intermediate federal judicial tribunal of review that is found in thirteen judicial districts, called circuits, in the United States.

Court of claims: A state judicial tribunal established as the forum in which to bring certain types of lawsuits against the state or its political subdivisions, such as a county. The former designation given to a federal tribunal created in 1855 by Congress with original jurisdiction—initial authority—to decide an action brought against the United States that is based upon the Constitution, federal law, any regulation of the executive department, or any express or implied contracts with the federal government.

Comptroller: An officer who conducts the fiscal affairs of a state or MUNICIPAL CORPORATION.

Conciliation: The process of adjusting or settling disputes in a friendly manner through extrajudicial means. Conciliation means bringing two opposing sides together to reach a compromise in an attempt to avoid taking a case to trial. ARBITRATION, in contrast, is a contractual remedy used to settle disputes out of court. In arbitration the two parties in controversy agree in advance to abide by the decision made by a third party called in as a mediator, whereas conciliation is less structured.

Congressional record: A daily publication of the federal government that details the legislative proceedings of Congress.

Constitutional law: The written text of the state and federal constitutions. The body of judicial precedent that has gradually developed through a process in which courts interpret, apply, and explain the meaning of particular constitutional provisions and principles during a legal proceeding. Executive, legislative, and judicial actions that conform with the norms prescribed by a constitutional provision.

Consumer credit: Short-term loans made to enable people to purchase goods or services primarily for personal, family, or household purposes.

Consumer protection: Consumer protection laws are federal and state statutes governing sales and credit practices involving consumer goods. Such statutes prohibit and regulate deceptive or UNCONSCIONABLE advertising and sales practices, product quality, credit financing and reporting, debt collection, leases, and other aspects of consumer transactions.

Corpus: *[Latin, Body, aggregate, or mass.]*

Correlative: Having a reciprocal relationship in that the existence of one relationship normally implies the existence of the other.

Criminal action: The procedure by which a person accused of committing a crime is charged, brought to trial, and judged.

Criminal law: A body of rules and statutes that defines conduct prohibited by the government because it threatens and harms public safety and welfare and that establishes punishment to be imposed for the commission of such acts.

Criminal procedure: The framework of laws and rules that govern the administration of justice in cases involving an individual who has been accused of a crime, beginning with the initial investigation of the crime and concluding either with the unconditional release of the accused by virtue of acquittal (a judgment of not guilty) or by the imposition of a term of punishment pursuant to a conviction for the crime.

Cruel and unusual punishment: Such punishment as would amount to torture or barbarity, any cruel and degrading punishment not known to the COMMON LAW, or any fine, penalty, confinement, or treatment that is so disproportionate to the offense as to shock the moral sense of the community.

Custodial interrogation: Questioning initiated by law enforcement officers after a person is taken into custody or otherwise deprived of his or her freedom in any significant way, thus requiring that the person be advised of his or her applicable constitutional rights.

Declaratory judgment: Statutory remedy for the determination of a JUSTICIABLE controversy where the plaintiff is in doubt as to his or her legal rights. A binding adjudication of the rights and status of litigants even though no consequential relief is awarded.

Defamation: Any intentional false communication, either written or spoken, that harms a person's reputation; decreases the respect, regard, or confidence in which a person is held; or induces disparaging, hostile, or disagreeable opinions or feelings against a person.

Default judgment: Judgment entered against a party who has failed to defend against a claim that has been brought by another party. Under rules of CIVIL PROCEDURE, when a party against whom a judgment for affirmative relief is sought has failed to plead (i.e., answer) or otherwise defend, the party is in default and a judgment by default may be entered either by the clerk or the court.

Demonstrative evidence: Evidence other than testimony that is presented during the course of a civil or criminal trial. Demonstrative evidence includes actual evidence (e.g., a set of bloody gloves from a murder scene) and illustrative evidence (e.g., photographs and charts).

Dicta: Opinions of a judge that do not embody the resolution or determination of the specific case before the court. Expressions in a court's opinion that go beyond the facts before the court and therefore are individual views of the author of the opinion and not binding in subsequent cases as legal precedent. The plural of *dictum.*

Directed verdict: A procedural device whereby the decision in a case is taken out of the hands of the jury by the judge.

Disfranchisement: The removal of the rights and privileges inherent in an association with a group; the taking away of the rights of a free citizen, especially the right to vote. Sometimes called disenfranchisement.

Disposition: Act of disposing; transferring to the care or possession of another. The parting with, alienation of, or giving up of property. The final settlement of a matter and, with reference to decisions announced by a court, a judge's ruling is commonly referred to as disposition, regardless of level of resolution. In CRIMINAL PROCEDURE, the sentencing or other final settlement of a criminal case. With respect to a mental state, means an attitude, prevailing tendency, or inclination.

District court: A designation of an inferior state court that exercises general jurisdiction that it has been granted by the constitution or statute which created it. A U.S. judicial tribunal with original jurisdiction to try cases or controversies that fall within its limited jurisdiction.

Docket: A written list of judicial proceedings set down for trial in a court.

Doing business: A qualification imposed in state LONG-ARM STATUTES governing the SERVICE OF PROCESS, the method by which a lawsuit is commenced, which requires nonresident corporations to engage in commercial transactions within state borders in order to be subject to the PERSONAL JURISDICTION of state courts.

Double jeopardy: A second prosecution for the same offense after acquittal or conviction or multiple punishments for same offense. The evil sought to be avoided by prohibiting double jeopardy is double trial and double conviction, not necessarily double punishment.

Due process of law: A fundamental, constitutional guarantee that all legal proceedings will be fair and that one will be given notice of the proceedings and an opportunity to be heard before the government acts to take away one's life, liberty, or property. Also, a constitutional guarantee that a law shall not be unreasonable, ARBITRARY, or capricious.

Dummy: Sham; make-believe; pretended; imitation. Person who serves in place of another, or who serves until the proper person is named or available to take his place (e.g., dummy corporate directors; dummy owners of real estate).

Duress: Unlawful pressure exerted upon a person to coerce that person to perform an act that he or she ordinarily would not perform.

DWI: An abbreviation for *driving while intoxicated,* which is an offense committed by an individual who operates a motor vehicle while under the influence of alcohol or DRUGS AND NARCOTICS.

Eminent domain: The power to take private property for public use by a state, municipality, or private person or corporation authorized to exercise functions of public character, following the payment of just compensation to the owner of that property.

En banc: *[Latin, French. In the bench.]* Full bench. Refers to a session where the entire membership of the court will participate in the decision rather than the regular quorum. In other countries, it is common for a court to have more members than are usually necessary to hear an appeal. In the United States, the Circuit Courts of Appeal usually sit in panels of judges but for important cases may expand the bench to a larger number, when the judges are said to be sitting *en banc.* Similarly, only one of the judges of the U.S. TAX COURT will typically hear and decide on a tax controversy. However, when the issues involved are unusually novel or of wide impact, the case will be heard and decided by the full court sitting *en banc.*

Endowment: A transfer, generally as a gift, of money or property to an institution for a particular purpose. The bestowal of money as a permanent fund, the income of which is to be used for the benefit of a charity, college, or other institution.

Entity: A real being; existence. An organization or being that possesses separate existence for tax purposes. Examples would be corporations, partnerships, estates, and trusts. The accounting entity for which accounting statements are prepared may not be the same as the entity defined by law.

Entrapment: The act of government agents or officials that induces a person to commit a crime he or she is not previously disposed to commit.

Entry of judgment: Formally recording the result of a lawsuit that is based upon the determination by the court of the facts and applicable law, and that makes the result effective for purposes of bringing an action to enforce it or to commence an appeal.

Equal protection: The constitutional guarantee that no person or class of persons shall be denied the same protection of the laws that is enjoyed by other persons or other classes in like circumstances in their lives, liberty, property, and pursuit of happiness. The Declaration of Independence states.

Estoppel: A legal principle that bars a party from denying or alleging a certain fact owing to that party's previous conduct, allegation, or denial.

Et seq.: An abbreviation for the Latin *et sequentes* or *et sequentia,* meaning "and the following."

Excise: A tax imposed on the performance of an act, the engaging in an occupation, or the enjoyment of a privilege. A tax on the manufacture, sale, or use of goods or on the carrying on of an occupation or activity, or a tax on the transfer of property. In current usage the term has been extended to include various license fees and practically every internal revenue tax except the INCOME TAX (e.g., federal alcohol and tobacco excise taxes).

Exclusionary rule: The principle based on federal CONSTITUTIONAL LAW that evidence illegally seized by law enforcement officers in violation of a suspect's right to be free from unreasonable SEARCHES AND SEIZURES cannot be used against the suspect in a criminal prosecution.

Exoneration: The removal of a burden, charge, responsibility, duty, or blame imposed by law. The right of a party who is secondarily liable for a debt, such as a surety, to be reimbursed by the party with primary liability for payment of an obligation that should have been paid by the first party.

Extrajudicial: That which is done, given, or effected outside the course of regular judicial proceedings. Not founded upon, or unconnected with, the action of a court of law, as in extrajudicial evidence or an extrajudicial oath.

Extraordinary remedy: The designation given to such writs as HABEAS CORPUS, MANDAMUS, and QUO WARRANTO, determined in special proceedings and granted only where absolutely necessary to protect the legal rights of a party in a particular case, as opposed to the customary relief obtained by the maintenance of an action.

Extraterritoriality: The operation of laws upon persons existing beyond the limits of the enacting state or nation but who are still amenable to its laws. Jurisdiction exercised by a nation in other countries by treaty, or by its own ministers or consuls in foreign lands.

Fair market value: The amount for which real property or PERSONAL PROPERTY would be sold in a voluntary transaction between a buyer and seller, neither of whom is under any obligation to buy or sell.

False advertising: "Any advertising or promotion that misrepresents the nature, characteristics, qualities or geographic origin of goods, services or commercial activities" (LANHAM ACT, 15 U.S.C.A. § 1125(a)).

False pretenses: False representations of material past or present facts, known by the wrongdoer to be false, and made with the intent to defraud a victim into passing title in property to the wrongdoer.

Federal courts: The U.S. judicial tribunals created by Article III of the Constitution, or by Congress, to hear and determine JUSTICIABLE controversies.

Federal question: An issue directly involving the U.S. Constitution, federal statutes, or treaties between the United States and a foreign country.

Federal Register: A daily publication that makes available to the public the rules, regulations, and other legal notices issued by federal administrative agencies.

Felony: A serious crime, characterized under federal law and many state statutes as any offense punishable by death or imprisonment in excess of one year.

Fiduciary: An individual in whom another has placed the utmost trust and confidence to manage and protect property or money. The relationship wherein one person has an obligation to act for another's benefit.

Filibuster: A tactic used by a legislative representative to hinder and delay consideration of and action to be taken on a proposed bill through prolonged, irrelevant, and procrastinating speeches on the floor of the House, Senate, or other legislative body.

Final decision: The resolution of a controversy by a court or series of courts from which no appeal may be taken and that precludes further action. The last act by a lower court that is required for the completion of a lawsuit, such as the handing down of a final judgment upon which an appeal to a higher court may be brought.

Finance charge: The amount owed to a lender by a purchaser-debtor to be allowed to pay for goods purchased over a series of installments, as opposed to one lump sum at the time of the sale or billing.

First impression: The initial presentation to, or examination by, a court of a particular QUESTION OF LAW.

First instance: The initial trial court where an action is brought.

Fiscal: Relating to finance or financial matters, such as money, taxes, or public or private revenues.

Foreclosure: A procedure by which the holder of a mortgage—an interest in land providing security for the performance of a duty or the payment of a debt—sells the property upon the failure of the debtor to pay the mortgage debt and, thereby, terminates his or her rights in the property.

Forensic: Belonging to courts of justice.

Forfeiture: The involuntary relinquishment of money or property without compensation as a consequence of a breach or nonperformance of some legal obligation or the commission of a crime. The loss of a corporate charter or franchise as a result of illegality, malfeasance, or NONFEASANCE. The surrender by an owner of his or her entire interest in real property, mandated by law as a punishment for illegal conduct or NEGLIGENCE. Under old ENGLISH LAW, the release of land by a tenant to the tenant's lord due to some breach of conduct, or the loss of goods or chattels (articles of PERSONAL PROPERTY) assessed as a penalty against the perpetrator of some crime or offense and as a recompense to the injured party.

Forthwith: Immediately; promptly; without delay; directly; within a reasonable time under the circumstances of the case.

Fraud: A false representation of a matter of fact—whether by words or by conduct, by false or misleading allegations, or by concealment of what should have been disclosed—that deceives and is intended to deceive another so that the individual will act upon it to her or his legal injury.

Fraudulent: The description of a willful act commenced with the SPECIFIC INTENT to deceive or cheat, in order to cause some financial detriment to another and to engender personal financial gain.

Freedom of speech: The right, guaranteed by the FIRST AMENDMENT to the U.S. Constitution, to express beliefs and ideas without unwarranted government restriction.

Friend of the court: A person who has a strong interest in a matter that is the subject of a lawsuit in which he or she is not a party.

Fruit of the poisonous tree: The principle that prohibits the use of secondary evidence in trial that was culled directly from primary evidence derived from an illegal SEARCH AND SEIZURE.

General jurisdiction: The legal authority of a court to entertain whatever type of case comes up within the geographical area over which its power extends.

General verdict: A decision by a jury that determines which side in a particular controversy wins, and in some cases, the amount of money in damages to be awarded.

General welfare: The concern of the government for the health, peace, morality, and safety of its citizens.

Genetic engineering: The human manipulation of the genetic material of a cell.

Good cause: Legally adequate or substantial grounds or reason to take a certain action.

Good faith: Honesty; a sincere intention to deal fairly with others.

Grand jury: A panel of citizens that is convened by a court to decide whether it is appropriate for the government to indict (proceed with a prosecution against) someone suspected of a crime.

Grand larceny: A category of larceny—the offense of illegally taking the property of another—in which the value of the property taken is greater than that set for petit larceny.

Gross negligence: An indifference to, and a blatant violation of, a legal duty with respect to the rights of others.

Guardian: A person lawfully invested with the power, and charged with the obligation, of taking care of and managing the property and rights of a person who, because of age, understanding, or self-control, is considered incapable of administering his or her own affairs.

Habeas corpus: *[Latin, You have the body.]* A writ (court order) that commands an individual or a government official who has restrained another to produce the prisoner at a designated time and place so that the court can determine the legality of custody and decide whether to order the prisoner's release.

Hearsay: A statement made out of court that is offered in court as evidence to prove the truth of the matter asserted.

Hot pursuit: A doctrine that provides that the police may enter the premises where they suspect a crime has been committed without a warrant when delay would endanger their lives or the lives of others and lead to the escape of the alleged perpetrator; also sometimes called fresh pursuit.

Husband and wife: A man and woman who are legally married to one another and are thereby given by law specific rights and duties resulting from that relationship.

Imputed: Attributed vicariously.

Incorporation doctrine: A constitutional doctrine whereby selected provisions of the BILL OF RIGHTS are made applicable to the states through the DUE PROCESS CLAUSE of the FOURTEENTH AMENDMENT.

Indicia: Signs; indications. Circumstances that point to the existence of a given fact as probable, but not certain. For example, *indicia of partnership* are any circumstances which would induce the belief that a given person was in reality, though not technically, a member of a given firm.

Individual retirement account: A means by which an individual can receive certain federal tax advantages while investing for retirement.

Interlocutory: Provisional; interim; temporary; not final; that which intervenes between the beginning and the end of a lawsuit or proceeding to either decide a particular point or matter that is not the final issue of the entire controversy or prevent irreparable harm during the pendency of the lawsuit.

Interrogatories: Written questions submitted to a party from his or her adversary to ascertain answers that are prepared in writing and signed under oath and that have relevance to the issues in a lawsuit.

Intervenor: An individual who is not already a party to an existing lawsuit but who makes himself or herself a party either by joining with the plaintiff or uniting with the defendant in resistance of the plaintiff's claims.

Involuntary manslaughter: The act of unlawfully killing another human being unintentionally.

Irreparable injury: Any harm or loss that is not easily repaired, restored, or compensated by monetary damages. A serious wrong, generally of a repeated and continuing nature, that has an equitable remedy of injunctive relief.

Irrevocable: Unable to cancel or recall; that which is unalterable or irreversible.

Issue preclusion: A concept that refers to the fact that a particular QUESTION OF FACT or law, one that has already been fully litigated by the parties in an action for which there has been a judgment on the merits, cannot be relitigated in any future action involving the same parties or their privies (persons who would be bound by the judgment rendered for the party).

Jeopardy: Danger; hazard; peril. In a criminal action, the danger of conviction and punishment confronting the defendant.

Joint venture: An association of two or more individuals or companies engaged in a solitary business enterprise for profit without actual partnership or incorporation; also called a joint adventure.

Judicial administration: The practices, procedures, and offices that deal with the management of the administrative systems of the courts.

Judicial review: A court's authority to examine an executive or legislative act and to invalidate that act if it is contrary to constitutional principles.

Juris doctor: The degree awarded to an individual upon the successful completion of law school.

Jurisprudence: From the Latin term *juris prudentia,* which means "the study, knowledge, or science of law"; in the United States, more broadly associated with the philosophy of law.

Just compensation: Equitable remuneration to the owner of private property that is expropriated for public use through condemnation, the implementation of the governmental power of EMINENT DOMAIN.

Justice of the peace: A judicial officer with limited power whose duties may include hearing cases that involve civil controversies, conserving the peace, performing judicial acts, hearing minor criminal complaints, and committing offenders.

Larceny: The unauthorized taking and removal of the PERSONAL PROPERTY of another by an individual who intends to permanently deprive the owner of it; a crime against the right of possession.

Law of nations: The body of customary rules that determine the rights and that regulate the intercourse of independent countries in peace and war.

Ledger: The principal book of accounts of a business enterprise in which all the daily transactions are entered under appropriate headings to reflect the debits and credits of each account.

Legal proceedings: All actions that are authorized or sanctioned by law and instituted in a court or a tribunal for the acquisition of rights or the enforcement of remedies.

Legal tender: All U.S. coins and currencies—regardless of when coined or issued—including (in terms of the FEDERAL RESERVE System) Federal Reserve notes and circulating notes of Federal Reserve banks and national banking associations that are used for all debts, public and private, public charges, taxes, duties, and dues.

Libelous: In the nature of a written DEFAMATION, a communication that tends to injure reputation.

Lien: A right given to another by the owner of property to secure a debt, or one created by law in favor of certain creditors.

Liquidate: To pay and settle the amount of a debt; to convert assets to cash; to aggregate the assets of an insolvent enterprise and calculate its liabilities in order to settle with the debtors and the creditors and apportion the remaining assets, if any, among the stockholders or owners of the corporation.

Liquidation: The collection of assets belonging to a debtor to be applied to the discharge of his or her outstanding debts.

Magistrate: Any individual who has the power of a public civil officer or inferior judicial officer, such as a JUSTICE OF THE PEACE.

Mail fraud: A crime in which the perpetrator develops a scheme using the mails to defraud another of money or property. This crime specifically requires the intent to defraud, and is a federal offense governed by section 1341 of title 18 of the U.S. Code. The mail fraud statute was first enacted in 1872 to prohibit illicit mailings with the Postal Service (formerly the Post Office) for the purpose of executing a fraudulent scheme.

Malfeasance: The commission of an act that is unequivocally illegal or completely wrongful.

Mandamus: *[Latin, We comand.]* A writ or order that is issued from a court of superior jurisdiction that commands an inferior tribunal, corporation, MUNICIPAL CORPORATION, or individual to perform, or refrain from performing, a particular act, the performance or omission of which is required by law as an obligation.

Market value: The highest price a willing buyer would pay and a willing seller would accept, both being fully informed, and the property being exposed for sale for a reasonable period of time. The market value may be different from the price a property can actually be sold for at a given time (market price). The market value of an article or piece of property is the price that it might be expected to bring if offered for sale in a fair market; not the price that might be obtained on a sale at public auction or a sale forced by the necessities of the owner, but such a price as would be fixed by negotiation and mutual agreement, after ample time to find a purchaser, as between a vendor who is willing (but not compelled) to sell and a purchaser who desires to buy but is not compelled to take the particular article or piece of property.

Mediation: A settlement of a dispute or controversy by setting up an independent person between two contending parties in order to aid them in the settlement of their disagreement.

Medicaid: A joint federal-state program that provides HEALTH CARE insurance to low-income persons.

Mental anguish: When connected with a physical injury, includes both the resultant mental sensation of pain and also the accompanying feelings of distress, fright, and anxiety. As an element of damages implies a relatively high degree of mental pain and distress; it is more than mere disappointment, anger, worry, resentment, or embarrassment, although it may include all of these, and it includes mental sensation of pain resulting from such painful emotions as grief, severe disappointment, indignation, wounded pride, shame, despair, and/or public humiliation. In other connections, and as a ground for DIVORCE or for compensable damages or an element of damages, it includes the mental suffering resulting from the excitation of the more poignant and painful emotions, such as grief, severe disappointment, indignation, wounded pride, shame, public humiliation, despair, etc.

Merit system: System used by federal and state governments for hiring and promoting governmental employees to civil service positions on the basis of competence.

Ministerial: Done under the direction of a supervisor; not involving discretion or policymaking.

Miscegenation: Mixture of races. A term formerly applied to marriage between persons of different races. Statutes prohibiting marriage between persons of different races have been held to be invalid as contrary to the EQUAL PROTECTION CLAUSE of the Constitution.

Misdemeanor: Offenses lower than felonies and generally those punishable by fine, penalty, FORFEITURE, or imprisonment other than in a penitentiary. Under federal law, and most state laws, any offense other than a felony is classified as a misdemeanor. Certain states also have various classes of misdemeanors (e.g., Class A, B, etc.).

Mitigating circumstances: Circumstances that may be considered by a court in determining culpability of a defendant or the extent of damages to be awarded to a plaintiff. Mitigating circumstances do not justify or excuse an offense but may reduce the severity of a charge. Similarly, a recognition of mitigating circumstances to reduce a damage award does not imply that the damages were not suffered but that they have been partially ameliorated.

Money laundering: The process of taking the proceeds of criminal activity and making them appear legal.

Monopoly: An economic advantage held by one or more persons or companies deriving from the exclusive power to carry on a particular business or trade or to manufacture and sell a particular item, thereby suppressing competition and allowing such persons or companies to raise the price of a product or service substantially above the price that would be established by a free market.

Mutual fund: A fund, in the form of an investment company, in which shareholders combine their money to invest in a variety of stocks, bonds, and money-market investments such as U.S. Treasury bills and bank certificates of deposit.

Of counsel: A term commonly applied in the PRACTICE OF LAW to an attorney who has been employed to aid in the preparation and management of a particular case but who is not the principal attorney in the action.

Of record: Entered on the appropriate official documents maintained by a governmental body and that are usually available for inspection by the public.

Omnibus: *[Latin, For all; containing two or more independent matters.]* A term frequently used in reference to a legislative bill comprised of two or more general subjects that is designed to compel the executive to approve provisions that he or she would otherwise reject but that he or she signs into law to prevent the defeat of the entire bill.

Open court: Common law requires a trial in open court; "open court" means a court to which the public has a right to be admitted. This term may mean either a court that has been formally convened and declared open for the transaction of its proper judicial business or a court that is freely open to spectators.

Ordinance: A law, statute, or regulation enacted by a MUNICIPAL CORPORATION.

Original jurisdiction: The authority of a tribunal to entertain a lawsuit, try it, and set forth a judgment on the law and facts.

Penny stocks: Inexpensive issues of stock, typically selling at less than $1 a share, in companies that often are newly formed or involved in highly speculative ventures.

Penology: The science of prison administration and rehabilitation of criminals.

Pension: A benefit, usually money, paid regularly to retired employees or their survivors by private businesses and federal, state, and local governments. Employers are not required to establish pension benefits but do so to attract qualified employees.

Per curiam: *[Latin, By the court.]* A phrase used to distinguish an opinion of the whole court from an opinion written by any one judge.

Personal jurisdiction: The power of a court to hear and determine a lawsuit involving a defendant by virtue of the defendant's having some contact with the place where the court is located.

Plurality: The opinion of an appellate court in which more justices join than in any concurring opinion.

Ponzi scheme: A fraudulent investment plan in which the investments of later investors are used to pay earlier investors, giving the appearance that the investments of the initial participants dramatically increase in value in a short amount of time.

Positive law: Those laws that have been duly enacted by a properly instituted and popularly recognized branch of government.

Power of sale: A clause commonly inserted in a mortgage and deed of trust that grants the creditor or trustee the right and authority, upon default in the payment of the debt, to advertise and sell the property at public auction, without resorting to a court for authorization to do so.

Prayer: The request contained in a bill in EQUITY that the court will grant the process, aid, or relief that the complainant desires.

Preemption: A doctrine based on the SUPREMACY CLAUSE of the U.S. Constitution that holds that certain matters are of such a national, as opposed to local, character that federal laws preempt or take precedence over state laws. As such, a state may not pass a law inconsistent with the federal law.

Preliminary hearing: A proceeding before a judicial officer in which the officer must decide whether a crime was committed, whether the crime occurred within the territorial jurisdiction of the court, and whether there is PROBABLE CAUSE to believe that the defendant committed the crime.

Preliminary injunction: A temporary order made by a court at the request of one party that prevents the other party from pursuing a particular course of conduct until the conclusion of a trial on the merits.

Preponderance of evidence: A standard of proof that must be met by a plaintiff if he or she is to win a civil action.

Prevailing party: The litigant who successfully brings or defends an action and, as a result, receives a favorable judgment or verdict.

Price-fixing: The organized setting of what the public will be charged for certain products or services agreed to by competitors in the marketplace in violation of the SHERMAN ANTI-TRUST ACT (15 U.S.C.A. § 1 et seq.).

Privileges and immunities: Concepts contained in the U.S. Constitution that place the citizens of each state on an equal basis with citizens of other states in respect to advantages resulting from citizenship in those states and citizenship in the United States.

Pro se: For one's own behalf; in person. Appearing for oneself, as in the case of one who does not retain a lawyer and appears for himself or herself in court.

Pro tem: *[Latin, For the time being.]* An abbreviation used for *pro tempore,* Latin for "temporary or provisional."

Probable cause: Apparent facts discovered through logical inquiry that would lead a reasonably intelligent and prudent person to believe that an accused person has committed a crime, thereby warranting his or her prosecution, or that a CAUSE OF ACTION has accrued, justifying a civil lawsuit.

Probate: The court process by which a will is proved valid or invalid. The legal process wherein the estate of a decedent is administered.

Proctor: A person appointed to manage the affairs of another or to represent another in a judgment.

Product liability: The responsibility of a manufacturer or vendor of goods to compensate for injury caused by defective merchandise that it has provided for sale.

Profanity: Irreverence towards sacred things; particularly, an irreverent or blasphemous use of the name of God. Vulgar, irreverent, or coarse language.

Protective order: A court order, direction, decree, or command to protect a person from further harassment, SERVICE OF PROCESS, or discovery.

Proximate cause: An act from which an injury results as a natural, direct, uninterrupted consequence and without which the injury would not have occurred.

Public figure: A description applied in LIBEL AND SLANDER actions, as well as in those alleging invasion of privacy, to anyone who has gained prominence in the community as a result of his or her name or exploits, whether willingly or unwillingly.

Public offering: An issue of SECURITIES offered for sale to the public.

Public policy: A principle that no person or government official can legally perform an act that tends to injure the public.

Punitive damages: Monetary compensation awarded to an injured party that goes beyond that which is necessary to compensate the individual for losses and that is intended to punish the wrongdoer.

Purview: The part of a statute or a law that delineates its purpose and scope.

Qui tam actions: Civil actions maintained by private persons on behalf of both themselves and the government to recover damages or to enforce penalties available under a statute prohibiting specified conduct. The term *qui tam* is short for the Latin *qui tam pro domino rege quam pro se ipso in hac parte sequitur*, which means "who brings the action for the king as well as for himself."

Ratification: The confirmation or adoption of an act that has already been performed.

Rational basis test: A judicial standard of review that examines whether a legislature had a reasonable and not an ARBITRARY basis for enacting a particular statute.

Reasonable person: A phrase frequently used in TORT and CRIMINAL LAW to denote a hypothetical person in society who exercises average care, skill, and judgment in conduct and who serves as a comparative standard for determining liability.

Rebuttable presumption: A conclusion as to the existence or nonexistence of a fact that a judge or jury must draw when certain evidence has been introduced and admitted as true in a lawsuit but that can be contradicted by evidence to the contrary.

Receiver: An archaic term, used in common law and CIVIL LAW countries, to designate an individual who holds and conceals stolen goods for thieves. Currently an independent individual appointed by a court to handle money or property during a lawsuit.

Recidivism: The behavior of a repeat or habitual criminal. A measurement of the rate at which offenders commit other crimes, either by arrest or conviction baselines, after being released from incarceration.

Redress: Compensation for injuries sustained; recovery or restitution for harm or injury; damages or equitable relief. Access to the courts to gain REPARATION for a wrong.

Reformation: A remedy utilized by the courts to correct a written instrument so that it conforms to the ORIGINAL INTENT of the parties to such an instrument.

Reparation: Compensation for an injury; redress for a wrong inflicted.

Repeal: The ANNULMENT or abrogation of a previously existing statute by the enactment of a later law that revokes the former law.

Res judicata: *[Latin, A thing adjudged.]* A rule that a final judgment on the merits by a court having jurisdiction is conclusive between the parties to a suit as to all matters that were litigated or that could have been litigated in that suit.

Rescission: The abrogation of a contract, effective from its inception, thereby restoring the parties to the positions they would have occupied if no contract had ever been formed.

Respondent: In EQUITY practice, the party who answers a bill or other proceeding in equity. The party against whom an appeal or motion, an application for a court order, is instituted and who is required to answer in order to protect his or her interests.

Restitution: In the context of CRIMINAL LAW, state programs under which an offender is required, as a condition of his or her sentence, to repay money or donate services to the victim or society; with respect to maritime law, the restoration of articles lost by jettison, done when the remainder of the cargo has been saved, at the general charge of the owners of the cargo; in the law of TORTS, or civil wrongs, a measure of damages; in regard to contract law, the restoration of a party injured by a breach of contract to the position that party occupied before she or he entered the contract.

Rider: A schedule or writing annexed to a document such as a legislative bill or insurance policy.

Right of action: The privilege of instituting a lawsuit arising from a particular transaction or state of facts, such as a suit that is based on a contract or a TORT, a civil wrong.

Ripeness: The mandate contained in Article III of the Constitution that requires an appellate court to consider whether a case has matured into a controversy worthy of adjudication before it can hear the case.

Robbery: The taking of money or goods in the possession of another, from his or her person or immediate presence, by force or intimidation.

Rule of law: Rule according to law; rule under law; or rule according to a higher law.

Scienter: *[Latin, Knowingly.]* Guilty knowledge that is sufficient to charge a person with the consequences of his or her acts.

Search and seizure: A hunt by law enforcement officials for property or communications believed to be evidence of crime, and the act of taking possession of this property.

Self-dealing: The conduct of a trustee, an attorney, or other fiduciary that consists of taking advantage of his or her position in a transaction and acting for his or her own interests rather than for the interests of the beneficiaries of the trust or the interests of his or her clients.

Sodomy: Anal or oral intercourse between human beings, or any sexual relations between a human being and an animal, the act of which may be punishable as a criminal offense.

Solicitation: Urgent request, plea, or entreaty; enticing, asking. The criminal offense of urging someone to commit an unlawful act.

Solicitor general: An officer of the U.S. DEPARTMENT OF JUSTICE who represents the U.S. government in cases before the U.S. Supreme Court.

Sovereign immunity: The legal protection that prevents a sovereign state or person from being sued without consent.

Split decision: A decision by an appellate court that is not unanimous.

State action: A requirement for claims that arise under the DUE PROCESS CLAUSE of the FOURTEENTH AMENDMENT and CIVIL RIGHTS legislation, for which a private citizen seeks relief in the form of damages or redress based on an improper intrusion by the government into his or her private life.

State interest: A broad term for any matter of public concern that is addressed by a government in law or policy.

Statute: An act of a legislature that declares, proscribes, or commands something; a specific law, expressed in writing.

Statute of limitations: A type of federal or state law that restricts the time within which legal proceedings may be brought.

Statutory: Created, defined, or relating to a statute; required by statute; conforming to a statute.

Statutory rape: Sexual intercourse by an adult with a person below a statutorily designated age.

Strict liability: Absolute legal responsibility for an injury that can be imposed on the wrongdoer without proof of carelessness or fault.

Strict scrutiny: A standard of JUDICIAL REVIEW for a challenged policy in which the court presumes the policy to be invalid unless the government can demonstrate a compelling interest to justify the policy.

Subject matter jurisdiction: The power of a court to hear and determine cases of the general class to which the proceedings in question belong.

Substantive law: The part of the law that creates, defines, and regulates rights, including, for example, the law of contracts, TORTS, wills, and real property; the essential substance of rights under law.

Summary judgment: A procedural device used during civil litigation to promptly and expeditiously dispose of a case without a trial. It is used when there is no dispute as to the material facts of the case and a party is entitled to judgment as a MATTER OF LAW.

Suspended sentence: A sentence given after the formal conviction of a crime that the convicted person is not required to serve.

Taxable income: Under the federal tax law, gross income reduced by adjustments and allowable deductions. It is the income against which tax rates are applied to compute an individual or entity's tax liability. The essence of taxable income is the accrual of some gain, profit, or benefit to a taxpayer.

Term of art: A word or phrase that has special meaning in a particular context.

Testament: Another name for a will.

Third party: A generic legal term for any individual who does not have a direct connection with a legal transaction but who might be affected by it.

Tort law: A body of rights, obligations, and remedies that is applied by courts in civil proceedings to provide relief for persons who have suffered harm from the wrongful acts of others. The person who sustains injury or suffers pecuniary damage as the result of tortious conduct is known as the plaintiff, and the person who is responsible for inflicting the injury and incurs liability for the damage is known as the defendant or tortfeasor.

Tribunal: A general term for a court, or the seat of a judge.

Trustee: An individual or corporation named by an individual, who sets aside property to be used for the benefit of another person, to manage the property as provided by the terms of the document that created the arrangement.

U.S. Code: A multivolume publication of the text of statutes enacted by Congress.

Unconscionable: Unusually harsh and shocking to the conscience; that which is so grossly unfair that a court will proscribe it.

Use tax: A charge imposed on the use or possession of PERSONAL PROPERTY.

Venue: A place, such as the territory from which residents are selected to serve as jurors.

Vicarious liability: The TORT doctrine that imposes responsibility upon one person for the failure of another, with whom the person has a special relationship (such as PARENT AND CHILD, employer and employee, or owner of vehicle and driver), to exercise such care as a reasonably prudent person would use under similar circumstances.

Without prejudice: Without any loss or waiver of rights or privileges.

Writ: An order issued by a court requiring that something be done or giving authority to do a specified act.

Wrongful death: The taking of the life of an individual resulting from the willful or negligent act of another person or persons.

Wrongful discharge: An at-will employee's CAUSE OF ACTION against his former employer, alleging that his discharge was in violation of state or federal antidiscrimination statutes, public policy, an implied contract, or an implied COVENANT of GOOD FAITH and fair dealing.

A.	Atlantic Reporter	ACS	Agricultural Cooperative Service
A. 2d	Atlantic Reporter, Second Series	ACT	American College Test
AA	Alcoholics Anonymous	Act'g Legal Adv.	Acting Legal Advisor
AAA	American Arbitration Association; Agricultural Adjustment Act of 1933	ACUS	Administrative Conference of the United States
AALS	Association of American Law Schools	ACYF	Administration on Children, Youth, and Families
AAPRP	All African People's Revolutionary Party	A.D. 2d	Appellate Division, Second Series, N.Y.
AARP	American Association of Retired Persons	ADA	Americans with Disabilities Act of 1990
AAS	American Anti-Slavery Society	ADAMHA	Alcohol, Drug Abuse, and Mental Health Administration
ABA	American Bar Association; Architectural Barriers Act of 1968; American Bankers Association	ADC	Aid to Dependent Children
		ADD	Administration on Developmental Disabilities
ABC	American Broadcasting Companies, Inc. (formerly American Broadcasting Corporation)	ADEA	Age Discrimination in Employment Act of 1967
		ADL	Anti-Defamation League
		ADR	Alternative dispute resolution
		AEC	Atomic Energy Commission
ABM	Antiballistic missile	AECB	Arms Export Control Board
ABM Treaty	Anti-Ballistic Missile Treaty of 1972	AEDPA	Antiterrorism and Effective Death Penalty Act
ABVP	Anti-Biased Violence Project	A.E.R.	All England Law Reports
A/C	Account	AFA	American Family Association; Alabama Freethought Association
A.C.	Appeal cases		
ACAA	Air Carrier Access Act		
ACCA	Armed Career Criminal Act of 1984	AFB	American Farm Bureau
		AFBF	American Farm Bureau Federation
ACF	Administration for Children and Families	AFDC	Aid to Families with Dependent Children
ACLU	American Civil Liberties Union	aff'd per cur.	Affirmed by the court
ACRS	Accelerated Cost Recovery System	AFIS	Automated fingerprint identification system

AFL	American Federation of Labor	ANA	Administration for Native Americans
AFL-CIO	American Federation of Labor and Congress of Industrial Organizations	Ann. Dig.	Annual Digest of Public International Law Cases
AFRes	Air Force Reserve	ANRA	American Newspaper Publishers Association
AFSC	American Friends Service Committee	ANSCA	Alaska Native Claims Act
AFSCME	American Federation of State, County, and Municipal Employees	ANZUS	Australia-New Zealand-United States Security Treaty Organization
AGRICOLA	Agricultural Online Access	AOA	Administration on Aging
AIA	Association of Insurance Attorneys	AOE	Arizonans for Official English
		AOL	America Online
AIB	American Institute for Banking	AP	Associated Press
		APA	Administrative Procedure Act of 1946
AID	Artificial insemination using a third-party donor's sperm; Agency for International Development	APHIS	Animal and Plant Health Inspection Service
		App. Div.	Appellate Division Reports, N.Y. Supreme Court
AIDS	Acquired immune deficiency syndrome	Arb. Trib., U.S.-British	Arbitration Tribunal, Claim Convention of 1853, United States and Great Britain Convention of 1853
AIH	Artificial insemination using the husband's sperm		
AIM	American Indian Movement	Ardcor	American Roller Die Corporation
AIPAC	American Israel Public Affairs Committee	ARPA	Advanced Research Projects Agency
AIUSA	Amnesty International, U.S.A. Affiliate	ARPANET	Advanced Research Projects Agency Network
AJS	American Judicature Society	ARS	Advanced Record System
ALA	American Library Association		
Alcoa	Aluminum Company of America	Art.	Article
		ARU	American Railway Union
ALEC	American Legislative Exchange Council	ASCME	American Federation of State, County, and Municipal Employees
ALF	Animal Liberation Front		
ALI	American Law Institute	ASCS	Agriculture Stabilization and Conservation Service
ALJ	Administrative law judge		
All E.R.	All England Law Reports	ASM	Available Seatmile
ALO	Agency Liaison	ASPCA	American Society for the Prevention of Cruelty to Animals
A.L.R.	American Law Reports		
ALY	*American Law Yearbook*		
AMA	American Medical Association	Asst. Att. Gen.	Assistant Attorney General
		AT&T	American Telephone and Telegraph
AMAA	Agricultural Marketing Agreement Act	ATFD	Alcohol, Tobacco and Firearms Division
Am. Dec.	American Decisions		
amdt.	Amendment	ATLA	Association of Trial Lawyers of America
Amer. St. Papers, For. Rels.	American State Papers, Legislative and Executive Documents of the Congress of the U.S., Class I, Foreign Relations, 1832–1859	ATO	Alpha Tau Omega
		ATTD	Alcohol and Tobacco Tax Division
		ATU	Alcohol Tax Unit
		AUAM	American Union against Militarism
AMS	Agricultural Marketing Service	AUM	Animal Unit Month
AMVETS	American Veterans (of World War II)	AZT	Azidothymidine
		BAC	Blood alcohol concentration

BALSA	Black-American Law Student Association	CAB	Civil Aeronautics Board; Corporation for American Banking
BATF	Bureau of Alcohol, Tobacco and Firearms	CAFE	Corporate average fuel economy
BBS	Bulletin Board System	Cal. 2d	California Reports, Second Series
BCCI	Bank of Credit and Commerce International	Cal. 3d	California Reports, Third Series
BEA	Bureau of Economic Analysis		
Bell's Cr. C.	Bell's English Crown Cases	CALR	Computer-assisted legal research
Bevans	United States Treaties, etc. *Treaties and Other International Agreements of the United States of America, 1776–1949* (compiled under the direction of Charles I. Bevans, 1968–76)	Cal. Rptr.	California Reporter
		CAP	Common Agricultural Policy
		CARA	Classification and Ratings Administration
		CATV	Community antenna television
		CBO	Congressional Budget Office
BFOQ	Bona fide occupational qualification	CBS	Columbia Broadcasting System
BI	Bureau of Investigation	CBOEC	Chicago Board of Election Commissioners
BIA	Bureau of Indian Affairs; Board of Immigration Appeals	CCC	Commodity Credit Corporation
BID	Business improvement district	CCDBG	Child Care and Development Block Grant of 1990
BJS	Bureau of Justice Statistics	C.C.D. Pa.	Circuit Court Decisions, Pennsylvania
Black.	Black's United States Supreme Court Reports	C.C.D. Va.	Circuit Court Decisions, Virginia
Blatchf.	Blatchford's United States Circuit Court Reports	CCEA	Cabinet Council on Economic Affairs
BLM	Bureau of Land Management		
BLS	Bureau of Labor Statistics	CCP	Chinese Communist Party
BMD	Ballistic missile defense	CCR	Center for Constitutional Rights
BNA	Bureau of National Affairs		
BOCA	Building Officials and Code Administrators International	C.C.R.I.	Circuit Court, Rhode Island
		CD	Certificate of deposit; compact disc
BOP	Bureau of Prisons	CDA	Communications Decency Act
BPP	Black Panther Party for Self-defense	CDBG	Community Development Block Grant Program
Brit. and For.	British and Foreign State Papers	CDC	Centers for Disease Control and Prevention; Community Development Corporation
BSA	Boy Scouts of America		
BTP	Beta Theta Pi		
Burr.	James Burrows, *Report of Cases Argued and Determined in the Court of King's Bench during the Time of Lord Mansfield* (1766–1780)	CDF	Children's Defense Fund
		CDL	Citizens for Decency through Law
		CD-ROM	Compact disc read-only memory
BVA	Board of Veterans Appeals	CDS	Community Dispute Services
c.	Chapter		
C³I	Command, Control, Communications, and Intelligence	CDW	Collision damage waiver
		CENTO	Central Treaty Organization
		CEO	Chief executive officer
C.A.	Court of Appeals	CEQ	Council on Environmental Quality
CAA	Clean Air Act		

CERCLA	Comprehensive Environmental Response, Compensation, and Liability Act of 1980	CLASP	Center for Law and Social Policy
cert.	*Certiorari*	CLE	Center for Law and Education; Continuing Legal Education
CETA	Comprehensive Employment and Training Act	CLEO	Council on Legal Education Opportunity; Chief Law Enforcement Officer
C & F	Cost and freight		
CFC	Chlorofluorocarbon	CLP	Communist Labor Party of America
CFE Treaty	Conventional Forces in Europe Treaty of 1990	CLS	Christian Legal Society; critical legal studies (movement); Critical Legal Studies (membership organization)
C.F. & I.	Cost, freight, and insurance		
C.F.R	Code of Federal Regulations		
CFNP	Community Food and Nutrition Program		
CFTA	Canadian Free Trade Agreement	C.M.A.	Court of Military Appeals
		CMEA	Council for Mutual Economic Assistance
CFTC	Commodity Futures Trading Commission	CMHS	Center for Mental Health Services
Ch.	Chancery Division, English Law Reports	C.M.R.	Court of Military Review
CHAMPVA	Civilian Health and Medical Program at the Veterans Administration	CNN	Cable News Network
		CNO	Chief of Naval Operations
		CNOL	Consolidated net operating loss
CHEP	Cuban/Haitian Entrant Program		
		CNR	Chicago and Northwestern Railway
CHINS	Children in need of supervision		
		CO	Conscientious Objector
CHIPS	Child in need of protective services	C.O.D.	Cash on delivery
		COGP	Commission on Government Procurement
Ch.N.Y.	Chancery Reports, New York		
Chr. Rob.	Christopher Robinson, *Reports of Cases Argued and Determined in the High Court of Admiralty* (1801–1808)	COINTELPRO	Counterintelligence Program
		Coke Rep.	Coke's English King's Bench Reports
		COLA	Cost-of-living adjustment
		COMCEN	Federal Communications Center
CIA	Central Intelligence Agency		
CID	Commercial Item Descriptions	Comp.	Compilation
		Conn.	Connecticut Reports
C.I.F.	Cost, insurance, and freight	CONTU	National Commission on New Technological Uses of Copyrighted Works
CINCNORAD	Commander in Chief, North American Air Defense Command		
		Conv.	Convention
C.I.O.	Congress of Industrial Organizations	COPA	Child Online Protection Act (1998)
CIPE	Center for International Private Enterprise	COPS	Community Oriented Policing Services
C.J.	Chief justice	Corbin	Arthur L. Corbin, *Corbin on Contracts: A Comprehensive Treatise on the Rules of Contract Law* (1950)
CJIS	Criminal Justice Information Services		
C.J.S.	Corpus Juris Secundum		
Claims Arb. under Spec. Conv., Nielsen's Rept.	Frederick Kenelm Nielsen, *American and British Claims Arbitration under the Special Agreement Concluded between the United States and Great Britain, August 18, 1910* (1926)	CORE	Congress on Racial Equality
		Cox's Crim. Cases	Cox's Criminal Cases (England)
		COYOTE	Call Off Your Old Tired Ethics
		CPA	Certified public accountant
		CPB	Corporation for Public Broadcasting, the
		CPI	Consumer Price Index

CPPA	Child Pornography Prevention Act	DAR	Daughters of the American Revolution
CPSC	Consumer Product Safety Commission	DARPA	Defense Advanced Research Projects Agency
Cranch	Cranch's United States Supreme Court Reports	DAVA	Defense Audiovisual Agency
		D.C.	United States District Court; District of Columbia
CRF	Constitutional Rights Foundation		
CRR	Center for Constitutional Rights	D.C. Del.	United States District Court, Delaware
CRS	Congressional Research Service; Community Relations Service	D.C. Mass.	United States District Court, Massachusetts
		D.C. Md.	United States District Court, Maryland
CRT	Critical race theory		
CSA	Community Services Administration	D.C.N.D.Cal.	United States District Court, Northern District, California
CSAP	Center for Substance Abuse Prevention		
		D.C.N.Y.	United States District Court, New York
CSAT	Center for Substance Abuse Treatment	D.C.Pa.	United States District Court, Pennsylvania
CSC	Civil Service Commission		
CSCE	Conference on Security and Cooperation in Europe	DCS	Deputy Chiefs of Staff
		DCZ	District of the Canal Zone
		DDT	Dichlorodipheny ltricloroethane
CSG	Council of State Governments		
		DEA	Drug Enforcement Administration
CSO	Community Service Organization		
		Decl. Lond.	Declaration of London, February 26, 1909
CSP	Center for the Study of the Presidency		
		Dev. & B.	Devereux & Battle's North Carolina Reports
C-SPAN	Cable-Satellite Public Affairs Network		
		DFL	Minnesota Democratic-Farmer-Labor
CSRS	Cooperative State Research Service		
		DFTA	Department for the Aging
CSWPL	Center on Social Welfare Policy and Law	Dig. U.S. Practice in Intl. Law	Digest of U.S. Practice in International Law
CTA	*Cum testamento annexo* (with the will attached)		
		Dist. Ct.	D.C. United States District Court, District of Columbia
Ct. Ap. D.C.	Court of Appeals, District of Columbia		
Ct. App. No. Ireland	Court of Appeals, Northern Ireland	D.L.R.	Dominion Law Reports (Canada)
Ct. Cl.	Court of Claims, United States	DMCA	Digital Millennium Copyright Act
Ct. Crim. Apps.	Court of Criminal Appeals (England)	DNA	Deoxyribonucleic acid
		Dnase	Deoxyribonuclease
Ct. of Sess., Scot.	Court of Sessions, Scotland	DNC	Democratic National Committee
CTI	Consolidated taxable income		
CU	Credit union	DOC	Department of Commerce
CUNY	City University of New York	DOD	Department of Defense
Cush.	Cushing's Massachusetts Reports	DODEA	Department of Defense Education Activity
CWA	Civil Works Administration; Clean Water Act	Dodson	Dodson's Reports, English Admiralty Courts
		DOE	Department of Energy
DACORB	Department of the Army Conscientious Objector Review Board	DOER	Department of Employee Relations
		DOJ	Department of Justice
Dall.	Dallas's Pennsylvania and United States Reports	DOL	Department of Labor

DOMA	Defense of Marriage Act of 1996	ERISA	Employee Retirement Income Security Act of 1974
DOS	Disk operating system		
DOT	Department of Transportation	ERS	Economic Research Service
		ERTA	Economic Recovery Tax Act of 1981
DPT	Diphtheria, pertussis, and tetanus	ESA	Endangered Species Act of 1973
DRI	Defense Research Institute		
DSAA	Defense Security Assistance Agency	ESF	Emergency support function; Economic Support Fund
DUI	Driving under the influence; driving under intoxication	ESRD	End-Stage Renal Disease Program
DVD	Digital versatile disc	ETA	Employment and Training Administration
DWI	Driving while intoxicated		
EAHCA	Education for All Handicapped Children Act of 1975	ETS	Environmental tobacco smoke
		et seq.	*Et sequentes* or *et sequentia* ("and the following")
EBT	Examination before trial		
E.coli	Escherichia coli	EU	European Union
ECPA	Electronic Communications Privacy Act of 1986	Euratom	European Atomic Energy Community
ECSC	Treaty of the European Coal and Steel Community	Eur. Ct. H.R.	European Court of Human Rights
EDA	Economic Development Administration	Ex.	English Exchequer Reports, Welsby, Hurlstone & Gordon
EDF	Environmental Defense Fund	Exch.	Exchequer Reports (Welsby, Hurlstone & Gordon)
E.D.N.Y.	Eastern District, New York		
EDP	Electronic data processing	Ex Com	Executive Committee of the National Security Council
E.D. Pa.	Eastern-District, Pennsylvania		
EDSC	Eastern District, South Carolina	Eximbank	Export-Import Bank of the United States
EDT	Eastern daylight time	F.	Federal Reporter
E.D. Va.	Eastern District, Virginia	F. 2d	Federal Reporter, Second Series
EEC	European Economic Community; European Economic Community Treaty	FAA	Federal Aviation Administration; Federal Arbitration Act
EEOC	Equal Employment Opportunity Commission	FAAA	Federal Alcohol Administration Act
EFF	Electronic Frontier Foundation	FACE	Freedom of Access to Clinic Entrances Act of 1994
EFT	Electronic funds transfer	FACT	Feminist Anti-Censorship Task Force
Eliz.	Queen Elizabeth (Great Britain)	FAIRA	Federal Agriculture Improvement and Reform Act of 1996
Em. App.	Temporary Emergency Court of Appeals		
ENE	Early neutral evaluation	FAMLA	Family and Medical Leave Act of 1993
Eng. Rep.	English Reports		
EOP	Executive Office of the President	Fannie Mae	Federal National Mortgage Association
EPA	Environmental Protection Agency; Equal Pay Act of 1963	FAO	Food and Agriculture Organization of the United Nations
ERA	Equal Rights Amendment	FAR	Federal Acquisition Regulations
ERDC	Energy Research and Development Commission	FAS	Foreign Agricultural Service
		FBA	Federal Bar Association

FBI	Federal Bureau of Investigation	FISA	Foreign Intelligence Surveillance Act of 1978
FCA	Farm Credit Administration	FISC	Foreign Intelligence Surveillance Court of Review
F. Cas.	Federal Cases		
FCC	Federal Communications Commission	FJC	Federal Judicial Center
FCIA	Foreign Credit Insurance Association	FLSA	Fair Labor Standards Act
		FMC	Federal Maritime Commission
FCIC	Federal Crop Insurance Corporation	FMCS	Federal Mediation and Conciliation Service
FCLAA	Federal Cigarette Labeling and Advertising Act	FmHA	Farmers Home Administration
FCRA	Fair Credit Reporting Act	FMLA	Family and Medical Leave Act of 1993
FCU	Federal credit unions		
FCUA	Federal Credit Union Act	FNMA	Federal National Mortgage Association, "Fannie Mae"
FCZ	Fishery Conservation Zone		
FDA	Food and Drug Administration	F.O.B.	Free on board
FDIC	Federal Deposit Insurance Corporation	FOIA	Freedom of Information Act
		FOMC	Federal Open Market Committee
FDPC	Federal Data Processing Center	FPA	Federal Power Act of 1935
FEC	Federal Election Commission	FPC	Federal Power Commission
FECA	Federal Election Campaign Act of 1971	FPMR	Federal Property Management Regulations
Fed. Cas.	Federal Cases	FPRS	Federal Property Resources Service
FEHA	Fair Employment and Housing Act	FR	Federal Register
FEHBA	Federal Employees Health Benefit Act	FRA	Federal Railroad Administration
FEMA	Federal Emergency Management Agency	FRB	Federal Reserve Board
		FRC	Federal Radio Commission
FERC	Federal Energy Regulatory Commission	F.R.D.	Federal Rules Decisions
		FSA	Family Support Act
FFB	Federal Financing Bank	FSB	Federal'naya Sluzhba Bezopasnosti (the Federal Security Service of Russia)
FFDC	Federal Food, Drug, and Cosmetics Act		
FGIS	Federal Grain Inspection Service	FSLIC	Federal Savings and Loan Insurance Corporation
FHA	Federal Housing Administration	FSQS	Food Safety and Quality Service
FHAA	Fair Housing Amendments Act of 1998	FSS	Federal Supply Service
FHWA	Federal Highway Administration	F. Supp.	Federal Supplement
		FTA	U.S.-Canada Free Trade Agreement of 1988
FIA	Federal Insurance Administration		
FIC	Federal Information Centers; Federation of Insurance Counsel	FTC	Federal Trade Commission
		FTCA	Federal Tort Claims Act
		FTS	Federal Telecommunications System
FICA	Federal Insurance Contributions Act	FTS2000	Federal Telecommunications System 2000
FIFRA	Federal Insecticide, Fungicide, and Rodenticide Act	FUCA	Federal Unemployment Compensation Act of 1988
		FUTA	Federal Unemployment Tax Act
FIP	Forestry Incentives Program		
FIRREA	Financial Institutions Reform, Recovery, and Enforcement Act of 1989	FWPCA	Federal Water Pollution Control Act of 1948
		FWS	Fish and Wildlife Service
		GAL	Guardian ad litem

GAO	General Accounting Office; Governmental Affairs Office	HEW	Department of Health, Education, and Welfare
GAOR	General Assembly Official Records, United Nations	HFCA	Health Care Financing Administration
GAAP	Generally accepted accounting principles	HGI	Handgun Control, Incorporated
GA Res.	General Assembly Resolution (United Nations)	HHS	Department of Health and Human Services
GATT	General Agreement on Tariffs and Trade	Hill	Hill's New York Reports
GCA	Gun Control Act	HIRE	Help through Industry Retraining and Employment
Gen. Cls. Comm.	General Claims Commission, United States and Panama; General Claims United States and Mexico	HIV	Human immunodeficiency virus
Geo. II	King George II (Great Britain)	H.L.	House of Lords Cases (England)
Geo. III	King George III (Great Britain)	H. Lords	House of Lords (England)
GHB	Gamma-hydroxybutrate	HMO	Health Maintenance Organization
GI	Government Issue	HNIS	Human Nutrition Information Service
GID	General Intelligence Division	Hong Kong L.R.	Hong Kong Law Reports
GM	General Motors	How.	Howard's United States Supreme Court Reports
GNMA	Government National Mortgage Association, "Ginnie Mae"	How. St. Trials	Howell's English State Trials
GNP	Gross national product	HUAC	House Un-American Activities Committee
GOP	Grand Old Party (Republican Party)	HUD	Department of Housing and Urban Development
GOPAC	Grand Old Party Action Committee	Hudson, Internatl. Legis.	Manley Ottmer Hudson, ed., *International Legislation: A Collection of the Texts of Multipartite International Instruments of General Interest Beginning with the Covenant of the League of Nations* (1931)
GPA	Office of Governmental and Public Affairs		
GPO	Government Printing Office		
GRAS	Generally recognized as safe		
Gr. Br., Crim. Ct. App.	Great Britain, Court of Criminal Appeals	Hudson, World Court Reps.	Manley Ottmer Hudson, ea., *World Court Reports* (1934–)
GRNL	Gay Rights-National Lobby		
GSA	General Services Administration	Hun	Hun's New York Supreme Court Reports
Hackworth	Green Haywood Hackworth, *Digest of International Law* (1940–1944)	Hunt's Rept.	Bert L. Hunt, *Report of the American and Panamanian General Claims Arbitration* (1934)
Hay and Marriott	Great Britain. High Court of Admiralty, *Decisions in the High Court of Admiralty during the Time of Sir George Hay and of Sir James Marriott, Late Judges of That Court* (1801)	IAEA	International Atomic Energy Agency
		IALL	International Association of Law Libraries
		IBA	International Bar Association
HBO	Home Box Office	IBM	International Business Machines
HCFA	Health Care Financing Administration	ICA	Interstate Commerce Act
H.Ct.	High Court	ICBM	Intercontinental ballistic missile
HDS	Office of Human Development Services	ICC	Interstate Commerce Commission; International Criminal Court
Hen. & M.	Hening & Munford's Virginia Reports		

ICJ	International Court of Justice	ITA	International Trade Administration
ICM	Institute for Court Management	ITI	Information Technology Integration
IDEA	Individuals with Disabilities Education Act of 1975	ITO	International Trade Organization
IDOP	International Dolphin Conservation Program	ITS	Information Technology Service
IEP	Individualized educational program	ITT	International Telephone and Telegraph Corporation
IFC	International Finance Corporation	ITU	International Telecommunication Union
IGRA	Indian Gaming Regulatory Act of 1988	IUD	Intrauterine device
IJA	Institute of Judicial Administration	IWC	International Whaling Commission
IJC	International Joint Commission	IWW	Industrial Workers of the World
ILC	International Law Commission	JAGC	Judge Advocate General's Corps
ILD	International Labor Defense	JCS	Joint Chiefs of Staff
Ill. Dec.	Illinois Decisions	JDL	Jewish Defense League
ILO	International Labor Organization	JNOV	Judgment *non obstante veredicto* ("judgment nothing to recommend it" or "judgment notwithstanding the verdict")
IMF	International Monetary Fund		
INA	Immigration and Nationality Act		
IND	Investigational new drug	JOBS	Jobs Opportunity and Basic Skills
INF Treaty	Intermediate-Range Nuclear Forces Treaty of 1987	John. Ch.	Johnson's New York Chancery Reports
INS	Immigration and Naturalization Service	Johns.	Johnson's Reports (New York)
INTELSAT	International Telecommunications Satellite Organization	JP	Justice of the peace
		K.B.	King's Bench Reports (England)
Interpol	International Criminal Police Organization	KFC	Kentucky Fried Chicken
Int'l. Law Reps.	International Law Reports	KGB	Komitet Gosudarstvennoi Bezopasnosti (the State Security Committee for countries in the former Soviet Union)
Intl. Legal Mats.	International Legal Materials		
IOC	International Olympic Committee		
IPDC	International Program for the Development of Communication	KKK	Ku Klux Klan
		KMT	Kuomintang (Chinese, "national people's party")
IPO	Intellectual Property Owners		
IPP	Independent power producer	LAD	Law Against Discrimination
IQ	Intelligence quotient	LAPD	Los Angeles Police Department
I.R.	Irish Reports		
IRA	Individual retirement account; Irish Republican Army	LC	Library of Congress
		LCHA	Longshoremen's and Harbor Workers Compensation Act of 1927
IRC	Internal Revenue Code		
IRCA	Immigration Reform and Control Act of 1986	LD50	Lethal dose 50
		LDEF	Legal Defense and Education Fund (NOW)
IRS	Internal Revenue Service		
ISO	Independent service organization	LDF	Legal Defense Fund, Legal Defense and Educational Fund of the NAACP
ISP	Internet service provider		
ISSN	International Standard Serial Numbers	LEAA	Law Enforcement Assistance Administration

L.Ed.	Lawyers' Edition Supreme Court Reports	Mercy	Movement Ensuring the Right to Choose for Yourself
LI	Letter of interpretation		
LLC	Limited Liability Company	Metc.	Metcalf's Massachusetts Reports
LLP	Limited Liability Partnership	MFDP	Mississippi Freedom Democratic party
LMSA	Labor-Management Services Administration	MGT	Management
LNTS	League of Nations Treaty Series	MHSS	Military Health Services System
Lofft's Rep.	Lofft's English King's Bench Reports	Miller	David Hunter Miller, ea., *Treaties and Other International Acts*
L.R.	Law Reports (English)		*of the United States*
LSAC	Law School Admission Council		*of America* (1931–1948)
LSAS	Law School Admission Service	Minn.	Minnesota Reports
		MINS	Minors in need of supervision
LSAT	Law School Aptitude Test		
LSC	Legal Services Corporation; Legal Services for Children	MIRV	Multiple independently targetable reentry vehicle
LSD	Lysergic acid diethylamide	MIRVed ICBM	Multiple independently targetable reentry vehicled intercontinental ballistic missile
LSDAS	Law School Data Assembly Service		
LTBT	Limited Test Ban Treaty		
LTC	Long Term Care	Misc.	Miscellaneous Reports, New York
MAD	Mutual assured destruction		
MADD	Mothers against Drunk Driving	Mixed Claims Comm., Report	Mixed Claims Commission, United States
MALDEF	Mexican American Legal Defense and Educational Fund	of Decs	and Germany, Report of Decisions
		M.J.	Military Justice Reporter
Malloy	William M. Malloy, ed., *Treaties, Conventions International Acts,*	MLAP	Migrant Legal Action Program
	Protocols, and Agreements	MLB	Major League Baseball
	between the United States	MLDP	Mississippi Loyalist Democratic Party
	of America and Other Powers (1910–1938)	MMI	Moslem Mosque, Incorporated
Martens	Georg Friedrich von Martens, ea., *Noveau recueil général*	MMPA	Marine Mammal Protection Act of 1972
	de traités et autres actes	Mo.	Missouri Reports
	relatifs aux rapports de droit	MOD	Masters of Deception
	international (Series I, 20 vols. [1843–1875]; Series II,	Mod.	Modern Reports, English King's Bench, etc.
	35 vols. [1876–1908];	Moore, Dig.	John Bassett Moore, *A Digest*
	Series III [1909–])	Intl. Law	*of International Law,* 8 vols.
Mass.	Massachusetts Reports		(1906)
MCC	Metropolitan Correctional Center	Moore, Intl. Arbs.	John Bassett Moore, *History and Digest of the*
MCCA	Medicare Catastrophic Coverage Act of 1988		*International Arbitrations to Which United States*
MCH	Maternal and Child Health Bureau		*Has Been a Party,* 6 vols. (1898)
MCRA	Medical Care Recovery Act of 1962	Morison	William Maxwell Morison, *The Scots Revised Report:*
MDA	Medical Devices Amendments of 1976		*Morison's Dictionary of Decisions* (1908–09)
Md. App.	Maryland, Appeal Cases	M.P.	Member of Parliament
M.D. Ga.	Middle District, Georgia	MP3	MPEG Audio Layer 3

MPAA	Motion Picture Association of America	NAWSA	National American Woman's Suffrage Association
MPAS	Michigan Protection and Advocacy Service	NBA	National Bar Association; National Basketball Association
MPEG	Motion Picture Experts Group	NBC	National Broadcasting Company
mpg	Miles per gallon		
MPPDA	Motion Picture Producers and Distributors of America	NBLSA	National Black Law Student Association
MPRSA	Marine Protection, Research, and Sanctuaries Act of 1972	NBS	National Bureau of Standards
		NCA	Noise Control Act; National Command Authorities
M.R.	Master of the Rolls	NCAA	National Collegiate Athletic Association
MS-DOS	Microsoft Disk Operating System	NCAC	National Coalition against Censorship
MSHA	Mine Safety and Health Administration	NCCB	National Consumer Cooperative Bank
MSPB	Merit Systems Protection Board	NCE	Northwest Community Exchange
MSSA	Military Selective Service Act	NCF	National Chamber Foundation
N/A	Not Available		
NAACP	National Association for the Advancement of Colored People	NCIP	National Crime Insurance Program
		NCJA	National Criminal Justice Association
NAAQS	National Ambient Air Quality Standards	NCLB	National Civil Liberties Bureau
NAB	National Association of Broadcasters	NCP	National contingency plan
NABSW	National Association of Black Social Workers	NCSC	National Center for State Courts
NACDL	National Association of Criminal Defense Lawyers	NCUA	National Credit Union Administration
		NDA	New drug application
NAFTA	North American Free Trade Agreement of 1993	N.D. Ill.	Northern District, Illinois
		NDU	National Defense University
NAGHSR	National Association of Governors' Highway Safety Representatives	N.D. Wash.	Northern District, Washington
		N.E.	North Eastern Reporter
NALA	National Association of Legal Assistants	N.E. 2d	North Eastern Reporter, Second Series
NAM	National Association of Manufacturers	NEA	National Endowment for the Arts; National Education Association
NAR	National Association of Realtors	NEH	National Endowment for the Humanities
NARAL	National Abortion and Reproductive Rights Action League	NEPA	National Environmental Protection Act; National Endowment Policy Act
NARF	Native American Rights Fund	NET Act	No Electronic Theft Act
NARS	National Archives and Record Service	NFIB	National Federation of Independent Businesses
NASA	National Aeronautics and Space Administration	NFIP	National Flood Insurance Program
NASD	National Association of Securities Dealers	NFL	National Football League
		NFPA	National Federation of Paralegal Associations
NATO	North Atlantic Treaty Organization	NGLTF	National Gay and Lesbian Task Force
NAVINFO	Navy Information Offices		

NHL	National Hockey League	NPL	National priorities list
NHRA	Nursing Home Reform Act of 1987	NPR	National Public Radio
NHTSA	National Highway Traffic Safety Administration	NPT	Nuclear Non-Proliferation Treaty of 1970
Nielsen's Rept.	Frederick Kenelm Nielsen, *American and British Claims Arbitration under the Special Agreement Concluded between the United States and Great Britain, August 18, 1910* (1926)	NRA	National Rifle Association; National Recovery Act
		NRC	Nuclear Regulatory Commission
		NRLC	National Right to Life Committee
		NRTA	National Retired Teachers Association
NIEO	New International Economic Order	NSA	National Security Agency
		NSC	National Security Council
NIGC	National Indian Gaming Commission	NSCLC	National Senior Citizens Law Center
NIH	National Institutes of Health	NSF	National Science Foundation
NIJ	National Institute of Justice	NSFNET	National Science Foundation Network
NIRA	National Industrial Recovery Act of 1933; National Industrial Recovery Administration	NSI	Network Solutions, Inc.
		NTIA	National Telecommunications and Information Administration
NIST	National Institute of Standards and Technology	NTID	National Technical Institute for the Deaf
NITA	National Telecommunications and Information Administration	NTIS	National Technical Information Service
		NTS	Naval Telecommunications System
N.J.	New Jersey Reports		
N.J. Super.	New Jersey Superior Court Reports	NTSB	National Transportation Safety Board
NLEA	Nutrition Labeling and Education Act of 1990	NVRA	National Voter Registration Act
NLRA	National Labor Relations Act	N.W.	North Western Reporter
NLRB	National Labor Relations Board	N.W. 2d	North Western Reporter, Second Series
NMFS	National Marine Fisheries Service	NWSA	National Woman Suffrage Association
No.	Number	N.Y.	New York Court of Appeals Reports
NOAA	National Oceanic and Atmospheric Administration	N.Y. 2d	New York Court of Appeals Reports, Second Series
NOC	National Olympic Committee	N.Y.S.	New York Supplement Reporter
NOI	Nation of Islam		
NOL	Net operating loss	N.Y.S. 2d	New York Supplement Reporter, Second Series
NORML	National Organization for the Reform of Marijuana Laws	NYSE	New York Stock Exchange
		NYSLA	New York State Liquor Authority
NOW	National Organization for Women	N.Y. Sup.	New York Supreme Court Reports
NOW LDEF	National Organization for Women Legal Defense and Education Fund	NYU	New York University
		OAAU	Organization of Afro American Unity
NOW/PAC	National Organization for Women Political Action Committee	OAP	Office of Administrative Procedure
NPDES	National Pollutant Discharge Elimination System	OAS	Organization of American States

OASDI	Old-age, Survivors, and Disability Insurance Benefits	OST	Office of the Secretary
		OT	Office of Transportation
OASHDS	Office of the Assistant Secretary for Human Development Services	OTA	Office of Technology Assessment
		OTC	Over-the-counter
OCC	Office of Comptroller of the Currency	OTS	Office of Thrift Supervisors
		OUI	Operating under the influence
OCED	Office of Comprehensive Employment Development	OVCI	Offshore Voluntary Compliance Initiative
OCHAMPUS	Office of Civilian Health and Medical Program of the Uniformed Services	OWBPA	Older Workers Benefit Protection Act
		OWRT	Office of Water Research and Technology
OCSE	Office of Child Support Enforcement	P.	Pacific Reporter
OEA	Organización de los Estados Americanos	P. 2d	Pacific Reporter, Second Series
OEM	Original Equipment Manufacturer	PAC	Political action committee
		Pa. Oyer and Terminer	Pennsylvania Oyer and Terminer Reports
OFCCP	Office of Federal Contract Compliance Programs	PATCO	Professional Air Traffic Controllers Organization
OFPP	Office of Federal Procurement Policy	PBGC	Pension Benefit Guaranty Corporation
OIC	Office of the Independent Counsel	PBS	Public Broadcasting Service; Public Buildings Service
OICD	Office of International Cooperation and Development	P.C.	Privy Council (English Law Reports)
OIG	Office of the Inspector General	PC	Personal computer; politically correct
OJARS	Office of Justice Assistance, Research, and Statistics	PCBs	Polychlorinated biphenyls
		PCIJ	Permanent Court of International Justice
OMB	Office of Management and Budget		Series A-Judgments and Orders (1922–30)
OMPC	Office of Management, Planning, and Communications		Series B-Advisory Opinions (1922–30)
ONP	Office of National Programs		Series A/B-Judgments, Orders, and Advisory Opinions (1931–40)
OPD	Office of Policy Development		
OPEC	Organization of Petroleum Exporting Countries		Series C-Pleadings, Oral Statements, and Documents relating to Judgments and Advisory Opinions (1923–42)
OPIC	Overseas Private Investment Corporation		
Ops. Atts. Gen.	Opinions of the Attorneys-General of the United States		Series D-Acts and Documents concerning the Organization of the World Court (1922–47)
Ops. Comms.	Opinions of the Commissioners		
OPSP	Office of Product Standards Policy		Series E-Annual Reports (1925–45)
O.R.	Ontario Reports		
OR	Official Records		
OSHA	Occupational Safety and Health Act	PCP	Phencyclidine
		P.D.	Probate Division, English Law Reports (1876–1890)
OSHRC	Occupational Safety and Health Review Commission	PDA	Pregnancy Discrimination Act of 1978
OSM	Office of Surface Mining	PD & R	Policy Development and Research
OSS	Office of Strategic Services		

Pepco	Potomac Electric Power Company	PURPA	Public Utilities Regulatory Policies Act
Perm. Ct. of Arb.	Permanent Court of Arbitration	PUSH	People United to Serve Humanity
PES	Post-Enumeration Survey	PUSH-Excel	PUSH for Excellence
Pet.	Peters' United States Supreme Court Reports	PWA	Public Works Administration
		PWSA	Ports and Waterways Safety Act of 1972
PETA	People for the Ethical Treatment of Animals	Q.B.	Queen's Bench (England)
PGA	Professional Golfers Association	QTIP	Qualified Terminable Interest Property
PGM	Program	Ralston's Rept.	Jackson Harvey Ralston, ed.,
PHA	Public Housing Agency		*Venezuelan Arbitrations*
Phila. Ct. of Oyer and Terminer	Philadelphia Court of Oyer and Terminer	RC	*of 1903* (1904)
			Regional Commissioner
PhRMA	Pharmaceutical Research and Manufacturers of America	RCRA	Resource Conservation and Recovery Act
		RCWP	Rural Clean Water Program
PHS	Public Health Service	RDA	Rural Development Administration
PIC	Private Industry Council		
PICJ	Permanent International Court of Justice	REA	Rural Electrification Administration
Pick.	Pickering's Massachusetts Reports	Rec. des Decs. des Trib. Arb. Mixtes	G. Gidel, ed., *Recueil des décisions des tribunaux arbitraux mixtes, institués par les traités de paix* (1922–30)
PIK	Payment in Kind		
PINS	Persons in need of supervision		
PIRG	Public Interest Research Group	Redmond	Vol. 3 of Charles I. Bevans, *Treaties and Other International Agreements of the United States of America, 1776–1949* (compiled by C. F. Redmond) (1969)
P.L.	Public Laws		
PLAN	Pro-Life Action Network		
PLC	Plaintiffs' Legal Committee		
PLE	Product liability expenses		
PLI	Practicing Law Institute		
PLL	Product liability loss	RESPA	Real Estate Settlement Procedure Act of 1974
PLLP	Professional Limited Liability Partnership		
		RFC	Reconstruction Finance Corporation
PLO	Palestine Liberation Organization	RFRA	Religious Freedom Restoration Act of 1993
PLRA	Prison Litigation Reform Act of 1995		
		RIAA	Recording Industry Association of America
PNET	Peaceful Nuclear Explosions Treaty		
		RICO	Racketeer Influenced and Corrupt Organizations
PONY	Prostitutes of New York		
POW-MIA	Prisoner of war-missing in action	RLUIPA	Religious Land Use and Institutionalized Persons Act
Pratt	Frederic Thomas Pratt, *Law of Contraband of War, with a Selection of Cases from Papers of the Right Honourable Sir George Lee* (1856)		
		RNC	Republican National Committee
		Roscoe	Edward Stanley Roscoe, ed., *Reports of Prize Cases Determined in the High Court Admiralty before the Lords Commissioners of Appeals in Prize Causes and before the judicial Committee of the Privy Council from 1745 to 1859* (1905)
PRIDE	Prostitution to Independence, Dignity, and Equality		
Proc.	Proceedings		
PRP	Potentially responsible party		
PSRO	Professional Standards Review Organization		
PTO	Patents and Trademark Office		

ROTC	Reserve Officers' Training Corps	S.E. 2d	South Eastern Reporter, Second Series
RPP	Representative Payee Program	SEA	Science and Education Administration
R.S.	Revised Statutes	SEATO	Southeast Asia Treaty Organization
RTC	Resolution Trust Corp.		
RUDs	Reservations, understandings, and declarations	SEC	Securities and Exchange Commission
Ryan White CARE Act	Ryan White Comprehensive AIDS Research Emergency Act of 1990	Sec.	Section
		SEEK	Search for Elevation, Education and Knowledge
SAC	Strategic Air Command		
SACB	Subversive Activities Control Board	SEOO	State Economic Opportunity Office
SADD	Students against Drunk Driving	SEP	Simplified employee pension plan
SAF	Student Activities Fund	Ser.	Series
SAIF	Savings Association Insurance Fund	Sess.	Session
		SGLI	Servicemen's Group Life Insurance
SALT	Strategic Arms Limitation Talks		
SALT I	Strategic Arms Limitation Talks of 1969–72	SIP	State implementation plan
		SLA	Symbionese Liberation Army
SAMHSA	Substance Abuse and Mental Health Services Administration	SLAPPs	Strategic Lawsuits Against Public Participation
		SLBM	Submarine-launched ballistic missile
Sandf.	Sandford's New York Superior Court Reports	SNCC	Student Nonviolent Coordinating Committee
S and L	Savings and loan	So.	Southern Reporter
SARA	Superfund Amendment and Reauthorization Act	So. 2d	Southern Reporter, Second Series
SAT	Scholastic Aptitude Test	SPA	Software Publisher's Association
Sawy.	Sawyer's United States Circuit Court Reports	Spec. Sess.	Special Session
SBA	Small Business Administration	SPLC	Southern Poverty Law Center
		SRA	Sentencing Reform Act of 1984
SBI	Small Business Institute		
SCCC	South Central Correctional Center	SS	*Schutzstaffel* (German, "Protection Echelon")
SCLC	Southern Christian Leadership Conference	SSA	Social Security Administration
Scott's Repts.	James Brown Scott, ed., *The Hague Court Reports*, 2 vols. (1916–32)	SSI	Supplemental Security Income
		START I	Strategic Arms Reduction Treaty of 1991
SCS	Soil Conservation Service; Social Conservative Service	START II	Strategic Arms Reduction Treaty of 1993
SCSEP	Senior Community Service Employment Program	Stat.	United States Statutes at Large
S.Ct.	Supreme Court Reporter	STS	Space Transportation Systems
S.D. Cal.	Southern District, California	St. Tr.	State Trials, English
S.D. Fla.	Southern District, Florida	STURAA	Surface Transportation and Uniform Relocation Assistance Act of 1987
S.D. Ga.	Southern District, Georgia		
SDI	Strategic Defense Initiative		
S.D. Me.	Southern District, Maine	Sup. Ct. of Justice, Mexico	Supreme Court of Justice, Mexico
S.D.N.Y.	Southern District, New York		
SDS	Students for a Democratic Society		
		Supp.	Supplement
S.E.	South Eastern Reporter	S.W.	South Western Reporter

S.W. 2d	South Western Reporter, Second Series	UFW	United Farm Workers
SWAPO	South-West Africa People's Organization	UHF	Ultrahigh frequency
		UIFSA	Uniform Interstate Family Support Act
SWAT	Special Weapons and Tactics	UIS	Unemployment Insurance Service
SWP	Socialist Workers Party		
TDP	Trade and Development Program	UMDA	Uniform Marriage and Divorce Act
Tex. Sup.	Texas Supreme Court Reports	UMTA	Urban Mass Transportation Administration
THAAD	Theater High-Altitude Area Defense System	U.N.	United Nations
		UNCITRAL	United Nations Commission on International Trade Law
THC	Tetrahydrocannabinol		
TI	Tobacco Institute	UNCTAD	United Nations Conference on Trade and Development
TIA	Trust Indenture Act of 1939		
TIAS	Treaties and Other International Acts Series (United States)	UN Doc.	United Nations Documents
		UNDP	United Nations Development Program
TNT	Trinitrotoluene		
TOP	Targeted Outreach Program	UNEF	United Nations Emergency Force
TPUS	Transportation and Public Utilities Service	UNESCO	United Nations Educational, Scientific, and Cultural Organization
TQM	Total Quality Management		
Tripartite Claims Comm., Decs. and Ops.	Tripartite Claims Commission (United States, Austria, and Hungary), Decisions and Opinions	UNICEF	United Nations Children's Fund (formerly United Nations International Children's Emergency Fund)
TRI-TAC	Joint Tactical Communications	UNIDO	United Nations Industrial and Development Organization
TRO	Temporary restraining order		
TS	Treaty Series, United States	Unif. L. Ann.	Uniform Laws Annotated
TSCA	Toxic Substance Control Act	UN Repts. Intl. Arb. Awards	United Nations Reports of International Arbitral Awards
TSDs	Transporters, storers, and disposers		
TSU	Texas Southern University		
TTBT	Threshold Test Ban Treaty	UNTS	United Nations Treaty Series
TV	Television	UPI	United Press International
TVA	Tennessee Valley Authority	URESA	Uniform Reciprocal Enforcement of Support Act
TWA	Trans World Airlines		
UAW	United Auto Workers; United Automobile, Aerospace, and Agricultural Implements Workers of America	U.S.	United States Reports
		U.S.A.	United States of America
		USAF	United States Air Force
		USA PATRIOT Act	Uniting and Strengthening America by Providing Appropriate Tools Required to Intercept and Obstruct Terrorism Act
U.C.C.	Uniform Commercial Code; Universal Copyright Convention		
U.C.C.C.	Uniform Consumer Credit Code		
UCCJA	Uniform Child Custody Jurisdiction Act	USF	U.S. Forestry Service
		U.S. App. D.C.	United States Court of Appeals for the District of Columbia
UCMJ	Uniform Code of Military Justice		
UCPP	Urban Crime Prevention Program	U.S.C.	United States Code; University of Southern California
UCS	United Counseling Service		
UDC	United Daughters of the Confederacy	U.S.C.A.	United States Code Annotated

U.S.C.C.A.N.	United States Code Congressional and Administrative News	Wall.	Wallace's United States Supreme Court Reports
USCMA	United States Court of Military Appeals	Wash. 2d	Washington Reports, Second Series
USDA	U.S. Department of Agriculture	WAVES	Women Accepted for Volunteer Service
USES	United States Employment Service	WCTU	Women's Christian Temperance Union
USFA	United States Fire Administration	W.D. Wash.	Western District, Washington
		W.D. Wis.	Western District, Wisconsin
USGA	United States Golf Association	WEAL	West's Encyclopedia of American Law; Women's Equity Action League
USICA	International Communication Agency, United States	Wend.	Wendell's New York Reports
		WFSE	Washington Federation of State Employees
USMS	U.S. Marshals Service	Wheat.	Wheaton's United States Supreme Court Reports
USOC	U.S. Olympic Committee		
USSC	U.S. Sentencing Commission	Wheel. Cr. Cases	Wheeler's New York Criminal Cases
USSG	United States Sentencing Guidelines	WHISPER	Women Hurt in Systems of Prostitution Engaged in Revolt
U.S.S.R.	Union of Soviet Socialist Republics	Whiteman	Marjorie Millace Whiteman, Digest of International Law, 15 vols. (1963–73)
UST	United States Treaties		
USTS	United States Travel Service	WHO	World Health Organization
v.	Versus	WIC	Women, Infants, and Children program
VA	Veterans Administration		
VAR	Veterans Affairs and Rehabilitation Commission	Will. and Mar.	King William and Queen Mary (Great Britain)
VAWA	Violence against Women Act	WIN	WESTLAW Is Natural; Whip Inflation Now; Work Incentive Program
VFW	Veterans of Foreign Wars		
VGLI	Veterans Group Life Insurance	WIPO	World Intellectual Property Organization
Vict.	Queen Victoria (Great Britain)	WIU	Workers' Industrial Union
VIN	Vehicle identification number	W.L.R.	Weekly Law Reports, England
VISTA	Volunteers in Service to America	WPA	Works Progress Administration
VJRA	Veterans Judicial Review Act of 1988	WPPDA	Welfare and Pension Plans Disclosure Act
V.L.A.	Volunteer Lawyers for the Arts	WTO	World Trade Organization
		WWI	World War I
VMI	Virginia Military Institute	WWII	World War II
VMLI	Veterans Mortgage Life Insurance	Yates Sel. Cas.	Yates's New York Select Cases
		YMCA	Young Men's Christian Association
VOCAL	Victims of Child Abuse Laws		
VRA	Voting Rights Act	YWCA	Young Women's Christian Association
WAC	Women's Army Corps		

TABLE OF
CASES CITED